FOUNDATIONS OF

Financial Literacy

12TH EDITION

Robert L. Dansby, PhD
Columbus, Georgia

Sally R. Campbell, M.Ed.
Winnetka, Illinois

Listed on
jumpstartclearinghouse.org

Publisher
The Goodheart-Willcox Company, Inc.
Tinley Park, Illinois
www.g-w.com

correlated to
you science

ISBN 979-8-88817-656-6

3 4 5 6 7 8 9 – 24 – 29 28 27 26 25 24

The Goodheart-Willcox Company, Inc. Brand Disclaimer: Brand names, company names, and illustrations for products and services included in this text are provided for educational purposes only and do not represent or imply endorsement or recommendation by the author or the publisher.

The Goodheart-Willcox Company, Inc. Safety Notice: The reader is expressly advised to carefully read, understand, and apply all safety precautions and warnings described in this book or that might also be indicated in undertaking the activities and exercises described herein to minimize risk of personal injury or injury to others. Common sense and good judgment should also be exercised and applied to help avoid all potential hazards. The reader should always refer to the appropriate manufacturer's technical information, directions, and recommendations; then proceed with care to follow specific equipment operating instructions. The reader should understand these notices and cautions are not exhaustive.

The publisher makes no warranty or representation whatsoever, either expressed or implied, including but not limited to equipment, procedures, and applications described or referred to herein, their quality, performance, merchantability, or fitness for a particular purpose. The publisher assumes no responsibility for any changes, errors, or omissions in this book. The publisher specifically disclaims any liability whatsoever, including any direct, indirect, incidental, consequential, special, or exemplary damages resulting, in whole or in part, from the reader's use or reliance upon the information, instructions, procedures, warnings, cautions, applications, or other matter contained in this book. The publisher assumes no responsibility for the activities of the reader.

The Goodheart-Willcox Company, Inc. Internet Disclaimer: The Internet resources and listings in this Goodheart-Willcox Publisher product are provided solely as a convenience to you. These resources and listings were reviewed at the time of publication to provide you with accurate, safe, and appropriate information. Goodheart-Willcox Publisher has no control over the referenced websites and, due to the dynamic nature of the Internet, is not responsible or liable for the content, products, or performance of links to other websites or resources. Goodheart-Willcox Publisher makes no representation, either expressed or implied, regarding the content of these websites, and such references do not constitute an endorsement or recommendation of the information or content presented. It is your responsibility to take all protective measures to guard against inappropriate content, viruses, or other destructive elements.

Image Credits. Front cover: SergeyBitos/Shutterstock.com; History of Finance: Pavel Mastepanov/Shutterstock.com; Economics in Action: ale1969/Shutterstock.com; Employability Skills: davooda/Shutterstock.com

Introduction

In today's fast-paced economy, becoming financially literate is more challenging than ever. *Foundations of Financial Literacy* helps you meet that challenge. This text provides a comprehensive framework for learning about personal financial responsibility. You can discover how to make wise financial decisions that will help you lead a productive life and achieve financial security.

As you progress through this textbook, you will learn how to make financial decisions related to earning money, spending money, and planning for your future. You will learn what you need to know when using credit, buying insurance, purchasing a car, and living on your own. An introduction to economics is presented to help you connect what you have learned about financial literacy to current national economic issues and to the global economy. A unit on career planning and digital citizenship will help you prepare for a career in the modern world.

Becoming financially capable can begin for you today by studying *Foundations of Financial Literacy.*

About the Authors

Robert (Bob) Dansby is an instructor of accounting, business, and personal finance at Chattahoochee Valley Community College in Alabama. He is the author of numerous textbooks and workbooks in the areas of accounting, cost accounting, managerial accounting, business math, and personal finance. Dr. Dansby has also written several articles for professional journals and served a five-year term as editor of the Georgia Business Education Association Journal. He holds a PhD in business education from Southern Illinois University at Carbondale.

Sally Campbell is a freelance writer and consultant in consumer economics. She has developed education materials, including teacher's guides, curriculum guides, textbooks, and student activity materials. Ms. Campbell has a master degree in education from St. Louis University and completed the Certified Financial Planning Professional Education Program of the College for Financial Planning.

Acknowledgments

The authors and publisher would like to thank the following individuals for their contribution of resource material, images, or other support in the development of *Foundations of Financial Literacy.*

Fletcher Woolsey, teacher of AP Microeconomics, AP United States Government and Politics, and Sociology at Cherry Creek High School in Greenwood Village, Colorado, for his work on *Personal Finance and Economics.* This supplement focuses on the relationship between economics and finance and shows students how they will use economic concepts in their own finances.

Reviewers

The authors and publisher wish to thank the following industry and teaching professionals for their valuable input into the development of *Foundations of Financial Literacy.*

Laura S. Beaton
GED Instructor
Mount Vernon Adult Complex
Henrico, Virginia

Bland D. Campbell
CTE Finance Teacher
Colonial Heights High School
Colonial Heights, Virginia

David M. Candelaria
Tech Coordinator, Department Chair
Career and Technical Education
Del Norte High School
Albuquerque, New Mexico

Suzanne Dowd, G-W Advisory Council
Team Leader, Family-Consumer Science Family-Consumer Science Teacher
Plano West Senior High School
Plano, Texas

Lynn Falk, G-W Advisory Council
Business Educator
Bemidji High School
Bemidji, Minnesota

Delia Fernandez, MBA, CFP®
President
Fernandez Financial Advisory, LLC
Los Alamitos, California

Laura Hildebran
Business Teacher
River Bend Middle School
Claremont, North Carolina

Clarissa R. Hobson
CFP®/Senior Financial Planning Advisor
Carnick & Kubik, LLC
Colorado Springs & Denver, Colorado

Michael Koch
Vice President
Insurance Services
Wilder, Kentucky

Karen Kurtz
Unified Arts Department Teacher
Westhill High School
Stamford, Connecticut

Christy R. Sellers
Business & IT Teacher
Robert E. Lee High School
Staunton, Virginia

Joy Shannahan
IBCC Coordinator/BIT-CTE Teacher
J.E.B. Stuart High School
Fairfax County Public Schools
Falls Church, Virginia

Randy R. Sims
Mortgage Loan Officer
Huntington National Bank
Columbus, Ohio

John L. Sorah, EdS
Financial Literacy Instructor
Mill Creek High School
Hochton, Georgia

Cynthia M. Sweeney
Business Teacher
J.M. Alexander Middle School
Charlotte-Mecklenburg Schools
Huntersville, North Carolina

Jenifer C. Richards
Business Education Teacher
Spartanburg High School
Spartanburg, South Carolina

Lois L. Richardson, G-W Advisory Council
Teacher, CTE
Copperas Cove High School
Copperas Cove, Texas

Carin Pankros Roman, CFP®
Financial Planner
CCP, Inc. Financial Planning Services
Palatine, Illinois

Alberto Velez
Business & Finance Teacher
Gladys Porter Early College High School
Brownsville, Texas

Rick V. Wall
Career & Technical Education Department Chair
Bailey Middle School
Cornelius, North Carolina

Warren Ward
Warren Ward Associates
Columbus, Indiana

Jason Weiss
CTAE Supervisor
Bibb County Board of Education
Macon, Georgia

Barbara Wiegand, G-W Advisory Council
FCS Instructor
Civic Memorial High School
Bethalto, Illinois

Credentialing Partners and Support

Goodheart-Willcox appreciates the value of industry credentials, certifications, and accreditation. We are pleased to partner with leading organizations to support students and programs in achieving credentials. Integrating industry-recognized credentialing into a career and technical education (CTE) program provides many benefits for the student and for the institution. By achieving third-party certificates, students gain confidence, have proof of a measurable level of knowledge and skills, and earn a valuable achievement to include in their résumés. For educators and administrators, industry-recognized credentials and accreditation validate learning, enhance the credibility of programs, and provide valuable data to measure student performance and help guide continuous program improvement.

Foundations of Financial Literacy is correlated to the Personal Financial Responsibility certification offered by Precision Exams by YouScience and to the National Standards for Personal Financial Education offered by Jump$tart.

Precision Exams by YouScience Certification

Goodheart-Willcox is pleased to partner with Precision Exams by YouScience, correlating select Goodheart-Willcox titles to Precision Exams certifications, to the benefit of states, instructors, and students working to achieve Precision Exams certifications.

Precisions Exams Standards and Career Skill Exams™ are created in concert with industry and subject matter experts to match real-world skills and marketplace demands. Students who pass the exam and performance portion of the exam can earn a Career Skills Certification™. For more information about Precision Exams by YouScience, including a complete listing of their 150+ Career Skills Exams™ and certificates, please visit www.youscience.com/certifications/career-clusters/.

Jump$tart Coalition for Personal Financial Literacy

Goodheart-Willcox is pleased to partner with the Jump$tart Coalition for Personal Financial Literacy to correlate Foundations of Financial Literacy with their National Standards in K–12 Personal Finance Education. The Jump$tart Coalition works to raise awareness about the importance of financial literacy and the need for financial education, especially among youth; fosters collaboration among financial literacy stakeholders; and promotes and supports effectiveness in financial education endeavors. For more information about Jump$tart, please visit www.jumpstart.org.

To see how *Foundations of Financial Literacy* correlates to credentialing and certification standards, visit the Correlations tab at www.g-w.com/foundations-financial-literacy-2024.

Guided Tour

The instructional design includes student-focused learning tools to help students succeed. This visual guide highlights the features designed for the textbook.

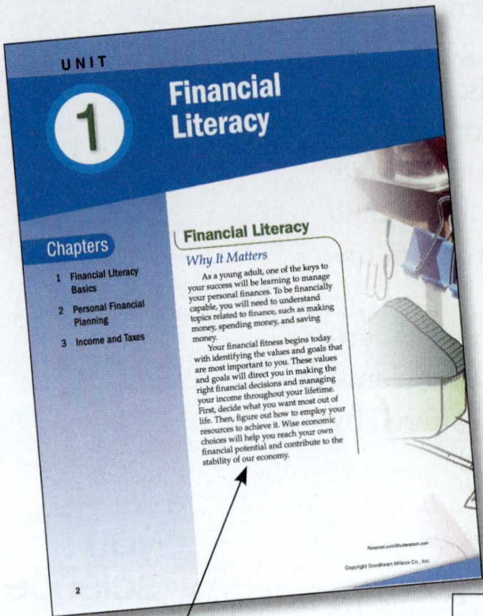

English/Language Arts standards for reading, writing, speaking, and listening are incorporated in **Reading Prep** activities, as well as in end-of-chapter applications.

Why It Matters introduces each unit to set the stage for learning about financial literacy.

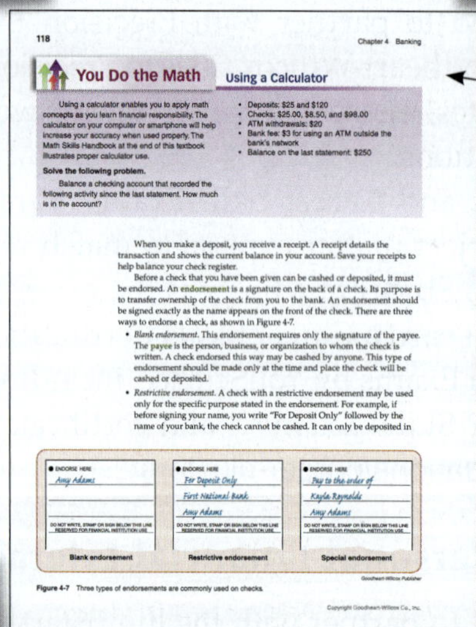

A **You Do the Math** activity in each chapter focuses on skills that are important to your understanding of math for business. You are given an opportunity to apply math concepts in the context of business applications.

The **Essential Question** at the beginning of each section will engage you as you uncover the important points presented in the content.

Employability Skills review essential soft skills for success in the workplace.

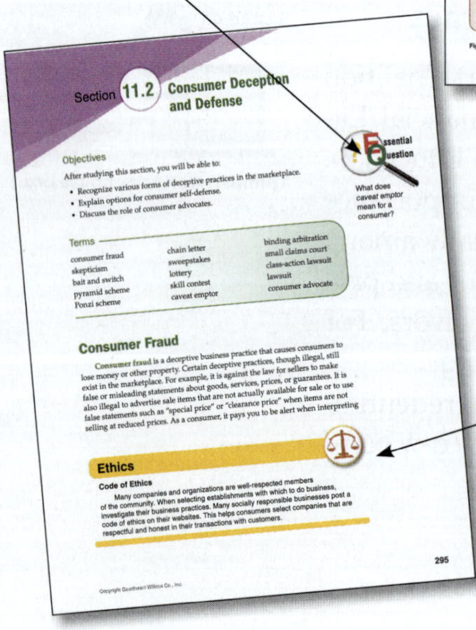

Ethics offers insight into ethical issues with which you will be confronted in the workplace.

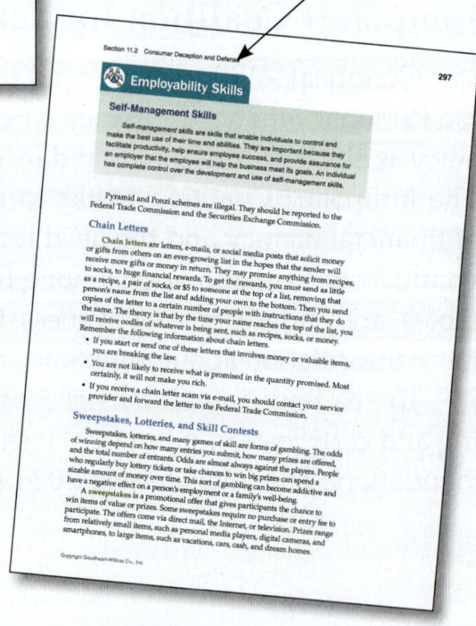

Exploring Careers features present information about potential career opportunities. By studying these, you can investigate career possibilities for your future.

Check Your Understanding questions at the end of each chapter section provide an opportunity to review what you have learned before moving on to additional content.

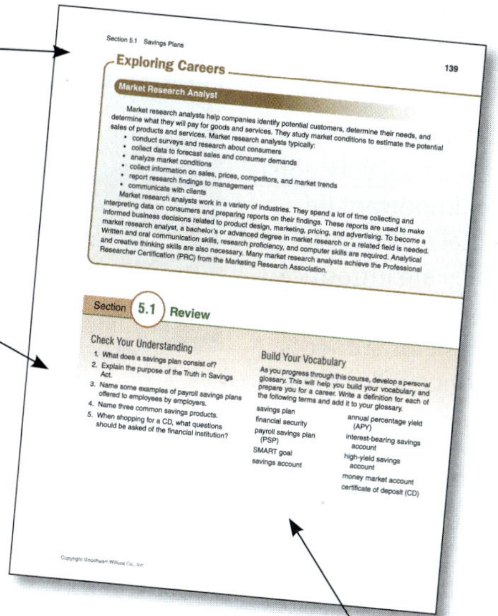

Review Your Knowledge activities cover the basic concepts presented in the chapter so you can evaluate your understanding of the material.

Build Your Vocabulary activities review the key terms presented in each section. By completing these activities, you will be able to demonstrate your understanding of vocabulary terms.

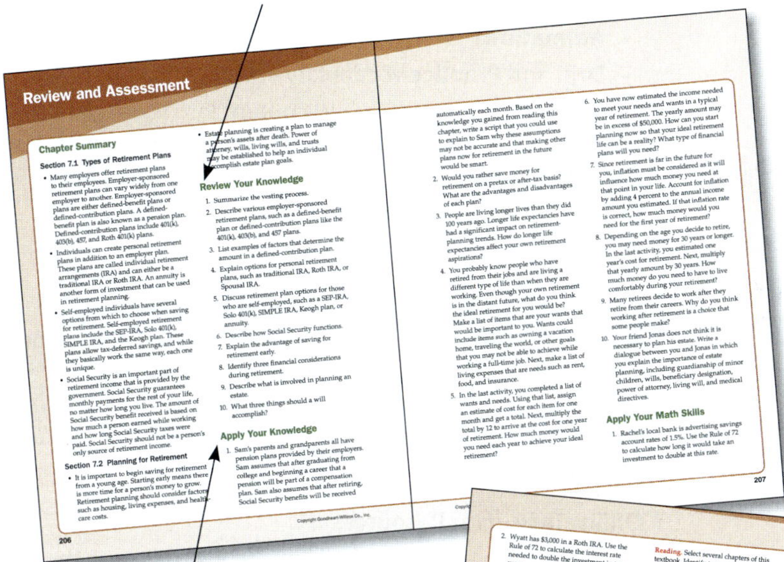

Teamwork activities encourage a collaborative experience to help you learn how to interact with other students in a productive manner.

Apply Your Knowledge activities challenge you to relate what you learned in the chapter with your own ideas, experiences, and goals.

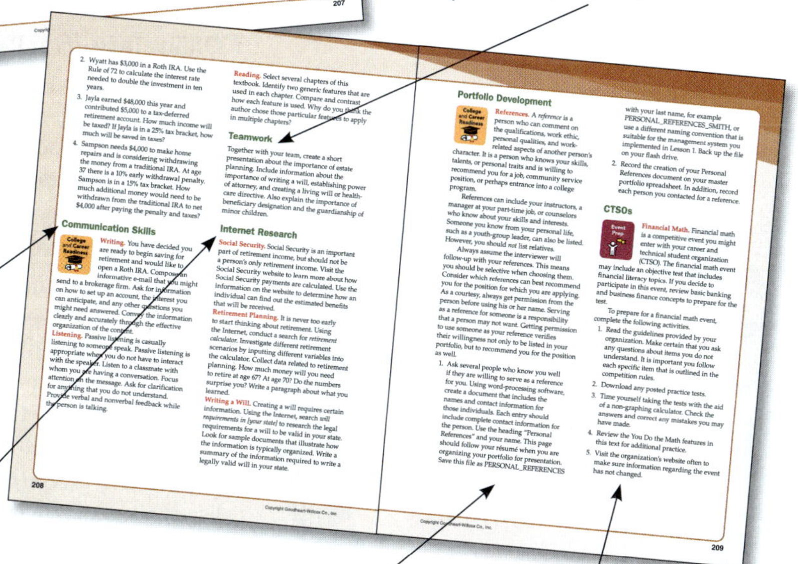

Communication Skills activities provide ways for you to demonstrate the literacy and career readiness skills you have mastered.

Internet Research activities at the end of each chapter provide opportunities to put critical research skills to work.

Portfolio Development activities provide guidance to create a personal portfolio for use when exploring volunteer, education and training, and career opportunities.

Event Prep presents information to use when preparing for competitive activities in career and technical student organization (CTSO) competitions.

TOOLS FOR STUDENT AND INSTRUCTOR SUCCESS

Student Tools

Student Text

Foundations of Financial Literacy is a contemporary text that presents the financial concepts that are vitally important in today's workplace. The basics of financial literacy are introduced in an easy-to-understand manner, which helps students connect the concepts to their everyday life.

Personal Finance and Economics

This supplement focuses on the relationship between economics and finance and shows students how they will use economic concepts in their own finances.

Workbook

- Hands-on practice includes questions and activities.
- Organized to follow the textbook lessons to help students achieve key learning outcomes.

Online Learning Suite

- Online student text and workbook, along with rich supplemental content, bring digital learning to the classroom.
- All instructional materials are accessible at home, at school, or on the go.

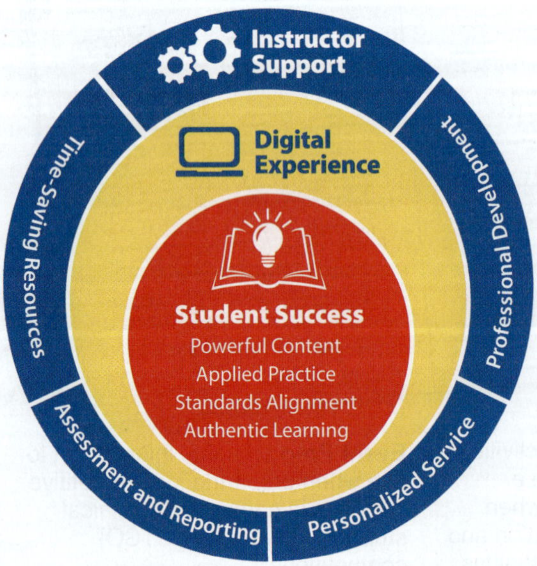

Instructor Tools

LMS Integration

Integrate Goodheart-Willcox content within your Learning Management System for a seamless user experience for both you and your students. LMS-ready content in Common Cartridge® format facilitates single sign-on integration and gives you control of student enrollment and data. With a Common Cartridge integration, you can access the LMS features and tools you are accustomed to using and G-W course resources in one convenient location—your LMS.

G-W Common Cartridge provides a complete learning package for you and your students. The included digital resources help your students remain engaged and learn effectively:

- **Digital Textbook**
- Online **Workbook content**
- **Videos**
- **Animations**
- **Drill and Practice** vocabulary activities

When you incorporate G-W content into your courses via Common Cartridge, you have the flexibility to customize and structure the content to meet the educational needs of your students. You may also choose to add your own content to the course.

For instructors, the Common Cartridge includes the Online Instructor Resources. QTI® question banks are available within the Online Instructor Resources for import into your LMS. These prebuilt assessments help you measure student knowledge and track results in your LMS gradebook. Questions and tests can be customized to meet your assessment needs.

Online Instructor Resources

- The **Instructor Resources** provide instructors with time-saving preparation tools such as answer keys, editable lesson plans, and other teaching aids.
- **Instructor's Presentations for PowerPoint®** are fully customizable, richly illustrated slides that help you teach and visually reinforce the key concepts from each chapter.
- Administer and manage assessments to meet your classroom needs using **Assessment Software with Question Banks**, which include hundreds of matching, completion, multiple choice, and short answer questions to assess student knowledge of the content in each chapter.

See www.g-w.com/foundations-financial-literacy-2024 for a list of all available resources.

Professional Development

- Expert content specialists
- Research-based pedagogy and instructional practices
- Options for virtual and in-person Professional Development

Brief Contents

Contents

Feature Contents

Focus on Finance

Case Study

History of Finance

Economics in Action

Employability Skills

You Do the Math

Exploring Careers

Ethics

UNIT

1 Financial Literacy

Chapters

Financial Literacy

Why It Matters

As a young adult, one of the keys to your success will be learning to manage your personal finances. To be financially capable, you will need to understand topics related to finance, such as making money, spending money, and saving money.

Your financial fitness begins today with identifying the values and goals that are most important to you. These values and goals will direct you in making the right financial decisions and managing your income throughout your lifetime. First, decide what you want most out of life. Then, figure out how to employ your resources to achieve it. Wise economic choices will help you reach your own financial potential and contribute to the stability of our economy.

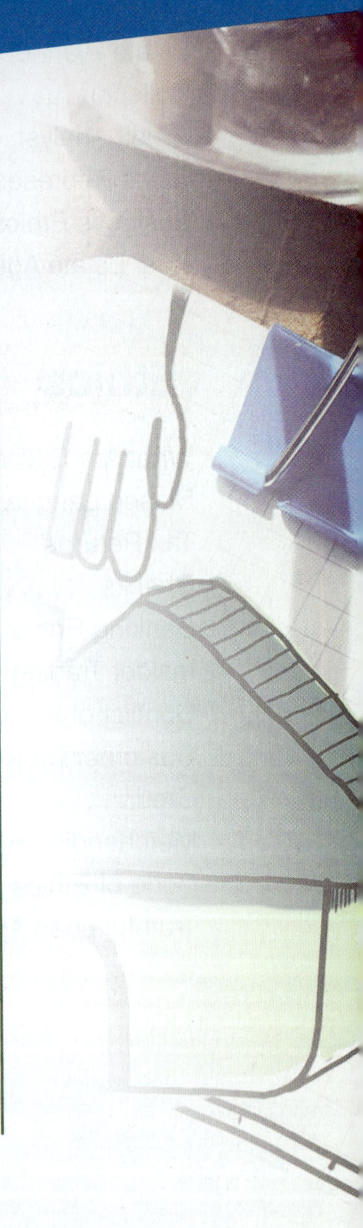

Rawpixel.com/Shutterstock.com

Big Idea

Enjoying financial security throughout life is an achievable goal.

CHAPTER

1 Financial Literacy Basics

One of the most important requirements for making personal finance decisions is knowing yourself. Financially capable individuals are well aware of the differences between needs and wants. Being *financially capable* means having the ability to understand basic topics related to finance, such as wisely making, spending, and saving money.

Values, ethics, and goals lie beneath your everyday decisions and overall behavior. Good management involves using resources (what you have) to reach goals (what you want). Economic decision-making tools include cost-benefit analysis and marginal analysis. Common sense is a decision-making tool as well. It reminds you to live within your means so you can enjoy financial security now and in the future. Making the best use of resources calls for planning, acting on your plan, and evaluating the results.

Focus on Finance

Financial Goals

Setting financial goals is an important step in creating financial independence. Without goals, you may find yourself spending money but not achieving the things that are most important to your well-being. Prioritizing your needs and wants, as well as your values, can help you:

- create a plan for independence;
- handle your income responsibly;
- spend less than you make;
- borrow no more than you can repay; and
- live within your means.

The sooner you put a plan in place, the sooner you can start making wise decisions and be on the road to financial independence and security.

College and Career Readiness

Reading Prep. As you read this chapter, determine the point of view or purpose of the author. What aspects of the text help to establish this purpose or point of view?

Sections

racorn/Shutterstock.com

Section 1.1 Introduction to Financial Literacy

Essential Question

Why is it important to plan your financial future?

Objectives

After studying this section, you will be able to:

- Explain the initial steps for creating a financial plan.
- Discuss the importance of setting goals as a part of financial planning.

Terms

financial literacy	consumer	ethics
personal financial planning	good	priority
financial plan	service	standard
need	values	resource
want	value system	goal

Planning Your Future

Some people always seem to know what they want and where they are going. They seem to know what is important and what is not worth serious attention. This sense of direction and purpose is often a key factor separating the people who achieve what they want from those who do not. The good news is that you can develop this sense of direction and purpose by developing multiple strategies for making choices. Planning your personal finances can help you reach important goals and achieve a sense of financial security over your lifetime.

MBI/Shutterstock.com

People who are financially competent determine the differences between needs and wants and spend accordingly.

To manage money successfully, you need to be educated about money matters. **Financial literacy** is the possession of a body of financial knowledge, a set of basic skills, and the ability to apply knowledge and skills to making informed, responsible financial choices. These financial choices should serve both your interests and the larger community and respond to the ever-changing economic environment.

Personal financial planning is the process of setting financial goals and developing plans to reach them while meeting financial needs.

Employability Skills

Employability skills, or *soft skills*, are the skills used to communicate and work well with others. These skills help an individual find a job, perform well in the workplace, and gain success in a job or career. Some soft skills are acquired through life experience and social interaction. They are not specific to one career and are transferable to any position.

The US Census Bureau reports that a person with a high school degree makes a lifetime average of $1.2 million, while a college graduate can expect lifetime earnings over $2 million. However, no matter how much you earn, you may not meet your financial needs if you do not have a plan for your future. It depends on your goals, expected income, and age. To achieve your goals, financial planning is essential in every phase of life. It is an evolving and ongoing process that can take you from where you are to where you wish to be financially. It is largely a matter of balancing money coming in and money going out over time. Some of the benefits of financial planning are shown in Figure 1-1.

A **financial plan** is an overview of an individual's current financial position and strategies to meet future financial aspirations. Creating a plan starts with analyzing your needs and wants, values, and ethics. It also takes into consideration your personal priorities, standards, and available resources.

Needs and Wants

Needs are necessities a person must have to survive. Examples include physical needs for food, clothing, and shelter. You also have psychological needs for a sense of safety, security, love, acceptance, approval, and success.

Wants are things that a person desires but can live without. For instance, you may want the latest smartphone or a ten-speed racing bike. However, these things are not necessary for your survival.

Benefits of Financial Planning
• Use financial resources effectively • Set and achieve goals for your future • Protect finances by making smart decisions • Achieve and maintain control of your life • Be prepared for emergencies • Accumulate wealth • Enjoy freedom from financial worry

Goodheart-Willcox Publisher

Figure 1-1 Financial planning has many lifelong benefits.

A **consumer** is an individual who purchases goods and services for personal use. **Goods** are *tangible* items that can be touched, used, and purchased, such as food or clothing. **Services** are *intangible* activities that another person usually performs for a fee, such as house cleaning or completing tax returns. Goods and services are purchased to meet a person's needs and wants.

Values

Values are principles and beliefs that a person considers important. They influence the way you live and think as well as your decisions and behavior. Values differ from person to person. Important values for many people relate to family, friends, good health, meaningful work, financial security, and inner peace.

Your values govern and direct your life even if you are unaware of them. Identifying and choosing your values deliberately can give you a sense of direction and control. To identify your values, make a list of things you think are most important in your life today. When you give the list some thought, you will probably find that your family, friends, education, and life experiences all influence your list of values. As you meet new people and have new experiences, what is important to you may change. As life unfolds, your values may change, too. Some become more important and others less so.

Kzenon/Shutterstock.com

A person's family often influences his or her values later in life.

As you make decisions and choices, you eventually create a value system. A **value system** is the overall structure of values and goals that guides a person's behavior and provides a sense of direction in life. For example, good school performance may score high in your value system. If so, you will try to participate in class, complete your homework, and prepare for exams. If loyalty to friends is high in your system, you will help your friends when they need you. If popularity ranks higher than loyalty, you may find it difficult to stand by an unpopular person or cause.

Ethics

Ethics are the moral principles or beliefs that direct a person's behavior. Ethics often conform to accepted standards of right and wrong. Ethical behavior calls for honesty, fairness, reliability, respect, courage, tolerance, civility, and compassion. These and other qualities make our lives with each other peaceful and safe. Ethical behavior is important not only in personal relationships but also in businesses and government.

Unethical behavior is usually considered wrong and is sometimes illegal. It includes things such as cheating on an exam, stealing office supplies from your employer, surfing the Internet on company time, or returning merchandise to a store for a refund after using it.

Financial planning requires the application of ethics and personal responsibility. You have an ethical obligation to plan for your financial future to the best of your ability. Ethical financial planning requires you to earn money for doing honest work. It also requires you to use the money in a way that sustains your life. For example, it would be unethical to incur unnecessary credit card debt without the intention of repaying it. When planning for your future, you should not assume someone else will provide for your health and well-being for the rest of your life. To purposefully avoid work and depend on someone else, or the government, to provide you with food and shelter could be considered unethical.

Priorities

A **priority** is a value or goal that is given more importance than other values and goals. Priorities are set by ranking goals in their order of importance. Identify the things that are important to you and rank each item from most to least important. This helps direct time, energy, and money to whatever you most want to achieve.

Whenever you decide one thing is more important than another, you are making a priority judgment. If you think it is important to enjoy your work, you may choose a job you like rather than a higher-paying job that does not appeal to you.

Some priorities are related to money and financial matters. These can have a major impact on the choices you make as a consumer and in your financial life.

Standards

A **standard** is an established measure of quality, value, or quantity. The word "standard" is used in many ways. Electrical products must meet certain safety standards before they receive a seal of approval. Doctors and lawyers must meet certain professional standards before they can practice.

Case Study *Making Decisions*

Maurice wants the lead in the school play. The problem is that rehearsal will be held two hours each weekday afternoon for the next three months. Getting the lead would make keeping an after-school job impossible. A manager would fill the position with another person, and getting the job back for summer would be highly improbable. No job would mean no money for college tuition.

Considering this is senior year, it is the last chance to be in a high school production. The best actors in the spring play sometimes are chosen for Summer Theater. This often leads to a career in drama, which Maurice has always wanted.

Case Review

1. What is the trade-off of keeping a part-time job?
2. What is the opportunity cost of participating in the play rather than taking a job?
3. What other alternatives might Maurice have?
4. How would you resolve this goal conflict if this were your decision?

Ethics

What Are Ethics?

Ethics are the moral principles or beliefs that direct a person's behavior. Ethics often conform to accepted standards of right and wrong. They are the set of rules that define what is wrong and right. Ethics help people make good decisions in both their personal and professional lives.

You set standards for the way you want to live, what you want to do, and the goods and services you want to buy. These standards depend on your values and goals. They often vary from situation to situation. For instance, if a big, perfect picture is a top priority when you buy a television, you may only settle for the best. Your standards for a TV would be high. If you just want a small TV that fits the corner of a workspace, your standards would call for something smaller and less pricey. Think about situations in which you look for the best and other situations when you just want what is good enough. A clear understanding of your standards in different situations will help you make financial decisions that are right for you.

Resources

A **resource** is a supply of something that can be used when needed. Resources are tools you can use to reach goals. Two types of resources are human and nonhuman resources.

Human resources are internal. They include energy, knowledge, experience, skills, talents, motivation, imagination, and determination. These resources vary greatly from one person to the next. The people in your life often serve as resources, too. Parents, friends, teachers, and neighbors are among the people who may be helpful resources.

Nonhuman resources are external, such as money, time, and equipment. It is easy to overlook some of these resources. People often do not see their possessions as resources or as a means to achieving goals. Consider the resource value of a computer, camera, car, time, and other things available for your use. You often can make use of public resources, such as libraries, parks, recreational facilities, schools, and public transportation.

As you plan the use of your resources, consider the following points.

- *Resources are scarce.* The amount of available time, energy, money, land, and other resources is limited. By planning, you can make the most of them.
- *Resources are manageable.* Resources can be managed to meet specific goals. For example, saving money or using credit lets you buy costly items you cannot purchase with a single paycheck. Planning your errands to follow direct routes and avoid backtracking saves time and fuel. Reading a book when you are on a bus or in a waiting room makes idle time productive.

- *Resources are related to one another.* Multiple resources can be combined to reach a specific goal. For example, you might use both savings and credit to buy a big-ticket item, such as a car. In addition, one resource may be needed to produce or make use of another. You could use your talent and skills to get a job and earn money. Finally, you can use one resource to make up for the lack of another. For example, if you have plenty of time and little money, you can check several stores for the best values before buying.

Everyone has different amounts and types of resources. Identifying all available resources will help you improve your management skills. Practicing good resource management will help you reach your goals.

Goals

After you have analyzed your needs and wants, values, and ethics, you can set goals for your financial plan. A **goal** is an objective to be attained in a specific amount of time. You will set and achieve many financial goals throughout your life. Creating financial goals is necessary so you can manage the money you earn.

You can set goals for almost anything in life. There are different types of goals, such as *to be* goals, *to do* goals, and *to have* goals.

To be goals are related to personality and character. You might want to be smart, popular, entertaining, reliable, relaxed, or competitive. This group of goals also includes career choices. You may want to be a teacher, an airline pilot, a scientist, or an artist. If you consider eventual job security important, completing

michaeljung/Shutterstock.com

After personal needs and wants, values, and ethics have been analyzed, goals can be set for a financial plan.

some type of career preparation program could be an important goal. This goal might motivate you to begin a savings program to pay for job training or higher education. You might also spend extra hours on homework in preparation for further education. Choosing a career is an important aspect of financial goals. Your career enables you to earn an income and live a life that you choose.

To do goals cover the endless list of things you might want to accomplish. You may want to learn to play the piano or speak a foreign language. You may want to go to college, travel, or get a job as soon as possible. You may want to see a particular movie or make the basketball team. These are all *to do* goals. Many of these goals require money, which will influence your financial planning.

To have goals are easy to identify and continually change. You may want to have a new watch, some new clothes, a car, a smartphone, or concert tickets. These goals also include the endless list of routine purchases, such as socks and toothpaste. They may include costly items for which you need to plan and save.

No one has the resources to reach all of his or her goals at one time. You can get the most from your resources by planning how and when to use them. This will help you gain more control over your life and achieve the goals most important to you as early as possible.

It is helpful to identify your goals and to rank them in order of importance. This helps direct time, energy, and money to the goals that are most important to you. As you set and rank your goals, ask yourself the following key questions.

Bullstar/Shutterstock.com

A library is an example of a nonhuman resource that is available at no charge to the community.

- *Is the goal realistic and possible?* Goals should be realistic in order for them to be met. Getting perfect grades is a realistic goal for some, not for others. Buying a car in two years is possible for some, but not for everyone. The important thing is not to let the impossible stand in the way of the possible.
- *Can I break big goals into smaller pieces?* Many goals, especially medium- and long-term goals, can be challenging. Tackle them by breaking them down into smaller, more-achievable goals. For example, saving $500 for summer camp may sound impossible. There are only five months until the money is due. However, you can focus on the smaller goal of saving $100 each month or even $25 each week.
- *Can I measure my progress?* Progress toward a goal should be measurable in dollars, grades, hours, points, or something specific. Otherwise, you do not know how well you are doing. For example, if your goal is to get an A in a class this semester, measure your progress weekly by tracking your grades for homework, quizzes, and exams. If your goal is to buy something, such as a laptop computer, measure your progress by the number of dollars you save. Seeing progress motivates you to continue working hard.

- *What will the goal cost in time, money, and effort?* After thinking it through, you may decide that some objectives are not worth what it takes to achieve them. For example, if you want to start a new business, a careful look at the time and the risks involved might change your mind. At the same time, potential rewards may keep you focused.
- *Will I still want the goal by the time I am able to reach it?* For instance, a high school senior may want a scooter for getting to and from school. If it requires a year or more of savings, the need may vanish by the time the money is available. The need for a car may become more important.

It pays to set worthwhile, realistic goals. Attaining them can give you a sense of satisfaction and accomplishment. Working toward unrealistic goals can cause frustration. Aiming at the impossible can prevent you from reaching what is possible.

Goals often are *interdependent*. This means you have to achieve one goal in order to reach another. For instance, you need to finish high school before going to college. You need to complete training before starting a career. You need to complete driver education before getting a driver's license.

Goals sometimes conflict with one another. For example, Alfonso has $1,200 and can afford to either buy a used car or take a one-week trip with friends. Alfonso must decide which of these conflicting goals has more personal value.

Judy also has conflicting goals. She wants to be on the girls' basketball team, which practices each day after school. At the same time, she wants to keep her part-time job after school. Judy cannot reach both her goals. She must decide which one is more important to her.

Life is full of conflicting goals and difficult choices. When your goals conflict, your priorities and values will help you choose wisely.

Section 1.1 Review

Check Your Understanding

1. What factors should be taken into consideration when creating a financial plan?
2. Name examples of positive ethical behavior.
3. How are priorities set?
4. List the two types of resources that can be used to meet goals.
5. What are three types of goals?

Build Your Vocabulary

As you progress through this course, develop a personal glossary. This will help you build your vocabulary and prepare you for a career. Write a definition for each of the following terms and add it to your glossary.

financial literacy
personal financial planning
financial plan
need
want
consumer
good
service
values
value system
ethics
priority
standard
resource
goal

Section 1.2 Managing Your Personal Finances

Essential Question

Why must financial strategies be applied when making choices about how to spend money?

Objectives

After studying this section, you will be able to:

- Discuss strategies for making financial decisions.
- List the steps used for systematic decision-making.
- Determine how to manage limited resources to reach personal goals.

Terms

financial competence	law of diminishing marginal utility	systematic decision-making
cost-benefit analysis	trade-off	management
marginal benefit	opportunity cost	personal information management (PIM)
marginal cost		

Making Economic Decisions

Every day you make countless decisions. Some are so routine that you hardly use any thought at all. Think about today. Before you left home, you decided when to get up, what to wear, what to eat, when to leave home, and how to get to school.

Think about choices you have made that did not work well for you. You made a promise you could not keep. You scheduled yourself to be in two places at the same time. You ran out of money before payday. Perhaps you acted in one of the following ways.

- *Out of habit.* Do you automatically get the same foods for lunch every day? Do you sit with the same group for lunch? Do you shop in the same stores?
- *On impulse.* Have you bought a pair of shoes on sale, even if they did not really fit? Did you ever go to a movie you did not care to see just because your friends were going?
- *By failing to act.* Have you settled for unemployment by not applying for summer jobs until they were all taken? Have you earned a poor grade by not studying for an exam? Have you been without money when you needed it because you failed to save?

For some choices, these methods work fine. However, mistakes with the major financial decisions in your life carry lasting consequences. Given their importance, these decisions call for systematic choices. **Financial competence** is having the ability to understand basic topics related to finance such as wisely making, spending, and saving money.

Individuals, families, businesses, and government apply multiple strategies when making decisions to satisfy needs and wants. Some of those strategies are cost-benefit analysis, marginal analysis, trade-offs, and opportunity costs. In other situations, sometimes common sense is the best strategy.

Cost-Benefit Analysis

Cost-benefit analysis is a method of weighing the costs against the benefits of an action, a purchase, or a financial decision. It shows that it is in your interest to take an action or make a purchase only if the benefits are at least as great as the costs.

For example, if you want to vacation in a distant place, you may need to decide whether to drive or fly. Flying costs $350 more than driving. It also saves you eight hours of driving time. Is the benefit of saving eight hours worth the cost of $350? The choice depends on the value you place on time saved and on how much money you can comfortably spend. The choice will be different for different people.

You can use cost-benefit analysis to decide whether or not college is worth its cost, whether a new car is worth a higher cost than a good used car, or whether a big wedding is worth its cost compared to the cost of a small, simple wedding. You simply calculate the cost, put a value on the benefits, and compare the results.

In some situations, you will be weighing dollar costs against social, psychological, or emotional benefits. A vacation presents pleasure, time with friends or family, adventure, and new experiences against the costs in time and money. Cost-benefit analysis makes these decisions more rational and well-reasoned.

VGStockStudio/Shutterstock.com

A cost-benefit analysis will help a person decide to take action only if the benefits are worth the costs.

This principle applies to economic decisions of individual consumers, businesses, and governments. It is a strategy to use to make decisions to satisfy needs and wants. Is the benefit worth the cost?

Marginal Analysis

Marginal analysis is also a powerful decision-making tool, particularly in business. It measures the added benefit, versus the added cost, of one more unit of a product. The change in total benefit of using one additional unit is the **marginal benefit**. The change in total cost of using one more unit is the **marginal cost**.

For example, suppose you are hungry and buy an apple. It tastes so good that you buy another and another. Will the second apple bring as much satisfaction as the first one? Probably not, because you are less hungry. The third apple will be even less satisfying. You would probably be willing to pay more for that first apple than for the second, more for the second than for the third. Eventually, you stop eating because you get little or no benefit since your stomach is full.

The economic **law of diminishing marginal utility** states that the marginal benefit of using each additional unit of something tends to decrease as the quantity used increases. The law applies to thrill rides, snacks, movie tickets, and many other experiences and purchases. It is particularly useful in business when measuring the cost of increasing production. By using marginal analysis, businesses can determine the right number of workers needed to maximize their profits. This principle also applies to economic decisions of individual consumers, families, businesses, and governments. It is another strategy used to make decisions to satisfy needs and wants.

Economics in Action

Marginal Analysis

Marginal analysis can help businesses use resources in the best way possible. For example, suppose five workers in a mask factory produce 100 medical-grade masks per day. Each worker makes 20 masks. They cut the material for the different parts of the mask first. Then they sew them together. The sewing room has five heavy-duty machines.

The manager hires two more workers but does not buy new machinery. The manager reasons that time used to cut the material can be done away from the sewing machines. This should leave some machines free for the new workers to sew more masks. The seven workers handle the new work arrangement well and produce 20 masks each, or 140 per day.

This success inspires the manager to add one more worker, but the manager does not get the predicted results. The number of masks produced is only 152, not the 160 expected. Workers averaged only 19 masks apiece. They must stand in line to use equipment, which slows them down. The manager realizes that increasing the total production by only 12 masks daily does not cover the cost of the eighth worker.

Trade-Offs and Opportunity Costs

The choices you make involve trade-offs and opportunity costs. A **trade-off** is the choice you give up when you make one choice over another. **Opportunity cost** is the value of the option you gave up.

When you make a choice, you trade off, or give up, the other choices you could have made. For example, there is a trade-off when you spend $50 to buy a jacket. The trade-off is the other ways the $50 could have been used. When you choose one of two options, the trade-off, or what you give up, is the opportunity cost of the choice you made. It is the consequence of an economic decision.

If you turn down an after-school job because you have to be at soccer practice, there is an opportunity cost. The opportunity cost of playing soccer is the after school job and the money you could have earned. The opportunity cost of working instead of playing soccer would be the pleasure and advantages you get from playing a team sport you love.

Opportunity cost can be measured in terms of dollars, time, enjoyment, or something else of value. The opportunity cost of a decision often varies from one person to the next. It depends on what the person who makes the decision values.

Opportunity costs should be analyzed in terms of spending and saving in order to properly achieve your short-term, medium-term, and long-term goals. Saving for a concert that is coming to town next month is a short-term goal. All spending you make in the next month has an opportunity cost related to saving money for the concert ticket. If you go to a movie with friends, the opportunity cost is the money you could have saved for the concert ticket. To have enough money to purchase a concert ticket, each opportunity cost must be analyzed in terms of how it affects your likelihood of achieving your short-term goal.

Saving money to buy a car in the next two years is a medium-term goal. Since cars cost much more than concert tickets, the consequences of opportunity costs are more significant. Bringing your lunch to school or work provides an opportunity to possibly save hundreds of dollars in two years. The opportunity cost of every purchase affects the likelihood of having enough money to buy the car you wish.

Saving for a home purchase and retirement are long-term goals. The opportunity costs associated with long-term goals can be significant. Buying a new car every two years could result in not saving enough for retirement. Not saving enough for retirement can have serious consequences for your future.

Opportunity cost applies to economic choices of families, businesses, and governments as well as individuals. Weighing opportunity costs is a valuable decision-making tool.

OLJ Studio/Shutterstock.com

The decisions a person makes today will affect personal finances tomorrow.

Common Sense

Even before applying laws of economics to help make financial decisions, one rule is obvious. You do not want to spend more than you can afford. The key to financial well-being is spending less than you earn. Living within your means is the only way to have financial peace of mind.

No matter how much money you have, you cannot afford everything you want. Consequently, you need to establish priorities and plan carefully. Needs should be covered before satisfying wants. If there are family responsibilities, the needs of the family generally come before the wants of individual family members.

Your financial future is in your hands. It pays to develop a clear understanding of your financial situation before making decisions that involve current or future money matters. Today's economic choices determine tomorrow's economic security.

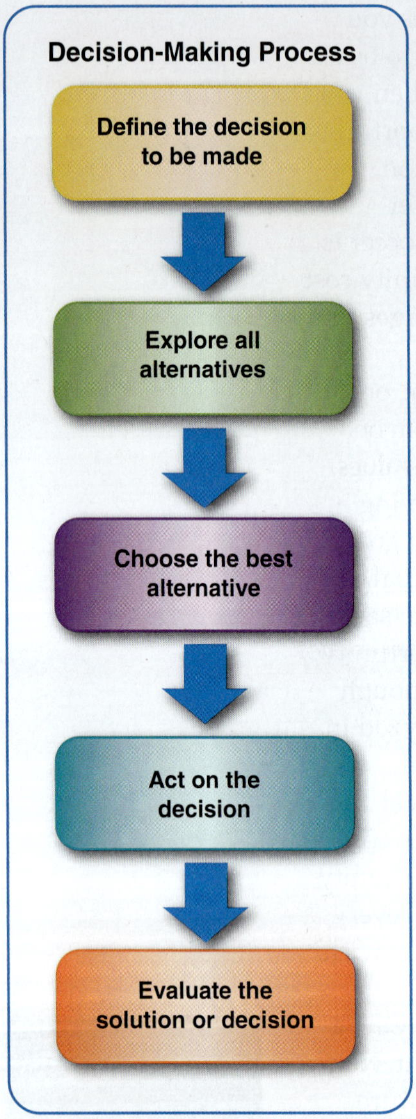

Goodheart-Willcox Publisher

Figure 1-2 The five steps of the decision-making process can be a helpful tool when making decisions.

Systematic Decision-Making

When deciding important matters, a systematic or rational decision-making process can help you arrive at the best course of action. **Systematic decision-making** is a process of choosing a course of action after evaluating available information and weighing the costs and benefits of alternative actions and their consequences. It involves five steps, as shown in Figure 1-2.

1. *Define the decision to be made.* You need a clear idea of the challenge in order to find the best approach. What is the issue? Perhaps you never have time to exercise. Identifying this problem can lead you to set an achievable goal, such as putting aside an hour each day for exercise.
2. *Explore all alternatives.* Analyze possible solutions to your problem. If you need to find an hour to exercise, identify and cut back on time killers. Can you free up an hour by limiting your Internet surfing and TV watching? Can you rearrange your schedule to gain time? Is there an after-school activity you can drop, or can you combine some of your activities?
3. *Choose the best alternative.* After considering all alternatives, decide which one best fits your situation. It may be one alternative or some combination.
4. *Act on the decision.* Carry out your plan. For example, if you decide to rearrange your schedule, write a plan for the new routine. Follow it for a few days to see how it works. You may need to make some adjustments. If you decide to limit phone time, it may help to tell friends when you will be taking calls and when you will not be available. Find reminders and aids to help you stick to your new schedule.
5. *Evaluate the solution or decision.* Evaluation is an ongoing process. As you carry out your plan, evaluate your progress toward your intended goal. Is the plan of action working? How can you improve it? The evaluation process can help you stay on track and make better future decisions.

Managing Resources

Managing personal finances requires that you manage the use of your resources to the best of your ability. **Management** is the process of organizing and using resources to achieve predetermined objectives. Whether you run a big corporation, an average household, or your own personal affairs, you need management skills to get things done. Management skills put you in control. You make the decisions. You carry them out. You benefit from the right choices and occasionally suffer from the mistakes.

Using a management system can help you manage human and nonhuman resources that are available for your use. **Personal information management (PIM)** is a system that individuals use to acquire, organize, maintain, retrieve, and use information. An example of a PIM system is Microsoft Outlook in which an individual can keep a schedule, record contact information, and complete other activities that help organize personal information. It helps users manage tasks, as well as personal responsibilities, to help manage resources.

Using systematic decision-making is an important part of management. However, management involves more than making decisions and solving problems. There are stages of management that must be applied, which include planning, action, and evaluation.

Planning

"A job well planned is a job half done." This familiar saying points out the importance of planning. Whether you want to reach a career goal or find a summer job, you need a plan. This applies to almost anything you want to achieve. For example, deciding what to wear to school may involve very little conscious planning. Choosing what to wear to a wedding or a job interview takes more thought. Building an appropriate wardrobe for your lifestyle can be a major planning challenge.

The planning phase of management involves identifying goals, obstacles, and resources. Consider these questions:

- What goals do you want to have or achieve?
- What obstacles stand between you and your goals? What must you overcome?
- What resources can you use to overcome the obstacles and reach your goals?

Figure 1-3 shows two goals and a plan for accomplishing each one. Listed with each goal are the obstacles and resources related to it. Try putting together a similar plan for achieving something you want, such as a summer job, racing bike, or part in your school play.

Action

Planning is of little value without action. Action involves putting your resources to work to overcome the obstacles that stand between you and your goals. Success depends on two key personal characteristics—determination and flexibility.

Determination keeps you focused on the final goal and helps you stick with the project to the end. Determination is especially necessary when things are not going so well. When working on a tough math assignment, you may feel like giving up. Determination keeps you working until the problem is solved.

Flexibility helps you adjust to new and unexpected situations. It helps you find ways to revise and improve your plans. Imagine that you have two goals for the weekend: earning money for a camping trip and writing a book report. You have a babysitting job on Saturday and plan to spend Sunday afternoon on the book report.

Goal Planning		
Goal	**Obstacles**	**Available Resources**
Plan #1 **Complete an English assignment on time**	• Time limitations • Lack of interest in the topic • Difficulty getting started • Tough grading by the English instructor	• Two free hours after school each day • Public library reference room • Knowledge of the topic and where to go for information • Detailed instructions from the English instructor • Writing and computer skills • Computer • Determination to finish on time and get a good grade
Plan #2 **Become president of the student body**	• Popularity of the other candidates • Difficulty in contacting all the voters • Limited time before the election • Lack of organization among supporters	• Knowledge of the job and its demands • Experience in student government • Organizational skills • Public speaking skills • Reputation for leadership • Energy and enthusiasm for planning and running the campaign • Knowledge of what the voters want • Broad support from both the student body and the faculty • Friends who are willing to help run the campaign • Use of school computers and graphics programs • Desire to win

Goodheart-Willcox Publisher

Figure 1-3 Listing goals, obstacles, and resources will help give perspective on what can be accomplished.

When you are called to babysit for much longer than expected, you revise your plans. You write the report while babysitting when the children are asleep. This frees time for something else on Sunday. Flexibility can work to your advantage in all kinds of situations.

Evaluation

Evaluation is a continuous process. When you evaluate a plan of action, you assess your progress as you go through all stages of the management process. What worked? What did not? How could you make it better next time? Evaluation also improves your management skills for future projects. Ongoing evaluation can help you develop better ways of using resources to reach goals. Consider the successes and failures in your planning. How can you do better in the future? Figure 1-4 illustrates the process of evaluation.

Process of Evaluation		
Evaluating Plans	**Evaluating Actions**	**Evaluating Results**
• What are the goals? • What obstacles stand in the way? • What resources are needed? • Are the needed resources available? • Are the goals realistic, given the obstacles and resources? • Are the goals worth the effort and resources required to attain them?	• Is the plan working? • Is there steady progress toward the goals? • Are resources being used to their best advantage? • Are top priority goals getting top priority attention? • Is there room for improvement in the original plans? What adjustments can be made? • Have new or unexpected developments created the need to change the original plans? What changes are needed?	• Were the goals achieved? • Was achieving the goals worth the effort and resources used? • Are the results satisfactory? • What key factors contributed to reaching or failing to reach the goals? • What were the weaknesses in the plans and actions? What were the strengths? • How can future plans be improved?

Goodheart-Willcox Publisher

Figure 1-4 Evaluation is an important stage of the management process.

Section 1.2 Review

Check Your Understanding

1. What are some of the *unplanned* ways people make decisions?
2. List four strategies that individuals, families, businesses, and government apply when making financial decisions.
3. What are the five steps in systematic decision-making?
4. Name three stages of management.
5. What two personal characteristics are key in reaching goals?

Build Your Vocabulary

As you progress through this course, develop a personal glossary. This will help you build your vocabulary and prepare you for a career. Write a definition for each of the following terms and add it to your glossary.

- financial competence
- cost-benefit analysis
- marginal benefit
- marginal cost
- law of diminishing marginal utility
- trade-off
- opportunity cost
- systematic decision-making
- management
- personal information management (PIM)

Section 1.3 Financial Influencers

Essential Question

What factors influence your financial future?

Objectives

After studying this section, you will be able to:

- Identify and explain factors that impact an individual's financial future.
- Discuss how the government influences the economy.
- Explain how globalization influences a person's finances.

Terms

economic condition	demographics	media
recession	culture	entitlement
inflation	technology	globalization
interest		

Your Financial Future

There are many important factors and forces that influence your financial life now and in the future. Government actions and advancing globalization affect personal finances as well. Individually and together, these factors will cause you to redefine your financial needs, priorities, and goals over time. Some of these factors include economic conditions, demographics, culture, and changing technology.

Economic Conditions

Economic conditions are the state of the economy at a given time. When the economy is on the upswing, people are generally optimistic. Businesses make money, grow, and hire more workers. People who want to work can find good jobs. Their future income is fairly secure and they can pay their bills. If they plan carefully, they can save and invest for the future. However, when the economy is plagued by economic conditions, such as recession, inflation, or interest rates going up or down, managing personal finances becomes important and challenging.

Recession is a period of slow or no economic growth. It can have a major impact on personal money management. This is especially true for those who are out of work or whose incomes are stagnant. Recessions spread uncertainty and pessimism over the entire economy. Consumers spend less and save more if possible. Businesses cut back and unemployment rises.

Inflation is a period of rising prices. It also relates to personal money management. As prices go up, the value of a dollar goes down. If income does not rise at the same rate that prices rise, buying power is reduced. Consumers cannot buy or save as much. Sound financial planning and saving can help you cope with challenging economic conditions.

Interest is the amount that is paid for using money. When money is deposited into a bank, the bank pays the depositor interest. The bank then takes that money and loans it to other consumers. Those who borrow that money pay the bank interest for using that money. If interest rates are high for borrowing money, consumers borrow less, which means they spend less.

Demographics

To some extent, the way you manage your money and your life in the years ahead will depend on demographics. **Demographics** are the statistical characteristics of a population. Vital statistics include records of births, deaths, and marriages. Social statistics include population breakdowns by age, sex, and race with geographic distributions and growth rates. Other socioeconomic statistics include education levels, income levels, employment, religion, crime, immigration, and ethnic representation. Consider some of the following trends and their economic implications.

- Couples are marrying and having children later in life.
- The percentage of single-parent families is growing.
- The average age of the overall population is increasing.
- Educational requirements for jobs are rising, and job markets are changing.
- Skilled workers are in greater demand.

Exploring Careers

Personal Financial Advisor

Personal financial advisors give financial advice to help clients plan for short- and long-term goals, such as saving for college and retirement. They recommend savings and investments choices to match their clients' goals. Personal financial advisors typically:

- discuss financial goals and money needs with clients
- answer questions about savings and investment options and potential risks
- recommend investment options to clients
- help clients plan for their financial futures
- monitor clients' accounts and determine if changes are needed
- research investment opportunities

Personal financial advisors often work at brokerage firms, banks, or insurance companies. They typically work full time and may meet with clients in the evenings or on weekends. The work is fast-paced and requires the advisor to stay current on financial products and tax laws.

A bachelor's degree in finance or a related area is usually required, and a master's degree and certification will increase chances for advancement. Advisors must be excellent communicators. Math and computer skills are essential, while attention to detail and initiative are also important traits.

- More young adults are living at home with their parents.
- The number of unmarried adults is increasing.
- More mothers are working away from home.
- The number of births to single mothers is increasing.

The US Census Bureau is a good place to look for the latest demographic statistics. Recent demographic trends have an impact on the overall economy and, in turn, on the financial life of individual consumers.

Culture

Most communities include a variety of racial and ethnic groups. Each group makes an impact on consumer attitudes and buying habits, community services, schools, and many other consumer and family issues. Relationships and marriages between people of different races, cultures, and religions are on the increase. This creates a blending of ethnic traditions, religious beliefs, languages, and concepts of family.

Culture is the beliefs, behaviors, and other characteristics common among members of a group or society. Cultural and ethnic traditions affect many everyday choices and routines. They may dictate the role each person plays in the family, who makes financial and spending decisions, whether both partners work, how the family uses credit, and how the family manages its money.

Kobby Dagan/Shutterstock.com

Culture may influence the way a person makes financial decisions.

Technology

Odua Images/Shutterstock.com

Media has a significant impact on the financial decisions people make.

New developments and discoveries in communication, medicine, science, and other areas change the way we live in the world and the economic decisions we make. For example, medical advances may result in longer, healthier lives for you and others. New findings on healthful lifestyles include fitness routines, nutritious diets, and stress reduction. You now know how to improve your own health and quality of life. However, living longer makes financial planning even more critical. Your savings must sustain you over a longer period of time.

Technology is the application of science and research to human life and environments. Technology brings changes in the way you live and deal with financial matters. Advanced technology creates new markets as well as provides more and cheaper goods and services for consumers. It also creates jobs in many new lines of work.

Technology has fueled *offshore outsourcing* in some fields. This is the business practice of moving factories and jobs overseas and across borders to take advantage of cheap labor and business-friendly government regulations. As a result, many American workers must compete for jobs with lower-paid workers in other countries. This situation has caused layoffs and unemployment, especially among those who work in manufacturing and information technology industries. Today and in the future, the higher-paying jobs will require higher levels of education and training. The right education has never been more important than in today's economy.

Media is forms of communication designed to reach a large number of people. Examples of media include television, radio, and the Internet. *Social media* refers to websites and apps that allow individual users to network online by creating and sharing content with one another. Media impacts individual, family, business, and government decisions by providing information for making financial decisions. It provides the latest information from around the world about consumer products, services, and issues. Consumers can compare prices, opportunities, and ways to spend money wisely without leaving home.

Consumers are able to take control of their finances through management apps downloaded on a phone, tablet, or computer. Apps are used to manage savings accounts, online banking, stock trades, and budgets. Often free, these apps enable consumers to have control of their finances as well as become more independent and wiser about financial decisions.

You Do the Math

Numeric Reasoning

Real numbers are all whole and fractional or decimal numbers on a continuous number line that are not imaginary. *Whole numbers* are numbers with no fractional or decimal portion. *Decimals* are numbers with digits to the right of the decimal point. An *imaginary number* is any number that results in a negative number when squared. An imaginary number always includes the notation *i*, such as 2i.

To add a positive number, move to the right on the number line. To subtract a positive number, move to the left on the number line.

Solve the following problems.

1. 5.87 + 4.956 + 2.011 + 4 =
2. 34 + 9 – 127 + 783 =
3. 112.058 + 2.1 + 93.237 =
4. 987 + 705 + 827 + 4 =
5. 73 + 8 – 12 =

Government and the Economy

It would be difficult to overstate the impact of government policies on the economy and, in turn, on consumers. Fiscal and monetary policies affect prices and wages, availability and cost of credit, job opportunities and employment trends, growth and international trade, and a host of other economic conditions.

In the area of consumer information, very few sources can provide more complete information than the government. An example is the Federal Trade Commission (FTC), which serves as a protector of both consumer and business rights. On its website, you will see the phrase "Protecting America's Consumers" as it provides important information, much of which can assist you in financial planning and money management.

Government programs provide direct public assistance for many people. An **entitlement** is a government program that provides financial benefits to eligible citizens based on their legal rights. Examples of entitlement programs include Medicaid, Medicare, and Social Security. These programs are called entitlements because as long as a citizen meets the eligibility requirements, he or she has a legal right to receive the program's benefits.

Assistance from entitlement programs plays an important role in personal financial planning for most citizens. Federal budgets typically change from year to year, as a result of the evolving economy. In recent years, these programs have represented over 60 percent of the federal budget.

However, as changes in these programs and tax laws occur, citizens will need to adjust their financial plans. Financial planning plays an important role in balancing the dependence on government programs and building future financial security.

Globalization and Your Finances

Globalization, with all its pros and cons, is today's reality. **Globalization** is the worldwide spread and integration of production, markets, communications, and technology. Your financial and consumer interests are linked to global trade and international economics. On the positive side, globalization gives you access to a vast diversity of goods and services through worldwide markets. News, entertainment, and information travel in seconds to every corner of the globe. Money is equally mobile.

Business competition on a global scale can bring price and quality advantages for consumers. The local and outside world links economic and cultural changes. Take a walk through your own home to see how many products, foods, music downloads, and furnishings came from other nations. As products, services, and ideas flow from country to country, you will have opportunities to share common experiences and to understand people from backgrounds and cultures different from your own.

Living in a global economy can bring job opportunities if you prepare to meet the demand in current job markets. It can be devastating for those whose job skills are no longer in demand or whose jobs have moved to other countries. As a young person entering the workforce, you will be competing with workers around the globe. You can benefit by getting the best training and education possible to meet the needs of current and future job markets.

Section 1.3 Review

Check Your Understanding

1. List four factors that impact an individual's financial future.
2. What economic conditions make managing personal finances important and challenging?
3. How does media impact financial decisions made by individuals, families, businesses, and the government?
4. Provide an example of an entitlement program.
5. How does globalization affect job opportunities as a person enters the workforce?

Build Your Vocabulary

As you progress through this course, develop a personal glossary. This will help you build your vocabulary and prepare you for a career. Write a definition for each of the following terms and add it to your glossary.

economic condition
recession
inflation
interest
demographics
culture
technology
media
entitlement
globalization

Review and Assessment

Chapter Summary

Section 1.1 Introduction to Financial Literacy

- Financial literacy is the possession of a body of financial knowledge, a set of basic skills, and the ability to apply knowledge and skills to make informed, responsible financial choices. Personal financial planning means setting financial goals and creating plans to achieve them. In order to begin planning and managing personal finances, it is important for a person to analyze personal needs, wants, values, and ethics. Personal priorities, standards, and available resources are also important factors to consider when making financial decisions.
- Setting financial goals can help a person achieve wants and needs in life. Common types of goals include *to be* goals, *to do* goals, and *to have* goals. It is important to evaluate goals as they are set and achieved over a person's lifetime.

Section 1.2 Managing Your Personal Finances

- Individuals, families, businesses, and governments apply multiple strategies when making decisions to satisfy needs and wants. Some of those strategies are cost-benefit analysis, marginal analysis, trade-offs, and opportunity costs. In other situations, sometimes common sense is the best strategy.
- By applying systematic decision-making, the best course of action can be chosen. The five steps in systematic decision-making are: define the decision to be made; explore all alternatives; choose the best alternative; act on the decision; and evaluate the solution or decision.
- Management is the process of organizing and using resources to achieve predetermined objectives. Using a personal information management system can help an individual manage tasks, as well as personal responsibilities. Using systematic decision-making is an important part of management as well as planning, action, and evaluation.

Section 1.3 Financial Influencers

- Factors and forces that influence an individual's financial future include economic, social, cultural, and technological forces. Governmental actions and advancing globalization affect personal finances as well.
- Governmental policies affect prices and wages, availability and cost of credit, employment opportunities and trends, growth and international trade, and a host of other economic conditions.
- Globalization is the worldwide spread and integration of production, markets, communications, and technology. Consumers have access to goods and services sold all over the globe. The increase in competition makes pricing and product quality more advantageous for the consumer. However, there is increased competition in current job markets as well.

Review Your Knowledge

1. Describe the initial steps for creating a financial plan.
2. Summarize the role of ethics and personal responsibility in financial planning.
3. Discuss the importance of setting goals as a part of financial planning.
4. What is one common sense rule that can be applied to financial decisions?
5. How can limited resources be managed to reach personal goals?
6. How do recessions affect the economy?
7. How are consumers affected by inflation?

8. Describe how the government influences the economy.
9. Explain the effect of offshore outsourcing on American workers.
10. Explain how globalization influences a person's finances.

Apply Your Knowledge

1. Financial planning provides benefits for families and individuals in personal ways. Name two personal benefits that you can experience through financial planning. Why are these benefits important to you?
2. As you enter the adult world, a financial plan is necessary to satisfy your individual needs and wants. Consider the values, ethics, and standards important to your life. How does this knowledge enable you to develop strategies for satisfying your needs and wants? Make a list of multiple strategies you currently use to make choices. Describe how you have applied one or more of these strategies to meet a need or want.
3. Families also need a financial plan in order to meet the needs and wants of their members. Which strategies can a family develop to satisfy needs and wants? How are these strategies impacted by the values, ethics, and standards of the family?
4. Identify three needs that you must regularly satisfy on your own. An example might be food, transportation, or money for school supplies. Which strategy, such as cost-benefit analysis, trade-off, opportunity cost, or marginal analysis, do you use to satisfy each need?
5. In many cases of problem solving, a process similar to the systematic decision-making process is used. This process typically includes steps such as identifying the problem, gathering information, listing and considering the options, considering advantages and disadvantages, choosing and implementing a solution, and evaluating the effectiveness of the solution. How can you apply the systematic decision-making process to help you solve problems?
6. Multiple strategies can be used when making decisions to satisfy needs and wants. Some of those strategies are cost-benefit analysis, marginal analysis, trade-offs, and opportunity costs. Select a need or want that a family may wish to satisfy. Explain how each of the strategies can be applied to analyze if and how the need or want can be met.
7. Being *financially capable* means having the ability to understand basic topics related to finance such as wisely making, spending, and saving money. Create a chart with three columns. Label the columns *Making Money*, *Spending Money*, and *Saving Money*. In each column, write bullet points on actions you can take to meet each objective in a responsible manner. Name your chart *Financial Capability Plan*. As you progress through this text, add new ideas that you learn as you read the chapters.
8. Individuals must take responsibility for the financial decisions they make. Describe the consequences that a person might experience if a decision relating to finances is made hastily without weighing the outcome.
9. Media influences consumer decisions in many ways. Make a list of the ways that television, the Internet, or other media influences decisions you make as an individual consumer. Next, make another list of media influences on family decisions. Discuss why you think the impact of media is positive in some instances and negative in other instances when making decisions.

10. Technology influences how families and consumers make decisions. Name four technological changes that have happened in your lifetime that made an impact on how we live as a society. Analyze how these changes influence your decision-making as well as that of your family. What do you think will be the next big technology advance that will change the way you meet your own needs and wants?

Apply Your Math Skills

1. Joe has $500 in spending money for the fall semester and needs to buy new athletic shoes for gym class. A plain pair costs $30 while a brand-name pair costs $75. Joe also wants $25 a week to buy lunch in the cafeteria every day. If the semester is 18 weeks long, can Joe afford to buy the name-brand shoes and eat in the cafeteria every day?
2. Alana has a summer job opportunity at a local day camp for young children. The job requires 30 hours of work per week for 10 weeks and pays $8 an hour after taxes. If Alana does not take the job, the summer is free for doing other fun activities with friends. What is the opportunity cost of not taking the job?

Communication Skills

College and Career Readiness

Reading. *Skimming* means to quickly glance through an entire document. Skimming will give you a preview of the material to help your comprehension when you read the chapter. You should notice headings, key words, phrases, and visual elements. The goal is to identify the main idea of the content. Skim this chapter. Provide an overview of what you read.

Speaking. Participate in a collaborative classroom discussion about financial competence. Ask questions that connect your ideas to the relevant evidence that has been presented.

Writing. Generate ideas for writing a paper that describes the concept of personal finance as you interpret it. Gather information to support your thoughts and ideas. Keep careful and accurate records of any sources that you use as references. Create the notes that you could use to write a paper to distribute for discussion with your classmates.

Teamwork

Working with a teammate, discuss how the decision-making process might help in establishing local, state, and federal governmental policies and budgets. Create a chart and list your ideas. Share your findings with your class. Relate the discussion to actual issues where possible.

Internet Research

Personal Information Management (PIM). Using the Internet, research personal information management (PIM) systems. Identify a system that would work for you. Explain how you can apply a PIM system to your daily schedule to help you plan, manage, and organize tasks and personal responsibilities.

Cost-Benefit Analysis. Paying for college can be a huge expense. Many college students receive grants, scholarships, and loans that help with costs. However, for this exercise, assume that you and your parents will be paying the entire cost. A number of websites, such as the College Board, offer online calculators that provide estimates of college costs. Use one of these sites to determine how much money you will need for college. Determine how much money you will need to save per month. Weigh these costs against the benefits of a college education.

Portfolio Development

College and Career Readiness

Overview. When applying for a job, a volunteer position, or entry into an educational institution, one way to demonstrate your qualifications is to present a portfolio to the interviewer. A *portfolio* is a selection of related materials that you collect and organize to demonstrate your job qualifications, skills, and talents. For example, a certification showing you have completed Microsoft Office Specialist training could help you get into an IT program. A portfolio is a *dynamic document*, which means it should be reviewed and updated regularly.

Visual artists and communication professionals have historically presented portfolios of their creative work when seeking jobs or admission to educational institutions. However, portfolios are now used in many professions. It is helpful to research and identify which type is appropriate for the industry in which you are interested in working after your educational career has ended.

Commonly used formats for a portfolio are print and electronic. A *print portfolio* is a hard-copy version that can be carried to an interview. It can be presented in a three-ring binder with divider tabs or any other method that works for you. An *electronic portfolio* is a digital version of a print portfolio. It can be saved to cloud-based storage services or flash drives. There are many creative ways to present an electronic portfolio. The method you choose should allow the viewer to navigate and find items easily. It is beneficial to have both types when applying to a school or for employment.

1. Research *Types of Portfolios* and select the one that is most appropriate for you and your career goals.
2. Consider and plan for the technology that might be needed for creating and scanning documents for an electronic portfolio. You may need access to desktop-publishing software, scanners, cameras, and other digital equipment or software.

CTSOs

Event Prep

Student Organizations. Career and technical student organizations (CTSOs) are a valuable asset to any educational program. These organizations support student learning and the application of skills learned in real-world situations. Competitive events may be written, oral, or a combination of both. There is a variety of organizations from which to select, depending on the goals of your educational program.

To prepare for any competitive event, complete the following activities.

1. Go to the website of your organization to find specific information for the events. Visit the site often as information changes quickly. If the organization has an app, download it to your digital device.
2. Read all the organization's guidelines closely. These rules and regulations must be strictly followed, or disqualification can occur.
3. Communication plays a role in all the competitive events, so read which communication skills are covered in the event you select. Research and preparation are important keys to a successful competition.
4. Select one or two events that are of interest to you. Print the information for the events and discuss your interest with your instructor.

CHAPTER

2 Personal Financial Planning

The first step toward a plan for financial security is the establishment of financial goals. Determining short-term and long-term financial goals can help you create a budget to keep your earnings and spending on target. Learning to follow a budget can bring you personal and financial satisfaction.

When you enter the adult world, your money management needs will grow. Many independent young adults face new financial responsibilities. Developing the skills to handle them now will pay off in the future.

Keep in mind that even with the most competent money management practices, you may face financial difficulties in the future. It is important to know how to prepare for possible problems and to deal with a financial crisis should the need arise.

Focus on Finance

Budgets

Where do you want to be financially in ten years? Can you see yourself owning a car and living in your own house? Will you have a great career and be on your way to financial security? In order to meet your goals, you will need to learn how to manage your personal finances.

Budgeting is one way to get started on the path to financial independence. Budgeting can help you:

- stay out of debt;
- pay your bills on time;
- create a savings account;
- finance your education; and
- buy a car.

Start budgeting today in order to have the future you want tomorrow.

College and Career Readiness

Reading Prep. Before you begin reading this chapter, consider how the author developed and presented information. How does the information in this chapter provide a foundation for the next chapter?

Sections

seyomedo/Shutterstock.com

Section 2.1 Personal Financial Landscape

Essential Question

Why is it important to create and maintain a budget?

Objectives

After studying this section, you will be able to:

- Identify steps to develop a budget based on personal goals.
- Explain how to create personal financial statements.
- Discuss the benefits of creating a good recordkeeping system for financial documents.
- Explain how money management software can assist in financial planning.

Terms

life span	discretionary expense	net worth
nature of financial planning	pay yourself first	asset
budget	wealth	liability
spreadsheet	emergency fund	net worth statement
income	charity	liquidity
expense	social responsibility	recordkeeping
fixed expense	data analysis	legal document
variable expense	discretionary income	money management software
	cash flow statement	

Budgets

In Chapter 1, you learned about the importance of financial planning. Planning allows you to meet changing needs and goals over your life span. A **life span** is the time between birth and death. Creating a financial plan helps you manage your personal finances throughout your life span and learn to achieve economic self-sufficiency.

The **nature of financial planning** is the development of a strategy to meet a person's financial needs over the course of a lifetime. Creating a financial plan is an important aspect of financial planning. A financial plan demonstrates an individual's ability to apply money management strategies. A first step in developing a financial plan begins with creating a budget. A **budget** is a plan for the use of money over time based on goals, expenses, and expected income. A budget can be of benefit by helping you make the most of your money and avoid financial problems. It is the tool that lets you take control of your finances. Planning helps you meet daily needs and achieve your future goals as well and maintain economic self-sufficiency.

You may choose to use a spreadsheet to create your budget. A **spreadsheet** is a software program that formats data in columns and rows and can perform calculations. Spreadsheets enable a computer to be used as a tool to enter, calculate, and analyze information.

Complete the steps that follow to create a budget tailored to your income and needs. These steps can help you create a simple, workable budget.

Step 1: Establish Financial Goals

Well-thought-out goals can help you direct your dollars to those things you consider most important. A goal can be short term, medium term, or long term. A *short-term goal* is a goal that you want to reach today or next week or in two or three months. For instance, saving money for a new camera may take a month or more. A *medium-term goal*, such as buying a car, may take one to three years to achieve. A *long-term goal*, such as completing school, starting a business, getting married, or buying a house, may take several years to achieve.

Make a list of your important personal financial goals. Include short-, medium-, and long-term goals, as shown in Figure 2-1. For example, having money for a movie this weekend is a fairly immediate goal. Saving for a ten-day camping trip next year is a medium-term goal. Paying for a new car or future education are long-term goals that require saving over a period of time.

Step 2: Estimate and Total Your Income

Determine if your budget period should be weekly, biweekly, or monthly. This will depend on when you receive most of your income. **Income** is any form of money received, such as an allowance, a paycheck, gifts, and gains from an investment. If you receive money weekly, it makes sense to budget on a weekly basis. If you receive a regular monthly paycheck and pay monthly bills, it may be easier to work with monthly figures.

Estimate your income for the budget period. Using a worksheet similar to the one in Figure 2-2, estimate how much money you normally receive from each source of income. Each amount will be recorded in the Income section of the worksheet in the Estimated column. If you are using a spreadsheet, enter a formula to sum the sections. If you are using a handwritten budget, use a calculator to total the amounts.

Financial Goals		
Short-Term	**When Wanted**	**Estimated Cost**
Boots	In 2 months	$ 65
Holiday gifts	In 3 months	$ 100
Summer trip	In 9 months	$ 350
Medium-Term	**When Wanted**	**Estimated Cost**
Laptop computer	In 1 year	$ 500
Used car	In 2 years	$ 6,000
Long-Term	**When Wanted**	**Estimated Cost**
College expenses	In 5 years	$32,000

Goodheart-Willcox Publisher

Figure 2-1 Organizing goals helps a person focus on spending plans.

Employability Skills

Humility

Humility means being modest. A person who possesses humility does not judge other people as less important or competent. Possessing humility does not mean to be meek or have diminished self-esteem or self-image. Instead, it means treating people respectfully, being confident in one's abilities, and behaving as a professional. When soft skills are mastered, some aspects of humility naturally happen. For example, simply saying "thank you" to someone demonstrates humility.

Step 3: Estimate and Total Your Expenses

After calculating income, estimate typical expenses per budget period. An **expense** is the cost of goods and services purchased. Generally, expenses will be either fixed or variable.

A **fixed expense** is a set amount that must be paid each budget period. These expenses may include items such as rent or mortgage payments, tuition, insurance premiums, or loan payments. Fixed expenses tend to increase in number and amount as you move into adult life. As a rule, fixed expenses must be paid when due. Therefore, it is important to list them first.

A **variable expense** is a cost that changes both in the amount and time it must be paid. Variable expenses include items such as food, clothing, and entertainment. These expenses may be necessary or discretionary. A **discretionary expense** is an amount spent for an item that a person could do without. For example, food is a necessary item. However, the cost of a dinner in an upscale restaurant is a discretionary expense. When you are short of cash, discretionary expenses offer the best opportunities for adjusting your spending.

Each month, you will likely purchase different items for personal use. Purchases should be identified and prioritized. Essential purchases are for items needed during the budget period. Nonessential purchases are for items you would like to have, but can wait if needed.

Essential purchases are the first priority. They include items needed for family, school, work, and overall well-being. A textbook needed for a class is an essential purchase and should take priority over a new pair of jeans that are currently on sale. After essential purchases are identified and prioritized, money remaining in the budget can be used for nonessential purchases. If there is not enough money left in the budget for nonessential purchases, they should wait until another budget period.

At this point in your life, you may receive basic necessities from your family or guardians and spend your money mainly on discretionary items, such as music, cell phone data, computer games, and movies. For adults, discretionary expenses often include vacations, gifts, expensive clothing, and other unnecessary goods and services.

Using the worksheet in Figure 2-2 as a guide, list each estimated fixed and variable expense in the Expenses section. Then enter the amount you spend on each one and total the sections. You may want to star discretionary items and start with them if you need to reduce your expenses.

Budget
Courtney Acorinti
Budget period ____________________

		Estimated		Actual	Variance
Income					
	Jobs				
	Babysitting	$25			
	Yard work	40			
	After-school job	200			
	Allowance	40			
	Gifts	10			
	Total Income		$315		
Expenses					
	Fixed Expenses				
	Bus pass	$15			
	Lunches	90			
	Savings	15			
	Total Fixed Expenses		$120		
	Variable Expenses				
	Snacks	$20			
	Movies/concerts/events	40			
	Clothes	50			
	Music downloads	25			
	Gifts	20			
	Magazines	15			
	Personal care products	25			
	Total Variable Expenses		$195		
	Total Expenses		$315		

Goodheart-Willcox Publisher

Figure 2-2 Estimated income and expenses should be entered in the estimated column of the budget.

Budgeting for Savings

In order to have cash available for unexpected emergencies, savings should be included in your budget. **Pay yourself first** is a personal financial strategy that can help you save money. By paying yourself first and putting money aside for saving, you begin building wealth for your future. The term **wealth** means an abundance of money and other assets.

Saving money is needed for major purchases and medium- and long-term goals. It is also necessary to save money to use in the event of a financial emergency. An **emergency fund** is an amount of money that can be easily accessed in case of a job layoff, illness, or unexpected expense.

It is a good idea to include savings as a fixed expense in your budget. For example, if you wish to take a camping trip in five months, estimate how much money you will need. If the trip will cost $360, figure out how much you will need to save per month or per week to pay for the trip.

- To calculate the monthly savings required, divide $360 by 5. You will need to save $72 each month.
- To calculate the weekly savings required, divide $360 by 20, the number of weeks in five months. You will need to save $18 per week.

This method can be used to plan for any expense if you know the amount you need and when you need it. When you build savings into your budget, you will be better able to deal with unexpected expenses and to reach important goals in your future. Paying yourself first is a strategy that can be used throughout your life span to help assure you have money for the things that you need.

Charitable Giving as an Expense

A **charity** usually refers to an organization that aids those in need, such as the homeless or victims of natural disasters. A *charitable contribution* is a donation of money or other property. According to the IRS, "a charitable contribution is a donation or gift to, or for the use of, a qualified organization. It is voluntary and is made without getting, or expecting to get, anything of equal value."

One benefit of making charitable contributions is a tax deduction on an individual's income tax return. Tax deductions can be made on an income tax return if the contribution meets specific standards set by the IRS. Taxes and tax deductions are covered in detail in Chapter 3.

FashionStock.com/Shutterstock.com

Philanthropy can be a donation of time as well as money.

Another benefit of charitable giving is the feeling of fulfilling social responsibility. **Social responsibility** is behaving with sensitivity to social, environmental, and economic issues. *Philanthropy* is the act of giving money, goods, or services to meet the needs of others and supporting organizations and causes that are important to an individual. Being socially responsible, or philanthropic, is also known to make individuals feel happier and relieve stress. Donating time or talent to an organization may not translate into a tax deduction. However, it may make a person feel positive about making a contribution to the betterment of society.

It pays to investigate before you give. Some charitable organizations are more efficient and effective than others. Some groups may pose as charities but use the funds they collect for personal gain. Be aware that there are times when only a portion of a contribution is tax deductible, especially if the contributor receives something in return. For example, buying tickets for a charitable dinner may require that the actual cost of the dinner is not deductible. Only the portion that is going to charity may qualify.

Step 4: Analyze Estimated Income and Expenses

Data is information. **Data analysis** is the process of studying data with the goal of discovering new information that can help with making decisions. Performing data analysis on your estimated income and expenses is necessary in order to evaluate your budget.

Do your total estimated expenses equal the total estimated income? Do you have money left over? If you have nothing left or are "in the hole," you need to find ways to increase income or reduce spending. To increase income, explore the following possibilities.

- Can you earn money by doing special jobs for your family or neighbors? For example, can you do the grocery shopping, wash windows, reorganize closets and cabinets, or do some yard work?
- Can you get a part-time job? Look for help wanted ads. Ask friends, coaches, neighbors, and store managers about job possibilities.
- If you have a job, can you negotiate an increase in wages? Is it possible to work more hours without sacrificing time you need for schoolwork and other important activities?

To reduce spending, study your record of expenses.

- Start with your discretionary expenses. Can you eliminate any items or reduce the cost of items you buy? Maybe you can cut back cell phone data usage. Perhaps you can check out books or movies at the library.
- Look at fixed and variable expenses. These expenses may be necessary, but can you reduce their cost by making substitutions? For example, try a generic shampoo instead of an expensive brand. Drink tap water instead of bottled water.
- Can you cut spending that does not bring you closer to achieving your goals? For example, if good health is a priority, you can walk instead of driving or taking the bus.

Step 5: Analyze Actual Income and Expenses

Now it is time to bring together your goals, income, and expenses into a budget. A budget reduces the temptation to spend carelessly. Figure 2-3 shows a completed budget.

When a budget period ends, fill in the Actual column and total each section. Then, subtract the Actual amount from the Estimated amount.

Budget			
Courtney Acorinti			
Budget period ______			
	Estimated	Actual	Variance
Income			
Jobs			
Babysitting	$25	$25	—
Yard work	40	40	—
After-school job	200	200	—
Allowance	40	40	—
Gifts	10	10	—
Total Income	$315	$315	
Expenses			
Fixed Expenses			
Bus pass	$15	$15	—
Lunches	90	90	—
Savings	15	15	—
Total Fixed Expenses	$120	$120	
Variable Expenses			
Snacks	$20	$20	—
Movies/concerts/events	40	25	15
Clothes	50	40	10
Music downloads	25	25	—
Gifts	20	20	—
Magazines	15	15	—
Personal care products	25	25	—
Total Variable Expenses	$195	$170	$25
Total Expenses	$315	$290	$25
Discretionary Income (Income – Expenses)	$0	$25	$25

Goodheart-Willcox Publisher

Figure 2-3 At the end of the budget period, the actual income and expenses can be recorded.

Enter the difference in the Variance column. A *variance* is the difference between the budgeted amount and the actual amount. Are there variances in any items?

When an actual expense is greater than budgeted amount, identify the cause. Did you ignore the budget? Was there an unexpected expense? Was your estimate too low? Adjust your budget to reflect actual income and spending. Try it for a few weeks. The points in Figure 2-4 can make a budget work better.

On the last line of the budget, the expenses should be subtracted from the income. The budget in Figure 2-3 shows a positive outcome. Courtney actually spent $25 less than what was estimated. When a budget has a positive outcome, the money left over can be considered discretionary income. **Discretionary income**, also known as *disposable income*, is the money that remains after a person has paid all expenses. If you have any discretionary income, you can save, invest, or spend it however you like.

From time to time, review and analyze your overall money management plan to make sure it is working for you. Reflect on your spending practices and evaluate how they influence your financial well-being. You can expect financial plans to change with significant events in your life. These events include going to college, starting a new job, leaving home, getting married, having children, and changing jobs.

Consider these questions as you analyze your budget.

- Is your financial plan working?
- Is your money doing what you want it to do?
- Are you reaching important goals?
- As you achieve goals, do you set new ones?
- Are you controlling your spending?
- Has your income or pattern of spending changed significantly?
- Are there changes in your life that call for adjustments in your financial planning?

When revisions are needed, make the necessary changes to update your budget. Recheck in a week or two to see if the new entries are an improvement. Monitor your finances carefully to make sure your income works well for you over the years.

Advice for Better Budgeting	
• Keep it simple.	• Be prepared for the unexpected.
• Write it down.	• Set goals.
• Be specific.	• Be prepared to revise.
• Be flexible.	• Prioritize your wants and needs.
• Be disciplined.	• Choose a method that works for you.
• Keep it all together.	• Be realistic.

Goodheart-Willcox Publisher

Figure 2-4 When planning a budget, keep these points in mind.

You Do the Math — Problem Solving and Reasoning

Word problems are exercises in which the problem is set up in text, rather than presented in mathematical notation. Many word problems tell a story. You must identify the elements of the math problem and solve it. There are many strategies for solving word problems. Some of the common strategies include making a list or table; working backward; guessing, checking, and revising; and substituting simpler numbers to solve the problem.

Solve the following problem.

Lena Chang, 23, lives alone in a rented apartment and earns $2,300 a month after taxes and payroll deductions. Personal assets include $1,500 in a savings account, $2,000 in stocks, and some jewelry worth about $1,000. The largest asset is a car that could sell today for $10,000. Lena still owes $15,000 on a student loan. Monthly expenses include:

- $200 savings
- $750 rent
- $250 student loan payment
- $250 utilities
- $200 gas, car insurance, and registration
- $230 groceries
- $50 donations to a charity
- $350 extras such as entertainment, eating out, and clothing

Is Lena's net worth statement positive or negative?

Personal Financial Statements

Personal financial statements show information about the financial status of an individual. When applying for credit, the creditor will require that information be given about your income, expenses, and other information. Financial statements report this type of information. Two examples are cash flow statements and net worth statements.

Cash Flow Statement

A **cash flow statement** is a summary of the amount of money received and the amount paid for goods and services during a specific period. The cash flow statement shown in Figure 2-5 appears very similar to the budget shown earlier. However, there are important differences. In the cash flow statement:

- income is called *Cash Inflow*;
- expenses are called *Cash Outflow*; and
- the term *Actual* heads the column of figures instead of *Planned*.

The cash flow statement goes beyond the budget to reflect actual money inflow and outflow for the month. Prepared at the end of the budget period, it shows real income and spending, not what was planned.

To get accurate figures for the statement, record cash inflows and outflows in an *income and expense log*, as shown in Figure 2-6. This log is basically a personal spending diary. Itemize your expenses and record exactly how much money came in. Keep these records until you reach the end of your budget period. You will find that recording cash inflows and outflows leads to more accurate budgeting. Once you finish the cash flow statement, you can prepare the budget for the next month more quickly.

Cash Flow Statement		
Month of October		
	Actual	
Category		
Cash Inflow (Income)		
Part-time jobs	$265	
(Babysitting, yard work, after-school job)		
Allowance	40	
Gifts	10	
Total Income		$315
Cash Outflow (Expenses)		
Fixed Expenses	$120	
(Bus pass, lunches, savings)		
Variable Expenses	$170	
(Snacks, clothes, cell phone, personal care products, movies/concerts/events)		
Total Expenses		290
Total Outflow		$290
Net Cash Flow		$25

Goodheart-Willcox Publisher

Figure 2-5 A cash flow statement is a summary of the amount of money received and the amount paid for goods and services during a specific period.

Ethics

Biased Language

As you go to work or school each day, you may encounter others who categorize people using biased words and comments. Using age, gender, race, disability, or ethnicity as a way to describe others is unethical and sometimes even illegal. Use bias-free language in all of your communications, whether verbal or printed, to show respect for others.

Income and Expense Log			
Date	Item	Income	Expenses
9/10	Bus fare (round trip)		$4.00
	Lunch		$5.15
	Snack		$2.05
9/11	Babysitting	$20.00	
	Snack		$3.50
	School supplies		$17.00
	Movie ticket		$7.00
9/12	Birthday gift	$25.00	
	New tennis shoes		$85.00

Goodheart-Willcox Publisher

Figure 2-6 Keeping a detailed log of your income and spending will help you develop a more accurate and realistic budget.

Net Worth Statement

Net worth is the difference between what is owned and what is owed. An **asset** is an item of value that is owned, such as cash, stocks, bonds, real estate, and personal possessions. A **liability** is a financial obligation that requires future payment. Liabilities include unpaid bills, credit card charges, mortgages, personal loans, and taxes. Your net worth is the difference between your assets and liabilities.

Experts advise evaluating your total financial situation at least annually. A net worth statement can help you do this accurately. A **net worth statement** is a written record of an individual's current financial situation. It measures financial standing at a particular point in time. A net worth statement is shown in Figure 2-7.

To create a net worth statement, list all of your assets and liabilities. Assets are divided into two basic categories:

- *Current assets* include cash and savings that can be converted to cash quickly and easily. These are also called *liquid assets*. **Liquidity** is the ease with which an asset can be converted into cash without losing value.

Net Worth Statement Courtney Acorinti December 31, 20--			
Assets		**Liabilities**	
Current Assets (bank account, savings account, college fund)	$9,200	Current Liabilities (credit card, medical bills)	$1,200
Fixed Assets (auto, personal property)	800	Long-Term Liabilities (auto loan, college loan)	8,000
		Total Liabilities	$9,200
		Net Worth	
		Net Worth (Assets – Liabilities)	800
Total Assets	$10,000	Total	$10,000

Goodheart-Willcox Publisher

Figure 2-7 A net worth statement is a written record of an individual's current financial situation.

- *Fixed assets* include investments, such as stocks, bonds, and invested funds, that are set aside for long-term goals, such as the education of children or retirement needs. Fixed assets also include a home, auto, personal possessions, and other durable goods that enrich your life through use.

Assets tend to change in value from year to year, so they should be listed at their current or market value. This amount is an estimated worth at the time the net worth statement is made.

Liabilities are also divided into two categories:

- *Current liabilities* are debts due soon, usually within the year. They include medical bills, taxes, unpaid bills from credit cards and charge accounts, and the amount you borrowed for lunch last week.
- *Long-term liabilities* include obligations to be paid over a long period of time, such as an auto loan or a home mortgage.

Subtract your total liabilities from your total assets. If you own more than you owe, you have a positive net worth. This means that you can meet your financial obligations and possibly reach some of your important financial goals.

If you owe more than you own, your net worth will be a negative figure. You need to find ways to reduce expenses or increase income. Start with a careful look at expenses. Try to reduce or eliminate all the items that are not essential. Pay credit debts and do not take on more credit obligations. Consider ways to increase income by working more hours or assuming more responsibilities on the job. A job change or additional training may also lead to higher income. Do all you can to create a positive net worth.

This may not seem necessary now, but as you move into the adult world, your circumstances can change rapidly. Tracking finances will become more complicated and more important. The net worth statement helps chart your financial future.

Wealthy individuals have assets far in excess of their liabilities. Wealth includes investments, property, a business, cash, and other items of value that contribute significantly to financial security and a high standard of living and giving.

Case Study *Making Plans*

At 28, Myra is a top-notch professional photographer and, as a single person, has no plans to marry or start a family in the near future. The photographer job pays $70,000 annually and has outstanding benefits including health, disability, and life insurance, as well as retirement contributions.

Being independent and having a successful career is an important financial dream for Myra. Currently, Myra lives in a rented apartment 20 miles from work. Living so far away is not convenient, as traffic is an issue each morning and evening. To be able to buy a home would be the answer to a long-term goal.

Case Review

1. What personal life situation changes could alter Myra's financial needs and plans?
2. What are some financial steps to take before purchasing a new home? What additional expenses will home ownership bring?
3. What are some key differences in financial planning for those with dependents and those without dependents?
4. How does an individual's age relate to financial planning and decisions?

Recordkeeping

As you enter the workplace and take on adult responsibilities, certain documents and papers will become important in managing your affairs. The process of setting up an organized system for important documents is called **recordkeeping**. Keeping track of financial records is an important part of money management. Well-ordered records can help you stay within your budget and make adjustments as needed. It is helpful to keep money management records over a period of time so you can review your current financial situation, evaluate your progress, and plan for the future.

Diego Cervo/Shutterstock.com

A budget is a tool that helps an individual take control of personal finances.

A recordkeeping system should be simple and convenient. A desk drawer, file cabinet, or fireproof box can be used to keep important papers together in one place. Some people keep their most important financial and legal documents in a safe deposit box at a financial institution with copies in their home files.

Information stored on your computer should be organized, secure, and password protected. Data may include bill payment records, contracts, tax forms, and e-mail correspondence related to financial and consumer matters. Financial software or web-based money management programs can guide you in setting up your financial affairs so you can locate information as you need it. To prevent losing important documents should your computer fail, backup copies should be placed on a USB flash drive or external hard drive or uploaded to the cloud. Up-to-date security software should be installed to protect against viruses and thieves who target financial information on unprotected websites.

Financial Records

Financial records related to your banking business and credit cards should be kept as well as records of income and spending.

- Savings and checking account numbers, names on each account, and the name of the financial institution where each account is located
- Credit card and charge account numbers, the name of issuer, expiration dates, names of persons authorized to use each account, and numbers to call for lost cards
- PINs (personal identification numbers) for cash or debit cards and passwords for online accounts

Income records to keep include:

- paycheck stubs;
- statements showing interest earned on savings accounts;
- records of dividends; and
- amounts of cash gifts, tips, and bonuses.

Spending records to keep include:

- bank statements and checkbook registers;
- receipts from purchases and bills paid;
- statements from credit accounts; and
- cash register receipts for big purchases.

Receipts serve as proof of payments. They are especially important for fixed expenses, such as loan payments, and for major purchases, such as a road bike. They also may be needed for warranty services, settling dispute, or exchanges.

Keeping receipts for minor purchases, such as cosmetics or movie tickets, is a good way to keep track of your spending. If you have trouble staying within your budget, you may want to record all purchases for a time. Then you will have a clear idea of where your money goes.

It is important to keep track of bills. Due dates for bills should be monitored so you can pay on time and avoid late fees. If you receive bills by mail, place them in a box or drawer until you are ready to pay them. The due dates and your paydays will dictate your bill scheduling. Pay the bills that are due first. Many people pay bills on a regular schedule, such as every Sunday night or at the end of the month. If you lose track of your bills, you run the risk of paying them late or not at all.

Documents

Important personal documents and information should be accessible by anyone you designate to handle your financial and legal affairs if you become unable to do so. A **legal document** is a paper that can be filed with a court officer or used to uphold an agreement in a court of law, such as a marriage certificate, auto loan, mortgage, or credit card agreement.

Examples of important documents to keep in a secure place are as follows.

- Personal information such as birth certificates, Social Security cards, medical records
- Savings and investment information such as securities and investment records, including stocks, bonds, and mutual funds
- Tax records such as income tax returns and Form W-2s
- Estate planning documents such as wills and trusts, adoption papers, insurance policies, mortgage papers, tax records, property deeds and titles, pension plans and employee benefit documents, business partners or co-owners, executors names and contact information for people responsible for the management of your affairs, including wishes you want carried out if you die, and instructions to be followed if you are incapacitated

gualtiero boffi/Shutterstock.com

A recordkeeping system should be simple and convenient, such as a desk drawer, file cabinet, or fireproof box to keep important papers together in one place.

- Valuable property and possessions inventories with locations, estimated market values, appraisals, and details of purchases

Some records may be printed (hard) copies and others may be digital. The important thing is to know where to find what you need when you need it.

When reviewing personal and legal documents relating to individual or family finances, each one should be evaluated for its importance. There are some personal documents that may not have any financial significance. These do not need to be part of your recordkeeping practices. However, most legal documents will be important for financial matters, and should be evaluated accordingly.

Money Management Software

Money management software is a computer program used to organize daily finances and keep track of income, spending, saving, debts, investments, and other financial data. It allows the user to track information and perform data analysis related to the individual's finances. It also provides a detailed picture of what is going on in your financial life.

Money management software allows the user to perform the following activities:

- Create a self-tailored budget and overall money management program.
- Enter income, expenses, and goals.
- Categorize expenses and evaluate spending patterns.
- Connect to and interact with checking, credit, savings, and investment accounts.
- Create budgets, cash flow statements, net worth statements, and other financial documents.
- Track spending and other financial transactions.
- Access financial records at any time.
- Manage and track investments.
- Prepare and file income tax returns.

There are many money management software programs from which to choose. These programs can be found by conducting an Internet search using the phrase *money management software*. Reading reviews of the most popular programs can help you decide which one would work well for you. These programs generally are very affordable, and some programs may even be free of charge.

wavebreakmedia/Shutterstock.com

Calculators and spreadsheet software can make analyzing personal financial data a manageable task.

Many programs are basic and easy to use; others are more advanced and intended for more experienced users. Some programs focus on basic budgeting, while others are intended for advanced investment tracking. Your choice will depend on the functions you want and your computer skills. It is a good idea to try a demo of a program before you decide whether it will work for you.

Money management software may be available as a web-based service. With a web-based service, your information is stored on a server rather than on your computer. Before enrolling in one of these programs, make sure the company is reputable and is certified as a secured site. If you prefer to store your information on your computer, there are programs you can download from a disc, from a website, or as an app.

Whether you are using a web-based program or one on your computer, appropriate virus checkers, malware protections, and backup systems should be installed for your data. Online money management, like many other online activities, requires confidential information regarding your finances. Take the necessary steps to ensure that your computer and your online connections are secure before providing sensitive personal information.

Section 2.1 Review

Check Your Understanding

1. When establishing a budget, what types of expenses should be tracked?
2. List examples of benefits of charitable giving.
3. List two examples of personal financial statements.
4. Why should an individual create a recordkeeping system for personal documents?
5. What are some tasks that can be performed using money management software?

Build Your Vocabulary

As you progress through this course, develop a personal glossary. This will help you build your vocabulary and prepare you for a career. Write a definition for each of the following terms and add it to your glossary.

- life span
- nature of financial planning
- budget
- spreadsheet
- income
- expense
- fixed expense
- variable expense
- discretionary expense
- pay yourself first
- wealth
- emergency fund
- charity
- social responsibility
- data analysis
- discretionary income
- cash flow statement
- net worth
- asset
- liability
- net worth statement
- liquidity
- recordkeeping
- legal document
- money management software

Section **2.2** **Young Adult and Family Finances**

Objectives

After you study this section, you will be able to:

- Identify financial tasks that young adults must learn to address.
- Analyze how the family life cycle influences financial decisions.
- List ways to avoid financial problems.

Essential Question

What type of financial decisions will you have to make when you start living on your own?

Terms

family life cycle

personal financial crisis

On Your Own

As you enter the adult world, your money management activities will expand. You may be eager to leave home and live on your own. Once independent, you may be surprised by the many expenses and responsibilities you must handle that were previously taken care of by your parents or guardians. Managing money well in order to remain independent becomes the number one financial challenge.

MBI/Shutterstock.com

Having an emergency fund is one way to prepare for unexpected financial issues, such as an unexpected automobile repair.

Young adults who are newly independent will face many new financial responsibilities. You will need to stay on top of fixed expenses, such as rent, taxes, insurance, car payments, utilities, cell phone, and other bills you may be paying for the first time. Planning the use of income to cover expenses will take on new meaning and importance. Following the steps for budgeting that were presented earlier in the chapter can guide you in setting up a budget that will work for you. Some of the financial tasks you will need to assume include:

- managing household expenses;
- paying bills on time;
- saving and investing for your future;

- protecting against financial losses; and
- computing and paying taxes.

If you choose to live with one or more roommates, you can reduce your overall costs by sharing expenses. Before moving in with roommates, it is a good idea to discuss financial and living arrangements in detail so each of you knows what to expect. Housing decisions are covered in Chapter 12.

Family Life Cycle

After a period of living alone or with roommates, many adults marry and start families. The **family life cycle** consists of the stages a family passes through over its lifetime. The five stages are *beginning, expanding, developing, launching,* and *aging.* There are typical patterns of social and financial behavior families follow at different periods in the life cycle. In each stage, there are family as well as personal expenses to cover. Perhaps the most important factors affecting family budgeting decisions will be age and stage in the family life cycle. Stages in the family life cycle are explained in detail in Figure 2-8. Your goals and needs, as well as earning and spending patterns, will change with each stage. Becoming familiar with these patterns can provide you with a framework for your own financial planning.

Financial Aspects of the Family Life Cycle		
Beginning Stage		
Stages in the Family Life Cycle	**Career and Income Characteristics**	**Typical Expenses and Obligations**
Marriage Getting started as a couple Establishing a home	Finishing education Making career decisions Entering the workforce Low or no income, with gradual increases	Living expenses Tuition and/or repayment of education loans Auto loan payments and insurance Life, health, and other insurance Home furnishings Savings and retirement contributions Income tax
Expanding Stage		
Stages in the Family Life Cycle	**Career and Income Characteristics**	**Typical Expenses and Obligations**
Infant years Birth/adoption of first child	Increasing income and job responsibilities One or two full-time incomes Decreased income if one parent leaves work for childbearing	Child care and baby equipment Education fund Increased insurance coverage Prenatal, birth, and postnatal health care Income taxes Retirement contributions

(Continued)

Goodheart-Willcox Publisher

Figure 2-8 Career and income characteristics, as well as typical expenses and obligations, tend to follow a pattern at different stages of the life cycle.

Financial Aspects of the Family Life Cycle		
Developing Stage		
Stages in the Family Life Cycle	**Career and Income Characteristics**	**Typical Expenses and Obligations**
Toddler, preschool, and elementary school years Children become primary focus	Job advancement likely Increasing income Increasing job responsibilities	Move to larger living space Additional home furnishings Property and income tax increases Increased living expenses Retirement contributions
Adolescent years Involvement in school activities Preparation for launching stage	Continuing job advancement or possible career change Possible return of parent to the workforce Income still increasing	School expenses for extracurricular activities Savings and investments Savings for education Charitable contributions Travel Adolescents' spending Income and property taxes
Launching Stage		
Stages in the Family Life Cycle	**Career and Income Characteristics**	**Typical Expenses and Obligations**
Children leave home Parents adjust to "empty nest"	Heavier job responsibilities Peak performance years Income may peak as well Benefits may increase Retirement planning becomes a priority	Home improvements or new, smaller home Replacement furnishings Education and tuition costs Travel Retirement savings Income and property taxes Weddings of children
Aging Stage		
Stages in the Family Life Cycle	**Career and Income Characteristics**	**Typical Expenses and Obligations**
Parents focus on each other Children marry Grandchildren arrive Elderly parents may require care	Job responsibilities and earnings begin to level off Retirement and estate planning take form	Travel, recreation, and adult education Care for aging parents Increased savings and investments Gifts to help children get established Income and property taxes Long-term care insurance
Retirement years Establishing new routines, interests, and hobbies Grandparenting	Part-time or volunteer work Social Security income Income from retirement savings Wills and estate plans are revised as needed	Health insurance Possible relocation to a retirement area Travel Health care and medications Taxes Long-term care

Figure 2-8 Continued.

Not every family follows the stages of the family life cycle in order. *Variations in the life cycle* are patterns that differ from typical families as shown in Figure 2-9. The number of children and spacing between them can cause the cycle to vary from family to family. Some families skip, overlap, or repeat stages of the family life cycle. For example, couples who do not have children skip the expanding, developing, and launching stages. Parents with children in school could have more children. This brings an overlap of the developing and expanding stages. Single parents who marry may repeat stages with their new spouses.

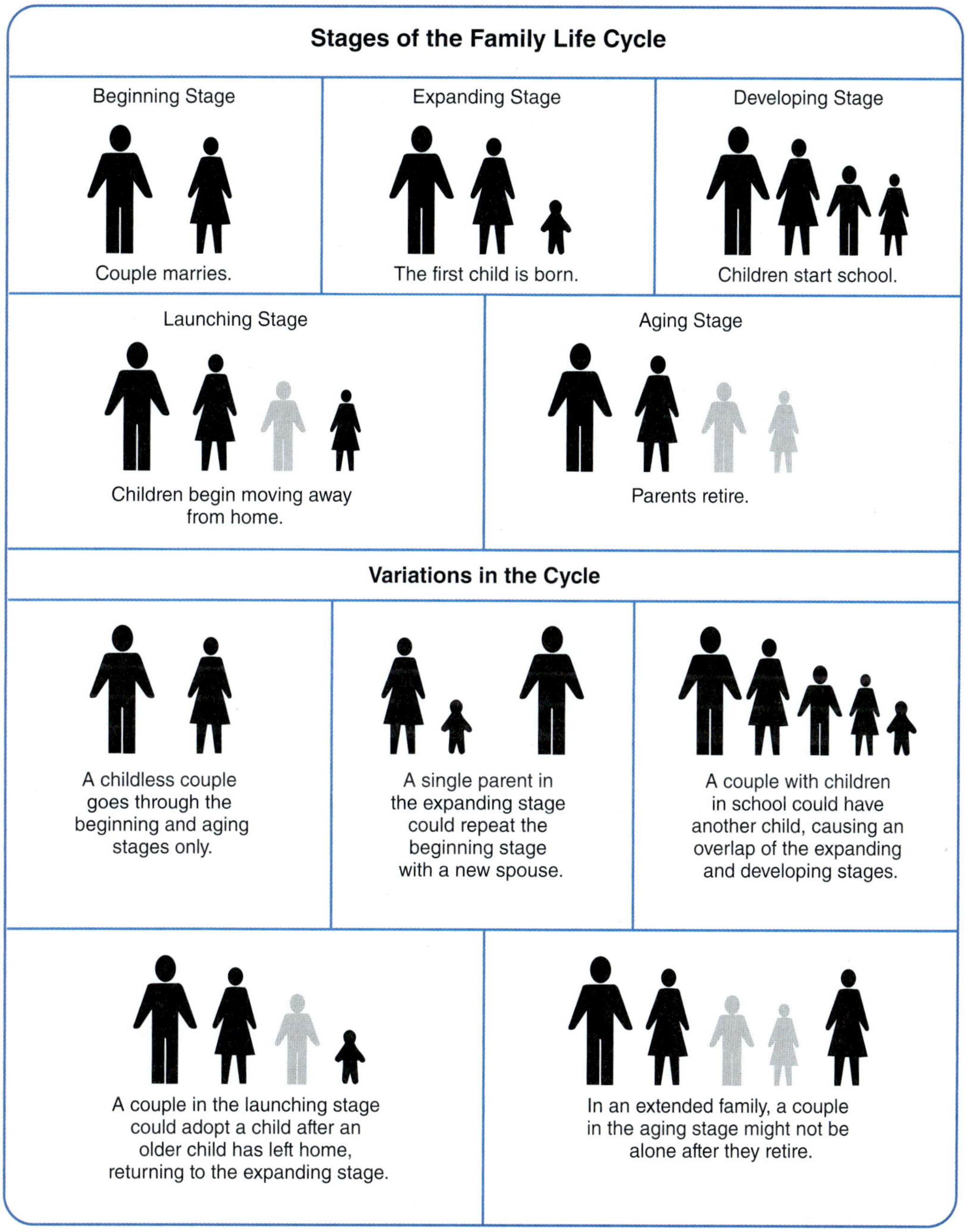

Goodheart-Willcox Publisher

Figure 2-9 Not all families progress through all stages of the family life cycle in the same way.

Economics in Action

COVID-19 Pandemic

When the COVID-19 pandemic hit in early 2020, the impact was felt by millions of people. Many people, young and old, struggled to find work. Businesses stopped hiring, and many employees lost their jobs. Demand dropped, and growth came to a near standstill. Financial institutions made fewer business and consumer loans. Credit sources disappeared.

When people lost their jobs or had hours reduced, entire families suffered. Long-term goals, such as higher education or starting a business, were put on hold. Many people lost employer-provided health insurance. Unemployment led to the inability to afford basic life necessities.

Loss of income meant lifestyle changes for almost everyone. There was less money and more anxiety. Retirement savings and home values dropped along with the stock market. People who were retired, or nearing retirement, were forced to work beyond their planned retirement age, if they could find work at all.

The pandemic left its mark on the population. It created health problems that affected millions of people. In addition, the economic impact was felt by every sector of the population. Corporate and small businesses struggled to stay open. Economic recovery is unpredictable after such a devastating event. The COVID-19 pandemic, similar to the 2007 Great Recession, will be felt for many years to come.

As family conditions change, financial planning concerns change, too. For example, single individuals and childless couples, single-parent families, and divorced or separated people have added considerations.

Singles and Childless Couples

Singles and couples with no dependents do not have the expenses related to raising children, such as school and medical expenses. Both groups may spend more throughout the life cycle on travel, leisure, and other extras. Some may choose to give more to charitable causes. Both groups often feel a greater responsibility to help their aging parents.

Single-Parent Families

Females lead most single-parent families. Their income is typically less than that of two-parent families and single-parent families led by males. Saving and planning for future security is sometimes difficult as these families struggle to meet current expenses. Government and community services and assistance can be very helpful for single-parent families.

Separated and Divorced Individuals

Separated and divorced people face a unique set of financial concerns. They may have the following expenses: legal fees, alimony, child support, and property settlement costs. The cost of establishing and maintaining a separate home may be another expense, especially if there are children involved. A divorce or separation may require additional furnishings and moving costs.

Personal Financial Problems

There may be times when financial disaster strikes because of circumstances beyond your control. A **personal financial crisis** is a major problem that changes a person or family's lifestyle and future. Examples include job loss, divorce, death, disability, serious illness, and natural disasters. When such events occur, you may need to make some serious changes in your financial planning and behavior. If debt problems reach the crisis stage, you need prompt, drastic action to correct the situation.

Handling Financial Problems

When a personal financial crisis arises, start by discussing the problem with adult members of the household, including older children. Make sure that everyone understands the potential impact on their standard of living and what they can do to help. For example, college-bound teens may need to consider work/study programs or a community college near enough to allow living at home while going to school. Knowing they have a stake in resolving the crisis will encourage cooperation of all family members and reduce conflict.

Make a list of financial and nonfinancial resources available to you. In analyzing your situation, consider the following steps to minimize negative financial consequences

Exploring Careers

Accountant

Most companies are in business to make money. As a result, knowing the financial standing of a company is important information. An accountant is responsible for understanding and assessing this information. Accountants also analyze financial information so they can advise business owners and managers. Business owners rely on accountants to help them make sound business decisions. Examples of tasks accountants perform include:

- gather information to prepare financial reports
- create and maintain financial reports
- analyze financial reports to create forecasts and budgets
- communicate the financial standing of the company to managers or business owners
- compute taxes owed and prepare tax returns

Accounting positions require a bachelor's degree in accounting, business administration, or a related field. Many companies require applicants to have a master's degree in a related field as well. The Certified Public Accountant (CPA) certification is also required for many accounting jobs.

- Accept and acknowledge the crisis.
- If debt is a part of the crisis, contact creditors promptly.
- Avoid making any new credit purchases.
- Look for reliable, affordable credit and financial counseling.
- Adjust spending habits and cut expenses.
- Look for every possible source of new income.
- Ask unemployed family members to seek work.
- Look for assistance from extended family, employers, insurance, government programs, and community or charitable organizations.
- Consider selling some assets, such as real estate, investments, autos, and valuable possessions.
- As a last resort, consider bankruptcy.

Some situations may call for the help of professionals. Consider consulting health-care providers, family counselors, financial advisors, and lawyers to determine the full scope of the crisis.

Kudla/Shutterstock.com

Individuals can avoid financial trouble by spending only what they can afford and keeping debt under control.

Avoiding Financial Problems

Preventive measures often help people and families avoid financial problems altogether. They also can minimize the impact of unavoidable problems, such as the loss of a job in a recession.

Having an emergency fund will help you to prepare for the unexpected. In hard times or during a recession, an emergency fund should equal 8 to 10 months' income. Other preventive measures include:

- sound money management;
- practical credit controls;
- regular savings;
- insurance protection;
- reasonable caution in financial matters; and
- regular family money management discussions.

Financial trouble can be avoided by living within your means and keeping debt under control. This involves taking responsibility for your life, including your financial choices and decisions. Preparation can help you weather a crisis situation if it arises. Getting the best education and job training possible are ways to be prepared. With a good education and job skills, you are better able to find work and advance on the job. Staying current in your field through continuing education and training programs also helps.

Section 2.2 Review

Check Your Understanding

1. What are the stages of the family life cycle?
2. Name three family conditions that may change and affect financial planning.
3. List examples of financial crisis that a person might face.
4. How many months' income should an emergency fund cover?
5. List three ways to minimize the negative consequences of a personal financial crisis.

Build Your Vocabulary

As you progress through this course, develop a personal glossary. This will help you build your vocabulary and prepare you for a career. Write a definition for each of the following terms and add it to your glossary.

family life cycle

personal financial crisis

Review and Assessment

Chapter Summary

Section 2.1 Personal Financial Landscape

- Creating a financial plan helps a person manage personal finances and learn to become economically self sufficient. A budget can be used to analyze income and expenses and to create a plan for achieving financial goals. Financial security requires financial literacy and life-long financial planning.
- Personal financial statements show information about the financial status of an individual. Two types of personal financial statements are a cash flow statement and net worth statement. A cash flow statement reflects actual cash inflow and outflow for a budgeting period. A net worth statement shows a person's current financial.
- Setting up an organized system for financial and legal documents, called recordkeeping, is an important part of effectively managing personal finances. Knowing what to keep and where to file important documents can help a person manage financial affairs.
- Money management software can help organize daily finances and keep track of income, spending, saving, debts, investments, and other financial data.

Section 2.2 Young Adult and Family Finances

- As an adult, your money management activities will expand to include keeping track of income and expenses, paying bills, saving, investing, and paying taxes.
- Age and stage in the family life cycle are important factors affecting family financial decisions. Variations in the family life cycle include singles, childless couples, single parent families, and divorced or separated adults. An individual's goals and needs will change with each stage.
- A person or family can often avoid financial trouble by living within their means, keeping debt under control, getting a good education and job training, and having an emergency fund.

Review Your Knowledge

1. Identify steps to develop a budget based on personal financial goals.
2. Explain the differences between fixed expenses and variable expenses and provide an example of each.
3. Explain how to create a cash flow statement.
4. Explain how to create a net worth statement.
5. Discuss the benefits of creating a good recordkeeping system for financial documents.
6. How can money management software assist an individual in financial planning?
7. Identify examples of financial tasks that young adults must address.
8. List an example of a variation in the family life cycle.
9. Analyze how the family life cycle influences financial decisions.
10. List ways to avoid financial problems.

Apply Your Knowledge

1. Financial resources must be managed to meet financial goals. Describe how an individual or family could evaluate and analyze their needs for personal and family financial planning and its importance.

Write a paragraph describing how you would evaluate your own individual need for financial planning.

2. Identify types of purchases and charitable donations. Rank them according to priority. What factors went into your organization of these expenses?
3. The first step in creating a budget is to establish personal financial goals. Think about the next 12 months. What are your short-, medium-, and long-term goals? Using Figure 2-1 as an example, create a list of your financial goals.
4. Create a budget for the upcoming month that will help you meet your personal financial goals. Using Figure 2-3 as an example, create a spreadsheet. If you do not have access to a computer, use a sheet of paper. Fill in headings for each type of information that should be entered. If the types of income and expenses you have are not the same as the example, enter ones more appropriate for you. Next, fill in the estimated column for income and expenses that you anticipate in the coming month.
5. At the end of the month, you will complete your budget. Using the spreadsheet you started in the last activity, enter the actual amounts you spent in the actual column. Next, analyze your budget. Did you have any discretionary income at the end of the month? Write a paragraph on what you learned from this activity.
6. Your net worth is the difference between what you own and what you owe. List all of the assets that you own and their current value. Examples include a savings account, mountain bike, or car. Next, list all of your liabilities. Examples include unpaid bills, a credit card balance, and money you owe to a friend. Using the net worth statement in Figure 2-7 as an example, organize this information into a net worth statement. Then, use a spreadsheet, a calculator, or money management software to calculate your net worth. Do you have a positive or negative net worth? Perform data analysis on your findings.
7. Financial management includes keeping records that cover your life span. Make a list of the types of documents you should keep and evaluate their importance. Ask your parent or guardians for a copy of each, and start a filing system for your records. What type of storage container will you use?
8. Keeping expense records is an important part of financial management. For the next month, keep a receipt for every purchase you make. If you buy something that doesn't come with a receipt, such as at a vending machine, create your own receipt on a piece of paper. Organize your receipts by date of purchase, category, or some other method. Put them in the filing system you created in the last activity. Analyze which expenses were planned and which ones were unplanned.
9. One of the benefits that comes from personal financial planning is economic self-sufficiency. Define what *economic self-sufficiency* means to you. Describe how you can maintain economic self-sufficiency throughout your adult life.
10. Financial planning is important at every stage of the family life cycle. Describe how family financial planning is affected by the family's size, their geographic location, and the members' stages in the life cycle.

Apply Your Math Skills

1. Pete is saving money to buy a used car in eight months and wants to save $5,000 for a down payment. Pete already has $1,400 saved for the car. How much money needs to be saved per month to meet the goal of saving $5,000?
2. Meredith's assets include a tablet computer worth $500; $1,250 in savings; a car worth $5,400; and $75 cash. Liabilities include a $1,700 tuition bill for one semester; $630 for textbooks paid for with a credit card; an $80 cell phone bill; and $10 borrowed from a friend. What is Meredith's current net worth? Is it positive or negative?

Communication Skills

College and Career Readiness

Writing. Rhetoric is the study of writing or speaking as a way of communicating information or persuading someone. Identify rhetoric that could be used to describe the family life cycle. Write a script for presenting the topic to your classmates.

Reading. Read a magazine, newspaper, or online article about the importance of personal finance for teens. Determine the central ideas of the article and review the conclusions made by the author. Provide an accurate summary of your reading, making sure to incorporate the *who, what, when, where, why,* and *how* of this situation.

Speaking. There will be many instances when you will be required to persuade the listener. When you persuade, you convince a person to take a proposed course of action. Prepare for a conversation with a friend about why keeping financial and personal records is important. Discuss the reasons for selecting a solid recordkeeping system and a safe storage option. Ask for assistance from a peer to help you plan a focused presentation that argues your case and shows solid reasoning that will influence the listener's understanding of the topic.

Teamwork

Consumers have a responsibility to live within their means. Work in a team with other students to discuss the following questions. When consumers have financial difficulties caused by overspending, what, if any, public assistance should be available to them? Is it ethical to create credit card debt to buy nonessentials, to buy a car you cannot afford, or to borrow money you cannot repay? Is it ethical for creditors to make credit readily available to borrowers who have limited ability to repay as agreed? Share your team's opinion with the class.

Internet Research

Money Management Software. Primary research is conducted by the writer in preparation for writing a report. Investigate several money management software programs online. Compare and contrast the key features of three of them. Write a report that discusses ways money management software could help you with financial planning and management over your lifetime.

Charitable Giving. There are many personal and financial benefits to charitable giving. Create a plan for charitable giving for the upcoming year by identifying one or two organizations you would like to support. Research these organizations to confirm they are the type of organization they claim to be. Next, investigate the ways in which charitable giving can create a tax benefit in your state.

Nature of Financial Planning. *Nature of financial planning* is a term that is used in personal finance. Using the Internet, research this phrase. Write a paragraph describing what it means to you.

Portfolio Development

College and Career Readiness

Objective. Before you begin collecting information, it is beneficial to write an objective for your portfolio. An *objective* is one or two complete sentences that state what you want to accomplish. Your objective will help keep you on track as you build your portfolio.

First, focus on your short-term and long-term goals. A *short-term goal* is a goal you would like to achieve in the next one to two years. A *long-term goal* is a goal you wish to accomplish in the next five to ten years. Your objective should be written in a way that allows you to achieve your goals. For example, if a short-term goal is to get accepted to a university within a year but your long-term goal is to work in a field closely related to your career interests, your objective could be: "I will gain acceptance to one of my top-choice universities within a year and will be working in my desired field within five years." By focusing on your goals, you will be able to write a descriptive objective for your portfolio.

When writing your objective, include enough details so you can easily judge when it is accomplished. Consider this objective: "I will try to get into college." This is too general. A better, more detailed objective might read: "I will get accepted into the undergraduate program at one of my top-three colleges of choice." Creating a clear objective is a good starting point when beginning to work on your portfolio.

1. Create a document with the heading "Portfolio Objective." Then create two subheadings, one that says "Short-Term Goals" and another that says "Long-Term Goals." List your goals under their respective headings. These are goals on which you should focus when writing your objective.
2. Next, write your portfolio objective based on those goals. Keep in mind that this objective will likely change as your ideas and goals evolve during the portfolio creation process.
3. Save this document as PORTFOLIO_OBJECTIVE with your last name, for example PORTFOLIO_OBJECTIVE_SMITH, or use a different naming convention that is suitable for the management system you put into place in Lesson 1.
4. Place this document as the first page of your portfolio to guide you as you build it. Remember to remove it when you organize the final product.
5. This is your first activity, so record it on the master portfolio spreadsheet. Title your first entry Portfolio Objective.

CTSOs

Event Prep

Performance. Some competitive events for CTSOs have a performance component. The activity could potentially be a decision-making scenario for which your team will provide a solution and present to the judges.

To prepare for the performance component of a presentation, complete the following activities.

1. On your CTSO's website, locate a rubric or scoring sheet for the event.
2. Confirm whether visual aids may be used in the presentation and the amount of setup time permitted.
3. Review the rules to confirm whether questions will be asked or if the team will need to defend a case or situation.
4. Make notes on index cards about important points to remember. Use these notes to study. You may also be able to use these notes during the event.
5. Practice the performance. You should introduce yourself, review the topic that is being presented, defend the topic being presented, and conclude with a summary.
6. After the practice performance is complete, ask for feedback from your instructor. You may also consider having a student audience listen and give feedback.

CHAPTER

3 Income and Taxes

In order to have money, people need to make money by working. Income gives individuals money to spend. When you begin working, an important financial responsibility is filing an income tax return. Reporting your income to the government ensures that each person has paid his or her fair share in taxes.

Taxes give the various levels of government their spending money, which is called *revenue*. A major way for a government to raise revenue is by taxing each person's income as well as the items they buy or own. The government then uses that revenue to provide public goods and services that benefit all. As a teen, you use some of those goods and services now, such as schools, libraries, parks, highways, and police protection. As an older adult, you will use other types of public goods and services, such as Social Security benefits.

Focus on Finance

Social Security Number

A Social Security number serves two major purposes. One, the Social Security Administration uses this number to keep a record of your covered earnings. These earnings determine the amount you will eventually receive in retirement, disability benefits, or benefits to your survivors if you die. Two, the IRS also uses your Social Security number as a taxpayer identification number on all tax returns and forms.

No two Social Security numbers are the same. Your number is yours alone. It prevents your records from being mixed up with the records of someone else who may have the same name. If you lose your card or change your name, contact the nearest Social Security office for a new card. Safeguard your Social Security number. Do not carry it with you or give it out unnecessarily. Criminals can use this number to steal your identity and damage your finances.

College and Career Readiness

Reading Prep. As you read the chapter, record any questions that come to mind. Indicate where the answer to each question can be found: within the text, by asking your teacher, in another book, on the Internet, or by reflecting on your own knowledge and experiences. Pursue the answers to your questions.

Sections

Dragon Images/Shutterstock.com

Section 3.1 Income

Objectives

After studying this section, you will be able to:

- List and explain examples of earned income.
- Identify common payroll deductions, and explain how net pay is determined.
- Summarize common types of employee benefits.
- Explain work-life balance.

Essential Question

Why is it important for a worker to understand how net income is calculated?

Terms

earned income	tip	FICA taxes
wage	bonus	employee benefit
overtime wage	payroll deduction	compensation
piecework	gross pay	work-life balance
salary	net pay	
commission	Form W-4	

Earned Income

There are many ways to earn income. Most people work for an employer. Others choose to work for themselves as self-employed individuals. **Earned income** is the income received from employment, including self-employment. Earned income includes wages, salaries, commissions, tips, bonuses and self-employment income.

Wages

A **wage** is payment for work that is usually calculated on an hourly, daily, or piecework basis. For example, an hourly wage is a fixed amount paid for each hour worked. A wage is paid on a schedule, such as every week or every two weeks.

Many unskilled and beginning workers are paid the minimum wage. The *minimum wage* is the lowest hourly wage employers can pay most workers by law. Workers who frequently receive minimum wage include food preparers in fast-food restaurants, store salespeople, and workers at a car wash. Contrary to popular belief, most minimum wage workers are adults, not teens.

The US government sets and enforces the minimum wage through the *Fair Labor Standards Act (FLSA)*. Periodically, Congress passes legislation raising the minimum wage so it keeps pace with cost-of-living increases. Some states require a higher minimum wage than the federal wage. If there is both a state and a federal minimum wage, workers get whichever wage is higher.

mangostock/Shutterstock.com

A minimum-wage job is often a starting point for young workers.

Most wage-earners are covered by the overtime provisions of the FLSA. **Overtime wage** is the amount paid for working time in a week that is beyond the standard 40-hour workweek. Eligible workers who put in more than 40 hours per week must receive overtime pay at least 1.5 times their regular hourly rate. For example, Sue Barnwell earns $10 an hour and worked a total of 44 hours last week. Sue's total earnings for the week are:

regular earnings:	40 hours	×	$10 per hour	=	$400
overtime rate:	$10 per hour	×	1.5	=	$15 per hour
overtime earnings:	4 hours	×	$15 per hour	=	$60
total earnings:	$400	+	$60	=	$460

Some employers pay overtime if an employee works more than eight hours in a day, even if the employee's total hours for the week do not exceed 40. Some employers also pay overtime for weekend and holiday work regardless of the total number of hours worked in the week.

Some employees covered by the FLSA are exempt from receiving the full minimum wage. For example, workers under the age of 20 who are receiving job training can be paid less than the minimum wage. However, this is only during their first 90 consecutive days on the job. High school students enrolled in career education classes can sometimes be paid less than full minimum wage. The Department of Labor in your state can answer questions about wage requirements.

Piecework is a wage based on a rate per unit of work completed. For example, garment workers may be paid by the number of garments completed. The total piecework wages, however, must add up to at least the minimum wage.

Salary

Salary is a fixed payment for work and is expressed as an annual figure. It is paid in periodic equal payments. The payment period is usually weekly, biweekly (every other week), semimonthly (twice a month), or monthly. For example, the salary for a job may be listed as $42,120 a year. However, a worker does not receive a lump sum payment of $42,120. Instead, the salary is divided into equal payments at regular intervals during the year. If the employer pays employees weekly, the worker would receive 52 checks of $810 ($42,120 ÷ 52) throughout the year. Figure 3-1 shows how $42,120 would be broken down and paid in the common pay periods.

Salaried workers are expected to put in as much time as it takes to do the job. Therefore, most salaried professionals like teachers, managers, and supervisors are not paid overtime.

Annual Salary of $42,120 in Common Pay Periods				
Pay Period	Salary	Number of Pay Periods in a Year	Calculation	Earnings per Pay Period
Weekly	$42,120	52	$42,120 ÷ 52	$ 810
Biweekly	$42,120	26	$42,120 ÷ 26	$1,620
Semimonthly	$42,120	24	$42,120 ÷ 24	$1,755
Monthly	$42,120	12	$42,120 ÷ 12	$3,510

Goodheart-Willcox Publisher

Figure 3-1 When there are more pay periods per year, the earnings for the pay period are smaller.

Commission

A **commission** is income paid as a percentage of sales made by a salesperson. Some people may work on a commission-only basis. Others may receive a combination of a base salary plus commission. Salespeople, who usually work on commission, sell cars, real estate, insurance, and other goods and services.

For a person working on commission, making many sales means income goes up. If customers do not buy, income shrinks. For many salespeople, income varies from month to month and year to year. A good salesperson generally earns more in commissions than in salary.

Tips

A **tip**, or *gratuity*, is money paid for service beyond what is required. A customer leaves a tip as a reward for good service. Tips are also given as incentives for workers to provide good service. This money belongs to workers, not their employers. This form of income is common for food servers, taxi drivers, hair stylists, and other service-industry workers.

According to the US Department of Labor, a tipped employee is one who engages in an occupation in which more than $30 of tips are customarily and regularly received per month. The FLSA requires that tipped employees be paid at least the minimum wage. However, the employer of a tipped employee is only required to pay $2.13 per hour in direct wages. If the $2.13 paid by the employer and the tips received by the employee do not equal the minimum wage, the employer must make up the difference.

Some state laws require an hourly direct wage higher than $2.13 for tipped employees. In those states, employers must pay the higher wage.

Bonus

A **bonus** is money added to an employee's base pay. It is usually a reward for performance or a share of business profits. Bonuses are incentives to encourage workers to perform better. Bonus income is usually based on worker performance, length of time with the company, or company performance.

Self-Employment Income

A growing proportion of the US workforce is self-employed. Unlike employees, who perform services for their employer, self-employed people work for themselves. The form of income earned is called *profit* or *self-employment income.*

This category of workers includes many entrepreneurs in the trades, such as plumbers, carpenters, and painters. Artists and consultants are often self-employed. A teenager who has a part-time job mowing lawns is self-employed.

One of the drawbacks of being self-employed is that you must arrange and pay for your own employment-related benefits. Some of these benefits, especially health care, are costly when purchased by individuals.

Payroll Deductions

The dollar figure on your paycheck is not the same as the dollar figure you are told when hired for a job. A **payroll deduction** is a subtraction from gross pay. Payroll deductions can lower a paycheck by 20 percent or more. The larger the deductions, the smaller the individual's net pay. This usually translates into less discretionary income for the taxpayer.

Some deductions are mandatory, such as Social Security taxes, Medicare taxes, and income taxes. Other deductions are voluntary, such as amounts for health insurance and retirement plans. Money withheld from an employee's paycheck is forwarded to the Internal Revenue Service (IRS) or other appropriate agencies.

Gross pay is total income before payroll deductions. **Net pay**, or *take-home pay,* is gross pay (plus bonuses) minus payroll deductions. For example, the pay stub in Figure 3-2 shows the worker earned a total of $345 in wages and overtime pay. This is gross pay, but the worker's net pay is only $286.75. Gross pay is reduced by payroll deductions.

Case Study *Tax Reality*

Alvin just started a summer job as an assistant at a local veterinarian's office. Working with animals is a nice job, and receiving a paycheck for doing something you enjoy is great. The job requires 30 hours per week and pays $240 per week. A check is issued every two weeks.

Alvin's first paycheck is much lower than the expected $480. The pay stub showed the following payroll deductions: $29.76 for Social Security tax, $6.96 for Medicare tax, $62.10 for federal withholding tax, and $28.80 for state income tax. It is disappointing to receive only $352.38 and have taxes deducted. No matter the disappointment, it is still a good opportunity to gain job experience.

Case Review

1. Do these figures surprise you? What has been your experience with payroll deductions?
2. Do you think it is fair to have to pay $127.62 in taxes every two weeks? Why or why not?
3. What benefits does a worker receive from the money that went to taxes? Does Alvin receive any direct benefits?
4. What information from the pay stub will be important when an income tax return is filed?

Town Department Store 111 Broadway Avenue Franklin, IL 65432		Pay Period: 03/08/-- through 03/21/--		Employee: Kristy A. James 1027 Cedar Street Franklin, IL 65432	
Gross Pay	**Federal Income Tax Withheld**	**State Income Tax Withheld**	**Social Security Tax Withheld**	**Medicare Tax Withheld**	**Net Pay**
$ 345.00	$ 18.06	$ 13.80	$ 21.39	$ 5.00	$ 286.75
Gross Pay Year-to-Date	**Federal Year-to-Date**	**State Year-to-Date**	**Social Security Year-to-Date**	**Medicare Year-to-Date**	**Net Pay Year-to-Date**
$ 8,484.50	$ 444.16	$ 339.38	$ 526.04	$ 123.03	$ 7,051.89

Goodheart-Willcox Publisher

Figure 3-2 This pay stub shows gross pay, payroll deductions, and net pay.

Federal, State, and Local Withholding Taxes

The federal income tax system is built on a *pay-as-you-earn* concept. This means a working person pays taxes from each paycheck instead of in one lump sum each year. State and local income taxes usually work this way, too.

The amount of income tax withheld from a paycheck depends on how much is earned and filing status. There are five filing statuses: single, married filing jointly, married filing separately, head of household, and qualifying widow(er) with dependent child.

Federal income taxes are used to provide for national programs such as national defense, foreign affairs, education, highway construction, veterans affairs, community development, law enforcement, and interest on the national debt.

State income taxes are used to pay for social services like public housing, welfare, and Medicaid. Other than that, the money usually goes to things like roads and services such as hospitals, education, and state police.

Local taxes are used to pay for police and fire services, education and health services, libraries, road maintenance, and other programs and projects that benefit the community.

When you begin a job, your employer will ask you to complete a Form W-4. **Form W-4** is the Employee's Withholding Certificate that helps an employer determine how much income tax to withhold from an employee's paychecks as payroll deductions. Figure 3-3 shows a completed Form W-4.

FICA Tax

Most workers in the United States are covered by the Federal Insurance Contributions Act (FICA). **FICA taxes** are taxes paid by the employee and employer used to finance the federal Social Security and Medicare programs. Total FICA taxes are 7.65 percent, which includes 6.2 percent for OASDI (old-age, survivors, and disability insurance) and 1.45 percent for Medicare.

Employers withhold FICA taxes from each employee's paycheck. There is an annual cap on the amount of income that is subject to the 6.2% OASDI portion of FICA taxes. However, there is no cap on income taxed for Medicare.

Form **W-4** | Department of the Treasury Internal Revenue Service

Employee's Withholding Certificate

▶ Complete Form W-4 so that your employer can withhold the correct federal income tax from your pay.
▶ Give Form W-4 to your employer.
▶ Your withholding is subject to review by the IRS.

OMB No. 1545-0074 | 20--

Step 1: Enter Personal Information

(a) First name and middle initial	Last name	(b) Social security number
Kristy A.	James	987-65-4321
Address: 1027 Cedar Street		▶ **Does your name match the name on your social security card?** If not, to ensure you get credit for your earnings, contact SSA at 800-772-1213 or go to *www.ssa.gov*.
City or town, state, and ZIP code: Franklin, IL 65432		

(c) [X] **Single or Married filing separately**
[ ] **Married filing jointly** (or Qualifying widow(er))
[ ] **Head of household** (Check only if you're unmarried and pay more than half the costs of keeping up a home for yourself and a qualifying individual.)

Complete Steps 2–4 ONLY if they apply to you; otherwise, skip to Step 5. See page 2 for more information on each step, who can claim exemption from withholding, when to use the online estimator, and privacy.

Step 5: Sign Here

Under penalties of perjury, I declare that this certificate, to the best of my knowledge and belief, is true, correct, and complete.

▶ Kristy A. James — **Employee's signature** (This form is not valid unless you sign it.)

▶ 01/02/-- — **Date**

Employers Only	Employer's name and address	First date of employment	Employer identification number (EIN)

For Privacy Act and Paperwork Reduction Act Notice, see page 3. Cat. No. 10220Q Form **W-4** (20--)

Source: United States Department of the Treasury, Internal Revenue Service

Goodheart-Willcox Publisher

Figure 3-3 Employees complete Form W-4 when starting a new job. It provides information used to determine how much federal tax to withhold from paychecks.

FICA is a matching tax. This means that employers must match the amount of FICA taxes that their employees pay. Employers add their share to the FICA tax and pay the total to the government under the employee's name and Social Security number.

Other Deductions

Voluntary deductions may be withheld for health care, dental care, vision care, retirement plans, and other insurance that employees purchase through their employers. These deductions might also include charitable contributions made through an employer.

Benefits

An **employee benefit**, or *fringe benefit*, is a form of noncash compensation received in addition to a wage or salary. **Compensation** is wages or salaries and benefits paid to employees. Some of the most valuable forms of payment to workers are noncash compensation. Employee benefits offer important financial advantages. When an employer provides a benefit, such as health insurance, the employee does not have to spend personal income. This can make it possible to have more discretionary income.

The availability of employee benefits and other extras depends on the company and type of work. Along with salary or wages, benefits contribute significantly to the financial well-being of workers and their families. Common types of employee benefits include:

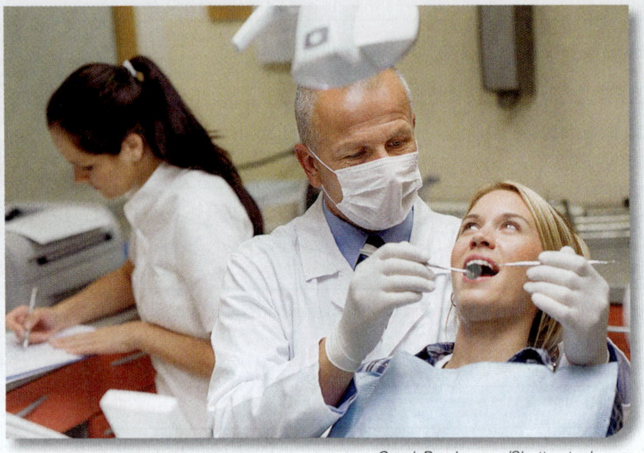

CandyBox Images/Shutterstock.com

Dental insurance is a fringe benefit often provided by employers.

- health insurance
- dental insurance
- retirement plan
- sick leave
- vacation time
- flexible work schedule
- childcare
- profit-sharing program
- opportunities for continuing education and professional development

Your employer can help you save money for the future. An employer-sponsored retirement savings plan is an investment program. One example is a 401(k) retirement savings plan. Money is withheld from the employee's gross pay and placed into a savings fund. Employers sometimes match employee contributions. However, with a few exceptions, money must stay in the account until retirement to avoid taxes and penalties. Chapter 7 presents more information about these plans and other valuable financial resources.

Work-Life Balance

Work-life balance is the amount of time an individual spends at work compared to the amount of time spent in a personal life. Less than a hundred years ago, most workers were expected to work six to seven days a week from sunrise to sunset. This left little time for life outside of work. Working that many hours was harmful to employee health and decreased job productivity.

Many organizations recognize that employees have responsibilities and obligations outside of work. To create a positive organizational culture, employees may be offered various ways to balance job responsibilities with family and life responsibilities. Some of the ways an organization may offer balance include personal leave, family leave, flextime, job sharing, and telecommuting.

- *Personal leave* is time off work that employees can use for personal reasons. In most organizations, personal time can be taken an hour at a time or days at a time.
- *Family leave* is time off work for certain life events. These may include the birth or adoption of a child, caring for a sick family member, and other family-related emergencies.
- *Flextime* is a policy allowing employees to adjust work schedules to better match personal schedules. For example, it is more practical for some employees to begin work early in the morning and leave early in the afternoon.
- *Job sharing* is an arrangement where two part-time employees handle the responsibilities of a single full-time position. Together, their hours and duties are equal to one full-time employee.
- *Telecommuting* is an arrangement where employees work away from the business site. Most telecommuters work from home and use technology to communicate with managers, coworkers, and customers.

Section 3.1 Review

Check Your Understanding

1. Name the US government law that sets and enforces the minimum wage.
2. What is income called when you earn it working for yourself rather than for a company?
3. Explain why the federal income tax system is known as a *pay-as-you-earn* system.
4. What is an employee benefit?
5. Name one of the ways an organization can offer work-life balance to its employees.

Build Your Vocabulary

As you progress through this course, develop a personal glossary. This will help you build your vocabulary and prepare you for a career. Write a definition for each of the following terms and add it to your glossary.

earned income
wage
overtime wage
piecework
salary
commission
tip
bonus
payroll deduction
gross pay
net pay
Form W-4
FICA taxes
employee benefit
compensation
work-life balance

Section 3.2 Tax Returns

Objectives

After completing this section, you will be able to:

- List examples of information needed to file an income tax return.
- Explain how to prepare a Form 1040.
- Identify sources of tax information and assistance.
- Summarize the tax audit process.

Essential Question

What information is required for an individual to complete a tax return?

Terms

tax return	capital gain	tax liability
voluntary compliance	taxable income	tax table
Form W-2	adjusted gross income	audit
gross income	net income	tax audit
unearned income	dependent	
dividend	standard deduction	

Income Tax Return Basics

The IRS is the government agency responsible for enforcing federal income tax laws. Approximately 200 million individuals file a tax return each year. A **tax return** is a report containing information used to calculate taxes owed by the taxpayer. Tax returns must also be filed with state governments. In many areas, a city tax return may need to be filed. Not filing a tax return is a crime.

The individual income tax is the federal government's largest source of revenue. The income tax system is based on voluntary compliance. **Voluntary compliance** means that the government expects individuals and businesses to voluntarily report all income that is subject to the income tax. Some income, such as wages, is reported by employers. However, other sources of income must be voluntarily reported by the taxpayer. This includes income from tips, gains from selling personal property, and income earned by independent consultants.

Who Must File

Individuals must file a tax return when their income reaches a level established by the IRS. If income is not high enough to file a tax return but income taxes were withheld, a return should be filed so a refund can be obtained. Refunds are never automatic. A tax return must be filed in order to receive a refund.

Employability Skills

Emotional Control

Emotional control is the process of directing one's feelings and reactions toward a desirable result that is socially acceptable. The lack of emotional control in a workplace situation can be cause for dismissal. Learning how to manage emotions helps a person think logically and act appropriately.

When to File

Tax returns must be filed no later than April 15 of the year after the income was earned. If April 15 falls on a Saturday, a Sunday, or a national holiday, the filing date is extended to the next business day. Those who file late are charged a penalty.

Hurst Photo/Shutterstock.com

A person must file an income tax return in order to receive a refund.

Filing Status

Filing status is a category that determines filing requirements, standard deduction, eligibility for certain credits, and the correct tax. It is based on your marital status on the last day of the tax year.

- *Single*. For individuals who are unmarried at the end of the year.
- *Married filing jointly (even if only one had income)*. For couples who are legally married on the last day of the tax year.
- *Married filing separately*. For legally married couples who choose to file separate returns.
- *Head of household (with qualifying person)*. For individuals who are unmarried at the end of the year and have at least one dependent child or other dependent relative.
- *Qualifying widow(er) with dependent child*. A special status for an individual with a dependent child whose spouse has died. This status is only available for two years after the death of a spouse if the taxpayer does not remarry during that two-year period.

It is important to choose the correct filing status. Choosing an incorrect filing status could result in an incorrect tax return.

Documentation

At the end of every year, each of your employers will send you a Form W-2, illustrated in Figure 3-4. **Form W-2** is a Wage and Tax Statement that shows an individual's earnings and the amounts of taxes withheld from the earned income during the current year. This statement will usually be mailed to your home by January 31 of the year following the year the income was earned.

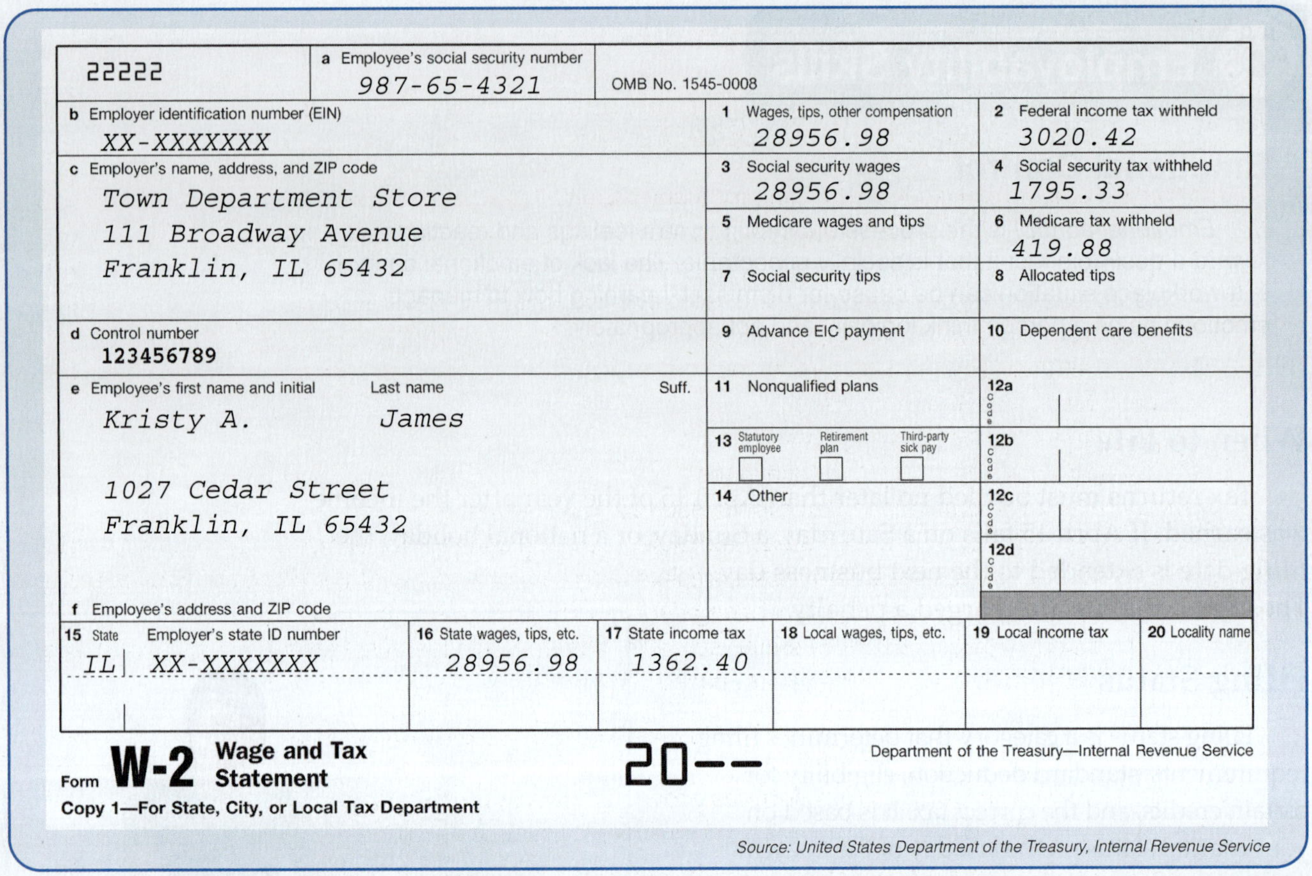

22222

a Employee's social security number 987-65-4321

OMB No. 1545-0008

b Employer identification number (EIN) XX-XXXXXXX

1 Wages, tips, other compensation 28956.98

2 Federal income tax withheld 3020.42

c Employer's name, address, and ZIP code
Town Department Store
111 Broadway Avenue
Franklin, IL 65432

3 Social security wages 28956.98

4 Social security tax withheld 1795.33

5 Medicare wages and tips

6 Medicare tax withheld 419.88

7 Social security tips

8 Allocated tips

d Control number 123456789

9 Advance EIC payment

10 Dependent care benefits

e Employee's first name and initial Kristy A. Last name James Suff.

11 Nonqualified plans

12a Code

13 Statutory employee / Retirement plan / Third-party sick pay

12b Code

14 Other

12c Code

12d Code

1027 Cedar Street
Franklin, IL 65432

f Employee's address and ZIP code

15 State	Employer's state ID number	16 State wages, tips, etc.	17 State income tax	18 Local wages, tips, etc.	19 Local income tax	20 Locality name
IL	XX-XXXXXXX	28956.98	1362.40			

Form **W-2** Wage and Tax Statement 20--

Department of the Treasury—Internal Revenue Service

Copy 1—For State, City, or Local Tax Department

Source: United States Department of the Treasury, Internal Revenue Service

Goodheart-Willcox Publisher

Figure 3-4 A Form W-2 shows how much an employee was paid during a year and the payroll deductions that were withheld.

You will receive a *Form 1099-MISC* if you earned income from contracted work, royalties, unemployment compensation, and other sources of nonemployee income.

Additional records and forms needed to prepare a return include:

- records of other income, such as from tips
- Social Security number and numbers of household members
- copies of tax returns from the previous year
- forms and instructions from the IRS

Taxpayers who choose to itemize deductions may also need these records:

- canceled checks and receipts for deductions or credits entered on a tax return
- itemized bills and receipts for deductible expenses
- records of interest paid on home mortgages
- real estate closing statements
- investment records, including purchase and sale dates, prices, gains, losses, and commissions

Income

A taxpayer must calculate the gross income for a tax return. **Gross income** is all the income an individual receives in a year including both earned and unearned income.

Exploring Careers

Tax Preparer

Preparing a tax return can be confusing for many people. A tax preparer completes tax returns for clients. This includes completing all supporting schedules, inserting all appropriate information, and calculating the amount of money to be paid to or received from the IRS. Preparers may specialize in one area, such as individual returns, business returns, estates and trusts, tax planning, and tax appeals. Examples of tasks that tax preparers perform include:

- consult and advise clients on their taxes
- research tax laws and regulations
- input data into computer programs
- help clients develop plans to reduce taxes
- prepare all tax documentation for clients, such as return forms

Tax preparer jobs typically require a bachelor's degree in accounting. To receive an Enrolled Agent (EA) designation from the IRS, tax preparers must complete five years of working for the IRS or an equivalency exam. A tax preparer spends a lot of time working directly with clients, so they must have excellent communication skills. They should have strong computer skills, knowledge of tax laws and regulations, and the ability to work without supervision in a fast-paced environment.

Unearned income is earnings from sources other than work. Monetary gifts, lottery winnings, or other contest winnings are examples. Unearned income includes interest on savings accounts, investments, and other bank accounts. Also included in unearned income is rent income. *Rent income* is payments received from rental property. Individuals who rent property to other people, such as an apartment in an apartment complex, earn a source of income.

Unearned income includes dividends and capital gains. **Dividends** are a portion of a corporation's earnings paid to its stockholders. A **capital gain** results when property, such as corporate stock, is sold for an amount greater than its cost. Social Security, retirement income, alimony, and unemployment compensation are also considered unearned income.

Taxes are not calculated based on gross income. **Taxable income** is the amount on which taxes are calculated. This amount can be reduced by adjustments. *Tax adjustments* are government-approved reductions in gross income. This helps to reduce the amount of tax that must be paid. For example, students or their parents can deduct the interest paid on student loans. **Adjusted gross income** is calculated by subtracting adjustments from total income.

Individuals who own businesses must also pay income taxes on earnings. Gross income in a business is the total income earned from business operations. **Net income** is gross income minus the expenses of operating the business. Income taxes are paid on net income.

Tax Forms

Prior to 2018, taxpayers chose to use the tax form best suited to their individual circumstances. The available forms included the 1040EZ, 1040A, and 1040 forms. However, the *Tax Cuts and Jobs Act of 2017* introduced many changes

MBI/Shutterstock.com

The Internal Revenue Service can provide assistance in filing a return.

to income tax laws in the United States. To simplify the tax-filing process, the US Treasury approved a new approach that reduced the number of forms from which taxpayers had to choose to one basic Form 1040 that all taxpayers use.

Form 1040 uses a "building block" approach. This means taxpayers with straightforward tax situations only need to file Form 1040. Taxpayers who have more-complicated tax situations need to provide supplemental information on additional numbered forms, called schedules, that relate to their specific circumstances.

The federal *Bipartisan Budget Act of 2018* required the IRS to create a tax form for seniors who do not have complicated tax returns. Effective January 1, 2020, taxpayers age 65 or older have the option to use Form 1040-SR, U.S. Tax Return for Seniors. Form 1040-SR is a one-page form that features larger font for better readability. It is similar to the old Form 1040EZ, but expanded to include Social Security benefits, pension income, and other forms of retirement income. Form 1040-SR, similar to Form 1040, uses the building-block approach and additional schedules can be attached, if needed. For married couples filing jointly, only one must be age 65 or over to use Form 1040-SR.

Taxpayers can file paper forms or electronically. Electronic filing, or *e-filing,* allows filing of an income tax return online. A variety of computer software programs are available that enable a return to be filed using a personal computer. E-filing programs provide information and advice with step-by-step directions for the filing process. The IRS also offers a free e-filling service for qualified filers.

Preparing a Form 1040

When preparing a tax return, a taxpayer should read and follow the instructions provided with the tax return form. Forms can change each year, so it is important to read the information that accompanies the return.

Step 1: Personal Information

The first step in completing a tax return is to fill in personal information. The first page of Form 1040, shown in Figure 3-5, asks for information about the taxpayer's filing status, name, Social Security number, address, dependents, and sources of income.

Kristy left the standard deduction section blank because she is single and cannot be claimed on her parent's tax return as a dependent. A **dependent** is an individual who relies on someone else for financial support, such as a child, a spouse, or an elderly parent. She does not have a spouse, so she left the spouse's information and standard deduction blank.

Form **1040** Department of the Treasury—Internal Revenue Service (99)
U.S. Individual Income Tax Return 20-- OMB No. 1545-0074 IRS Use Only—Do not write or staple in this space.

Filing Status Check only one box. ☐ Single ☐ Married filing jointly ☐ Married filing separately (MFS) ☐ Head of household (HOH) ☐ Qualifying widow(er) (QW)
If you checked the MFS box, enter the name of your spouse. If you checked the HOH or QW box, enter the child's name if the qualifying person is a child but not your dependent ▶

Your first name and middle initial	Last name	Your social security number
Kristy A.	James	987 65 4321
If joint return, spouse's first name and middle initial	Last name	Spouse's social security number

Home address (number and street). If you have a P.O. box, see instructions.		Apt. no.	Presidential Election Campaign
1027 Cedar Street			Check here if you, or your spouse if filing jointly, want $3 to go to this fund. Checking a box below will not change your tax or refund. ☐ You ☐ Spouse
City, town, or post office. If you have a foreign address, also complete spaces below.	State	ZIP code	
Franklin	IL	65432	
Foreign country name	Foreign province/state/county	Foreign postal code	

At any time during 20--, did you receive, sell, send, exchange, or otherwise acquire any financial interest in any virtual currency? ☐ Yes ☐ No

Standard Deduction **Someone can claim:** ☐ You as a dependent ☐ Your spouse as a dependent
☐ Spouse itemizes on a separate return or you were a dual-status alien

Age/Blindness **You:** ☐ Were born before January 2, 1956 ☐ Are blind **Spouse:** ☐ Was born before January 2, 1956 ☐ Is blind

Dependents (see instructions): If more than four dependents, see instructions and check here ▶ ☐

(1) First name Last name	(2) Social security number	(3) Relationship to you	(4) ✔ if qualifies for (see instructions): Child tax credit	Credit for other dependents
			☐	☐
			☐	☐
			☐	☐
			☐	☐

Attach Sch. B if required.

Standard Deduction for— • Single or Married filing separately, $12,400 • Married filing jointly or Qualifying widow(er), $24,800 • Head of household, $18,650 • If you checked any box under *Standard Deduction*, see instructions.

1	Wages, salaries, tips, etc. Attach Form(s) W-2			1	28,956.98
2a	Tax-exempt interest	2a	b Taxable interest	2b	850.00
3a	Qualified dividends	3a	b Ordinary dividends	3b	
4a	IRA distributions	4a	b Taxable amount	4b	
5a	Pensions and annuities	5a	b Taxable amount	5b	
6a	Social security benefits	6a	b Taxable amount	6b	
7	Capital gain or (loss). Attach Schedule D if required. If not required, check here ▶ ☐			7	
8	Other income from Schedule 1, line 9			8	
9	Add lines 1, 2b, 3b, 4b, 5b, 6b, 7, and 8. This is your **total income** ▶			9	29,806.98
10	Adjustments to income:				
a	From Schedule 1, line 22	10a			
b	Charitable contributions if you take the standard deduction. See instructions	10b			
c	Add lines 10a and 10b. These are your **total adjustments to income** ▶			10c	
11	Subtract line 10c from line 9. This is your **adjusted gross income** ▶			11	29,806.98
12	**Standard deduction or itemized deductions** (from Schedule A)			12	12,400.00
13	Qualified business income deduction. Attach Form 8995 or Form 8995-A			13	
14	Add lines 12 and 13			14	12,400.00
15	**Taxable income.** Subtract line 14 from line 11. If zero or less, enter -0-			15	17,406.98

For Disclosure, Privacy Act, and Paperwork Reduction Act Notice, see separate instructions. Cat. No. 11320B Form **1040** (20--)

Source: United States Department of the Treasury, Internal Revenue Service

Goodheart-Willcox Publisher

Figure 3-5 The 1040 replaced all other tax forms.

Step 2: Income

The lower part of page 1 requests detailed information about the taxpayer's income. Line 1 requests income from wages, salaries, and tips. Here, Kristy entered $28,956.98 as her total salary for the year.

This information is on her Form W-2 Wage and Tax Statement previously shown in Figure 3-4. At the end of the fiscal year, employers send employees a Form W-2 that shows earnings and the amounts of income, Social Security, and Medicare taxes withheld from the employee's earned income during the year.

Kristy had additional taxable income of $850.00 in interest income, which she entered on line 2b. Having no other income, she totaled her income and entered the number on line 9. Total income is commonly called *gross income*. Gross income is income before deductions.

History of Finance

Taxes

The nation's first income tax was created with the passage of The Revenue Act of 1862 to support the Civil War effort. In 1866, revenue collections reached the highest point in the nation's history. The Revenue Act also established the office of Commissioner of Internal Revenue. The Commissioner was given the power to assess, levy, and collect taxes. The Commissioner was also given the right to prosecute people who did not pay taxes and seize their property and income. Today, these powers and authority are vested in the Internal Revenue Service and remain very much the same.

In 1868, Congress eliminated the income tax due to public opposition. The income tax was revived in 1894 in order to reduce taxes paid on imported goods. In 1895, however, the US Supreme Court declared that the income tax was unconstitutional because it was not apportioned among the states as required by the Constitution.

In 1913, the Sixteenth Amendment made the income tax permanent. The amendment gives Congress legal authority to tax the incomes of both individuals and corporations. The withholding tax on wages was introduced in 1943 to speed up revenue collections needed to support the nation's involvement in World War II.

Step 3: Standard Deduction

Line 12 is used to record a taxpayer's standard deduction. The **standard deduction** is a dollar amount that non-itemizers may subtract from their income before income tax is applied. Taxpayers may choose either itemized deductions or the standard deduction, but usually choose whichever results in the lesser amount of tax payable. It will vary according to the taxpayer's filing status (single, married, or head of household). Kristy is single, so she entered $12,400. Kristy also entered the amount on line 14 because she had no business income deduction. The amount is deducted from line 11 to arrive at her taxable income on line 15. Taxable income is gross income minus allowed deductions.

Step 4: Payments and Tax

The amount of **tax liability,** which is tax owed, is found on the tax tables available on the IRS website. **Tax tables** are government-issued tables that show a taxpayer's total tax obligation for a year based on the amount of total taxable income. Tax tables are updated each year. A partial tax table is shown in Figure 3-7. Kristy's taxable income ($17,406.98) falls in the income bracket *At least 17,400, But less than 17,450.* The tax in that bracket for a single person is $1,897. Kristy entered that amount on line 16 of Form 1040. She does not owe any other taxes, so she repeats that amount on line 24.

On line 25a, Kristy entered the amount of federal tax withheld from her salary as recorded on her Form W-2. The amount was $3,020.42. She repeated that amount on line 25d and line 33. If line 33 is more than line 24, the taxpayer is due a refund. Kristy received a refund of $1,123.42.

Form 1040 (20--) Page **2**

16	**Tax** (see instructions). Check if any from Form(s): **1** ☐ 8814 **2** ☐ 4972 **3** ☐ ______	16	1,897.00
17	Amount from Schedule 2, line 3	17	
18	Add lines 16 and 17	18	
19	Child tax credit or credit for other dependents	19	
20	Amount from Schedule 3, line 7	20	
21	Add lines 19 and 20	21	
22	Subtract line 21 from line 18. If zero or less, enter -0-	22	
23	Other taxes, including self-employment tax, from Schedule 2, line 10	23	
24	Add lines 22 and 23. This is your **total tax** ▶	24	1,897.00
25	Federal income tax withheld from:		
a	Form(s) W-2 — 25a 3,020.42		
b	Form(s) 1099 — 25b		
c	Other forms (see instructions) — 25c		
d	Add lines 25a through 25c	25d	3,020.42
26	20-- estimated tax payments and amount applied from 20-- return	26	
27	Earned income credit (EIC) — 27		
28	Additional child tax credit. Attach Schedule 8812 — 28		
29	American opportunity credit from Form 8863, line 8 — 29		
30	Recovery rebate credit. See instructions — 30		
31	Amount from Schedule 3, line 13 — 31		
32	Add lines 27 through 31. These are your **total other payments and refundable credits** ▶	32	
33	Add lines 25d, 26, and 32. These are your **total payments** ▶	33	3,020.42

• If you have a qualifying child, attach Sch. EIC.
• If you have nontaxable combat pay, see instructions.

Refund

34	If line 33 is more than line 24, subtract line 24 from line 33. This is the amount you **overpaid**	34	
35a	Amount of line 34 you want **refunded to you.** If Form 8888 is attached, check here ▶ ☐	35a	1,123.42
▶ b	Routing number ______ ▶ c Type: ☐ Checking ☐ Savings		
▶ d	Account number ______		
36	Amount of line 34 you want **applied to your 2021 estimated tax** ▶ — 36		

Direct deposit? See instructions.

Amount You Owe

For details on how to pay, see instructions.

37	Subtract line 33 from line 24. This is the **amount you owe now** ▶	37	
	Note: Schedule H and Schedule SE filers, line 37 may not represent all of the taxes you owe for 20--. See Schedule 3, line 12e, and its instructions for details.		
38	Estimated tax penalty (see instructions) ▶ — 38		

Third Party Designee

Do you want to allow another person to discuss this return with the IRS? See instructions ▶ ☐ **Yes.** Complete below. ☐ **No**

Designee's name ▶ Phone no. ▶ Personal identification number (PIN) ▶

Sign Here

Under penalties of perjury, I declare that I have examined this return and accompanying schedules and statements, and to the best of my knowledge and belief, they are true, correct, and complete. Declaration of preparer (other than taxpayer) is based on all information of which preparer has any knowledge.

Joint return? See instructions. Keep a copy for your records.

Your signature	Date	Your occupation	If the IRS sent you an Identity Protection PIN, enter it here (see inst.) ▶
Kristy A James	03/01/--		
Spouse's signature. If a joint return, **both** must sign.	Date	Spouse's occupation	If the IRS sent your spouse an Identity Protection PIN, enter it here (see inst.) ▶
Phone no.	Email address		

Paid Preparer Use Only

Preparer's name	Preparer's signature	Date	PTIN	Check if: ☐ Self-employed
Firm's name ▶			Phone no.	
Firm's address ▶			Firm's EIN ▶	

Go to *www.irs.gov/Form1040* for instructions and the latest information. Form **1040** (20--)

Source: United States Department of the Treasury, Internal Revenue Service

Goodheart-Willcox Publisher

Figure 3-6 Page two Form 1040.

Step 5: Signature

A return must be signed before it can be processed, and an unsigned return will be returned for a signature. If a refund is due, this could delay the return by several weeks. If taxes are owed, it could result in penalties and interest owed. Kristy signed her name on the appropriate line and dated the return.

If Kristy hired a tax preparer, that person would complete the section Paid Preparer Use Only. Since she completed her own return, this section was left blank.

Sources of Tax Information and Assistance

Many sources are available for tax planning information and assistance in filing a return. As income increases, finances become more complicated. There are professionals who can advise on tax matters.

Ethics

Tax Returns

It is unethical to file a fraudulent tax return. In a fraudulent tax return, a person deliberately reports information that is not correct. A person who intentionally files a tax return that is not accurate may be subject to penalties, interest, and possibly prison time.

- *Internal Revenue Service (IRS).* The IRS publishes free instruction booklets annually. The office also operates a system of recorded phone messages with tax information on a variety of questions. The agency offers a website and a toll-free hotline for specific questions. Walk-in service is available at some IRS offices across the country.
- *Volunteer Income Tax Assistance (VITA) Program.* The VITA Program is an IRS service that offers free tax help to lower-income people who need assistance in preparing their tax returns. IRS-certified volunteers provide free basic income tax return preparation to qualified individuals in local communities. VITA sites are generally located at community and neighborhood centers, libraries, schools, shopping malls, and other convenient locations. Most locations also offer free electronic filing.
- *Tax Counseling for the Elderly (TCE) Program.* The IRS TCE Program provides free tax assistance to individuals who are age 60 and older. Certified by the IRS, TCE volunteers provide fee tax assistance to elderly individuals who qualify for the service. Tax assistance is provided at community locations across the nation. Many of these community locations also offer free electronic filing services.
- *Tax Preparation Services.* Many tax attorneys and certified public accountants specialize in tax matters. They prepare tax returns based on records and receipts provided by the taxpayer.
- *Tax Preparation Guides.* Each year, tax guides are published by various sources and are available for purchase. These guides are also available at many public libraries.

If line 15 (taxable income) is—		And you are—			
At least	But less than	Single	Married filing jointly *	Married filing sepa rately	Head of a house-hold
		Your tax is—			
17,000	17,050	1,849	1,703	1,849	1,766
17,050	17,100	1,855	1,708	1,855	1,772
17,100	17,150	1,861	1,713	1,861	1,778
17,150	17,200	1,867	1,718	1,867	1,784
17,200	17,250	1,873	1,723	1,873	1,790
17,250	17,300	1,879	1,728	1,879	1,796
17,300	17,350	1,885	1,733	1,885	1,802
17,350	17,400	1,891	1,738	1,891	1,808
17,400	17,450	1,897	1,743	1,897	1,814
17,450	17,500	1,903	1,748	1,903	1,820
17,500	17,550	1,909	1,753	1,909	1,826
17,550	17,600	1,915	1,758	1,915	1,832
17,600	17,650	1,921	1,763	1,921	1,838
17,650	17,700	1,927	1,768	1,927	1,844
17,700	17,750	1,933	1,773	1,933	1,850
17,750	17,800	1,939	1,778	1,939	1,856
17,800	17,850	1,949	1,783	1,945	1,862
17,850	17,900	1,951	1,788	1,951	1,868
17,900	17,950	1,957	1,793	1,957	1,874
17,950	18,000	1,963	1,798	1,963	1,880

Source: US Department of the Treasury/Internal Revenue Service

Goodheart-Willcox Publisher

Figure 3-7 A 1040 tax table categorizes levels of taxable income with the corresponding tax amounts.

IRS Audits

An **audit** is the review of financial records and statements to make sure the information is accurate as reported. A **tax audit** is a detailed examination of a tax return by the IRS. In 2015, the IRS audited approximately 1.2 percent of the more than 141.5 million returns filed. The *Internal Revenue Service Reform Act of 1998* guarantees taxpayers due process in their dealings with the IRS. The IRS must provide a detailed statement of your rights and the IRS's obligations during the audit, appeals, refund, and collection process. You have the right to make an audio recording of any audit interview conducted by the IRS.

If the IRS audits your return, you have to prove the accuracy of your reported income, tax deductions, adjustments, credits, and other details on your tax return. You are expected to answer the IRS agent's questions honestly and completely, providing documentation when necessary.

If you disagree with the outcome of a tax audit, you have the right to a conference at the Regional Appeals Office. From there, you can take your case to the US Tax Court, the US Court of Federal Claims, or even the US Supreme Court. In the end, you have to pay any additional taxes, interest, and penalties that are assigned.

It is important to provide accurate information on a tax return form. Being *accurate* means to give factual, error-free information. Providing *inaccurate* information could extend the processing of the tax return, delay the tax refund, and may prompt the IRS to investigate the tax return.

It is easy to make an error when recording numbers. To ensure accuracy, entries and calculations should be double-checked. Being accurate also means recording truthful information. Intentionally providing false information on a tax return form is a crime. An individual caught providing false information faces financial penalties, fines, and even criminal prosecution.

Section 3.2 Review

Check Your Understanding

1. Who must file an income tax return?
2. To simplify the tax-filing process, the US Treasury approved one form for all to complete a tax return. What is the name of that form?
3. Differentiate between gross, net, and taxable income.
4. What kind of information does the Internal Revenue Service (IRS) provide taxpayers?
5. Why is accuracy important when filing an income tax return?

Build Your Vocabulary

As you progress through this course, develop a personal glossary. This will help you build your vocabulary and prepare you for a career. Write a definition for each of the following terms and add it to your glossary.

tax return
voluntary compliance
Form W-2
gross income
unearned income
dividend
capital gain
taxable income
adjusted gross income
net income
dependent
standard deduction
tax liability
tax table
audit
tax audit

Section 3.3 Government Spending

Essential Question

Why do state, local, and federal government agencies impose taxes on taxpayers?

Objectives

After studying this section, you will be able to:

- Explain the purpose of federal, state, and local taxes.
- Define types of tax classifications.
- Discuss the federal tax code.
- Explain the Social Security program.

Terms

levy	Medicaid	indirect tax
mandatory expenditure	transfer payment	progressive tax
Social Security	discretionary expenditure	regressive tax
Medicare	direct tax	proportional tax
disability		

Government Spending

Paying for governmental operations, facilities, and services is the primary purpose of taxes. The government provides goods and services that benefit the public. Examples include fire and police protection, schools, highways, airports, parks, and water and sewage treatment. Federal, state, and local governments generate revenue by taxing individuals and businesses. To **levy** a tax means to use legal authority to impose a payment. At present, most taxpayers spend a sizable share of their dollars to pay their income tax, Social Security tax, and other taxes.

Harry Hu/Shutterstock.com

Police services and protection are an example of a public service provided by the government.

In addition to providing goods and services necessary for society, legislators may raise or lower taxes for many reasons.

- *Stabilize the economy.* Governments may use taxes to promote economic stability, fight inflation, or slow a recession. This helps achieve the United States' greater goals of stable prices, full employment, and steady economic growth.
- *Address social challenges.* Some tax dollars are used to provide services and opportunities for populations in need. Food stamps, housing subsidies, and veterans'

educational benefits are examples of such programs. A less obvious but very important way that governments address social needs is by supporting an economy that raises the standard of living for people in the country. Less government assistance is needed when people have the ability to improve their financial situations.

- *Influence taxpayer behavior.* By removing taxes from some items and taxing others, the government tries to change peoples' behaviors. For example, the federal government and most state governments allow taxpayers to deduct certain charitable donations. This lowers the taxpayer's taxes and, as a result, encourages giving. The government adds tax on alcohol and tobacco products, which increases their cost and discourages people from using them.

Tax revenue is used to run federal, state, and local governments. However, since resources are limited, each level of government must make choices. Like individuals and families, governments create a budget for spending. Federal, state, and local government spending reflects the needs, priorities, and goals of the people living within each government level.

Federal Government Spending

Taxation is the primary source of revenue for the federal government. Sources of the federal government's revenue are shown in Figure 3-8. In those years when the government spends more than it collects, it must borrow money. This is called *deficit spending*, and it increases the national debt. The US Treasury divides all spending into three categories: mandatory spending, discretionary spending, and interest on the national debt.

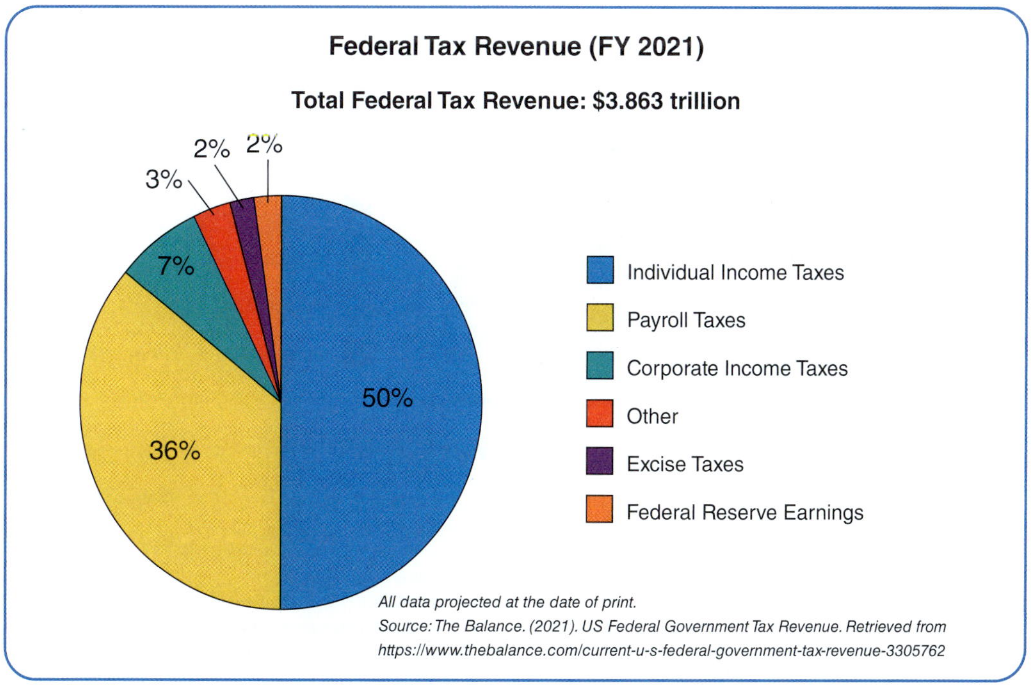

Goodheart-Willcox Publisher

Figure 3-8 Federal government dollars come from a variety of taxes.

Mandatory Spending

A large percentage of federal spending is for mandatory expense items. **Mandatory expenditures** are those Congress legislated into law. These expenditures must be paid for each year. If enough tax dollars are not available, the government must borrow the money to meet these commitments. Figure 3-9 shows a summary of mandatory federal spending.

About 78 percent of mandatory expenditures are for entitlements. The largest entitlement program is Social Security, followed by Medicare.

Social Security is a federal program that provides income when earnings are reduced or stopped because of retirement, serious illness or injury, or death. In the case of death, benefits are provided to survivors of the deceased. Benefits are funded by a payroll tax on workers' income and matching contributions from employers.

Medicare is a federal health insurance program that provides benefits for people 65 years or older or those with disabilities. A **disability** is a limitation that affects a person's ability to function in major life activities. The Medicare program is funded by the Medicare tax, which is part of the Federal Insurance Contributions Act (FICA). Medicare taxes are paid by employers and employees.

Medicaid is a public insurance program that provides health coverage to low-income families and individuals. The program includes children, parents, pregnant women, seniors, and people with disabilities. Medicaid is funded jointly by the federal government and the individual states. Each state operates its own Medicaid program within federal guidelines. The annual income limitation to qualify for Medicaid benefits is based on the current *federal poverty level (FPL)*. Annual earnings limit and amount of benefits is set by the individual states.

Other entitlement programs include federal employee retirement benefits, veterans' pensions and medical care, nutrition assistance, unemployment

Mandatory Federal Spending (FY 2021)

Total Mandatory Spending: $2.966 trillion

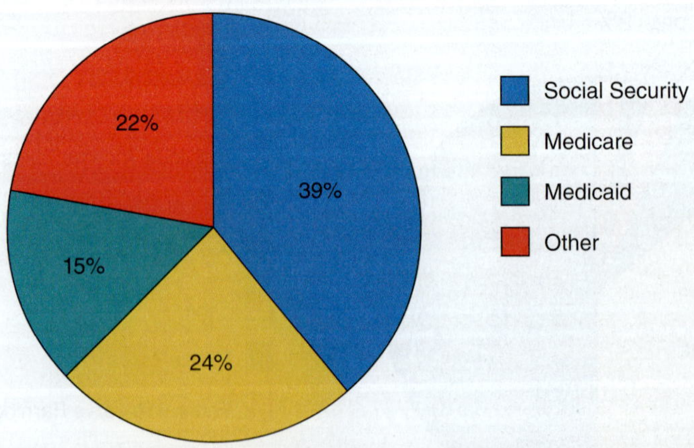

All data projected at the date of print.
Source: The Balance. (2021). Current Federal Mandatory Spending. Retrieved from https://www.thebalance.com/current-federal-mandatory-spending-3305772

Goodheart-Willcox Publisher

Figure 3-9 Mandatory expenditures of the US Federal Government can be broken up into four major categories.

compensation, and housing assistance. Money received from entitlement programs is considered income. However, income from these sources is usually not taxable. Instead, a payment of this type is called a transfer payment. A **transfer payment** is a payment made to an individual from the federal government through various social benefit programs.

Discretionary Spending

Discretionary spending is the portion of the budget that Congress spends through annual appropriations. A **discretionary expenditure** is an expense item that can be adjusted according to needs and revenues. National defense and nondefense discretionary spending are the two main categories for the government. Money for national defense is used to equip the armed forces and pay for military personnel, research, and technology. When the nation goes to war or enters a military conflict, defense spending is increased.

Nondefense discretionary spending includes the cost of government operations and a wide array of programs. The federal government also provides funds to state and local governments for certain programs. Figure 3-10 shows a summary of federal discretionary spending.

Interest on National Debt

Even though the government classifies interest on the national debt as a separate category, it is a mandatory expense item. This interest must be paid, even if the government must borrow money to pay it. The interest is paid to

Federal Discretionary Spending (FY 2021)

Total Discretionary Spending: $1.485 trillion

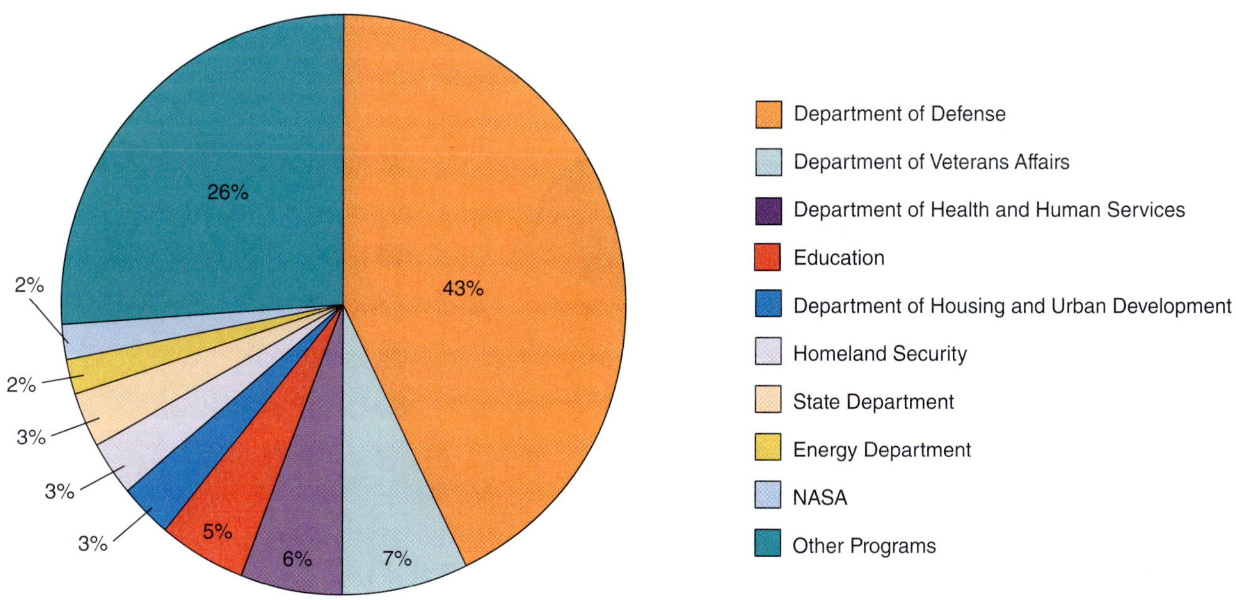

All data projected at the date of print.
Source: The Balance. (2021). Current U.S. Discretionary Spending. Retrieved from https://www.thebalance.com/current-us-discretionary-federal-budget-and-spending-3306308

Goodheart-Willcox Publisher

Figure 3-10 Discretionary spending includes national defense, government operations, and a wide array of programs.

financial institutions, foreign investors and governments, and individuals who buy government securities. In essence, these institutions and individuals lend money to the federal government, and taxpayers pay the interest.

State and Local Government Spending

Both taxation and government spending vary widely from state to state and city to city. However, the sources of revenues and categories of expenditures are similar.

Sales, real estate, and personal property taxes make up a large part of state and local revenues. Most states and localities also rely on personal and corporate income tax for a large share of their revenues. These taxes are important to the economy and are used mainly to pay for public education, highways, and public assistance programs run by the state. Figure 3-11 shows government taxing and spending at the state and local levels.

Types of Taxes

Taxes are paid on income, purchases, property, and wealth. Different types of taxes apply to these taxable items. More than one government body can tax the same item. For example, all levels of government have the power to tax personal income. Some of the specific taxes are described as follows.

- *Personal income tax is levied on earnings.* Most earned and unearned income is subject to the federal income tax. Most states also tax the income of residents.

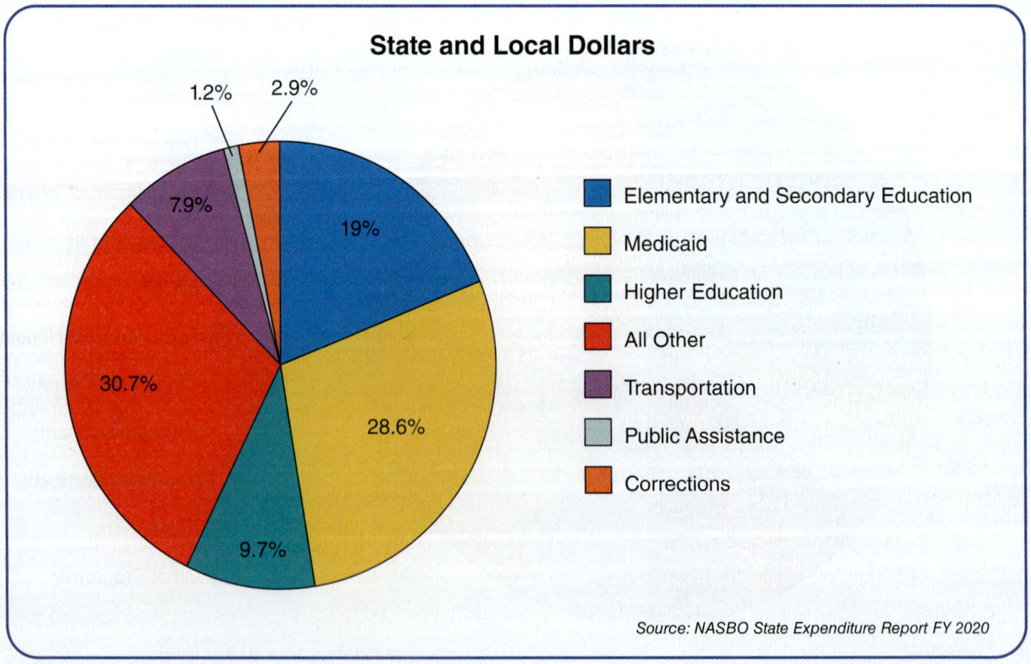

Goodheart-Willcox Publisher

Figure 3-11 State and local dollars are mostly spent on education and health care.

- *Sales tax is levied by state and local governments on purchases of goods and services.* All but five states have a general sales tax on the goods and services people buy. In many states, food and drugs are exempt from this tax. This eases the burden of sales tax on low-income individuals.
- *Excise tax is levied by federal and state governments on the sale and transfer of certain items.* Examples include cigarettes, alcoholic beverages, air travel, telephone services, gasoline, firearms, and certain luxury items.
- *Property tax is levied on property owned.* It includes real estate property tax and personal property tax. *Real estate tax* is based on the value of land and buildings owned. This is an important source of revenue for local and state governments. Rates vary greatly from area to area and state to state. *Personal property taxes* are assessed in some states on items such as cars, boats, furniture, and other assets.
- *Wealth tax is levied on assets.* There are two main types of wealth taxes. Estates worth over a certain amount are subject to *estate tax*. This is a tax imposed by the federal government on assets left by an individual at the time of his or her death. This tax must be paid out of the estate before assets are distributed. *Gift tax* is levied by the federal government on donors or givers who transfer assets over a given amount to others. The regulations regarding gift tax change from time to time when new tax laws are passed.

There are different classifications of taxes. Examples are direct and indirect taxes and progressive, regressive, and proportional taxes.

Direct and Indirect Taxes

One tax classification is related to how taxes are paid. A **direct tax** is paid directly to the government by the taxpayer. Personal income tax is a direct tax. An **indirect tax** is a tax levied on one person or entity, but shifted to or paid by another. Sales tax is one example. It is imposed on the seller of goods and services but paid by the consumer.

Progressive, Regressive, and Proportional Taxes

Another classification of taxes is related to how the tax rate is applied. A **progressive tax** imposes a higher tax rate on those with higher incomes. Income tax is one type of progressive taxation. As earners' incomes increase, their tax rates increase. In recent years, tax rates ranged from 10 to 39.6 percent. Progressive tax rates change with new tax laws. However, lower rates always apply to lower incomes, and rates increase as income increases.

A **regressive tax** has the effect of imposing a higher tax rate on those with lower incomes. A **proportional tax** imposes the same tax rate on all individuals or entities regardless of differences in income or ability to pay. This is sometimes called a *flat tax*. Sales tax is one example of proportional tax in that the same rate is applied to the purchases of all consumers.

michaeljung/Shutterstock.com

Sales tax is one example of proportional tax in that the same rate is applied to the purchases of all consumers.

However, it also is considered a regressive tax in that it takes a higher percentage of income from consumers with lower incomes.

For example, two consumers buy a computer for $1,000. Both pay a 7 percent sales tax that comes to $70. The tax is proportional since both pay the same rate. However, if one buyer has an annual income of $30,000 and the other has an annual income of $60,000, the sales tax could be considered regressive because the $70 sales tax represents a higher percentage of the lower income.

Federal Tax Code

When the federal income tax system was created in 1914, the tax code was 14 pages long. Today the US tax code contains thousands of pages of complex rules and provisions. The IRS publishes over 450 tax forms and almost 300 forms to explain them. There are also 50 state tax systems and over 80,000 local taxing agencies. Each one has its own set of laws and regulations.

As the cost of providing government services increases, taxes increase. As legislators periodically revise and review the tax code, the tax system becomes more and more complex. In recent years, tax reform legislation has occupied both state and federal lawmakers. Citizens concerned about rising taxes have pushed for measures that limit new taxes.

The federal tax code changes periodically. Congress struggles to meet the need for revenues with a level of taxation voters will accept. Legislators propose new tax laws to increase revenues, to make the tax burden fairer, and to achieve desired economic outcomes.

Since major changes in tax policies can cause major changes in the economy, any new tax legislation needs to be thought out carefully. Now tax proposals and policies are evaluated on effectiveness, fairness, and impact.

- *Effectiveness.* Will a new or changed tax law produce adequate revenues? Tax revenues should be great enough to achieve the goals of the tax proposal. Ideally, revenues should be considerably higher than the cost of administering, enforcing, and collecting the taxes.
- *Fairness.* Is the tax fair? To be fair, a tax must fit the taxpayer's ability to pay. Tax rates should be no greater than required for essential government services and operations. In addition, the burden should be distributed fairly among taxpayers.
- *Impact.* Is the economic impact of tax legislation minimal or beneficial? Almost all tax legislation shapes the economy to some degree. Tax laws should achieve positive economic goals or at least keep negative results to a minimum.

Tax laws should not cause major economic problems or seriously interfere with the economy. For example, an increase in federal income tax during a recession would lower consumer demand at a time when the economy needs the stimulus of greater demand. Eliminating the tax advantages of retirement accounts could reduce savings rates at a time when savings are needed for business growth and expansion.

You Do the Math Multiplication

To multiply whole numbers and decimals, place the numbers, called the *factors*, in pairs in a vertical list. When multiplying a percentage, move the decimal two places to the left. To find the number of decimal places needed in the final product, add the number of places in each number. Two decimal places plus three decimal places means the product must have five decimal places.

Solve the following problems.

1. Shelia earns $12 an hour and is covered by the Fair Labor Standards Act. Last week, Shelia worked 42 hours. What is the gross pay for the week?
2. You live in an area that has a general sales tax rate of 8.5 percent on most purchases. How much sales tax would you pay for the following goods and services from area stores?

   A. $150 jacket

   B. $30 haircut

   C. $2 magazine

   The tax rate in a neighboring county is 7 percent. How much can you save on each item by crossing the county line to do your shopping?

Social Security

President Franklin Roosevelt signed the Social Security Act into law in 1935. Medicare became part of the law in 1965. The Social Security Administration manages the Social Security program. Today, the program covers almost everyone who works. The tax is figured as a percentage of an employee's income and withheld from gross pay. FICA, or Federal Insurance Contributions Act, is the law that requires the collection of Social Security payroll taxes.

Social Security Benefits

When you begin working, your Social Security taxes pay for the benefits others receive. When you retire, or if you become disabled or die, other workers pay Social Security taxes to cover benefits to you and your family. Before a worker or a worker's family can receive benefits, the worker must have paid Social Security taxes for a certain length of time.

As you work, you earn Social Security credits, usually at a rate of four per year. The number of credits required to receive Social Security benefits varies. Most workers need 40 credits or 10 years of work to qualify for benefits. Younger workers who become disabled may require fewer credits to qualify. The benefit amount depends on the worker's age and average earnings over a period of years. It is a good idea to check your Social Security record every few years to make sure your earnings are being credited to your record. You can get a free postcard form at any Social Security office for this purpose.

Social Security benefits do not start automatically. When a person becomes eligible, the benefits must be applied for at the nearest Social Security office. The Social Security Administration calculates benefits and issues monthly payments.

The types of benefits provided by the Social Security program include retirement, disability, survivors', and divorced people's benefits.

Retirement Benefits

Workers become eligible for full retirement benefits at age 67. Early retirement can begin as early as age 62, but with reduced retirement benefit payments. Benefits may also be paid to these members of a retired worker's family:

- unmarried children under 18 (under 19 if full-time high school students) or over 18 with a serious disability beginning before age 22
- spouse who is age 62 or older
- spouse of any age if caring for a retired worker's child who is under age 16 or disabled

Retirees need to contact the Social Security office in their area several months before retirement. This will give the office plenty of time to calculate benefits and begin payments as soon as retiring workers are eligible.

Disability Benefits

A worker who becomes disabled before retirement age may receive disability benefits. Getting these benefits often involves an extensive application process. A worker must present concrete evidence that the disability prevents him or her from earning a living. The Social Security Administration will review a worker's medical records and other information to determine eligibility. Monthly disability benefits may also be paid to a worker's family members.

Survivors' Benefits

If a worker dies, benefits may be paid to certain members of the worker's family. A single, lump-sum payment may also be made when a worker dies. This payment usually goes to the surviving spouse. Monthly benefits may be paid to these family members of a deceased worker:

- unmarried children under age 18 (19 if full-time high school students) or over 18 if severely disabled, with the disability occurring before age 22
- spouse 60 or older (50 if disabled)
- spouse at any age who is caring for a worker's child under age 16 or disabled
- spouse 50 or older who becomes disabled
- parents who depend on the worker for half or more of their support

Divorced People's Benefits

A former spouse can be eligible for benefits on a worker's record under certain circumstances. This eligibility does not affect the amount of benefits the worker and the worker's family are entitled to receive. To qualify for benefits, a former spouse must satisfy these requirements:

- married to the worker at least 10 years
- at least 62 years old
- not eligible individually or on someone else's Social Security record

Future of Social Security

The sound future of Social Security depends on responsible fiscal action today. People are living longer lives. By 2030, there will be almost twice as many Americans of retirement age as there were in 1999. Presently, about three workers pay Social Security taxes for each person who is receiving benefits. By 2030, that number will decrease to two workers to every beneficiary. In 2010, the payments from the fund exceeded tax collections. While the system has some reserves, the fund will be exhausted in 2031 unless Social Security reforms are enacted soon.

If benefit payments exceed tax collection, the Social Security trust fund will be depleted. There will be no money in the fund to support all the persons who have paid into it. Dealing with this problem will require increasing taxes, decreasing benefits, or both. In the 1980s, Congress called for taxing some retirees' benefits and raising the retirement age. This was done, but it was not enough. Among the other solutions proposed are plans to:

- reduce the automatic cost-of-living allowance (COLAs) increases in benefits;
- raise taxes on benefits to higher-income recipients;
- cut benefits for higher-income recipients;
- raise the retirement age again;
- increase Social Security tax contributions;
- invest Social Security trust fund surpluses in the stock market; and
- permit individuals to invest a portion of their Social Security taxes in personal retirement accounts

As policymakers work toward reform, it will be important to provide dependable benefits regardless of changes in the economy and financial markets. Benefits must continue for the retirees, people with disabilities, and low-income individuals who currently receive payments. One of every three people getting benefits in the current system is not a retiree.

Continued funding of the system will likely require increasing revenues and reducing benefits. It also will require fiscal responsibility, a curb on deficit spending, and a reduction of the national debt.

Section 3.3 Review

Check Your Understanding

1. What is the primary purpose of taxes?
2. What is deficit spending?
3. Describe transfer payments as a source of income. Provide an example of a transfer payment.
4. List the classifications that are used for taxes.
5. What types of benefits are included in the Social Security program?

Build Your Vocabulary

As you progress through this course, develop a personal glossary. This will help you build your vocabulary and prepare you for a career. Write a definition for each of the following terms and add it to your glossary.

levy
mandatory expenditure
Social Security
Medicare
disability
Medicaid
transfer payment
discretionary expenditure
direct tax
indirect tax
progressive tax
regressive tax
proportional tax

Review and Assessment

Chapter Summary

Section 3.1 Income

- Earned income is the income received from employment or from self-employment. Examples of earned income include wages, salary, commission, tips, bonuses, and self-employment income.
- The federal income tax system is built on a pay-as-you-earn concept. This means a working person pays taxes from each paycheck instead of in one lump sum each year. After these taxes are deducted from a person's paycheck, the remaining amount is called net pay. Net pay is gross pay minus payroll deductions for items such as Social Security taxes, Medicare taxes, and income taxes.
- Compensation is the payment and benefits received for work performed. Employee benefits are a form of noncash compensation received in addition to a wage or salary. Common types of employee benefits include paid vacation, paid sick leave, health insurance plans, and retirement savings plans.
- Work-life balance is important for many workers. Personal leave, family leave, flextime, job sharing, and telecommuting are examples of options employers give their employees to balance home and work life.

Section 3.2 Tax Returns

- People who earn money in the United States are required to file an income tax return every year. A tax return is a report containing information used to calculate taxes owed by the taxpayer. The IRS provides specific guidelines that describe who needs to file, date for filing, and other income tax basics needed to file a return.
- When preparing a tax return, the instructions should be followed as provided with the tax return form. Instructions on the form will help the taxpayer calculate taxable income and tax liability for the year. If the amount of taxes already paid is more than the amount owed, the taxpayer will receive a refund. If the amount is less, the taxpayer must pay the difference. A return must always be signed before it can be processed.
- There are professionals and services available for tax planning and filing assistance. The IRS, Volunteer Income Tax Assistance Program, Tax Counseling for the Elderly Program, tax preparation services, and tax preparation guides are all available for taxpayers to use when filing income tax.
- An audit is the review of financial records and statements to make sure information is accurate as reported. A tax audit is a detailed examination of a tax return by the IRS. When a person is the subject of an audit, due process is guaranteed by the Internal Revenue Service Reform Act of 1998.

Section 3.3 Government Spending

- Paying for government operations, facilities, and services is the primary purpose of taxes. Most taxpayers spend a sizable portion of their dollars to pay income tax, Social Security tax, and other taxes.
- Taxes are paid on income, purchases, property, and wealth. Different types of taxes apply to these taxable items. There are different classifications of taxes. Examples are direct and indirect taxes and progressive, regressive, and proportional taxes.
- The federal tax code changes periodically. Congress struggles to meet the need for revenues with a level of taxation voters will accept. Legislators propose new tax laws to increase revenues, to make the tax burden fairer, and to achieve desired economic outcomes.
- Social Security provides income when earnings stop for certain reasons. Retirement, disability, survivors', and

divorced people's benefits may be provided to those who pay into Social Security during their working years.

Review Your Knowledge

1. Earned income includes wages and salaries. Describe each. What are examples of other forms of earned income?
2. Identify common payroll deductions, and explain how net pay is determined.
3. List common types of employee benefits.
4. Describe examples of information needed to file an income tax return.
5. Unearned income includes dividends, capital gains, interest, and rent income. Describe each type of unearned income.
6. Explain how to prepare a Form 1040.
7. Identify sources of tax information and assistance.
8. Explain the tax audit process.
9. Relate taxation to government spending.
10. Discuss the federal tax code.

Apply Your Knowledge

1. US citizens pay tax on income as well as purchases that they make. What types of taxes have you paid in the last year? Were the taxes on purchases or income?
2. It is important to examine how personal financial decisions are used to achieve goals. One way a person can do this is to examine a pay stub. Analyze the pay stub shown in Figure 3-2 by answering the following questions.
   A. What is the gross pay for the pay period?
   B. How much federal income tax was withheld?
   C. What was the net pay?
   D. What is the year-to-date gross pay?
   E. Based on this pay stub, how is this person's discretionary income impacted by taxes? How might this affect financial decisions?
3. Employee benefits are valuable forms of noncash payment to many employees. Describe how employee benefits are an important factor in a person or family's financial planning.
4. Review the list in Section 3.1 of ways an organization may offer work-life balance to its employees. Which item on this list would be the most attractive to you if you were a job seeker? Discuss why you made this choice.
5. Many sources of personal information must be used to complete an income tax return. Make a list of the documentation that you or a member of your household will need to complete an income tax return this year.
6. Create a chart with two columns. In column one, write the heading *Local Taxes*. In column two, write the heading *Economic Importance*. In the first column, record examples of local taxes in your area, such as property taxes. In column two, explain why these taxes are important to the economy.
7. Create a chart with two columns. In column one, write the heading *State Taxes*. In column two, write the heading *Economic Importance*. In the first column, record examples of state taxes, such as sales tax. In column two, explain why these taxes are important to the economy.
8. Create a chart with two columns. In column one, write the heading *National Taxes*. In column two, write the heading *Economic Importance*. In the first column,

record examples of national taxes such as income tax. In column two, explain why these taxes are important to the economy.

9. A progressive tax levies a higher tax rate on people with higher incomes. A proportional tax, or flat tax, levies the same tax rate on every taxpayer, regardless of income. Which tax do you think is more fair to the consumer? On what did you base your decision?
10. Federal income tax must be paid by all taxpayers, but state, county, and city income taxes vary by location. What income taxes are levied where you live? List each tax and where the revenue for each is used in the community.

Apply Your Math Skills

1. Suzanne worked 40 hours during a week plus 4 overtime hours with an hourly rate of $15.75. What was the gross pay before overtime pay? What were the total gross earnings for the week? Suzanne had to pay state taxes of $47.03, federal taxes of $137.57, local taxes of $19.60, and did not have any other deductions. What was the net pay for the week?
2. FICA taxes are withheld from each employee's paycheck at a rate of 6.2 percent of gross pay. In addition, employers must match the amount of FICA taxes that their employees pay. How much is deducted from Micah's paycheck for FICA taxes if gross pay is $750 each week? What is the employer's annual matching amount for Micah?
3. Using the tax table in Figure 3-7 and the following personal information, calculate the amount of John's tax refund or balance due.
    - Age: 24
    - Filing status: Single
    - Earnings:
        - Form W-2 showed $29,900 in earnings
        - Form 1099 from the bank showed $90 in interest income
    - Taxes withheld: Form W-2 showed $2,812 in federal income tax withholding

Communication Skills

College and Career Readiness

Writing. Generate ideas that relate to the importance of using accurate information. Make a list of reasons you would provide to a coworker while explaining why accurate information is important when filing an income tax return.

Reading. *Reading for detail* involves reading all words and phrases, considering their meanings, and determining how they combine with other elements to convey ideas. Using this approach, read the first section in this chapter. Consider the way the words are used by the author in each paragraph. After you have finished, determine if you have a good grasp of the content by using reading for detail as your goal.

Speaking. Participate in a one-on-one communication with a classmate about the benefits of using electronic filing for personal income tax. Keep in mind that your style of presentation can influence the opinion of the listener.

Teamwork

Social Security taxes pay for the benefits that eligible individuals receive. Working with your team, create a poster that illustrates the different ways Social Security can benefit workers and their families. Share your poster with the class.

Internet Research

Completing a Form W-4. The website of the Internal Revenue Service provides tax forms and information for individuals and businesses. Navigate to the IRS website and download a Form W-4. You may print the form or complete the form online. However, omit your Social Security number.

Preparing an Individual Tax Return. Navigate to the Internal Revenue Service website and download a 1040 form. You may print the form or complete the process online. Next, you will complete an imaginary income tax return. Follow the instructions that accompany the form for completing a 1040. However, omit your Social Security number. Assume your wages were reported on a W-2 statement from your employer. Your total wages were $30,150. Federal tax withheld was $3,100. State income tax was $1,400. Claim that you are single and no one can claim you on another income tax return. Follow the steps in this chapter for completing a return. What is your refund?

Portfolio Development

College and Career Readiness

File Structure. After you have chosen a portfolio type, determine a strategy for storing and organizing the materials. Think of this step in portfolio creation as building a pool of documents from which you can add to your portfolio. The file structure is similar for both hard-copy and electronic portfolios.

First, you need a place to store each item. Hard-copy documents can be stored in folders or in a three-ring binder. For digital files, ask your instructor about the best place to save your documents. This could be on the school's network or a flash drive of your own.

Next, decide how to organize related files into categories and subcategories. The names for folders and files should be descriptive but not too long. For example, you may label a folder *Certificates* with one subfolder named *Community Service Certificates* and a second subfolder that says *School Certificates*. Appropriate certificates would be saved in their respective subfolder.

1. Decide on the file structure for your documents.
2. Create folders and subfolders on the school's network drive or flash drive on which you will save your files.

CTSOs

Event Prep

Ethics. Many competitive CTSO events include an ethics component that covers multiple topics. The ethics component of an event may be part of an objective test. However, ethics may also be a part of the competition in which teams participate to defend a given position on an ethical dilemma or topic.

To prepare for an ethics event, complete the following activities.

1. Read the guidelines provided by your organization.
2. Make notes on index cards about important points to remember. Use these notes to study.
3. To get an overview of various ethical situations that individuals encounter, read each of the Ethics features that appear throughout this text.
4. Ask someone to practice role-playing with you by asking questions or taking the other side of an argument.
5. Use the Internet to find more information about ethical issues. Find and review ethics cases that involve business situations.

UNIT

2 Protecting Your Finances

Chapters

Financial Literacy

Why It Matters

Earning money from a career that is personally satisfying is the first step in gaining financial independence. However, your financial success depends less on how much money you make than on how well you manage it. Wealth does not always come from just a paycheck. It usually comes from the ability to manage your finances and make your money work for you.

Learning to manage your cash is an important component of being financially capable. Financial institutions are available and willing to help you establish checking and savings accounts to help you reach your personal goals. When you are ready to make investments, professionals are available to guide you in making decisions about stocks, bonds, and retirement options for your future.

Illustration Forest/Shutterstock.com

Big Idea

Careful decisions and wise use of resources can help you achieve your financial goals.

CHAPTER

4 Banking

Financial institutions make it possible to conduct economic activity on a daily basis in today's modern and increasingly high-tech world. Through their many products and services, they facilitate financial exchange for consumers. Financial institutions also keep money circulating throughout the global economy. The availability and circulation of money is the basis for all economic growth. Without money, the economy would grind to a halt.

Banking products are an important part of financial management for consumers. Consumers use checking accounts, debit cards, savings accounts, and many other products to facilitate their daily economic activities. Banking services assist consumers in managing their finances and reaching their financial goals.

Focus on Finance

Check Cashing

Check-cashing services are businesses that provide certain financial services for a fee. Even though they are not considered financial institutions, they are still regulated by law. A check-cashing service cannot cash a check, or checks, that total more than $1,000 per day for an individual. Most states regulate check-cashing services to protect consumers against fraud and abuse by these services.

People who use check-cashing services generally do not have a bank account and need cash immediately. Financial experts advise avoiding check-cashing services for two reasons. One, they are not federally insured. Two, they charge high fees, which quickly surpass bank fees. By contrast, many banks offer free checking and low-cost services if the account balance stays above a certain level. Many check-cashing services also make payday loans, which are even more costly. For most consumer needs, bank accounts are less costly and more reliable.

College and Career Readiness

Reading Prep. Read the chapter title and tell a classmate what you have experienced or already know about the topic. Write a paragraph describing what you would like to learn about the topic. After reading the chapter, share two things you have learned with the classmate.

Sections

kurhan/Shutterstock.com

Section 4.1 Financial Service Providers

Essential Question

Why are financial institutions necessary in our economy?

Objectives

After studying this section, you will be able to:

- Identify types of financial institutions.
- Describe banking products and services.
- Explain how to select a financial institution at which to open an account.

Terms

financial institution	Internet bank	savings account
financial exchange	savings and loan association (S & L)	overdraft
money	credit union	stop-payment order
bank	check	electronic funds transfer (EFT)
charter	checking account	Federal Deposit Insurance Corporation (FDIC)
commercial bank	debit card	
community bank	credit card	
mutual savings bank		

Types of Financial Institutions

A **financial institution** is an organization that provides services related to money. Our economic system could not function without them. Financial institutions serve the primary purpose of keeping money flowing throughout the economy among consumers, businesses, and governments.

Financial institutions are considered either depository or nondepository institutions. A *depository institution* accepts money from customers and deposits it into the customer's account. An example is a bank or credit union. A *nondepository institution* does not accept deposits from customers, but accepts money to invest in business deals or to provide a service. An example is an insurance company that sells services to its customers.

Virtually all businesses and individuals look to financial institutions for help with financial exchange and money management. **Financial exchange** is the process of transferring money from one individual or organization to another. **Money** is anything of value that is accepted in return for goods or services. Money is also known as *currency*, which includes paper money and coins. Paper money is produced by the US Treasury. Coins are produced by the United States Mint.

R. MACKAY PHOTOGRAPHY, LLC/Shutterstock.com

Money is known as *currency*, which includes paper money and coins.

Money is exchanged for consumer, business, and government transactions. Paper money and coins are probably the most common forms of financial exchange. However, not all financial exchange involves actual cash. Many people prefer not to carry cash in their wallets for various reasons. Sometimes it is more convenient to carry a credit card than the bulk that paper money and coins create. By not carrying cash, an individual may be safer from theft or losing money.

When money is deposited in a bank, it does not sit in a vault. The financial institution lends the money to other consumers, businesses, and government organizations.

- Consumers borrow money to finance cars, homes, college tuition, and other needs.
- Businesses borrow money to pay for new equipment and expansion.
- State and local governments borrow to build new highways, schools, and hospitals.

The interaction that financial institutions create among consumers, businesses, and governments keeps the economy alive, as shown in Figure 4-1.

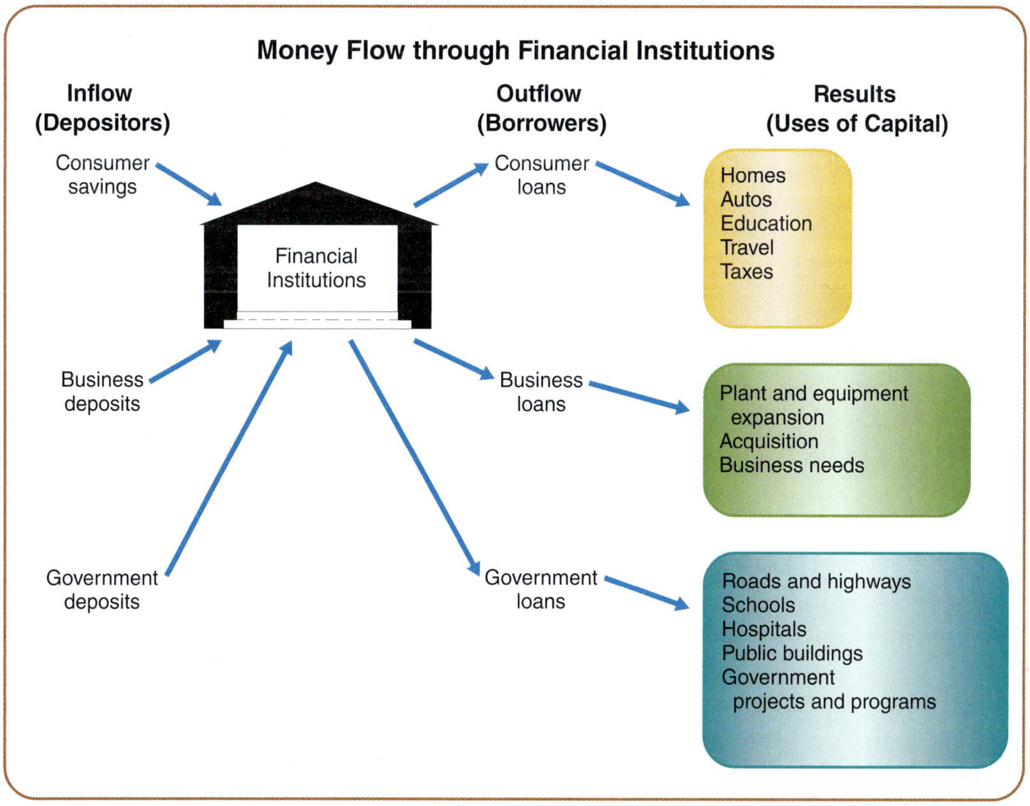

Goodheart-Willcox Publisher

Figure 4-1 Financial institutions keep money flowing through the economy among consumers, businesses, and government.

Without financial institutions, consumers would probably keep their cash under a mattress or locked in a safe. Money could not circulate easily. The nation's money supply would shrink. Funds would not be available for consumer borrowing and spending. Demand for goods and services would fall. Businesses could not get money to modernize factories and develop new products. The economy would slow down. Jobs would become scarce. The economy depends on the flow of money and the services financial institutions provide.

There are different types of financial institutions that meet specific needs for their customers. Examples of financial institutions include banks, credit unions, and savings and loans (S & Ls).

Banks

A **bank** is a financial institution that receives, lends, exchanges, and safeguards money. In the United States, banks must have a charter in order to do business. A **charter** is the license authorizing a bank to operate. Federally chartered banks are called *national banks* and may use the word "national" in their names. These banks must comply with federal banking regulations. State-chartered banks are regulated by state banking commissions. The most common types of banks are commercial banks, community banks, mutual savings banks, and Internet banks.

Commercial Banks

A **commercial bank** is a business in which the primary function is to receive, transfer, and lend money to individuals, businesses, and governments. Commercial banks are owned by investors called *stockholders* or *shareholders*. Commercial banks are often called *full-service banks*. They offer a wide range of financial services, including checking, savings, and lending. Many commercial banks, such as Bank of America and Wells Fargo, are large businesses that operate on a multistate or multinational level. Commercial banks may be chartered by the federal government or by a state government.

JStone/Shutterstock.com

A depository institution, such as Chase bank, accepts money from customers and deposits it into the customer's account.

Community Banks

A **community bank** is a type of commercial bank that is locally owned and operated. All lending decisions are made by bank loan officers who live locally and understand the financial needs of people in the community. It is often easier to obtain a loan from a community bank than from a larger bank.

Community banks offer all standard banking services, including checking, savings, loans, and safe-deposit boxes. Community banks are governed by the same laws that govern the multistate and multinational banks.

Mutual Savings Banks

A **mutual savings bank** is a financial institution that is owned by its depositors. Earnings are distributed to depositors after operating expenses are deducted and reserve funds are set aside as needed. These earnings are distributed as dividends in proportion to the amount of business a depositor does with the bank. *Dividends* are a portion of the bank's earnings paid to depositors. Therefore, depositors who have larger deposits receive a greater amount of dividends than those with smaller deposits.

Traditionally, mutual savings banks received and paid dividends on deposits and made home mortgage and improvement loans. Now, they offer a wider variety of financial services.

Mutual savings banks are governed by a board of trustees who perform their duties in accordance with the bank's charter. Only state governments charter mutual savings banks. They exist in only 17 states, mostly in the northeast.

Internet Banks

An **Internet bank** is a financial institution that provides banking services exclusively online. They are also known as *virtual banks*. Customers access the bank's website to make electronic deposits and withdrawals, transfer funds, or check account balances.

Internet banks have minimal operating expenses because they do not maintain or staff physical banks or branch offices. Their lower overhead costs allow them to pay higher interest rates on savings accounts. The higher yield is the primary advantage of online-only savings accounts. A recent national survey revealed that the average savings interest rate offered by Internet banks was nearly three times the rate offered by traditional banks.

Another advantage of virtual banks is that most of their services are free of service charges. Many offer free checking and low minimum account balances. Figure 4-2 lists some questions to ask when considering the use of an Internet bank.

Case Study *Online Banking*

Alyssa is eager to try online banking. It sounds like a great idea to be able to track accounts from home, as well as pay bills online.

Signing up for an account was easy. After visiting the bank's website, selecting a username, password, and security code, access for the online account is ready.

Alyssa is able to schedule rent and insurance premiums payments online but wants to pay other bills as they are received. Direct deposit for paychecks is a great service, and the ability to review the account in real time is helpful. All in all, Alyssa feels in control over personal financial affairs now.

Case Review

1. Would you conduct your financial business online? Why or why not?
2. What questions would you ask before signing up for online banking services?
3. What are some advantages of online banking?
4. Can you identify any disadvantages of online banking?

Questions to Ask When Considering an Internet Bank
• Are the accounts insured by the FDIC? • What is the process to make deposits? • How easily and quickly can money be withdrawn? • How do rates and yields compare from bank to bank? • Does the bank have reliable online security for protecting personal information? • How prompt and thorough is the bank in responding to customer questions and concerns? • Can an online account be linked with an individual's local bank to make transfers? • What other banking services are available?

Goodheart-Willcox Publisher

Figure 4-2 Asking these questions can help a person evaluate an Internet bank.

Savings and Loan Associations

A **savings and loan association (S & L)** is a financial institution that offers most of the services commercial banks do. Savings and loan associations previously only made mortgage loans and paid dividends on depositors' savings. They may be state or federally chartered. There are two types of savings and loan associations.

- *Mutual savings and loan associations.* These S & Ls are owned by and operated for the benefit of their depositors. These depositors receive dividends on their savings.
- *Stock savings and loan associations.* These S & Ls are owned by stockholders. Like commercial banks, these companies operate for profit.

Savings and loan associations may pay slightly higher interest rates on savings than banks.

Credit Unions

A **credit union** is a nonprofit financial cooperative owned by and operated for the benefit of its members. Its services are offered only to members. Traditionally, membership is gained through affiliation with an employer, union, religious organization, community organization, or some other group. In recent years, however, some credit unions have started offering membership on a basis other than job or group affiliation. One criterion may be based on geography, such as living in a specific community or within a certain ZIP code.

Since credit unions are nonprofit organizations, they pay no federal income taxes. Members often run them, and operating costs may be relatively low. For these reasons, successful credit unions can lend funds to members at slightly lower rates than other financial institutions. They may also pay slightly higher interest rates on savings. They offer most of the services banks and other financial institutions provide.

Large credit unions are usually run by professional management. Credit unions may be either federally or state chartered. The *National Credit Union Administration (NCUA)* grants federal charters and supervises credit unions across the country. "People helping people" is the stated mission of the credit union industry.

Banking Products and Services

Consumers typically look to a financial institution to help manage their money. The variety of products and services offered to customers by financial institutions are called *banking products and services.*

Banking Products

Banking products help facilitate financial exchange between consumers and businesses. Examples of banking products include checking accounts, bank cards, and savings accounts.

Checking Accounts

A **check** is a written order for the bank to pay a specific amount to the person to whom the check is written. A **checking account** is a bank account that allows the owner to make deposits, write checks, and withdraw money. Checking accounts are also called *demand deposit accounts* because cash can be withdrawn or checks written on demand.

Bank Cards

Banks and credit unions issue various types of cards to account holders. Debit cards are generally issued automatically to checking account customers. To obtain a credit card, an application must be completed to determine creditworthiness. Not everyone will be approved for the same bank cards or rates. The two basic types of bank cards are debit cards and credit cards.

Debit Cards. A **debit card** is a card that allows the holder to electronically access funds in an account at an ATM or to pay for goods and services from a business. Using a debit card has the same result as writing a check, because the amount of the purchase comes directly from the checking account. These transactions are automatic and deducted almost immediately from the account. A debit card can also be used at most ATMs to make withdrawals and deposits, and to transfer money from one account to another.

Dual-purpose debit cards can also be used for credit purchases. A purchase can be made by swiping the card through a *point-of-sale (POS)* terminal at the merchant's checkout counter. The cardholder will be asked if the purchase is to be recorded as a debit or as a credit. If debit is chosen, a PIN is entered to authorize the transaction. The money comes directly from the checking account. If credit is chosen, a sales slip is signed rather than entering a PIN. The transaction is treated as a credit purchase. The money still comes from the checking account, but it may be several days before the merchant receives the money.

Dragon Images/Shutterstock.com

Employees at a community bank are often familiar with their clients and the needs of the community.

An advantage of using debit cards is the convenience that they provide. Carrying a debit card is safer than carrying cash and more convenient than writing a check. A disadvantage of a debit card is that when it is used as cash, the money is immediately withdrawn from the checking account. It is important that these transactions are recorded in the check register so the account is not overdrawn.

Credit Cards. A **credit card** is a plastic card that allows the holder to make credit purchases up to an authorized amount. Most banks and credit unions offer credit cards, such as Visa and MasterCard. A credit card is not given automatically to customers in the same way that a debit card is issued. Issuing a credit card requires the customer to apply and meet certain conditions. Unlike debit cards, money does not come directly out of a checking account when a purchase is made. Instead, monthly payments are made based on the balance of the account. Interest is charged on the average unpaid monthly balance for all credit cards. Credit cards are discussed in Chapter 8.

Savings Account

A **savings account** is a bank account used by depositors to accumulate money for future use. Having this type of account is a good way to get in the habit of saving money.

Financial institutions offer several different types of savings accounts. These accounts are *liquid*, which means that money can be easily accessed. However, a disadvantage of savings accounts is that they typically pay low interest. Savings accounts are covered in Chapter 5.

Banking Services

Kostsov/Shutterstock.com

Many bank customers use safe-deposit boxes to store valuable items and documents.

In order to take advantage of banking services, an individual must own an account at the bank, such as a checking or savings account. Examples of banking services are safe-deposit boxes, loans, account services, and various special payment services.

Safe-Deposit Boxes

Some financial institutions rent boxes within their vaults to customers for the storage of valuables. Jewelry, birth records, insurance policies, and other important items are often kept in safe-deposit boxes. Rental charges for these boxes vary. The contents of a safe-deposit box are *not* insured by the FDIC. However, some banks provide insurance if the contents of a box is lost or destroyed.

Loans

Making loans has always been one of the primary services provided by banks and other financial institutions. Individuals can borrow money to finance the purchase of cars, homes, and other items. Owners of businesses can borrow money for many reasons, such as to expand operations, purchase inventory, develop new products, and buy new equipment.

Ethics

Checks

When writing a check, the amount of the check should be covered by the amount of money in the drawer's account. If there is not enough money in the account to cover the check amount, the check will bounce. Keeping a checking account up-to-date and balanced will help prevent this from happening by mistake. Intentionally writing a check that will bounce is unethical and illegal. Intent to defraud the payee can cause the writer of the check to face criminal penalties.

Overdraft Protection

Although overdrafts are not encouraged, some banks offer *overdraft protection*. An **overdraft** is a check written for an amount greater than the balance of the account. This is often called a *bounced check*. Banks charge an insufficient funds fee to cover an overdraft transaction. This fee can be costly. With overdraft protection service, a financial institution will honor a check even if it exceeds the account balance. Money from the customer's savings account is automatically moved to the checking account to cover the amount of the check. However, this service is not free. A charge is applied to the account for each instance.

Consumers must sign up for overdraft protection service with their bank. The *Consumer Overdraft Protection Fair Practices Act of 2009* requires consumers to sign an agreement with their depository institutions to cover and charge for overdrafts.

Stop-Payment Order

A **stop-payment order** is a request for a financial institution to refuse to honor a check written, if the check has not already cleared the account and been paid. This service is useful to prevent others from cashing a check if it is lost or stolen. A stop-payment order is also useful when there is a grievance about goods or services paid for by check. The best way to place a stop-payment order is to go directly to the bank and make the request in person. A stop-payment order may also be made by phone. Forms and processes provided by the bank must be followed.

Special Payment Services

Banks offer services that provide customers with alternative ways of making payments. Some examples of payment services offered by financial institutions include cashier's checks, certified checks, money orders, and traveler's checks.

- A *cashier's check* is a special type of check that the bank guarantees to pay. A cashier's check is purchased from a bank and used to make a payment to a person or a business. A cashier's check cannot be forged and will not bounce.
- A *certified check* is a personal check that the bank certifies is genuine and that there is enough money in the account to cover the check. A written check is taken to the bank where a bank official signs and stamps the word *certified* on it. The money is immediately deducted from the account and becomes unavailable for any other purpose.

Syda Productions/Shutterstock.com

Many people purchase traveler's checks from their bank before setting out on vacation.

- A *money order* is a payment order for a specific amount of money payable to a specific payee. People who do not have checking accounts may use money orders to safely send payments by mail. Money orders do not contain personal information, and the purchaser is not responsible if one is lost or stolen.
- A *traveler's check* is a special form of check that functions as cash. Traveler's checks can be cashed at many places around the world. If the checks are lost or stolen, they can be replaced at the nearest bank or by the agency selling them.

Electronic Banking Options

There are many alternative ways to carry out traditional banking activities. Electronic banking is a popular banking service offered by most financial institutions when a customer opens a checking account.

Online Banking

Online banking services allow bank customers to conduct financial transactions on a secure website owned by the financial institution. With online banking, account holders can:

- pay bills
- transfer money between accounts
- view account balances and statements
- access accounts 24 hours a day
- view checks and deposits
- review account history

Most online banking sites allow the account holder to download or export banking data to money management systems, such as Quicken® and Moneydance®.

There are some disadvantages of online banking that should be considered. Among these are security and data integrity. Security is a concern when making any type of transaction over the Internet. Antivirus software and firewalls should be kept up-to-date when using online banking. Financial institutions typically have backup systems and protocols in place, but data loss can still occur. Keeping hard copies of records and statements is a good practice to adopt when banking online.

Electronic Funds Transfer

An **electronic funds transfer (EFT)** is the movement of money over an online network from one financial institution to another. EFT is safe, secure, efficient, and faster than sending and receiving paper check payments. While the actual costs fluctuate, EFT transactions are less expensive than paper check transfers overall. Businesses, governments, and individuals can benefit from the savings in using EFT.

Economics in Action

2020 COVID-19 Shutdown

In early spring 2020, the world was plunged into a pandemic caused by a highly contagious strain of the coronavirus called COVID-19. In an effort to slow spread of the virus, government leaders established social distancing guidelines, and most ordered a shutdown of all businesses except those considered essential. Individuals were required to stay in their homes except to buy essential items such as groceries and medicine. The shutdown of businesses caused significant harm to the nation's economy, and many businesses failed. Some businesses that survived the shutdown were forced to lay off part, or all, of their employees. As a result, the nation's unemployment rate reached a level not seen since the Great Depression of 1933.

To address the problem, Congress acted quickly and passed several legislative acts to provide financial assistance for individuals and businesses. Financial assistance came in various forms, including grants for public health agencies, small business loans, COVID-19 testing, enhanced unemployment insurance, and stimulus checks for most Americans.

As an additional measure to address the economic slowdown, the Federal Reserve System lowered interest rates and increased the money supply to banks. These measures were taken to protect the American people and reopen businesses. Without open businesses, there is no economy.

Customers using the EFT service can arrange to have paychecks, Social Security checks, and other payments deposited directly into their accounts. Recurring bills, such as car payments and utility bills, can be automatically paid. Using EFT in these ways can make managing money more convenient.

Mobile Banking

Many banks also offer mobile banking services. By downloading an application (app) from the bank, a customer can use a digital device for banking transactions. Typical mobile banking services include quick access to an account and a variety of other banking services.

Peer-to-Peer (P2P) Payments

Some banks offer a service called peer-to-peer payment. *Peer-to-peer (P2P) payments* are a way to immediately transfer money from one person to another. Instead of mailing cash or a check to someone, a virtual check can be sent through e-mail or a mobile app. The receiver gets an e-mail or text message notification with a code from the P2P system, such as PayPal™. The code allows the recipient to transfer the money into an account.

MBI/Shutterstock.com

Mobile banking allows an individual to complete banking transactions from almost anywhere.

Automated Teller Machines

For the convenience of their customers, most banks and credit unions provide automated teller machines (ATMs). An ATM can be used to check account balances, make cash withdrawals and deposits, and move money from one account to another. To use an ATM, customers must have a debit card or ATM card issued by the bank. Generally, an ATM owned by the customer's bank can be used at no charge. There is usually a charge for any transaction made at an ATM not owned by or affiliated with the customer's bank. Since money is withdrawn at ATMs, consider the suggested safety advice shown in Figure 4-3.

Selecting a Financial Institution

When selecting a financial institution, compare and evaluate different types, including local banks, credit unions, savings and loan associations, and other providers of financial services. Commercial banks and credit unions are popular choices when individuals are opening their first checking account. These institutions generally offer savings accounts, online banking, and other types of banking products and services.

Financial institutions offer benefits to customers to encourage them to open accounts and use the services they provide. Some benefits that may be offered include the following.

- no monthly fees
- no minimum balance
- no limit on number of transactions
- free ATM access fees
- online banking
- mobile banking
- overdraft protection

Safety Advice for Using an ATM
• Memorize your personal identification number (PIN). Do not tell anyone your PIN or carry it with you. If someone stole both your card and PIN, that person would have complete access to your account.
• Protect your privacy. Do not let anyone see you enter your PIN. If a friend is standing too close, politely ask the person to step back. If a stranger is too close, cancel your transaction and use the ATM at another time.
• Watch for suspicious people. Criminals may target ATMs as easy places to steal money. Before approaching, see if anyone is standing around. If so, use another machine or return later.
• Use an ATM in a well-lighted area. Generally, avoid nighttime use, but if necessary, choose a machine in a grocery store or other high-traffic area. If you are at the bank at night, choose a drive-up ATM rather than a walk-up machine.
• Make transactions at walk-up ATMs quickly. Approach the ATM with your card out and ready. Then, leave the area immediately and count your money later.

Goodheart-Willcox Publisher

Figure 4-3 Following these guidelines can help a banking customer avoid being a target for theft at an ATM.

Benefits can save a customer time and money. However, for many people, location, interest rates, and safety are the most important considerations to evaluate when selecting a financial institution.

Location

For individuals who prefer to have face-to-face interaction with bank employees, the financial institution should be conveniently located near home or work and have convenient hours. For those who prefer not to visit a facility, online banking and mobile services should be an option. Bank-owned ATMs should be in convenient locations and available at no charge if automated banking is preferred.

Interest Rates

Financial institutions should be evaluated on interest rates that are offered. Interest rates should be competitive, especially on savings accounts. Checking accounts generally offer low rates, but these amounts should be compared and evaluated. The rates offered on savings accounts should also be evaluated in the event that you decide to open another type of account.

Safety

When selecting a financial institution, it is important to know your money is safe. The **Federal Deposit Insurance Corporation (FDIC)** is an independent agency created by the federal government to protect bank customers by insuring their deposits. The FDIC insures accounts in banks and savings and loan associations that choose to enroll in the program. However, the FDIC provides no coverage for investment products. The FDIC also examines and supervises financial institution policies and operations.

The goal of the FDIC is to help maintain consumer and business confidence in the banking system. When customer deposits are federally insured, it means the bank and savings and loan associations are regularly checked. The institution must pass ongoing examinations of its financial holdings, operations, and management. FDIC insurance guarantees that depositors are protected if the bank fails or cannot repay deposits on demand.

Prior to the Great Recession that started in late 2007, the FDIC insured each customer's deposits in a given bank up to $100,000. To improve confidence in US banks during the recession, the coverage was raised to $250,000 in 2008. This increase was initially intended to be temporary, but was made permanent in 2010 as part of the *Dodd-Frank Wall Street Reform and Consumer Protection Act*.

For example, Bill Jones has $240,000 deposited in savings and $10,000 deposited in a checking account at a local bank. If the bank were to fail, the FDIC would return the entire $250,000 to Bill. On the other hand, if Bill has $256,000 in checking and savings deposits, FDIC insurance covers all but $6,000.

Haslam Photography/Shutterstock.com

A sign stating "Insured by FDIC" should appear by the front window or near each teller station of a financial institution.

It is possible for Bill to have multiple types of accounts at the bank. In this case, the total of Bill's accounts is insured up to $250,000. If Bill opens an account at another bank, the FDIC also insures this account up to $250,000. The law applies to individual owners of the account.

The *National Credit Union Administration (NCUA)* insures customer deposits in credit union accounts. Similar to banks insured by the FDIC, each credit union customer is insured up to $250,000 in all federally chartered and many state-chartered credit unions.

A sign stating "Insured by FDIC" or "Insured by NCUA" should appear by the front window or near each teller station of a financial institution. An account without insurance could be subject to loss should a financial crisis occur. Since the FDIC's creation in 1933, not one person has lost one cent of an insured deposit when a bank failed.

Section 4.1 Review

Check Your Understanding

1. What is the primary function of financial institutions in the economy?
2. Provide examples of common financial institutions that serve consumers.
3. How does overdraft protection work?
4. List some of the criteria that can be used to select a financial institution.
5. What service does the FDIC provide for depositors of money in qualified financial institutions?

Build Your Vocabulary

As you progress through this course, develop a personal glossary. This will help you build your vocabulary and prepare you for a career. Write a definition for each of the following terms and add it to your glossary.

financial institution
financial exchange
money
bank
charter
commercial bank
community bank
mutual savings bank
Internet bank
savings and loan association (S & L)
credit union
check
checking account
debit card
credit card
savings account
overdraft
stop-payment order
electronic funds transfer (EFT)
Federal Deposit Insurance Corporation (FDIC)

Section 4.2 Checking Accounts

Objectives

After studying this section, you will be able to:

- Describe different types of personal checking accounts.
- Explain how to open and use a checking account.

Essential Question

What factors should be considered when opening a personal checking account?

Terms

check register	payee	reconcile
endorsement	bank statement	bank reconciliation

Personal Checking Accounts

When earning a regular income, the first financial service many people need is a checking account. A checking account offers many benefits. This type of account is a safe place to keep money. It provides a convenient way to buy goods and services and pay bills. It also provides a record of deposits and receipts of payments. Responsible use of a checking account aids in money management. It also helps you build a sound credit rating.

Financial institutions use different names to describe checking account services they offer. However, there are three common types of checking accounts: basic, interest-bearing, and lifeline.

A *basic checking account* permits the user to deposit and withdraw money and write checks. It usually requires a minimum balance to avoid service charges. If the balance falls below the minimum, a fee is charged. There may also be a monthly service charge and a fee per check. Fees vary from one financial institution to another. Many banks offer a student checking account with minimal fees. This may be a good option for students opening their first checking account.

JohnKwan/Shutterstock.com

Bank reconciliation should be done on a regular basis to make sure the checking account is accurate.

An *interest-bearing checking account* is a combination savings and checking account. Money earns interest and checks can be written on the account. In credit unions, these accounts are called *share drafts*. In banks and S & Ls, they are called *negotiable orders of withdrawal* or *NOW accounts*. Financial institutions offer this type of account with varying interest rates, minimum-balance requirements, and service charges.

Lifeline checking accounts are intended for low-income customers. In some states, banks are required by law to make these accounts available. They feature low minimum deposit and minimum balance requirements, low monthly fees, and limits on the number of checks that may be written per month. Electronic services may also be limited, unless the account holder pays additional fees.

When shopping for a checking account, researching these topics can help you make a choice that works for you.

- *Restrictions and Penalties.* Ask about minimum balance requirements, withdrawal limitations, and penalties for overdrafts or late payments on credit accounts. These items can increase the cost of services and make managing your money more complicated.
- *Fees and Charges.* Ask about all fees and charges associated with the type of account you want. These may include a maintenance fee, charges for ATM use, low-balance penalties, check-writing fees, and check-printing costs. These charges can vary among institutions and different types of accounts. Higher minimum balance accounts usually reduce or eliminate these fees.
- *Interest Rates.* Compare the interest rates on interest-bearing checking accounts. In addition, examine the rates charged to borrow money or use a bank credit card. Look for high interest rates on savings and low interest rates for using credit.

Using a Checking Account

Once the financial institution is chosen and the type of account is selected, the checking account can be established for use. The first step is to open the account. The next step is to deposit money so that checks can be written.

Opening a Checking Account

Opening a checking account requires only a few simple steps. Some banks require a parent or guardian to be listed on an account for an individual under 18 years old. The bank will require the owner of the account to provide personal information, such as a Social Security number, birth date, and address. The bank will also request a personal ID to confirm identity. A signature card, shown in Figure 4-4, will need to be signed. This is the only signature the financial institution will honor on checks and withdrawal slips. If the account will be accessed on a mobile device or a computer, you may be asked to supply answers to security questions to verify your identity when the account is used.

If you want someone else to have check-cashing privileges on your account, that person also needs to sign a signature card. This may be helpful if you want someone else to be able to access your account in the event that you are unable to do so. If you share an account with a parent or a spouse, it becomes a *joint account*. This requires a clear understanding of who will write checks and how records of transactions will be kept.

Exploring Careers

Bank Teller

When a person walks into a bank, the first person encountered is likely a bank teller. Bank tellers assist in the services offered at the bank and help customers with their existing accounts. Tellers handle cash transactions, communicate with the customers, and balance the cash drawer at the end of the day. Examples of tasks bank tellers perform include:

- cash checks and pay out the corresponding money
- receive checks and cash for deposit
- enter customer transactions into computers
- examine checks for endorsements and verify information
- count currency, coins, and checks received
- receive and count daily inventories of cash, drafts, and traveler's checks
- prepare and verify cashier's checks

Bank teller jobs often require a high school diploma, though a college degree is preferred. Tellers receive training in bank policies and procedures including emergency operations. Tellers must have excellent math skills as well as good communication skills, people skills, honesty, and integrity.

Signature Card

Submit one card to establish an optional check redemption privilege, which allows you to write checks against your account.			
Name of Account			
Account Number		Date	
The registered owner(s) of this account must sign below. By signing this card, the signatory(ies) agree(s) to all the terms and conditions set forth on the reverse side of this card.			
Signature		Signature	
Signature		Signature	
Institutional Accounts: ❑ Check here if any two signatures are required on checks ❑ Check here if only one signature is required on checks		Joint Tenancy Accounts: ❑ Check here if both signatures are required on checks ❑ Check here if only one signature is required on checks	

Goodheart-Willcox Publisher

Figure 4-4 A signature card is completed when a checking account is opened. This is the signature that should be used for all transactions on the bank account.

Employability Skills

Professionalism

Professionalism is the act of exhibiting appropriate character, judgment, and behavior by a person trained to perform a job. It is a person's conduct while at work or representing an employer. Professionalism extends to every job, career, and industry. It means conducting oneself in a manner that exhibits responsibility, integrity, and excellence.

When you open a checking account, you receive a book of checks. They will be printed with your name, address, and account number. The checkbook includes a check register, as shown in Figure 4-5. A **check register** is a record of

Check Register

RECORD ALL CHARGES OR CREDITS THAT AFFECT YOUR ACCOUNT

NUMBER	DATE	CODE	DESCRIPTION OF TRANSACTION	PAYMENT/DEBIT (–)		✓ T	FEE (IF ANY) (–)	PAYMENT/ CREDIT (+)		BALANCE $	
	3/1		Opening balance		00			100	00	100	00
										100	00
101	3/2		Lee's Grocery	15	32					15	32
			Groceries							84	68
	3/3		Cash withdrawal	20	00					20	00
										64	68
102	3/4		The Book Shelf	11	75					11	75
			Calendar							52	93
	3/6	DC	No Limits	35	13					35	13
			Jeans							17	80
	3/8	D	Deposit					130	00	130	00
										147	80
103	3/9		Lee's Grocery	18	35					18	35
			Groceries							129	45
	3/11	AP	Unified Utilities	23	07					23	07
			Electric bill							106	38
	3/14	DC	Mary's Dept. Store	34	60					34	60
			Navy shirt							71	78
104	3/16		Richard's Records	21	20					21	20

Goodheart-Willcox Publisher

Figure 4-5 All checks, debits, ATM transactions, and deposits should be recorded in a checkbook register.

account deposits, withdrawals, checks, fees, and interest. It is important to keep track of all your transactions so you know how much you have in your account.

You may be offered credit, debit, and ATM cards when you open a checking account. Inquire about the service fees associated with using ATM and debit cards and any limits applying to their use.

Making Deposits

To deposit money in your account, fill out a deposit slip as a record of the transaction. A *deposit slip* states what is being deposited (currency, coins, or checks) and the amount of each item, as shown in Figure 4-6. Follow these steps when completing a deposit slip:

1. Write the date.
2. Enter the amount of money being deposited in checks, currency, and coins. If you need more room, you may continue listing checks on the back of the deposit slip.
3. Total the amount of currency, coins, and checks to be deposited. Write this number after the word *Subtotal.*
4. If you want to withdraw cash at the same time you make a deposit, enter the amount after the words *Less cash received*. You must sign the slip if you want cash back from your deposit.
5. Subtract the amount received from the subtotal.
6. Enter the amount deposited after words *Total deposit.*
7. Record the deposited amount in your check register. Calculate the new balance in your check register.

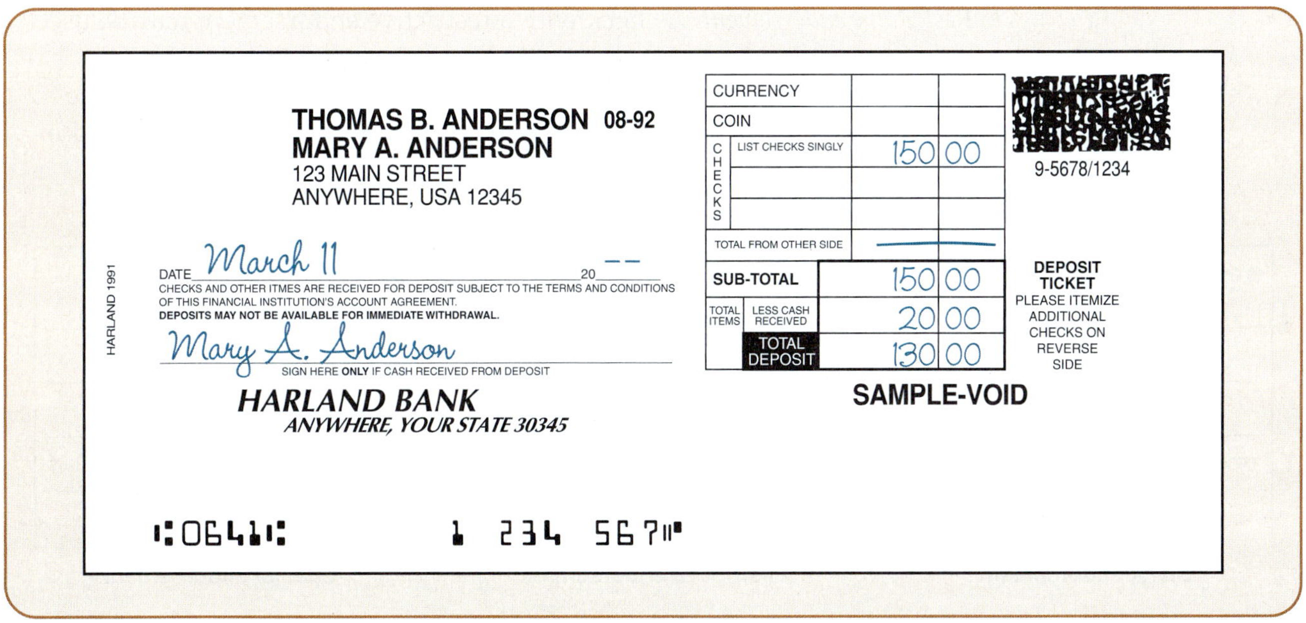
THOMAS B. ANDERSON 08-92
MARY A. ANDERSON
123 MAIN STREET
ANYWHERE, USA 12345

DATE March 11 20 --
CHECKS AND OTHER ITMES ARE RECEIVED FOR DEPOSIT SUBJECT TO THE TERMS AND CONDITIONS OF THIS FINANCIAL INSTITUTION'S ACCOUNT AGREEMENT.
DEPOSITS MAY NOT BE AVAILABLE FOR IMMEDIATE WITHDRAWAL.
Mary A. Anderson
SIGN HERE ONLY IF CASH RECEIVED FROM DEPOSIT

HARLAND BANK
ANYWHERE, YOUR STATE 30345

HARLAND 1991

CURRENCY		
COIN		
CHECKS — LIST CHECKS SINGLY	150	00
TOTAL FROM OTHER SIDE	—	—
SUB-TOTAL	150	00
TOTAL ITEMS — LESS CASH RECEIVED	20	00
TOTAL DEPOSIT	130	00

9-5678/1234

DEPOSIT TICKET
PLEASE ITEMIZE ADDITIONAL CHECKS ON REVERSE SIDE

SAMPLE-VOID

⑆0641⑆ 1 234 567⑈

Goodheart-Willcox Publisher

Figure 4-6 A deposit slip is a record of money put into an account.

You Do the Math
Using a Calculator

Using a calculator enables you to apply math concepts as you learn financial responsibility. The calculator on your computer or smartphone will help increase your accuracy when used properly. The Math Skills Handbook at the end of this textbook illustrates proper calculator use.

Solve the following problem.

Balance a checking account that recorded the following activity since the last statement. How much is in the account?

- Deposits: \$25 and \$120
- Checks: \$25.00, \$8.50, and \$98.00
- ATM withdrawals: \$20
- Bank fee: \$3 for using an ATM outside the bank's network
- Balance on the last statement: \$250

When you make a deposit, you receive a receipt. A receipt details the transaction and shows the current balance in your account. Save your receipts to help balance your check register.

Before a check that you have been given can be cashed or deposited, it must be endorsed. An **endorsement** is a signature on the back of a check. Its purpose is to transfer ownership of the check from you to the bank. An endorsement should be signed exactly as the name appears on the front of the check. There are three ways to endorse a check, as shown in Figure 4-7.

- *Blank endorsement.* This endorsement requires only the signature of the payee. The **payee** is the person, business, or organization to whom the check is written. A check endorsed this way may be cashed by anyone. This type of endorsement should be made only at the time and place the check will be cashed or deposited.
- *Restrictive endorsement.* A check with a restrictive endorsement may be used only for the specific purpose stated in the endorsement. For example, if before signing your name, you write "For Deposit Only" followed by the name of your bank, the check cannot be cashed. It can only be deposited in

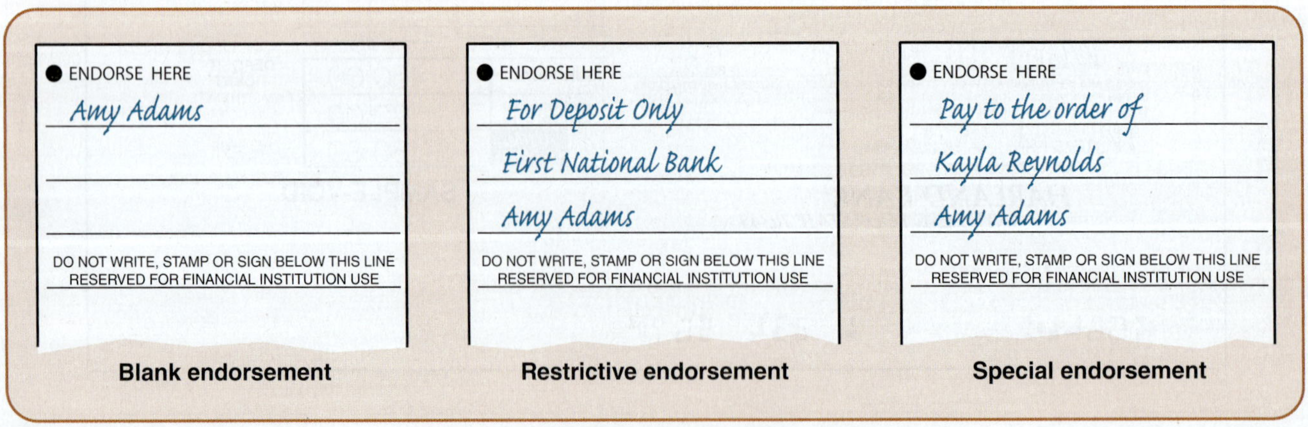

Goodheart-Willcox Publisher

Figure 4-7 Three types of endorsements are commonly used on checks.

your account. Restrictive endorsements are often used when banking by mail, depositing at an ATM, or when someone else is depositing a check for you.

- *Special endorsement.* A special endorsement is used to transfer a check to another party. Only the person named in the endorsement can cash the check. To use a special endorsement, the words "Pay to the order of" are written. This indicates the name of the party to receive the check.

Writing Checks

For checks to be processed, they must be written correctly. When writing a check, enter the following items in the correct spaces. A completed check is shown in Figure 4-8.

- date
- name of the payee
- amount of the check in numbers
- amount of the check in words
- reason for writing the check on the *Memo* line (optional)
- signature of the drawer (person writing the check)

Checks should be written in black ink. Corrections should never be made on a check. Instead, the check should be voided and a new one written. Record a destroyed check in the check register by writing its number and the word "void."

The check number, date, payee, and amount should be recorded in the check register. The new balance in the account should then be calculated. To avoid

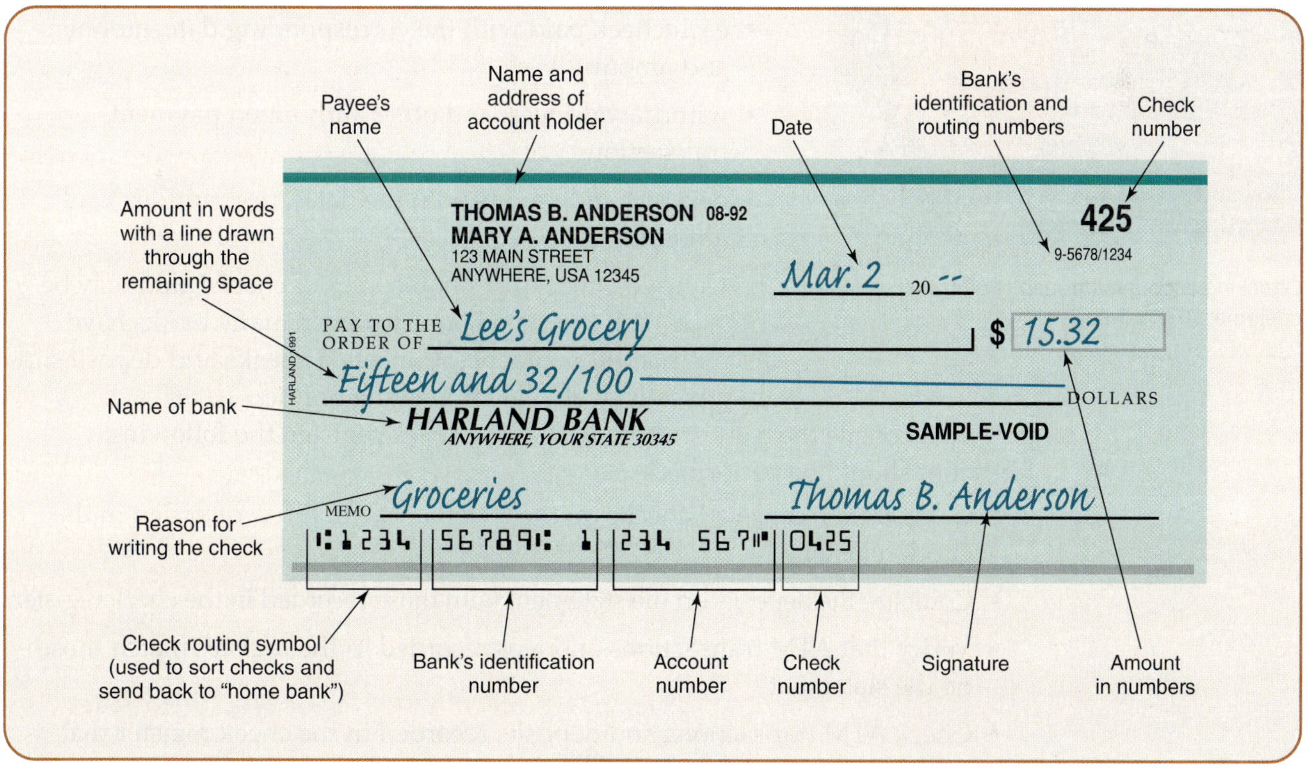

Goodheart-Willcox Publisher

Figure 4-8 Checks should be written neatly and carefully to avoid mistakes in processing the payment.

errors in a checking account balance, all transactions and fees should also be recorded in the check register.

Never postdate a check. A *postdated check* is a check written with a future date. Some people postdate a check because they will not have enough money in their account to cover the check until a later date. However, there is no guarantee that the person will hold the check until the date on the check. If the check is cashed early and there is not enough money in the account to cover the payment, you will be overdrawn.

Managing a Checking Account

Most financial institutions send a bank statement to customers each month. A **bank statement** is a record of checks, ATM transactions, deposits, and charges on an account, as shown in Figure 4-9. Some banks still send statements through the mail. However, many banks encourage customers to access statements online.

When the bank statement is received, it should be reconciled. **Reconcile** means to compare items to make sure they are in agreement with each other. A **bank reconciliation** is the process of comparing the check register with the bank statement. After the process is completed, the final balance on each should be the same. This is also known as *balancing the checkbook.*

AlikeYou/Shutterstock.com

Checking accounts frequently offer the customer ATM privileges.

A bank statement usually begins with a summary of the account. It shows the beginning balance, total amount of checks cleared and other payments made, total amount of deposits and credits, and ending balance. The summary is followed by a detailed listing of these items:

- each check paid with the corresponding date, number, and amount
- withdrawals, fees, and other authorized payment transactions
- deposits and credits with the dates, descriptions, and amounts

Canceled checks or photocopies of checks paid may be enclosed with the statement. However, many banks have discontinued this practice. Cancelled checks and deposit slips are typically available for viewing online.

To reconcile the bank statement with the check register, the following activities should be performed.

- Compare the canceled checks on the statement with those recorded in the check register.
- Compare the deposits on the statement with those recorded in the check register.
- Verify that ATM transactions and fees recorded in the register match those on the statement.
- Check ATM transactions and deposits recorded in the check register that have not yet appeared on the statement.

National Bank
Anytown, USA

ACCOUNT NUMBER
123-45-67-8
PAGE 1
NO. OF CHECKS 10

THIS STATEMENT DATE AND BALANCE		DEBITS AMOUNT	NUMBER	SERVICE CHARGE
3/31/--	$48.73	$246.29	10	5.00

LAST STATEMENT DATE AND BALANCE		CREDITS AMOUNT	NUMBER
2/28/--	$50.02	$250.00	2

STATEMENT OF ACCOUNT

Sarah Student
2647 Evergreen Drive
Anytown, U.S.A.

DAY	REF CHECKS AND OTHER DEBITS	AMT	REF CHECKS AND OTHER DEBITS	AMT	DEPOSITS AND OTHER CREDITS	DAILY BALANCE
3/2	488	15.32				34.70
3/4	489	25.00				9.70
3/9	490	5.25				4.45
3/11					130.00	134.45
3/15	ATM, National Bank	80.00				54.45
3/16	492	23.07				31.38
3/21	493	18.35				13.03
3/23					120.00	133.03
3/25	494	34.60				98.43
3/26	495	12.20				86.23
3/28	496	7.50				78.73
3/30	497	25.00				53.73
3/30		5.00	SERVICE CHARGE			48.73

Goodheart-Willcox Publisher

Figure 4-9 A bank statement is a record of all the transactions on an account during the statement period.

- Confirm debit card purchases.
- Add any interest earned on the account to the check register balance.
- Determine if all checks written have cleared the account.

- Subtract service charges listed on the statement from the balance shown in the register.

The bank should be contacted if the bank statement lists questionable fees or items of which there are no records.

Many bank statements include reconciliation worksheets that can be used for this purpose, as shown in Figure 4-10. The worksheet can be completed with the following steps.

RECONCILIATION WORKSHEET

MONTH March -- , 20 --

BANK BALANCE shown on this statement $ 48.73

ADD+

$ 125.00

DEPOSITS made but not shown on statement because made or received after date of this statement.

TOTAL $ 173.73

SUBTRACT–

CHECKS OUTSTANDING .... $ 68.40

BALANCE............... $ 105.33

The above balance should be same as the up-to-date balance in your checkbook.

CHECKS AND DEBITS OUTSTANDING
(Written but not shown on statement because not yet received by Bank.)

NO.		
498	28	40
499	15	00
ATM	25	00
TOTAL	68	40

Goodheart-Willcox Publisher

Figure 4-10 This type of worksheet and directions for reconciling an account appear on the back of most bank statements.

1. Write in the closing balance as shown on the bank statement.
2. Record deposits made that are not listed on the statement.
3. Add the amount from steps 1 and 2 and record the total.
4. Record the number and amount of any checks and ATM withdrawals not included on the statement. These amounts should be added together and entered as a total outstanding amount.

The balance on your reconciliation should match the current balance in your check register. If they do not agree, review the process. If the figures still do not agree or come close, you may want to contact your bank for help.

Section 4.2 Review

Check Your Understanding

1. Why might a person want to have a checking account?
2. Name three common types of checking accounts.
3. List the information that must be written on a check in order for it to be processed.
4. Which type of endorsement should be used when someone else is handling the check?
5. What is the goal of conducting a bank reconciliation?

Build Your Vocabulary

As you progress through this course, develop a personal glossary. This will help you build your vocabulary and prepare you for a career. Write a definition for each of the following terms and add it to your glossary.

check register
endorsement
payee
bank statement
reconcile
bank reconciliation

Review and Assessment

Chapter Summary

Section 4.1 Financial Service Providers

- Financial institutions provide services related to money and help keep the economic system functioning. Virtually all businesses and individuals look to financial institutions for help with financial exchange and money management. Types of financial institutions include banks, credit unions, and savings and loan associations.
- Financial institutions offer a variety of banking products and services. Banking products include checking accounts, bank cards, and savings plans. Banking services are available only to bank customers and may include safe-deposit boxes, loans, overdraft protection, stop-payment orders, special payment services, and electronic banking.
- When selecting a financial institution, the institution should be evaluated for its location, interest rates, and benefits. It is important that the choice of a financial institution meets the customer's personal needs. The financial institution should also be federally insured.

Section 4.2 Checking Accounts

- The first financial service many people need is a checking account, which is a bank account that allows an individual to make deposits, write checks, and withdraw money.
- After a checking account is opened, money can be deposited so that the account may be used. All checking transactions should be recorded in the checkbook so that the balance is accurate at all times. At the end of the time period, the checkbook should be balanced and the account reconciled with statements from the financial institution.

Review Your Knowledge

1. Briefly describe commercial banks, community banks, mutual savings banks, Internet banks, savings and loan associations, and credit unions.
2. List examples of banking products that facilitate financial exchange.
3. List examples of banking services that financial institutions might provide customers.
4. Explain electronic banking options and list examples.
5. What did the Dodd-Frank Wall Street Reform and Consumer Protection Act provide?
6. What is the purpose of a checking account?
7. When shopping for a checking account, which topics should be researched?
8. Explain procedures for using a checking account.
9. What are the three ways to endorse a check?
10. What information is typically included on a bank statement?

Apply Your Knowledge

1. Create a chart with three columns to compare types of financial institutions. In column one, list the following financial providers: commercial banks, community banks, mutual savings banks, Internet banks, savings and loan associations, and credit unions. In column two, write the major benefits that each institution provides its customers. In column three, evaluate each provider based on benefits it provides. Compare and contrast each.

Which institution would you prefer to use? Write a paragraph to explain your reasoning.

2. On a piece of paper, list the following forms of financial exchange: cash, credit cards, debit cards, and electronic fund transfer. Describe each form of financial exchange, explain how it is used, and list its advantages and disadvantages.
3. Compare and contrast paper money with coins. How are they similar? How are they different?
4. Electronic banking options are becoming standard in most financial institutions. Do you think that electronic banking is a safe practice? Why or why not?
5. Many people use online or mobile banking for most of their banking transactions. If this statement is true, why would the location of the financial institution be an important factor in evaluating where to bank?
6. There are three basic types of endorsements. Which endorsement would you use most to cash a check? Why do you think the endorsement type you chose is the best one to use?
7. Make a list of the benefits a consumer realizes by maintaining a checking account. Compare and contrast each benefit. Which are the benefits that are most important to you personally?
8. Reconciling a bank statement is an important financial management practice to make sure accounts are up-to-date and accurate. Using the bank statement in Figure 4-9, interpret what the statement reveals. Write a paragraph about your findings.
9. Reconciling a checkbook is part of good money management. Write a script that you would use to demonstrate to a friend how to balance a checkbook.
10. Do you think it is important to reconcile a check register with a checking account statement each month? Why or why not?

Apply Your Math Skills

1. The previous month's balance in William's checking account is $480. William makes the following transactions throughout the month of January. Using this list of transactions, balance William's check register. What is the beginning balance for the next month?
   - January 5: Deposit of $100.
   - January 7: Debit card purchase of $43.12 at Food Center.
   - January 10: Check #289 for $17.34 to Commonwealth Electric for electric bill.
   - January 15: Deposit paycheck of $325.80
   - January 21: ATM withdrawal of $20 for birthday gift.
   - January 30: Check #290 for $600 to landlord for February rent.
2. Alex's bank statement shows a beginning balance of $573.28 and the following transactions:
   - three deposits: $25, $150, and $30
   - posted checks: number 110 for $45.00, number 111 for $500, and number 113 for $10.75
   - ATM withdrawal of $10
   - service fee of $2.

   Alex's checkbook also lists a deposit for $300 and check number 112 written for $54.87. Using the bank reconciliation worksheet in

Figure 4-10 as an example, reconcile the bank statement and find the ending balance.

Communication Skills

Writing. As a student and worker, financial institutions will play an important part in your life. Describe ways you would use financial institutions in the workplace. Then describe ways you would use financial institutions in your private life. What do these two uses have in common?

Reading. In order to retain information that you read, it is necessary to focus and read with a purpose. The Focus on Finance feature in this chapter discusses check cashing services. Read the feature with the intention of focusing on each word that is written. After you have finished, close the book. Can you remember what you read?

Listening. Engage in a conversation with a classmate with whom you do not regularly interact. Ask them how they typically use banking products and services. Keep the conversation general so as not to reveal personal details to each other. For example, neither of you should discuss personal banking details, only the types of accounts you typically use. Actively listen to what they share. Next, summarize and retell what the person conveyed in conversation to you. Did you really hear what they said?

Teamwork

Working with your team, create a checklist for comparing financial institutions. List 10 or more specific benefits a consumer should consider when selecting a financial institution. Using word-processing software, insert blank lines or boxes before each criterion for the consumer to check. Duplicate these for your classmates. Did anyone have other suggestions to make?

Internet Research

Opening a Student Checking Account. Search the Internet to find a bank that offers student checking accounts. Record the URL of the website for the bank. Examine the requirements for opening a basic checking account with no limit on the number of checks written. As a practice exercise, write the information on a separate sheet of paper that is requested for opening a checking account. Do not write your social security number on this sheet of paper. If the website permits, practice completing the application online.

Maintaining a Student Checking Account. In the last exercise, you chose a bank at which you could potentially open a student checking account. List the requirements for maintaining a basic checking account with the bank. Identify the benefits and restrictions that must be followed.

Portfolio Development

Hard-Copy Organization. As you collect materials for your portfolio, you will need an effective strategy to keep the items clean, safe, and organized for assembly at the appropriate time. Structure and organization are important when working on an ongoing project that includes multiple pieces. Photocopy each document that you want to include and file the original in a safe place for future reference. Never include an original document in a portfolio.

Plan to keep similar items together and label each category of items. For example, store documents that illustrate your writing skills together. Use notes clipped to the documents to identify each item and state why it is included in the portfolio. For example, a note might say, "Newsletter that illustrates desktop-publishing skills."

A large manila envelope works well to keep hard copies of documents, photos, awards, and other items safe. File folders and three-ring binders with divider tabs also work well.

1. Create a master spreadsheet to track each component that you add to your portfolio. Save the spreadsheet as MASTER_PORTFOLIO with your last name, for example MASTER_PORTFOLIO_SMITH, or use a different naming convention that is suitable for your management system. Ask your instructor where you should save your file. It is recommended to use a flash drive as a backup, in addition to the school network, so that you have access to your information at all times.
2. Decide on a management system that works for you as you collect items. You may list each document alphabetically, by category, date, or other convention that helps you keep track of each document you are including. For each activity you complete, remember to update the spreadsheet.

CTSOs

Teamwork. Some competitive events for CTSOs have a teamwork component. If it is a team event, it is important that the competing team prepare to operate as a cohesive unit.

To prepare for teamwork activities, complete the following activities.

1. Review the rules to confirm whether questions will be asked or if the team will need to defend a case or situation.
2. Practice performing as a team by completing the team activities at the end of each chapter in this text. This will help members learn how to interact with each other and participate effectively.
3. Locate a rubric or scoring sheet for the event on your organization's website to see how the team will be judged.
4. Confirm whether visual aids may be used in the presentation and the amount of setup time permitted.
5. Make notes on index cards about important points to remember. Team members should exchange note cards so that each evaluates the other person's notes. Use these notes to study. You may also be able to use these notes during the event.
6. Assign each team member a role for the presentation. Practice performing as a team. Each team member should introduce himself or herself, review the case, make suggestions for the case, and conclude with a summary.
7. Ask your instructor to play the role of competition judge as your team reviews the case. After the presentation is complete, ask for feedback from your instructor. You may also consider having a student audience to listen and give feedback.

CHAPTER

5 Savings

Being financially secure throughout your life is an achievable goal. However, the money you spend today cannot be saved for what you might need tomorrow. Steps to financial security begin with creating a savings plan. Regular savings build the foundation for you to acquire most of the things you need and want in life. Establishing a routine for saving can lead to money for college, your first car, your first home, financial assistance to your family, and a comfortable retirement.

Financial institutions offer a variety of savings products to begin the path to financial security. It is a great advantage to begin your savings program when you are young. The more money you put away, and the longer time you have to save, the more interest you will earn. It is never too early to start saving for your future.

Focus on Finance

Savings Accounts

There are four primary factors to consider when opening your first savings account.

- *Convenience.* You will probably make frequent trips to your bank, so select a bank that is convenient to where you live or work.
- *Competitive interest rates.* Shop around for the highest interest rate available. The higher the interest rate, the more you earn.
- *Low minimum balance.* It takes time to build your savings. As a result, you want a bank that allows a low balance.
- *No inactivity fees.* Look for a bank that is not going to charge you for periods of inactivity.

Many banks offer special savings plans for students that offer low fees and low minimum balances. Typical features of plans for young savers include a $5 minimum to open an account; no monthly service charges; and unlimited withdrawals.

College and Career Readiness

Reading Prep. Arrange a study session to read the chapter aloud with a classmate. Take turns reading each section. Stop at the end of each section to identify and discuss its main points. Take notes during your study session to prepare for class discussions and quizzes.

Sections

Syda Productions/Shutterstock.com

Section 5.1 Savings Plans

Objectives

After studying this section, you will be able to:

- Explain how to create a savings plan.
- Describe various types of savings instruments that are available from financial institutions.

Essential Question

Why is it important to create a savings plan for your future?

Terms

savings plan
financial security
payroll savings plan (PSP)
SMART goal
savings account
annual percentage yield (APY)
interest-bearing savings account
high-yield savings account
money market account
certificate of deposit (CD)

Creating a Savings Plan

A **savings plan** is a strategy for using money to reach important goals and to advance a person's financial security. **Financial security** is the ability for an individual to meet essential needs without taking on more debt than can be repaid. Financial security enables you to afford the goods and services you need and want. It also enables you to have money to use as a cushion for emergencies, for savings to reach important goals, for insurance to cover financial losses, and for investments to grow in worth.

Cheryl Savan/Shutterstock.com

"Pay yourself first" is a strategy that assures savings will grow.

Creating a savings plan involves a careful look at your current finances and your important objectives. Money is a limited resource. Every decision to spend or save has an opportunity cost. The money spent today cannot meet tomorrow's needs and wants. The opportunity cost of current spending is reduced future spending power. Current spending also costs you the opportunity to earn interest on savings.

A *financial plan* is an overview of an individual's current financial position and strategies to meet future financial aspirations. A personal savings plan is a vital part of an overall financial plan. It consists of budgeting for savings, creating an emergency fund, and setting goals for savings to meet your needs.

Budget for Saving

First, you need to have money that can be set aside for savings. Review the budgeting section in Chapter 2. Follow the steps outlined to create a simple, workable budget. This will show how much money you can use to start a savings program. Once you budget for savings, the following strategies can help make your savings grow.

- *Pay yourself first.* Rather than waiting until all bills are paid and placing the leftover money into savings, set aside money for your savings first.
- *Budget for savings.* Make saving a regular part of your bill-paying routine. When you receive extra money, like a gift, a bonus, or a tax refund, add it to your savings.
- *Let your savings grow.* Savings will not grow if you are constantly dipping into them. If the temptation is too great, perhaps you can choose a savings plan that makes withdrawal difficult.
- *Reduce spending; increase saving.* Keep an income and expense log as described in Chapter 2. This log will show you where your money goes. Look for places where you can cut spending and add to your savings.

Saving money can be challenging, especially when you begin your first job. If your employer offers automatic savings options, this can be a good way to get started saving money for your future. A **payroll savings plan (PSP)** is a program in which an employee authorizes the employer to make regular deductions from each paycheck to automatically deposit in a designated savings plan. The employee signs up for the program and authorizes an amount of money to be deducted from each paycheck and deposited to a specific account. Some employers allow employees to divide the direct deposit of their paychecks into multiple accounts, such as a checking account or savings account. Examples of payroll savings plans include:

- retirement funds, such as a 401(k), into which employers sometimes provide matching funds
- electronic savings bonds purchased through the US Treasury
- traditional savings accounts

Most individuals become accustomed to the automatic deposit and seldom miss the money from their paychecks. Automatic deductions are a good way to become disciplined to save your money and have a positive effect on your financial well-being. It is another application of the strategy to *pay yourself first.*

Create an Emergency Fund

The first savings goal is to build an emergency fund. An *emergency fund* is an amount of money that can be easily accessed in case of a job layoff, illness, or unexpected expense. Since most emergencies are unplanned, the money should be kept in an account that allows you to make withdrawals quickly and without a fee. A basic bank savings account, discussed later in the chapter, is a good choice for an emergency fund.

The amount of money in this fund varies depending on your needs. However, a common guideline is that you keep enough money in the emergency fund to cover living expenses for 8 to 10 months. This would include rent or mortgage payments, car and other loan payments, taxes, utilities, food, and all other expenses.

Set Goals for Saving

Once you have an emergency fund, you can save for other things. It is easier to save if you have clearly defined goals. Begin with a list of what you want to achieve with your money. What would persuade you to give up spending now so you can save enough for the future? Next, create SMART goals as shown in Figure 5-1. A **SMART goal** is something a person wants to achieve stated in terms that are specific, measurable, achievable, realistic, and time related.

Specific

Savings goals should be straightforward and emphasize what you want to happen. Outline the goal in exact terms. "Saving $1,200 for a ski trip next winter" is more specific than "saving money to travel sometime in the future." Likewise, "saving $50 a month to buy a computer next summer" is more specific than "putting money aside in case it is needed next year." When goals are stated in specific terms, you can more easily focus your efforts and track your progress.

Measurable

You need to know when you reach your goal. If the goal is to save enough money to buy a laptop computer, decide how to determine the point at which the goal is reached. Since laptops can range in price from $400 for a basic model to over $4,000 for a powerful gaming model, decide which type of laptop will meet your needs and when you wish to make the purchase. For example, assume that in one year you would like to purchase a particular make of laptop that currently sells for $799. Research helps determine that, due to improved technology, the computer you want will probably sell for around $600 a year from now.

Goodheart-Willcox Publisher

Figure 5-1 SMART goals are specific, measurable, achievable, realistic, and time related.

Case Study *Savings Accounts*

Now that Marcus has a summer job, it seems like a good idea to open a savings account and start saving for college. The bank that the family uses seems like an obvious choice. Unfortunately, the interest rates are unimpressive.

While Marcus surfs the Internet, an ad pops up for online high-yield savings accounts. These online accounts pay higher interest than does the family bank.

Moving the money to an Internet bank might be a good idea, but Marcus is worried about security. After further research, it is apparent that Internet banks are covered by FDIC insurance.

Opening an online-only savings account is easy, and transferring funds electronically between banks is quick and efficient.

Case Review

1. What risks, if any, is Marcus taking by opening a savings account with an Internet bank?
2. What do you think of the decision to move a savings into an online-only account?
3. What research would you conduct before opening an online-only savings account?
4. Would you choose to open an online-only savings account? Why or why not?

You now have a measurable goal. You know that you must save $50 a month for the 12-month period established as the time frame for the purchase.

Achievable

Goals need to be reasonable in order to be achievable. If you are saving money for the purchase of your first home, for example, consider how much money is needed for the down payment and the amount of monthly payments. Owning a $1 million home on the beach may be very appealing. However, it is not an achievable goal for most first-time homebuyers. Set your sights on a home you can afford and create a savings plan that will allow you to achieve that goal. Do not set yourself up for failure by setting goals that are out of reach.

Antonio Guillem/Shutterstock.com

Creating a savings plan can help an individual reach important goals and advance a person's financial security.

Realistic

Consider your income and expenses, your life situation, and any likely changes. Set up financial goals that can be achieved based on these realities. For example, suppose you can save $300 monthly and you want to buy a car within two years without getting a loan. Buying a used car is a realistic goal while buying a new luxury car is not.

Time Related

Goals and objectives should be put into a time frame. Goals should have starting points, ending points, and fixed time periods. When will you need your savings? This will vary for different goals.

It is never too soon to start saving for the goods and services you want for your future. Once you know what you want your money to do for you, you can take realistic steps to reach your financial goals.

History of Finance

Wealth

Early banks only did business with wealthy people. Wealth was held in the form of coins, jewels, gold ornaments, fine rugs, silk goods, and other tangible objects of value. Most homes in the ancient world did not have a safe place to store such valuable goods, however. This led to many people storing their wealth in temples where it could be safely kept and easily watched over.

By the Middle Ages, global exploration had led to the establishment of trade routes that linked many parts of the world. Traditional objects of wealth could no longer be safely and practically transported for long distances. Shipwrecks and pirates were a constant threat.

As a result, early banks issued letters of intent to pay, which were usually printed on durable parchment paper. These letters could easily travel safely with their owners around the world. They are considered a predecessor to *banknotes*, or paper currency. Along with the letters, a banking network was established. This allowed people to redeem their letters for the stated value in gold or silver coins.

Savings Products

There are a variety of savings products and plans available at most financial institutions. A **savings account** is an account designed for accumulating money for future use. Important factors to consider when opening a savings account are shown in Figure 5-2.

The *Truth in Savings Act* requires financial institutions to provide clear information about the costs and terms of interest-earning accounts in uniform terms. The purpose of this act is to help consumers compare savings products and make informed decisions. The **annual percentage yield (APY)** is the rate of yearly earnings from an account, including compound interest. This figure is useful in comparing accounts. The act requires advertising and any materials describing savings products to include the following information:

- minimum amount required to open the account
- interest rate
- annual percentage yield (APY) and the period during which that APY is in effect
- minimum deposit, time requirements, and other terms the saver must meet to earn the stated APY
- description of any fees, conditions, and penalties that could lower the yield

As you compare savings products and plans, it is important to make sure your money is safe. The Federal Deposit Insurance Corporation (FDIC) insures deposits up to $250,000 in many financial institutions. The National Credit Union Administration (NCUA) insures deposits in most credit unions up to $250,000.

Choosing a Savings Product
To decide which form of saving is best for you, consider the following questions. • How much can you save regularly each week or month? • When and how often do you expect to deposit money? • When and how often do you expect to withdraw savings? • Do you have a specific goal, such as an amount you want to save within a given time? • Are you saving for a specific purpose or purchase? • Is it important to be able to convert savings to cash quickly and conveniently?

Goodheart-Willcox Publisher

Figure 5-2 Answering these questions can help evaluate savings product options.

Another important consideration is liquidity. *Liquidity* is the ease with which an asset can be converted into cash without losing value. You may want part of your savings to be liquid, or be "ready money" for emergencies or other needs. However, more interest is usually earned when money is left on deposit for a longer period of time.

For the best earnings on your savings, look for the following.

- *Highest annual interest rate.* The higher the interest rate, the more interest your money will earn.
- *Highest APY.* The higher the rate, the more your money will earn.
- *Most frequent compounding of interest.* The more frequently interest is compounded, the more interest your savings will earn.
- *Shortest interest periods.* Interest periods may be monthly, quarterly, semiannually, or annually. Generally, shorter interest periods offer more flexibility for depositing and withdrawing money without loss of interest.
- *Fewest restrictions and penalties on the account.* Restrictions and penalties can affect both your earnings and your use of the account. For example, savings accounts may involve a minimum deposit or balance requirements.
- *Lowest fees.* Even small fees can add up over time. A financial institution may charge a fee every time you write a check on an account, for example.

Typically, interest is calculated on an account's balance at regular intervals. Find out when interest is calculated to maximize the interest rate. If you withdraw savings just before interest is credited, you may not receive the full interest on your savings. Some financial institutions offer a *grace period.* During this time, you can receive full earnings on deposits or withdrawals. The grace period often extends from five days before to five days after the crediting date. You may withdraw or deposit money during the grace period and still receive interest for the entire period.

How you save depends on your short- and long-term goals, your income, and the amount you have available to save. Often, savers will have more than one type of savings account. Common savings products include interest-bearing savings accounts, money market deposit accounts, and certificates, all of which are FDIC insured. A summary of savings choices is shown in Figure 5-3.

Choosing a Savings Product		
Type of Account	**Advantages**	**Disadvantages**
Passbook Savings Account	• Instantaneous recordkeeping • No or low minimum balance • Money is readily available	• May only allow in-bank transactions • Passbook can be lost or stolen • Not offered by all banks
Statement Savings Account	• No passbook needed • Low or no minimum balance • ATM cards often offered	• Interest rates only slightly better than passbook accounts
Online Savings Account	• Higher interest rates and lower fees than traditional banks • Convenient	• Lack of personal contact • Account may be inaccessible if bank goes offline
High-Yield Savings Account	• Higher interest rates than passbook or statement accounts	• Higher initial deposit • Higher minimum balance • Withdrawals may be limited
Money Market Account (MMA)	• Higher interest rates • Higher liquidity • Free checking often offered • Higher interest rates for larger deposits	• Higher initial deposits • Limited number of checks each month • Minimum amount for each check can be as high as $500
Certificate of Deposit (CD)	• Highest interest rates of FDIC-insured products • Interest rates increase with longer terms	• No liquidity • Fixed interest rate • Penalty for early withdrawal
Jumbo Certificate of Deposit	• Higher interest rates than regular CDs • Tiered interest rates based on the amount deposited.	• High minimum deposit • No liquidity • Penalty for early withdrawal
Reward Savings Account	• Cash or a non-cash gift for opening the account • Interest rates may be higher than regular savings accounts	• Higher minimum deposit • Rewards are often on a one-time basis

Goodheart-Willcox Publisher

Figure 5-3 Savings products should be compared to determine which one meets your needs.

Interest-Bearing Savings Accounts

An **interest-bearing savings account** is a type of demand deposit account that pays interest and allows for regular deposits and withdrawals. Interest-bearing savings accounts have no set maturity date. This means that you do not have to wait until the end of a certain period of time to have access to your money. Instead, you can make withdrawals whenever you choose, and you are also able to close the account when you wish. Common types of interest-bearing accounts are passbook, statement, online-only, and high-yield savings accounts.

Passbook Savings Accounts

Passbook savings accounts, also called *regular savings accounts*, pay interest and allow deposits and withdrawals. These savings accounts generally offer the lowest interest earnings of all savings options. They also have the most liquidity of savings options. Passbook accounts usually allow unlimited withdrawals, have few fees, and require a low or no minimum balance.

With this type of account, a booklet (passbook) is used to record deposits, withdrawals, interest earned, and the current balance. This booklet is presented to a bank teller each time a bank transaction is conducted.

Passbook accounts are most suitable for customers who wish to deal in person with a bank teller. It also works well for customers who conduct a relatively small number of transactions, such as children opening their first accounts. However, the popularity of passbook accounts has dropped since the introduction of ATMs and online banking.

Statement Savings Accounts

A *statement savings account* is an account for which the bank sends a statement that summarizes the activity of the account for a specific period of time, usually a month. The statement lists all deposits, withdrawals, and interest earned for the period covered by the statement. As with passbook accounts, statement accounts usually allow unlimited withdrawals, have few fees, require a low or no minimum balance, and have a low interest rate. Most basic savings accounts today are statement accounts.

Online-Only Savings Accounts

A savings account with an Internet bank generally offers a higher yield than other financial institutions. Online accounts usually allow limited withdrawals, have few fees, and may require a minimum balance. ATM use may be free. Typically, the bank sends a monthly or quarterly e-mail to customers with a link to the customer's account.

High-Yield Savings Accounts

As the name implies, a **high-yield savings account** is an account that pays a higher interest rate than passbook and statement savings accounts. To get the higher rate, however, the bank requires a larger initial deposit and a higher minimum balance. The number of withdrawals in a year may also be limited. A monthly statement is usually sent to the depositor.

Money Market Accounts

A **money market account** is a type of savings account that typically pays a higher interest rate than regular savings accounts. However, money market accounts (MMAs) have a higher minimum balance—usually $500 but possibly as much as $10,000. Some MMAs pay a flat rate of interest regardless of the balance, while others use a tier structure that pays a higher interest rate on accounts with higher balances.

Most MMAs offer check-writing privileges. When an MMA is opened, the bank issues a checkbook to the depositor so that checks can be written against the balance in the account. However, there is a limit to the number of checks that can be written in a month. Also, there is a minimum amount for each check, which can be as much as $500.

Certificates of Deposit

A **certificate of deposit (CD)** is a savings account that requires a deposit of a fixed amount of money for a fixed period of time, known as a term. When the term is up, the money can be kept in the CD, deposited in another CD, or taken out. A CD is sometimes called a *time deposit* or *time account*.

Certificates of deposit may offer a fixed annual rate of interest or a variable or floating interest rate. A variable rate moves up and down (floats) with market rates. Usually, it is tied to a specific market rate, such as the rate on US Treasury Bills.

Since CDs require you to commit your money for a period of time, they pay a higher rate of interest than money market and savings accounts. The longer you agree to hold a CD, the higher the rate of interest you can earn. For example, a five-year CD will yield a higher annual rate of interest than a two-year CD.

CDs are not liquid. In order to get the highest interest earnings, the money must be left in the account until the term is up. This term may be as little as one month or as much as seven years. If CDs are cashed before the time period is over, a significant amount of interest is lost. Also, there is a penalty for early withdrawal. When shopping for a CD, ask the following questions.

- What is the current APY?
- What is the maturity date?
- What is the dollar amount of earnings if the certificate is held to maturity?
- What happens to the CD at maturity? Will the money earn interest at the regular savings account rate? Will it be automatically reinvested in another CD? Will the financial institution hold it with no interest until hearing from you?
- Will you receive notice of the maturity date in advance? This notice gives you time to decide how to put the money to work again.

Jumbo Certificates of Deposit

A *jumbo certificate of deposit* is a CD that requires a larger minimum balance than a regular CD. In return for the larger minimum balance, a jumbo CD usually pays a higher interest rate than a regular CD. Traditionally, the minimum amount to open a jumbo CD was $100,000. However, in recent years, some banks have lowered the minimum amount. Like regular CDs, there is a substantial penalty for early withdrawal in a jumbo CD.

Rewards Savings Accounts

A *rewards savings account* is the same as ordinary savings account, except the bank offers an extra reward for opening it. The reward may be in the form of cash, a non-cash gift, or a gift card. A rewards savings account may pay a higher interest rate than a regular checking account. However, it often requires a larger minimum balance compared to regular savings accounts. Some banks have structured award accounts where the value of the award is based on the amount deposited. The reward is often on a one-time basis.

Exploring Careers

Market Research Analyst

Market research analysts help companies identify potential customers, determine their needs, and determine what they will pay for goods and services. They study market conditions to estimate the potential sales of products and services. Market research analysts typically:

- conduct surveys and research about consumers
- collect data to forecast sales and consumer demands
- analyze market conditions
- collect information on sales, prices, competitors, and market trends
- report research findings to management
- communicate with clients

Market research analysts work in a variety of industries. They spend a lot of time collecting and interpreting data on consumers and preparing reports on their findings. These reports are used to make informed business decisions related to product design, marketing, pricing, and advertising. To become a market research analyst, a bachelor's or advanced degree in market research or a related field is needed. Written and oral communication skills, research proficiency, and computer skills are required. Analytical and creative thinking skills are also necessary. Many market research analysts achieve the Professional Researcher Certification (PRC) from the Marketing Research Association.

Section 5.1 Review

Check Your Understanding

1. What does a savings plan consist of?
2. Explain the purpose of the Truth in Savings Act.
3. Name some examples of payroll savings plans offered to employees by employers.
4. Name three common savings products.
5. When shopping for a CD, what questions should be asked of the financial institution?

Build Your Vocabulary

As you progress through this course, develop a personal glossary. This will help you build your vocabulary and prepare you for a career. Write a definition for each of the following terms and add it to your glossary.

- savings plan
- financial security
- payroll savings plan (PSP)
- SMART goal
- savings account
- annual percentage yield (APY)
- interest-bearing savings account
- high-yield savings account
- money market account
- certificate of deposit (CD)

Section 5.2 Maximizing Savings

Essential Question

In what ways do you think an individual can maximize savings?

Objectives

After studying this section, you will be able to:

- Explain how interest is earned on savings instruments.
- Describe how to choose a savings plan.

Terms

time value of money	compound interest	brokerage firm
principal	future value	tax-exempt
simple interest	Rule of 72	tax-deferred

Earning Interest

Interest is the amount that is paid for using money. The value of money is generally stable. However, it can lose some of its purchasing power over time. For example, $10 buys less today than it did a generation ago. Money saved today is worth more than the same amount received in the future. The **time value of money** is the idea that money decreases in value over time. This is because money received today can be invested or deposited in the bank to earn interest.

Remember that when you earn interest, you are being paid to save. The more interest you earn, the more you are paid. You can maximize your savings by considering the following.

- *Total amount deposited.* The **principal** is the amount of money originally deposited. When more money is deposited, more interest can be earned.
- *Time span of the deposit.* The longer money remains in savings without withdrawals, the more money is accumulated.
- *Interest rate.* The higher the interest rate, the more you stand to gain.

In addition, the *interest type* determines the amount of interest earned. There are two types of interest: simple interest and compound interest.

Calculating Simple Interest

Simple interest is interest earned only on the principal. The principal does not include interest earned. The formula is based on the principal, interest rate, and time the money will be on deposit. The formula is as follows.

Employability Skills

Self-Awareness

Self-awareness is a sense of being aware of one's feelings, behaviors, needs, and other elements that make up the whole person. Being self-aware in the workplace helps a person deal better with stress, manage time better, and be open to constructive criticism.

$$\text{Principal (P)} \times \text{Rate (R)} \times \text{Time (T)} = \text{Interest}$$

For example, if a person deposits $100 in a bank at 5 percent interest for 1 year, $5 interest will be earned.

$$\$100 \times .05 \times 1 = \$5$$

The amount of interest earned is added to the principal. The formula is as follows.

$$\text{Principal (P)} + \text{Interest (I)} = \text{New Account Balance}$$
$$\$100 + \$5 = \$105$$

At the end of the year, the account will be worth $105.

Calculating Compound Interest

Compound interest is an amount calculated using the principal plus the interest it earns. The interest previously earned is included in the total before new interest earnings are computed. Earning interest on the interest makes money grow faster. *Frequency of compounding* also increases the amount of interest earned. The more often interest is compounded, the faster savings grow. Compounding may be done on a daily, quarterly, monthly, or semiannual basis. Over time, compound interest increases the value of your savings.

Calculating compound interest involves the following steps.

1. Multiply the deposit by the annual interest rate.
2. Divide the answer from Step 1 by the rate of compounding. For monthly compounding, divide by 12; for quarterly, divide by 4; for semiannual, divide by 2; for daily, divide by 365.
3. Add the answer from Step 2 to the deposit amount. The result is the new balance with interest.

These steps are shown in Figure 5-4, which illustrates calculating monthly compounding. For example, the savings plan shows a single deposit of $100 and an annual interest rate of 5 percent. Therefore, the deposit amount at the end of month 12 is $105.12.

Using Future Value Tables

A future value table provides an easy way to calculate compound interest earnings at different interest rates and times. **Future value** is the value of an amount of money invested with compound interest at the end of a specified time period.

You Do the Math

Exponents

Compound interest is *exponential*. This means that previously earned interest itself earns interest in the future. This can be thought of as *interest on interest*. The future value of a balance with compound interest is calculated by multiplying the present value by one plus the annual interest rate taken to the power of the number of terms.

$FV = PV \times (1 + r)^n$

In this equation, *FV* is the future value, *PV* is the present value, *r* is the annual interest rate, and *n* is the period of time over which interest is compounded.

Solve the following problems.

1. Susan has placed $10,000 in a certificate of deposit (CD) that earns 3.78 percent interest per year. The term of the CD is three years. How much money will have been earned at the end of the term?
2. Elijah started a college fund of $25,000 for a term of five years. The interest rate is 2.9 percent annually. How much interest will have been earned at the end of the term?

Calculating Compound Interest			
Month	Step 1 Deposit × Annual Interest Rate	Step 2 Step 1 Answer ÷ Rate of Compounding	Step 3 Deposit + Step 2 Answer = New Balance with Interest
1	$100 × 5% = $5.00	$5 ÷ 12 = $0.42	$100 + $0.42 = $100.42
2	$100.42 × 5% = $5.02	$5.02 ÷ 12 = $0.42	$100.42 + $0.42 = $100.84
3	$100.84 × 5% = $5.04	$5.04 ÷ 12 = $0.42	$100.84 + $0.42 = $101.26
4	$101.26 × 5% = $5.06	$5.06 ÷ 12 = $0.42	$101.26 + $0.42 = $101.68
5	$101.68 × 5% = $5.08	$5.08 ÷ 12 = $0.42	$101.68 + $0.42 = $102.10
6	$102.10 × 5% = $5.11	$5.11 ÷ 12 = $0.43	$102.10 + $0.43 = $102.53
7	$102.53 × 5% = $5.13	$5.13 ÷ 12 = $0.43	$102.53 + $0.43 = $102.96
8	$102.96 × 5% = $5.15	$5.15 ÷ 12 = $0.43	$102.96 + $0.43 = $103.39
9	$103.39 × 5% = $5.17	$5.17 ÷ 12 = $0.43	$103.39 + $0.43 = $103.82
10	$103.82 × 5% = $5.19	$5.19 ÷ 12 = $0.43	$103.82 + $0.43 = $104.25
11	$104.25 × 5% = $5.21	$5.21 ÷ 12 = $0.43	$104.25 + $0.43 = $104.68
12	$104.68 × 5% = $5.23	$5.23 ÷ 12 = $0.44	$104.68 + $0.44 = $105.12

Goodheart-Willcox Publisher

Figure 5-4 After one year, a single deposit of $100, earning an annual interest rate of 5 percent compounded monthly, will increase to $105.12.

Future value tables usually show compound interest earnings for either a series of equal annual deposits or a single deposit, as shown in Figure 5-5.

For example, find the future value of a single $100 deposit after 5 years at a 3 percent interest rate. Look across the *5 Years* row to the number in the *3%* column.

Future Value of $1 (Single Deposit)								
Years	Annual Interest Rate							
	1%	2%	3%	4%	5%	6%	7%	8%
1	1.0100	1.0200	1.0300	1.0400	1.0500	1.0600	1.0700	1.0800
2	1.0201	1.0404	1.0609	1.0816	1.1025	1.1236	1.1449	1.1664
3	1.0303	1.0612	1.0927	1.1249	1.1576	1.1910	1.2250	1.2597
4	1.0406	1.0824	1.1255	1.1699	1.2155	1.2625	1.3108	1.3605
5	1.0510	1.1041	1.1593	1.2167	1.2763	1.3382	1.4026	1.4693
6	1.0615	1.1262	1.1941	1.2653	1.3401	1.4185	1.5007	1.5869
7	1.0721	1.1487	1.2299	1.3159	1.4071	1.5036	1.6058	1.7138
8	1.0829	1.1717	1.2668	1.3686	1.4775	1.5938	1.7182	1.8509
9	1.0937	1.1951	1.3048	1.4233	1.5513	1.6895	1.8385	1.9990
10	1.1046	1.2190	1.3439	1.4802	1.6289	1.7908	1.9672	2.1589

Goodheart-Willcox Publisher

Figure 5-5 This table shows the future value (with compounding) of a single deposit of $1.

You will find 1.1593. Now, multiply 1.1593 by $100. The $100 deposit would be worth $115.93.

Suppose you made a single deposit of $1,000 instead of $100. To find the future value after 5 years at 3 percent interest, multiply by $1,000. The $1,000 would grow by $159.30 and be worth $1,159.30.

Applying the Rule of 72

If you do not have a future value table, you can use the Rule of 72 to estimate the amount of time or interest it will take for your savings to double in value. The **Rule of 72** is an equation that estimates how long it will take to double an investment with a fixed interest rate.

To calculate the number of years in which your savings will double, divide 72 by the rate of interest. For example, if you deposit $1,000 at a rate of 4 percent, divide 72 by 4. The result is 18. In 18 years, your $1,000 will be worth approximately $2,000.

To find the annual interest rate needed to double your savings, divide 72 by the number of years. For example, if your savings were in an account for 20 years, divide 72 by 20. The result is 3.6. Your savings must be in an account paying 3.6 percent for it to double in 20 years.

Choosing a Savings Plan

When selecting a savings plan, compare and evaluate different types, including local banks, credit unions, and savings and loan associations. Other institutions offer savings plan options, too, such as insurance companies or

MJTH/Shutterstock.com

The Rule of 72 can be used to estimate the amount of time or interest it will take for your savings to double in value.

brokerage firms. A **brokerage firm** is a financial institution that facilitates the purchase and sale of financial securities by buyers and sellers. Brokerage firms usually pay higher interest rates on savings accounts than traditional banks and credit unions. However, the accounts may not be insured by the FDIC. Brokerage accounts are covered in Chapter 6.

Interest is always a primary consideration when opening an account. However, inflation, liquidity, safety, and fees should also be evaluated.

Inflation

When planning for the future, keep in mind that inflation reduces the value of your savings. The goods and services you wish to buy with your savings next year will cost more money than they cost today. Try to find a savings plan that pays a higher interest than the rate of inflation.

Due to inflation, a dollar buys less this year than it did last year. The inflation rate varies from quarter to quarter and year to year. An inflation calculator tells how much buying power a sum of money will lose between two points in time. One such calculator is available on the Bureau of Labor Statistics website.

Taxes also erode savings. Taxes on the money you earn can take 25 percent or more of your income. Taxes can be minimized by putting money into tax-exempt or tax-deferred savings.

- **Tax-exempt** means free of certain taxes. Certain savings accounts for education expenses are tax-exempt.
- **Tax-deferred** means that taxes on the principal and/or earnings are delayed until the funds are withdrawn. Retirement savings accounts are a common example. Taxes are deferred until withdrawals begin at retirement.

When taxes are reduced or deferred, you are able to accumulate more money over time. Many employers offer tax-exempt or tax-deferred savings plans. Retirement plans help employees by allowing them to shift some of their tax liability to the future.

You must pay taxes on the interest earned by your savings. After the end of the year, you should receive a *Form 1099-INT* from each financial institution that holds your savings. It will state the total interest earned that year and reported when filing your taxes.

Liquidity

The level of liquidity should be considered for a savings plan. If there is a chance that the money in the account might be needed in the near future, the account must be flexible enough that it can be accessed or closed without paying large penalties.

Ethics

Banking Errors

Even though banks use computers to process customer transactions, they still make occasional errors. If your bank were to accidently put money into your account that you did not deposit, it would be unethical to withdraw and spend the money.

Opportunity costs may need to be evaluated when opening an account. For example, a regular savings account comes with a lower interest rate than a CD. However, there are no penalties when a savings account is closed.

Safety

Knowing that your money is safe is an important factor when selecting a financial institution. The Federal Deposit Insurance Corporation (FDIC), Savings Association Insurance Fund (SAIF), and National Credit Union Administration (NCUA) are three organizations that guarantee accounts up to a certain amount are safe from bank failures. Before opening an account with a financial institution, find out whether your deposits will be insured by one of these three organizations.

Fees

It is important to understand any fees that may be imposed on the account. These include fees for making deposits or withdrawing money. It also can include a service charge for accounts that fall below a minimum balance. These charges can add up quickly. Always remember it is important to read the fine print when opening an account. If you have questions about the details of how a savings product works, ask a member of the bank's staff to help clarify the information.

Section 5.2 Review

Check Your Understanding

1. List three factors to consider to maximize interest on your savings.
2. What information is typically shown on a future value table?
3. List four factors that can affect the amount of interest earned on a savings account.
4. List factors that should be considered when choosing a savings plan.
5. How can taxes be minimized on the money a person earns?

Build Your Vocabulary

As you progress through this course, develop a personal glossary. This will help you build your vocabulary and prepare you for a career. Write a definition for each of the following terms and add it to your glossary.

- time value of money
- principal
- simple interest
- compound interest
- future value
- Rule of 72
- brokerage firm
- tax-exempt
- tax-deferred

Review and Assessment

Chapter Summary

Section 5.1 Savings Plans

- Steps to financial security begin with creating a savings plan. A savings plan is a strategy for using money to reach important goals. Creating a savings plan involves budgeting for savings, creating an emergency fund, and creating SMART goals for saving.
- There are a variety of savings products and plans from which to choose. Examples include interest-bearing savings accounts, money market accounts (MMA), and certificates of deposit (CD). Key features to look for when deciding when and where to save include the interest rate, annual percentage yield (APY), lowest fees, and fewest account restrictions.

Section 5.2 Maximizing Savings

- The amount of interest earned on savings accounts depends on the amount of money deposited, the interest rate, and the amount of time the money remains on deposit. The type of interest earned, simple or compound, also influences earnings. Future value tables and the Rule of 72 can be used to calculate interest earnings.
- When choosing a savings plan, interest is a major consideration. However, inflation, liquidity, safety, and fees should also be considered.

Review Your Knowledge

1. Name several strategies to help make savings grow.
2. How do automatic savings options, such as employer sponsored payroll savings plans, help individuals save money?
3. How does creating SMART goals help a person reach savings objectives?
4. Describe how passbook savings accounts work.
5. Describe the advantages and disadvantages of using a certificate of deposit (CD) to save money.
6. Describe two types of interest.
7. Summarize how to calculate compound interest.
8. Explain how to use the Rule of 72.
9. What is the purpose of a Form 1099-INT?
10. How does inflation affect the value of savings?

Apply Your Knowledge

1. Why is *pay yourself first* an important strategy to apply when creating a saving plan? Explain how you can implement this strategy in your own life.
2. Savings plans can be impacted by economic factors that are out of your control. Take a look at the current economic conditions in the United States. People generally save when the economy is stable rather than when it is in flux. How does the job market and worker earnings in the current economy influence an individual's savings plans?
3. Savings options come with risks. One such risk is liquidity and the fact that some savings options are liquid and others are not. Why would it be important for you personally to have a savings option that is liquid? What type of savings option would you choose in the current economy if liquidity was an important factor to analyze?
4. When shopping for a savings account, details to evaluate include: annual interest rate; APY; frequency of compounding;

length of interest period; restrictions and penalties; and fees. Which of these factors is most important to you when choosing a savings account? Explain why you chose one factor as being more important than the others.

5. Implementing a savings program can benefit individuals and families by helping them meet savings goals across the life span. Describe the evidence and data that you would need to collect in order to convince a friend to implement a savings program. Why would a future values chart be one type of evidence of data?
6. Saving money is an important aspect of personal financial planning. Make a list of benefits that you think you would experience by creating a personal savings plan. Why is each of these important for your future?
7. Select one short-, medium-, and long-term savings goal that you have for yourself. Using the SMART goal model, identify how each of these three goals is specific, measurable, attainable, realistic, and timely.
8. Assume you are saving for a down payment on your first car, which you plan to buy in one year. What savings instrument would you choose to accumulate money for the down payment? Explain your choice.
9. When selecting a financial institution or savings product, the interest rate is one consideration. Explain the importance of compound interest when evaluating interest rates. Why is interest one of the main considerations when evaluating service providers?
10. The *time value of money* is the idea that money decreases in value over time. Why is money that you have now worth more than it would be in the future? Assume you made a loan of $100 to a friend. Why would you want your friend to repay you as soon as possible?

Apply Your Math Skills

1. Natalie wants to deposit $2,000 into a savings account at a 1.25 percent interest rate. The interest is compounded every six months. How much interest will be earned over two years?
2. Josiah has $750 to put in a savings account at a rate of 3 percent. Using the Rule of 72, calculate the number of years it will take for $750 to double in value.
3. Gwen has $4,500 to put in a certificate of deposit (CD) while studying at a university. The bank is offering a rate of 2 percent on CDs. Use the Future Value Table in Figure 5-5 to help calculate the amount of interest that would be earned if this amount was put in a CD for 4 years at an annual interest rate of 2 percent.

Communication Skills

College and Career Readiness

Speaking. A presentation is usually a speech given to a group of people. This chapter discussed different ways to start a savings plan. Plan and deliver a speech to your peers about ideas and ways to start a savings plan. Be clear in your perspective for the idea and demonstrate solid reasoning.

Reading. Active reading is processing the words, phrases, and sentences you read. Active reading is a complex task that involves concentration. Apply active reading skills and read the History of Finance feature in this chapter. What was the purpose of the article? Who was the intended audience?

Writing. Generate ideas for writing a paper that describes the concept of savings as you interpret it. Gather information to support your thoughts and ideas. Keep careful and accurate records of any sources that you use as references. Create the notes that you could use to write a paper to distribute for discussion with your classmates.

Teamwork

A savings plan is crucial for every consumer. Working with a teammate, develop a saver's guide covering local places to save, types of savings accounts, safety and liquidity of saved funds, and questions to ask before committing your money to an account. Create a handout that summarizes the information you discovered.

Internet Research

Electronic Savings Bonds. Conduct an Internet search for *Treasury Direct electronic savings bonds*. Explore the Treasury Direct website to find the information to the following questions. What are the different kinds of savings bonds? How are they similar? How are they different? How are they purchased? How are they redeemed?

Financial Calculators. Using the Internet, locate financial calculators that compound interest over a period of years. You may use the phrases *daily compound interest calculator* or *future value calculator* to find one that you are comfortable using. When you find one that you like, insert $1,000; interest rate 10 percent; 20 years. Was it easy or difficult to use?

Online-Only Savings Accounts. Use the Internet to investigate online-only savings accounts. Compare two or three accounts at different Internet banks and answer the following questions: What are some of the features of these accounts? How do online-only savings accounts differ from the accounts the local banks offer? What are some of the advantages and disadvantages of online-only savings accounts? How can you open an online-only savings account?

Portfolio Development

College and Career Readiness

Electronic Organization. Before you begin collecting items for an electronic portfolio, you will need to decide how you are going to present the final product. There are many creative ways to present an electronic portfolio. The method you choose should allow the viewer to navigate and find items easily. For example, you could create an electronic presentation with slides for each section. The slides could have links to documents, videos, graphics, or sound files. Alternatively, you could use a CD or a flash drive to present the material.

Websites are another option for presenting an electronic portfolio. You could create a personal website to host the files and have a main page with links to various sections. Each section page could have links to pages with your documents, videos, graphics, or sound files. Be sure you read and understand the user agreement for any site on which you place your materials.

1. If you have not already done so, create a master spreadsheet to track each component that you add to your portfolio. Save the spreadsheet as MASTER_PORTFOLIO with your last name, for example MASTER_PORTFOLIO_SMITH, or use a different naming convention that is suitable for your management system. Ask your instructor where you should save your file. It is recommended to use a flash drive as a backup, in addition to the school network, so that you have access to your information at all times.
2. Decide on a management system that works for you as you collect digital files. You may list each document alphabetically, by category, date, or other convention that helps you keep track of each document you are including. For each activity you complete, remember to update the spreadsheet.

3. Begin collecting hard-copy files you will need to scan into the computer. As you scan each file, place it in the appropriate folder or subfolder established in a previous portfolio activity. Remember, you can always add additional folders or subfolders as needed. When finished, update your spreadsheet.

CTSOs

Event Prep

Objective Test. Some competitive events for CTSOs require that entrants complete an objective component of the event. This event will typically be an objective test that includes terminology and concepts related to a selected subject area. Participants are usually allowed one hour to complete the objective test component of the event. The Global Business event may also include a team activity, case, or role play.

To prepare for an objective test, complete the following activities.

1. Read the guidelines provided by your organization.
2. Visit the organization's website and look for objective tests that were used in previous years. Many organizations post these tests for students to use as practice for future competitions.
3. Look for the evaluation criteria or rubric for the event. This will help you determine what the judge will be looking for in your presentation.
4. Create flash cards for each vocabulary term with its definition on the other side. Ask a friend to use these cards to review with you.
5. Ask your instructor to give you practice tests for this chapter of the text that would prepare you for the subject area of the event. It is important that you are familiar with answering multiple choice and true/false questions. Have someone time you as you take a practice test.

CHAPTER

6 Investing

In order to make money grow to meet financial goals, many people choose to invest with the goal of creating wealth. An investment plan is an important part of an individual's overall financial plan. There are many different ways to approach investing. Some people buy stocks, bonds, or mutual funds as a part of their plan. Others choose to invest in real estate or valuable goods. These decisions fluctuate depending on the investor's income and stage in the life cycle.

Investments generally offer greater returns for your money than a savings account. However, they also present an element of risk. With careful and consistent financial decisions, you can have money for things such as education, travel, and an overall increase in your standard of living.

Focus on Finance

Investments

If you are a student, you may think you cannot start a portfolio and make an investment. However, the truth is, even if you have $100 you can make an investment and start a portfolio. How can you do that? There are several investments you can make to get started.

- *Stocks.* Technically, there is no minimum number of shares you must purchase from a publicly traded company.
- *Bonds.* Treasury bonds are interest-bearing bonds that pay semiannual interest. Maturity and interest rates may fluctuate.
- *Mutual Funds.* Mutual funds are a great way to create retirement funds or educational funds. Many banks sell mutual funds.

Think big, even if you must start small. Before you know it, you will be on your way to creating an investment portfolio that will get you started on a solid financial path that will help you reach your goals.

College and Career Readiness

Reading Prep. Before reading the chapter, skim the photos and their captions. As you read, determine how these concepts contribute to the ideas presented in the text.

Sections

Andresr/Shutterstock.com

Section 6.1 Investments

Essential Question

What are the benefits of investing?

Objectives

After studying this section, you will be able to:

- Explain the concept of investing.
- Identify benefits gained from investing.

Terms

investing	investment portfolio	appreciation
risk	volatility	inflation
risk tolerance	rate of return	capital loss
diversification	level of risk	capital gain
personal investment plan	yield	

Investing Basics

Understanding when to put money into savings and when to invest will help you make sound financial decisions. **Investing** is purchasing a financial product or valuable item with the goal of increasing wealth over time in spite of possible loss. A *short-term investment* is one held for a year or less. Short-term investments typically have lower returns than long-term investments. A *long-term investment* is held for more than a year, often many years.

Risk

Stephen Coburn/Shutterstock.com

Investing comes with high risks and the possibility of high reward.

Investments generally offer greater returns or profit on money than savings. However, they also present an element of risk. **Risk** is a measure of the likelihood that something will be lost. When you invest, you risk losing some or all of your money. Investments are *not* insured. However, when you save, the savings are guaranteed. Loss up to $250,000 per person per ownership category, or account type, for each insured financial institution is guaranteed.

Risk tolerance is the amount of uncertainty a person is willing to handle. The level of risk a person is willing to take varies from person to person. It may be based on a person's level of income, whether or not the person has a family or other dependents, and even personality. Some people have a personality that allows them to take more risks while others are more conservative and take few risks. Each person must determine personal emotional and financial risk tolerance, and choose investments accordingly. Risk tolerance changes over time depending on an individual's investment goals and objectives, earning power, and stage in the life cycle.

However, sometimes people make poor choices when investing. For example, when there is a downturn in the market, some people react on emotion and sell, afraid they will lose more money. If your situation allows for it, the better approach is to ride out the downturn and wait for the market to improve.

Careful investing for long-term financial goals may reduce risk. With wise investing, financial gains usually exceed losses over time. You are ready to invest when you meet all of the following conditions.

- You pay your essential living expenses and have discretionary income left over.
- You do not have excessive debt.
- You are not paying finance charges, which may be higher than any earnings on an investment.
- You have adequate insurance protection.
- You have an emergency fund with savings of eight to ten months of living expenses.

Diversifying can lower risk. **Diversification** is spreading risk by putting money in different types of investments. If one investment doesn't perform well, there is a chance that another investment will perform well. By diversifying, you avoid "putting all your eggs in one basket," which reduces your overall risk.

Investment Plan

A **personal investment plan** outlines how to develop investment growth. For example, you may plan to set aside a given amount to invest every week or every month. A personal investment plan is an important step in meeting long-term goals and achieving financial security. It is an evolving document that should be reviewed on a regular basis.

There are many formats and methods that can be used to create an investment plan. Figure 6-1 shows an example of steps to take in creating an investment plan.

An investment plan can be part of your overall financial plan. A *financial plan* is an overview of an individual's current financial position and strategies to meet future financial aspirations.

Investment Portfolio

An **investment portfolio** is a collection of the investments a person has made. Selecting investments to meet individual goals and objectives requires careful study. Investments are characterized by these four factors:

- degree of volatility;
- rate of return;
- risk; and
- liquidity.

Creating an Investment Plan	
1. Write SMART goals.	Define short-term and long-term investment goals. Is your goal to invest for the short term, such as purchasing a car? Or for the long term, such as purchasing a house or planning for retirement?
2. Determine the date you will need funds from your investments.	The date you need the money will determine what types of investments to make. Low-risk investments, such as bank CDs, are usually purchased for short-term goals. For long-term goals, stocks and other higher growth investments are usually purchased.
3. Research investment opportunities.	Make a list of appropriate investments that will allow you to meet your goals.
4. Decide how much risk you are willing to take.	Weigh the pros and cons of risk taking. High-risk investments normally grow faster than low-risk investments. However, high-risk investments typically lose more in a bad economy.
5. Determine how much money is needed for investing.	Set up an investment plan and start investing to reach your target goal. Most investment plans can be funded on a monthly basis.
6. Review the plan regularly.	Review investment plans at least once a year to determine if you are on track to achieve your goals.
7. Use your funds.	Withdraw money from the plan to meet your goal.

Goodheart-Willcox Publisher

Figure 6-1 Creating a personal investment plan is important in meeting financial goals.

Volatility is quick and unexpected changes in value or price. The change can be either positive or negative. Investments with a high degree of volatility can present greater uncertainty as to risk and return.

The **rate of return** is the amount earned on an investment for a given period of time. It is often expressed as a percentage. An investment should show a history of growth.

The **level of risk** is the degree to which an investment may deviate from its rate of return. Low-risk investments generally offer lower returns, but provide more security. High-risk investments offer the possibility of big gains, but also are more likely to experience losses. Most investments fall somewhere between these extremes.

Liquidity is the ease with which an investment can be converted to cash without losing value. High-liquidity investments are actively traded on security exchanges and are usually sold with nothing more than a phone call or a click of a mouse. Low-liquidity investments, such as art, antiques, coins, gold, and real estate, are often more difficult to sell.

Benefits of Investing

Each individual investigates personal financial goals when developing an investment plan. For example, if earning income is important to you, look for investments with high yields. An investment's **yield** is the amount of money earned on the investment, usually expressed as an annual percentage. If growth is more important, invest in companies that put earnings back into research, development, and expansion. Some of the benefits of investing include increasing

Ethics

Insider Trading

Insider trading is when an employee uses private company information to purchase company stock or other securities for personal gain. This activity is unethical and illegal. It can be difficult to contain information, but employees must know the consequences of insider trading and refrain from this unethical behavior.

wealth, earning a steady income, beating inflation, taking advantage of tax benefits, and preserving wealth in unstable economic times.

Increase Wealth

Many people have long-term goals and needs of building wealth. Investments can help reach that goal. Having enough money to be financially secure enables a person to live a comfortable life. However, building wealth requires a plan. Some people invest with the intention of holding on to the investment and allowing its value to grow over time. Growth, or **appreciation**, is an increase in the value of an investment. Various types of investments grow at different rates.

Earn a Steady Income

Some types of investments provide a steady stream of income to the investor. One example of such income is the interest received from bonds issued by the federal government. Other types of investments can also provide steady income. For example, owners of rental property can earn income from rent collected from tenants.

Beat Inflation

Inflation is the overall rise in prices. Inflation reduces the value of money and the return on investments. Due to inflation, a dollar will buy less next year than it did this year. To beat inflation, the rate of return earned on an investment needs to be higher than the rate of inflation. In periods of low interest rates, it is difficult to beat inflation with bank savings accounts. If the return on an investment is high enough, the investment earnings can outpace inflation.

Take Advantage of Tax Benefits

The purpose of investing is to earn money and build a secure future. Just as the money earned from a job is subject to income tax, money earned from investments is subject to state and federal taxes.

However, the earnings from some investments are *tax exempt*, such as interest received from bonds issued by state and local governments. When earnings from an investment are not taxed, the investor has more money available for personal use or to make additional investments.

Some investments are *tax deferred*, such as most retirement accounts. A tax-deferred investment is one where no taxes are paid as the investment earns income and grows in value. Instead, taxes are paid only when withdrawals are

AN NGUYEN/Shutterstock.com

One of the benefits of investing is the potential to create wealth for future purchases such as a college education.

made from the account. As a result, the values of tax-deferred investments usually grow more quickly than taxable ones.

Another possible tax benefit of investments is being able to deduct capital losses from income when you file your tax return. A **capital loss** is a loss of money that occurs when the selling price of an investment is less than the purchase price. On the other hand, a **capital gain** is income that results from selling an asset for more than the purchase price. Capital gains are taxable by the federal government and most state governments. However, capital gains on the sale of assets owned for more than a year are taxed at a lower rate than ordinary income.

Tax-reduction strategies vary greatly from investor to investor and from year to year as tax laws change. Certain investments are especially important for those in high tax brackets. A competent tax accountant, lawyer, or financial planner should be consulted for tax advice.

Preserve Wealth in Unstable Economic Times

Both investments and cash can lose value quickly during times of inflation or political and economic instability. Choosing a variety of investments helps protect your portfolio during periods of economic uncertainty. For example, when the US economy is not doing well, many investors add stocks of companies located in other countries. A diversified portfolio should contain investments in US stocks, international stocks, bonds, and real estate. Many investors also allocate a small portion of their portfolios to precious metals, such as gold and silver.

Section 6.1 Review

Check Your Understanding

1. What makes investments different from savings?
2. Investments are characterized by what four factors?
3. List some examples of the benefits of investing.
4. How does an investment beat inflation?
5. What is a tax-deferred investment?

Build Your Vocabulary

As you progress through this course, develop a personal glossary. This will help you build your vocabulary and prepare you for a career. Write a definition for each of the following terms and add it to your glossary.

investing
risk
risk tolerance
diversification
personal investment plan
investment portfolio
volatility
rate of return
level of risk
yield
appreciation
inflation
capital loss
capital gain

Section 6.2 **Types of Investments**

Objectives

After studying this section, you will be able to:

- Describe stocks as a type of security.
- Describe types of bonds that can be purchased as an investment strategy.
- Discuss mutual funds as a type of security.
- List and describe alternative types of investments.

Essential Question

What types of investment options do you think are available for consumers?

Terms

securities
stock
dividend
common stock
proxy
preferred stock
stock trade
primary market
initial public offering (IPO)
secondary market
securities exchange
market value
OTC market
bond
Treasury bill
Treasury note
Treasury bond
Series EE bond
Series I bond
mutual fund
net asset value (NAV)
money market mutual fund
real estate investment trust (REIT)

Stocks

Prudent investors have multiple strategies for investment. One investment strategy is to purchase securities. **Securities** are financial assets issued by corporations, governments, and other organizations. Stocks are an example of securities.

A **stock** is a share in the ownership of a corporation. Corporations sell stock to raise money for start-up costs, ongoing activities, and expansion. When an individual purchases stock, the person becomes a *stockholder*, or *shareholder*, of the corporation. A stockholder has an ownership interest in the company. The more stock owned, the greater the ownership interest.

Many investors buy stocks in hopes the stock will grow in value, or *appreciate*. Stock that has grown in value can be sold at a gain or held for additional growth. Appreciated stocks can also be donated to charities or left to family members. If increased wealth and stock value appreciation is the reason you are buying stock, look for opportunity to buy low and sell high.

A **dividend** is a portion of a company's earnings that is paid to stockholders. Dividends are paid only when declared by the company's board of directors.

Songquan Deng/Shutterstock.com

The New York Stock Exchange (NYSE) in New York City is the oldest continually operating stock exchange in the United States.

The *board of directors* is a group of individuals who represent stockholders and oversee the major policy decisions of the company. Most corporations that pay dividends pay them on a quarterly basis.

Dividends are not guaranteed. They are only paid when the board of directors believes it is in the best interest of the company. Instead of paying dividends, some companies put profits back into the company in the hope of increasing its growth and stock value.

Dividends are a source of income for an investor and a benefit of investing. If steady income is the reason you are buying stock, check the dividend policy of the company before you buy. For example, The Coca-Cola Company has paid a quarterly dividend since 1920 and has increased its dividend in each of the last 58 years. Likewise, Proctor & Gamble, makers of Pampers diapers and many other consumer products, has paid a dividend every year for over 129 consecutive years and has raised its dividend in each of the last 63 years.

However, Alphabet (Google) has never paid a dividend. Even though Alphabet is an exceptionally profitable company, it is a young company; its cash is being used to fuel the growth of the company. This is typically the case. Young, growth-oriented companies usually pay no or little dividends. As a company grows and experiences more consistent profits, however, it usually starts to pay a dividend to its stockholders. For example, Microsoft was founded on April 4, 1975, but it did not pay its first dividend until 2003.

Stock Classifications

Corporations can issue various types of stock. The most popular types of stock are common stock and preferred stock.

When a corporation issues only one type of stock, it is called common stock. **Common stock** is stock that has voting rights and receives dividends when declared by the company. Each share of common stock has equal rights with all other shares in the issue. Typical rights of common stockholders are the right to vote in corporate matters and the right to receive dividends when they are declared by the board of directors. Typically, common stockholders receive one vote per share, so a stockholder holding 100 common shares would have 100 votes.

Since common stockholders have voting rights, they elect the company's board of directors. Common stockholders can also vote on other important matters, such as major expansion projects. Common stockholders may vote in person at the company's annual stockholders' meeting. Stockholders unable to attend the meeting can vote their shares by proxy. A **proxy** is a stockholder's written authorization to have someone else cast a vote on the stockholder's behalf. The proxy form, called a *proxy statement*, is mailed to the stockholder who completes it and mails it back to the corporation. Proxy votes can also be cast electronically.

Case Study *Investing*

Michael and Brandy received 100 shares of Springfield Tool Company stock as a wedding gift from the family. The current price of the stock is $19.88 per share. The 100 shares are worth $1,988 but could be worth less tomorrow.

Other company stock prices are higher and have better performance records. Brandy wants to sign up with an online brokerage firm to sell the shares. With the proceeds, they can buy higher-priced stock in companies that have performed better in recent years. Michael is wary of online brokerage firms and is hesitant to sell the stock because they have never invested before.

Case Review

1. Would you conduct your financial business online? Why or why not?
2. What questions would you ask before signing up for online financial services?
3. What are some of the advantages of online financial services?
4. Can you identify any disadvantages of online financial services?

Most common stockholders vote their shares by proxy rather than attending the annual stockholders' meeting.

In addition to common stock, some corporations also issue preferred stock. **Preferred stock** is a type of stock that pays a regular dividend at a fixed rate. The price of common stock usually moves up and down more than preferred stock. However, preferred stock typically does not increase in value as much as common stock. All preferred dividends must be paid before common stockholders receive a dividend. However, preferred stockholders usually do not have voting privileges.

If a company closes its doors, stockholders may lose their investment in the company along with any unpaid dividends. However, being a stockholder does not make an individual responsible for the company's debts if it goes out of business. The company's creditors cannot come after stockholders for payment. If the company were to fail, the first in line for payment from the company's assets are creditors. Next, preferred stockholders' claims are met. Only then are the claims of common stockholders met. Since it is paid before common stock, preferred stock is generally considered a more conservative, safer investment with less risk than common stock.

Stock Categories

When evaluating stock investments, investors often classify stocks into various categories. Besides the common or preferred categories, you may see stock described as blue chip, income, growth, defensive, cyclical, or penny stock. Additional stock categories exist, each presenting different levels of risk and volatility. Choosing a combination of stocks with varying degrees of risk can reduce overall risk.

Blue-chip stocks are from large and well-established companies that have demonstrated they can withstand downturns in the economy. These stocks are generally more expensive than other categories of stock. However, they have track records of paying regular dividends and are considered relatively safe and stable investments. The term "blue chip" comes from the blue-colored poker chip, which is typically the most valuable chip in the card game of poker.

Income stocks are from companies with a history of paying above-average dividends. These stocks are for investors who want a consistent source of income, such as retirees.

Growth stocks are from companies that put a premium on long-term growth. Most or all profits are put back into the company, and often there are no dividends. Growth stocks are for investors who plan to buy and hold their stocks for long-term gains.

Defensive stocks are from companies whose sales are relatively stable across the ups and downs of the economy. These companies often sell necessities, such as food, health care, and utilities.

Cyclical stocks are from companies whose sales are sensitive to economic ups and downs. The companies provide goods and services, such as cars or spa sessions, that consumers buy when economic conditions are good. Consumers spend less in these areas during economic downturns, so these companies earn less money. This, in turn, affects the stock price and dividend.

Penny stocks are issued by companies with questionable earnings forecasts. These stocks are inexpensive, but risky. However, if the company becomes successful, investors can get above-average returns. Penny stocks can cost as little as a few cents or as much as $10 per share.

Many stocks fall into more than one category. For example, The Coca-Cola Company is a blue-chip stock. However, since the company pays an above-average and consistent dividend, it can also be considered a growth stock and income stock.

Stock Trading

A **stock trade** is the purchase or sale of shares of stock. Stock trades occur either in the primary market or the secondary market.

Primary Market

The **primary market**, also called the *new-issues market*, exists when a company first sells stock to the public. An **initial public offering (IPO)** is a company's first sale of stock to the public. Companies usually make an IPO to raise capital for expansion or to become publicly traded. The company works with one or more investment banks that help determine the type of stock to issue, the price, and the best time to make the offering. The banks charge a commission to sell the securities to investors. A *commission* is an amount of money paid to an organization or employee for facilitating or conducting a sale. The money raised from the sale of IPO stock, minus the bank's commission, goes to the company. IPO stocks can be risky

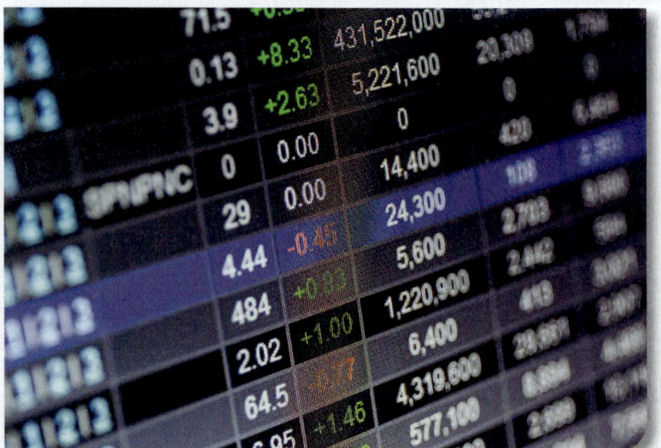

Gotzila Freedom/Shutterstock.com

The National Association of Securities Dealers Automated Quotations (NASDAQ), an American-based electronic network for trading securities, lists the securities of more than 3,000 companies worldwide.

Exploring Careers

Stockbroker

Stockbrokers are salespeople who buy and sell securities for clients. They advise clients on appropriate investments based on the clients' needs and financial conditions. Clients may be individuals, groups, or businesses. Stockbrokers typically:

- contact prospective clients to present information and explain available services
- counsel clients on investment opportunities and market conditions
- buy and sell securities, such as stocks and bonds
- buy and sell commodities, such as cotton, corn, oil, and gold
- monitor financial markets and the performance of individual securities
- analyze company finances and make recommendations to clients

Stockbrokers usually work in fast-paced office environments. They are subject to the regulations of the SEC, the stock exchanges, the firms for which they work, and state requirements. To become a stockbroker, a bachelor degree in business or accounting is necessary. Stockbrokers must also pass the General Securities Representative Qualification Examination Series 7 and any additional state exams. Sales skills are very beneficial.

investments because the company is often a young business without a long track record of success.

Secondary Market

Stocks issued through an IPO can later be bought and sold by individual investors in the secondary market. The **secondary market** exists when investors purchase securities from other investors rather than from the issuing company. In other words, in the secondary market, stockholders are buying and selling among themselves. For example, stock issued by Google in its 2004 IPO can never be issued again as new stock. However, the IPO shares can be bought and sold many times in the secondary market. The majority of stock market activity occurs in the secondary market. The major secondary markets in the United States are the *New York Stock Exchange (NYSE)* and the *National Association of Securities Dealers Automated Quotations (NASDAQ).*

Assume Kelly Larson had the good fortune to buy 100 shares of Google stock for $100 per share when the company held its IPO on August 19, 2004. Kelly bought these shares in the primary market. When the stock soared to $600 per share, Kelly sold the shares and made a profit of $50,000. The shares were sold in the secondary market. In addition, the person who bought Kelly's shares can choose a time to sell them. This is how the secondary market works. Shares of stock that Google issued in its IPO can be bought and sold over and over again in the secondary market. The shares Google sold in its IPO can never be sold in the primary market again.

Some companies, such as Aflac, Microsoft, and Walmart, have direct-stock-investment plans that allow investors to buy shares directly from the company.

However, most stock trades in the secondary market are made through organized security exchanges.

Securities Exchange. A **securities exchange** is a secondary market where securities are bought and sold through stockbrokers. A *stockbroker* is an agent who executes stock trades for clients. The stockbroker's role is that of a go-between who brings buyers and sellers together. Brokers are licensed by the *Financial Industry Regulatory Authority (FINRA)* to trade securities. Usually, stockbrokers charge a commission on both buying and selling transactions.

Minerva Studio/Shutterstock.com

Stock trades occur in the primary or secondary market.

A securities exchange does not own stock. Instead, it serves as a market that connects buyers and sellers. The companies that initially issued the stock are not involved in these transactions and receive no additional money from the trades.

The NYSE is a traditional brick-and-mortar securities exchange located on Wall Street in Manhattan, New York. It is the largest securities exchange in the world. Unlike newer exchanges, it still uses a large trading floor where brokers conduct transactions.

The NASDAQ is an American-based electronic network for trading securities. NASDAQ lists the securities of more than 3,000 companies worldwide. Think of the NASDAQ as a giant electronic flea market where investors all over the world can buy and sell securities. International securities exchanges make it easier and less expensive to invest in foreign companies and for foreign investors to invest in US companies.

Over-the-Counter (OTC) Markets. Stocks that are not listed on securities exchanges can be bought and sold at over-the-counter (OTC) markets. **OTC markets** are virtual markets where stockbrokers conduct business through an electronic network of computers and telephones. Other types of securities are also traded on OTC markets. OTC markets lack many of the rules and regulations imposed on stockbrokers in securities exchanges. Investors need to be especially alert when trading OTC stock because there can be a high level of risk involved. The largest OTC markets in the United States are NASDAQ's Over-the-Counter Bulletin Board (OTCBB) and Pink Sheets.

Stock Quotes

A *stock quote* is the price of a stock on a securities exchange at a given point in time. They are sometimes called *stock listings*. Stock quotes allow people to follow the daily ups and downs of stock prices.

To follow a particular stock, you need to know the stock's ticker symbol. The *ticker symbol*, also known as a *trading symbol*, is a series of letters that identify the company. Stocks listed on the NYSE use one, two, or three letters as a symbol. For example, the ticker symbol for Ford Motor Company is F, for MasterCard Inc. is MA, and for Walmart Stores Inc. is WMT. Most companies listed on the NASDAQ use four letters as a symbol. For example, the ticker symbol of Apple, Inc. is AAPL and of Starbucks is SBUX.

Stock quotes appear in the financial section of the *Wall Street Journal* and other major newspapers, similar to Figure 6-2. Listings are also available on the Internet.

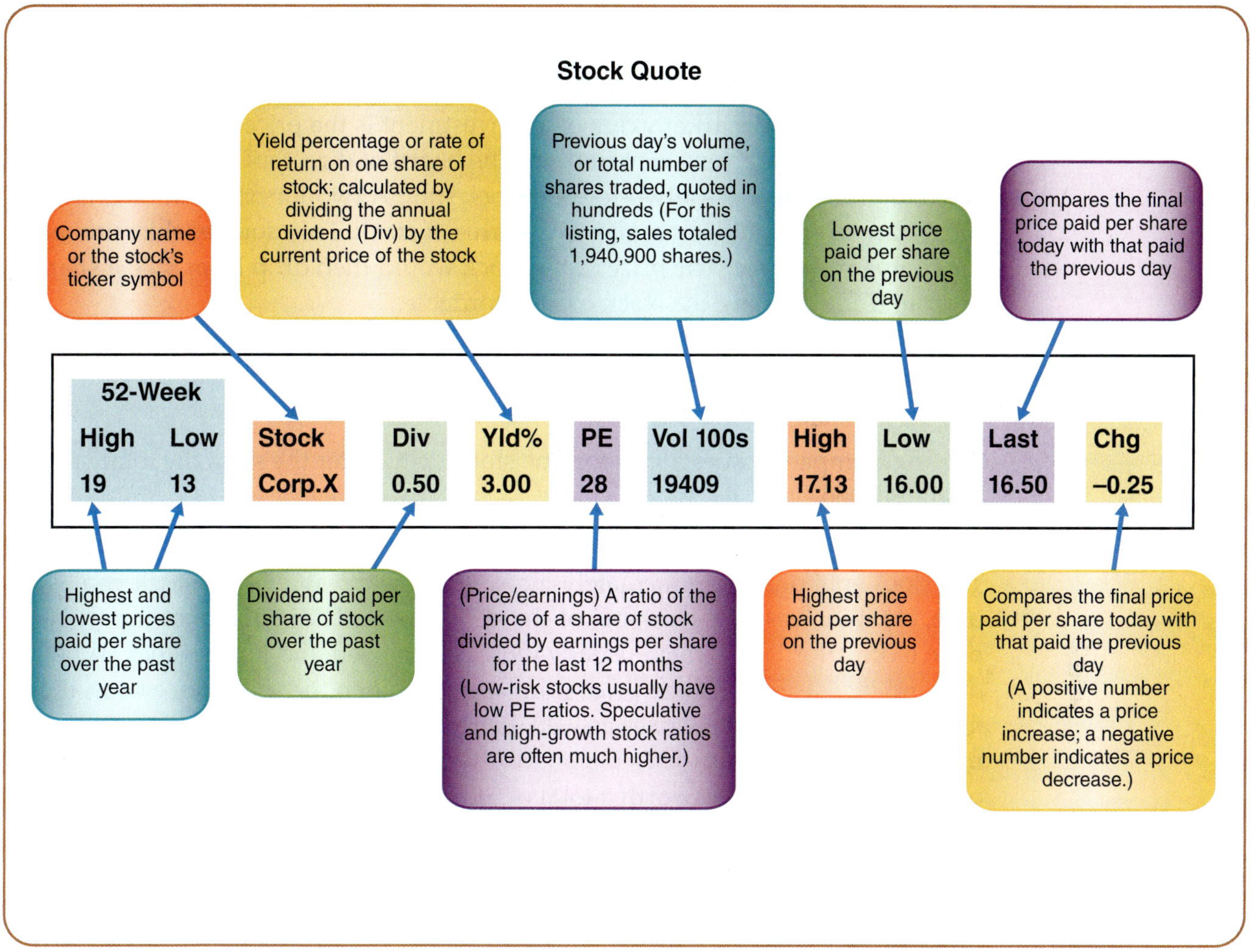

Goodheart-Willcox Publisher

Figure 6-2 Stock quotes provide essential information for investing in securities and following those you own.

You can quickly and easily find stock quotes on financial websites. Stock quotes contain valuable financial information. The current yield (Yld%) and the price/earnings ratio (PE) help investors determine the health or weakness of a company and the value of its investments.

The current price for a given stock is based on many factors. For example, the stock market often reacts to news. If the government announces interest rates will be reduced, the market may react in a positive manner, and stock prices may go up. On the other hand, if a particular company experiences something negative, such as being hacked, that company's stock may go down in price.

Stock Splits

When a corporation is doing well, its stock usually increases in value because investors are willing to pay more for the stock. When a stock's value grows very quickly, the company's board of director's may decide the stock is getting too expensive for employees and average investors to buy on a regular basis. As a result, a corporation may decide to split its stock to create more shares, which brings the share price down. Every major corporation in the United States has split its stock at least once. The Coca-Cola Company has split its shares 10 times since the company went public in 1919.

For example, assume the stock of Sterling Company has a market value of \$100 per share. The **market value** of an investment is the price at which it can be bought or sold at a given point in time. The board of directors thinks this price is too high and declares a two-for-one stock split. A two-for-one split means that each share of stock now becomes two shares of stock. This doubles the number of the company's shares. The price of the stock would then drop from \$100 a share to around \$50, making the stock more affordable.

Assume you own 100 shares of Sterling Company stock. Before the split, the total value of the stock was \$10,000.

100 shares × \$100 = \$10,000

Sterling Company issues a two-for-one stock split. After the split, the total value is still \$10,000.

200 shares × \$50 = \$10,000

The stock split did not immediately increase the total value of the stock you own, but it increased the number of shares you own. The split makes the share price more affordable, which usually increases the demand for the stock. When demand increases, the share price usually rises. When the share price rises, the total value of your shares rises as well. For example, Sterling Company stock might increase in value to \$53 per share after the stock split. The same number of shares would then be worth a total of \$10,600. This is a profit of \$600 for the stockholder if the stock is sold.

A split can be in any proportion a company chooses, such as four-for-one, three-for-one, and three-for-two. In 2015, for example, Netflix split its stock on a seven-for-one basis.

Bonds

Bonds are another type of security. A **bond** is a certificate of debt issued by a corporation or government. Information stated on a bond includes the following.

- *Maturity date* is the date a bond is repaid to the bondholder; it is the date bondholders get their money back.
- *Face value,* or principal, is the amount for which a bond is issued and on which interest payments are figured; at maturity, the bondholder receives the face value.
- *Yield* is the percentage of a return on an investment.

Other important terms relating to bonds include coupon rate, market value, and current yield.

Coupon rate is the annual rate of interest the issuer promises to pay on the face value. *Market value* is the amount for which a bond sells. It may be more, less, or the same as the face value. *Current yield* is the annual interest or coupon rate divided by the market price of a bond.

To acquire a bond, the common expression is "buy it." However, when you "buy" a bond, you are lending money to the issuer of the bond. Until the bond matures, you, the bondholder, are a creditor. The issuer owes you the amount of the loan plus interest. The three major issuers of bonds are corporations, municipalities, and the federal government.

Corporate Bonds

Corporate bonds are issued by corporations that need money to operate and expand. The quality, coupon rates, and yields of these bonds vary with the financial soundness of the issuing corporation. Yields and market prices move up and down as market interest rates change.

Most corporate bonds are bought and sold through brokers. Some bonds are bought and sold on securities exchanges and are listed in newspapers and online. High-grade corporate bonds are considered safer investments than stocks because they are debt instruments. If a company goes bankrupt, it must pay its debts first.

Municipal Bonds

Municipal bonds are issued by state, county, and city governments. Coupon rates and yields depend on market rates and the financial soundness of the issuing municipality. Interest on these bonds is exempt from federal income tax and, in some cases, state and local taxes as well. This makes municipal bonds attractive to upper-income investors in high tax brackets.

Most municipal bonds are bought and sold by brokers. Some municipalities may allow investors to purchase bonds directly from the local government. Corporate and municipal bond listings are in the financial sections of major newspapers and online. Look for certain key information when reviewing bond quotes, as illustrated in Figure 6-3.

Bond Quote

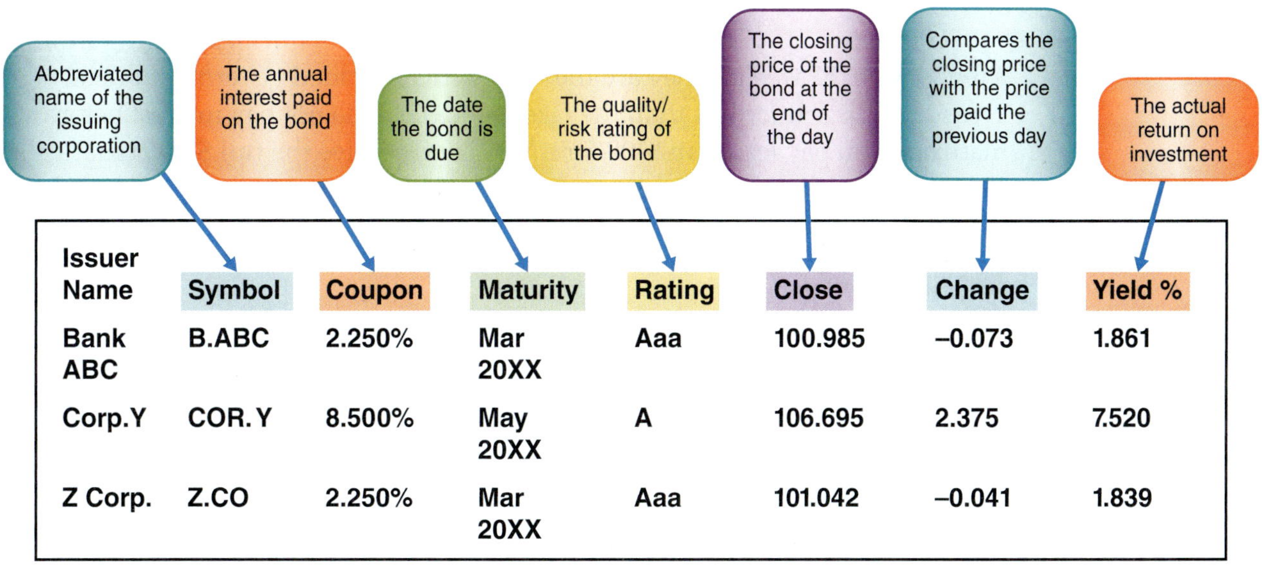

Issuer Name	Symbol	Coupon	Maturity	Rating	Close	Change	Yield %
Bank ABC	B.ABC	2.250%	Mar 20XX	Aaa	100.985	–0.073	1.861
Corp.Y	COR.Y	8.500%	May 20XX	A	106.695	2.375	7.520
Z Corp.	Z.CO	2.250%	Mar 20XX	Aaa	101.042	–0.041	1.839

Goodheart-Willcox Publisher

Figure 6-3 Corporate bond quotes provide the information needed to track bond yields and prices in the marketplace.

Rating	Bond Credit Quality
AAA	Highest
AA	Superior
A	Satisfactory
BBB	Adequate
BB	Speculative
B	Highly speculative
CCC	Very highly speculative
CC	Extremely speculative
C	Extremely speculative, behind on interest payments
D	In default

Goodheart-Willcox Publisher

Figure 6-4 Standard & Poor's bond rating categories range from AAA (best) to D (worst).

Corporate and municipal bonds are rated for quality and risk. The most common rating system is by Standard and Poor, illustrated in Figure 6-4. The first four rating categories—AAA, AA, A, and BBB—are recommended for conservative investors. The next four categories—BB, B, CCC, and CC—are considered too risky for average investors. The last two categories—C and D—are for exceptionally risky bonds that are behind on interest payments, in default, or both. Only professional investors should consider bonds in these categories.

Government Securities and Bonds

US governmental obligations are the safest debt instruments because they are backed by the federal government. The US government issues treasury bills, treasury notes, and treasury bonds in increments of $100. These securities can be purchased at government auctions. They can also be purchased through a bank, broker, or dealer. However, a fee, or commission, is usually charged.

The US government also issues savings bonds in various amounts. Savings bonds are popular because they can be purchased for as little as $25. They can be purchased without a fee directly from the US Treasury. However, savings bonds can no longer be purchased at financial institutions.

US governmental notes and bonds can be a sound investment for many types of investors. When you buy one, you lend money to the federal government.

Treasury Bills

Treasury bills (T-bills) are short-term debts with maturities ranging from a few days to 52 weeks. They are the most actively traded government debt. Treasury bills sell for less than the face value. They do not pay interest before maturity. You pay less than $100 for a T-bill and receive the full $100 at maturity. The difference between the price you pay and the amount you receive at maturity is the interest.

Treasury Notes

Treasury notes (T-notes) are short-term securities with maturities of two, three, five, seven, or ten years. They are sold in increments of $100. Interest is paid every six months on treasury notes. Most treasury notes are sold electronically. However, they may be issued as paper certificates.

Treasury Bonds

Treasury bonds (T-bonds) are long-term investments with maturities of 30 years. They are sold in increments of $100. Buyers receive interest payments every six months. Most treasury bonds are sold electronically. However, they may be issued as paper certificates.

US Savings Bonds

There are other choices of investments that offer less liquidity and commitment of funds for a longer period of time. A popular choice is US savings bonds. Two types of US savings bonds are *Series EE Bonds* and *Series I Bonds*. Neither is insured by the FDIC. However, both are backed by the full faith and credit of the US government. As a result, they are considered exceptionally safe.

The US Treasury Department only issues electronic savings bonds through the TreasuryDirect website. Paper bonds are no longer issued. Those currently holding paper savings bonds can continue to redeem them at most banks and credit unions. Paper bonds that have not matured, but have been lost, stolen, or destroyed, can be reissued in paper or electronic form.

Africa Studio/Shutterstock.com

Creating a personal investment plan is one way an individual can take control of the future.

Series EE Bonds. A **Series EE Bond** earns a fixed rate of interest for up to 30 years. Series EE Bonds are purchased at full face value in amounts of $25 or more, to the penny. *Face value*, or principal, is the amount for which a bond is issued and on which interest payments are figured. A bond with a face value of $25 is purchased for $25. *To the penny* means it is not necessary to invest full dollar amounts. If you so choose, you could invest $25.01. The maximum that can be purchased in one year is $10,000.

The interest rate is based on market yields of treasury notes and other considerations related to savings bonds. New rates are announced on May 1 and November 1 each year. If you redeem series EE Bonds in the first five years, you will forfeit the last three months' interest. If you redeem them after five years, there is no penalty.

Series I Bonds. A **Series I Bond** earns interest based on combining a fixed interest rate and the inflation rate. The Secretary of Treasury determines the fixed interest rate. The interest rate in effect at the time of purchase applies for the life of an I Bond. The inflation rate is based on the *Consumer Price Index*, a figure that represents prices consumers pay for goods and services. Every six months, the inflation rate on Series I Bonds changes. When interest rates are low and inflation is not a threat, the return on Series I Bonds is relatively low. However, they are good insurance against inflation.

Series I Bonds are sold at face value in denominations ranging from $25 to $10,000. An individual can purchase up to $10,000 per year directly from TreasuryDirect. Also, you can purchase up to $5,000 per year in Series I Bonds as a result of an income tax refund.

Mutual Funds

A **mutual fund** is an investment created by pooling the money of many people and investing it in a collection of securities. Think of a mutual fund as

Employability Skills

Professional Image

An *image* is the perception others have of a person based on that person's dress, behavior, and speech. It is what people remember about a person from business, professional, and even social interactions. A *professional image* is the image projected by an individual in the professional world. A positive professional image projects honesty, skill, courtesy, and respect for others.

a "basket" of securities. Professional managers at investment firms purchase securities and place them in the basket. Shares of ownership in the basket are then sold to investors. Each investor in the fund owns a tiny part of every security in the basket. Mutual funds may invest in stocks, bonds, commodities, gold, and other securities.

Types of Mutual Funds

The two basic types of mutual funds are closed-end or open-end. A *closed-end fund* offers a fixed number of shares. These shares are traded like stocks on securities exchanges and secondary markets. You buy and sell shares in these funds through investment brokers, not through an investment company.

An *open-end fund* has an unlimited number of shares. It sells and redeems shares at their net asset value. **Net asset value (NAV)** is the total of the fund's assets minus its liabilities divided by the number of the shares the fund has outstanding. Most mutual funds are open-end funds.

Open-end mutual funds may be load or no-load funds. *Load funds* charge a sales commission of up to eight percent of the amount you invest when you buy shares. The average commission is three to five percent. A *front-end load* is deducted when you buy shares in the fund. For example, if you invest $1,000 in a fund with a five percent front-end load, a $50 commission ($1,000 × 5 percent) will be deducted from your $1,000 investment. The difference, $950, then goes into your account. A *back-end load* is deducted when you sell the shares. In this example, the $50 commission will come out of the proceeds when you sell your shares.

A *no-load fund* is one sold without a sales commission. These do not charge sales commissions when you buy shares. However, some funds charge fees when the shares are sold or redeemed. Most mutual funds today are sold without a load.

Several different types of mutual funds are available:

- income funds
- balanced funds
- growth funds
- specialized funds
- money market mutual funds

Income funds buy conservative bonds and stocks that pay regular dividends. Their primary goal is to provide current income. *Balanced funds* invest in common stock, preferred stock, and bonds. Their goal is to provide a lower-risk investment opportunity with moderate growth and dividend income. *Growth funds* invest in securities that are expected to increase in value. They emphasize growth over income, but involve more risk. *Specialized funds* invest in securities of certain industries or sectors, such as all technology or all health-care companies. They may also invest in certain types of securities, such as all municipal bonds or all common stock. Some concentrate on foreign securities.

Another type of mutual fund is the money market mutual fund. A **money market mutual fund** is a type of mutual fund that deals only in interest-paying, short-term investments, such as US treasury securities, certificates of deposit, and commercial paper. *Commercial paper* is a short-term note issued by a major corporation. The funds are managed and sold by investment companies, brokerage firms, and other financial institutions. The interest earned, minus management fees for operating the fund, is passed along to the depositors. Interest rates on money market mutual funds can go up or down based on current interest rates.

Mutual funds are often divided into families. Each fund has its own name and investment objectives. Mutual fund quotes display the names of individual funds listed within each family, as shown in Figure 6-5.

Advantages of Mutual Funds

There are some key advantages to investing in mutual funds, especially for the beginning investor. These advantages include:

- professional management;
- diversification; and
- liquidity.

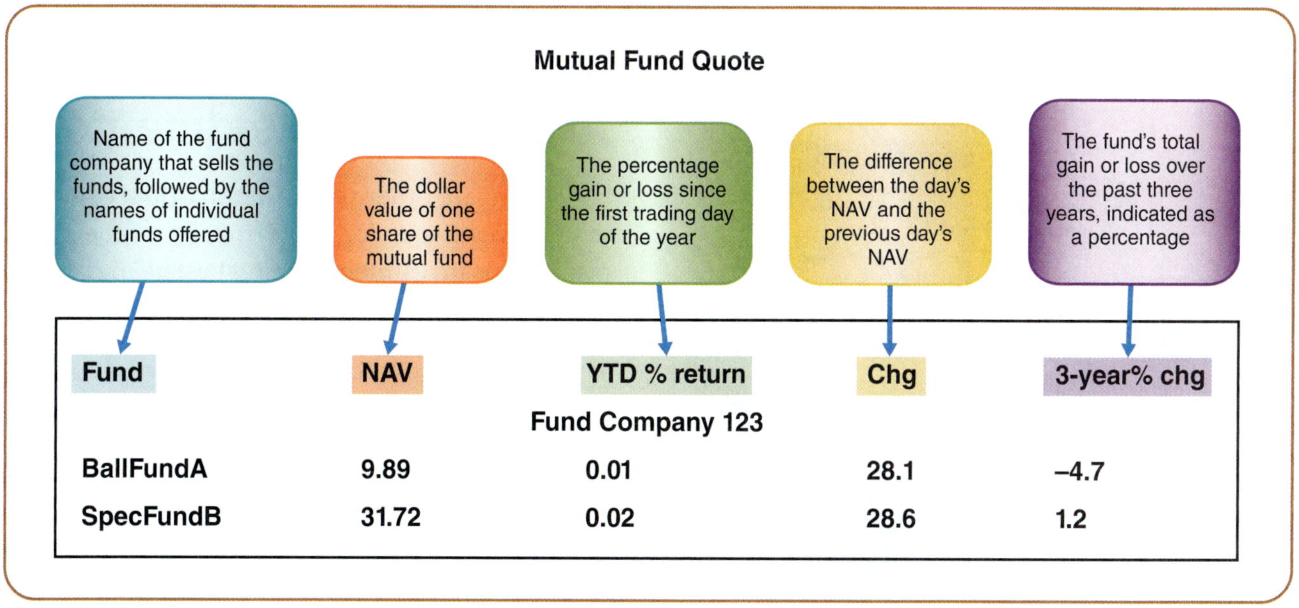

Goodheart-Willcox Publisher

Figure 6-5 Mutual funds quotes appear in the financial pages of major newspapers and online.

Mutual funds are managed by professional investors who carefully follow the markets and are assisted by a team of researchers. Mutual funds also offer diversification in a single investment. When you invest in several securities, you spread your risks. Mutual fund shares are easy to buy and sell, which means they have high liquidity. To buy or sell shares in a fund, you simply call the mutual fund company and make the transaction. Most transactions can also be done over the Internet.

Investing in money market mutual funds has many advantages. These funds provide investors with high yields when interest rates are high. They can be liquidated at any time since they have no term or maturity date. No interest penalties apply for early withdrawals. They can be used as collateral for loans.

Disadvantages of Mutual Funds

Mutual funds also have some disadvantages. These include:

- management fees;
- sales commissions;
- lack of personal control; and
- minimum investment.

Mutual fund managers charge fees to pay for research, administration, sales, and other operating expenses. Fees are not paid by investors, but instead they are deducted directly from the fund's earnings. Additionally, mutual funds can have a load, or sales commission. When investing in mutual funds, you give up control over the selection and timing of your investments. The fund managers make these decisions. Some mutual funds require a minimum investment of $1,000 or more. However, there are many mutual funds with minimum investments as low as $100.

Money market mutual funds have some disadvantages, too. The rate paid on money market mutual funds changes daily. If money market rates drop, so does the rate of return. Unlike money market deposit accounts issued by banks, money market mutual funds are not FDIC-insured.

Andy Dean Photography/Shutterstock.com

Municipal bonds are used to fund projects such as schools or roads.

Alternative Investments

There are other ways an individual can make investments for the future. Two other options for investments are real estate and valuable goods.

Real Estate

Buying real estate, such as land or buildings, is another strategy to invest for future profit. This type of investment usually requires enough money for a down payment plus a long-term loan.

For most people, buying a home is their first experience in real estate. When the real estate market is strong, owning a home can increase your net worth and protect against inflation. Property usually, but not always, increases in value over time. During the Great Recession of the early 21st century, property values in many areas dramatically decreased. Some people found themselves owing more for the property than the market value of the property. Most financial experts advise thinking of a home first in terms of a place to live and second as an investment.

Buying land or buildings for investment purposes is not for amateurs. Before investing in real estate for profit, buyers need to know about property values and property management. They also need to learn about mortgages, down payments, taxes, titles, insurance, and the legal aspects of leases and property ownership. These considerations are described in Chapter 12.

A **real estate investment trust (REIT)** is a company that owns income-earning real estate, such as apartments, shopping malls, office buildings, or hotels. Purchasing shares in a REIT is a way to invest in real estate without the complications and financial commitment of owning property. The government requires that REITs distribute at least 90 percent of their profits to shareholders through dividends. Shares of many REITs are traded on securities exchanges.

Real estate mutual funds are another way to indirectly invest in real estate. These funds may include a mixture of securities from REITs, commercial developers, and other types of real estate companies.

Investing in REITs and real estate mutual funds requires less capital and offers more liquidity than purchasing property. Changes in interest rates, housing prices, and demand for housing can affect the rate of return. As with other securities, investors should research before investing and carefully review prospectuses and annual reports. Prospectuses and annual reports are discussed in Section 6.3.

Valuable Goods

Individuals have collected precious goods and objects for thousands of years and continue to do so today. These items can be attractive investments because their value is not eroded by inflation as money can be. Valuable goods include:

- collectibles;
- precious metals; and
- gemstones.

Keith Bell/Shutterstock.com

Investments can take many forms, including this collectible 1931 Ford automobile.

Collectibles are objects purchased for the pleasure of ownership and because they are expected to increase in value. Common collectibles include rare coins, books, stamps, art, antiques, sports memorabilia, and vintage automobiles.

Precious metals include gold, silver, platinum, and other metals. These are purchased from banks and dealers in the form of jewelry, coins, or bars. Gold lasts forever and it does not tarnish, corrode, or degrade. Gold is in demand worldwide and is a way to diversify an investment portfolio. Prices for precious metals, particularly gold, silver, platinum, and copper, are posted on business websites. Prices for these goods are often volatile.

Gemstones include diamonds, emeralds, sapphires, and other precious gems. They are collected as stones or as pieces of jewelry.

Consider the risks before you choose these investments. They are less liquid than stocks, bonds, and mutual funds. Like real estate, valuable goods can be difficult to sell quickly. When collectors are ready or forced to sell these assets, they sometimes must accept less than what they originally paid. These valuable goods can also be hard to store and protect from damage and theft.

Judging the worth of valuable goods is often difficult unless you have expert knowledge and considerable experience. Before buying valuable goods for investments, consult a reputable professional with experience in estimating value. Ask for a formal appraisal before making a significant investment in collectibles. Only then are you safe in purchasing these items from dealers and online auction sites.

There is no guaranteed return on investments in valuable goods. Putting money into a savings account generates interest. Over time, investing in securities usually pays off. Historically, real estate goes up in value. However, the rate of return on collectibles, precious metals, and gems is less predictable than these other investments.

Section 6.2 Review

Check Your Understanding

1. Name two stock classifications.
2. What are the two markets in which stocks are sold?
3. List the three major issuers of bonds.
4. What are three advantages of mutual funds?
5. Name two alternative investment options.

Build Your Vocabulary

As you progress through this course, develop a personal glossary. This will help you build your vocabulary and prepare you for a career. Write a definition for each of the following terms and add it to your glossary.

securities
stock
dividend
common stock
proxy
preferred stock
stock trade
primary market
initial public offering (IPO)
secondary market
securities exchange
market value
OTC market
bond
Treasury bill
Treasury note
Treasury bond
Series EE bond
Series I bond
mutual fund
net asset value (NAV)
money market mutual fund
real estate investment trust (REIT)

Section 6.3 Investment Resources

Objectives

After studying this section, you will be able to:

- Identify sources of investment information.
- Describe factors that affect investment performance.
- Explain different investment strategies.
- List ways securities can be acquired.

Essential Question

How can a person tell when an investment is a good one?

Terms

prospectus
business cycle
bull market
bear market
dollar-cost averaging
brokerage firm
investment club
dividend reinvestment plan (DRIP)

Investment Information

Building a diversified portfolio involves gathering information, considering strategies, and selecting investment methods. A professional should be consulted for advice on complex investments. A list of financial experts is shown in Figure 6-6. Common sources of information on investments are online resources, annual reports, and prospectuses.

Online Resources

Investment-related websites provide useful information about individual securities and market movements. Company websites usually post investor information or press releases to evaluate the company's investment potential.

In the United States, financial markets have general regulatory oversight from two governmental bodies, the *Commodity Futures Trading Commission (CFTC)* and the *Securities and Exchange Commission (SEC)*. Both have similar goals: to ensure that investors and traders have adequate information to make decisions and to prevent fraud and abuse.

The SEC is the governmental agency that regulates the securities industry. Its mission is to combat fraud as well as to ensure that the securities markets operate efficiently and fairly. All publicly traded companies are required to file financial statements and documents with the SEC. The SEC manages the *Electronic Data Gathering, Analysis, and Retrieval (EDGAR)* database and keeps it up to date as a guide for investors. Visit www.sec.gov to explore this database.

Financial Experts		
Job Title	**Description**	**Credentials**
Accountant	• Keep, audit, and inspect financial records of individuals and businesses • Prepare financial reports and tax returns	• Certified Public Accountant (CPA) indicates an accountant is certified by the American Institute of Certified Public Accountants
Financial planner	• Assist consumers in forming a financial program • Give advice on insurance, savings, investments, taxes, retirement, and estate planning	• Certified Financial Planner (CFP) indicates completion of training and certification administered by the Certified Financial Planner Board of Standards, Inc. • Chartered Financial Consultant (ChFC) may be used by those who have completed additional education and training • Financial planners are not required by law to be certified or licensed
Investment broker-dealer	• Buy and sell securities and other investment products	• Individuals must be registered with the Securities and Exchange Commission (SEC) and the Financial Industry Regulatory Authority (FINRA)
Registered representative	• Work for broker-dealers as salespeople, commonly known as brokers	• Individuals must be registered with FINRA and licensed by the appropriate state securities regulator
Investment advisor	• Provide information and advice on different types of securities	• Advisors managing over $25 million in client accounts must be registered with the SEC. Advisors managing less must be registered with the state securities regulator

Goodheart-Willcox Publisher

Figure 6-6 Consulting an experienced professional can help in managing financial and legal matters.

Annual Reports

The websites of most publicly traded corporations offer access to annual and quarterly reports. These reports can be used to assess the financial health of the company. One piece of information in annual reports is *earnings per share (EPS).* EPS is the earnings of the company divided by the number of its common shares. When earnings per share increase from year to year, it is an indication the company is doing well. Earnings per share are the total corporate earnings, after taxes, divided by the total number of shares.

Prospectuses

A **prospectus** is a legal document that gives a detailed description of a security. When an investor buys a security, the issuer must provide a prospectus. You may also get a copy if you are considering buying a security. A prospectus can usually be found on a company's website or the SEC's EDGAR database.

A prospectus lists company officers, describes business history and operations, and outlines plans for the future. It also includes financial information on:

- risks;
- performance summary;
- fees and expenses; and
- management.

The risks section spells out the ways an investor can lose money by investing in the security. The performance summary section indicates how the investment has performed and how its performance compares with that of similar investments. The *performance* of an investment refers to how much the investment has grown in value and how much income the investment has generated. However, the past performance of the investment does not necessarily indicate future results. The fees and expenses section outlines any costs you must pay when buying, selling, or redeeming shares. The management section identifies the qualifications and experience of the directors and officers of the company or fund.

Factors Affecting the Value and Performance of Investments

The *market value* of an investment is the price at which it can be bought or sold at a given point in time. In a market economy, the laws of supply and demand have a great impact on the market value of stocks and many other investments. For example, a corporation issues a fixed number of shares in its IPO. If the corporation is doing well, and its products are in demand, investors are usually eager to buy the stock. The increased demand from investors pushes

Economics in Action

Tax Revenues

To operate, federal, state, and local governments depend on revenue from various forms of taxes. During an economic recession, tax revenues fall as business activity slows and unemployment rises.

The 2020 COVID-19 pandemic and the resulting shutdown of businesses triggered a severe budget crisis in state and local governments. Tax revenues declined sharply as businesses closed or operated at reduced hours, and millions of people were suddenly unemployed. As a result, state governments and many local governments faced budget shortfalls because tax revenues were not sufficient to cover the costs of operating.

Almost all states have balanced-budget laws, which means money cannot be borrowed to cover budget shortfalls. Suddenly faced with dramatic cuts in vital services, state governments looked to the federal government for assistance. Congress quickly responded and passed several legislative acts. An early, but important, legislative act was the March 27, 2020, enactment of the Coronavirus Aid, Relief, and Economic Security (CARES) Act. This act provided over $2 trillion in economic relief for American workers, families, and small businesses. The CARES Act also established the Paycheck Protection Program to provide small businesses with the resources they needed to maintain their payroll, hire back employees who may have been laid off, and cover applicable overhead.

up the price of stock. On the other hand, when the corporation is not doing well, there may be more sellers of stock than buyers. This, in turn, pushes down the price of the stock. Other factors that affect the value and performance of an investment include economic indicators, product innovation, governmental actions, and transactional costs.

Economic Indicators

How well an investment performs depends largely on the overall strength of the economy. In a strong and growing economy, investors have confidence their investments will do well. As a result, buyers outnumber sellers and investments tend to grow in value. On the other hand, in a weak and declining economy, investors lose confidence. Sellers outnumber buyers, which pushes down the value of most types of investments.

The strength of an economy can be measured using certain indicators. An *indicator* is a sign that shows the condition or existence of something. Some of the most widely followed indicators of the economy are gross domestic product (GDP), rate of inflation, interest rates, unemployment rate, and the stock and bond markets. Economic indicators that affect investments are business cycle fluctuations, interest rate fluctuations, stock market fluctuations, and the exchange-rate risk.

Business Cycle Fluctuations

A **business cycle** is the fluctuations between periods of economic growth and slowdown. When the economy is growing, most businesses and investors do well. However, when economic growth slows, many businesses and investors lose money as sales decline. Being aware of the ups and downs of the economy can help investors make wise choices.

Interest Rate Fluctuations

Fluctuations in interest rates affect the value of securities and other investments. Bonds and real estate are directly affected by the ups and downs of interest rates. For example, as interest rates rise, bond prices fall. This is because investors can receive higher returns by investing in bonds with the new higher rates. Conversely, as interest rates fall, bond prices rise. Real estate sales increase as interest rates fall and suffer when they rise. Business growth generally is greater when interest rates are low and lesser when rates increase.

Stock Market Fluctuations

Bull and *bear* are terms used to describe the strength or weakness of the stock market. A **bull market** is an extended period of rising stock prices, which comes with high consumer confidence and optimism. The sense of optimism often encourages the exploration of other investment opportunities, including real estate and valuable goods.

A **bear market** is an extended period of falling stock prices, which comes with uncertainty and pessimism. During bear markets, investors feel insecure and wary about the economy. Fearing further drops in the value of their investments, they often sell the investments. However, this is often a buying opportunity for those willing to take the risk because prices are low.

You Do the Math — Rounding

Many times, you will not need as precise a number as a calculation provides. For example, when working with decimals, especially multiplication and division operations, the final answer may have several more decimal places than you need.

To round a number, locate the value place to which you want to round. Then, look at the digit to the right of this place. If the digit to the right is 5 or greater, add 1 to the value place to which you are rounding. If the digit to the right is less than 5, do nothing to the value place to which you are rounding.

Solve the following problems.

1. Assume you invest $1,000 each quarter at the following stock prices. How many shares of stock will you own at the end of the year? Round your answer to three decimal places.
   - First quarter: $20 per share
   - Second quarter: $25 per share
   - Third quarter: $35 per share
   - Fourth quarter: $30 per share
2. What is the average cost of all shares purchased throughout the year? Round your answer to the nearest penny. This demonstrates how dollar-cost averaging balances out the highs and lows of stock prices.

Exchange-Rate Risk

For investors who trade securities of companies in other countries, the currency exchange rate needs to be considered. The currency exchange rate is how much one US dollar is equal to in another currency, such as euros. It may be necessary to exchange US dollars for another currency. Dividends and gains or losses may be presented in foreign currency. The ups and downs of the exchange rate, whether buying or selling, become a potential risk for the investor.

Product Innovation

Historically, investors who financed winning products in their infancy, such as the automobile, microwave oven, and cell phone, made high profits. Those who invested in products that did not succeed lost their money. For most investors, the results of investing in new products fall somewhere between high profits and high losses.

Business failure is caused by many factors, ranging from poor management to new competition to governmental regulations. Technological advancement can cause new companies and industries to spring up while making outdated companies obsolete.

Governmental Actions

Actions by governments can impact the value of an investment in a positive or negative way. Product recalls, new regulations, and increased taxes often have a negative impact on company stock. Trade barriers protecting US companies from foreign competition often improve the outlook of stock in protected industries.

Transactional Costs

Another factor that affects the performance of an investment is the costs associated with owning it. There are fees for buying and selling financial assets. These are called *transactional costs*. The bank or broker through which the sale or purchase occurs charges a fee or commission. In real estate investing, there are costs such as title searches, appraisal fees, and closing costs. Mutual funds charge an annual fee for managing the money invested in the fund. These fees are charged even if a mutual fund declines in value.

Transactional costs reduce the overall return on the investment. Over time, high transactional costs can add up to thousands of dollars in fees, not to mention the opportunity cost of not being able to invest the money spent on fees.

Investment Strategies

Smart investing is a balancing act. It requires balancing risks against returns. Figure 6-7 shows how different types of investments carry varying levels of risk. As people get closer to retirement, they need to choose more conservative investments to preserve principal and provide income. Younger investors can usually take more risks than older investors. A young investor has many wage-earning years ahead. Investing at an early age allows you to benefit from two common investment strategies: buy and hold and dollar-cost averaging.

Buy and Hold

Buy and hold is the strategy of buying securities and holding them for long-term gains as opposed to frequent trading. An investor using this strategy stays

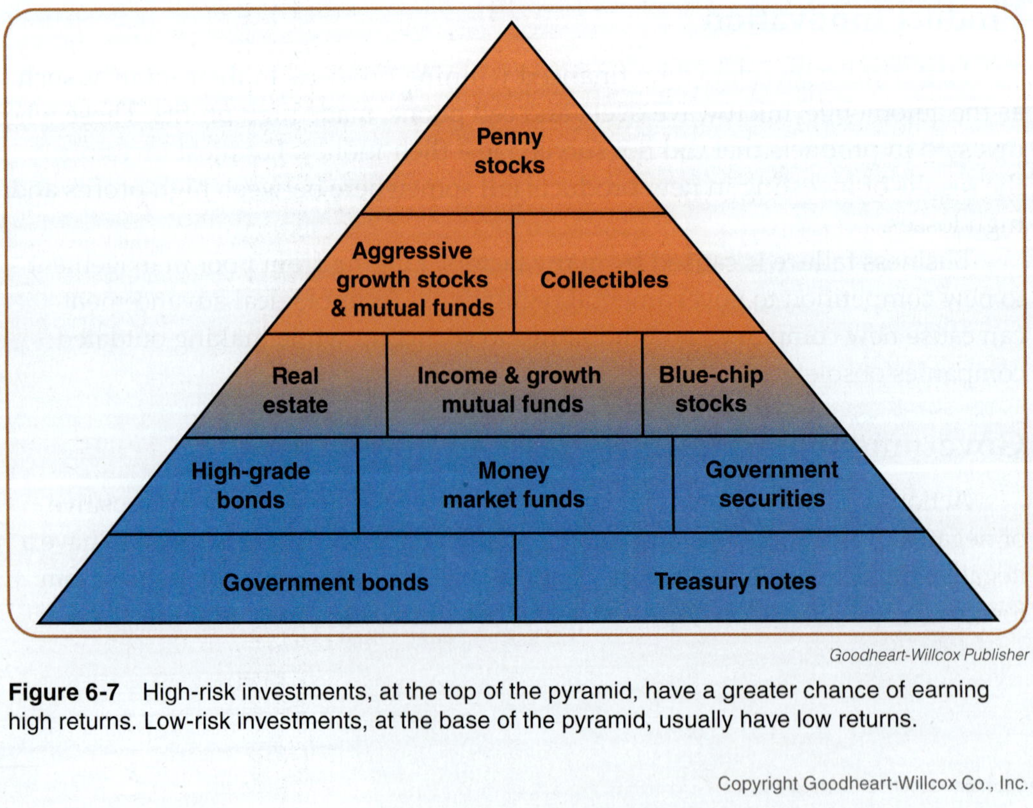

Goodheart-Willcox Publisher

Figure 6-7 High-risk investments, at the top of the pyramid, have a greater chance of earning high returns. Low-risk investments, at the base of the pyramid, usually have low returns.

invested during market fluctuations. Investors who sell stocks when they drop in value lose money. Investors who hold stocks usually gain in the long run.

If your stock earns dividends, money will be earned over the years you own the stock. Also, if you hold a stock for a period of time, the company may split its stock, increasing your holdings.

Buy and hold does not mean buy and forget. Investments should be checked periodically to know how well they are performing. When an investment is not performing well, it may be time to sell and reinvest in a more promising company. An accountant or tax professional should be consulted to evaluate the tax implications of selling.

Dollar-Cost Averaging

Dollar-cost averaging is a strategy of investing a fixed dollar amount at regular intervals, such as monthly, without regard to the price of the investment at the time you buy it. You buy more shares when the price is low and fewer when it is high. This buying strategy reduces the risk of investing a lump sum when it may not be the best time to buy.

Dollar-cost averaging offers the added advantage of convenience. You can set up an automatic payment and make it a part of your overall budget. It helps make a habit of investing affordable amounts of money. Brokerage firms, mutual funds, and retirement accounts all offer opportunities for dollar-cost averaging. Often, you can invest as little as $25 monthly.

Buying Securities

Once you have decided on specific securities you wish to buy, it is time to decide how to buy them. There are several ways to acquire securities. They can be acquired through brokerage firms, investment clubs, or as a DRIP.

Brokerage Firms

To buy stocks, bonds, and other securities, you may open an account with a brokerage or securities firm. A **brokerage firm** is a financial institution that facilitates the purchase and sale of financial securities by buyers and sellers. The main mission of a brokerage firm is to process buy and sell orders for its customers.

To open a brokerage account, complete an application with a firm. Once the application is accepted, the broker is called with orders to buy and sell. Most firms also offer online services.

Full-service brokerage firms maintain research departments to follow market trends and individual securities. In addition, they provide investment advice, portfolio management, and other services. The commission you pay covers the cost of trading and support services provided by the firm. Both experienced and beginning investors can benefit from the expertise of full-service brokerage firms.

Discount brokerage firms execute orders to buy and sell securities, but offer few other services. For instance, a discount brokerage firm does not offer investment advice. The commission is considerably lower than that charged by a full-service broker. However, you will need to do your own research and investment planning when buying from a discount broker. Some experienced investors may prefer to use discount brokers to save money on commissions.

Online brokerage firms have a network of computer systems that allow investors to place buy and sell orders 24 hours a day. Use the following guidelines when investing through an online brokerage firm.

- Use reputable brokers.
- Study investment information.
- Keep investment documents.
- Track performance.

When investing directly online, no one will be supervising your account. This makes it essential to follow market trends and prices of securities you own.

Deal only with people and companies who are reputable and legitimate. Brokers and securities firms can be researched with your state securities regulator or the SEC. Trustworthy brokers will also be members of the Financial Industry Regulatory Authority (FINRA) and Securities Investor Protection Corporation (SIPC). The FINRA, which was mentioned earlier in the chapter, holds brokers accountable for fairness and honesty, while the SIPC serves the securities industry in much the same way as the FDIC serves the banking industry by providing account insurance to investors. Obtain and review material such as a prospectus, an annual report, and recent company news.

Before placing an order, know exactly what you are buying and what risks are involved. Obtain and keep written confirmations of your buy and sell orders and their completion. File all of your investment records and information in a safe place where you can locate them easily. These records are needed to file a tax return. Follow the performance of your investments. Prices can rise and fall swiftly in active markets. Buy and sell at the most advantageous times.

When securities are purchased online or by phone, specific types of orders are needed to conduct trades. These include market orders, limit orders, and stop orders. A *market order* instructs your broker to buy or sell a stock at the best price available. Stock prices can change between the time you place an order and the time it is executed. A *limit order* instructs your broker to buy or sell a certain stock at a set price or better. If the broker cannot buy or sell at the price you request, the order will not be executed. A *stop order* instructs your broker to buy or sell a stock when and if it reaches a specific price. It will be carried out only when the stock reaches the target price. This type of order helps you protect gains and limit losses.

Investment Clubs

An **investment club** is a group of people who work together to learn about securities and to invest their pooled funds. Members attend regular meetings, pay dues, and elect officers. Members research and follow stocks under consideration or in the club's portfolio. They also buy and sell securities by vote of the majority. Most investment clubs become legal partnerships for the purpose of filing income taxes and meeting Internal Revenue Service requirements.

An investment club can be a good way to start investing. It offers the opportunity to invest on a small scale while learning. If you can find a few friends who are interested in learning to invest, you may consider forming an investment club.

The National Association of Investors Corporation provides information on starting and running a successful club. You will also find similar information from the SEC and Investment Club Central.

DRIPs

A **dividend reinvestment plan (DRIP)** allows investors to reinvest cash dividends by purchasing additional shares of stock. DRIPs offer a way to bypass brokers and commissions and invest directly in a company. Dividends are automatically reinvested. Many companies offer DRIPs to the public.

To enroll in a DRIP, become a stockholder by purchasing at least one share of stock in your own name. Then go to the Investor Relations section of the company's website for instructions and an application. Often you can make automatic weekly or monthly stock purchases in amounts as little as $25. Some even offer a three to five percent discount from the current market price of the security.

When you wish to sell shares, it may take a few days to complete the transaction. There may also be a fee for selling. Accurate records should be kept of dividends, gains, and losses for income tax purposes.

Section 6.3 Review

Check Your Understanding

1. Name several sources of investment information.
2. Which two governmental bodies regulate financial markets?
3. Explain what is meant by *bull* and *bear* markets.
4. Name two common investment strategies.
5. List ways securities can be purchased.

Build Your Vocabulary

As you progress through this course, develop a personal glossary. This will help you build your vocabulary and prepare you for a career. Write a definition for each of the following terms and add it to your glossary.

prospectus
business cycle
bull market
bear market
dollar-cost averaging
brokerage firm
investment club
dividend reinvestment plan (DRIP)

Review and Assessment

Chapter Summary

Section 6.1 Investments

- Investing is purchasing a financial product or valuable item with the goal of increasing wealth over time in spite of possible loss. It offers the opportunity to accumulate money to meet future needs and goals. A personal investment plan is an important part of a financial plan.
- Each person creates an investment plan to reach specific financial goals or meet certain needs. Benefits of investing include increasing wealth, earning a steady income, beating inflation, taking advantage of tax benefits, and preserving wealth in unstable economic times.

Section 6.2 Types of Investments

- A stock is a share in the ownership of a corporation. Stock can be classified as common or preferred stock. When a company first sells stock to the public in an initial public offering (IPO), it is considered a primary market. Stock can then be resold to other investors in several secondary markets.
- A bond is a certificate of debt issued by a corporation or government. The three major issuers of bonds are corporations, municipalities, and the federal government. Corporate bonds are issued by corporations that need money to operate and expand. Municipal bonds are issued by state, county, and city governments. US government bonds include treasury bills, treasury notes, treasury bonds, Series EE bonds, and Series I bonds.
- A mutual fund is an investment created by pooling the money of many people and investing it in a collection of securities. The two basic types of mutual funds are closed-end or open-end. Mutual funds can also be load or no-load.
- Alternative options for investments include real estate and valuable goods. Purchasing stock in a real estate investment trust (REIT) or real estate mutual fund is a way to invest in real estate without the complications and financial commitment of owning property. Purchasing valuable goods like collectibles, precious metals, and gemstones is another way to invest.

Section 6.3 Investment Resources

- Successful investors diversify their portfolios. Building a diversified portfolio involves gathering information, considering strategies, and selecting investment methods. Common sources of information on investments are online resources, annual reports, prospectuses, and market quotes.
- Certain information can help predict investment return. Examples of economic indicators are business cycle fluctuations, interest rate fluctuations, stock market fluctuations, market fluctuations, product innovations, governmental actions, and the exchange-rate risk.
- Investing at an early age allows you to benefit from two common investment strategies: buy and hold and dollar-cost averaging. Buy and hold is the strategy of buying securities and holding them for long-term gains as opposed to frequent trading. Dollar-cost averaging is a strategy of investing a fixed dollar amount at regular intervals without regard to the price of the investment at the time you buy it.
- To buy stocks, bonds, and other securities, you may open an account with a brokerage or securities firm, join an investment club, or take part in a dividend reinvestment plan (DRIP).

Review Your Knowledge

1. Explain the concept of investing.
2. Discuss the benefits an individual could gain from investing.
3. Explain the difference between common stock and preferred stock.

4. Describe types of bonds that can be purchased as an investment strategy.
5. Discuss mutual funds as a type of security.
6. List and describe alternative types of investments.
7. Identify sources of information when researching investment opportunities.
8. Describe examples of factors that affect investment performance.
9. Describe some of the ways securities can be acquired.
10. What are some guidelines to follow when investing through an online brokerage firm?

Apply Your Knowledge

1. Investments include stocks, bonds, mutual funds, real estate property, and valuable goods. Create a three-column chart. In the first column, list each type of investment. In the second column, list the advantages of each investment. In the third column, list the disadvantages of each. Evaluate the different types of investments. Which one do you think is the better investment in the current economy? Write a paragraph to explain your reasoning.
2. Investment goals change depending on your earning power and stage in the life cycle. How much money do you have now that you could invest today? List your short-term and long-term needs for this money. They could be paying for college, buying a car, or other activity for which funding needs to be planned. Investigate your long-term needs for money in your future.
3. Based on the list of long-term needs you established in the last activity, state your financial goals. How can you accomplish these goals?
4. You have now investigated your long-term needs and written your financial goals. The next step is to decide how to invest your money for future growth. What is your risk tolerance for investing the money? Are you willing to take chances on your investment or are you looking for something that will be a consistent return? Analyze your risk tolerance.
5. Successful investing often results in earning capital gains. Name some examples of investments that qualify for capital gains or capital loss. Which one of the investments you listed would you be willing to take a risk on and purchase?
6. You have some money that you want to invest in the stock market. However, you are aware of the economic indicators that affect the value and performance of investments: business cycle fluctuations, interest rate fluctuations, stock market fluctuations, and the exchange-rate risk. Which of these factors do you think are important in today's economy for those who are making investments?
7. Two common investment strategies are *buy and hold* and *dollar cost-averaging*. Create a chart to compare and contrast these investment strategies.
8. Is it wise for young adults to take bigger risks in hopes of earning higher returns than older adults? Write several paragraphs to explain your opinion.
9. Make a list of personal and financial factors that a 40-year-old should consider when making investments for retirement. Assume that this individual has not made any previous plans to date. When you have finished with your list, create a checklist of your top ten factors to consider when making investments for retirement.
10. Create a three-column chart. Label the first column *Full-Service Brokerage Firm*. Label the second column *Discount Brokerage Firm*. Label the third column *Online Brokerage Firm*. Write the characteristics of each type of brokerage firm in its column. Compare the three types of firms. Which type of brokerage firm would you use and why?

Apply Your Math Skills

1. Helena purchased 200 shares of a company's stock for $17.50 per share. A year later, the stock was sold for $20 per share. How much money did Helena make from the sale of the stocks?
2. Kamil owns 70 shares of stock in Star Industries. Star Industries pays an annual dividend of $1.30 per share. How much money will Kamil make when the dividend is paid out for the year?
3. Josie inherits $5,000 and decides to put it into a retirement account that has 6% interest with a plan to add $1,000 a year in order to retire at the age of 65. Analyze and compare the difference in the amount Josie will have in the account if $1,000 per year is added starting at age 25 versus starting at the age of 40.

Communication Skills

College and Career Readiness

Speaking. Select three of your classmates to participate in a discussion panel. Acting as the team leader, name each person to a specific task such as timekeeper, recorder, etc. Discuss the topic of earning a steady income as one benefit of investing. Dividends and capital gains can be a source of income for investors. Keep the panel on task and promote democratic discussion about sources of income for investors. The recorder should make notes of important information that was discussed. The notes should be edited and a final document created for distribution to the class.

Reading. After you have read this chapter, identify the explicit details, as well as the author's main idea for the chapter. Apply appropriate reading techniques to identify the main ideas and purpose of the information that is presented about investments. Draw conclusions about the author's purpose. Share your findings with the class.

Writing. Attending to your personal and financial well-being is an important step in becoming a contributing member of society. Why do you think it is important to create an investment plan while you are still in high school? What advantages can starting a plan now provide you as an adult?

Teamwork

Form a team of classmates and develop a plan for investing $5,000 over the length of this course. Use the Internet, current financial publications, and books on financial planning for information on developing your plan. Factors to identify and consider include your objectives, types of investments, expected returns, risk tolerance, liquidity, and diversification. Describe your plan in terms of these factors. In the final week of class, compare your team's plans with those of other teams in the class.

Internet Research

Publicly Traded Stock. Using the Internet, research a publicly traded stock on the NASDAQ or New York Stock Exchange. Record the daily closing value each day for two weeks. Compare the value on day 1 with the value on day 14. How did the stock perform?

Investment Advice. There are many sources of investment advice available. Use the Internet to research how to be a prudent investor in the stock market. Make a list of some of the advice that you found. Cite each source.

US Government Bonds. The US government offers multiple investment instruments that consumers can purchase. Examples are Treasury Bills, Treasury Notes, Treasury Bonds, Series EE Bonds, and Series I Bonds. Using the Internet, navigate to the TreasuryDirect website. Research the characteristics of each type of investment listed here. Then, compare and contrast each type. Create a chart to summarize your findings.

Investment Options. Stocks, bonds, and mutual funds are traditional ways to invest. Real estate and valuable goods offer some alternatives as investments. Select examples of other investment options, rather than stocks or bonds, that you would consider purchasing. Using the Internet, research how your investments options appreciate or depreciate. What did you learn about your choices?

Portfolio Development

Checklist. Once you have established a method of collecting and organizing your documents, you will need to ensure nothing is left out or forgotten. Remember, a portfolio is a living document—one that is often customized for each job or academic program to which you apply. Unfortunately, this makes it easy to misplace, lose, or forget relevant information. It is helpful to use the master list of documents you created in a previous portfolio activity to serve as a checklist of components to be included in your portfolio. The checklist can also be used to record ideas for additional documents and other items that you may choose to include. It should *not* be included in your final portfolio, however.

Your checklist will likely need to be updated for each school or employer who will see your portfolio. Modifying your master list to appeal to each instance will result in greater chances of success. For example, if you were applying to a visual arts program at a university specialized in art, you would likely not present the same portfolio as if you were applying for a part-time job creating graphics for a marketing company.

As you move copies of documents from their original location to your customized portfolio, check the document off your list. This will help you make sure all relevant items are included.

1. Ask your instructor for a checklist. If one is not provided, use the Internet and research Student Portfolio checklists. Find an example that works for your purpose.
2. Print the master list of documents you created in a previous portfolio activity and compare that to the checklist you obtained in step 1. Make any necessary adjustments.
3. Using the master list, sample checklist, and any pertinent notes you made while comparing the two, create a checklist to serve as a roadmap for your portfolio.

CTSOs

Parliamentary Procedures. The *Parliamentary Procedure* competitive event is an event in which the participants must demonstrate understanding of parliamentary procedures such as *Roberts Rules of Order.* This is a team event in which the group will demonstrate how to conduct an effective meeting. An objective test may be administered to each person on the team that will be evaluated and included in the overall team score.

To prepare for the parliamentary procedure, complete the following activities.

1. Read the guidelines provided by your organization.
2. Study parliamentary procedure principles by reviewing *Roberts Rules of Order.*
3. Practice proper procedures for conducting a meeting. Assign each team member a role for the presentation.
4. Visit the organization's website and look for the evaluation criteria or rubric for the event. This will help you determine what the judges will be looking for in your presentation.

CHAPTER

7 Retirement and Estate Planning

A key element of financial security is retirement planning. Saving for retirement early means you have more time for your money to grow. By the time you retire, you could need to provide income for yourself for 30 to 40 more years. This many years requires early planning, careful investment, periodic review, and proper adjustments to meet changing needs. Starting a retirement investment plan early is the most effective way to provide enough money to live comfortably during retirement.

Estate planning is also an important part of an overall financial plan. It allows you to decide how your assets should be managed after your death, make plans for any dependents, and minimize taxes. Some of the tools necessary to complete an estate plan include power of attorney, wills, living wills, and trusts.

Focus on Finance

Estate Tax

Your *estate* is everything you own or have a financial interest in when you die. Your estate may include cash, real estate, insurance policies, business interests, valuable goods, and other assets. In most cases, when a person dies, the estate passes to the person's heirs, such as children or grandchildren.

In some cases, tax must be paid on the estate before it can be transferred. This is called the *estate tax*. In order to determine the estate tax owed, the fair-market value of the estate must be determined. The *fair-market value* of an asset is what the asset can be sold for at that point in time, not what you paid for it or what you think it is worth. The estate tax is then calculated on this value or a portion of this value. For example, in 2020, only the portion of an estate exceeding $7,222,200 was taxed. Typically, no estate tax is paid if the estate is left to a spouse or a charity.

College and Career Readiness

Reading Prep. Before reading this chapter, flip through the pages and make notes of the major headings. Analyze the structure of the relationships of the headings with the concepts in the chapter.

Sections

George Dolgikh/Shutterstock.com

Section 7.1 Types of Retirement Plans

Essential Question

What does *retirement planning* mean?

Objectives

After studying this section, you will be able to:

- Describe various employer-sponsored retirement plans.
- Explain options for personal retirement plans.
- Discuss retirement plan options for those who are self-employed.
- Identify examples of governmental pension plans.

Terms

retirement	required minimum distribution (RMD)	spousal IRA
vesting	403(b) plan	traditional IRA
rollover	457 plan	Roth IRA
defined-benefit plan	Roth 401(k)	annuity
defined-contribution plan	individual retirement account (IRA)	SEP-IRA
401(k) plan		Solo 401(k)
		SIMPLE IRA

Employer-Sponsored Retirement Plans

Retirement is the period of life after ending a working or professional career. The word "retirement" can also be used to refer to the money a person has saved to be used during this period of life.

Many employers offer retirement plans to their employees. These plans can vary greatly from employer to employer, but all must meet the standards set forth in the *Employee Retirement Income Security Act (ERISA).* This 1974 law sets standards for pension and retirement plans to guarantee that workers receive the benefits to which they are entitled.

Vesting requirements are an important part of ERISA. **Vesting** is the process of determining when money that has been set aside in a retirement plan belongs to an employee. Once vested, an employee is entitled to the promised benefits even if the employee leaves the company before retirement.

The vesting period is gradual and varies from employer to employer. Typically, after seven to ten years, the employee becomes *fully vested.* Once fully vested, the employee has a legal claim to 100 percent of promised benefits.

Alexander Chaikin/Shutterstock.com

Planning for retirement at an early age can help an individual enjoy financial freedom.

Case Study *Estate Planning*

Kelly and Jerome owned a successful office-supply business. Over the years, they made enough money to buy a house, raise two children, and travel.

Sadly, Jerome died a few years before they were ready to retire. Neither could face the thought that one of them would die, so they had not created wills or done any tax planning. Since there was no will, Jerome's estate was divided according to state law, and half of the estate went to their children. The amount left over is not enough to allow Kelly to live comfortably for long, especially since there is no legal right to the children's inheritance and there are taxes to pay.

Case Review

1. When does it become important to prepare a will and complete estate planning?
2. Why is a will important even to those who do not have large amounts of money or property?
3. What are some estate-planning steps that can ease financial burdens following the death of a loved one?
4. What advice would you have given to Jerome and Kelly before they reached retirement age?

Most employer-sponsored retirement plans are portable. You can take your retirement savings with you if you leave your job. A **rollover** is the process of moving retirement savings from one qualified account to another qualified account without incurring penalties and taxes. There are strict regulations on rollovers. You can learn more about retirement plan rollovers on the IRS website.

There are two common types of employer-sponsored retirement plans. These are the defined-benefit plan and the defined-contribution plan.

Defined-Benefit Plans

A **defined-benefit plan** is a retirement plan that makes regular payments, usually monthly, to a retiree until the person's death. It is also known as a *pension plan*. In some plans, payments will continue to a spouse or other beneficiary after the death of the retiree.

At retirement, payments from the plan are calculated using a formula that is typically based on a combination of the employee's salary and years of service to the organization. Defined-benefit plans are usually funded by contributions from both the employer and the employee. However, some plans are fully funded by the employer. Money contributed to the plan is professionally managed.

Most defined-benefit plans establish a *normal retirement age*, which is the age an employee can retire and receive full benefits. Depending on the organization, the normal retirement age is usually between 60 and 65 years of age. However, the age for full Social Security retirement benefits is 67 for individuals born in 1960 and later.

Defined-benefit plans are normally the most advantageous plans for employees, because a person cannot outlive a pension. Persons who have pensions collect the benefits their entire lives. However, these plans are usually expensive for the employer to fund. Because of the expense, many private-sector employers have moved away from defined-benefit plans.

Defined-Contribution Plans

A **defined-contribution plan** is a retirement plan in which an employee and/or employer contributes to the employee's individual account under the defined plan. The amount contributed is typically either a percentage of an employee's salary or a specific dollar amount. The employee's contribution may be deducted from earnings as part of a *payroll savings plan (PSP)*. In a PSP program, the employee authorizes the employer to make regular deductions from each paycheck to automatically deposit in a designated account.

In some cases, employers will match a certain percentage of the employee's contribution. The combined funds are then invested in a variety of options made available by the employer. The amount in the defined-contribution plan at retirement depends on several factors:

- how much the employee saves in the plan
- how much the employer contributes to the plan
- how long the funds are invested
- how well those investments perform

Unlike pensions, the money in defined-contribution plans does not necessarily last a lifetime. Retirees who do not adequately fund their plans risk running out of money. Common defined-contribution plans are the 401(k), 403(b), and 457 plans.

401(k) Plans

A **401(k) plan** is an employer-sponsored retirement plan that allows an individual to deposit earnings into a tax-deferred investment. It is a well-known retirement savings plan. The plan is funded with an individual's pretax salary contributions that are often matched by contributions from an employer. Some employers match employee contributions on a dollar-for-dollar basis. However, most match only a lesser percentage of the employee contribution.

Typical 401(k) plans offer several different investment options from which employees can choose, such as stock-based mutual funds, bond-based mutual funds, and money-market funds. Many companies also allow employees to purchase company stock and hold it in the 401(k) plan.

Investing in a 401(k) plan can be a good way to save for retirement, especially when employers match contributions. The great advantage of a 401(k) plan is tax-deferred growth of savings. *Tax-deferred* means that the account holder does not have to pay taxes on the money in the 401(k) account until it is withdrawn. When taxes are deferred, money is not coming out of the account each year to pay taxes. This leaves more money to be invested and grow in value.

Money can be withdrawn from a 401(k) plan without a penalty the year in which the holder turns 59 1/2. Withdrawals before this age are considered *early withdrawals* and are usually subject to a 10 percent penalty by the IRS. The penalty for early withdrawals is in addition to income taxes that must be paid on the withdrawal. Taxes must be paid on the withdrawals since the contributions were pretax dollars. The money withdrawn from the account must be reported as income on a federal income tax form. Some states also tax 401(k) withdrawals as income.

The holder of a 401(k) plan must start taking withdrawals after 72. At this age, required minimum distribution rules must be followed. The **required minimum distribution (RMD)** is the minimum amount that must be withdrawn

You Do the Math Percentages

Many calculations related to retirement planning are based on percentages. A percentage is a part of 100 and is the same as a fraction or decimal. For example, 15 percent is the same as 15 ÷100, which is .15. To calculate the percentage of a number, change the percentage to a decimal and multiply by the number. For example:

15 percent of 200 = 15 ÷ 100 × 200 or .15 × 200 = 30

Solve the following problems.

1. Riley has been working as a high school principal for 30 years. The formula for calculating retirement pensions in the school system is based on 2 percent multiplied by each year worked. What is the percentage that will be used to calculate Riley's retirement pension?
2. The annual retirement pension received is based on the average salary earned over Riley's career. If the average salary is $50,000, what will be the annual retirement pension?

from a retirement plan each year. A table for RMDs can be found on the IRS website.

You can withdraw more than the RMD in any year. If a RMD is not made, or too little is withdrawn, the IRS fines the taxpayer 50 percent of the amount that should have been withdrawn. However, there are some exceptions to this law. The RMD rule does not apply to those still working full time at age 72. Examples of other situations when this law does not apply include:

- a worker becomes disabled and leaves the workforce;
- a worker retires and leaves the workforce at age 55;
- a worker dies and the account is paid to a beneficiary; and
- the withdrawal is for a major medical expense.

403(b) Plans

A **403(b) plan** is retirement plan available to employees of nonprofit organizations such as public schools, colleges, hospitals, and public libraries. It has many of the same characteristics as the 401(k) plan. Participants in a 403(b) plan are allowed to set aside money for retirement on a pretax basis, and the money grows tax-deferred until withdrawals are made. Like the 401(k) plan, the 403(b) plan allows workers to choose from a variety of investment options. For instance, a typical 403(b) plan includes several stock-based and bond-based mutual funds. Unlike the 401(k) plan, however, the 403(b) plan does not allow participants to invest in individual stocks. Workers with 403(b) plans are also subject to RMD rules.

lightpoet/Shutterstock.com

Many nonprofit employers, such as schools, offer 403(b) plans for their employees.

Dmitry Kalinovsky/Shutterstock.com

A 457 plan is a type of defined-contribution retirement plan that is available primarily to governmental employees, such as police and firefighters.

457 Plans

A **457 plan** is a type of defined-contribution retirement plan that does not have RMD rules and is available primarily to governmental employees. However, certain nonprofit organizations, such as public schools, are also authorized to offer 457 plans. They work much the same way as 401(k) plans. The employee contributes part of each paycheck to the plan. The money is automatically deducted from each paycheck before taxes are deducted. The money grows tax-deferred until it is withdrawn. With a 457 plan, however, there are no employer-matched contributions.

Unlike 401(k) and 403(b) plans, the IRS does not impose a 10 percent penalty on employees who leave a job and start taking withdrawals from a 457 plan before age 59 1/2. However, withdrawals are subject to federal and state income taxes. Withdrawals can be taken in a lump sum or in annual installments.

Roth 401(k) Plans

Introduced in 2006, the Roth 401(k) is the newest form of defined-contribution plans. A **Roth 401(k) plan** is an employer-sponsored retirement plan in which contributions are made with after-tax earnings, but withdrawals are not taxed. The Roth 401(k) plan is similar to the traditional 401(k) plan. However, contributions to a Roth 401(k) plan are made on an after-tax basis. An *after-tax basis* means that the employer does not deduct Roth 401(k) contributions from the employee's paycheck before taxes are calculated. As a result, there is no immediate tax benefit for contributing to a Roth 401(k) plan. However, the tax advantages come in retirement. Withdrawals from a Roth 401(k) plan are tax-free as long as the account holder has had the account for five years and is at least 59 1/2 when withdrawals are made.

Younger workers benefit the most from a Roth 401(k) because they will have many years of tax-free growth during their working years and tax-free income in retirement. However, the employer must offer the plan. Currently only one out of every two employers offers this type of plan. Additionally, workers already contributing to traditional 401(k) plans have been reluctant to switch to the Roth version. As the benefits of the Roth version become more commonplace and new employees enter the workforce, the Roth 401(k) is likely to grow in popularity. Roth 401(k) plans are subject to RMD rules.

Personal Retirement Plans

Individuals who do not have an employer-sponsored retirement plan can create a personal retirement plan. Individuals with employer-sponsored plans can also create a personal retirement plan if they want the added security of two retirement plans. Many workers have both an employer-sponsored retirement plan and a personal retirement plan.

An **individual retirement account (IRA)** is a personal account for setting money aside for retirement. Unlike employer-sponsored retirement plans, in which the investment options are chosen by the employer, an individual has total control of where money is invested in an IRA. There are many places where an IRA can be set up. For example, a bank, an insurance company, a mutual fund company, and a brokerage firm may offer IRAs.

An IRA is *not* an investment. It is an account that contains the investments chosen by the account holder. Many types of investments can be held in an IRA, including individual stocks, bonds, mutual funds, exchange-traded funds, REITs, certificates of deposit, and even real estate. Professional advice should be sought when making a selection of investments.

There are two primary types of IRAs: a traditional IRA and a Roth IRA. The process of setting up a traditional IRA and a Roth IRA is identical. When filling out an application, simply check a box to designate whether it should be treated as traditional or Roth.

To contribute to a traditional or Roth IRA, you must have earned income. *Earned income* is money received for work. Examples include wages, salaries, commissions, tips, and self-employment income. The income can be earned on a full- or part-time basis.

An exception to the earned-income rule is the spousal IRA. A **spousal IRA** is a type of individual retirement account that allows a working spouse to contribute to the retirement savings of a nonworking spouse. Spousal IRAs can be either traditional or Roth IRAs and are subject to the same rules as traditional and Roth IRAs. To qualify for a spousal IRA, the couple must be legally married and file a joint tax return.

Traditional IRA

A **traditional IRA** is an individual retirement arrangement in which contributions are tax-deductible, but withdrawals are taxed. This type of IRA allows individuals to contribute pretax income to investments that grow tax-deferred. Contributions to a traditional IRA are tax-deductible. This means that the amount you contribute each year can be deducted from your income when you file an income tax return. However, when you retire, money withdrawn from a traditional IRA will be taxed.

The maximum amount that can be contributed each year to a traditional IRA is periodically adjusted for inflation. The current limit is $6,000 for a person under age 50 and $7,000 for a person over age 50.

Withdrawals from a traditional IRA before age 59 1/2 are considered early withdrawals and are typically subject to a 10-percent penalty by the IRS. Withdraws after 59 1/2 are penalty-free. However, amounts withdrawn must be reported as ordinary income when federal and state tax returns are filed. Holders of traditional IRAs are subject to the required minimum distribution (RMD) rule and must start distributions at age 72.

Roth IRA

A **Roth IRA** is an individual retirement arrangement in which individuals contribute after-tax income, but qualified withdrawals are not taxed. *After-tax income* means Roth IRA contributions cannot be deducted on a tax return. Qualified withdrawals occur when you retire. However, there are other withdrawals that may be qualified, such as withdrawing money for a first-time home purchase or to cover the college expenses of a child. Currently, the same limits on traditional IRAs apply to Roth IRAs.

Another benefit of Roth IRAs is that the RMD rule does not apply. As a result, when Roth IRA holders turn 72, they do not have to worry about making annual withdrawals. Instead, they can let their balances grow and make withdrawals at a later date, or leave a larger balance to beneficiaries. However, the RMD rule applies to the beneficiaries of an inherited Roth IRA.

Annuities

An annuity is another form of investment that can be used in personal retirement planning. An **annuity** is a contract with an insurance company that provides regular income for a set period of time, usually for life. There are two basic types of annuities: immediate and tax-deferred.

An *immediate annuity* is an annuity contract purchased with a lump sum of money. Usually within a month after purchase, the insurance company starts making monthly payments to the purchaser, called the *annuitant*. In most cases, the monthly payments will continue for the life of the annuitant. However, some immediate annuities pay for a specific period of time, such as 20 years. Some immediate annuities can be purchased with a death benefit. With a death benefit, payments will continue to a named beneficiary after the death of the annuitant. If the contract does not contain a death benefit, the insurance company keeps any money not withdrawn at the death of the annuitant.

A *tax-deferred annuity* is an annuity contract in which money is invested and the interest it earns grows tax-deferred until it is withdrawn. Most withdrawals are in the form of monthly payments taken in retirement. Money can be invested in a tax-deferred annuity in a lump sum or in installments over a period of years.

Neither immediate nor tax-deferred annuities are guaranteed by any governmental agency. Instead, the guarantee of payments is based on the financial strength of the insurance company. As a result, anyone considering the purchase of an annuity should shop around and consider the financial strength of the issuing company.

Small Business and Self-Employed Retirement Plans

Self-employed individuals have several options from which to choose when saving for retirement. All plans allow tax-deferred savings and basically work the same way. However, each plan has unique features. Professional advice should be sought before opening an account. Self-employed retirement plans include the SEP-IRA, Solo 401(k) plan, SIMPLE IRA, and Keogh plan as well as annuities.

SEP-IRA

A Simplified Employer Pension Individual Retirement Account, or **SEP-IRA,** is a tax-deferred retirement plan that allows a business owner to open an IRA and make tax-deductible contributions. The amount a self-employed person can contribute each year to a SEP-IRA is 25 percent of net profit up to a maximum limit, currently $57,000.

If a self-employed person chooses, a SEP-IRA can also be created for employees of the self-employed person. In this case, the SEP-IRA works like a grouping of traditional IRAs. A SEP-IRA can be set up at any financial institution that offers the option. The employer then contributes to each employee's account while the employees make no contribution. Earnings grow tax-deferred until money is withdrawn at retirement.

In addition to self-employed individuals, anyone with freelance income can open a SEP-IRA. A *freelancer* is anyone who earns income independent of an employer but is not organized as a business.

Pavel Vinnik/Shutterstock.com

Self-employed individuals have multiple options from which to choose when saving for retirement.

Solo 401(k) Plan

The **Solo 401(k) plan**, also called an *Individual 401(k) plan*, is a self-employed retirement plan that allows tax-deductible contributions for employers and employees. The unique feature of the Solo 401(k) plan is the matching contribution levels allowed for a business in which the only employees are a married couple. Each can contribute 25 percent of compensation up to the annual income limit, currently $57,000 each. This could potentially result in more retirement savings than possible with other plans. Created by the *Economic Growth and Tax Relief Reconciliation Act of 2001 (EGTRRA)*, the Solo 401(k) plan is the newest retirement plan for self-employed individuals.

SIMPLE IRA

A Savings Incentive Match Plan for Employees of Small Employers, or **SIMPLE IRA,** is a tax-deferred retirement plan for businesses with 100 or fewer employees. This plan was created to make it easier for small businesses to create and maintain an employee retirement program. Start-up and operating costs are low, and business owners do not have to file annual reports with the IRS. A SIMPLE IRA can be set up only at banks, mutual fund companies, insurance companies, and certain other financial institutions approved by the IRS. Additionally, an employer cannot have another plan if the SIMPLE plan is chosen.

Keogh Plan

A *Keogh plan*, also called an *HR 10*, is a type of personal retirement plan for the self-employed. Keogh plans can invest in the same set of securities as 401(k) plans and IRAs, including stocks, bonds, and mutual funds. Contributions are taxable and the required minimum distribution (RMD) rules apply. Withdrawals cannot be made before age 59 1/2 without penalties, and withdrawals must begin at 72.

Introduced in 1962, the Keogh plan is the oldest of the self-employment plans. However, Keogh plans require more detailed recordkeeping than other plans. As a result, they have lost popularity since the introduction of SEP and SIMPLE IRAs.

Governmental Pension Plans

For most Americans, Social Security is an important part of retirement income. *Social Security* is a pension plan run by the federal government and based on payments an individual makes throughout the years while working. Social Security guarantees monthly payments for the rest of your life, no matter how long you live. Additionally, Social Security provides for annual increases in benefits to reflect the level of inflation. However, Social Security should not be the only source of retirement income. Instead, it should supplement your other sources of retirement savings.

The amount of the Social Security benefit you receive is based on two factors: how much you earned during the 35 working years in which you earned the most, up to an annual maximum; and how many years you were employed and

History of Finance

Social Security

In the United States, programs for providing financial or economic security have appeared and disappeared over the years, from military pensions for Revolutionary War and Civil War soldiers to private-company pension plans and state-sponsored "old age" welfare pensions. By 1935, there were 30 states with some form of "old age" welfare pension.

During the Great Depression in the 1930s, there was still no national program for providing financial security in old age. Millions of people were out of work, and most elderly people had to depend on others for living expenses. As a result, there was increased public interest in programs to provide financial security.

The national program known as Social Security was adopted in 1935. From 1937 when Social Security was implemented until 1940, a person would receive a single lump-sum payment. Beginning in 1940, payments became monthly.

The first person to apply for a Social Security benefit was Ernest Ackerman. He retired one day after the program started. In his one day in the program, five cents were withheld from his paycheck. In return, he received a lump-sum benefit payment of 17 cents.

paid into Social Security. The minimum number of years that must be worked to qualify for Social Security is 10 years. Reduced benefits can start at age 62. However, benefits starting at 62 are only about 25 percent of what they would be at full retirement age. For those born after 1960, full retirement age is 67, as shown in Figure 7-1. Your Social Security benefit increases each year you wait to begin receiving a benefit past your full retirement age up to age 70. It is important that individuals read the information provided on the Social Security website in advance of retirement so that the procedures for applying are followed.

Age to Receive Full Social Security Benefits	
Year of Birth	**Full Retirement Age**
1943–1954	66
1955	66 and 2 months
1956	66 and 4 months
1957	66 and 6 months
1958	66 and 8 months
1959	66 and 10 months
1960 and later	67

Source: Internal Revenue Service; Goodheart-Willcox Publisher

Figure 7-1 The age to receive full Social Security benefits depends on the year the recipient was born.

Most public employees, such as governmental employees, teachers, police officers, and firefighters, are not eligible for Social Security. There are other governmental plans for which some individuals qualify. There are special retirement plans for some federal workers that are not covered by Social Security. The Veteran's Administration provides pensions for survivors of those who die while serving in the armed forces. Also, most state and local governments have retirement plans for their employees.

Section 7.1 Review

Check Your Understanding

1. Name the two categories of employer-sponsored retirement plans.
2. What is the difference between a traditional IRA and a Roth IRA?
3. What is meant by *required minimum distribution*?
4. List examples of retirement plans that self-employed people can use.
5. On what two factors are a Social Security benefit based?

Build Your Vocabulary

As you progress through this course, develop a personal glossary. This will help you build your vocabulary and prepare you for a career. Write a definition for each of the following terms and add it to your glossary.

- retirement
- vesting
- rollover
- defined-benefit plan
- defined-contribution plan
- 401(k) plan
- required minimum distribution (RMD)
- 403(b) plan
- 457 plan
- Roth 401(k)
- individual retirement account (IRA)
- spousal IRA
- traditional IRA
- Roth IRA
- annuity
- SEP-IRA
- Solo 401(k) plan
- SIMPLE IRA

Section 7.2 Planning for Retirement

Essential Question

Why should a young person begin planning for retirement now?

Objectives

After studying this section, you will be able to:

- Explain the importance of planning for retirement.
- Describe what is involved in planning an estate.

Terms

estate	beneficiary	probate
power of attorney	trustee	living will
will	codicil	trust

Retirement Planning

As a young person, saving for retirement is probably not on your mind. However, the sooner you start saving for retirement, the better. Starting early means you have more time for your money to grow. For example, Figure 7-2 shows the results of three individuals who created Roth IRAs. Allison started contributing $3,000 a year to an account starting at age 25. If the contributions continue until age 65, the value of the account will grow to $839,343. Bill also started contributing $3,000 to an account at age 25, but stopped ten years later at age 35. If Bill makes no additional contributions, the account will grow to $472,000 by age 65. Taylor started contributing $3,000 to an account at age 35. If the contributions continue for the next 30 years, the account value will grow to $367,038 by age 65.

Allison's account had the greatest growth because contributions started early and continued until retirement. While Bill only contributed for 10 years, the account still grew more than Taylor's because the account was started ten years earlier. Starting early is important because each year's gains can generate their own gains in later years.

Financial experts recommend that, when possible, individuals have both an employer-sponsored retirement plan and a personal retirement plan. If similar contributions had been made to a 401(k) plan with employer-matching contributions, the account values in the previous examples would have been much higher.

Retirement planning is a key element of financial security. Recent trends indicate more people are retiring earlier and living longer. Early retirees could need income for as long as 30 to 40 years. Providing income for this many years requires planning, careful and early investment, periodic reviews, and proper adjustments to meet changing needs. The rule of thumb is you will need roughly

Benefits of Starting a Retirement Account Early			
Investor	**Contributions**	**Total Invested**	**Value at Age 65**
Allison	Age 25–65: $3,000 a year for 40 years	$120,000	$839,343
Bill	Age 25–35: $3,000 a year for 10 years Age 35–65: No contributions for 30 years	$30,000	$472,000
Taylor	Age 25–35: No contributions for 10 years Age 35–65: $3,000 a year for 30 years	$90,000	$367,038

Assumes 8 percent annual rate of return.

Goodheart-Willcox Publisher

Figure 7-2 This chart reflects the value advantage of starting a retirement plan at an early age.

70 to 80 percent of your preretirement income to live comfortably in retirement. Typical sources of income for retirees are a:

- defined-contributions plan, such as 401(k) and 403(b);
- personal retirement plan, such as IRAs, self-employment plans, and annuities; and
- governmental plan, such as Social Security.

Financial experts use these sources to form the "three-legged stool for retirement," as illustrated in Figure 7-3.

Retirees may also have other sources of income, such as personal savings accounts and outside investments. Personal savings accounts earn interest income, which can be withdrawn on a regular basis. *Outside investments* are investments that are not held in a retirement account. Examples include stocks, bonds, mutual funds, and REITS. Stocks, mutual funds, and REITS usually pay dividends on a quarterly basis. Bonds usually pay interest semiannually.

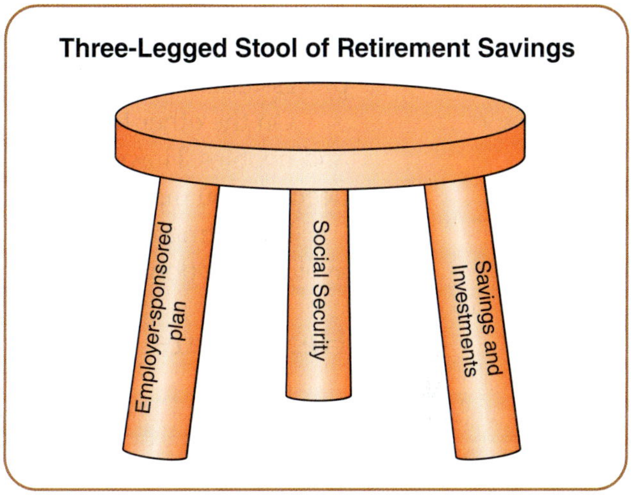

Goodheart-Willcox Publisher

Figure 7-3 Financial experts include an employer-sponsored plan, personal savings and investments, and Social Security as the "three-legged stool for retirement."

Several aspects of a person's financial situation should be considered when earning stops and retirement starts. Included factors are housing, living expenses, and health-care costs.

Housing

Many Americans downsize their homes in retirement. Larger, more expensive homes are sold and smaller, less expensive homes or condominiums are purchased with the proceeds. Many retirees also move to parts of the country where taxes, utilities, and other costs are lower.

Paying off a home mortgage before retirement is also an important consideration. Having an $800 monthly mortgage paid off is equivalent to earning an extra $800 a month.

Employability Skills

Listening

Hearing is a physical process. *Listening* is an intellectual process that combines hearing with evaluating. The inability to listen carefully usually results in misunderstood instructions and missed opportunities, which can hinder a company's productivity. Listening requires discipline. Companies lose millions of dollars every year because employees are not listening to what is being said by customers, managers, or peers. Paying attention is important in the workplace. Not learning how to listen effectively can cause an employee to be terminated.

Living Expenses

A large part of retirement planning is estimating expenses in retirement. Start by looking at your current expenses and estimate how they will change. You will likely spend less for clothing and dry cleaning, taxes, transportation, professional dues, and eating out during retirement.

On the other hand, you will likely spend more on leisure activities, travel, and hobbies. However, these expenses are optional and can be scaled back if needed. You may also pay more for utilities if you will be home more often.

Budgeting is centered on predictable income and expenses that cannot be avoided. Optional expenses are then considered with any discretionary income.

Health Care

For most people, health-care costs increase steadily with age. Between the ages 50 and 64, health-care costs represent about nine percent of the average person's budget. However, the number doubles to 18 percent after age 85.

For many retirees, health care is the single highest expense. As a result, adequate health insurance is a necessity. Retirees age 65 and over can participate in the federal Medicare program. However, Medicare only pays about 80 percent of most health-related issues. Retirees must therefore have a Medicare supplement policy.

Long-term care in a nursing home or other long-term-care facility is a substantial cost. Consequently, many people purchase long-term-care insurance as part of retirement planning. This type of insurance costs more the longer you wait to purchase it. Purchasing long-term-care insurance in your twenties or thirties will cost much less than purchasing it in your fifties or sixties.

Working while Retired

A growing number of retirees are supplementing their retirement income by working part-time. These people are considered *semiretired*.

Some have to work because of shortfalls in retirement savings. The Great Recession caused a huge loss in the value of investments. As a result, some retirees whose accounts were not well diversified lost a significant portion of their retirement savings. For many, returning to work was the only way to make ends meet.

However, many retirees continue to work by choice, not by necessity. For them, a job is more than a paycheck. It provides happiness and a sense of purpose. Many love their jobs and enjoy the social interaction with fellow employees. Some working retirees stay on the same job, but with a reduction in hours. Others find new jobs, and many start businesses. According to the US Bureau of Labor Statistics, the number of people aged 75 and older in the workforce is expected to grow 86 percent by the year 2024.

Estate Planning

Estate planning is part of an overall financial plan. An **estate** consists of the assets and liabilities a person leaves after death. Assets include personal property and real estate, money, securities, jewelry, family heirlooms, and insurance benefits. *Estate planning* is the active management of these assets with instructions for managing and distributing them when the owner dies. An estate plan allows people to accomplish these goals:

- decide how their assets should be managed after death
- provide for dependents and the guardianship of minor children
- minimize tax liabilities
- name an executor
- assign a power of attorney
- prepare a will
- prepare a trust

There are many estate-planning tools available to guide the process. Some of these tools include power of attorney, wills, living wills, and trusts. Generally, it is wise to ask a lawyer for professional advice about legal documents that are used for planning your estate.

NotarYES/Shutterstock.com

In most states, people must be at least 18 to make a will.

Power of Attorney

A **power of attorney** is a legal document that gives a person the power to act for another person regarding financial and legal matters. If you become unable to make decisions due to health or other reasons, the person to whom you have given power of attorney can sign documents and make legal decisions in your place.

Wills

A **will**, or *last will and testament*, is a legal document that states a person's wishes for an estate after death. A will should clearly outline a person's wishes for the transfer of any assets. Figure 7-4 shows a typical will. Anyone who has property to leave or other rights to distribute should prepare a will. In most states, people must be at least 18 to make a will and must be of sound mind. *Of sound mind* means the person must know what is occurring and be mentally competent.

LAST WILL AND TESTAMENT
OF
THOMAS GEROLD VIATOR

I, Thomas Gerold Viator, of Rockford, Illinois, being of sound mind, declare this to be my Last Will and Testament and revoke my former Wills and Codicils.

ARTICLE I
IDENTIFICATION OF FAMILY

I am married to Anita Margaret Viator and all references in this Will to "my spouse" are references to Anita Margaret Viator.

I currently have no children, but all references in this Will to "my children" are references to any children born to me or adopted by me after the signing of this Will.

ARTICLE II
PAYMENT OF DEBTS AND EXPENSES

I direct that my just debts, funeral expenses and expenses of last illness be first paid from my estate.

ARTICLE III
DISPOSITION OF PROPERTY

Residuary Estate. I direct that my residuary estate be distributed to:

50% - my spouse, Anita Margaret Viator. If my spouse does not survive me, this share shall be distributed proportionately to the other distributee(s) listed under this provision.

50% - my Trustee, to be retained, managed and distributed under the provisions of Article IV (Trust for Children).

100 - *Percent Total*

ARTICLE IV
TRUST FOR CHILDREN

A. Purpose. The primary purpose of this Trust is to provide for the health, support, maintenance, and education of any children born to me or adopted by me after the signing of this Will. The provisions of this Trust also provide for the distribution of my residuary estate. If the Trustee is the beneficiary of any life insurance policy on my life, any pension plan or any other contract, the proceeds of such policy, plan or contract shall be treated by my Trustee as though received as a part of my residuary estate.

Goodheart-Willcox Publisher

Figure 7-4 A will guarantees the settlement of an estate according to the wishes of the deceased person.

A will guarantees the settlement of an estate according to the wishes of the deceased person. This makes the process simpler for beneficiaries. A **beneficiary** of a will is a person or group who receives the deceased person's assets. Beneficiaries who are family members are called *heirs*. Friends may be listed as beneficiaries, as well as a favorite charity, a college, or some other organization.

A will should do at least three things:

- name beneficiaries
- name an executor
- name a guardian

Exploring Careers

Estate Planner

Estate planners are financial advisors who help individuals manage personal assets, such as investments, savings, and real estate. They have a particular focus on transferring and protecting these assets after the client dies. Estate planners typically:

- discuss end-of-life financial issues, such as wills, trusts, and debilitating medical issues
- provide advice on how to best manage a client's wealth
- provide advice on local, state, and federal taxes as related to wealth management
- review a client's financial documents after death, such as insurance policies, a last will and testament, and outstanding debts

Estate planners often work at legal firms, banks, or insurance companies, but many are self-employed. They typically work full time and may meet with clients in the evenings or on weekends. About 30 percent of estate planners work more than 40 hours a week. However, the work of estate planners is typically less stressful than that of other careers in the financial industry.

A bachelor degree in finance, law, or a related area is usually required, and a master degree and certification are often preferred if not required. Good math, computer, and communication skills are essential, while attention to detail and initiative are also important traits.

Before writing a will, it is necessary to determine which individuals or organizations will be beneficiaries and receive the deceased's assets. The executor handles paying funeral expenses, medical bills, taxes, and other liabilities. The executor also performs other duties outlined in the will. A guardian is a person responsible for the care of any beneficiaries who are young children. A guardian may also manage an estate on behalf of the dependents, or a trustee may be named to do this. A **trustee** is a person or institution named to manage assets on behalf of the beneficiaries.

A will must be signed in the presence of witnesses. If you change your will after it has been signed, an amendment called a codicil is added. A **codicil** is a document that explains, changes, or deletes provisions in a will. The codicil must also be signed in the presence of witnesses. If major changes are needed in an existing will, it may be preferable to write a new will. In this case, it is important to add a clause that cancels all previous wills and codicils.

The cost of preparing a will varies. The more complex the estate, the more expensive the will may be to prepare. You can write your own will. A do-it-yourself kit that contains basic information and sample formats may cost less than $20. However, such a kit is unwise for large estates, situations with many tax issues, or when there are complicated instructions for distributing assets.

Since legal requirements for wills vary from state to state and may change with new laws, consulting an attorney who specializes in estate planning is a wise choice. This is especially true for people who own their own businesses or have estates that total more than $1 million in value. Attorney fees vary, and consumers can usually arrange a free consultation with a lawyer. The local chapter of the American Bar Association is a good source for a directory of attorneys.

Ethics

Conflict of Interest

Retirement and estate planners must be aware of conflicts of interest. A *conflict of interest* occurs when two parties have different goals or when a person can benefit from the actions of his or her position. For example, while a married couple may seem to have the same goals, it is possible for each to have very different goals. The planner must be aware of potential differences between what each person wants when representing both spouses. The same is true when representing parents and children.

When people die without a will, it is called *dying intestate*. When there is no will, property is divided according to state laws. This is not ideal because it can take a lot of time, and the government decides how to distribute assets.

Probate is a legal process of settling the affairs of an estate, paying final expenses, and distributing the balance of money and property to beneficiaries. A *probate court* is the governmental institution that processes a deceased individual's will and estate. The probate procedure requires:

- proof the will is valid;
- an inventory and identification of the deceased person's assets and property;
- property appraisals;
- settlement of debts and taxes; and
- distribution of property according to terms of the will.

Probate can be a costly and time-consuming process that involves paperwork, court appearances, and lawyers. Probate fees are paid out of the estate before assets are distributed. The process can take several months, a year, or longer. The executor of the estate must manage the assets during this period. These proceedings are a matter of public record. If the value of an estate exceeds a limit set by law, the estate is subject to a federal tax called the *estate tax*. Currently, value of property that can be inherited before the estate tax applies is $5,430,000 per individual. This amount is usually adjusted each year to reflect inflation.

Living Wills

A **living will** is a statement of instructions for specific medical treatment if a person becomes unable to make medical decisions related to deathbed concerns. It is also known as a *health-care directive*. The primary purpose is to make known the medical treatments the individual wishes to receive in the case of incapacitating injury or illness. It also outlines desires about medically prolonging the person's life. Creating a living will is a serious and very personal step to take. It should be discussed with family members, loved ones, and your physician.

Trusts

A **trust** is an arrangement through which a person transfers assets to a trustee, who then oversees and manages the assets on behalf of beneficiaries.

The creator of a trust is the *grantor*. The grantor decides which assets to transfer to the trust. Trusts are used to achieve different goals. People can use a trust to:

- provide income and asset management for beneficiaries;
- set forth specific provisions for the support and education of minor children or dependents with disabilities;
- have a plan in place for managing financial affairs if they should become incapacitated or unable to manage for themselves;
- minimize estate and gift taxes; and
- protect their privacy and avoid probate court.

In addition to a will, you may need one or more trusts, particularly if your estate is complex or if you wish to make special arrangements for its settlement. Establishing a trust can avoid the lengthy and costly process of probate. A trustee is appointed to manage the assets according to terms outlined in the trust. Beneficiaries are named who are to receive the assets and when they will receive them.

Unlike a will, a trust does not have to be probated. This means assets can easily pass to beneficiaries without court involvement. Another advantage of a trust is that it prevents the court from taking control of a person's assets should the person become incapacitated.

A trust can be either a living trust or a testamentary trust. A *living trust* is set up during an individual's lifetime and provides for the management of assets before death and for the distribution of assets as directed after death. Prior to death, you may serve as grantor, trustee, and beneficiary of the trust. A *testamentary trust* is set up under the terms of an individual's will and becomes effective when then the person dies.

When setting up a trust, you will need to decide whether the agreement is irrevocable or revocable. With an *irrevocable trust*, the terms of the trust cannot be changed or ended. A *revocable trust*, on the other hand, is one in which the terms can be changed or ended.

Section 7.2 Review

Check Your Understanding

1. What is the benefit of saving for retirement from an early age?
2. List typical sources of retirement income.
3. What aspects of a person's financial situation should be considered when planning for retirement?
4. List some of the goals that an estate plan helps people accomplish.
5. Name examples of planning tools that are available for people who are planning their estate.

Build Your Vocabulary

As you progress through this course, develop a personal glossary. This will help you build your vocabulary and prepare you for a career. Write a definition for each of the following terms and add it to your glossary.

- estate
- power of attorney
- will
- beneficiary
- trustee
- codicil
- probate
- living will
- trust

Review and Assessment

Chapter Summary

Section 7.1 Types of Retirement Plans

- Many employers offer retirement plans to their employees. Employer-sponsored retirement plans can vary widely from one employer to another. Employer-sponsored plans are either defined-benefit plans or defined-contribution plans. A defined-benefit plan is also known as a pension plan. Defined-contribution plans include 401(k), 403(b), 457, and Roth 401(k) plans.
- Individuals can create personal retirement plans in addition to an employer plan. These plans are called individual retirement arrangements (IRA) and can either be a traditional IRA or Roth IRA. An annuity is another form of investment that can be used in retirement planning.
- Self-employed individuals have several options from which to choose when saving for retirement. Self-employed retirement plans include the SEP-IRA, Solo 401(k), SIMPLE IRA, and the Keogh plan. These plans allow tax-deferred savings, and while they basically work the same way, each one is unique.
- Social Security is an important part of retirement income that is provided by the government. Social Security guarantees monthly payments for the rest of your life, no matter how long you live. The amount of Social Security benefit received is based on how much a person earned while working and how long Social Security taxes were paid. Social Security should not be a person's only source of retirement income.

Section 7.2 Planning for Retirement

- It is important to begin saving for retirement from a young age. Starting early means there is more time for a person's money to grow. Retirement planning should consider factors such as housing, living expenses, and health-care costs.
- Estate planning is creating a plan to manage a person's assets after death. Power of attorney, wills, living wills, and trusts may be established to help an individual accomplish estate plan goals.

Review Your Knowledge

1. Summarize the vesting process.
2. Describe various employer-sponsored retirement plans, such as a defined-benefit plan or defined-contribution plans like the 401(k), 403(b), and 457 plans.
3. List examples of factors that determine the amount in a defined-contribution plan.
4. Explain options for personal retirement plans, such as traditional IRA, Roth IRA, or Spousal IRA.
5. Discuss retirement plan options for those who are self-employed, such as a SEP-IRA, Solo 401(k), SIMPLE IRA, Keogh plan, or annuity.
6. Describe how Social Security functions.
7. Explain the advantage of saving for retirement early.
8. Identify three financial considerations during retirement.
9. Describe what is involved in planning an estate.
10. What three things should a will accomplish?

Apply Your Knowledge

1. Sam's parents and grandparents all have pension plans provided by their employers. Sam assumes that after graduating from college and beginning a career that a pension will be part of a compensation plan. Sam also assumes that after retiring, Social Security benefits will be received

automatically each month. Based on the knowledge you gained from reading this chapter, write a script that you could use to explain to Sam why these assumptions may not be accurate and that making other plans now for retirement in the future would be smart.

2. Would you rather save money for retirement on a pretax or after-tax basis? What are the advantages and disadvantages of each plan?
3. People are living longer lives than they did 100 years ago. Longer life expectancies have had a significant impact on retirement-planning trends. How do longer life expectancies affect your own retirement aspirations?
4. You probably know people who have retired from their jobs and are living a different type of life than when they are working. Even though your own retirement is in the distant future, what do you think the ideal retirement for you would be? Make a list of items that are your wants that would be important to you. Wants could include items such as owning a vacation home, traveling the world, or other goals that you may not be able to achieve while working a full-time job. Next, make a list of living expenses that are needs such as rent, food, and insurance.
5. In the last activity, you completed a list of wants and needs. Using that list, assign an estimate of cost for each item for one month and get a total. Next, multiply the total by 12 to arrive at the cost for one year of retirement. How much money would you need each year to achieve your ideal retirement?
6. You have now estimated the income needed to meet your needs and wants in a typical year of retirement. The yearly amount may be in excess of $50,000. How can you start planning now so that your ideal retirement life can be a reality? What type of financial plans will you need?
7. Since retirement is far in the future for you, inflation must be considered as it will influence how much money you need at that point in your life. Account for inflation by adding 4 percent to the annual income amount you estimated. If that inflation rate is correct, how much money would you need for the first year of retirement?
8. Depending on the age you decide to retire, you may need money for 30 years or longer. In the last activity, you estimated one year's cost for retirement. Next, multiply that yearly amount by 30 years. How much money do you need to have to live comfortably during your retirement?
9. Many retirees decide to work after they retire from their careers. Why do you think working after retirement is a choice that some people make?
10. Your friend Jonas does not think it is necessary to plan his estate. Write a dialogue between you and Jonas in which you explain the importance of estate planning, including guardianship of minor children, wills, beneficiary designation, power of attorney, living will, and medical directives.

Apply Your Math Skills

1. Rachel's local bank is advertising savings account rates of 1.5%. Use the Rule of 72 to calculate how long it would take an investment to double at this rate.

2. Wyatt has $3,000 in a Roth IRA. Use the Rule of 72 to calculate the interest rate needed to double the investment in ten years.
3. Jayla earned $48,000 this year and contributed $5,000 to a tax-deferred retirement account. How much income will be taxed? If Jayla is in a 25% tax bracket, how much will be saved in taxes?
4. Sampson needs $4,000 to make home repairs and is considering withdrawing the money from a traditional IRA. At age 37 there is a 10% early withdrawal penalty. Sampson is in a 15% tax bracket. How much additional money would need to be withdrawn from the traditional IRA to net $4,000 after paying the penalty and taxes?

Communication Skills

College and Career Readiness

Writing. You have decided you are ready to begin saving for retirement and would like to open a Roth IRA. Compose an informative e-mail that you might send to a brokerage firm. Ask for information on how to set up an account, the interest you can anticipate, and any other questions you might need answered. Convey the information clearly and accurately through the effective organization of the content.

Listening. Passive listening is casually listening to someone speak. Passive listening is appropriate when you do not have to interact with the speaker. Listen to a classmate with whom you are having a conversation. Focus attention on the message. Ask for clarification for anything that you do not understand. Provide verbal and nonverbal feedback while the person is talking.

Reading. Select several chapters of this textbook. Identify two generic features that are used in each chapter. Compare and contrast how each feature is used. Why do you think the author chose those particular features to apply in multiple chapters?

Teamwork

Together with your team, create a short presentation about the importance of estate planning. Include information about the importance of writing a will, establishing power of attorney, and creating a living will or health-care directive. Also explain the importance of beneficiary designation and the guardianship of minor children.

Internet Research

Social Security. Social Security is an important part of retirement income, but should not be a person's only retirement income. Visit the Social Security website to learn more about how Social Security payments are calculated. Use the information on the website to determine how an individual can find out the estimated benefits that will be received.

Retirement Planning. It is never too early to start thinking about retirement. Using the Internet, conduct a search for *retirement calculator*. Investigate different retirement scenarios by inputting different variables into the calculator. Collect data related to retirement planning. How much money will you need to retire at age 67? At age 70? Do the numbers surprise you? Write a paragraph about what you learned.

Writing a Will. Creating a will requires certain information. Using the Internet, search *will requirements in [your state]* to research the legal requirements for a will to be valid in your state. Look for sample documents that illustrate how the information is typically organized. Write a summary of the information required to write a legally valid will in your state.

Portfolio Development

College and Career Readiness

References. A *reference* is a person who can comment on the qualifications, work ethic, personal qualities, and work-related aspects of another person's character. It is a person who knows your skills, talents, or personal traits and is willing to recommend you for a job, community service position, or perhaps entrance into a college program.

References can include your instructors, a manager at your part-time job, or counselors who know about your skills and interests. Someone you know from your personal life, such as a youth-group leader, can also be listed. However, you should *not* list relatives.

Always assume the interviewer will follow-up with your references. This means you should be selective when choosing them. Consider which references can best recommend you for the position for which you are applying. As a courtesy, always get permission from the person before using his or her name. Serving as a reference for someone is a responsibility that a person may not want. Getting permission to use someone as your reference verifies their willingness not only to be listed in your portfolio, but to recommend you for the position as well.

1. Ask several people who know you well if they are willing to serve as a reference for you. Using word-processing software, create a document that includes the names and contact information for those individuals. Each entry should include complete contact information for the person. Use the heading "Personal References" and your name. This page should follow your résumé when you are organizing your portfolio for presentation. Save this file as PERSONAL_REFERENCES with your last name, for example PERSONAL_REFERENCES_SMITH, or use a different naming convention that is suitable for the management system you implemented in Lesson 1. Back up the file on your flash drive.
2. Record the creation of your Personal References document on your master portfolio spreadsheet. In addition, record each person you contacted for a reference.

CTSOs

Event Prep

Financial Math. Financial math is a competitive event you might enter with your career and technical student organization (CTSO). The financial math event may include an objective test that includes financial literacy topics. If you decide to participate in this event, review basic banking and business finance concepts to prepare for the test.

To prepare for a financial math event, complete the following activities.

1. Read the guidelines provided by your organization. Make certain that you ask any questions about items you do not understand. It is important you follow each specific item that is outlined in the competition rules.
2. Download any posted practice tests.
3. Time yourself taking the tests with the aid of a non-graphing calculator. Check the answers and correct any mistakes you may have made.
4. Review the You Do the Math features in this text for additional practice.
5. Visit the organization's website often to make sure information regarding the event has not changed.

UNIT

3 Managing Your Spending

Chapters

Financial Literacy

Why It Matters

Credit is a medium of exchange in our economy. It allows the purchaser to buy goods and services today and pay for them later. Used carefully and wisely, it can help the consumer get more of what is needed when it is needed. Misused credit can lead to financial disaster.

Poor purchasing decisions can be made when using cash or credit. However, applying a systematic decision-making process can help consumers make wise spending decisions without exceeding their financial limits.

Enjoying freedom to make spending decisions comes with personal rights and responsibilities. Financially capable individuals understand that laws and regulations are in place to protect the buyer and seller. These laws must be respected in order for our economy to operate effectively.

Jiratsung/Shutterstock.com

Big Idea

To save money and build wealth, spend less than you earn.

CHAPTER

8 Credit

Credit serves as a medium of exchange that allows individuals, businesses, and governmental agencies to buy goods or services now and pay for them later. Financially capable people are aware of the importance of obtaining and using credit. Wise use of credit allows for an increased standard of living and the ability to acquire the necessities and luxuries of life. On the other hand, unwise use of credit can have a negative effect on a person's quality of life and lead to financial problems.

Creditors lend to people who are creditworthy and earn good credit ratings. Credit ratings are the evaluation of a person's willingness and ability to pay debts. A good credit report helps an individual to obtain credit from reputable businesses and avoid easy-access credit traps.

Focus on Finance

Predatory Lending

Predatory lending is a policy of making loans to high-risk borrowers who are unlikely to be able to repay. Predatory lenders prey on senior citizens, low-income individuals, and others who lack financial knowledge. These loans can be payday loans, mortgages, or other consumer credit. The interest rates are exceedingly high and may increase over the life of the loan, causing the monthly payment to increase substantially each month.

When borrowers find they cannot make the larger monthly payments, the lender offers to refinance the loan. While this may lower the monthly payments, it increases the debt. The refinancing terms put the borrower deeper in debt, which frequently leads to foreclosure or other financial trouble. Always read the fine print on any credit cards, mortgages, or other consumer loans and make sure you understand the terms.

College and Career Readiness

Reading Prep. As you read this chapter, take time to answer the Section Review questions. Were you able to answer the questions without referring to the chapter content?

Sections

Phuong D. Nguyen/Shutterstock.com

Section 8.1 Consumer Credit

Essential Question

Why do individual consumers use credit for purchasing goods and services?

Objectives

After studying this section, you will be able to:

- Summarize the purpose of credit.
- Identify the difference between closed-end credit and open-end credit.
- Describe the meaning of *creditworthiness.*
- Explain the role performed by credit bureaus.

Terms

credit	principal	cosigner
creditor	collateral	creditworthy
debtor	secured credit	credit bureau
consumer credit	finance charge	credit history
contract	open-end credit	credit report
acceleration clause	revolving credit account	low-risk borrower
closed-end credit	line of credit	credit score
installment loan	unsecured credit	credit rating
down payment		

Credit

Credit is an agreement between two parties in which one party lends money or provides goods or services to another party with the understanding that payment will be made at a later date. In every credit transaction, there is a party who extends credit and a party who receives credit. The party extending credit is known as the **creditor**, or the *lender.* The creditor is the party to whom money is owed. The party receiving credit is known as the **debtor**, or the *borrower.* The debtor is the party who owes money to the creditor.

All credit is based on trust. The creditor believes there is a high likelihood the debtor can and will pay what is owed. For example, suppose you go out to eat with friends. One friend does not have enough money and asks to borrow some of yours. If you trust that friend and can spare the money, you will probably lend it.

Credit also has an element of risk. When you lend a friend money, a DVD, or a shirt, you risk that the item will not be returned. An unpaid debt between friends can harm a friendship. If a friend does not pay you back, you will probably not lend to that friend again.

Andy Dean Photography/Shutterstock.com

Learning to manage credit is an important life skill.

Using credit to buy goods and services is generally more costly than using cash, because fees are often added to the amount owed. Using credit is costly in another way, too. When you use credit, you spend future income. This means part of your future earnings must be used to pay what you owe. The use of credit reduces income you could spend on other purchases.

Purpose of Credit

The purpose of credit is to serve as a *medium of exchange* that allows individuals, businesses, and governmental agencies to buy goods or services now and pay for them later. Without credit, purchases would have to be made with cash. This could prevent businesses or individuals from buying goods and services needed to operate on a daily basis.

Consumer credit is credit granted to individual consumers by a retail business. It is the use of credit to purchase goods or services primarily for personal, family, or household use. Consumer credit plays an important role in the economy. It provides the extra buying power needed to support mass production and distribution of goods and services. Therefore, credit helps make more goods and services available to consumers at lower prices.

Credit also plays an important role in personal economics. Used carefully and wisely, it can help people get more of the things they need when they need them. Misused credit can lead to financial disaster. It is important for your own financial well-being to learn how to manage your use of credit.

Contracts

Before credit is extended, the borrower must sign a **contract**, which is a legally binding agreement between the borrower and the lender. The contract states the amount of credit extended, interest rate, payment schedule, and other provisions of the agreement. The terms outlined in a written agreement are legally binding. They can be enforced if the borrower or the lender fails to carry out the terms of the contract.

All blank spaces should be filled and none left open for someone to fill later. The annual percentage rate and dollar costs should be stated clearly and accurately. Terms that are not understood should be questioned.

A contract states fees, penalties, and consequences of failing to carry out all the terms of the agreement. It should describe the action the creditor can take if payments are late or missed by the creditor. Some contracts may have an acceleration clause. An **acceleration clause** is a statement in a contract that allows the creditor to require full and immediate payment of the entire balance if a payment is missed or the individual fails to abide by the terms of the contract.

Questions should also be asked if payment can be made in advance. If so, confirm if part of the finance charges will be refunded.

Be wary of add-on clauses that allow additional items to be purchased before paying in full for goods that have already been purchased. The clause may allow the seller to hold a security interest in the items purchased first until the later purchases are paid in full. For example, suppose you buy a washer and dryer but before paying for them, you buy a refrigerator. The seller can hold the title to the washer and dryer until you also pay for the refrigerator.

Types of Credit

Various types of credit are available to individuals and businesses. The most common types are closed-end credit and open-end credit.

Closed-End Credit

Closed-end credit is a loan for an agreed amount of money that must be repaid with interest by a specified date or according to a defined schedule. Closed-end credit is given for a specific purpose and is used to acquire more expensive items, such as cars, homes, furniture, major home appliances, and student loans.

Most closed-end credit is offered in the form of installment loans. An **installment loan** is a loan for a specific amount of money that is repaid with interest in regular payments, or *installments*. Examples of installment loans are auto loans and mortgages to purchase property. Figure 8-1 compares types of loans available to consumers.

Installment loans usually require a down payment at the time of purchase. A **down payment** is a portion of the purchase price paid up front. The **principal** is the amount of money borrowed. For example, if you purchase a car that costs $9,000 and pay $1,000 as a down payment, the principal of the loan would be the remaining $8,000.

Types of Consumer Loans		
Loan	**Purpose**	**Secured or Unsecured**
Auto loan	Purchase an automobile	Secured
Student loan	Fund a college education	Unsecured
Home loan (mortgage)	Purchase a home	Secured
Home equity loan	Make home improvements	Secured
Consolidation loan	Combine several existing loans or credit card bills into one loan with one payment	Secured or Unsecured

Goodheart-Willcox Publisher

Figure 8-1 This compares examples of common consumer loans.

Installment loans also require collateral. **Collateral** is property that a borrower promises to give up in the event the loan is not repaid. Loans that require collateral are known as **secured credit**. In the case of the auto loan, the collateral is the auto.

Before the loan is made, the borrower must sign a contract. The finance charge is stated on the contract. A **finance charge** is the total amount paid by a borrower to a lender for the use of credit. Finance charges include interest and other fees associated with the loan. *Interest* is the total amount paid by a borrower to a lender for the use of credit. *Fees* include charges for miscellaneous costs incurred by the bank to process the loan.

Exploring Careers

Collector

When individuals or businesses do not pay their bills, other businesses suffer. Collectors find and contact people who are behind on their bills. They arrange to have the person or business pay the money owed. Collectors use mail, telephone, or in-person visits in order to solicit payment. If payment is not provided, the person in this job starts the process to stop the service or reclaim the product or property. Examples of tasks collectors perform include:

- find customers who have delinquent accounts
- use mail, telephone, e-mail, or personal visits to solicit payment
- work with customers to create a plan for repayment
- use a computer to find and monitor overdue accounts
- monitor the efforts to collect on accounts

Most collector positions require a minimum of a high school diploma. Some positions provide training on the specific computer software used to record the status of collection accounts. Interpersonal skills are needed, as well as general computer skills.

An *amortization table* is a schedule that shows the amount of interest and principal for each installment so the loan can be repaid within a specific period of time. The amortization table in Figure 8-2 shows an installment loan with a principal of $1,000 using an interest rate of 9 percent that will be paid off in 12 months. The total amount of interest paid is $49.42 for the use of the money.

Open-End Credit

Open-end credit is an agreement that allows the borrower to use a specific amount of credit over a period of time. A maximum amount of credit is established, along with a repayment schedule. Common examples of open-end credit are:

- credit cards issued by banks;
- credit cards issued by department stores and oil companies;
- overdraft protection on checking accounts; and
- home equity lines of credit.

The borrower has a specified amount of credit that can be used at any time. Monthly payments are made against the balance owed. Because the account does not automatically close when the balance is paid off, it is referred to as a revolving account. A **revolving credit account** is a type of open-end credit agreement that offers a choice of paying in full each month or spreading payments over a period of time. Most credit cards are revolving credit accounts.

Amortization Table				
Month	Payment	Principal	9% Interest	Principal Balance
1	$87.45	$79.95	$7.50	$920.05
2	87.45	80.55	6.90	839.50
3	87.45	81.15	6.30	758.35
4	87.45	81.76	5.69	676.59
5	87.45	82.38	5.07	594.21
6	87.45	82.99	4.46	511.22
7	87.45	83.62	3.83	427.60
8	87.45	84.24	3.21	343.36
9	87.45	84.87	2.58	258.49
10	87.45	85.51	1.94	172.98
11	87.45	86.15	1.30	86.83
12	87.48	86.83	0.65	0.00

Goodheart-Willcox Publisher

Figure 8-2 An amortization table shows the amount of interest and principal applied with each payment scheduled during the period of a loan.

A typical revolving credit account places a limit on the total amount owed at any one time. Any number of purchases may be made at any time as long as the credit limit is not exceeded. This type of credit is available through many retailers and through issuers of credit cards, such as Visa, MasterCard, and Discover. The cards can be used to buy goods and services from any seller who honors the card. If the account is not paid in full, there is a finance charge. A minimum payment must be paid each month. For small balances, the minimum payment is usually a set amount, such as $10. For larger balances, the minimum payment is usually a percentage of the unpaid balance.

A line of credit is another example of open-end credit. A **line of credit** is a preapproved maximum amount that an individual can borrow. As long as that amount is not exceeded, the borrower can continue charging purchases and repaying on a regular schedule.

Open-end credit is typically unsecured. **Unsecured credit** is credit granted based on a signed credit agreement. It is also called a *signature loan*. No collateral is required, just the promise to pay and the signature of the borrower. Unsecured loans usually have higher interest rates than secured loans.

It is often difficult to obtain an unsecured loan unless you have established credit. However, you may be able to get an unsecured loan if you have a cosigner. A **cosigner** is a responsible person who signs the loan along with the person to whom the loan is granted. By signing the loan, the cosigner promises to repay the loan if the borrower fails to pay.

Creditworthiness

Creditors want to lend to applicants who are creditworthy. **Creditworthy** means having the assets, income, and willingness to repay debt. Creditworthiness is measured by the *three Cs of credit* which are character, capacity, and capital.

- *Character.* Current debt, payment history, and credit scores are considered when evaluating the financial character of an individual.
- *Capacity.* Lenders review finances to determine if the individual receives a regular paycheck and how long the person has been employed.
- *Capital.* All of an individual's assets and liabilities are evaluated to determine net worth.

You may find it difficult to get credit at first and show you are creditworthy. This is because creditors want evidence that you can and will pay your debts. Steps you can take to build a sound financial reputation are as follows.

- *Start with a job.* Prove that you can earn money.
- *Open a savings account.* Saving regularly shows a responsible attitude toward financial matters. Your savings also may serve as collateral for a loan.

VGstockstudio/Shutterstock.com

Proving the ability to earn money is the first step to establishing credit.

Economics in Action

Excessive Credit

The use of credit is good for the economy. It allows consumers to buy goods and services now and pay for them in the future. It benefits businesses by providing funds for creation and expansion and increasing profits through sales growth and interest on unpaid customer balances. Credit benefits governments, too, through the use of borrowed money for major projects, such as road construction.

However, excessive use of credit can throw the economy off balance and lead to higher inflation and a reduction in economic growth. When consumers use credit, it increases the demand for products they are buying. If the demand increases faster than the supply, prices will also increase. Excessive credit use also leads to higher monthly payments by consumers, which reduces spending for other important reasons, such as health care and retirement savings.

When businesses overuse credit, they can expand too quickly and significantly increase operating costs. This could significantly reduce profits if sales were to decline. The overuse of business and government credit can also cause demand for goods and services to increase more quickly than supply. The result is higher inflation, higher interest rates, a weakened economy, and fewer job opportunities.

- *Open a checking account.* A well-managed checking account shows you have experience in handling money. A checking account is often overlooked when people are trying to establish credit.
- *Get a credit card.* Apply to a local department store or an oil company for a credit card. If you are granted credit, make small purchases and pay promptly. This will give you a record of steady payments.

You may also ask a parent or other family member to add you as an authorized user of one of their credit cards. This means their record of the account is copied to your credit report. If your parents or other family members are not comfortable letting you have a credit card with their account, simply have them destroy the card as soon as it arrives. You will still get the favorable credit reporting every month, even though you do not personally use the card.

If you have never used credit, you will need to establish a credit rating. Begin establishing a good credit rating as early as you can. The longer you wait, the more difficult it becomes to find a lender willing to extend credit to you. Without an established credit history, you will also pay a higher rate of interest to lenders willing to give you a loan.

Credit Bureaus

A **credit bureau** is an organization that collects information about the financial and credit transactions of consumers. It is also called a *credit reporting agency*. There are three major national credit bureaus: Equifax; Experian; and TransUnion, LLC.

The role of credit bureaus is to accumulate credit histories for all individuals who use credit. A **credit history** is an individual's credit and financial behavior over a period of years. It includes every credit account ever opened and outstanding balances on current credit accounts. It also lists negative information, such as delinquent or late payments, bankruptcies, foreclosures, and overdue taxes. Businesses notify the credit reporting agencies when a consumer opens a new account, closes an account, or skips or makes late payments.

Using this information, credit bureaus generate credit reports, credit scores, and credit ratings. These agencies then sell the reports to creditors and a variety of other businesses.

Credit Report

A **credit report** is a record of a person's credit history. The *Fair Credit Reporting Act (FCRA)* requires each of the credit reporting agencies to provide consumers with a free copy of a credit report, when requested, once every 12 months. A request must include the individual's social security number and date of birth.

The information on credit reports may differ depending on the agency. A credit report should be carefully reviewed on a regular basis and checked for key information in each section as described in Figure 8-3. If errors are found, the credit reporting agency should be contacted for instructions on filing a dispute. The agency must respond to the dispute.

How to Read a Credit Report	
Section	**What to Check**
Personal information	Verify your personal information, such as your name, address, phone number, date of birth, and Social Security number.
Credit summary	This section summarizes your revolving and installment accounts and any home loans. Check the balances and your total amount of outstanding debt.
Account information (also called *Credit Items*)	Make sure all accounts listed belong to you. This section may be lengthy, but it is important to check all details for accuracy, including payment history, balance, and account status. Late payments and accounts taken over by collection agencies appear in this section.
Public records (also called *Negative Information* or *Negative Items*)	Any bankruptcies, garnishments, or liens are shown here. Ideally, this section should be blank.
Inquiries (also called *Credit History Requests*)	Look over the list of creditors that recently viewed your credit report. Applying for a credit card, taking out a loan, submitting an apartment application, or applying for insurance can trigger inquiries.

Goodheart-Willcox Publisher

Figure 8-3 A credit report should be checked to make sure key information is accurate.

Case Study *Credit Cards*

Damian sees credit as a useful tool and realizes the importance of establishing credit for many reasons, including the ability to get loans in the future. Besides, it is not realistic to buy everything with cash. By using a credit card sparingly, using it for necessities only, and keeping track of charges, debt can be kept to a repayable amount.

Damian's first purchase using a credit card was a pair of waterproof boots, which were on sale, but cost more than the amount of cash on hand. Waiting until payday would have meant the sale on the boots would be over. Using the credit card wisely saved $20.

Case Review

1. How does offering credit work in the interest of sellers?
2. How can the use of credit work for consumers? How can it create problems?
3. What did you learn from Damian's example?
4. How can Damian enjoy the benefits and avoid the problems of using credit?

A credit report is important because it shows how an individual manages financial responsibilities. It is one of the criteria that largely determines whether an individual can get credit. An individual with a good credit report is a *low-risk borrower.* **Low-risk borrowers** are those who are most likely to pay their debts. An individual with a poor credit report is a *high-risk borrower.* High-risk borrowers have established a record of not paying bills on time and are risks for creditors. These people will have trouble getting credit and may have to pay higher finance charges. Most lenders will charge a higher interest rate to justify the additional risk.

Before making credit available, a creditor reviews the borrower's financial history. Just as you may not lend money to someone who does not repay debts, creditors will not lend to a person with a poor credit reputation. Before making a loan offer, creditors already know the likelihood of the borrower defaulting on the loan. If risk of default is high, most reliable creditors will not lend. Less reputable creditors may lend but with a much higher finance charge and unfavorable terms.

Credit Scores

Creditors also evaluate creditworthiness by looking at credit scores. A **credit score** is a numerical measure of a loan applicant's creditworthiness at a particular point in time. In order to earn a FICO score, an individual consumer needs to have six months of credit history. FICO scores are only assigned to individuals rather than businesses or government.

A credit score is generated primarily by credit reporting agencies. A credit score, like a credit report, may differ from one credit reporting agency to another. Each agency has access to different information and uses different mathematical formulas to calculate scores. However, the scores for the same person are usually similar.

The credit score is also known as the *FICO score,* named for the Fair Isaac Corporation that developed the scoring system. A FICO score is assigned as points and is calculated based on five categories of information, as shown in Figure 8-4. This information is described as follows:

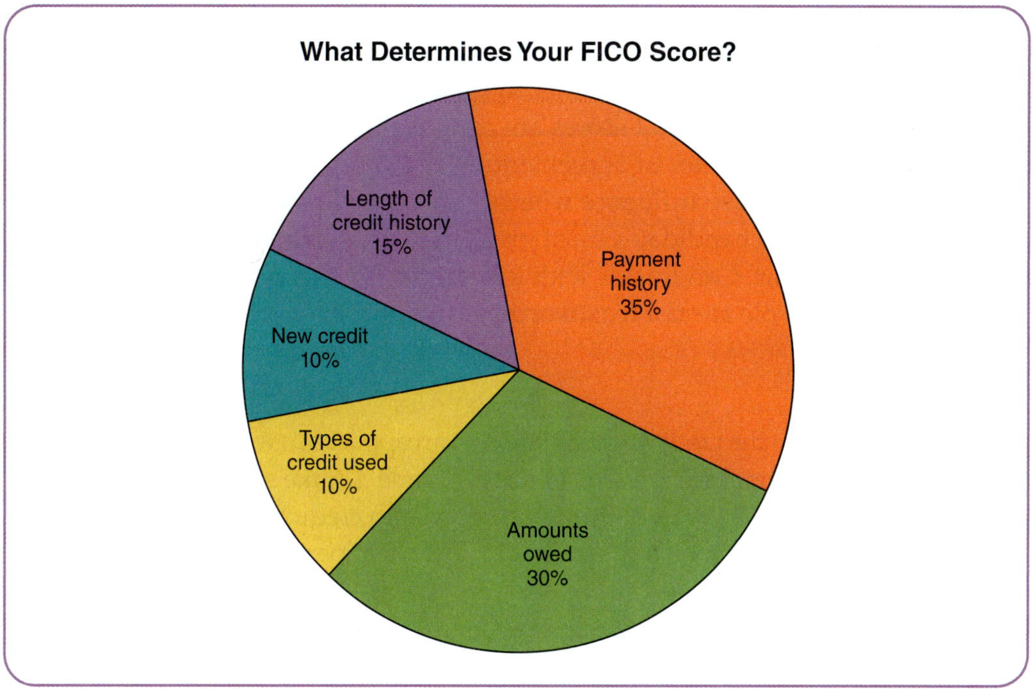

Goodheart-Willcox Publisher

Figure 8-4 Consumer FICO credit scores consider length of credit history, payment history, amounts owed, types of credit used, and new credit.

- *Payment history.* An individual will score high for payment history if there is a record of paying bills on time.
- *Amounts owed.* This category determines debt-to-credit-limit ratio. Debt is the total of all amount owed on credit cards, car loans, home loans, and other items. The credit limit is the total amount allowed under credit card maximums and the original loan amounts. A lower ratio is best.
- *Length of credit history.* The longer the credit card accounts have been well managed, the better the credit history will be.
- *New credit.* Multiple applications for new credit accounts can have a negative effect on a credit score.
- *Types of credit used.* Having a mix of loans and credit cards is slightly favored over using only one type of credit.

Collateral does not directly enter into consideration for a credit score. However, it can indirectly help you acquire credit and increase your credit rating if the collateral is used to obtain a loan, and payments on the loan are made regularly and timely.

The higher a credit score, the greater a person's creditworthiness and the ability to obtain credit. A person with a high credit score is considered a low-risk borrower. Examples of FICO scores are shown in Figure 8-5.

FICO Scores

Credit Score	Rating
800–850	Excellent
740–799	Very Good
670–739	Average
580–669	Fair
300–579	Poor

Goodheart-Willcox Publisher

Figure 8-5 FICO scores are the global standard for measuring credit risk in the banking, mortgage, credit card, auto, and retail industries.

Credit scores are sources of information for other types of businesses such as auto and homeowners' insurance companies and phone companies. These businesses use scores to decide whether to issue a policy or provide a service. Applicants who have low credit scores are considered risks for not making regular payments on policies or agreements.

Credit scores can also influence whether a job candidate is hired for a position. Employment candidates must give employers written permission to request a credit report. Candidates with low scores may sway an employer to think that those people are not trustworthy or responsible.

Credit Ratings

A **credit rating** is the creditor's evaluation of an applicant's willingness and ability to pay debts and is typically expressed as a letter grade. Unlike a FICO score that requires an individual to have a minimum three month credit history, a VantageScore can often be calculated as soon as a new credit account appears on a credit report.

The VantageScore is a credit rating model that was developed through a joint venture of the three major credit bureaus. This score is sometimes thought of as the more consistent scoring scale for evaluating creditworthiness. The most current version of the VantageScore was created in 2017. These ratings are evaluated based on the following criteria as illustrated in Figure 8-6.

- *Total Credit Usage, Balance, and Available Credit* is considered extremely influential for the rating. Keeping revolving credit balances under 30 percent is helpful.
- *Credit Mix and Experience* is highly influential. Maintaining a good mix of credit over time is a way to improve a score.

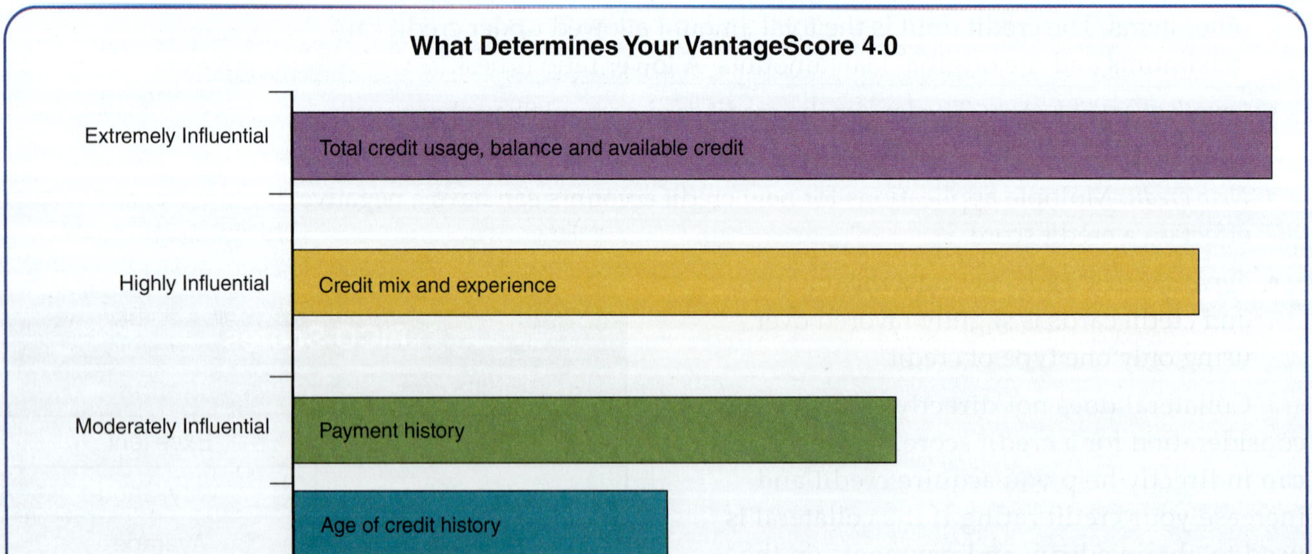

Goodheart-Willcox Publisher

Figure 8-6 The VantageScore credit rating takes payment history, percent of credit used, age and type of credit, total balance owed, available credit, and recent credit inquiries into consideration.

- *Payment History* is moderately influential. Paying all bills on time improves a score.
- *Age of Credit History* is less influential. Keeping accounts open for longer periods of time improves a score.
- *New Accounts* is also less influential. Opening too many accounts too quickly has a negative impact on a credit rating.

The VantageScore 4.0 scale uses the same point range as the FICO scores, as shown in Figure 8-7. The score is based on a mathematical model that combines the credit files from all three credit bureaus to establish a formula to assign a rating.

VantageScore 4.0	
Score	**Rating**
750–850	Excellent
700–749	Good
650–699	Fair
550–649	Poor
300–549	Very Poor

Goodheart-Willcox Publisher

Figure 8-7 The VantageScore© credit rating uses the same point range as FICO scores.

Section 8.1 Review

Check Your Understanding

1. What is the purpose of credit in our economy?
2. Name two types of credit.
3. List the three Cs of credit.
4. Name three credit bureaus.
5. On what information is a FICO score calculated?

Build Your Vocabulary

As you progress through this course, develop a personal glossary. This will help you build your vocabulary and prepare you for a career. Write a definition for each of the following terms and add it to your glossary.

credit
creditor
debtor
consumer credit
contract
acceleration clause
closed-end credit
installment loan
down payment
principal
collateral
secured credit
finance charge
open-end credit
revolving credit account
line of credit
unsecured credit
cosigner
creditworthy
credit bureau
credit history
credit report
low-risk borrower
credit score
credit rating

Section 8.2 Using Credit

Essential Question

What is included in the cost of credit?

Objectives

After studying this section, you will be able to:

- Explain the cost of credit.
- Discuss examples of easy-access credit traps.
- Describe types of credit cards and factors to consider when choosing a credit card.

Terms

annual percentage rate (APR)
easy-access credit
payday loan
title loan
pawnshop
rent-to-own agreement
cash advance
subprime credit card
grace period

Cost of Credit

Using credit is not free, and it can come with hefty charges. When you borrow $10 from a friend, you probably repay the friend an even $10. However, if you borrow money from a financial institution or make credit purchases of goods or services, you usually pay finance charges because you have the use of the lender's money.

As stated earlier, the *finance charge* is the total cost of using credit. Finance charges include interest and other fees associated with the loan. Two types of interest used when computing finance charges are annual percentage rate and simple interest.

Annual Percentage Rate (APR)

An **annual percentage rate (APR)** is the annual cost of credit a lender charges for extending credit. In addition to the interest rate, the APR factors in all other fees and charges that otherwise may be hidden from the borrower. This makes the APR a more accurate measure of the cost of credit because it reveals the true rate of interest. This helps consumers compare different loans and other sources of credit. Money lenders and credit card companies are required by law to state the APR when they advertise a rate.

micro10x/Shutterstock.com

Be aware of the fees associated with using credit—credit is not free money.

The total amount paid for the use of credit is based primarily on three factors:

- *Interest rate charged.* The APR is based on several factors, such as the type of loan, the current market rate of interest, and credit score.
- *Amount of credit used.* Interest is money paid for the use of someone else's money. The more that is borrowed or charged, the more interest is paid.
- *Length of the repayment period.* The more time taken to repay the money borrowed or to pay for credit purchases, the longer you have the use of the lender's money. The longer the period of a loan, the greater the amount of interest that will be owed.

Consumer credit transactions are regulated on the federal and state levels. Credit laws address finance charges, late fees, cash advances, and other issues to protect consumers. Businesses that extend credit must comply with both federal laws and laws issued by the state in which the businesses operate.

Simple Interest

In Chapter 5 you learned about simple interest. *Simple interest* is one formula used when calculating the cost of credit. The formula is based on the principal, interest rate, and length of time of the loan. The formula is as follows.

Principal (P) × Rate (R) × Time (T) = Interest (I)

You Do the Math Integers

Integers are positive and negative whole numbers and zero. In other words, they are not decimals or fractions.

Solve the following problems.

1. How long will it take to pay off a $1,000 credit card balance with an annual 18 percent interest rate if you make no additional purchases and make the minimum monthly payment (typically $10)? Go online and find a credit card interest calculator. Use the calculator to illustrate the benefits of paying more than the minimum due on a credit card. Enter the following numbers into the calculator:
   - Amount charged: $1,000
   - Annual interest rate: 18 percent
   - Minimum payment percent: 4 percent
   - Leave minimum payment blank

   Compute the results. How much time and money can you save by paying more than the required 4 percent each month?
2. Fiona's credit card balance is $5,000. The APR is 18 percent and the minimum payment is 5 percent of the balance. What is the minimum payment due? How much of the minimum payment goes to interest? How much of the payment goes to the principal? If Fiona makes the minimum payment this month and does not use the card to make any more purchases, what will the balance be next month? What is the minimum payment due next month?

For example, simple interest of 12 percent means that $12 interest will be paid per year on each $100 borrowed. If you pay for a $700 vehicle repair using a credit card that charges a 12 percent annual interest rate, the repair will actually cost $784.

$$\begin{aligned} \text{Principal} \times \text{Rate} \times \text{Time} &= \text{Interest (I)} \\ \$700 \times .12 \times 1 \text{ year} &= \$84 \\ \text{Principal} + \text{Interest} &= \text{Repayment amount} \\ \$700 + \$84 &= \$784 \end{aligned}$$

Simple interest is typically not used for installment credit. As you've learned, *installment credit* usually requires a down payment and is used for major purchases. The down payment is deducted from the price. The price less the down payment is used to calculate the finance charges.

Credit cards may also charge an annual fee for the privilege of using the card. These fees can be as much as $50 or more. Confirm the fees that can be charged to your account and how you can avoid these charges. These charges may include fees for:

- late payments;
- exceeding a credit limit;
- cash advances; and
- balance transfers.

Easy-Access Credit Traps

Easy-access credit is a short-term loan at a high interest rate that is granted regardless of the borrower's credit history. Even people who are high-risk borrowers can get these loans if the practice is considered legal in their state. This type of credit often poses danger to an individual's financial health.

One example of a risky, easy-access form of credit is a payday loan. A **payday loan** is a short-term, high-interest loan that usually must be repaid on the borrower's next payday. Repayment is guaranteed by the borrower's personal check at the time of the loan or by access to the borrower's bank account.

Payday loans are designed to be repaid in two weeks. However, many people cannot repay the loan in that time period and may be forced to take out another loan to pay off the first one. This creates a long-term debt cycle that can be difficult for a person to end. Late payments and continuous debt can harm credit scores and the ability to get future credit.

Payday loans are expensive and interest rates are high. Finance charges for a payday loan are often $15 or more weekly for every $100 borrowed. At this rate, if you borrow $1,000, you would pay $150 in finance charges each week. If you borrowed the money for four weeks, the finance charges would be $600!

Another example of easy-access credit is a title loan. A **title loan** is a secured, short-term loan made using a borrower's vehicle as collateral. The conditions of the loan temporarily transfers ownership of the car to the lender. Once the loan is repaid, the title is returned to the borrower, and vehicle ownership is reclaimed. However, if the borrower fails to repay the loan, the lender can sell the vehicle to make up for the lack of repayment. These loans, like payday loans, carry high interest rates. In addition, the borrower risks losing the vehicle if the terms of the contract are not met.

Some individuals who are looking for a quick loan use a pawnshop. **Pawnshops** are businesses that give customers high-interest loans with personal property, such as jewelry, held as collateral. Some pawnshops offer payday loans, too.

People who may not be able to qualify for a traditional loan to purchase furniture or appliances may choose to rent–to-own. **Rent-to-own agreements** are arrangements in which a consumer pays rent for the use of a product and eventually owns it. The advantage is little or no initial payment is required. The disadvantage to the consumer is paying much more than the product's purchase price by the time the final payment is made.

Ethics

Customer Data

Some financial institutions use their websites to gather personal and confidential information from customers, such as credit card numbers or phone numbers. Sharing or tampering with personal information is not only unethical, but may also be illegal. Protecting customer data helps the business protect its reputation and its customers.

Credit Cards

Credit cards are most often used as a medium of financial exchange to buy consumer goods and services. The most obvious purpose of a credit card is to purchase goods and services. Credit card purchases allow an individual to track spending. The receipts from credit purchases can be used in the event a return is needed or if a good needs to be replaced due to some defect.

Credit cards can also be used to get a cash advance. A **cash advance** is a loan against the available credit on an individual's account. Sometimes the credit card company will automatically mail checks to use for cash advances. Interest charges on cash advances begin immediately when a check is cashed. Even if the amount is paid by the due date for the credit account, interest will still be owed. There is also a transaction fee on the amount borrowed, and the interest rate may be higher than the rate for regular credit card purchases. A cash advance may not be the best option for borrowing money.

Types of Credit Cards

Three common types of credit cards are general-purpose cards, store credit cards, and travel and entertainment cards.

- *General-purpose cards*, such as Visa or MasterCard, are issued by banks, credit unions, and other financial institutions. They are often referred to as *bank cards*. These credit cards can be used around the world at the many places where they are accepted. Very often, these cards can also be used like a debit card, allowing cash to be withdrawn at automated teller machines. They carry a credit limit and require minimum monthly payments. Finance charges and other fees vary.
- *Store credit cards*, which are issued primarily by major department store chains, permit purchases to be charged only with the merchant issuing the card. Normally, there is a credit limit and a required minimum payment amount each month. Finance charges vary.
- *Travel and entertainment cards* usually require that the entire balance be paid each month. Some cards may allow payment over a longer period for travel- and vacation-related expenses, such as airfare, tours, cruises, and hotel bills. On these balances, a high interest rate is often charged and requires minimum monthly payments.

Susan Law Cain/Shutterstock.com

Macy's is an example of a department store that has its own credit card for which customers can apply.

Subprime credit cards are cards offered to people who have a poor credit history. Often they carry very high interest rates, large annual fees, sign-up fees, participation fees, late payment penalties, and other charges. The credit limits are generally low, usually $250 to $300. Some card issuers limit the credit to an amount equaling the deposit made in a collateral savings account. In other words, if you deposit $300, that is your credit limit; deposit $5,000, and that is your limit.

Subprime cards generally are easy to get, but they are very costly. For example, suppose you are issued a card with a $300 limit. It comes with a sign-up fee of $85, a monthly

Employability Skills

Networking

Networking means talking with people you know and developing new relationships that can lead to potential career or job opportunities. A *professional network* is a group of professionals you know and who know you. These are the people who are supportive in your career endeavors and may or may not be social friends. Networking can lead to job opportunities. The more contacts you make, the greater your opportunities for finding career ideas.

participation fee of $8, and an annual fee of $50. This leaves $157 of credit for the first month after sign-up. Terms vary with different credit card issuers. Be wary because you almost always lose more than you gain with a subprime credit card. It is better to deal only with reputable creditors.

Shopping for a Credit Card

Shopping for credit is as important as shopping for the goods and services you buy with it. Since credit cards are a form of unsecured credit, credit card companies are allowed to charge a higher interest rate. The annual rate can range from around 10 percent to over 30 percent. The more money that is borrowed, the more that is paid in finance charges. The higher the annual percentage rate, the higher the finance charges. The more time taken to repay, the more that is paid in finance charges.

Some credit card companies offer new customers *introductory offers*. These include items such as special interest rates or interest-free periods. At the end of the introductory period, these rates can increase to high interest rates and other charges for the credit card holder. Consumers should be cautious as some of these offers are marketing strategies to gain new customers for the creditor.

By law, credit card offers must include certain *disclosures* or credit terms, as illustrated in Figure 8-8. Before accepting and using any of these cards, you need to read the fine print on any contract you sign and ask questions. Knowing the exact cost of credit can help you compare finance charges and find the best deal. It also helps you decide how much credit you can afford to use.

Some credit cards have a grace period. A **grace period** is the time between the billing date and the start of interest charges. You have that time to pay the full balance without interest. In a few states, a grace period is mandatory on any new charges made each month. Interest may only be calculated on outstanding balances from the prior month. There are no interest charges on credit card balances that are paid in full by the due date each month.

When applying for a credit card, an individual is required to complete an application with the financial institution. The application will be verified, and a credit report and credit scores will be reviewed. The credit card company will then decide if the person is a good credit risk and if credit will be granted.

The *Equal Credit Opportunity Act (ECOA)* requires that all consumers are treated equally when applying for credit. If your application is denied, contact

Credit Card Disclosures	
Annual percentage rate (APR) for purchases	0% until 11/1/-- after that, 12.9%–22.9%
Other APRs	Cash-advance APR: 24.9% Balance-transfer APR: 17.9% Penalty rate: 24.9%. See explanation below.*
Variable-rate information	Your APR for purchase transactions may vary. The rate is determined monthly by adding 5.9% to the prime rate.**
Grace period for repayment of balances for purchases	25 days on average
Method of computing the balance for purchases	Average daily balance (excluding new purchases)
Annual fees	None
Minimum finance charge	$0.50
Transaction fee for cash advances: 3% of the amount advanced Balance-transfer fee: 3% of the amount transferred Late-payment fee: $25 Over-the-credit-limit fee: $25	

* Explanation of penalty. If your payment arrives more than 10 days late two times within a six-month period, the penalty rate will apply.

** The prime rate used to determine your APR is the rate published in *The Wall Street Journal* on the 10th day of the prior month.

Federal Reserve Board
Adapted from Learn More About Your Offer; FederalReserve.gov

Figure 8-8 On credit card application forms, disclosures are usually shown in a box similar to this one.

the financial institution for an explanation. You are entitled to know the specific details pertaining to credit rejection.

Credit Card Statements

Monthly statements are sent each month for a credit card account, as shown in Figure 8-9. Most credit card companies allow the consumer to choose to receive a printed statement or an online statement. The statement should be reconciled against receipts for charges, payments, and credits. In addition to the date, amount, and business related to each purchase, the statement should show the following information:

- date that payments are due
- minimum payment due
- new balance and previous balance
- total amount of new purchases, fees, and advances
- finance charges as a dollar amount, as well as the periodic and corresponding annual percentage rate

Credit Card Statement

Account Statement

For the period ending Aug 9, 20-- Days in billing cycle: 31 Account Number: XXXX-XXXX-XXXX-XXXX
Questions or lost/stolen card? Call Customer Service 1-800-555-1234 Page: 1 of 4

Summary of Account Activity

Previous Balance	$0.00
Payments	$0.00
Other Credits/Adjustments	$0.00
Purchases	+$152.33
Cash Advances	$0.00
Fees Charged	$0.00
Interest Charged	$0.00
Total New Balance	**$152.33**
Past Due Amount	$0.00
Credit Limit	$3000.00
Credit Available	$2847.00

Payment Information

Total New Balance	**$152.33**
Minimum Payment Due	**$5.00**
Payment Due Date	**Sep 9, 20--**

Late Payment Warning: If we do not receive your minimum payment by the date listed above, you may have to pay a Late Payment Fee of up to $25.00.

Minimum Payment Warning: If you make only the minimum payment each period, you will pay more in interest and it will take you longer to pay off your balance. For example:

If you make no additional charges using this card and each month you pay...	You will pay off the balance shown on this Statement in about...	And you will end up paying an estimated total of...
Only the minimum payment	5 years	$275
$6	3 years	$217 (Savings=$58)

If you are experiencing financial difficulty and would like information about credit counseling or debt management services, you may call 1-800-123-4567.

Goodheart-Willcox Publisher

Figure 8-9 A credit card statement is issued on a monthly basis by the lender.

- total amount of payments and credits
- total amount of credit available on the account

Compare the statement each month against your own record of charges, payments, and credits.

Section 8.2 Review

Check Your Understanding

1. What are two types of interest used when computing finance charges?
2. The total paid for the use of credit is based primarily on what three factors?
3. State the formula for simple interest.
4. List examples of easy-access credit sources.
5. What are three common types of credit cards?

Build Your Vocabulary

As you progress through this course, develop a personal glossary. This will help you build your vocabulary and prepare you for a career. Write a definition for each of the following terms and add it to your glossary.

annual percentage rate (APR)
easy-access credit
payday loan
title loan
pawnshop
rent-to-own agreement
cash advance
subprime credit card
grace period

Review and Assessment

Chapter Summary

Section 8.1 Consumer Credit

- Credit is an agreement between two parties in which one party lends money or provides goods or services to another party with the understanding that payment will be made at a later date. The party extending credit is known as the creditor, or the lender. The party receiving credit is known as the debtor, or the borrower. All credit is based on trust and has an accompanying element of risk.
- The most common types are closed-end credit and open-end credit. An example of closed-end credit is an installment loan, which often requires collateral to make it a secured loan. Open-end credit is typically unsecured. An example of open-end credit is a credit card.
- Being creditworthy means having the assets, income, and willingness to repay debt. Creditworthiness is measured by the three Cs of credit. Establishing credit is important because it provides a sound financial reputation which assures creditors that debt will be paid.
- Credit bureaus are responsible for collecting information about the financial and credit transactions of consumers. They accumulate the credit history of individuals and sell the reports to creditors.

Section 8.2 Using Credit

- Financial institutions charge fees for the use of credit. Two types of interest used when computing finance charges are annual percentage rate and simple interest.
- Easy-access credit traps often pose a danger to financial health. These short-term loans at high interest rates are granted to borrowers regardless of credit history. However, many borrowers cannot repay the money and are quickly sunk into serious, compounding debt.
- Credit cards are most often used as a medium of financial exchange to buy consumer goods and services. They allow the cardholder to buy goods and services on a time-payment plan. There are three common types of credit cards: general-purpose cards, store credit cards, and travel and entertainment cards.

Review Your Knowledge

1. Summarize the importance of credit.
2. Explain how credit cards serve as a medium of exchange.
3. Identify the similarities and differences between closed-end and open-end credit.
4. Describe the meaning of *creditworthiness.*
5. Explain the role of credit bureaus.
6. Describe the cost of credit.
7. Discuss the risks a person takes with using a payday loan.
8. Explain the risks a person takes with using a title loan.
9. List and describe three different types of credit cards.
10. What are important factors to consider when shopping for a credit card?

Apply Your Knowledge

1. When you use credit, an opportunity cost presents itself as well as a trade-off. What is the opportunity cost of using credit to purchase a new coat? What is the trade-off?
2. Individuals who are considered low-risk borrowers exhibit financial capability. Those who are high-risk borrowers fail to exhibit financial responsibility. Create a chart with two columns. In the first column, insert the heading *Low-Risk Borrower.* In the second column, insert

the heading *High-Risk Borrower.* Under each of the headings, enter behavior that an individual displays that earns that distinction. For example, a low-risk borrower pays bills on time; a high-risk borrower is late with bill payment.

3. Interview a friend and explain the risks of payday loans. Ask the person these questions:
   A. Do you know the purpose of a payday loan?
   B. Do you understand the risks involved with a payday loan?
4. Your friend needs to borrow money and has a car that is fairly new and is paid for. However, having a low credit score makes the bank think your friend is not creditworthy. Your friend has been told that people with low credit scores can qualify quickly for a title loan. What words of caution about title loans would you give this friend?
5. Credit cards serve as a convenient form of financial exchange. Make a list of different types of purchases for which a credit card is a better choice than cash. For each purchase you list, write the costs and benefits of using credit.
6. Why do you think it is important to monitor credit reports regularly and to address errors?
7. Read the following passage from a credit card contract. Analyze what the information means and explain what the consequences would be to the cardholder.

   We may increase the APRs on new transactions up to the penalty APR, based on your creditworthiness, each time a minimum payment due is not received by its applicable due date. We may elect to set your APRs for all transactions (including purchases, balance transfers, direct deposits, and cash advances) to different penalty APRs. We will provide you with a minimum of 45 days notice. An increased penalty APR will remain in effect indefinitely.
8. Often, credit card companies increase the credit limit of card holders who have reached their credit limit and are only paying the minimum payment every month. Why would credit card companies have a policy such as this one?
9. According to the Fair Isaac Corporation (FICO), the average credit score in America is 706. Evaluate this score using Figure 8-5. Would a person with this score be considered a high-risk borrower or a low-risk borrower?
10. Do you have a credit card? If so, which type of card do you have and how did you make a choice of types of credit cards? If you do not have a credit card, select one that you plan on applying for and explain why you chose that one.

Apply Your Math Skills

1. Pablo has an excellent FICO score at 810 and is approved to borrow $9,000 at 4.6%. Pablo's friend, Abraham, has a much lower score of 500 and will have to pay 12% for a loan of the same amount. How much less will Pablo pay in simple interest in one year with the better credit score than Abraham will pay?
2. Ashlee's credit card company charges a $30 fee for exceeding the credit limit and a $50 fee for a late payment. If Ashlee does both in the same month, how much will be paid in fees?

Communication Skills

Writing. Successful employees also are responsible citizens. Make a list of five things that you can do to show that you are financially responsible when using credit. When you are finished, write a paragraph that supports your reasoning for each item you chose.

Listening. Hearing is a physical process. Listening combines hearing with evaluation. Listen to your instructor presenting a lesson. Analyze the effectiveness of the presentation. Listen carefully and take notes about the main points. Then organize the key information that you heard.

Speaking. Etiquette is the art of using good manners in any situation. Etiquette is especially important when making phone calls since the two parties cannot interact face-to-face. Create a script for a telephone conversation to convince a loan officer that you are a good candidate for an automobile loan. Make a list of the important facts that support why you should be granted a loan. Use "please" and "thank you" when appropriate. Ask a classmate to assume the role of the loan officer. Practice your telephone conversation. How would you rate your use of good manners? How does your classmate rate your speech?

Teamwork

Work with a teammate to create two charts: one to list the pros and cons of installment credit and one to list the pros and cons of revolving credit. Compare and contrast the two charts. Present your visuals to the class.

Internet Research

Credit Reports and Scores. Visit the website of Annual Credit Report.com, which is the only source for free credit reports authorized by federal law. Read and analyze the information about the process to get a credit report and score. Synthesize and organize the information so that you may present it to your class.

Consumer Loans. Consumers have many choices from which to choose when credit is needed for making a purchase, as shown in Figure 8-1. Using the Internet, conduct a search for *types of consumer loans*. Compare and contrast secure loans (collateral) and unsecured loans (no collateral). Which consumer loan would you select if you needed money to finance your college education? What criteria did you use?

Credit Scores and Ratings. Borrowers need to be informed of the differences between a FICO score and VantageScore rating. Conduct an Internet search on FICO scores and VantageScore 4.0. Summarize what you learn about the differences between the two scores.

Portfolio Development

Recommendations. After you have created a list of references, you will need to obtain letters of recommendation. A *letter of recommendation* is a letter in which your qualities and abilities to perform in a specific capacity are assessed by a person you know well. It highlights your achievements in your academic or professional career. The letter is usually written by an instructor, supervisor, or someone else who is familiar with your qualifications for a given job or application. The purpose of the letter is to advocate for you as a candidate.

A letter of recommendation will probably be written by a person who also agrees to serve as a reference for you. However, it is not required that your letters of recommendation come from your references. For example, if you are applying for enrollment into an academic program, you may choose to use your managers or former employers as references but elect to have a teacher write a letter of recommendation. This allows people from both your professional and academic careers to vouch for your abilities. Two or three letters of recommendation are sufficient.

1. Contact several people from your references and ask if they are willing to write a letter of recommendation for you. For those contacts who agree to write letters, suggest to them a date by which you would like to receive it. Writing the letter can, and should, take some time, so plan in advance. When organizing your portfolio, it is suggested that these letters follow your personal references document.

CTSOs

Extemporaneous Speaking. Extemporaneous speaking is a competitive event you might enter with your CTSO. This event allows you to display your communication skills, specifically your ability to organize and deliver an oral presentation. At the competition, you will be given several topics from which to choose. You will also be given a time limit to create and deliver the speech. You will be evaluated on your verbal and nonverbal skills as well as the tone and projection of your voice.

To prepare for an extemporaneous speaking event, complete the following activities.

1. Ask your instructor for several practice topics so you can practice making impromptu speeches.
2. Once you have a practice topic, jot down the ideas and points to cover. An important part of making this type of presentation is that you will have only a few minutes to prepare. Being able to write down your main ideas quickly will enable you to focus on what you will actually say in the presentation.
3. Practice the presentation. You should introduce yourself, review the topic that is being presented, defend the topic, and conclude with a summary.
4. Ask your instructor to play the role of competition judge as you give the presentation. Afterward, ask for feedback from your instructor. You may also consider having a student audience listen and give feedback.
5. For the event, bring paper and pencils to record notes. Supplies may or may not be provided.

CHAPTER

9 Credit Management

Managing your credit is an important skill that will help you be in control of your financial future. Learning how to use credit wisely today will pay dividends tomorrow.

When you use a credit card, it is necessary to keep track of your spending. Never spend more than you can afford. Always be prepared to pay the balance in full when the statement arrives. Carrying unpaid balances forward from month to month can create credit card debt that is difficult to control.

Be aware of where your credit card is at all times. Never let a friend use your card. Avoid giving your credit card number to anyone on the phone or online unless you know the person or company well. By monitoring your card at all times, you can avoid becoming a victim of credit fraud.

Focus on Finance

Credit Card Debt

With the help of a credit card, we can purchase what we want, when we want. There is no need to wait and save money to buy something that seems important today. For credit card users, this can work if the credit card amount is paid in full each month. If there are no plans to pay in full each month, credit card debt can get out of hand.

As an example, 18-year-old Samantha charged $1,500 worth of merchandise at the local mall. The credit card carries a 19 percent interest rate. If the minimum amount of $60 is paid each month, Samantha will be more than 26 years old by the time the debt is paid in full. That's 106 payments and more than $889 extra in interest, assuming there are not any other charges on the card. That means that Samantha would still be paying for merchandise that was bought at age 18 and was probably worn out before Samantha reached age 26.

College and Career Readiness

Reading Prep. Before reading this chapter, review the objectives. Based on this information, write down two or three items that you think are important to note while you are reading.

Sections

Syda Productions/Shutterstock.com

Section 9.1 Wise Credit Use

Essential Question

Why is it important for a consumer to manage personal credit?

Objectives

After studying this section, you will be able to:

- Discuss ways to manage credit.
- Identify different financial problems caused by the misuse of credit.
- Explain the consequences of filing for bankruptcy.

Terms

debt	collection agency	bankruptcy
debt load	repossession	Chapter 7 bankruptcy
20/10 rule	foreclosure	Chapter 13 bankruptcy
financial personality	lien	
credit counseling service	garnishment	

Managing Credit

Credit can make it possible for you to spend more than you earn on a temporary basis. With careful planning, credit can help you get more of the things you need when you need them. Without planning, credit can create serious, long-lasting financial and legal problems. Using credit requires personal responsibility as well as responsibility to the creditor.

Debt is something that is owed that will decrease future earnings. **Debt load** is the amount of debt a consumer has at a given point in time. A common guideline for using credit is the 20/10 rule. The **20/10 rule** states that an individual should never borrow more than 20 percent of annual take-home pay. That amount is the maximum debt load. Monthly payments should be less than 10 percent of the monthly take-home pay. The 20/10 rule does not apply to home mortgages.

To avoid credit card debt, financial experts recommend that credit cards *should not be used* for everyday purchases such as lunch or entertainment. Credit cards *should be used* primarily for emergencies. Financial experts also suggest that, when possible, the balance should be paid in full each month. If the balance cannot be paid in full, at the least, the minimum payment should be made. The credit card company establishes the minimum payment, and it appears on each monthly statement. Figure 9-1 shows an example of a credit card statement. Note the minimum payment due and the number of years to pay off the debt.

New Balance	$3,997.16
Minimum Payment Due	$53.30
Payment Due Date	10/20/--*

*Late Payment Warning: If we do not receive your Minimum Payment Due by the Payment Due Date listed above, you may have to pay a late fee of up to $42.00 and your Purchase APR may be increased to the Penalty APR of 29.25%.

Minimum Payment Warning: If you make only the minimum payment each period, you will pay more in interest, and it will take you longer to pay off your balance. For example:

If you make no additional charges and each month you pay...	You will pay off the balance shown on this statement in about...	And you will pay an estimated total of...
Only the Minimum Payment Due	17 years	$5,126.29
$92	4 years	$4,325.14 (Savings = $801.15)

Goodheart-Willcox Publisher

Figure 9-1 A credit card statement must contain certain information that is essential to the consumer.

It can take years to pay off the balance on a credit card. For example, suppose a college student charged food and entertainment expenses for a semester and has a $5,000 credit card balance with an interest rate of 18 percent. If the student made monthly payments of $90, it would take 10 years to pay off the balance. The interest over that time would be $5,843.89! If the student made additional purchases, it would take even longer to pay off the balance. As a result, many consumers never pay off their credit cards balances.

It is smart to use credit in some situations but not in others. Several advantages of using credit are as follows.

- *Use of goods and services as you pay for them.* Being able to wear a coat or drive a car while you are paying for it can be a big plus. You have immediate access to an item you need even though you do not have the money to pay cash for it. This is a common reason for using credit.
- *Opportunity to buy costly items.* Many people find it difficult or impossible to save enough to pay for a car or house in one payment. With credit, you can buy costly goods and services as you need them and pay for them over a period of time. Borrowing is sometimes the only way consumers can pay for major purchases, such as a car.
- *Source of cash for emergency or unexpected expenses.* Even the best money managers encounter unexpected expenses, such as a major car repair. A common way to handle sudden needs for cash is having a line of credit, which is a preapproved amount that an individual can borrow.

- *Convenience and safety.* Credit eliminates the need to carry large amounts of cash and provides a sense of security. It provides a record of purchases. It usually simplifies telephone, mail, and Internet shopping as well as necessary returns and exchanges.
- *Taking advantage of sales.* Credit allows you to take advantage of sale prices on goods or services you need when you do not have enough cash at the time of the sale.
- *Long-range goals.* Credit can help consumers make purchases that are part of a long-range financial plan, such as paying for education, furniture, or a vacation.

To use credit wisely, it is necessary to be aware of its disadvantages as well as its advantages. Consider the negative aspects when you are deciding how and when to use credit.

- *Reduction of future spendable income.* By using credit, you spend future income. You thereby reduce the amount of money you can spend later.
- *Expense.* Using credit usually costs money. The more credit you use and the more time you take to repay, the more you will pay in interest and finance charges. This reduces the amount you will have to spend for other goods and services.
- *Overspending.* Credit makes it easy to spend money you do not have. It can be difficult to resist buying what you cannot afford or can do without when you have ready credit.
- *Risk of serious consequences.* Failure to pay debts on time and in full can cause serious financial problems.

To learn how to manage credit, it is important to be aware of your financial habits and spending. It is important to understand your own financial personality, be aware of overspending habits, and recognize alternatives to using credit.

Know Your Financial Personality

A **financial personality** is a combination of an individual's attitudes about money and spending patterns. Financial personality is expressed by the way a person handles cash and credit. Financial personalities vary greatly. Some people spend money freely. Others find it hard to part with a dollar. Some people think through each purchase, while others buy on impulse. The questions in Figure 9-2 can help define a person's financial personality.

If you answered "yes" to most of these questions, credit is probably a safe tool for you to use. If you answered "no" to most questions, credit may not be a good option for you.

What Is Your Financial Personality?

- Do you find it easy to control spending?
- Do you save regularly?
- Do you follow a spending plan?
- Do you consider purchases carefully, particularly major purchases?
- Do you pay bills promptly?
- Do you buy only what you can afford?
- Do you make long-range financial plans?
- Do you handle financial matters with confidence?
- Do you see credit as a tool to use with care and caution?

Goodheart-Willcox Publisher

Figure 9-2 Asking these questions allows you to determine your financial personality.

Be Aware of Overspending

Many credit problems result from poor money management. The development of good management skills can help you avoid serious credit problems. Since overspending is easy with a credit card, it is important to keep track of your charges and account balance.

- Try not to use more credit than you can pay off each month.
- Make installment payments on time.
- Avoid using cash advances from the credit card company.
- Avoid using credit cards for buying items you do not need.

Creating a credit plan can help avoid the pitfalls of overspending and overusing credit.

Featureflash/Shutterstock.com

Credit cards should not be used for wants, such as attending a concert by a favorite performer.

Look for Credit Alternatives

Usually there are three alternatives to using credit. You may choose to not make the purchase; to pay with savings; or to postpone buying now and buy later with cash. The choice you make will depend on what you want to buy and what you want to achieve with your cash and your credit.

- *How important is making the purchase?* If you can do without something, you might be wise not to buy it. Is having the purchase now instead of later worth the extra price you pay for credit?
- *Are you willing to use all or some of your savings to buy now?* Unless you have planned to use money you have saved to make the purchase, reducing or eliminating your savings could be risky. Often it is difficult to replace the savings used for unplanned purchases. You may be left unprepared for unexpected emergencies or financial difficulties.
- *Can you save your money and buy later?* This choice will depend on how long you can wait to make the purchase. It will also depend on your ability to save money. Many people find it easier to make monthly credit payments than to put money in savings.

By waiting and saving, you may miss the satisfaction or pleasure of having what you want now. For example, suppose you want to take a vacation with friends. They are leaving next month for a week at the beach. According to your savings plan, you need three more months to save enough money for the trip. If you wait three months, you will not be able to share the vacation with your friends. In this case, you may decide to use credit to help you finance the vacation.

On the other hand, waiting may help you get more satisfaction from a purchase. Suppose you want to buy a pool table. You want it now, but you do not have enough money. Also, you are not sure what type of pool table you want. You decide to wait and save. As you are saving, you do some comparison shopping.

You decide what features you want and where to get the best deal. When you finally buy the pool table, your satisfaction is greater than if you had rushed into a credit purchase. A waiting period can make the purchase more valuable to you.

Credit Problems

Used unwisely, credit can lead to serious financial difficulties. The chart in Figure 9-3 lists some of the danger signals that warn credit users of trouble ahead. The consequences of having a poor credit report are severe and impact more than the ability to get credit. A person with a low credit score may:

- be unable to get loans and credit cards;
- pay higher interest rates for credit;
- have fewer housing choices because property owners check credit reports and reject people with low scores;
- have fewer job prospects because employers avoid job candidates with financial problems; and
- pay higher insurance premiums.

Accurate negative information, such as missed or late payments, may remain on a credit report for seven years.

Credit Warning Signals

- Stalling one creditor to pay another.
- Receiving past due notices with billing statements.
- Paying only the minimum required each month.
- Charging more than the amount you can pay each month.
- Not paying off credit account balances.
- Routinely running out of money before payday.
- Using credit cards or cash advances for everyday living expenses.

Goodheart-Willcox Publisher

Figure 9-3 Be aware of these warning signals when using credit.

If you have trouble paying your bills, notify creditors promptly. Many reputable creditors will work with you. They may help you by renegotiating repayment schedules or setting up a repayment program you can handle. They may be willing to extend your repayment schedules to lower the size of your monthly payments. Of course, this will cost you more in credit charges in the long run, but it may help you get through a difficult period.

Credit Counseling Services

Eliminating debt may require professional help. One reliable source of help for people with credit problems is a credit counseling service. A **credit counseling service** is an organization that provides debt and financial management advice and services to people with debt problems at little or no cost. The National Foundation for Consumer Credit sponsors several hundred credit counseling services throughout the United States and Canada. The service helps a debtor with a stable income work out a practical financial program for repaying debts. The service also helps the debtor plan and control current expenses to avoid further debts.

A credit counseling agency may recommend that you enroll in a *debt management plan (DMP)*. In a DMP, you deposit money each month with the credit counseling organization. It uses your deposits to pay your unsecured debts, like your credit card bills, student loans, and medical bills, according to a payment schedule the counselor develops with you and your creditors. Your creditors may agree to lower your interest rates or waive certain fees. A DMP requires you to make regular, timely payments; it could take 48 months or more to complete your DMP.

MBI/Shutterstock.com

Credit counseling can provide debt and financial management advice and services to people with debt problems at little or no cost.

Be cautious of "credit doctors" and for-profit credit repair clinics that promise to fix your credit rating for a fee. A company that charges high fees or demands that the debtor pay them rather than their creditors should be avoided. Debtors should pay little or nothing for the help they receive. Claims that are too good to be true indicate a problem. The claim might be a guarantee that they can make debt disappear or dramatically reduce total debt. Also be suspicious of those who claim an ability to remove accurate negative information from credit reports.

Consumers can contact their local consumer protection agency to get a referral to a reputable consumer credit counseling service. The US Trustee Program of the Department of Justice maintains a list of credit counseling agencies approved for pre-bankruptcy counseling.

Collection Agencies

When debts go unpaid, businesses and creditors often hire collection agencies. A **collection agency** is a business that specializes in debt collection.

Exploring Careers

Credit Analyst

When a credit application is submitted, the business or financial institution must assess the risks involved. This assessment is done by a credit analyst. Credit analysts study credit and financial data to decide if and how much credit should be extended. They examine financial records, advise on financial matters, and prepare reports to illustrate the degree of risk involved in extending credit to a particular person or business. Financial analysis software is typically used to assist in this process. Examples of tasks that credit analysts perform include:

- analyze credit data to determine the risk involved in extending credit
- evaluate the financial status of customers
- resolve complaints and verify transactions

Most credit analyst positions require a bachelor or master degree. A strong background in mathematics, economics, and accounting is necessary. Credit analysts must also have critical-thinking, decision-making, and communication skills.

Often, the agency receives a portion of the money collected as payment. In order to get full payments from you, collection agencies use every lawful means possible. The nonstop pressure they apply causes many debtors to pay in full.

Repossession of Property

Repossession is the taking of collateral when a borrower fails to repay a loan. For example, companies that repossess autos may tow the cars away without notice. The cars are auctioned and the money goes toward paying the debt.

Perhaps the most serious type of repossession is foreclosure. **Foreclosure** is the forced sale of property. The property, usually a home, is taken by the lender because the debtor failed to make loan payments. The residents receive a court order to remove their possessions and leave by a specific date.

The two main types of foreclosure are judicial foreclosure and nonjudicial foreclosure. In *judicial foreclosure*, the lender sells the property under court supervision. In *nonjudicial foreclosure*, the lender is allowed to advertise and sell the property at a public auction without court supervision. Each state specifies the rules and procedures to follow in a nonjudicial foreclosure.

Liens

A **lien** is a legal claim on a borrower's property by a creditor who is owed money. For example, if a person fails to pay state taxes, the state can put a lien on that person's home. Though the borrower still has possession of the home, they

History of Finance

Crisis of Ethics

In the years prior to the Great Recession, many consumers overstated their income to qualify for larger mortgages and buy more expensive homes than they could really afford. Eager to make money, financial institutions relaxed the requirements to qualify for these loans and encouraged consumers to take on too much debt. Lenders also encouraged those who already owned homes to take out a second mortgage. This caused people to use their homes as a "piggy bank" to buy cars, take expensive vacations, and buy stocks. The federal government also encouraged lenders to grant loans in the belief that everyone has a right to own a home. The result of this easy credit policy was the creation of risky debt.

The lenders who granted the subprime loans quickly sold them to other companies. These subprime mortgages were then bundled into investment packages and sold to investors. The lenders collected large commissions from the creation and sale of the investments.

In mid-2007, the economy slowed down and thousands of people defaulted on their mortgages. The bundled investments were suddenly worth much less than what the investors had paid, and many people and financial institutions lost large amounts of money. These defaults were a major cause of the Great Recession that followed.

are legally unable to sell or take out a loan on the home until the lien is paid in full.

Garnishment of Wages

The court may order garnishment of a debtor's earnings. **Garnishment** is a legal procedure requiring a portion of the debtor's pay to be set aside by the person's employer to pay creditors. This reduces the amount of the debtor's paychecks. Some employers fire employees who have repeated garnishments.

Bankruptcy

For those who are overwhelmed by debt, the US Bankruptcy Code allows for a fresh start. **Bankruptcy** is a legal state in which the courts excuse a debtor from repaying some or all debt. In return, the debtor must give up certain assets and possessions. The most common types of bankruptcy are Chapter 7 bankruptcy and Chapter 13 bankruptcy.

Chapter 7 bankruptcy eliminates most types of debt and stays on a person's credit report for ten years. It is the most common type of bankruptcy filed. A person must pass a *means test* before being approved for Chapter 7 bankruptcy. The means test involves the court looking at the person's income and debt and determining if the person will be approved to file for Chapter 7. If approved, the court declares the person unable to meet financial obligations. Most debts are discharged or forgiven. This is also referred to as *straight bankruptcy* or *liquidation bankruptcy*. The court then takes and sells the debtor's property and possessions. Proceeds from the sale are divided among the creditors. You may be able to keep your home and car as these are basic needs for survival.

Andy Dean Photography/Shutterstock.com

Foreclosure is the forced sale of a property by the lender because the borrower failed to make loan payments.

Chapter 13 bankruptcy, sometimes called *Wage Earner's Bankruptcy*, permits debtors with regular incomes to pay all or a portion of their debts under the protection and supervision of the court. The court sets up a three- to five-year repayment schedule. It also establishes the monthly amount to be paid toward debts. Once the court accepts the debtor's petition, creditors may not take action against the debtor. This plan has three advantages over straight bankruptcy. The debtor fulfills credit obligations, keeps most personal property and possessions, and maintains a reasonably sound credit rating.

Some types of debt cannot be wiped out by declaring bankruptcy. These include most student loans, alimony, child support, and many types of taxes. Also, the *Bankruptcy Abuse Prevention and Consumer Protection Act of 2005* placed restrictions on discharging credit card debt through bankruptcy.

You Do the Math

Statistical Reasoning

There are three measures of the center of a data set. The *mode* is the value that occurs most frequently in the data set. The *median* is the value that is equidistant from the highest and lowest values in the data set. Median is found by putting all the numbers in order from lowest to highest and finding the middle value. The *mean* is the average of all values in the data set. Mean is calculated by adding all values and dividing that sum by the total number of values.

Solve the following problems.

1. A recent survey of gasoline prices for a region reported these prices per gallon: $3.49, $3.67, $3.52, $3.58, and $3.56. What is the mean price per gallon?
2. A business ships telephone headsets all across the country. The various shipping costs it charged last week are: $0.99, $1.05, $0.75, $1.07, $0.99, $1.05, $1.05, and $1.07. What is the mode shipping charge?
3. For the data in #2, what is the mean shipping charge?

The consequences of filing bankruptcy can haunt a debtor for many years. Chapter 7 bankruptcy stays on a consumer's credit report for 10 years from the filing date. Chapter 13 bankruptcy stays on a consumer's credit report for seven years from the filing date. The person may be denied loans or credit cards or only be granted credit at inflated interest rates. The person may be denied a job, a business loan, insurance, or housing by anyone who sees the credit report. Bankruptcy should be considered a last resort.

Section 9.1 Review

Check Your Understanding

1. List four advantages of using credit.
2. List three alternatives to using credit.
3. How long does accurate negative information stay on a person's credit report?
4. What should a person do if paying bills becomes difficult?
5. What are two common types of bankruptcy?

Build Your Vocabulary

As you progress through this course, develop a personal glossary. This will help you build your vocabulary and prepare you for a career. Write a definition for each of the following terms and add it to your glossary.

- debt
- debt load
- 20/10 rule
- financial personality
- credit counseling service
- collection agency
- repossession
- foreclosure
- lien
- garnishment
- bankruptcy
- Chapter 7 bankruptcy
- Chapter 13 bankruptcy

Section 9.2 Consumer Protection

Objectives

After studying this section, you will be able to:

- Identify the laws that govern the use of credit.
- Explain credit fraud.

Essential Question

How do credit laws protect consumers?

Term

credit fraud

Consumer Credit Laws

Over the years, a number of federal laws have been passed to protect consumers when they use credit. Many state governments have also passed laws to protect consumers from illegal or unfair lending practices. Figure 9-4 summarizes these laws.

Truth in Lending Act

The *Truth in Lending Act*, passed in 1968, requires creditors to tell consumers what credit will cost them before they use it. Under this law, credit contracts and agreements must include:

- the amount financed or borrowed;
- the total number, amount, and due dates of payments;
- the finance charge in dollar amount and annual percentage rate;
- all charges not included in the finance charge;
- penalties or charges for late payment, default, or prepayment; and
- a description of any security held by the creditor.

wavebreakmedia/Shutterstock.com

The Truth in Lending Act requires lenders to tell borrowers what credit will cost them before they use it.

For merchandise purchased on credit, creditors must provide additional information. This includes a description of the merchandise, cash price, deferred payment price, and down payment or trade-in. The Truth in Lending Act also prohibits creditors from issuing credit cards you have not requested. The Truth in Lending Act takes precedence over state laws regarding credit and lending.

Credit Laws		
Law	**Year**	**Description**
Truth in Lending Act	1968	Requires businesses and financial institutions to disclose precise credit terms and costs
Fair Credit Reporting Act	1970	Gives consumers the right to receive a copy of their credit reports and to dispute inaccurate information within it
Equal Credit Opportunity Act	1974	Prohibits creditors from discriminating against an applicant on the basis of race, color, religion, national origin, gender, marital status, age, or whether the applicant receives public assistance as income
Fair Credit Billing Act	1974	Protects consumers from billing errors and provides outlets to challenge incorrect statements
Preservation of Consumers' Claims and Defenses Ruling	1975	Protects debtors from being forced to pay for goods and services when they have a legitimate dispute with the seller of those goods or services
Fair Debt Collection Practices Act	1977	Establishes legal protection against abusive debt collection practices
Electronic Funds Transfer Act	1978	Protects consumers in their use of electronic funds transfer
Bankruptcy Abuse Prevention and Consumer Protection Act	2005	Designed to make the bankruptcy system fairer to both debtors and creditors, but has been met with criticism for disproportionately benefiting the credit card industry
Credit Card Accountability Responsibility and Disclosure Act	2009	Makes the rates and fees of credit cards more transparent and prohibits unfair practices related to credit card rates and fees
Dodd-Frank Wall Street Reform and Consumer Protection Act	2010	Established the Financial Stability Oversight Council and Orderly Liquidation Authority and Consumer Financial Protection Bureau

Goodheart-Willcox Publisher

Figure 9-4 Consumer credit transactions are regulated by federal and state credit laws.

Equal Credit Opportunity Act

The *Equal Credit Opportunity Act*, passed in 1974, prohibits credit grantors from discriminating against consumers on the basis of sex, marital status, race, national origin, religion, age, or the receipt of public assistance. This means credit can be denied only for financial reasons and not for any of the factors listed above. When applicants are turned down, creditors must provide a written explanation of why credit was denied.

Fair Credit Reporting Act

Passed in 1970 and revised in 1977, the *Fair Credit Reporting Act* requires accuracy and privacy of information contained in credit reports. If you are refused credit because of information supplied by a credit reporting agency, this law gives you the right to:

- receive the name and address of the reporting agency that sent the report;

- find out from the reporting agency what facts are on file, the source of the information, and who has received the information;
- require a recheck of any information you find to be false;
- receive a corrected report if errors are found; and
- require the agency to send the corrected report to all creditors who received false information.

dboystudio/Shutterstock.com

The Fair Credit Reporting Act requires accuracy and privacy of information contained in credit reports.

Fair Credit Billing Act

The *Fair Credit Billing Act* protects consumers against unfair billing practices. It outlines the procedures to follow in resolving billing errors or disputes. The law requires creditors to send customers a written explanation of steps to take when questions arise concerning bills. The customer has 60 days after receiving a bill to notify the creditor of an error. The creditor must answer within 30 days. Within 90 days, the creditor must either correct the bill or explain if it is accurate. Creditors may take no collection action on amounts in question until billing disputes are resolved. However, the customer must pay any amount not in question.

Fair Debt Collection Practices Act

The *Fair Debt Collection Practices Act* (FDCP) protects consumers against unfair methods of collecting debts. The aims of the act are to eliminate abusive practices, encourage fair collection, and to provide consumers the ability to dispute information or obtain information to ensure accuracy. According to this law, debt collectors may not:

- reveal or publicize a debtor's debt to other people;
- contact debtors at inconvenient times (before 8 a.m. or after 9 p.m.) or places (such as work);
- use threats or abusive language;
- make annoying, repeated, or anonymous phone calls;
- make false or misleading statements about the collector's identity or the consequences of nonpayment; or
- collect unauthorized fees or charge debtors for calls and telegrams.

Electronic Funds Transfer Act

Electronic funds transfer (EFT) systems use electronic impulses to activate financial transactions instead of cash, checks, or paper records. The *Electronic Funds Transfer Act* protects consumers in these transactions in the following ways.

- Prohibits the distribution of unrequested EFT cards. You receive a card only if you ask for it.

- Requires issuers of EFT cards to provide cardholders with written information outlining their rights and responsibilities for the card and its use.
- Limits the liability for unauthorized transfers up to $50. The cardholder must notify the issuer of card loss or misuse within two business days.
- Requires issuers to provide cardholders with printed receipts of EFT transactions.
- Requires issuers to promptly investigate and correct EFT errors.

Preservation of Consumers' Claims and Defenses Ruling

The *Preservation of Consumers' Claims and Defenses Ruling* was issued by the Federal Trade Commission. It protects debtors from being forced to pay for goods and services when they have a legitimate dispute with the seller of those goods or services.

This protection applies when a retailer sells consumer credit obligations or contracts to a third party creditor. The consumer then owes the third party. If the goods or services purchased with credit are unsatisfactory, the debtor still owes the third party rather than the seller. For this reason, the seller does not feel obligated to correct any problems with the goods or services.

This ruling greatly limits the *holder-in-due-course doctrine*. That doctrine says the holder of a consumer contract has a right to collect a debt regardless of any unfair practices on the part of the seller. Here is an example to show how the rule protects you. Suppose you buy a $500 TV from the Viewing Center. You sign an installment contract calling for 18 monthly payments. The Viewing Center offers credit through a sales finance company. Therefore, you owe the finance company rather than the seller.

After the television is delivered, you find that it does not work. You can get sound but no picture. When you complain, the seller refuses to correct the problem. You threaten nonpayment. The seller says that is not the Viewing Center's problem because you owe the finance company.

Case Study Credit Card Management

During college, Thad opened a credit card that was to be used for textbooks. The card was managed with help from family members. Now out of school, it is a struggle for Thad to maintain good financial practices.

Thad uses a credit card instead of money for regular, everyday purchases, such as gas and groceries. The credit card is also used on student loan payments, rent, and a car payment, so more debt has accumulated quickly. The current minimum monthly payment is $149, and the balance on the card is $12,348 at 19 percent interest. The ultimate goal is to get the card balance to zero, but bad habits are hard to break.

Case Review

1. What are Thad's options to reduce debt?
2. What is the easiest way for Thad to eliminate credit card debt?
3. What type of purchases should Thad have been making with the credit card?
4. How would you resolve Thad's situation if it were up to you?

Ethics

Credit

It is unethical to purposely incur debt with the intention to file bankruptcy to avoid paying what is owed. Businesses extended credit to you in good faith. If you do not pay your bills, the creditor suffers the loss of income. By filing bankruptcy, you will jeopardize your financial future and will have difficulty getting credit in the future.

You complain to the finance company, but they tell you the television is the seller's responsibility. Legally, you owe the finance company regardless of the seller's performance.

The Preservation of Consumers' Claims and Defenses Ruling protects you in this type of situation. Under the ruling, you have a right to a legal defense in court if you refuse to pay a creditor because you have a dispute with a seller.

Bankruptcy Abuse Prevention and Consumer Protection Act

The main goal of the *Bankruptcy Abuse Prevention and Consumer Protection Act*, passed in 2005, was to make the bankruptcy system fairer to both debtors and creditors. However, it has been criticized for disproportionately benefiting the credit card industry.

The law made filing for Chapter 7 bankruptcy more difficult. Those who are allowed to file must pass a means test that takes into account factors such as income and assets. Those who do not pass the means test must file for Chapter 13 bankruptcy, which requires some repayment of debt. Another provision of the law requires debtors to get credit and financial counseling before filing for bankruptcy.

Credit Card Accountability and Disclosure Act of 2009

Also called the *Credit CARD Act of 2009*, this statute limited how credit card companies can charge consumers, but did not include price controls, fee limits, or caps on interest rates. It stated that credit companies must give their borrowers at least 21 days from the date the bill is mailed to pay their statement. The Credit CARD Act also states that companies cannot retroactively increase rates, companies must apply payments to a consumer's highest interest rate balance first, fees on cards given to those with bad credit are restricted, and applicants under the age of 21 are required to have proof of independent income or a cosigner. It also prohibits companies from mailing offers to customers under the age of 21 and from offering free T-shirts or other incentives to sign up at university-sponsored events.

Dodd-Frank Wall Street Reform and Consumer Protection Act

Passed in 2010, the Dodd-Frank Act increased regulation of the banking and financial services industry. Dodd-Frank was passed in response to the 2008 financial crisis and established multiple governmental agencies such as the Financial Stability Oversight Council and Orderly Liquidation Authority, which monitors the financial well-being of companies whose failure would negatively impact the nation's economy.

Employability Skills

Punctuality

Employees are expected to be on time to begin work each day. Employees should be at their workspaces, ready to work when the workday begins. It is not acceptable to arrive at the starting time, hang up your coat, talk to co-workers, and then go to the workstation. If the start time is 8:00 a.m., work should begin at 8:00 a.m. rather than 8:15 a.m. It is equally important to be on time to meetings scheduled throughout the day.

Those in favor of the act believe it will help prevent another financial crisis like that of 2008. Critics think it hurts economic growth and could lead to higher unemployment, lower wages, and less competiveness of US firms in foreign markets. Siding with the critics, Congress passed a bill in 2018 called the Economic Growth, Regulatory Relief, and Consumer Protection Act, which loosened some key provisions of the Dodd-Frank Act.

Credit Fraud

Credit fraud is the fraudulent use of someone else's credit information. It usually involves purchasing goods or services and charging them to an innocent person. Credit cards should be safeguarded.

- Do not throw away credit card receipts or monthly statements without shredding them.
- Permission should not be given to others to use your credit card or credit card number.
- Periodically, order a copy of your credit report from a credit-reporting agency. Promptly resolve any errors or negative results in the report.
- Carry only the credit cards you really need and use.
- Call credit card companies and other issuers promptly to report missing cards, and follow the call with written confirmation.
- Keep a list of all your credit cards with account numbers, expiration dates, and toll-free customer service phone numbers.
- File a police report if you are a victim of theft.
- Destroy cards that have expired.
- Do not give credit card information to people or businesses you do not know.
- Make online purchases only from companies that are reputable and that have a website that is secure with https:// in the URL. The "s" stands for secure.

bikeriderlondon/Shutterstock.com

Shredding credit card statements and other confidential papers can help a person avoid credit fraud.

If a person's credit cards are lost or stolen, the law offers some protection. The cardholder is responsible for only $50 in charges per card if someone else uses the cards. However, if a cardholder notifies the companies that issued the cards before someone else uses them, the cardholder cannot be held responsible for any charges. Figure 9-5 contains a list of ways that an identity thief can obtain your personal information.

Ways Identity Thieves Can Obtain Your Personal Information

- Stealing your wallet or purse.
- Stealing your mail and gaining access to bank statements, credit card statements, and brokerage account statements.
- Going through your trash and dumpster diving.
- Stealing personal information from business databases (for example, businesses such as medical care providers, lenders, and car dealers often have much of your personal information on file).
- Hacking into your personal computer or sending fraudulent e-mails.
- Bribing people who have access to your personal information.
- Using a cell phone camera to take pictures of your driver's license, credit card, or debit card.
- Diverting your mail to another address by filing a change of address form with the post office.
- Stealing your PIN at a gas station or grocery store point-of-sale (POS) system.
- Cloning your credit card number at restaurants and other businesses where sales are rung up out of your sight.
- Using a skimmer, which is a hard-to-detect electronic reader that criminals place on top of card readers that are built into gas pumps. The skimmer is able to copy card and PIN numbers, giving criminals free access to victims' accounts without interfering with the legitimate purchase of gas.

Goodheart-Willcox Publisher

Figure 9-5 There are many ways a person's identity can be stolen.

Section 9.2 Review

Check Your Understanding

1. What federal law requires lenders to fully disclose to consumers the terms and total cost of credit before a credit agreement is finalized?
2. What federal law was passed to prohibit creditors from discriminating against consumers?
3. What federal law was passed to eliminate abusive collection practices by debt collectors?
4. Which ruling, issued by the FTC, protects debtors from being forced to pay for products when they have a legitimate dispute with the product's seller?
5. What protection does the law offer if a person's credit cards are lost or stolen?

Build Your Vocabulary

As you progress through this course, develop a personal glossary. This will help you build your vocabulary and prepare you for a career. Write a definition for the following term and add it to your glossary.

credit fraud

Review and Assessment

Chapter Summary

Section 9.1 Wise Credit Use

- There are many ways to manage credit to avoid debt. One common guideline is the 20/10 rule. When managing credit, it is also helpful to know the applicable financial personality, be aware of overspending, recognize alternatives to using credit, and understand the importance of checking a credit report regularly.
- Misusing credit can lead to many serious financial problems. A person with a low credit score may be unable to get loans or credit cards, pay higher interest rates, and have fewer job prospects. If debt builds, borrowers must face collection agencies, repossession of property, and possibly bankruptcy.
- Two common types of bankruptcy include Chapter 7 and Chapter 13. Both forms are meant to help those in debt regain financial stability. However, bankruptcy can stay on an individual's credit report for up to 10 years so it is better to seek other alternatives first, such as a credit counseling service.

Section 9.2 Consumer Protection

- A number of federal laws have been passed to protect consumers when they use credit. Many state governments also have laws to protect consumers from illegal or unfair lending practices.
- Credit fraud usually involves purchasing goods or services and charging them to another person. Identity theft and phishing are two common types of credit fraud.

Review Your Knowledge

1. List advantages and disadvantages of using credit.
2. Discuss three ways to help manage credit.
3. Identify financial problems caused by the misuse of credit.
4. Explain the consequences of filing for bankruptcy.
5. What are some of the unfair lending practices that consumers are protected from by consumer credit laws?
6. What are your rights, according to the Fair Credit Reporting Act, if you are refused credit due to information supplied by a credit reporting agency?
7. List five ways the Electronic Funds Transfer Act protects consumers.
8. What are examples of methods of collecting debts that are prohibited by the Fair Debt Collection Practices Act?
9. Identify three ways you can protect yourself from identity theft.
10. Explain credit fraud.

Apply Your Knowledge

1. Make a list of purchases for which you would be comfortable using credit. Next, make a list of purchases you would *not* be comfortable making using credit. In your opinion, are there any exceptions to the advice, "credit cards should be used primarily for emergencies"? What could be the consequences of using credit for things that you listed?
2. There are many good reasons to use credit. However, when used unwisely, a person can create serious financial problems. What advice would you have for a friend who just opened a credit card for the first time?
3. Understanding your financial personality can help you as you start using credit for personal purchases. Using the Financial Personality questions in Figure 9-2, use a sheet of paper to answer the questions

honestly about yourself. After you are finished, evaluate your answers. Do you think you understand the importance of using credit wisely?

4. Deciding to use credit creates trade-offs and opportunity costs. The choice you make depends on three things: How important is making the purchase? Are you willing to use all or some of your savings to buy now? Can you save your money and buy later? Consider the use of credit for something expensive you would enjoy, such as an article of designer clothing or a vacation. Evaluate whether you should use credit to pay for it by answering these three questions. Did you decide to purchase in the near future or wait?
5. Do you think it is a good idea to only make the monthly minimum payment on credit bills? Why or why not?
6. Vince applied for credit at a local store to purchase a new flat-screen television. The salesperson said a down payment is not required and that monthly payments would be minimal. When Vince got the payment book for the loan, the amount of interest to be paid and how long it would take to pay off the loan was startling. The Truth in Lending Act requires creditors to tell consumers what credit will cost before they use it. What questions should Vince have asked before signing for the loan? Now that the purchase is complete and the loan extended, is there any recourse to this transaction?
7. The Fair Credit Billing Act protects consumers against unfair billing practices. It outlines the procedures to follow in resolving billing errors or disputes. You received your monthly credit card statement in the mail. While reviewing it, you notice that the statement shows a purchase you did not make. Write a letter to the credit card company to dispute the charge. In your letter, explain why you feel the charge is an error and the way you want this situation to be resolved.
8. The Fair Debt Collection Practices Act establishes legal protection from abusive or threatening debt collection practices. What should you do if a creditor is harassing you for late payment of a bill?
9. Bankruptcy is a serious step and should be taken only when it is the last resort. Compare and contrast Chapter 7 and Chapter 13 bankruptcy. What would you tell a person who is considering bankruptcy about the seriousness of the decision?
10. A friend of yours is throwing all of the statements for bills that have been paid in the trash. You reminded your friend to be careful about how the account numbers and personal information are disposed of because of the potential for credit fraud. Write dialog between you and your friend to raise awareness of the dangers of credit card fraud. Explain strategies that can be used to control personal information.

Apply Your Math Skills

1. The 20/10 rule states that an individual should never borrow more than 20 percent of annual take-home pay. Lupe's monthly take-home pay is $3,500. Calculate 20 percent of Lupe's annual net income to find a safe debt load. Next, determine the maximum monthly payment amount by calculating 10 percent of Lupe's monthly income.
2. Sidney has been considering the purchase of a used car that costs $10,000. Using the 20/10 rule, calculate how much money must be made to be able to comfortably afford to buy the car.

3. Marcus makes $400 every two weeks and uses a check cashing system to cash the check every payday. The system takes 1% of each paycheck in return for the service. If Marcus does this every two weeks for 3 years, how much money is lost to the check cashing store?

Communication Skills

Speaking. Select three of your classmates to participate in a group discussion. Acting as the team leader, name each person to a specific task such as time-keeper, recorder, etc. Discuss credit fraud as a group. Gain consensus from the other members on how to avoid being a victim of credit fraud. Keep the panel on task and promote democratic discussion.

Listening. Engage in a conversation with someone you have not spoken with before. Ask how the person manages personal credit. Actively listen to what that person is sharing. Build on those ideas by sharing your own. Try this again with other people you have not spoken to before. How clearly were the different people able to articulate themselves? How do you think having a conversation with someone you do not normally speak with is different from a conversation you might have with a friend or family member you speak with every day?

Reading. Analyze the quality of the information about using visuals that you found in this chapter. Is the information coherent? Is concrete evidence presented? Report your findings to the class.

Teamwork

With a small group of classmates, discuss how you will use credit in the future. What types of businesses will be involved in your use of credit? What is the maximum amount of credit debt you are willing to carry? Why did you choose that amount? Be prepared to share your discussion findings with the class.

Internet Research

Financial Calculator. Primary research is conducted by gathering information. Using the Internet, conduct a search for a credit card payment calculator. How many months would it take to pay $1,000 at an interest rate of 15% if you made monthly payments of $25? In general, how many months, or years, does it take to pay off credit?

Teen Credit Cards. How difficult is it for teens to obtain a credit card? Visit the website of a local bank and read the application process for credit cards. Do they offer credit cards to teens? What are the qualifications? Share your findings with the class.

Bankruptcy. Bankruptcy should only be considered a last resort when attempting to resolve financial problems. Conduct an Internet search for *bankruptcy laws*. Investigate how bankruptcy laws can help individuals get out of debt, as well as the specific consequences of declaring bankruptcy. Next, conduct an Internet search for avoiding bankruptcy. How can a person in financial distress avoid bankruptcy?

Portfolio Development

Testimonials. A *testimonial* is a formal statement from a teacher, customer, or other professional that certifies a person's qualifications or character. A testimonial focuses on a specific action a person executed that was exceptional in nature. The person writing the testimonial may not know you personally, but is validating the work or service you provided.

For example, if you work part-time at a computer store and help a customer set up a computer, the customer may be very happy with your work and may contact your supervisor through an e-mail with a testimonial that conveys appreciation for your work. If your employer forwards any positive written customer comments about you, save these for inclusion in your portfolio.

You may also have testimonials from instructors who made complimentary remarks on a paper you wrote or a project in which you participated. A former employer may have sent you an e-mail with congratulations on a personal accomplishment of yours. These are all testimonials that validate your abilities.

Newspaper articles that summarize a contribution, service, or personal accomplishment are also testimonials of your character, skills, and talents. Include newspaper articles in which you are the subject.

You can also include employer evaluations in your portfolio. Evaluations serve as a snapshot of your performance as an employee. They reflect your work habits, strengths, and contributions to an employer. If you decide to include an evaluation, be selective in the one you choose.

1. Sort through testimonials you have collected. Include assignments that have an instructor's written comments about your work. Print any e-mails from community members or other professionals who complimented your actions on something you did for that person. Attach notes to each document to identify (1) what it is and (2) why it is included in the portfolio. For example, a note on a research paper you wrote might say, "Research paper, Professor Dansby commenting on my writing skills." Be sure to update your master portfolio spreadsheet as you add testimonials to your portfolio.
2. If you have any evaluations from supervisors of any jobs you may have, review and decide if these would be appropriate to include.

CTSOs

Event Prep

Written Events. Many competitive events for career and technical student organizations (CTSOs) require students to write a paper and submit it either before the competition or when the student arrives at the event. Written events can be lengthy and take a lot of time to prepare, so it is important to start early.

To prepare for a written event, complete the following activities.

1. Read the guidelines provided by the organization. The topic to be researched will be specified in detail. Also, all final format guidelines will be given, including how to organize and submit the paper. Make certain you ask questions about any points you do not understand.
2. Do your research early. Research may take days or weeks, and you do not want to rush the process.
3. Set a deadline for yourself so that you write at a comfortable pace.
4. After you write the first draft, ask an instructor to review it for you and give feedback.
5. Once you have the final version, go through the checklist for the event to make sure you have covered all of the details. Your score will be penalized if you do not follow instructions.
6. To practice, visit your organization's website and select a written event in which you might be interested. Research the topic and then complete an outline. Create a checklist of guidelines that you must follow for this event. After you have completed these steps, decide if this is the event or topic that interests you. If you are still interested, move forward and start the writing process.

CHAPTER

10 Consumer Purchasing

Smart purchasing decisions can make $50 seem like $100. Individuals who study the marketplace, research products, and weigh marketing influences that influence consumer purchasing can get the most out of their dollars.

Applying a systematic decision-making process can help a person create an intelligent spending plan. A spending plan helps a consumer avoid impulse buying and make wise choices. It also helps analyze trade-offs and opportunity costs so that purchases stay within the budget.

Knowing what you want and seeking out reliable consumer information can help you make the right spending choices. Using these strategies can make your shopping experiences rewarding rather than frustrating.

Focus on Finance

Impulse Buying

Do you find yourself buying products you do not need? Impulse buying is making an unplanned purchase in the spur of the moment. To help avoid impulse buying, make a list of what you need and what you want. Identify why some of the products are needs and what consequences would come if you did not buy these products. You may decide some items on the list are not needs but wants.

Once you finalize your list, stay focused. If possible, pay with cash. Using credit can influence you to overspend. Using cash instead will help you control spending on things that you really do not need.

Life is not all about saving; it is also about enjoying things that make you happy. By making good buying decisions, you can enjoy purchasing items that will bring you real satisfaction.

College and Career Readiness

Reading Prep. Examine the visuals in the chapter before you read it. Write down questions you have about them. Try and answer the questions as you read.

Sections

Section 10.1	The Marketplace
Section 10.2	Consumer Purchasing Strategies

Andresr/Shutterstock.com

Section 10.1 The Marketplace

Essential Question

What is a marketplace in the free enterprise economy?

Objectives

After studying this section, you will be able to:

- Describe the marketplace in which consumers purchase goods and services.
- Identify different promotional strategies used by businesses to encourage consumers to purchase.

Terms

marketplace	consumer cooperative	coupon
brick-and-mortar store	price	rebate
telemarketing	promotion	loss leader
e-commerce	advertising	game of chance
m-commerce	deceptive advertising	high-pressure selling
t-commerce	buying incentive	conflict of interest

Marketplace

The **marketplace** is anywhere buyers and sellers meet to exchange goods, services, and money. Our free enterprise economy is characterized by free economic choice, the profit motive, and competition. Within the framework of these three characteristics, the forces of supply and demand create a vast arena of sellers and buyers.

Businesses in the marketplace can operate out of traditional brick-and-mortar stores. They can also operate as nontraditional enterprises.

Brick-and-Mortar Stores

Retail stores that sell directly from a physical location are **brick-and-mortar stores**. Stores may be independently owned and centered in one region, or they may be chain stores located across the country.

- *Department stores* sell a wide variety of goods and services in a single store. Departments include clothing, cosmetics, linens, shoes, jewelry, and more. These stores offer one-stop shopping plus a variety of customer services.
- *Specialty shops* sell a specific type of merchandise, such as shoes, toys, or gifts, or services, such as haircuts or portrait photography. Generally, these stores offer a broad selection of their specialty. The salespersons are well informed about goods and services they sell.

- *Superstores* specialize in specific products, such as electronics, sporting goods, foods, or office supplies. Others sell a wide variety of merchandise similar to the department stores.
- *Warehouse clubs* sell memberships to customers who want buying privileges. They usually offer a wide variety of wholesale merchandise at relatively low prices.
- *Discount stores* sell certain lines of merchandise at relatively low prices. Services such as deliveries, credit, and returns may be limited.

Deymos.HR/Shutterstock.com

A marketplace is anywhere buyers and sellers meet to exchange goods, services, and money.

- *Factory outlets* sell brand-name merchandise directly to consumers. Frequently, a variety of factory outlets will be located in an outlet mall. Outlet prices are usually lower than prices for the same merchandise in other stores.
- *Resale shops* sell used merchandise. Extras, such as warranties, guarantees, exchanges, and credit privileges, are rare; prices may be exceptionally low. It is important to inspect merchandise carefully to be sure items are in good condition. Thrift shops and consignment shops are two kinds of specialty resale shops.

Alternative Marketplaces

Nontraditional sellers provide goods and services without a brick-and-mortar location. Shopping from home saves time, energy, and fuel. However, the seller cannot be seen in person and the product cannot be inspected prior to purchase. Shipping costs are usually added to the price of the item in addition to local sales taxes.

Catalogs

Customers can use *catalogs* to order goods and services featured on their pages. It is important to check the reliability of the seller and to understand the policies on returns or exchanges.

Telemarketing

Telemarketing is the sale of merchandise by phone. Telemarketers sell everything from kitchen appliances to insurance to burial plots. Consumer protection laws require telemarketers to state clearly the company and caller name, the purpose of the call, and the type of goods or services being offered. They may not call before 8:00 a.m. or after 9:00 p.m. or misrepresent the goods and services they are selling.

If you do not wish to receive telemarketing calls, place your phone number on the Federal Trade Commission's *National Do Not Call Registry*. It is free to register a telephone number. Telemarketers are not allowed to call registered numbers.

Case Study Consumer Decisions

Morris needs a sleeping bag for a camping trip right after graduation. Research uncovers a website that advertises high-quality sleeping bags at reduced prices. The company also has a brick-and-mortar store that carries the same merchandise at a temporary discount. The store has a $150 down sleeping bag reduced to $100, a savings of $50.

Susan sees a similar website with marked-down sleeping bags. Being a planner, it makes sense to buy a sleeping bag now for the family camping trip next summer. The sleeping bag was originally $120 and reduced to $80. It seems like a good bargain although it costs one paycheck. However, the camping trip never occurs. The sleeping bag is still in a closet with the tags on. Susan loses $80.

Case Review

1. Explain whether Morris benefited from the sales promotion.
2. Explain whether Susan benefited from the sales promotion.
3. How could Morris apply the steps of the systematic decision-making process to the decision to purchase a sleeping bag?
4. How could Susan apply the steps of the systematic decision-making process to the decision to purchase a sleeping bag?

E-commerce

E-commerce (electronic commerce) is buying and selling goods and services over the Internet, as well as transferring money or data. It is used by both consumers and businesses to make purchases, trade merchandise, and countless other transactions for which products, services, or data are involved.

Some people look at e-commerce as online shopping; however, it is broader than just shopping. The word *commerce* is sometimes used interchangeably for the word *business*. For example, the web page of a business or organization is typically referred to as the *e-commerce site* as it provides information about the company business as well as potentially offering product or services for purchase.

M-commerce (mobile commerce) is any business activity that transpires using a mobile device. It is not limited to buying and selling goods and services but includes business transactions such as banking. Digital devices, such as cell phones and tablets, enable a user to conduct transactions anytime and anywhere that is convenient.

T-commerce (TV commerce) is buying and selling products and services using an interactive or smart television. The goal of t-commerce is to provide consumers the ability to purchase items they see marketed on television using a remote or other devices connected to their television.

Online Auctions

Online auctions offer items for sale to the highest bidder. Auctions are announced, and bidding closes at a preset time. The highest bidder is then able to purchase the item. Auction rules and regulations are typically provided to those who want to participate.

In person-to-person online auctions, buyers and sellers connect at the close by e-mail or telephone to arrange payment and delivery. In business-to-person auctions, the auction site controls payment and delivery arrangements.

You Do the Math Multiplication

The number that is going to be multiplied by another number is called the *multiplicand*. The number by which the multiplicand is multiplied is called the *multiplier*. Many times, you will not need as precise of a number as the calculation provides. To round a number, locate the value place to which you want to round. Then, look at the digit to the right of this place. If the digit to the right is less than 5, do nothing to the value place to which you are rounding.

Solve the following problems.

1. A bike shop has a bicycle on clearance sale for $265. That same bike is available from a web-based business for $220. The sales tax rate for both is 6 percent. The Internet business charges $25 for shipping and handling. The bike shop bicycles are assembled free of charge. The bike available online is shipped unassembled. It costs $35 to have someone put it together. Which offer is a better deal?
2. Store A has flip-flops on sale at two pairs for $5.50. Store B has them on sale for 25 percent off their normal price of $3.50 a pair. Store C gives you one free pair of flip-flops if you buy a pair at the regular price of $5.
   A. How much do the flip-flops cost per pair at each store?
   B. Which store has flip-flops at the lowest price per pair?
   C. Which store charges the highest price?

Before buying or selling at an online auction site, download a copy of the Federal Trade Commission publication entitled *Internet Auctions, A Guide for Buyers and Sellers*. This publication details auction rules, payment options, types of fraud, tips for buyers and sellers, and information on where to find help if problems with a transaction occur. Educating yourself is the best way to protect yourself against potential incidents of theft or fraud.

Consumer Cooperatives

A **consumer cooperative** is a nonretail association owned and operated by a group of members for their own benefit rather than for profit. Members contribute services and pay dues to participate in the cooperative. Prices usually are lower than in retail stores. However, merchandise and customer services are limited to what the membership can provide.

Marketing Strategies That Influence Consumer Purchasing

Businesses in the marketplace exist to sell products and make a profit. The purpose of the market is to arrive at a transaction and price that is acceptable to both seller and buyer. Businesses use a number of marketing strategies to increase sales and profits. Examples of strategies include price, sales promotions, and personal selling.

Price

Price is the amount of money requested in exchange for a product. The *selling price* is the price a consumer will pay for a product.

Many economic factors affect the prices of products. When the supply of a specific item is greater than demand, prices fall. When demand is greater than the supply, prices rise. Rising prices tend to encourage more production and increase supply, which lowers demand. Falling prices tend to discourage production and decrease supply, which increases demand. To encourage purchases, retailers sometimes use these psychological pricing strategies.

- *Odd pricing* is when the price ends in an odd number, such as $19.99. Consumers perceive the price to be lower than it actually is.
- *Even pricing* is when the price ends in an even number, usually zero. Customers perceive products with even prices to be of high quality.
- *Prestige pricing* sets prices high to send the message of status and quality.
- *Buy one, get one (BOGO) pricing* gives customers a free or discounted product when another one is purchased for the full price. This makes customers feel like they are getting a bargain.
- *Price lining* sets various levels of prices on similar products to convey different levels of quality. For example, three similar styles of athletic shoes might sell for $40, $50, and $60, conveying "good," "better," and "best," respectively.
- *Bundle pricing* combines two or more products for one price, which is usually lower than if the items were purchased separately. This strategy conveys value and money saved.

lightpoet/Shutterstock.com

Many economic factors affect the prices of products, such as supply and demand.

Promotion

Promotion is the process of communicating with potential customers in an effort to influence their buying behavior. Types of promotion include advertising, sales promotions, and selling.

Advertising

Advertising is any paid public announcement promoting the sale of a good or service. The goal of the advertiser is to send a message to the consumer in the hopes of making a sale. There are two types of advertising: product and institutional. *Product advertising* sells a product. *Institutional advertising* promotes an organization, such as a business, rather than just the product.

Direct mail advertising includes advertising circulars, catalogs, coupons, and other unsolicited offers that arrive through mail or another delivery service.

Some techniques used by advertisers to convince consumers to buy their products are as follows.

- *Green ads* associate the use of a good or service with saving the planet, conserving resources, or some other environmental benefit. Key words may include *natural*, *organic*, *pure*, *green*, and *healthful*.

- *Humor* uses a funny character, picture, or situation to get attention.
- *Insecurity* appeals to the consumer desire to be popular and attractive.
- *Testimonials* show real people using a good or service.
- *Celebrity endorsements* use famous personalities to promote products.
- *Bandwagon* commercials try to show that a product is fashionable or trendy; everyone is buying it.
- *Puffery* uses exaggerated claims about a good or service.
- *Nostalgia* is associating a good or service with the "good old days," childhood memories, or a time when life was simpler and more satisfying.
- *Statistics* that are shocking or provocative may be used in advertisements.

There is an art to reading an ad or hearing a commercial. Look for information you can use, such as:

- factual descriptions of goods or services offered for sale;
- listings and demonstrations of special product features and qualities;
- descriptions of the differences between advertised items and similar ones on the market; and
- details on prices, availability, places to buy, special offers, and terms of sale.

Words or terms that should alert a consumer to possible deception are *free*, *one-time offer*, and *valued at*. When an offer sounds too good to be true, it probably is.

Although law prohibits false and misleading advertising, expect some exaggerated claims. **Deceptive advertising** is information that purposely misleads a consumer through dishonest claims. Illegal or unethical businesses should be reported to the local Better Business Bureau, chamber of commerce, or office of the Federal Trade Commission.

An *infomercial* is a paid television program designed to sell a service or good. The aim is to sell directly to the viewer via interactive television or by telephone. Infomercials are usually program-length advertisements that resemble actual television programming. The products being promoted, such as cosmetics, kitchenwares, or exercise equipment, are often demonstrated. Sellers may offer easy payments, risk-free trials, or claim limited availability to encourage viewers to buy immediately. While infomercials can offer valuable product information, conduct your own research before deciding to buy.

Sales Promotions

Businesses hold special sales and promotions to attract customers and increase sales. When price reductions and promotions increase sales and profits, they benefit the seller. By purchasing a necessary item on sale, the consumer benefits as well. However, if special sales persuade you to buy what you do not need, you lose. To take advantage of sales and promotions, follow these suggestions.

- Know your wants and needs with or without sales.
- Stay within your budget.
- Anticipate reduced prices, such as preseason specials and end-of-season sales.
- Control the urge to buy what you do not need or want just because it is on sale.

Consumers should know the meaning of the terms frequently used to sell merchandise. Some of these terms are explained in Figure 10-1.

Buying Incentives. A **buying incentive** is a special offer by sellers designed to help sell goods and services. They include loyalty cards, coupons, contests, games, rebates, premiums, and prizes. Consumers benefit from this form of selling as long as they limit purchases to the goods and services that are ordinarily needed. It is unwise for a consumer to buy something that is not really wanted or needed just to get loyalty points, use a coupon, or win a prize.

A **coupon** is a printed or electronic offer giving a discount for goods or services bought before a certain date. Coupons are given as incentives to purchase a new product or increase sales of established products. They are often found in magazines, newspapers, and e-mail blasts. They can also sometimes be found on store websites.

A **rebate** is a cash back offer. For example, a seller advertises a $75 rebate on the purchase of a $600 television. Ideally, the buyer sends the proof-of-purchase to the manufacturer and receives the $75 rebate. However, rebates usually come with rules and deadlines and sometimes have complicated instructions. Before you make a spending decision because of a rebate, study the offer carefully.

Two-for-one offers, bargain buys, and other forms of special pricing are also buying incentives. Some sellers offer loss leaders to bring customers into the store. A **loss leader** is an item priced at or below cost to attract buyers in the expectation that they will purchase other merchandise as well.

Contests and sweepstakes are games of chance sponsored by a business to engage prospective customers. **Game of chance** means that the participant must wager something to win. The wager might mean that a customer must buy a chance to win or submit personal information to enter. Contests require customer participation so the business can capture data for future campaigns or customer research.

Customer loyalty programs are popular buying incentives. These programs usually issue a frequent buyer card to the customer. The customer can then earn points with each purchase for future gifts or discounts at the store.

Sales Terms	
Term	**Description**
clearance sale	Merchandise price has been reduced from previous prices
closeout sale	Merchandise is being discontinued or is no longer being produced
going-out-of-business sale	Seller is closing its business and selling goods at reduced prices to hasten the closing; sellers cannot legally use this phrase if they are not closing
introductory offer	New merchandise is selling at a price that will increase after the initial offer
liquidation	Merchandise is selling at reduced prices in order to aid in converting inventory to cash

Goodheart-Willcox Publisher

Figure 10-1 These terms are frequently used to sell merchandise to consumers.

Exploring Careers

Sales Representative

Wholesale companies and manufacturers need people to present products to potential buyers in a positive way. Sales representatives present, demonstrate, and sell the company's products to both businesses and individuals. Some examples of tasks that sales representatives perform include:

- identify potential customers by following leads, attending trade shows and conferences, and using business directories
- monitor competitors' products, prices, and sales statistics
- determine which products to recommend based on customer needs and interests
- demonstrate products and explain their features
- provide price quotes, terms, warranties, and potential delivery dates

Sales representatives usually work in a specific territory which may require frequent traveling to maintain. They must have an excellent knowledge not only of their own products, but also of competitors' products, and should understand the principles of promoting and selling products. Sales representatives should enjoy working with people and need to have good communication skills. Most jobs in this field require on-the-job experience, training in a vocational school, or an associate degree.

Packaging and Displays. Packaging can be a powerful selling tool. In addition to appearance, products may sell for their convenience features or their ecological claims. Convenience innovations include boil-in-the-bag foods, juice boxes, squeezable bottles and tubes, resealable bags, pull-tab cans, and spray containers. Ecological selling terms include *recyclable* and *sustainable*.

Experts carefully plan and study every aspect of a product's presentation, from its color and size to its name and labels. Studies indicate that items displayed at floor level attract the least notice. When the same products are raised to waist level, sales increase by almost 60 percent. At eye level, they jump almost 80 percent.

Products a consumer is likely to buy without thinking are often placed near the checkout counter. These products may also be in display racks in the aisles where they can be picked up with ease.

Staples in the supermarket, such as dairy products, breads, meat, poultry, and produce, will be located well into the store. Nonessentials will be near the front. This way, consumers are drawn into and through the store and are likely to see and buy more products than intended.

Selling

In a system where the survival of a business depends largely on attracting consumers, selling plays an important role. Selling directly to customers is an important strategy that influences consumer purchasing. Knowledgeable salespeople should know how different brands and models compare and what features are most important. They should also know when new merchandise is

mangostock/Shutterstock.com

An important strategy that influences consumer purchasing is personal selling.

expected, when sales are scheduled, and a host of other facts that can help you make sound buying decisions.

While most businesses are honest and fair, some may use questionable selling methods to increase their sales and profits. **High-pressure selling** is attempting to convince a buyer to make a quick decision. To a certain extent, a conflict of interest exists between buyers and sellers because they both want different things. A **conflict of interest** is a situation in which a buyer and a seller have competing goals. Businesses want to sell as many products as they can at the highest price they can get. They want to be able to pay business expenses and make a good profit. Consumers want the product that best fits their needs at the lowest possible price. They want to have money left over to spend on other items. In other words, sellers want to get the highest price possible for all their products, while consumers want the best quality at the lowest price.

The free-market system helps resolve the conflict of interest between sellers and buyers. Both profits earned by the seller and prices paid by the buyer are tied to the forces of supply and demand. Everyone depends on these forces to achieve the proper balance between profits and prices. The system strives to create a supply of goods and services to meet demand at prices that will keep the producer in business and the buyer able to buy.

Section 10.1 Review

Check Your Understanding

1. What is the difference between brick-and-mortar stores and nontraditional sellers?
2. List some examples of traditional brick-and-mortar stores.
3. What are some examples of marketing strategies that businesses use to persuade customers to purchase?
4. Name two types of advertising that businesses use to persuade customers to purchase.
5. What is the difference between a coupon and a rebate offer?

Build Your Vocabulary

As you progress through this course, develop a personal glossary. This will help you build your vocabulary and prepare you for a career. Write a definition for each of the following terms and add it to your glossary.

marketplace	advertising
brick-and-mortar store	deceptive advertising
telemarketing	buying incentive
e-commerce	coupon
m-commerce	rebate
t-commerce	loss leader
consumer cooperative	game of chance
price	high-pressure selling
promotion	conflict of interest

Section 10.2

Consumer Purchasing Strategies

Objectives

After studying this section, you will be able to:

- Explain how to research and evaluate information about a good or service.
- List and explain the steps of the decision-making process as they apply to consumer purchases.
- Discuss the importance of planning before making a purchase.

Essential Question

Why is it important to use a systematic decision-making process when making purchases of goods or services?

Terms

research	overspending	implied fitness
comparison shopping	spending plan	express warranty
unit price	durable goods	full warranty
labeling law	nondurable goods	limited warranty
testing and rating service	warranty	extended warranty
review	implied warranty	obsolete
impulse buying	implied merchantability	

Conducting Research

The marketplace offers consumers both the privilege and the challenge of making free economic choices. You are free to choose how to earn a living and what to do with your money. You can choose to pay cash or use credit. You can decide to spend or save. Free choice offers the opportunity to decide for yourself how to get the most of your money.

Syda Productions/Shutterstock.com

Consumers who have used a product can tell you about their personal experiences with goods, services, and sellers.

One way to have a positive impact on the costs and benefits related to purchasing is to perform research before you buy. **Research** is the process of gathering information. The information needed to be an informed consumer includes constantly changing facts and figures. Products, services, laws, and economic conditions can change substantially from year to year. There is no substitute for reliable information. As goods, services, and markets become more varied and complex, knowledge is ever more important.

Another method of learning about products is to comparison shop. **Comparison shopping** is the process of gathering information about products to find the best option among similar products. When comparison shopping, look at the price, quality, performance, and other information that is important to you. The **unit price** of a product is the cost per unit, weight, or measure. The unit price is usually listed on the shelf where products are displayed. Unit pricing helps a consumer find the best values by comparing the price per unit of similar items. When comparison shopping, also consider store policies concerning returns, exchanges, credit, and customer satisfaction.

Finding Information

Knowing how to find, evaluate, and use available information can help you become a wise consumer. Information needed to make the best buying decisions comes from a variety of sources.

- *Labels and Hangtags.* Information about the content, quality, performance, care, and maintenance of products appears on labels and hangtags. A **labeling law** is a governmental regulation that requires certain information be placed on labels for certain products. Governmental labeling requirements are described in Figure 10-2.
- *Testing and Rating Services.* A **testing and rating service** is a group or organization that tests products and rates them according to certain criteria. They evaluate features and compare different models and brands of similar goods and services. Figure 10-3 lists questions to ask when evaluating the testing and rating of a product. Two common forms of testing and rating results are seals of approval or certification and ratings in consumer publications. A common seal is shown and explained in Figure 10-4.
- *Customer Reviews.* A **review** is a critical report about an item. Friends, relatives, neighbors, and other consumers who have used a good or service

Governmental Labeling Requirements

- Clothing and textile products must be labeled with clear and complete care information, fiber content, the name of the distributor or manufacturer, and the country of origin.
- Food packages must carry a list of ingredients, the name and address of the manufacturer, the quantity by weight and number of servings, and specific nutritional information. Look also for the nutritive values, grade and quality levels, expiration dates, and preparation and storage instructions.
- Drugs and cosmetics must be labeled with ingredients, directions for use, and cautions against misuse. Laundry supplies, household cleaning agents, pesticides, and herbicides must be labeled with directions for safe use and disposal. They also should contain warnings against hazards of misuse.
- Products intended for use by children should include age-of-user advice on their labels, such as "suitable for ages four to six" or "not recommended for children under three years old."

Goodheart-Willcox Publisher

Figure 10-2 Labeling laws are governmental regulations that require specific information to be stated on the labels of different types of products.

can tell you about their personal experiences with goods, services, and sellers. Many websites have reviews of products that have been posted by other customers.

Evaluating Information

When researching a product, begin by seeking material that is up to date and easy to understand. Research may reveal recent developments on the product, such as a new software update that has been released. It may help to consider the subjects that are being discussed. For example, if there have been media reports of a car manufacturer not honoring warranties, consider not buying products made by that company. It is also important to evaluate whether the information found is complete. Does it tell what you need to know?

When evaluating information, consider the source. Consider the reliability and credibility of the sources you use. Spending decisions, especially major ones, should be based on information that is accurate and complete. Ask yourself these questions.

- What are the source's credentials?
- What is the reputation of the source of information?
- Is the source from the mainstream media or unknown?
- Is the information current?

Evaluating Testing and Rating Services
• Who sponsored or conducted the testing? Are the ratings objective? • Were product performance and important features tested? • What test methods were used and under what conditions? • What do the test results or ratings mean? • When were the products tested, and which models were included? • What important factors are not included in testing?

Goodheart-Willcox Publisher

Figure 10-3 Before relying on information from testing and rating services, answer these questions.

The Seal	Where It Is Found	What It Means
	On appliances, computer equipment, furnaces, heaters, fuses, smoke detectors, fire extinguishers, and thousands of other products.	Products passed initial tests and periodic factory evaluations, indicating they continue to meet UL standards for safety.

Goodheart-Willcox Publisher

Figure 10-4 The Underwriters Laboratories, Inc. seal indicates that an appliance meets specific performance and safety standards.

- If data are presented, how were they collected and what is the source?
- Can the information be validated through other reliable sources?

Determine whether the information is intended to inform the buyer or to sell a product. Both news articles and advertisements can offer useful information, but ads generally present only positive, sometimes exaggerated facts. If your main source of product information is intended to sell the product, such as a manufacturer's website, attempt to find an objective review.

Applying Systematic Decision-Making

Consumers in the free marketplace make their own spending choices. The way they make these choices determines what their money will buy. Getting the most satisfaction for the dollars spent requires careful decision-making in the marketplace.

As you learned in Chapter 1, systematic decision-making can help when facing important choices. It is a process of choosing a course of action after evaluating information, weighing the costs and benefits of alternative actions, and considering the consequences.

Every economic decision has consequences. The choices consumers make involve trade-offs and opportunity costs. A *trade-off* is the choice given up when a different choice is made. An *opportunity cost* is the value of the option that was given up. Since money is a limited resource, spending it now means trading off the opportunity to spend it later. Spending money on one purchase means giving up the opportunity to spend that money on something else. The decision-making process in Figure 10-5 is a useful tool for making these purchasing decisions.

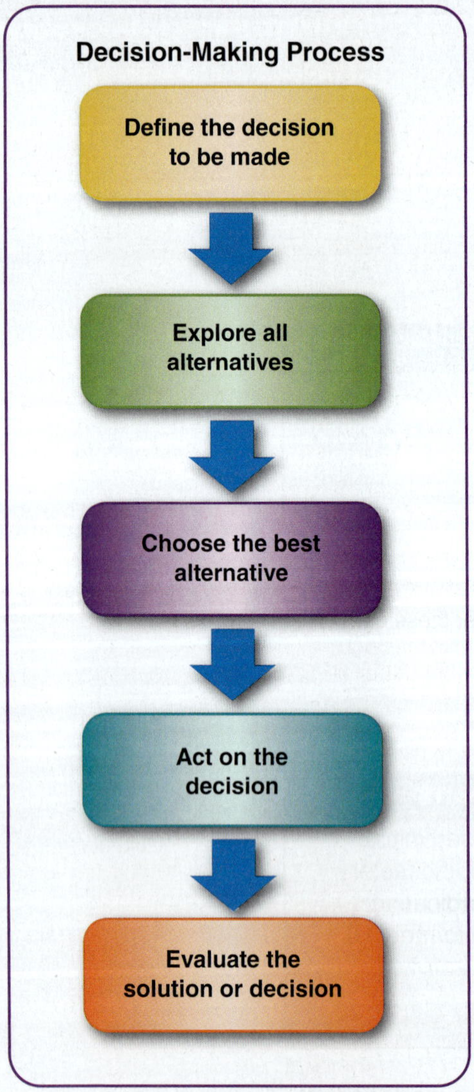

Goodheart-Willcox Publisher

Figure 10-5 The five steps of the decision-making process can be a helpful tool when making decisions.

Step 1: Identify the Decision to Be Made

To begin the decision-making process, identify the decision that needs to be made. In a purchasing situation, the decision is to identify what you want to purchase. Goods and services are purchased to meet a person's needs and wants. *Needs* are necessities a person must have to survive. *Wants* are things that a person desires but can live without. Once you have identified the purchase, you can determine whether it meets a need or want. When it comes to spending, you may treat needs and wants differently. For example, you might choose to spend more for a high-quality brand that satisfies a need and less on an item that satisfies a want. Some decisions are simple and routine, such as what brand of cereal to buy. Other decisions are complicated and take much thought, like buying a used car.

Your values will also play a role in decision making. *Values* are principles and beliefs that a person considers important.

Economics in Action

Consumer Spending

Except for a few brief periods, the late 20th and early 21st centuries were prosperous times for most Americans. Unemployment and inflation were low. Climbing stock market levels created wealth for most investors. Homeowners benefited from rising property values. Taxes were low. During these prosperous times, Americans spent more than they saved. Consumer spending was high, and people used credit to buy more goods and services.

In 2020, the US economy went into a recession. Businesses suffered and laid off workers. Unemployment climbed. Consumers stopped spending and focused on paying off debt and saving money. People delayed major purchases with hopes of better times ahead.

Although saving is a good financial strategy for individuals, strong consumer spending is crucial to the health of the American economy in a recession. Spending helps create demand for goods and services and contributes to the profit and success of businesses. Individual spending may not be major in creating a demand for a specific product. However, as a group, consumers determine the success or failure of specific businesses.

Some values are related to money and can have a major impact on the choices you make.

Step 2: Explore the Alternatives

Explore the alternatives for the purchase and research choices. Businesses compete with one another and as a result, the same or similar goods and services are sold by a wide variety of businesses. Comparison shopping will help you evaluate the pros and cons of each option. Choosing a reliable seller and finding the best product for the best price is a challenge. It is necessary to learn something about the sellers as well as the products.

Your income and overall budget will have a significant impact on the options available to you. While exploring alternatives, consider your overall financial situation and the value you place on responsible spending decisions. A cost-benefit analysis will weigh the costs of purchasing the product against the benefits of owning it. If you are considering two or more options, decide what the trade-off is of buying one product over the others. Purchase the product only if the benefits are at least as great as the costs.

When considering the alternatives, also take into consideration your personal priorities, standards, and available resources. Each of these factors will affect how you choose to allocate your money to satisfy needs and wants.

Step 3: Make a Choice

Once the research is complete and you are ready to make the purchase, you can decide where to purchase the product and method of payment. Using credit will add to the overall cost of the purchase. Before making a commitment, figure

Ethics

Merchandise Returns

It is unethical to return the merchandise to the store that you have already used. Do not repackage the item and pretend that you have not used it. Unless the merchant states that used products are permissible to be returned, accept your loss and keep the item you purchased.

out how much more money it will cost to buy using credit. You may decide to wait and save up until you can pay for the purchase with cash.

Step 4: Implement the Decision

Once the decision is made, implement the decision by making the purchase. Follow any instructions that come with products regarding use, care, and maintenance. This will extend the useful life of the purchase and your satisfaction having made it. Receipts, sales slips, and any other paperwork for possible returns or exchanges should be kept to ensure the product is eligible for warranty protection.

Step 5: Evaluate the Purchase

After you have used the goods or services for some time, evaluate the product and your decision-making process. Are you satisfied with your choice? What did you learn that will be helpful when you are ready to make another major purchase? What would you do differently? Review the purchase to see if you met the goal that you intended and whether the purchase meets your expectations.

Planning to Spend

Some of the worst consumer problems are caused by lack of planning. When consumers fail to plan ahead, they lack direction for their spending. They do not set goals for the use of income or build savings for future needs. Lack of planning also makes it difficult to control the use of credit. Consumers who do not plan ahead often have trouble paying routine monthly bills.

Poor planners often find it difficult to save enough for big expenses, such as a car, a home, an education, or retirement. They often make purchases that do not meet their needs and wants. Careful planning is the only way you can take charge of your financial well-being. It allows you to match the highs and lows of expenses with the highs and lows of income over a lifetime. Even informed consumers sometimes indulge in impulsive or thoughtless spending. Others habitually overspend, which can lead to debts that are difficult to repay.

Impulse buying is making a purchase without first considering needs, goals, or the consequences of spending money. When done regularly, this type of spending can consume a sizable amount of money. Thoughtful spending will leave more money for needs and wants that are truly important.

Overspending is spending more money than a person can afford to spend. Overspending happens easily when using credit cards. You cannot spend more cash than you have with you. You think more carefully before making a purchase. A budget or spending plan can help control spending.

Making sound spending decisions works to your advantage. A **spending plan** is a strategy to help an individual make smart choices and get the most out of money. This type of planning provides a framework for making decisions. Spending plans need to fit into an overall budget that is tailored to an individual's specific income and needs. A spending plan can incorporate both routine buying decisions, like groceries, as well as big purchases.

The following are some ways to implement a spending plan.

- Keep track of both cash and credit spending. When using credit, keep track of purchases and limit total charges to an amount you can pay on time.
- When paying by mail, send a check or money order; never send cash. This is safer and it gives you a record of the payment.
- Use product information before making a final decision. Read labels, hangtags, seals, and manuals for quality and performance features. Look for information about the price and any extra costs for delivery, installation, upkeep, and servicing.
- For certain goods, it may pay to buy in quantity. When buying in quantity, make sure the merchandise will keep. Only buy what you can conveniently use and store.
- Try to plan purchases to match the timing of sales. Seasonal sales usually offer the best buys. Ask about return and exchange policies on sale items. If a product is marked "second," "irregular," or "as is," it may be flawed in some way.
- Consider the value of time and energy as well as money. The price of a product may be less at a local retail store than on the Internet. Ordering the product online, however, may be worth saving the time rather than paying a lower price.
- When purchasing food, refer to *2020-2025 Dietary Guidelines for Americans* developed by the US Department of Agriculture to help you make healthful choices.
- When eating out, you pay for someone to buy, prepare, and serve the food. Consider how much and how often you want to pay someone else to purchase and cook food for you. Before choosing a restaurant, find out about the type of food served and the prices. Websites often provide menus with prices.

Purchasing goods and services can be a large part of a person's budget. **Durable goods** are items that do not wear out quickly. An item is considered a durable good when it can be used for three years or more. Examples include autos, appliances, and furniture. **Nondurable goods** are items that are used up immediately in one use or that will wear out in fewer than three years. Examples of nondurable goods include food, cosmetics, fuel, paper products, and clothing. When deciding how to spend your money, consider how long you will use the product and when it must be replaced.

Africa Studio/Shutterstock.com

Furniture is an example of durable goods.

When making major purchases, review warranties, service contracts, and product safety. Also consider product obsolescence and when and if the product will be out of style as soon as you purchase it.

Warranties

A **warranty** is a guarantee that a product will meet certain performance and quality standards. The warranty provides for specific remedies if the product does not live up to stated promises. Warranties are normally included in the purchase price. Most warranties cover products for a stated period of time, such as 90 days or one year. Warranties do not protect against failure caused by misuse of a product. Proof of purchase is usually needed to receive warranty service.

By law, a consumer has the right to read product warranty promises before purchasing an item. Product warranties can be implied warranties or expressed warranties. Additional warranty coverage can also be purchased separately.

Implied Warranties

An **implied warranty** is an unwritten promise about a product and its use. Two types of implied warranties that apply to most products are those of implied merchantability and implied fitness.

Implied merchantability is an unwritten guarantee that a product is what it is called and does what its name implies. A computer printer must print documents; a heater must produce heat. The product must be in working order.

Implied fitness is an unwritten promise that a product must be fit for any performance or purpose promised by the seller. If a salesperson or hangtag suggests roller skates are for outdoor use, they must be fit for outdoor skating. Implied warranties apply to the condition of a product at the point-of-sale.

They cover defects that are present but may not be obvious at the time of purchase.

takayuki/Shutterstock.com

A warranty is a guarantee that a product will meet certain performance and quality standards.

Express Warranties

An **express warranty** is one that is clearly stated and can be written or verbal. Express warranties may be full or limited. A **full warranty** completely covers the repair or replacement of any defect in a product. A full warranty must provide the following:

- free repair or replacement of defective products or parts
- repair or replacement within a reasonable time
- no unreasonable demands on you as a condition of receiving repairs or replacement
- replacement if a number of attempted repairs fail
- transfer of coverage to a new owner if the product changes hands during the warranty period

A **limited warranty** is a guarantee for service, repairs, and replacements only under certain conditions. The purchaser may be required to pay labor costs or handling charges. It may only cover repairs and not replacement. It may also require return of the product to the seller or an authorized service center for warranty servicing.

Extended Warranties

On major appliances, autos, or electronic products, the seller often offers an extended warranty for an additional cost. An **extended warranty** covers servicing and repairs that may be required after the initial warranty expires. An extended warranty is also known as a *warranty service contract*. Before you buy this type of protection, consider the following questions.

- Does it cover services already guaranteed in the original warranty?
- What is the cost? Is it necessary to pay a deductible?
- What is covered by the agreement and what must be done to obtain the services promised? Must proof of maintenance be submitted?
- What would repair services cost without it? Is it less expensive to simply replace the product if it fails?
- Who provides the warranty service? How can that person or company be contacted?
- Will the offer be available for purchase at a later date or after the manufacturer warranty expires?

Extended warranties are often expensive. It might be more economical to buy one directly from the manufacturer rather than the retailer. They are often available for both electronic products and home appliances. These contracts cover repair services that may be needed beyond the warranty period. For appliances, warranty servicing usually is adequate.

Employability Skills

Cultural Competency

Cultural competency is the acknowledgement of cultural differences and the ability to adapt one's communication style to successfully send and receive messages despite those differences. The first step in becoming culturally competent involves recognizing cultural barriers. Being aware of potential disruptions is the best way to prevent or avoid them. The second step of cultural competency involves the willingness to adapt to those barriers.

Product Safety

Electronics and home appliances should have seals and labels showing that products meet safety standards. For example, the UL seal of Underwriters Laboratories, Inc. indicates that products have been tested for electrical, thermal, and fire hazards.

Product Obsolescence

Most products eventually break or outlive their usefulness, making them obsolete. **Obsolete** means something is no longer useful because a newer version exists. Obsolescence gives manufacturers the opportunity to introduce new products and increase sales. Consumers benefit when obsolete products are replaced by something better. "Better" can mean cheaper, more powerful, more efficient, or with more features.

NAR studio/Shutterstock.com

Products become obsolete when they are replaced by something cheaper, more powerful, more efficient, or with more features.

Obsolescence also benefits producers because it stimulates demand. The more often consumers replace an outdated product with a new one, the more they buy overall. Consumer electronic products are especially susceptible to obsolescence because of the constant new developments in technology. Companies also strive to outdo each other in competitive markets. Every company wants to introduce something new.

Planned obsolescence occurs when products are designed to become obsolete or to break down after a certain amount of time or use. Obsolescence is created in the following ways.

- *Discontinued parts, refills, or service.* If consumers cannot have a product fixed, they are forced to buy a new one.
- *Discontinued upgrades.* Consumers must buy a new product when the older one cannot use the latest upgrades and applications. For example, newer computer software programs often require more memory than older computers possess.
- *Parts wear out or break.* Use of cheap, breakable parts during manufacturing can cause a product to wear out sooner.
- *Superficial design changes.* Consumers may be convinced they need to buy new products because they are better looking, more fashionable, or trendy. In the clothing and footwear market, for example, new trends quickly make current fashions obsolete.

Because there are new product developments each year, find out what is new on the market before buying. Carefully consider the benefits versus the costs before upgrading to a new model or product.

Section 10.2 Review

Check Your Understanding

1. What are some sources of information a consumer can use when conducting research on products?
2. List the steps in the decision-making process.
3. Name two basic types of product warranties.
4. What is covered by an extended warranty?
5. Provide an example of how a seller creates obsolescence.

Build Your Vocabulary

As you progress through this course, develop a personal glossary. This will help you build your vocabulary and prepare you for a career. Write a definition for each of the following terms and add it to your glossary.

research
comparison shopping
unit price
labeling law
testing and rating service
review
impulse buying
overspending
spending plan
durable goods
nondurable goods
warranty
implied warranty
implied merchantability
implied fitness
express warranty
full warranty
limited warranty
extended warranty
obsolete

Review and Assessment

Chapter Summary

Section 10.1 The Marketplace

- Buyers and sellers meet to exchange goods, services, and money in the marketplace. Within the marketplace, businesses can operate out of traditional brick-and-mortar stores. They can also be nontraditional sellers which include catalogs, telemarketing, t-commerce, m-commerce, e-commerce, Internet auctions, and consumer cooperatives.
- Marketing strategies that influence consumer purchasing include pricing and promotions. While many economic factors affect the price of products, sellers often employ psychological pricing practices to entice buyers. Promotion is the process of communicating with potential customers in an effort to influence their buying behavior. Types of promotion include advertising, sales promotions, and selling.

Section 10.2 Consumer Purchasing Strategies

- One way to have a positive impact on the costs and benefits related to purchasing is to perform research before you buy. Comparison shopping is one way to gather information about products to find the best option. Labels and hangtags, testing and rating services, and customer reviews are also sources of information. Knowing how to find, evaluate, and use available information can help you become a wise consumer.
- Consumers make spending choices that determine what their money will buy. Getting the most satisfaction for the dollars spent requires careful action in the marketplace. Systematic decision-making can be applied to purchasing decisions to assure that the best choice has been made.
- A spending plan provides a framework for making decisions. Planning for the use of money can help prevent consumer mistakes such as impulse buying and overspending. Before making a decision, consider how warranties, service contracts, product safety, and product obsolescence may affect the decision to buy.

Review Your Knowledge

1. Describe the marketplace in which consumers purchase goods.
2. What are some pricing techniques used by businesses to encourage customers to purchase product?
3. Identify and explain three types of promotion used by businesses.
4. List and describe some of the advertising techniques used to convince consumers to buy a product.
5. Provide examples of buying incentives.
6. Describe the role selling plays in persuading customers to purchase products.
7. Explain how a consumer can evaluate information about a good or service.
8. List and explain the steps of the decision-making process as they apply to consumer purchases.
9. Describe ways to implement a spending plan.
10. Explain the two categories of product warranties.

Apply Your Knowledge

1. The marketplace is anywhere buyers and sellers meet to exchange goods, services, and money. At what types of businesses

in the marketplace do you or the members of your household typically shop? Which types do you prefer, and why?

2. In the marketplace, the goal of sellers is to influence buyers to spend their money. What marketing strategies used by businesses affect your spending habits?
3. Psychological pricing strategies include odd, even, prestige, buy-one-get-one, and bundle strategies. Make a list of these strategies. Next to each one, identify how it influences a person's buying behavior. Then list a store or other seller that uses this strategy.
4. Advertising techniques include green ads, humor, insecurity, testimonials, celebrity endorsements, bandwagon, puffery, nostalgia, and statistics. Think about one of your favorite advertisements, such as a television commercial, billboard, or magazine ad. Write down the product and the type of advertisement. Identify the techniques used in this ad. What did the advertisement do that was effective in gaining your attention?
5. You need to purchase a new home appliance, such as a refrigerator. Create a list of criteria that could be used to select a product to purchase. Once you have your list finalized, explain how you will conduct research to decide which model or brand is the better choice. What sources of information will you use?
6. Every economic decision has consequences. A *trade-off* is the choice given up when a different choice is made. Give an example of a trade-off that you made recently when you chose the purchase of one item over another item, such as clothing or recreation. What decision-making strategy did you use? What were the consequences?
7. An *opportunity cost* is the value of the option that was given up. Spending money on one purchase means giving up the opportunity to spend that money on something else. Give an example of a purchase that you made that involved an opportunity cost. How did you reach the conclusion that the purchase was worth the cost? What were the consequences?
8. The decision-making process can be applied to purchases made to satisfy individual needs and wants, or the needs and wants of a family. You want to purchase a new tablet computer. Using the decision-making process in Figure 10-5, describe the specific actions you would take in each step as you analyze your decision to make a purchase. What was the outcome of this exercise? What did you decide to purchase and why?
9. Comparison shopping is often an important part of the decision-making process. Briefly explain the methods you would use to comparison shop for the following items. Include how the price of the item and your available income would affect your decision.
   A. a new backpack
   B. concert tickets
   C. weekly groceries
   D. a video gaming console
   E. a used car
   F. a house
10. Extended warranties are often available for expensive purchases. Under what circumstances would you personally purchase an extended warranty? Would it be related to the cost of replacing an item if it stopped working? Explain your logic.

Apply Your Math Skills

1. Cody is shopping at a warehouse club for pasta and wants to determine which of the following choices has the lowest unit price (per ounce).
   - Eight 16-oz packages of penne pasta for $9.99
   - Four 14.5-oz packages of whole-grain rotini for $5.99
   - Ten 14-oz packages of spaghetti for $9.99
2. Annie scheduled a cruise vacation for $1,545 and paid for the trip with a credit card. The first payment was missed and a penalty of 27.99% is received on the outstanding balance. How much will the cruise actually cost now?

Communication Skills

College and Career Readiness

Speaking. *Impromptu speaking* is speaking without preliminary planning of what you are going to say. Present an impromptu speech about product obsolescence. Give an example of a product that might be current today but out of favor next year. Express your opinion of the effect that product obsolescence has on the consumer.

Listening. Active listening is fully participating as you process what others are saying. Practice active listening skills while participating in a one-on-one discussion with a classmate on product safety. Consider the person's point of view, reasoning, stance, word choice, tone, points of emphasis, and organization. What did you learn from this activity?

Reading. Now that you have completed reading multiple chapters in this text, analyze the themes and structures that the author used. Create a concept map that illustrates how the themes of this text are related.

Teamwork

Working with your team, ask each team member to bring in an example of a warranty on an item that has recently been purchased. Create a list of questions that should be used to evaluate the warranty. Did each of the warranties meet the criteria the team created?

Internet Research

Marketplace. The coronavirus pandemic had a direct impact on the marketplace and the way in which consumers shopped. Research the *coronavirus pandemic 2020 and the marketplace.* Discuss how consumer shopping in 2020 is the same or different today. What changes did brick-and-mortar stores, as well as nontraditional sellers, experience and how did they adjust?

Centers for Disease Control and Prevention (CDC). The CDC is a governmental office responsible for controlling the introduction and spread of infectious diseases, and provides consultation and assistance to other nations and international agencies to assist in improving their disease prevention and control, environmental health, and health promotion activities. Visit the CDC website. What types of information does the CDC provide to help you become a better consumer?

Portfolio Development

College and Career Readiness

Schoolwork. Academic samples are important to include in a portfolio in order to show your accomplishments in school. Include items related to your schoolwork that support your portfolio objective and the job or program for which you are presenting your portfolio. These items might be report cards, completed assignments, lists of classes, or honor roll reports. Diplomas should also be included.

This is a particularly important part of a portfolio, especially for those interested in visual mediums of work, such as graphic design or sculpting. Samples of work completed for school are just as valuable as samples of work done for payment. For example, if a school assignment required you to design a menu for a fake restaurant, including the assignment shows your ability to design both visual and textual media. Even if your interest is not in visual art or something similar, showing your ability to create good work in that area demonstrates a variety of skills and well-roundedness.

1. Create a Microsoft Word document that lists notable classes you have taken and activities you have completed. Use the heading "Schoolwork" on the document along with your name.
2. Scan hard-copy documents related to your schoolwork, such as report cards, to serve as samples. Place each document in an appropriate folder.
3. Place the hard copy documents in the container for future reference.
4. Update your spreadsheet.

CTSOs

Public Speaking. Public speaking is a competitive event you might enter with your CTSO. This event allows you to showcase your communication skills of speaking, organizing, and making an oral presentation. This is usually a timed event you can prepare for before the competition. You will have time to research, prepare, and practice before going to the competition. Review the specific guidelines and rules for this event for direction as to topics and props you will be allowed to use.

To prepare for a public speaking event, complete the following activities.

1. Read the guidelines provided by your organization. Review the topics from which you may choose to make a speech.
2. Locate a rubric or scoring sheet for the event on your organization's website.
3. Confirm whether visual aids may be used in the presentation and the amount of setup time permitted.
4. Review the rules to confirm if questions will be asked or if you will need to defend a case or situation.
5. Make notes on index cards about important points to remember. Use these notes to study. You may also be able to use these notes during the event.
6. Practice the presentation. You should introduce yourself, review the topic that is being presented, defend the topic, and conclude with a summary.
7. After the practice presentation is complete, ask for feedback from your instructor. You may consider also having a student audience listen and give feedback.

CHAPTER 11

Consumer Power

You live in a market economy. Your economic activities such as spending, saving, and voting, all make a difference. Consumers are powerful. Collective consumer behavior makes an impact on overall economic conditions and prosperity, or lack of it.

While our economy offers economic freedom to consumers, it also presents challenges. Consumers are guaranteed certain rights in the marketplace, but they also have responsibilities to know and exercise these rights. For example, you have the right to safe goods and services. However, you are responsible for using products as directed and for heeding safety precautions and warnings. You have the right to be heard and the responsibility to speak out when there is a problem with goods, services, or sellers. The way in which individuals perform these activities determines how they will live and how well the economic system works.

Focus on Finance

Trial Offers

Companies often offer free trials of goods and services to consumers as an attempt to get more customers. If presented with a trial offer, pay close attention to the terms and conditions before agreeing to the offer.

Consumers who accept free trial offers for items such as streaming services or apps are often required to provide credit card information to start the service. However, it is not always made clear that cancellation must be made at the end of the trial period to avoid future charges on the credit card. Cancellation of a trial service is always required if the service is no longer wanted.

Before accepting a free trial offer, ask questions about how to cancel. Visit the website of the Federal Trade Commission (FTC) for more information before accepting free offers.

College and Career Readiness

Reading Prep. Skim the chapter by reading the first sentence of each paragraph. Use this information to create an outline for the chapter before you read it.

Sections

auremar/Shutterstock.com

Section 11.1 Consumer Rights

Essential Question

Why do consumer rights come with responsibilities?

Objectives

After studying this section, you will be able to:

- Summarize the Consumer Bill of Rights.
- Define consumer laws.

Terms

redress

consumer protection laws

Consumer Bill of Rights

In a message to Congress in 1962, President John F. Kennedy outlined four basic consumer rights. In 1985, the United Nations General Assembly added four more rights. These eight rights are now called the *Consumer Bill of Rights*. The original four basic consumer rights are:

- the right to safety;
- the right to be informed;
- the right to choose; and
- the right to be heard.

John F. Kennedy Presidential Library & Museum

President John F. Kennedy worked for many people's rights, including consumer rights.

The four additional rights that were added in 1985 are:

- the right to satisfaction of basic needs;
- the right to redress;
- the right to consumer education; and
- the right to a healthful environment.

These eight consumer rights have been endorsed by the United Nations and affirmed by Consumers International, a worldwide consumer organization. Each of these rights carries economic responsibilities. Together they form the basis for fairness in the marketplace.

Safety

In our free market economy, consumers have the right to protection against goods, production processes, and services that could be hazardous to life, health, and finances. The government plays an important role in establishing and enforcing safety standards. The *Consumer Product Safety Commission (CPSC)* protects the public from unreasonable risks of injury or death associated with the use of consumer products. The *Food and Drug Administration (FDA)* protects public health by ensuring the safety of human and veterinary drugs, biological products, and medical devices as well as safety of our nation's food supply, cosmetics, and products that emit radiation. Other federal agencies oversee consumer financial services.

Consumers are responsible to read and follow directions for safe use, care, storage, and disposal of products. Figure 11-1 shows warning labels required on products containing hazardous substances. Consumers are responsible for reporting product-related health and safety problems to sellers and manufacturers, as well as to the governmental agency that can take prompt action to prevent injury or accident.

Truthful Information

Consumers are entitled to accurate information on which to base their buying decisions. The government protects this right through various agencies and regulations. The law requires labels with specific consumer information on certain products. It also mandates specific facts to be clearly stated on any contracts you may be required to sign. In addition, the government prohibits false and misleading advertising. With the right to truthful information comes the responsibility to seek, evaluate, and use available consumer information.

Choice

Consumers have the right to choose from a variety of quality goods and services at competitive prices and are free to decide where to shop. Laws protect free choice in the marketplace by prohibiting practices such as monopolies and price fixing.

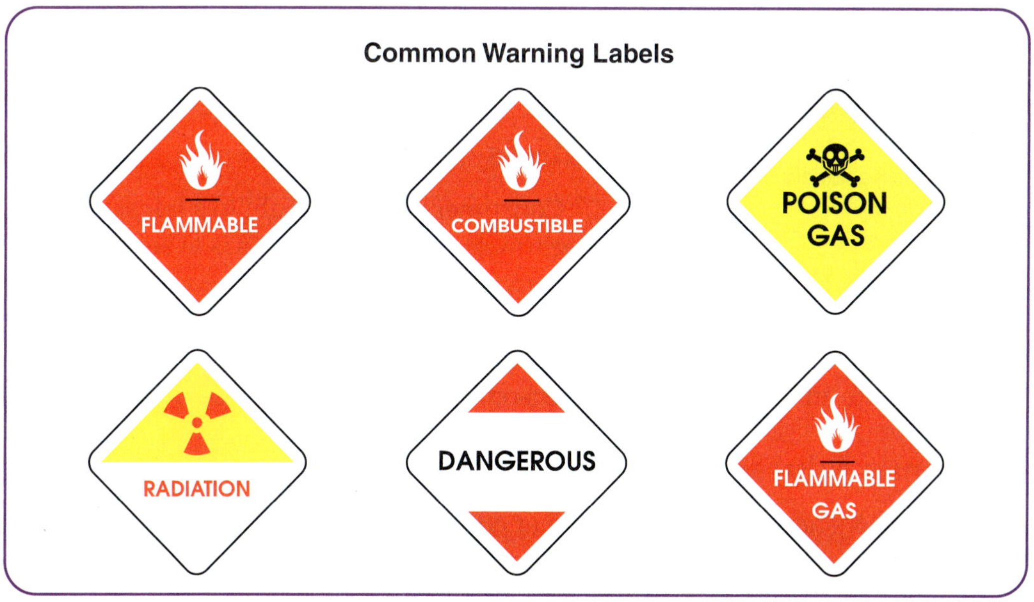

Goodheart-Willcox Publisher

Figure 11-1 Labels are required on products containing hazardous substances.

Consumers are responsible for choosing goods and services that will best meet their needs at prices they can pay. Consumers have an obligation to deal with reliable, reputable businesses for their own protection and for the overall good of the marketplace. Every buying choice expresses approval of the purchase and the seller. It pays to be aware of the messages you send with the dollars you spend.

Voice

When consumers have legitimate problems or concerns, they have the right to speak up, to be heard, and to receive a reasonable response to their concerns. Both businesses and governments have a responsibility to respond. Consumers are responsible for speaking out and expressing concerns to appropriate business and governmental representatives. This means learning and using appropriate and effective means of communication.

Satisfaction of Basic Needs

Consumers have the right to access goods and services required to meet basic needs. These include adequate food, shelter, clothing, health care, education, and sanitation. These basics should be available to all consumers. Governments play a role both in defining basic needs and helping citizens satisfy them. Various programs, such as public housing, Medicare, Medicaid, Social Security, schools and hospitals, sewer and sanitation systems, and fire and police protection, help satisfy basic needs. Responsibility for satisfying basic needs includes putting essential needs ahead of wants when spending, learning about and taking advantage of services available in the marketplace or provided by governments, and getting the training and education needed to earn a living wage.

06photo/Shutterstock.com

Consumers have the right to choose from a variety of quality goods and services at competitive prices.

Redress

Consumers have the right to a fair settlement of legitimate disputes. **Redress** is to set right or make up for a mistake. This correction includes some form of compensation for misrepresentation, shoddy goods, or unsatisfactory services. Consumers share some of the responsibility to present disputes clearly to the appropriate authorities and make reasonable demands.

Consumer Education

Consumers have a right to consumer education. This involves training in the knowledge and skills needed to make informed, confident choices in the marketplace. Consumers can fulfill their responsibilities related to this right by

Exploring Careers

Business Ethics Consultant

A business ethics consultant assesses the culture and values of a company or organization to determine whether its practices and policies meet ethical standards. They also assist businesses in developing an ethical culture and value system. Business ethics consultants typically:

- ensure an organization conforms to laws and regulations
- solve problems that occur within the organization
- advise on crisis control when problems occur with customers and governmental agencies
- implement training programs in corporate culture and core values
- educate employees in the legal and ethical interests of the organization

Business ethics consultants may work in corporations or nonprofit organizations or as independent agents. Career opportunities for business ethics consultants are expanding. They work in a variety of fields, including finance, health care, and communications. A bachelor or master degree in business administration is needed. Knowledge of regulations and compliance procedures for the field in which one works is crucial. Oral and written communication skills are very important.

taking consumer education or financial literacy courses and by keeping up-to-date on consumer issues.

Healthful Environment

Consumers have a right to live and work in an environment that is nonthreatening to the well-being of present and future generations. This means having pure water and air, safe and responsible waste disposal, preservation of natural resources, and respect for the earth and overall environment.

Consumer Protection Laws

Consumer protection laws are laws that govern sales and credit practices involving consumer goods and services. They protect against deceptive advertising, unfair trade practices, and a variety of other issues. In the United States, there are many laws at both the federal and state levels that protect the consumer.

The *Federal Trade Commission (FTC)* is an independent federal agency. Its mission is to promote consumer protection and eliminate anticompetitive business practices. The FTC protects consumers by stopping unfair, deceptive, or fraudulent practices. They conduct investigations, sue companies and people who violate the law, and develop rules for the marketplace. The FTC educates consumers and businesses about their rights and responsibilities. Consumers who are educated about the law can experience positive economic effects. Understanding their rights helps consumers make wiser decisions as they spend their dollars.

The FTC promotes fair competition for businesses, which also creates economic benefits for consumers. For service providers, laws and regulations pertaining to competition keep prices low and the quality of service high. For sellers of goods, competition keeps prices low and choice of products diverse. The FTC protects against practices that create negative economic effects, such as business practices that result in high price, low quality, and few choices.

The FTC helps ensure that markets are open and free. It challenges anticompetitive practices that could harm consumers by resulting in higher prices, lower quality, fewer choices, or reduced rates of innovation. The FTC monitors business practices and challenges them when appropriate to ensure that the market works according to consumer preferences, not illegal practices.

Some of the laws protecting consumers are found in Figure 11-2. Recent examples include Patient's Bill of Rights, Airline Passenger Bill of Rights, and Credit Cardholders Bill of Rights.

Consumer Protection Laws

Law	Year	Description
Federal Trade Commission Act	1914	Established the Federal Trade Commission (FTC); regulates trade and prevents unfair competition
Federal Food, Drug, and Cosmetic Act	1938	Gives the US Food and Drug Administration the power to oversee the safety of all food, drugs, and cosmetics
Fair Packaging and Labeling Act	1966	Requires that product labels identify the product and list the manufacturer's name and location and net amount of contents
Truth-in-Lending Act	1968	Requires the disclosure of all finance charges on consumer credit agreements and in the advertising for credit plans
Child Protection and Toy Safety Act	1969	Protects children from toys and other products that contain thermal, electrical, or mechanical hazards
Fair Credit Reporting Act	1970	Gives individuals the right to examine and correct their own credit history records
Consumer Product Safety Act	1972	Gives the Consumer Product Safety Commission the power to protect the public against risks of injury or death from unsafe products
Nutrition Labeling and Education Act	1990	Requires food labels to list the amount of calories, fat, cholesterol, sodium, and fiber per serving
Health Insurance Portability and Accountability Act	1996	Protects health insurance coverage for employees who leave their jobs, sets standards for electronic health care information, and requires health information to be confidential
Do-Not-Call Implementation Act	2003	Established the National Do Not Call Registry; stops telemarketers from making unwanted calls to consumers
Country of Origin Labeling Law	2009	Requires that product labels list a product's country of origin

Goodheart-Willcox Publisher

Figure 11-2 Consumer protection laws are in place to ensure fair treatment of individuals.

History of Finance

Food and Drug Safety

Before the early 1900s, consumers did not know what was in many foods and medicines, and producers did not have to tell them. Unethical businesspeople cut costs by adding inferior or harmful ingredients. They also made false "cure-all" claims about their products. It took public outrage and decades of effort by many groups to create laws that banned such practices.

In 1906, Congress passed the *Pure Food and Drug Act*. The law required drug labels to list addictive or dangerous ingredients. It also established a small federal agency of scientists and public health inspectors to inspect food and drugs. This agency eventually became the Food and Drug Administration (FDA).

The law was replaced in 1938 with the passage of the comprehensive *Federal Food, Drug, and Cosmetic Act*, which gave new power to the FDA to oversee the safety of food, drugs, and cosmetics. Today the agency has regulatory power over all food, drugs, cosmetics, tobacco products, bottled water, medical devices, and the nation's blood supply.

Patient's Bill of Rights

The *Patient Protection and Affordable Care Act (PPACA)* includes the *Patient's Bill of Rights*, which put an end to unfair insurance company practices. The Patient's Bill of Rights accomplishes the following.

- Provides for coverage of pre-existing conditions.
- Prohibits arbitrary withdrawal of insurance coverage.
- Bans lifetime coverage limitations.
- Grants the right to choose a doctor within your insurance network.
- Bans restrictions on emergency room care.
- Guarantees the patient's right to appeal insurance company decisions.
- Makes young adults under 26 eligible for coverage under a parent's insurance.
- Provides for coverage of certain preventive care.
- Requires a review of premium increases.

The Patient's Bill of Rights put an end to some of the worst insurance abuses and put consumers, not insurance companies, in control of their health care.

Airline Passenger Bill of Rights

Over the years, airline passengers have complained frequently about airline services. A consumer advocacy group, Flyers Rights, has worked for legislation to provide passenger rights. Current provisions in the *Airline Passenger Bill of Rights* include:

- restrictions on the number and length of tarmac delays;
- prominent listing of all ticket costs and fees, eliminating the hidden costs of flying;

michaeljung/Shutterstock.com

The Airline Passenger Bill of Rights provides significant economic benefits for passengers.

- compensation to passengers who are bumped;
- refunds of baggage fees for lost luggage; and
- changes in reservations within 24 hours of booking without penalties.

Some of these benefits provide significant economic benefits for passengers, including the compensation for being bumped from a flight and the refunding of baggage fees for lost luggage. Passengers should understand their economic rights before reserving a flight.

Credit Cardholders Bill of Rights

A law known as the *Credit Card Accountability, Responsibility, and Disclosure (CARD) Act of 2009* applies to existing credit card accounts as well as new accounts. The legislation requires credit providers to mail bills at least 21 days before the due dates. They also must give at least 45 days' advance notice of rate hikes or any other important changes to the credit card agreement and at least 30 days' notice prior to an account closure. The law includes special provisions regarding credit cards issued to minors. Credit providers may not offer credit card accounts to minors who have no proof of financial means to pay debts incurred unless there is a cosigner over age 21 who has the ability to pay. The law also requires any advertisements for free credit reports to make clear that free credit reports are available under federal law.

Section 11.1 Review

Check Your Understanding

1. List each of the eight components of the Consumer Bill of Rights.
2. Who is responsible for reading and following directions for the safe use of products?
3. What is the mission of the Federal Trade Commission (FTC)?
4. Name three examples of recent consumer laws.
5. What does the Patient's Bill of Rights provide?

Build Your Vocabulary

As you progress through this course, develop a personal glossary. This will help you build your vocabulary and prepare you for a career. Write a definition for each of the following terms and add it to your glossary.

redress

consumer protection laws

Section 11.2 Consumer Deception and Defense

Objectives

After studying this section, you will be able to:

- Recognize various forms of deceptive practices in the marketplace.
- Explain options for consumer self-defense.
- Discuss the role of consumer advocates.

Essential Question

What does *caveat emptor* mean for a consumer?

Terms

consumer fraud	chain letter	binding arbitration
skepticism	sweepstakes	small claims court
bait and switch	lottery	class-action lawsuit
pyramid scheme	skill contest	lawsuit
Ponzi scheme	caveat emptor	consumer advocate

Consumer Fraud

Consumer fraud is a deceptive business practice that causes consumers to lose money or other property. Certain deceptive practices, though illegal, still exist in the marketplace. For example, it is against the law for sellers to make false or misleading statements about goods, services, prices, or guarantees. It is also illegal to advertise sale items that are not actually available for sale or to use false statements such as "special price" or "clearance price" when items are not selling at reduced prices. As a consumer, it pays you to be alert when interpreting

Ethics

Code of Ethics

Many companies and organizations are well-respected members of the community. When selecting establishments with which to do business, investigate their business practices. Many socially responsible businesses post a code of ethics on their websites. This helps consumers select companies that are respectful and honest in their transactions with customers.

advertising and sellers' claims. **Skepticism** means having a degree of doubt. It is important to be skeptical when looking at promotions and sales alerts from a company. Some common deceptive techniques are bait and switch; pyramid and Ponzi schemes; chain letters; and sweepstakes, lotteries, and skill contests.

George Rudy/Shutterstock.com

Bait and switch happens when a seller claims to be out of an item advertised at an attractive price and attempts to sell a more expensive one as a substitute.

Bait and Switch

Bait and switch is a strategy that involves advertising one item and then substituting another item. An item is advertised at a very attractive price to attract customers. When customers come to buy the item, the seller claims to be out of that item and attempts to sell a substitute. The substitute may be a more expensive item, or it may be an inferior product offered at the same price. This technique is against the law. Bait and switch selling should be reported to the Federal Trade Commission or state consumer fraud agency.

Pyramid and Ponzi Schemes

Pyramid and Ponzi schemes are similarly deceptive. Both promise investors big returns with low risk. A **pyramid scheme** is a fraudulent investment plan. The pyramid scheme calls for each participant to invest a given amount of money and sign up a certain number of additional participants to do the same. The only way to produce the promised profits is to recruit new participants who will recruit others. The many at the bottom of the pyramid end up paying money to the few at the top. Eventually, the pyramid collapses because there are not enough new investors to pay all the earlier investors.

Warning signs of pyramid schemes include the following.

- The promise of quick, easy money and high returns on your investment.
- A large initial investment required to participate.
- No available money-back or exit plan.
- An unknown promoter or company making the offer with no detailed information available.
- Profits dependent on recruiting new members into the plan.
- A sense that the program is not legitimate.

A **Ponzi scheme** is an investment operation in which money from new investors is used to pay earlier investors. The operation works as long as new investors contribute money. Ponzi scheme organizers promise to invest in high-return, low-risk opportunities. In fact, however, they focus on attracting new investors to pay earlier investors and to cover their own personal expenses. These schemes are illegal, fraudulent operations. One of the most famous Ponzi schemes was run by Bernie Madoff who pled guilty in March 2009 to 11 federal felonies.

Employability Skills

Self-Management Skills

Self-management skills are skills that enable individuals to control and make the best use of their time and abilities. They are important because they facilitate productivity, help ensure employee success, and provide assurance for an employer that the employee will help the business meet its goals. An individual has complete control over the development and use of self-management skills.

Pyramid and Ponzi schemes are illegal. They should be reported to the Federal Trade Commission and the Securities Exchange Commission.

Chain Letters

Chain letters are letters, e-mails, or social media posts that solicit money or gifts from others on an ever-growing list in the hopes that the sender will receive more gifts or money in return. They may promise anything from recipes, to socks, to huge financial rewards. To get the rewards, you must send as little as a recipe, a pair of socks, or $5 to someone at the top of a list, removing that person's name from the list and adding your own to the bottom. Then you send copies of the letter to a certain number of people with instructions that they do the same. The theory is that by the time your name reaches the top of the list, you will receive oodles of whatever is being sent, such as recipes, socks, or money. Remember the following information about chain letters.

- If you start or send one of these letters that involves money or valuable items, you are breaking the law.
- You are not likely to receive what is promised in the quantity promised. Most certainly, it will not make you rich.
- If you receive a chain letter scam via e-mail, you should contact your service provider and forward the letter to the Federal Trade Commission.

Sweepstakes, Lotteries, and Skill Contests

Sweepstakes, lotteries, and many games of skill are forms of gambling. The odds of winning depend on how many entries you submit, how many prizes are offered, and the total number of entrants. Odds are almost always against the players. People who regularly buy lottery tickets or take chances to win big prizes can spend a sizable amount of money over time. This sort of gambling can become addictive and have a negative effect on a person's employment or a family's well-being.

A **sweepstakes** is a promotional offer that gives participants the chance to win items of value or prizes. Some sweepstakes require no purchase or entry fee to participate. The offers come via direct mail, the Internet, or television. Prizes range from relatively small items, such as personal media players, digital cameras, and smartphones, to large items, such as vacations, cars, cash, and dream homes.

Lotteries are similar to sweepstakes except prizes are awarded to participants by chance in exchange for some form of payment. Most states run lotteries to help fund governmental operations. Critics of public lotteries claim that they prey on the poor. On the other hand, state lotteries often benefit public schools and other necessary public services.

Skill contests offer the opportunity to win prizes by skill, such as writing an essay or submitting a photo, rather than by chance. There may be an entry fee or purchase required to enter the contest.

The law regulates these types of promotions, but you also need to be alert on your own behalf. Before you enter a sweepstakes, lottery, or skill contest for a chance to win prizes, follow these guidelines.

- Look for a full description and an estimate of the value of any prize or winning.
- Find out exactly who sponsors the offer and what the sponsor stands to gain.
- Read and be sure you understand all the rules, including small print.
- Know exactly what is required to participate.
- Know all the fees, charges, or expenses involved in participating.
- Find out the tax consequences attached to big winnings.

Consumer Self-Defense

Looking after your own interests is an essential consumer skill. Most sellers are honest and reputable, and most products are what they claim to be. Consumer self-defense involves following up when goods and services do not meet your expectations or the seller's claims. It calls for settling differences with sellers and seeking the help of third-party consumer advocates when necessary. Consumer self-defense may require legal action when all else fails.

There are times when you need to apply the principle of caveat emptor. **Caveat emptor** is a Latin phrase that means *let the buyer beware.* The risk in the transaction is on the buyer's side. If you have any question about a seller's reliability or the quality of a product, proceed with caution. This is particularly true when a sizable amount of money is involved or when you are signing a contract. Examples of consumer self-defense strategies include exercising the right of refusal, filing a complaint, and seeking a resolution.

Lisa S./Shutterstock.com

Sometimes legal action is necessary to settle a dispute.

Exercising the Right of Refusal

A consumer self-defense strategy is to exercise the right of refusal. It pays to exercise the right of refusal when sellers promote items you do not need, do not want, or cannot afford. As long as the economic system guarantees free economic choice, no one can make you buy what you do not need or want. You always have the ultimate right of refusal. Use this right to protect your financial interests.

Case Study Consumer Information

Leticia saves $250 to buy a smartphone and a service plan with unlimited texting and data. At a local cell phone store, the phone costs more than $300. A two-year service plan is $45 per month for unlimited talking and texting, plus three gigabytes of data. There is also a $99 activation fee. If an optional service plan is purchased, the cost of the phone is $19 per month rather than the upfront cost of $300.

Paying $45 a month is a lot of money and requires time to think it over. However, the salesperson cautions that the prices will not last forever and urges Leticia to make a decision soon.

Case Review

1. How might Leticia have prepared for a trip to the cell phone store?
2. What costs associated with owning a smartphone should have been anticipated before going to the cell phone store?
3. What are some ways the cost of the smartphone can be reduced?
4. What advice would you give Leticia?

On a larger scale, you can use the right of refusal to influence demand in the marketplace. Collectively, consumers have the power to strengthen the demand for what they buy and to weaken the demand for what they refuse. The economic system, as well as your own financial welfare, depends on the intelligent use of the power of refusal.

Filing a Complaint

The art of complaining is an essential consumer self-defense tool. You can often handle simple exchanges and returns of unsatisfactory merchandise by taking purchases back to the seller and explaining your dissatisfaction. Most reliable merchants take care of simple matters on the spot. When problems are more involved or complicated, a formal complaint can be made as follows.

- *Put your complaint in writing.* Explain the problem clearly, rationally, and briefly. Include important facts, figures, and dates along with copies of receipts.
- *Be prompt.* Do not wait weeks to act. Put your case in writing right away, and send it by registered mail. The receiver must sign for a registered letter, and you receive a record of its delivery.
- *Direct your complaint to the right person and place.* If an adjustment requires approval from higher up, the department or store manager is the person to see. Contact the credit department for billing errors and other credit problems. Complain to top management if a problem is serious or is not solved at lower levels.
- *Be specific and factual.* Clearly identify the good or service in question and describe the problem. Include the date and place of purchase, the product name and model number, and the purchase price. Include your account number or the last four digits of your credit card number if the purchase was charged.

You Do the Math — Number Sense

Number sense is an ability to use and understand numbers to make judgments and solve problems. For example, suppose you want to add three basketball scores: 35, 21, and 18.

First, add 30 + 20 + 10 = 60.

Then, add 5 + 1 + 8 = 14.

Finally, combine these two sums to find the answer: 60 + 14 = 74.

Solve the following problem.

Molly wants to purchase several items of clothing but is not sure a budget of $95 before tax will cover all three pieces. The prices of the three items are $16, $42, and $35. How can Molly figure the total cost of the three items without using a calculator?

- *Be reasonable.* You are more likely to get a satisfactory response if you state your problem reasonably and sympathize with the reader. For example, you might write, "I realize it takes time to correct a computer error, but...." Or you might say, "I know it must be difficult to give one-day service on appliances, but...." Threatening or sarcastic letters rarely lead to satisfactory solutions.
- *Suggest a solution.* You may not always get your way, but it helps to outline the solution you are seeking. Do you expect a repair, a replacement, a refund, or an apology?
- *Be professional.* Keep a written record of phone conversations with the date, the name of the other party, and promises made or action to be taken. Keep important receipts and records together. You may need to furnish papers or documents, such as sales slips, bills, receipts, warranties, and previous correspondence. Send copies of these papers and keep the originals.
- *Be persistent.* Most problems can be solved with one letter directed to the right person. However, if you do not get the desired results, write a follow-up letter. Enclose a copy of earlier correspondence and indicate a date by which you expect some action. If a third letter is necessary, include copies of the previous letters and outline the action you will take if the matter is not settled by a certain date. You may want to copy a consumer protection agency or organization with your third letter.

Seeking Resolution

If filing a complaint does not resolve a problem, the problem may require some form of legal action. However, legal action is costly and time consuming, and a favorable outcome is not guaranteed. For these reasons, most consumers only consider it as a last resort. Options to seek resolution include the following.

- *Binding arbitration.* **Binding arbitration** is a method of settling disagreements through an objective third party. Once both parties agree to arbitrate, each presents a case to the arbitrator. The arbitrator's decision is final and legally binding. Arbitrators are chosen from a pool of volunteers or professionals, depending on the program. Binding arbitration is quick, low cost, relatively simple, and informal.

- *Small claims court.* A **small claims court** is a part of the court system that offers a simple, prompt, and inexpensive way to settle minor differences involving small amounts of money. Procedures are relaxed, and consumers normally represent themselves without a lawyer. They collect and bring documentation and evidence to support their cases. Claim amounts are limited to a maximum of $1,200 in some states and up to $5,000 in others. Since procedures vary from state to state, contact your local courthouse for more information.
- *Class-action lawsuits.* A **class-action lawsuit** is a legal court action brought by a group of individuals who have been similarly wronged. The court permits members of a common class to pool their grievances and sue for damages on behalf of the entire class or group. Laws governing this type of lawsuit vary from state to state.
- *Individual lawsuits.* A **lawsuit** is a civil action brought by a person (a *plaintiff*) against another party (the *defendant*). The plaintiff claims to be damaged or negatively impacted by actions of the defendant. The plaintiff seeks a legal remedy to be determined by the court, and if successful, a judgment will be entered in the plaintiff's favor. The judgment may involve court orders to enforce the plaintiff's rights or to award damages to the plaintiff. The court may also issue an order to prevent or compel specific action by the defendant.

If money is a stumbling block to seeking resolution, there are other alternatives that can be taken by a consumer. Legal clinics and legal aid societies provide low-cost or free services for consumers who meet the qualifications for assistance.

Consumer Advocates

While consumer rights have been declared and defined in local, federal, and international forums, you still may find your rights denied or diminished in some situations. When this happens and the difference cannot be settled directly with sellers, it often helps to contact outside agencies. Both governmental agencies and private organizations offer consumers assistance with problems in the marketplace. A **consumer advocate** is a group or an individual who promotes consumer rights. Advocates address consumer interests in various areas, such as health and safety, education, redress, truthful advertising, fairness in the marketplace,

Gil C/Shutterstock.com

The Better Business Bureau (BBB) is a consumer advocacy group that offers dispute resolution programs.

and environmental protection. Consumer advocates include governmental agencies as well as private organizations.

Governmental Agencies

When dealing with dishonest and fraudulent business practices, contact the appropriate governmental regulatory agency. Most federal agencies will have local or regional offices. In addition, local and state governments provide regulatory and law enforcement functions to deal with fraud in the marketplace. Figure 11-3 lists some of the federal governmental agencies that provide services and protection for consumers.

Private Organizations

Consumer advocacy comes from a variety of other sources and offers a range of services to consumers. The advocacy groups fall primarily into the following categories.

- *Better Business Bureaus (BBBs).* These are nonprofit organizations supported largely by local businesses. They promote ethical business practices and, in some cases, offer dispute resolution programs.

Governmental Agencies
• United States Department of Agriculture
• Consumer Product Safety Commission
• Environmental Protection Agency
• Federal Trade Commission
• Food and Drug Administration
• Health and Human Services
• Housing and Urban Development
• National Institutes of Health
• United States Postal Service
• United States Department of Justice
• United States Department of Transportation
• Securities and Exchange Commission
• Social Security Administration

Goodheart-Willcox Publisher

Figure 11-3 There are governmental agencies that provide services and protect consumers.

- *Consumer organizations.* Consumer interest groups advocate for consumer causes and provide educational materials and information on goods and services. Many of these groups are nonprofit organizations that work actively on behalf of consumers. One example is the Consumers Union, which publishes *Consumer Reports.*
- *Trade associations and dispute resolution programs.* Many companies that produce or sell the same types of goods and services often belong to an industry association. These associations often act as go-betweens for the companies they represent and consumers. They provide consumer information on goods and services and may offer dispute settlement programs. One example is the Major Appliance Consumer Action Board. This board is a group of representatives from the home appliances industry that helps resolve consumer complaints.
- *Corporate consumer departments.* Many companies operate consumer affairs departments that deal with consumer concerns and resolve disputes. When you cannot get satisfaction at the point of sale, try contacting the consumer affairs or customer relations department at the company headquarters.

Section 11.2 Review

Check Your Understanding

1. List examples of deceptive practices consumers may encounter in the marketplace.
2. What does consumer self-defense involve?
3. List examples of consumer self-defense strategies.
4. What are some of the various areas in which consumer advocates address consumer interests?
5. Name a private organization that acts as a consumer advocate.

Build Your Vocabulary

As you progress through this course, develop a personal glossary. This will help you build your vocabulary and prepare you for a career. Write a definition for each of the following terms and add it to your glossary.

consumer fraud
skepticism
bait and switch
pyramid scheme
Ponzi scheme
chain letter
sweepstakes
lottery
skill contest
caveat emptor
binding arbitration
small claims court
class-action lawsuit
lawsuit
consumer advocate

Review and Assessment

Chapter Summary

Section 11.1 Consumer Rights

- In 1962, President John F. Kennedy outlined four basic consumer rights. In 1985, the United Nations General Assembly added four more rights. These rights are called the Consumer Bill of Rights.
- Consumer protection laws are laws that govern sales and credit practices involving consumer goods. In the United States, there are many federal and state laws that protect consumers. These laws protect against fraudulent advertising, unfair trade practices, and a variety of other issues.

Section 11.2 Consumer Deception and Defense

- Certain deceptive practices, though illegal, still exist in the marketplace. Some common deceptive techniques are bait and switch; pyramid and Ponzi schemes; chain letters; and sweepstakes, lotteries, and skill contests.
- Consumer self-defense involves following up when goods and services do not meet your expectations or the seller's claims. Examples of consumer self-defense strategies include exercising the right of refusal, filing a complaint, and seeking a resolution.
- A consumer advocate is a group or an individual who promotes consumer rights. Both governmental agencies and private organizations offer consumers assistance with problems in the marketplace.

Review Your Knowledge

1. Summarize the Consumer Bill of Rights.
2. Explain what it means to have the consumer right to safety.
3. Describe a consumer's responsibility to the satisfaction of personal basic needs.
4. What is the purpose of consumer protection laws?
5. How does the Federal Trade Commission (FTC) ensure that markets are open and free?
6. What are some of the warning signs of a pyramid scheme?
7. List some of the precautions a consumer should take before entering a sweepstakes, lottery, or skill contest.
8. Summarize how to make a successful complaint to a company.
9. What options are available to consumers who cannot afford legal services?
10. Explain the role of consumer advocates.

Apply Your Knowledge

1. Consumers have protected economic rights, but along with those rights, come economic responsibilities. Create a chart with two columns. Label the first column *Consumer Bill of Rights* and list each of the eight rights. Label the second column *Economic Rights*. In this column, analyze each of the economic rights as it applies to individuals as consumers.

2. In the previous activity, you analyzed each economic right from the Consumer Bill of Rights. Using the chart you created, add a third column and label it *Economic Responsibilities*. For each of the eight rights, analyze the economic responsibilities of individuals as consumers.
3. How do consumers benefit from laws and regulations? Analyze the economic effects of laws and regulations that pertain to consumers. Write a paragraph expressing your opinion.
4. What is the economic effect of laws and regulations on service providers like the airline industry? Analyze the economic benefits from laws and regulations gained by both the provider and the consumer.
5. Describe a situation in which a specific consumer protection law worked for you. What was the law and how were you protected?
6. Select a specific consumer protection law and apply a cost-benefit analysis to it. Consider costs and benefits for the consumer, businesses involved, and governmental enforcement agencies.
7. What do you see as the pros and cons of state lotteries? Make a list to share with your classmates.
8. Describe a situation in which you complained or wanted to complain about a good or service. How did you go about complaining? Or, if you did not complain, explain why.
9. Have you or someone you know ever experienced consumer fraud? Identify the type of fraud that was committed and explain the situation.
10. Are consumer advocates necessary in today's marketplace? Explain why or why not.

Apply Your Math Skills

1. Melanie purchased an airplane ticket to visit a college across the country. At the airport, passengers found out that the airline sold more tickets for the flight than there were seats available. A group of 18 passengers are going to be bumped from the flight. The airline offers $640 compensation to any passenger who gets bumped. How much money is the airline going to spend to compensate these passengers?
2. Davis purchased a dishwasher from a department store for $600 and has had to have the appliance repaired three times in six months. The repair company charges $90 for any service visit and performs repairs at a rate of $30 per hour. The first service call took 3 hours. The second service call took 1 hour, and required a new part that cost $70. The third service call took 1.5 hours. How much money should a letter to the manufacturer asking to be reimbursed for the cost of these repairs request?

Communication Skills

Reading. The ability to read and interpret information is an important workplace skill. As a consumer, it is important that you understand your consumer rights. Read the Consumer Bill of Rights section in this chapter. Interpret the information in each of the individual rights. How do these rights influence consumer behavior?

Speaking. It is important to be prepared when you are speaking to an individual or to an audience. Style and content influences how the listener understands your message. Create a script about how to be a successful complainer as a consumer who needs assistance. Make use of visuals or demonstrations to enhance the presentation. Adjust your presentation length to fit the attention of the audience.

Listening. Active listeners know when to comment and when to remain silent. Practice your listening skills while your instructor presents this chapter. Participate when appropriate and build on the ideas presented. Respond appropriately to the presentation.

Teamwork

Working as a team, consider a consumer who, having gone to the store to buy an advertised product, realizes the store doesn't really have that product. The consumer realizes that the store has set up a bait and switch tactic to draw customers. What steps should the consumer take?

Internet Research

Better Business Bureau (BBB). The Better Business Bureau (BBB) is a national consumer advocacy organization. Using the Internet, visit the website for the Better Business Bureau (BBB). How does the BBB help consumers? Describe three ways in which consumers can utilize the BBB to assist with consumer disputes.

Consumer Privacy Bill of Rights. President Obama introduced the Consumer Privacy Bill of Rights Act of 2015. Using the Internet, research the history of the content of this act and its status today. Summarize your findings.

Portfolio Development

Writing Samples. As you collect academic samples to include in your portfolio, you may want to emphasize samples of your best writing. Writing skills are necessary for success in every part of life including academics and career. Regardless of occupation, industry, or position, at some point, every job will require written communication. Even jobs that are not done on a computer require writing skills. For example, an automotive mechanic or welder will undoubtedly have to write or summarize the scope of work for a given job. It is important to demonstrate your ability to communicate ideas and information through the written word.

As you review documents, collect those that highlight your writing skills. Select items you have written, such as essays, stories, or poems.

Each person is different in terms of writing styles. Some can be as unique as a fingerprint. Focus on selecting items that not only positively demonstrate your writing abilities but also provide a glimpse of your signature writing style.

1. Select writing examples that demonstrate your writing style. Be critical and choose your best creative writing sample, an article you have written for the school newspaper, or other documents of which you are proud.
2. For each document, attach a note that (1) describes what the sample is and (2) states why it is included in your portfolio. For example, a note on an article you wrote for the school newspaper might say, "Example of journalistic and investigative reporting skills."
3. Update your master portfolio spreadsheet to include your academic work samples.

CTSOs

Event Prep

Case Study. A case study presentation may be part of a CTSO competitive event. The activity may be a decision-making scenario for which your team will provide a solution. The presentation will be interactive with the judges.

To prepare for a case study event, complete the following activities.

1. Conduct an Internet search for *case studies*. Your team should select a case that seems appropriate to use as a practice activity. Look for a case that is no more than a page long. Read the case and discuss it with your team members. What are the important points of the case?
2. Make notes on index cards about important points to remember. Team members should exchange note cards so that each evaluates the other person's notes. Use these notes to study. You may also be able to use these notes during the event.
3. Assign each team member a role for the presentation. Ask your instructor to play the role of competition judge as your team reviews the case.
4. Each team member should introduce himself or herself, review the case, make suggestions for the case, and conclude with a summary.
5. After the presentation is complete, ask for feedback from your instructor. You may also consider having a student audience listen and give feedback.

UNIT

4 Purchasing and Protecting Your Assets

Chapters

Financial Literacy

Why It Matters

As a consumer, you make decisions every day related to routine spending for food, clothing, health care, and personal needs. Most consumers also face some big spending decisions involving the choices of housing and automobiles. These assets can be some of the most costly items in a person's budget. In a world of so many choices, you want to get the most for your dollars. You accomplish this goal by prioritizing your needs and wants and spending within your means.

Once you purchase personal assets, such as a house or car, they need protection against risk. Loss of property can be financially devastating. You can minimize your risks by purchasing insurance for your apartment or home and auto.

everything possible/Shutterstock.com

Big Idea

Smart financial decisions and risk management can lead to financial security.

CHAPTER

12 Housing Decisions

The word *home* has different meanings for different people. To some people, a home is a base of operations—a headquarters. To others, a home is a secure shelter from an unfriendly world. It may be a place to relax and entertain, or simply a wise investment. A home may mean all of this and more. It is whatever people make it.

Over the years, you will probably spend a large portion of your income on a place to live. There are many options for the type of housing you choose and whether you rent space or purchase a home. Some of your decisions will depend on your lifestyle, where you are in your life cycle, and a multitude of other factors. Understanding the options can help with the decision-making process. The home you choose will influence the way you live, the people you meet, and your overall sense of well-being.

Focus on Finance

Mortgage Calculators

Buying a residence is a big step in life. Before beginning the home-buying process, make sure you can financially afford a mortgage. Mortgage calculators are normally user-friendly, and most are available for free online. Using a mortgage calculator early in the buying process can save a potential homebuyer a lot of time and money.

A mortgage calculator estimates monthly payments, total cost of the loan, amount of interest over the life of the loan, and other valuable information. In order to use a mortgage calculator, the down payment amount, principal, interest rate, and the length of the loan is entered. The mortgage calculator will then do the work to calculate financial information.

Using a mortgage calculator can help you decide if a mortgage is affordable for your budget. Of course, there are many other factors to consider, such as your credit rating, salary, and other personal financial details. However, this is the first step in deciding if a mortgage is the right decision.

College and Career Readiness

Reading Prep. Skim the Review Your Knowledge questions at the end of the chapter. Use them to help you focus on the most important concepts as you read the chapter.

Sections

Section 12.1 Renting a Residence

Section 12.2 Purchasing a Home

Blend Images/Shutterstock.com

Section 12.1 Renting a Residence

Essential Question

Why would a person choose to rent rather than buy a home?

Objectives

After studying this section, you will be able to:

- Compare the advantages and disadvantages of renting a place to live.
- Explain the process of finding and renting a residence.
- Describe how to prepare to move into a new residence.

Terms

apartment	lessor	rental inventory checklist
lease	security deposit	eviction
lessee	rental agreement	

Your First Apartment

If you live with your parents or guardians, you may look forward to moving out on your own in the future. At different times in your life, you will most likely choose different types and styles of housing. Your choices will be based on what you need and want, what you can afford, what is available, and whether you want to be a renter or a homeowner.

Your first adult residence might be on campus in a dormitory at a university. If you belong to a sorority or fraternity, you may choose to live in a house the organization owns or rents. Or, you might decide to live in an apartment.

XiXinXing/Shutterstock.com

A young person's first adult residence might be in a dormitory at a university.

An **apartment** is a group of rooms designed for use as a private living space. Most apartments have a kitchen, a living room, one or more bedrooms, and one or more bathrooms. A *studio apartment* is an apartment that has a bathroom and one large room that serves as the living room, bedroom, and kitchen. Studio apartments are smaller than traditional apartments, but they generally cost less. An *apartment complex* is a large group of multi-family dwellings where residents share common areas, such as a lobby, grounds, laundry facilities, and other building facilities.

Case Study *Housing Options*

Tatyana is starting college this upcoming semester but does not live close enough to the school to live with family and commute. Renting a two-bedroom apartment costs $900 a month with a refundable security deposit of $450. The utilities are included in the rent. It is necessary to find a roommate with whom to share expenses before the school year starts.

The other option is for Tatyana to live in a dorm room. The dorm cost would be added to the tuition bill. To live in the dorm would cost $6,800 for the school year, but it includes an unlimited meal plan.

Case Review

1. Which housing would you recommend?
2. How could finding a roommate for an apartment help with expenses?
3. What are the potential advantages and disadvantages of living with a roommate?
4. What are the potential advantages and disadvantages of adding living expenses to a tuition bill?

Rental houses and condominiums are sometimes practical and offer the comforts of living in a space that might offer a garage, basement, and other spaces that an apartment may not offer. However, renting a house may be more expensive than an apartment because of the location and space offered.

Roommates

Many young people, especially during difficult financial times, do not have the funds to move out on their own. Some college students and young adults make living expenses more affordable by sharing housing with roommates.

Prospective roommates should have a clear understanding of financial obligations and house rules before moving in together. The following questions should be discussed before signing the lease.

- When is rent due? What is each person's share of the rent?
- Is there a security deposit? How will it be divided if there are charges for damage to the residence?
- How long will each person live in the apartment? Who will pay the rent for the rest of the lease if someone moves out early?
- How are utility bills to be divided?
- Will furniture, televisions, and appliances be shared? If they are damaged, who will pay for repair or replacement?
- Will food and meals be shared? How will food costs be divided?
- How will housework be divided?
- Which part of the apartment is public and which parts are private?
- Will guests be allowed? If so, how often?

These issues should be discussed honestly with a potential roommate before renting a residence.

Renting Advantages and Disadvantages

Renting a living space offers certain advantages over owning a home. Some of the advantages include the following.

- *More free time.* Since renters are often not responsible for home maintenance, such as landscaping and home repairs, they have more free time.
- *Fewer financial responsibilities.* Rent is generally lower than a mortgage payment. Renters do not have to pay property taxes, pay for major repairs and maintenance, or purchase major appliances.
- *Less financial risk.* Renters do not need to worry about property values or the inability to pay a mortgage.
- *Greater mobility.* Renters can usually move at the end of their lease if they give a month's notice.

However, there are certain disadvantages of renting a residence. Some of those disadvantages are as follows.

- *Little control.* Renters have less control over their living space. At the end of a lease period, property owners can raise the rent or ask them to move out. They may not be allowed to own pets, hang pictures on the walls, or paint and decorate. Some renters have irresponsible property owners who do not maintain properties or make needed repairs. Inadequate heat, hot water, and pest control are just a few of the problems these renters endure.
- *No tax benefits.* Because rent payments are not tax deductible, there are no tax benefits from renting.
- *No investment.* Buying a home is an investment and renting is not. Rent payments do not benefit renters beyond providing a place to live. Instead, they go into the pockets of property owners.

Georgejmclittle/Shutterstock.com

There are many apps available for apartment hunting that can assist with the search for an apartment.

Rental Process

When finding a place to live, establishing a budget will determine what type of residence you can get for what you can afford. Before you begin looking for an apartment, consider how much your budget will allow. In addition to a monthly payment, some apartments require that the renter pay for utilities. Renters insurance should also be considered to cover personal property.

Next, location is one of the most important considerations. Will you be working, going to school, or getting married? Very often, a job or school will dictate in part where you live.

Once you have narrowed your search to particular communities or areas, you can begin looking for available rentals. You might begin

You Do the Math — Geometric Reasoning

The area of a two-dimensional shape considers measurements of its perimeter. The area of a rectangle, for example, is calculated by multiplying the length of two sides that meet at a right angle. The area of a circle is calculated by multiplying the constant *pi* (3.14) by the radius of the circle squared. To calculate the volume of a cylinder, multiply its height by the area of its base.

Solve the following problems.

1. Catalina must calculate the area of the living room in order to estimate the cost of carpet. The room measures 17 feet by 23 feet. What is the area of the living room?
2. Tim must order paint for a new home. The paint comes in buckets that are 12 inches in diameter and 2 feet in height. What is the volume of paint in each bucket?
3. Geoff must buy enough plywood to cover the floor in a room that is 12 feet by 25 feet. One sheet of plywood is 4 feet by 8 feet. How many sheets of plywood must be purchased? Round up to the nearest whole sheet.

by reading classified ads online or in local newspapers. Or, you might use an app designed for apartment seekers. These apps can be used on a computer or digital device. Often, local stores and restaurants have community bulletin boards where ads may be posted. You can also talk to family, friends, or acquaintances who live in the area.

After you find a place in which you are interested, if possible, find an opportunity to talk with several tenants. There are some questions that only those who live in a building can answer accurately. For example, are apartments warm enough in winter and cool enough in summer? Are other tenants agreeable? Is the noise level acceptable, and is privacy adequate? Find out if current tenants are satisfied with maintenance and repairs, building services, security, and the overall atmosphere.

Lease and Rental Agreements

When you find a place you are interested in renting, the apartment management will require you to complete an application. You will be asked for the name, address, and phone number of your employer; financial information; names and contact information of references; and a list of previous addresses and landlords. You may also be requested to give your Social Security number, pay a fee, and give permission for your credit report or credit score to be requested. Property owners are allowed to request a credit report on prospective tenants. Property owners usually will not rent to people with low credit scores.

If your application is approved, you will probably be asked to sign a lease to begin renting. A **lease** is a contract that specifies the conditions, terms, and rent for the use of an asset, as illustrated in Figure 12-1. The term of a lease varies, but 6-month or 12-month leases are common.

The lease must be signed by the **lessee**, the person who rents the property, and the **lessor**, the person who owns the property. An apartment lease explains the legal rights and responsibilities of both a tenant and a property owner.

WB-20 APARTMENT LEASE
Approved by Wisconsin Real Estate Examining Board

Nelco Forms
P.O. Box 10208
Green Bay, WI 54307-0208

APARTMENT LEASE

This lease of the apartment identified below is entered into by and between the Landlord and Tenant (referred to in the singular whether one or more) on the following terms and conditions:

PARTIES

Tenant: Raoul Doe
Ilse Doe

Landlord: Sawdusky Realty

Agent for maintenance, management:
name Mike Manning
address 1210 Fixit St.
Anytown, USA

Agent for collection of rents:
name Lisa Brown
address 1000 Collect St.
Anytown, USA

APARTMENT ADDRESS

Building address:
street 1000 Collect St.
city, village/town Anytown,
county Anycoanty State St

Agent for service of process:
name Myra Lee
address 508 Process St.
Anytown USA

Apartment number: 208

TERM

Lease term: 8/1/-- to 8/1/-- ~~Month to Month~~ (strike if not applicable)
First day of lease term: 8/1/-- Last day of lease term: 8/1/-- One Year Later

RENTALS

Apartment: $ 950.00 per mo. Other: Garage Sp. $ 30 per mo
Payable at Apt. 101, 1000 collect St. on or before the First day of each Month during the term of this lease.

UTILITIES

Utility charges, other than telephone, are included in the rent, except: Heat And Electricty which Tenant shall pay promptly when due. If charges not included in the rent are not separately metered, they shall be allocated on the basis of: Separate meters are installed

SPECIAL CONDITIONS

Special conditions: No Pets

RENEWAL OF LEASE TERM

(Strike clause 1 or 2; if neither is striken clause 2 controls.)

1. This lease shall be automatically renewed, without notice from either party, on identical terms for a like successive lease term unless either party shall, at least 45 days before the expiration of the lease, notify the other in writing of the termination of the lease. However, Landlord must, at least 15 days but not more than 30 days prior to the time specified for giving the notice as herein set forth notify Tenant in writing of the above provision for automatic renewal or extension.
2. ~~This lease shall be automatically renewed, without notice from either party, on identical terms, except that it shall be a month-to-month tenancy.~~

ASSIGNMENT SUBLETTING

Tenant shall not assign this lease nor sublet the premises or any part thereof without the prior written consent of Landlord. If Landlord permits an assignment or a sublease, such permission shall in no way relieve Tenant of Tenant's liability under this lease.

SECURITY DEPOSIT

Upon execution of this lease Tenant paid a security deposit in the amount of $ 950.00 to be held by Sawdusky Realty.
If the person holding the security deposit is a licensed real estate broker, acting as agent, it shall be held in the broker's trust account. The deposit, less any amounts withheld, will be returned in person or mailed to Tenant's last known address within 21 days after Tenant vacates the premises. If any portion of the deposit is withheld, Landlord will provide an accompanying itemized statement specifically describing any damages and accounting for any amount withheld. Failure to return the deposit or provide a written accounting within 21 days will result in the waiver of any claim against the deposit. The reasonable cost of repairing any damages caused by Tenant, normal wear and tear excepted, will be deducted from the security deposit. Tenant has 7 days after the beginning of the lease term to notify Landlord in writing of damages or defects in the premises; no deduction from Tenant's security deposit shall be made for any damages or defects of which notification is given. Landlord will give Tenant a written description of any physical damages charged to the previous tenant's security deposit as soon as such description is available. (If none, so specify________.) (Strike paragraph if no security deposit is paid.)

ASSIGNMENT SUBLETTING

LANDLORD'S RIGHT TO ENTER

VACATION OF PREMISES

Tenant agrees to vacate the premises at the end of the lease term or the extended lease term, and promptly deliver the keys to Landlord.

LANDLORD'S RIGHT TO ENTER

Landlord may enter the premises at reasonable times and with 12 hours advance notice, with or without Tenant's permission to inspect the premises, make repairs, show the premises to prospective tenants or purchasers, or to comply with any applicable law or regulation. Landlord may enter with less than 12 hours advance notice upon specific consent of Tenant. No advance notice is required for entry in a health or safety emergency or where entry is necessary to preserve and protect the premises from damage in Tenant's absence.

ABANDONMENT BY TENANT

If Tenant shall abandon the premises before the expiration of the lease term, Landlord shall make reasonable efforts to re-lease premises and shall apply any rent received, less costs of re-leasing, to the rent due or to become due on this lease, and Tenant shall remain liable for any deficiency. If Tenant is absent from the premises for three successive weeks without notifying Landlord in writing of such absence, Landlord, at Landlord's sole option, may deem the premises abandoned.

DISPOSAL OF TENANT'S PROPERTY

If Tenant shall leave any property on the premises after vacation or abandonment of the premises, Tenant shall be deemed to have abandoned the property, and Landlord shall have the right to dispose of the property as provided by law.

TENANT OBLIGATIONS

During the lease term, as a condition to Tenant's continuing right to use and occupy the premises, Tenant agrees and promises:

USE

1. To use the premises for residential purposes only by Tenant and Tenant's immediate family.
2. Not to make or permit use of the premises for any unlawful purpose or any purpose that will injure the reputation of the premises or the building of which they are a part.
3. Not to use or keep in or about the premises anything which would adversely affect coverage of the premises or the building of which they are a part under a standard fire and extended insurance policy.
4. Not to make excessive noise or engage in activities which unduly disturb neighbors or other tenants in the building which the premises are located.

PETS

5. Not to keep in or about the premises any pet unless specifically authorized as a special condition in this lease.

GOVT. REG.

6. To obey all lawful orders, rules and regulations of all governmental authorities.

MAINTENANCE IMPROVEMENTS

7. To keep the premises in clean and tenantable condition and in as good repair as at the beginning of the lease term, normal wear and tear excepted.
8. If obligated to pay for heat for the premises, to maintain a reasonable amount of heat in cold weather to prevent damage to the premises, and if damage results from Tenant's failure to maintain a reasonable amount of heat Tenant shall be liable for this damage.

WB20 NTF 0074

Goodheart-Willcox Publisher

Figure 12-1 A lease clearly states the rights and responsibilities of both the landlord and the tenant.

Renters are usually expected to pay the first month's rent and a security deposit at the time the lease is signed. A **security deposit** is an amount a renter pays to help protect the property owner against financial losses in case the renter damages the property or fails to pay rent. It usually must be paid before moving into a rental unit. The amount of the security deposit generally is one or two month's rent. For example, if the monthly rent is $800, a renter may need to pay a security deposit of two months' rent, $1,600. This would mean that the renter must pay $2,400 ($800 first month's rent + $1,600 security deposit) before moving in. The deposit should be returned when the lease expires provided there is no damage to the property.

A lease is a legal document. Before signing, read it carefully and be prepared to ask for the following information.

- *Rent.* How much is the rent and when must it be paid? What are the penalties for late payment?
- *Security deposit.* Is a security deposit required? If so, how much is it? Will it draw interest? How do you get the deposit back? Under what circumstances may the property owner keep part or all of it?
- *Utilities.* What utilities are included in the rent? How much should you expect to pay for utilities that are not included? Ask to see a record of previous billings.
- *Furnishings, appliances, services.* What furnishings and appliances are included? What building services and facilities are available? What is included in the rent and what costs extra?
- *Lease period.* What are the beginning and ending dates of the lease? When must rent payments begin? When must the lease be renewed or notice given that it will not be renewed? What happens if you move out before the lease expires? What are the conditions for subletting or assigning the lease to someone else?

A lease clearly states the rights and responsibilities of both the property owner and tenant.

- *Upkeep, maintenance, repairs.* What does the property owner maintain, and what must be maintained by the renter? What should either party do if the other fails to carry out upkeep and maintenance responsibilities? How is the property owner or rental agent contacted in case of emergencies, questions, problems, or complaints?
- *Legal remedies.* Does the lease outline ways, such as arbitration or legal action, to handle disagreements between the renter and the property owner? Who pays the legal costs of settling differences?
- *Other conditions of use.* Can the property be decorated by painting the walls or hanging pictures? If shelving, carpet, or equipment is installed, can it be removed later? Are pets allowed? Are roommates allowed?

Before signing, make sure all spaces in the lease are filled in accurately, including dates, dollar amounts, addresses, and names. All verbal agreements should be written into the lease. You should understand all clauses, obligations, and consequences. Make sure you receive a copy of the signed document and keep it in a safe place.

scyther5/Shutterstock.com

A rental agreement is a contract that allows the tenant to move out any time as long as the required notice is given.

The longer the term of a lease, the lower the rent typically is. For example, the rent under a 12-month lease is usually lower than a 6-month lease. However, you may not want to be under a lease contract for that long. An option is to find a property that allows you to have a rental agreement rather than a lease. A **rental agreement** is a written agreement that permits the tenant to move out at any time as long as the required notice is given. Rental agreements usually run month-to-month. This means you can continue renting as long as you pay your monthly rent, but you can move out any time after giving a one-month notice.

The downside of a month-to-month rental agreement is the cost. Since month-to-month rentals are more likely to experience more frequent periods of vacancy than a leased property, the property owner usually wants a higher amount of rent.

Renter Rights

There are a variety of federal, state, and local laws and regulations that protect renters. For example, Title VIII of the *Civil Rights Act of 1968*, also called the *Fair Housing Act*, prohibits discrimination against consumers who are looking to buy, rent, or get financing for a dwelling. Consumers cannot be discriminated against because of race, color, national origin, religion, sex, familial status, or disability.

Other laws state that property owners cannot enter a renter's dwelling without permission except in the case of an emergency. If property owners need to access a unit to do maintenance, they are required to give tenants a certain amount of notice.

The lease protects renters as well as property owners. The rent that is stated in the current lease cannot be raised until the lease period is over. Some cities have laws that limit how much property owners can raise the rent on their tenants. If heat is included in the rent, it must be provided when temperatures are low. Property owners are required to install fire alarms.

When you gain access to your new residence, conduct an inspection and complete a rental inventory checklist. The **rental inventory checklist**, which may be supplied by the property owner, is a detailed list of property items and their condition. Make a note of problems on the inventory checklist or the lease, such as a scratched floor, a dirty oven, and a dripping faucet. The property owner should fix some of these right away. Other problems should be documented so you are not charged for them when you move out. Take the time to fill out the form carefully and thoroughly and make a copy for yourself. Renters should purchase renters insurance to protect against losses due to theft, fire, or other damages.

Employability Skills

Appropriate Language

When speaking to others at work, use respectful and polite language at all times. Use polite phrases such as "please," "thank you," and "you are welcome" whenever possible. Choose words that show respect to others. Never use profane words or phrases. To do so is inappropriate and unacceptable workplace behavior.

Renter Responsibilities

Tenants also have responsibilities to their neighbors and property owners. The main responsibility is to pay the rent on time. Failure to pay rent can result in late fees, termination of the contract, or eviction. **Eviction** is the legal process of removing a tenant who is not paying rent from a rental property if the tenant does not leave voluntarily. Evictions are often reported to credit bureaus, which could lower the tenant's credit score and make it hard to obtain another lease.

Tenants are expected to:

- meet the terms of the lease;
- keep the dwellings clean and free of pests;
- prevent damage to the property;
- report problems, such as leaks or broken windows, right away;
- avoid noise and behaviors that could disturb neighbors;
- give notice before they move out as required in the lease; and
- clean up before moving out.

The renter is also responsible for taking reasonable care of the rental unit and paying any utility bills that are not included in the rent. In turn, the property owner is responsible for making the property habitable and providing the tenant quiet and peaceful possession of the property.

Moving Into a New Residence

For some people, finding a place to live is easy compared with moving their belongings. People who do not own much furniture often move themselves. A borrowed or rented truck and a few friends can accomplish a move in an afternoon. As you move into your new place, you may decide that additional items must be purchased to make the residence complete.

As you accumulate furniture and possessions, moving becomes more complicated and expensive. Moving a short distance away can be handled by local movers. Moving to another state requires a national carrier. Consider and compare all the possibilities.

If you hire a mover, check out the moving company thoroughly. Many consumer complaints involve moves and moving companies. Contact the Better Business Bureau to check for complaints against the company. Talk to friends and

Economics in Action

Housing Demand

Supply and demand of housing in the United States is influenced by many factors. Examples of obvious influences include demographics, income, and credit. Each play a role in determining how much housing is needed.

Demographics include population size and growth. The more people who want to live in an area, the higher the demand for housing. The number of families versus single people in an area also determines how much and what type of housing is needed.

The income level of the population influences the cost of real estate available for purchase. Areas in which people have higher incomes typically demand more expensive homes. Areas with lower incomes typically demand homes that are less expensive.

Cost of credit and its availability influences how much housing is needed. When interest rates are low, housing demand typically increases. Lower interest rates potentially translate into lower mortgage payments. More people are willing to buy when house payments are more affordable. When interest rates are high, the trend can be the opposite and housing demand can decrease or remain stable.

Kues/Shutterstock.com

If using a mover, it is wise to create an inventory of your possessions before the move.

acquaintances to get the names of movers they used with good results. If you use a mover, follow these guidelines to make a move go smoothly.

- *Get rid of excess belongings.* The more items you move, the more you pay. Get rid of items you do not need or want before moving. Items in good condition can be donated.
- *Get cost estimates from several movers.* Be sure estimates include everything that is to be moved. Find out what services are included in the estimates. Rates for interstate moves are regulated by laws and are based on weight and distance. Packing and other services add to the cost.
- *Time the move for better rates.* If you have a choice, move between mid-October and mid-April. You often get better service and lower rates than in the peak moving months of summer. The middle of a month is better than the first or last days of a month.
- *Collect information to help you move.* Most major carriers offer helpful publications for planning a move and settling in a new area. Interstate movers are required to give you a copy of the pamphlet *Your Rights and Responsibilities When You Move.* Carriers should also give you information about filing claims in case of loss or damage to your possessions.
- *Check insurance coverage.* A mover's liability for your possessions is limited to an amount per unit of weight. This often is less than replacement value for most items. Find out what additional protection is available if you need it. Make sure your possessions are adequately insured before you move.

Before your move, take an inventory of your possessions. As you pack, label moving cartons with a list of contents and their intended location in your new home. Supervise both pickup and delivery to be sure everything is moved and delivered to your new address.

Read the shipping order and bill of lading carefully. A *bill of lading* is a receipt listing the goods shipped. Make sure these forms accurately state pickup and delivery dates, estimated charges, and services to be performed. They should also state any special agreements or arrangements between you and the mover.

Be prepared to pay for your move on delivery with a certified check. Ask for an itemized receipt. In the event of loss or damage to your possessions, file reimbursement claims promptly.

After you move into your apartment, you may find you need items such as towels, bedding, and kitchen utensils. Great places to look for bargains include:

- garage and yard sales;
- flea markets;
- secondhand stores;
- furniture warehouses;
- online discounters; and
- estate sales.

As you add furniture, look for items that are multiuse. For example, a sofa bed can serve as a couch and also as a bed if you have overnight company. Likewise, lightweight chairs can be carried from room to room, allowing them to be used for different purposes. Add other furnishings as you can afford them.

Consider purchasing renters insurance. This type of insurance covers the losses of a renter's personal property and possessions such as furniture, clothing, and electronics. Chapter 14 covers insurance in more detail.

Section 12.1 Review

Check Your Understanding

1. What are some of the advantages of renting a living space?
2. Before signing a lease, what questions should you ask about the lease?
3. Name some of the responsibilities associated with being a tenant.
4. List some guidelines that can be followed to make a move go smoothly.
5. What is a bill of lading?

Build Your Vocabulary

As you progress through this course, develop a personal glossary. This will help you build your vocabulary and prepare you for a career. Write a definition for each of the following terms and add it to your glossary.

apartment
lease
lessee
lessor
security deposit
rental agreement
rental inventory checklist
eviction

Section 12.2 Purchasing a Home

Objectives

After studying this section, you will be able to:

- Explain the transition from renting to home ownership.
- Determine the factors that must be considered when purchasing a home.
- Describe the home-buying process.
- Explain how to apply for a mortgage.
- Describe different types of mortgages.

Essential Question

Why would a person choose to buy a home rather than rent?

Terms

equity
negotiation
asking price
market value
purchase agreement
contingency clause
earnest money
mortgage
loan application package
amortization
private mortgage insurance (PMI)
closing costs
appraisal
point
title
escrow account
assessed value
fixed-rate mortgage
adjustable-rate mortgage (ARM)
graduated payment mortgage
subprime mortgage
home equity loan

Home Ownership

Home ownership is a big step for many people. Giving up the comfort of renting requires planning. Renters are not responsible for maintaining the buildings or grounds of the property. It can be a comfortable situation to not have to worry about these tasks or to spend time and money on them. However, most people want to buy their own home at some point in their lives. Moving from an apartment you rent into a home that you purchase involves some transition.

Transition from Renting to Ownership

Transitioning from renting to owning requires planning. For some, renting may be the better decision than buying. A factor to consider when making the financial decision to buy is how long you will live in the property. Most financial experts agree that if you are going to live in the property for at least five years, buying makes more financial sense. However, if you plan to live in the property for fewer than five years, renting makes more financial sense.

Ethics

Truthful Loan Application

It is unethical and illegal to record false information on a mortgage application. Even the slightest exaggeration can result in the applicant losing the loan and ending in a lawsuit. If the lender is affiliated with the US government, the falsified application can be considered a federal offense. If the lender is FDIC-insured or the mortgage is processed through the Federal Housing Administration, resulting fines can cost up to $1 million and prison time.

From a budgeting perspective, new homeowners should not underestimate the expenses involved in owning a home. Money management skills must be applied, and budgets should be planned for the potential increase in monthly costs for home ownership in comparison to renting. Since housing is generally a monthly expenditure, begin by figuring a reasonable monthly housing allowance that you can afford. Housing costs include mortgage payments, utilities, property taxes, and homeowners insurance. In addition, housing experts recommend setting aside 1 to 3 percent of the purchase price each year to cover maintenance and repairs, which are also classified as housing costs. Most financial advisors suggest that total monthly housing costs should be no more than one-third of monthly take-home pay. *Take-home pay* is the amount of money you receive after taxes and other deductions are subtracted from your paycheck.

The initial costs that occur when purchasing a home should also be part of your budget. When planning the purchase of a new home, analyze the financial aspects of the purchase. If you plan to buy a home, you will need to determine a purchase price, down payment, closing costs, and mortgage you can handle over a long period of time. The cost of moving and furnishing your home should also be factored in the expenses.

Home ownership also includes personal responsibility that a renter may not have. In a rental apartment, it is largely a matter of keeping the space clean and caring for the appliances. If problems arise with the heating, air conditioning, plumbing, or major appliances, the property owner is usually responsible. When you buy a home, you become your own property owner and your responsibilities increase dramatically. Owning a home means that you have to shovel snow, cut the grass, and keep the property looking presentable, as well as cover the finances.

Advantages and Disadvantages of Home Ownership

Home ownership is a goal of many people. Buying a home can be a smart move for the following reasons.

- *Increased wealth.* Over time, the value of most homes *appreciates,* or increases in market value. For example, if you buy a home for $125,000 and three years later the home is worth $150,000, your property has appreciated by $25,000. **Equity** is the difference between the market value of property and the amount owed on the property. As a homeowner, you build equity as your home appreciates in value and your home loan is paid down. You are buying something you often can resell, perhaps for a profit.

Olesia Bilkei/Shutterstock.com

Homeowners build equity as the home appreciates in value and the loan is paid down.

- *Tax benefits.* Home mortgage interest and property taxes paid on a home are deductible expenses when figuring federal and state income taxes. Rent payments are not tax deductible.
- *Greater control.* When you buy a home, you generally have the freedom to make most of the decisions concerning your property, such as what color to paint it, where to hang pictures, and whether to put in a swimming pool. Condominiums and some housing subdivisions have rules that limit homeowners' freedoms.

However, there are disadvantages of buying a home which include the following.

- *Less mobility.* Moving usually involves selling a home, which is often complicated and time consuming. In a slow real estate market, it can take many months to sell a house or condominium.
- *Greater costs and financial responsibilities.* When purchasing a home, most homeowners make a down payment. Monthly costs include mortgage payments, homeowners insurance, and property taxes. Owners are also responsible for repair and maintenance costs.
- *Greater financial risk.* Although property values generally rise over time, homeowners risk losing money if property values drop or if they cannot keep up with mortgage payments. People who do not pay their mortgage can lose their homes.

Selecting a Home

Buying a home is an exciting event. For many people, owning a home gives a sense of permanence and financial security. It is a source of pride and satisfaction. When looking for a potential home to purchase, research location and type of home that fits your needs.

Location

As with renting a living space, location is one of the most important factors when purchasing a home. Would you prefer a lifestyle of living in the country, a small town, a city, or a suburb? Young, single persons or childless couples may prefer living in the heart of a city. Families with young children may want to live in a suburb or small town where there is more space and a stronger sense of community. Do you want to live close to your family or friends? Your answers to these and similar questions will help guide your choice of location.

The following sources can provide helpful information about specific regions and communities:

- chambers of commerce
- local newspapers and magazines
- long-time and new residents of an area

- travel books and almanacs
- community organizations in the area
- real estate brokers
- online sources

Research a location carefully before you purchase a home. Moving into a place that does not suit you can be costly in terms of happiness, time, and money. Employment, cost of living, climate, and the community in which you wish to live should be reviewed.

Employment Opportunities. Most people buy houses close to their employment. If you are employed, looking for housing close to your job may be a priority. If you are looking for employment, local or state employment offices and chambers of commerce are places to check out career opportunities in different areas. You can also find job listings and career opportunities for different areas and in different fields online.

Cost of Living. What is the average cost of housing in different areas? The Bureau of Labor Statistics publishes cost of living figures for different cities and parts of the country. What are the rates for home and car insurance? What are the sales, income, and real estate tax rates? The cost of maintaining similar lifestyles in different areas can vary greatly.

Climate. Do you prefer to live in a warmer climate? Would you rather experience snow in the winter? A world almanac or the National Climatic Center of the US Department of Commerce can provide weather statistics for different cities. These statistics include average high and low temperatures, rainfall and snowfall, humidity, and wind speed.

Community. Check out the community services and facilities. Is fire and police protection adequate? Does the community provide trash pickup, recycling, and snow removal? Look for services and activities that are important to you. Will you have access to a public library, churches, parks, and athletic facilities? Are there a variety of shops and stores?

The education system is important because its quality affects local property values. It is also important if you have children. Find out whether the schools in the area are noted for quality education.

Once you have narrowed your choices to a specific region or city, you can begin evaluating different neighborhoods. Appearance is one of the most obvious factors to consider in a neighborhood. Are the buildings attractive? Are both private and public areas well kept? Is the street layout attractive and functional?

What is the overall character of the neighborhood? Does it appear residential, commercial, industrial, or mixed? What zoning laws and building codes apply to the neighborhood? Is the area relatively free of

Sandra R. Barba/Shutterstock.com

Some communities often include features such as golf courses, tennis courts, clubhouses, walking trails, and parks.

heavy traffic, noise, and air pollution? How would you assess property values now and in the future? Does the neighborhood seem safe and crime-free? Local newspapers and law enforcement agencies may have information about crime rates.

You may want to research the ages, interests, occupations, and educational backgrounds of the people in the area. Is the overall income level similar to your own? Are most people living in the area single or married? Are there children in the neighborhood? Are there enough similarities to make life comfortable and enough differences to make it interesting?

Type of Home

Selecting your first home is an important decision. It is important to choose a residence that is conveniently designed for your lifestyle and housing needs.

A *single-family home* is a detached house, usually with a front and back yard, a driveway, and often an attached carport or garage. Single-family residences are built in a variety of ways.

- *Custom-built.* Homes are usually designed by architects to meet the specific needs and wishes of their clients. A contractor is hired to build the house according to an architect's plan. This can be a costly and lengthy project.
- *Tract.* Neighborhoods of new homes are built by developers who erect many houses at once within a given area. These houses are built from similar plans in order to keep costs down. They are less expensive and builders often make minor alterations to meet individual buyers' needs.
- *Manufactured.* A manufactured home is built in a factory and shipped to the home site where it is erected. These houses are relatively inexpensive. However, over time they may decrease rather than increase in value. The homeowner may purchase the lot that the manufactured home rests on. The lot may also be owned by a business that charges the homeowner a monthly rent.

A *condominium,* commonly referred to as a *condo,* is a form of multi-family housing in which a person typically owns the unit being occupied. The common grounds and building structure are jointly owned by the owners of the individual units. Owners pay a monthly assessment or maintenance fee to cover the costs of operating, maintaining, and repairing the shared property. The owners generally elect a board of managers to make policy and management decisions for the shared property.

A *landominium,* also called a *planned unit development,* is a type of residential property in which the homeowner owns both the home and the land on which the home is built. Landominium communities often include features such as golf courses, tennis courts, clubhouses, walking trails, and parks. A landominium owner may be responsible for windows, patio doors, decks, skylights, and walkways on the property. Like a condo, a landominium is part of a community where the landscaping, maintenance, and other services are provided by a homeowners' association. Unlike a condo, however, common areas, such as clubhouses and golf courses, are owned by the homeowners' association, not jointly by the residents.

A *housing cooperative,* commonly called a *co-op,* is a form of home ownership in which a person buys shares in a corporation that owns the apartment building. The size and type of apartment the buyer lives in is based on the number of shares purchased. As with a condo, owners of a co-op pay a monthly fee that covers their share of maintenance and service costs. The fee also covers the building mortgage and taxes.

Similar to condos and co-ops, a *townhouse* is a home that is attached to adjacent houses. The owner of a townhouse typically also owns the land on which the unit is built. Townhouses can be grouped together as a small number of units, such as a row of five to ten homes. Townhouses can also be part of a huge townhouse complex. Owners of townhouses often do not pay a monthly maintenance fee and are responsible for all inside and outside maintenance costs.

When buying a condominium, landominium, cooperative, or townhouse, it is important to do some thorough research. The soundness of this type of investment depends greatly on the management, restrictions, operating policies, and types of people involved in both ownership and management. When buying a residence, a checklist like the one in Figure 12-2 can help you with an initial evaluation.

Home-Buying Process

Buying a home involves many decisions. Once you have decided on budget, location, and specifications for the house, you can begin your search. When you are ready to buy a house, you must negotiate the offer. Then, you will sign a purchase agreement.

Find a Home

Many consumers looking to buy a home work with real estate brokers. A *real estate broker* is a person licensed to arrange for the purchase and sale of real estate

Checklist for Single-Family Home			
Outside House and Yard	**Outside Construction**	**Inside Construction**	**Living Space**
• Attractive and well-designed • Appropriate drainage of rain and moisture • Mature, healthy trees • Well-kept driveway, walkways, patio, and porch • Convenient parking • Sheltered, well-lighted entryway	• Durable siding in good condition • Solid brick and masonry free of cracks • Solid foundation walls • Weather-stripped windows and doors • Noncorrosive gutters and downspouts • Copper or aluminum flashing used over doors, windows, and roof joints • Screens and storm windows	• Smooth walls with invisible nails and taping • Well-done carpentry work • Properly fitted, easy-to-operate windows • Smooth, level floors • Dry basement with adequate drainage • Sturdy stairways with railings • Leakproof roof in good condition	• Convenient work areas (kitchen, laundry room, workshop) • Private, quiet bedrooms • Comfortable social areas (living and dining room, play space, porch or patio) • Adequate storage in closets, cabinets, attic, basement, and garage • Windows provide air, light, and ventilation

Goodheart-Willcox Publisher

Figure 12-2 A checklist can help a home buyer evaluate the condition of a home for sale.

for a fee or commission. Many people look at as many as 50 homes before they buy. Using a broker can save time for the buyer as brokers set up appointments to tour houses, help find financing, and negotiate the sale.

Real estate brokers usually employ *sales agents* to work for them. When a homeowner lists a home with a broker, the broker or a sales agent provides a variety of sales services. This person helps the homeowner price the home, advertise it, show it, and negotiate the sale with a prospective buyer. Brokers and agents post their listings online on sites such as the *Multiple Listing Service (MLS)*. Good brokers or agents know the territory in which they work. They have multiple contacts with people in the community and with other professionals in the business.

For their services, brokers and agents receive a commission, usually between 3 and 6 percent of the home's final sale price. The seller usually pays the commission.

People searching for a home may also work with exclusive buyer agents. An *exclusive buyer agent* is a real estate agent who works for the buyer and not the seller. An experienced broker or agent can provide valuable information about the real estate market, including home prices, zoning laws, and property taxes. An agent or broker can help buyers find neighborhoods that best meet their search criteria.

Negotiate an Offer

Billion Photos/Shutterstock.com

Buying a home usually requires that some negotiation take place.

Buying a home is not like going to a department store to buy a jacket. For most offers, there is usually some negotiation between the buyer and the seller. **Negotiation** is discussion with the goal of reaching an agreement.

Homebuyers usually do not pay the initial asking price. The **asking price** is the price the seller wishes to receive from the sale of the property. The **market value** is the price at which something can be bought or sold at a given point in time. In real estate, it is the price at which a seller is willing to sell and a buyer is willing to buy. If the property is an exceptional value and others are also submitting offers, it may be wise to submit the asking price or near the asking price.

For example, assume the asking price for a home is $200,000. You negotiate and offer less, perhaps 5 percent or $10,000 less. The seller can accept or reject your offer of $190,000. The seller may also reject your offer but counter with another price, such as $195,000. Now you must decide whether to accept the new price or make another offer.

There are many reasons to negotiate an offer less than the asking price. A buyer may offer less in these situations:

- the property needs repairs
- the home has not sold despite being on the market a long time
- other comparable homes nearby sold for much less
- the seller is desperate to sell
- the buyer is flexible about the move-in date

Exploring Careers

Real Estate Agent

Real estate agents help clients buy, sell, and rent properties. Real estate agents work through real estate brokers who are licensed to manage their own real estate businesses. Most real estate agents sell residential property. However, some sell commercial, industrial, agricultural, or other types of property. Real estate agents typically:

- solicit clients to buy, sell, and rent properties
- help sellers set the price of a property
- advise clients on mortgages and market conditions
- take prospective buyers or renters to tour properties
- promote properties through open houses, advertising, and listing services
- prepare documents, such as purchase offers
- attend closings with clients

Real estate agents often work more than 40 hours a week and have irregular schedules. The majority of their earnings comes from commissions. As a result, earnings can fluctuate each year. A high school diploma or equivalent is required to be a real estate agent. Agents must also pass a certification exam. Real estate agents must be able to work independently. Strong interpersonal, communication, selling, problem-solving, and negotiation skills are essential.

- the market for selling homes is bad, and there are many homes on the market
- there are a number of foreclosures in the neighborhood and in the area

Before making an offer, a buyer should research the sale price of comparable homes in the area. For example, if you are interested in a three-bedroom, two-bath home with a two-car garage, look for other homes of that description that have sold in the previous months in that neighborhood. What were the asking prices and the prices paid? The prices paid can serve as a guide to formulate a bid for a similar property. A real estate broker can do this research for you.

Sign a Purchase Agreement

When a buyer has reached an offer price, an agent or real estate attorney can draw up a purchase agreement. When the buyer agrees to buy and the seller agrees to sell, they both sign a purchase agreement. A **purchase agreement** is a contract between a homebuyer and a seller that includes a description of the real estate, its location, the purchase price, the possession date, and any other conditions and terms of the sale. Sometimes this contract is called a *sales agreement*.

The agreement should state all the conditions and terms of the sale. For example, if the seller agrees to make any home repairs, these should be stated in the agreement. If the owner promises to leave the draperies, dishwasher, range, and refrigerator, these should also be listed and described.

A home purchase agreement may contain a contingency clause. A **contingency clause** is part of a contract that calls for certain requirements to be met before the contract is binding. For example, the validity of the agreement may depend upon obtaining a mortgage within a certain period of time or at a certain rate. It may be made contingent upon the sale of the buyer's current home.

A common contingency in a purchase agreement is that the home must pass an inspection by a home inspector hired by the buyer. For a fee, home inspectors examine the home for problems that may affect the value of the home or require costly repair. These problems include cracks in the foundation, a leaky roof, and plumbing and electrical problems. Inspectors also check to make sure appliances work.

Buyers who live in areas where termites thrive or where mold is common may also have the home inspected for these problems by specialists. Specialized inspectors can be hired to find problems related to lead or asbestos exposure. If problems are found, buyers can ask sellers to fix them before they purchase the home. Buyers can also use the inspection findings to negotiate a reduction in the sale price.

When a buyer signs a purchase agreement, earnest money must be paid to the seller. **Earnest money** is a deposit made by a buyer when signing a purchase agreement to show that the offer is serious. It is usually a percentage of the home price and is applied toward the down payment at the closing of the sale. Earnest money prohibits the seller from selling the home to someone else. Buyers can lose the earnest money if they fail to go through with the agreement.

Apply for a Mortgage

Some homebuyers pay cash for a home. However, most homebuyers obtain loans to finance home purchases. A **mortgage** is a type of secured loan used for buying property. The lender is usually a bank or a mortgage company. As with other types of loans, the borrower promises to repay the lender the loan amount plus interest. The mortgage is paid in monthly installments over a set number of years. A loan repayment schedule, usually monthly payments, is created by the lender.

Loan Application Package

Applying for a mortgage is similar to applying for other types of consumer loans, as discussed in Chapter 8. To apply for a mortgage, you must submit a loan application package. A **loan application package** is the loan application and supporting documents for the loan.

The first step is to complete an application for the lender. The *Uniform Residential Loan Application (URLA)* is used for home mortgages. The information that is requested on the application is listed in Figure 12-3.

In accordance with the *USA PATRIOT Act*, federal law requires all financial institutions to obtain, verify, and record information that identifies each individual applying for a loan. The personal information provided on the loan application will be evaluated according to certain criteria including the creditworthiness of the applicant. Being creditworthy means that the person has the assets, income, and willingness to repay debt. A person's credit report will be requested from one of the credit bureaus and will be used as loan evaluation criteria.

The application also requests information about the property. The property for which the mortgage is being requested must be acceptable to the lender.

Uniform Residential Loan Application	
Section	**Information Requested**
Section I	Borrower Information
Section II	Financial Information—Assets and Liabilities
Section III	Financial Information—Real Estate
Section IV	Loan and Property Information
Section V	Declarations (questions about the property, your funding, and your past financial history)
Section VI	Acknowledgements and Agreements (requires signatures)
Section VII	Military Service
Section VIII	Demographic Information
Section IX	Loan Originator Information (to be completed by the loan agency)

Goodheart-Willcox Publisher

Figure 12-3 The Uniform Residential Loan Application (URLA) is used on all mortgage loan purchases.

The lender determines whether the property could be resold in the event that the borrower defaults. Each financial institution has guidelines on the type of property acceptable for a loan. The value of the property is also reviewed. A loan will not usually be granted for more than the appraised value of the property. Additional information about the property will be required as criteria for loan approval.

When you submit the application, you will be requested to provide personal information for the loan application package similar to those items listed in Figure 12-4. These items may take some time to gather, so allow adequate time to assemble these documents. You will also be asked for the signed sales contract for the property you are purchasing. In addition, there may also be a fee required for processing the application.

Once you submit the application package, the lender must make certain disclosures about privacy policies and other legal documents that the borrower must sign. The US Department of Housing and Urban Development (HUD) publishes a booklet entitled *Shopping for Your Home Loan: HUD's Settlement Costs Booklet*, which must be provided to the applicant.

The mortgage loan terms you are quoted often apply only at the time you apply for the mortgage. These terms may change by the time your mortgage is approved. You may want to ask for a *mortgage lock-in*, sometimes called a *rate lock* or *rate commitment*. This is a promise from the lender to honor the quoted rates and terms while your application is being processed.

After all disclosures are made and all documents signed, the lender will begin processing the application. Part of the process includes requesting a credit report for the

Loan Application Package
• Completed Uniform Residential Loan Application • Purchase contract • Two forms of identification • Income tax returns • Pay stubs • Savings account records • Declarations such as bankruptcy • Records of other property owned

Goodheart-Willcox Publisher

Figure 12-4 A loan application package requires these documents.

borrower from one of the three credit bureaus. Credit reports are covered in Chapter 8.

Mortgage Payments

The lender will create a loan payment schedule. **Amortization** is the process of paying back a loan in equal monthly installments. Each installment decreases the outstanding loan amount, or principal, each month. Most home mortgages are amortized for 30 years. In the beginning, payments are applied largely to interest. As the loan is repaid, an increasing amount of each payment is applied to the principal. This means the borrower builds up *equity*, or ownership, in the property as the loan is repaid.

The amount of a monthly mortgage payment depends on four factors: the size of the mortgage, down payment, interest rate, and term of the loan.

Size of Mortgage

Many homebuyers, especially first-time homebuyers, overestimate what they can afford and take out a mortgage that results in payments that are difficult to make. Most mortgage lenders require that the buyer spend no more than 28 percent of gross monthly income on mortgage, property tax, and home insurance payments. For example, if Mike McKenzie has total monthly earnings of \$3,000, the monthly mortgage payment should not exceed \$840 (\$3,000 × .28).

Down Payment

The larger the down payment, the less the monthly payments and total interest charges will be. If a down payment is less than 20 percent of the purchase price, most lenders will require the borrower to obtain private mortgage insurance. **Private mortgage insurance (PMI)** is an insurance policy that protects the lender from loss if the borrower defaults on the loan and the home goes into foreclosure. The reason for PMI is that if borrower is unable to make a down payment of 20 percent or more, lenders will typically look at the loan as a riskier investment. By requiring PMI, the bank is guaranteed an added layer of protection. The PMI payment is usually paid monthly as part of the overall mortgage payment.

After the borrower has paid between 20 and 25 percent of the home's purchase price, PMI is not required. The *Homeowners Protection Act of 1998* requires the automatic termination of PMI when the equity in the home reaches 22 percent of the property's value at the time the mortgage was taken. Homeowners can request early termination of PMI if they can provide proof that the equity in their home has risen to 22 percent of the property's current market value. Many borrowers either forget or do not know that PMI can be dropped once a home's value reaches the accepted level.

Interest Rate

The interest rate has a significant impact on the amount of a monthly mortgage payment. For example, monthly principal and interest payments (rounded to an even dollar amount) on a \$150,000, 30-year mortgage at various interest rates are shown in Figure 12-5.

A higher interest rate not only increases the amount of a monthly mortgage, but also adds thousands of dollars to the total interest paid over the life of a loan. Interest rates can vary greatly from year to year. If you buy when interest rates are high, you may have to look at lower-priced homes. If you buy when interest rates are low, you may be able to afford a more expensive home. A credit score is one of the most significant factors in determining the interest rate a borrower receives.

When inflation is higher or expected to rise in the near future, mortgage rates will increase because the value of the dollar is decreasing at a higher rate. On the other hand, when the economy is in recession and homes sales are sluggish, interest rates fall. The Great Recession led to a collapse in the housing market. Home prices dramatically fell, and interest rates fell to the lowest on record. The graph in Figure 12-6 shows the drop in interest rates as home sales remained sluggish for years after the start of the financial crisis.

Interest Rates versus Monthly Payment Amounts	
Interest Rate	**Monthly Payment**
4%	$716
5%	$805
6%	$899
7%	$998
8%	$1,101

Figures based on a $150,000, 30-year mortgage.

Goodheart-Willcox Publisher

Figure 12-5 Monthly mortgage payments depend on the rate of interest on the loan.

Term of the Loan

Interest is a factor of time. The longer a home is financed, the more interest will be paid over the term of the loan. Historically, the 30-year mortgage has been the most popular. However, taking out a mortgage for a shorter period means that you do not have the use of the lender's money as long. Therefore, you get a better interest rate. Most lenders offer a variety of terms for a mortgage. In addition to the two most popular terms, 30-year and 15-year, other common terms offered are 10-year, 20-year, and 25-year.

For example, assume Becky and James Quinn are borrowing $150,000 to purchase their first home. They have been quoted a rate of 4.00 percent on a 30-year mortgage and 3.25 percent on a 15-year mortgage. Figure 12-7 compares the monthly payment and total interest paid on the two loans.

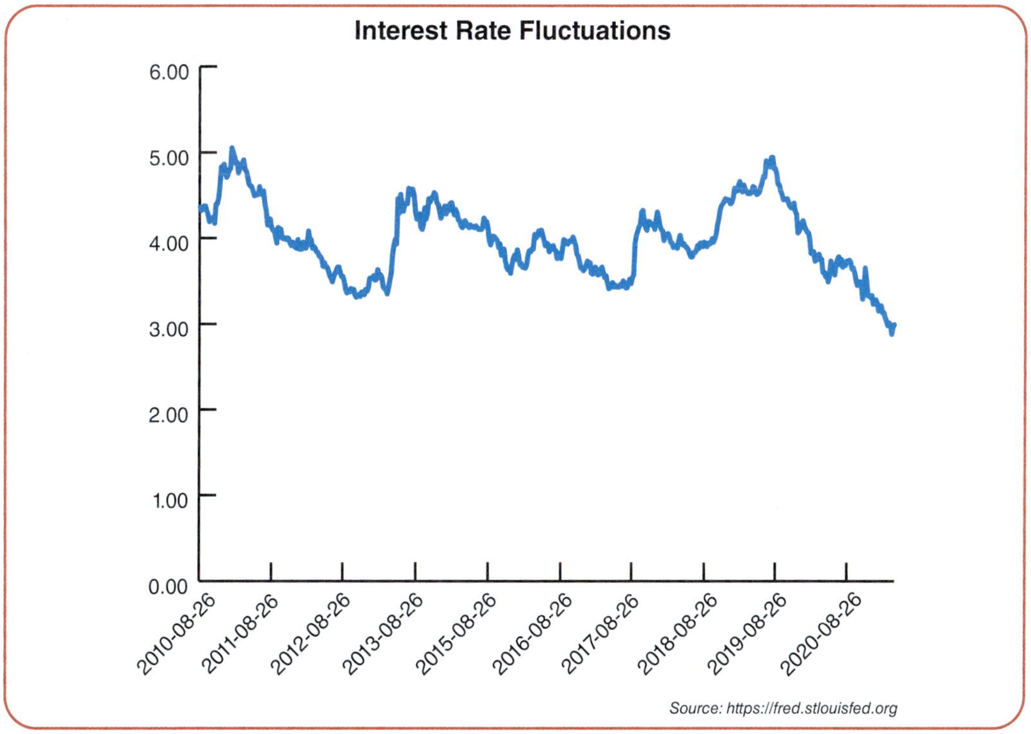

Goodheart-Willcox Publisher

Figure 12-6 Interest rates on 30-year fixed rate mortgages can fluctuate drastically.

Mortgage Rates					
Term of Loan	Amount of Loan	Rate	Monthly Payment	Total Payments	Total Interest
30-Year	$150,000	4.00%	$716	$257,805	$107,805
15-Year	$150,000	3.25%	$1,054	$189,721	$39,721

Goodheart-Willcox Publisher

Figure 12-7 A 15-year mortgage can save money over a 30-year mortgage.

As you can see, a 30-year mortgage results in monthly principal and interest payments of $716. Over the life of the loan, however, a total of $107,805 in interest will be paid. The $1,054 monthly payment with the 15-year mortgage is substantially higher. However, over the life of the loan, only $39,721 in interest will be paid. As a result, the 15-year mortgage will save Becky and James $68,084 ($107,805 – $39,721) in interest.

Closing Costs

After the seller accepts a buyer's offer, both parties set a deadline to finalize the sale of the home. This is called the *closing date*. Before the closing date, the buyer must obtain a mortgage.

On this day, the buyer, seller, lender's representative, real estate agents, and sometimes attorneys for the buyer or seller meet to sign documents and to settle all outstanding matters. The buyer gives the seller a certified check for the down payment. Other fees must be paid.

A **closing cost** is a fee or settlement charge that must be paid before the sale of a home is final. As of January 1, 2010, HUD requires lenders and brokers to give homebuyers a standard *good faith estimate (GFE)* when they apply for a mortgage. This form clearly states important loan terms and closing costs. It makes it easy to compare from lender to lender the actual and estimated costs of obtaining a mortgage and closing on the purchase of a home. The good faith estimate will include fees for many of the costs that are associated with applying for the loan. These fees are described as follows.

- *Credit report.* Credit report fees are charged to the borrower. When someone applies for a mortgage, the lender orders the borrower's credit report and/or credit score.
- *Loan application.* Loan application fees are charged by most lenders to process new loan applications.
- *Property survey.* A property survey is a map of the property drawn by a surveyor to show size, boundaries, and characteristics of a property. Lenders usually require a survey to make sure the building is on the land according to its legal description. It is normally the seller's responsibility to hire a surveyor and pay for a survey.
- *Appraisal.* An **appraisal** is a written estimate of the value of the real estate. The buyer usually pays the appraisal fee. Before approving a mortgage loan, the lender will usually require an appraisal. It helps the lender decide if the home is worth its price and if the mortgage is a good investment.

- *Points.* A **point** is a fee charged by lenders at closing and equals one percent of the mortgage. Points are prepaid interest. By prepaying some of the interest, the home buyer gets a lower interest rate. A lower interest rate, in turn, means lower monthly payments. Each point reduces in the interest rate by .25 percent. Most lenders charge one to three points. Two points on a $100,000 mortgage comes to $2,000. Points are also called *discount points.*
- *Title search and title insurance.* A **title** is a legal document that proves ownership of property. An *abstract of title* is a summary of the public records regarding the ownership of a property. The buyer should have an attorney or title insurance company review the abstract of title to be sure that the seller is the legal owner and that the property is free of debts or title problems. The title company also offers *title insurance,* which is a type of insurance that protects the buyer if problems with the title arise after the purchase. The buyer usually pays the title search fee and the one-time fee for title insurance.
- *Recording the deed.* Recording fees must be paid to record the deed. This document transfers the ownership of the property from the seller to the buyer.

Sean Locke Photography/Shutterstock.com

Home inspectors examine a home for problems that may affect the value of the home or require costly repair.

Other expenses due at or after closing are commissions paid to real estate brokers and fees for attorneys' services.

Some lenders require buyers to set up escrow accounts to cover real estate taxes and property insurance. An **escrow account** is an account for holding money in trust for others. Part of the insurance and taxes each month are paid with the mortgage payment. The lender will then take the escrowed money and pay the taxes and insurance when they are due.

Real estate taxes are based on the assessed value of the property. The **assessed value** is the dollar amount assigned to a residence for tax purposes. It is usually a percentage of the market value. Property insurance is required in order to obtain a mortgage. The bank wants to be assured that if something happens to the property, its interests are covered.

Types of Mortgages

Home financing alternatives vary from state to state and lender to lender. Sources of home loans include commercial banks, savings banks, mortgage companies, and credit unions. At least three sources should be researched to compare rates and terms. Types of mortgages on the market today include the following.

- *Fixed-rate mortgage.* A **fixed-rate mortgage** is a mortgage with a guaranteed fixed or unchanging interest rate for the life of the loan. These loans are normally written with 20-, 25-, or 30-year repayment periods. However, shorter-term, fixed-rate loans are another alternative. Fifteen-year mortgages dramatically increase monthly payments, but they bring an equally dramatic reduction in total interest charges.

- *Adjustable-rate mortgage.* An **adjustable-rate mortgage (ARM)** is a mortgage with an interest rate that can be adjusted up or down periodically. The adjustments are made according to a national rate index and other predetermined factors. These loans are often offered at lower interest rates than fixed-rate mortgages. However, borrowers take the risk that interest rates and loan payments will increase when adjustments are made.
- *Graduated payment mortgage.* A **graduated payment mortgage** is a mortgage that allows the buyer to pay low monthly payments at first and higher payments in the future. It has the advantage of low monthly payments in the early years of the loan. Those who take this type of mortgage generally expect their earnings to increase.
- *Subprime mortgage.* A **subprime mortgage** is a mortgage made by lenders who charge higher-than-prime rates to borrowers who have poor or no credit ratings. Often, these borrowers do not qualify for mortgages from other lenders. Subprime lenders often bundle these mortgages together and sell them to financial institutions that are willing to absorb the risks.
- *Home equity loan.* A **home equity loan**, also called a *second mortgage*, is a type of loan in which the borrower uses the equity in a home as collateral for the loan. These loans can be used by homeowners to pay for home improvements, vacations, college costs, and other debts, such as medical bills and credit cards. In a home equity loan, the home serves as collateral. If the homeowner cannot repay the debt, the lender can repossess the home.

There are also government-sponsored mortgages for those who qualify. Examples of government-sponsored mortgages are as follows.

- *First-time homebuyer programs.* First-time homebuyer programs provide buyers with assistance, including financial incentives, to buy a home. These incentives include reduced down payments, tax breaks, and lowered requirements for obtaining credit.
- *FHA-insured loans.* An FHA-insured loan is guaranteed by the Federal Housing Administration (FHA) and helps people with low and moderate incomes purchase homes. The FHA makes no loans, but it insures lenders against borrowers' defaults. The maximum loan amounts are determined by a formula based on average cost of homes in the area. Down payment for FHA-insured loans can be as low as 3 percent. Borrowers can take up to 30 years to repay. Interest rates may be lower than for conventional loans because the government insures the lender. The home being bought and certain loan terms must meet FHA standards.
- *VA-guaranteed loans.* A VA-guaranteed loan is insured by the Veterans Administration. Only veterans of the US Armed Forces are eligible for these loans. They are long-term, fixed-rate mortgages. The Veterans Administration sets rates. There are no down payment requirements. Interest rates usually are lower than the current market rate. Borrowers can take up to 30 years to repay.

You can save money on a mortgage by making a bigger down payment or locking in a lower interest rate. Other strategies are described in Figure 12-8.

How to Save Money on a Mortgage
• *Avoid paying private mortgage insurance (PMI).* PMI payments are in addition to what you already pay for the principal, interest, and insurance. Not needing PMI means the monthly payment amount will be less.
• *Make an additional mortgage payment each year.* This can result in thousands of dollars of interest savings because the loan will be paid off early.
• *Pay additional amounts against the principal.* Since the interest is calculated on the principal, the interest payment will decrease as the principal decreases.
• *Refinance your mortgage if rates drop.* If interest rates drop below the rate you obtained for your mortgage, refinancing at a lower rate can save you money on monthly payments. However, refinancing costs money for processing the loan. Refinance only if the savings are more than the costs.

Goodheart-Willcox Publisher

Figure 12-8 These strategies can be used to save money on a mortgage.

Section 12.2 Review

Check Your Understanding

1. What are some of the advantages of owning a home?
2. List examples of the different types of homes available to buy.
3. What is the role of a real estate broker?
4. What four factors affect the amount of a person's mortgage payment?
5. What is the difference between a fixed-rate mortgage and an adjustable-rate mortgage?

Build Your Vocabulary

As you progress through this course, develop a personal glossary. This will help you build your vocabulary and prepare you for a career. Write a definition for each of the following terms and add it to your glossary.

equity
negotiation
asking price
market value
purchase agreement
contingency clause
earnest money
mortgage
loan application package
amortization
private mortgage insurance (PMI)
closing costs
appraisal
point
title
escrow account
assessed value
fixed-rate mortgage
adjustable-rate mortgage (ARM)
graduated payment mortgage
subprime mortgage
home equity loan

Review and Assessment

Chapter Summary

Section 12.1 Renting a Residence

- Your first adult residence might be on campus at a university. Or, you might decide to live in an apartment or rent a house. Rent is expensive, so it might be necessary to have roommates to share the cost. As a young person, there are many advantages to renting over home ownership. However, there are disadvantages that should also be considered.
- Following the rental process can help you find a place that works for you and your budget. When you find a place, you probably will be required to sign a lease or rental agreement. It is important to be a good tenant and respect your rights and responsibilities as a renter.
- Planning your move can save problems later. Take an inventory of your possessions before you move. After you move, create a list of items you need that you don't currently own. A list can help you furnish your place with the necessities for apartment living.

Section 12.2 Purchasing a Home

- Buying a home necessitates transition from renting to purchasing. There are many financial and personal responsibilities that come with home ownership. In addition, there are advantages and disadvantages that should be considered before purchasing a home. When searching for a house you would like to purchase, consider location and type of home at the beginning of the process.
- The homebuying process includes finding a home, negotiating a price, and signing a purchase agreement.
- After a home has been chosen, it will be necessary to apply for a mortgage. The lender will have a loan application package that you will complete. The mortgage payments will be calculated based on the amount, time, and interest rate for the loan. Once the process is complete, the transaction will be closed and the borrower receives title to the property.
- There are various types of mortgages that are available. The borrower should research all options before settling on one type of loan.

Review Your Knowledge

1. Compare the advantages and disadvantages of renting a place to live.
2. Summarize and explain the rights consumers have when renting a residence.
3. Explain the process of finding and renting a residence.
4. Summarize and explain the responsibilities that come with renting a residence.
5. Describe how to prepare to move into a new residence.
6. Explain the transition from renting to home ownership.
7. Determine the factors that must be considered when purchasing a home.
8. Describe the home-buying process.
9. Explain how to apply for a mortgage.
10. Describe three different types of mortgages.

Apply Your Knowledge

1. Renting housing is costly and impacts the budget of an individual or family. Make a list of the costs that are associated with renting a residence. Include items such as deposits, rent, utilities, and any other expenses you think you would incur as a renter. Create a checklist of these items and insert an amount of money that you think each would cost. Analyze each line item. What do you think your monthly living expenses would be for an apartment?

2. Living with roommates requires that each person understand obligations. What topics do you think are important for roommates to discuss before moving into an apartment? Are some more important than others? Make a list of topics you would discuss when considering moving in with a friend.
3. Steven is starting college in the fall and will be attending a local technical school while also working at a part-time job. Some friends are renting a house and have asked Steven to move in with them. There are two options: moving into a house with friends as roommates, or living with parents and siblings. Examine the advantages and disadvantages of both options. Make a list of pros and cons for each living situation for Steven.
4. An apartment lease is a legal contract between the lessee and the lessor. Assume you are going to college and will be renting a house with several roommates. Describe the legal aspects that each of you assumes when signing a lease.
5. Sometimes, legal documents use words or phrases that are difficult for the average person to understand. Review the lease shown in Figure 12-1. Carefully read through and evaluate this lease. Make a list of the important points you learned.
6. When signing a lease, you are entering into a legal contract with the property owner. Create a two-column chart. Label the first column *Legal Responsibilities of Lessee*. In this column, list what the tenant is contractually bound to do by the terms of the lease. Label the second column *Legal Responsibilities of Lessor*. In this column, list what the property owner is contractually bound to do by the terms of the lease.
7. Start the process of planning ahead for your first move from your home into an apartment or dorm for your first year of college. Make a list of all the items you own that you would move with you. Next, make a list of additional items you think you will need that you do not currently own. These could include towels, bedding, and other items necessary for daily living. After you complete your list, estimate the amount of money that will be needed for these purchases.
8. Transitioning from paying rent each month to the financial responsibilities of home ownership can be overwhelming. Create a plan that could be used to help a person transition to home ownership. Identify money-management techniques that can be used to help an individual experience a smooth transition from renting to home ownership.
9. Suppose you are applying for a mortgage loan for $125,000. The lending agent with whom you are working states that an adjustable-rate mortgage (ARM) would give you the lowest possible monthly payment during the first three years of the mortgage. Would you consider an ARM? Why or why not?
10. There are many financial aspects of purchasing a house. Create a list of expenses you think are involved in each of these steps of the home-buying process: finding a home; applying for a loan; moving into a home; furnishing a home; maintaining a home; and insurance, taxes, utilities. Create a detailed list and analyze each line item.

Apply Your Math Skills

1. Financial experts recommend that housing not exceed 1/3 of an individual's monthly take-home pay. Using the monthly payments shown in Figure 12-5, calculate what an individual's monthly take-home pay would need to be for each payment to be affordable.

2. Cassie is buying a condo for $137,500 and has enough money saved up to pay a 20% down payment. How much is the down payment? What is the amount of the mortgage?

Communication Skills

College and Career Readiness

Reading. Review the vocabulary list at the beginning of this chapter. *Sight words* are those words that you recognize automatically. Identify the sight words with which you are familiar. For those words that are unfamiliar, write context clues that will help you decide the meaning of those words.

Writing. Standard English means that word choice, sentence structure, paragraphs, and the format of communication follow standard conventions used by those who speak English. Using standard English, write several paragraphs to describe your ideal house to live in as an adult. Include the type of home, number of bedrooms and baths, and other amenities and requirements that you would have. Edit and revise your work until the ideas are refined and clear to the reader.

Listening. *Hearing* is a physical process. *Listening* is an intellectual process that combines hearing with evaluating. Practice listening while your instructor presents this lesson. Focus on the message and monitor for understanding.

Teamwork

Working with a teammate, create a budget that two roommates could use when sharing an apartment. Include rent, utilities, food, insurance, and any other costs you might have. How much will it cost per month for the apartment?

Internet Research

Renter's Rights. Consumers who rent a living space are entitled to certain rights under the Fair Housing Act. Use the Internet to research this law. Explore the consumer rights associated with renting a residence. Next, conduct Internet research for renter's rights in your state. How are your state's laws the same as the federal Fair Housing Act? How are they different?

Mortgage Rates. Visit the websites of several banks and other mortgage lenders. What is the current mortgage rate today? Next, research what the mortgage rate was on this date last year. How do they compare?

Mortgage Calculator. The purchase of a long-term asset, such as a house, usually requires that an individual take out a mortgage. Mortgage payments generally extend over a 30-year period. The amount of the mortgage is amortized over that span of time. Conduct an Internet search for a mortgage calculator. Assume you are financing a home for $200,000 over 30 years with a 10 percent down payment. Use a current interest rate. What is the monthly payment amount? Create a home loan payment schedule for the life of the loan.

Purchase Agreement. There are many legal aspects to buying a home for which an attorney or real estate professional should be hired. Some of the legal documents involved when purchasing a home include a purchase agreement, property title, and HUD documentation. Using the Internet, research the legal documents that are required to purchase a home. Create a list of each document and analyze the legal purpose of each.

Loan Application Package. Lenders typically guide potential customers through the loan application process on their website. Select a bank or other financial institution and visit its website. Search for the home loan application package on the site. Summarize each component of the loan application package. Next, print the Uniform Residential Loan Application. What information does this application require that will be used as loan evaluation criteria?

Portfolio Development

College and Career Readiness

Transcripts. A *transcript* is an official academic record of the courses a student has completed, the school where the courses were taken, grades received, dates the courses were taken, and a cumulative grade point average (GPA). Including a transcript as part of your portfolio provides evidence of your scholastic achievements. Transcripts reflect academic successes and confirm the candidate's statements that courses of study have been completed as indicated on a résumé. It is a given that universities will want to see your transcripts, but employers may also ask for a transcript at some point in the interviewing process. By including a copy in your portfolio, it shows organization and anticipation on the part of the candidate, which are signs of leadership.

When you contact your school for a copy of your transcript, you will likely be asked if you want an unofficial or official copy. An unofficial copy can generally be received by a student at no cost. For an official transcript, there may be a small fee requested. However, some schools may not release official transcripts to students. Each school has different guidelines regarding transcripts, so check with your advisor regarding transcript policies.

1. Determine if you should request an unofficial or official transcript.
2. Contact and obtain transcripts from your school. This may require a wait time, so plan accordingly.
3. Add dates for when you requested and received your transcript to your master portfolio spreadsheet.

CTSOs

Event Prep

Communication Skills. Competitive events may also judge communications skills. Presenters must be able to exchange information with the judges in a clear, concise manner. This requirement is in keeping with the mission of CTSOs: to prepare students for professional careers in business. Communication skills will be judged for both the written and oral presentation. The evaluation will include all aspects of effective writing, speaking, and listening skills.

To prepare for the business communications portion of an event, complete the following activities.

1. Visit the organization's website and look for specific communication skills that will be judged as a part of a competitive event.
2. Spend time to review the essential principles of business communication, such as grammar, spelling, proofreading, capitalization, and punctuation.
3. If you are making a written presentation, ask an instructor to evaluate your writing. Review and apply the feedback so that your writing sample appears professional and correct.
4. If you are making an oral presentation, ask an instructor to review and listen for errors in grammar or sentence structure. After you have received comments, adjust and make the presentation several times until you are comfortable with your presentation.
5. Review the Communication Skills activities that appear at the end of each chapter of this text as a way to practice your reading, writing, listening, and speaking skills.
6. To practice listening skills, ask your instructor to give you a set of directions. Then, without assistance, repeat those directions to your instructor. Did you listen closely enough to be able to do what was instructed?

CHAPTER

13 Purchasing a Car

As you learned in Chapter 10, studying the marketplace and researching products can help consumers get the most out of their dollars. Knowing and understanding consumer protection for buyers is also important when making a purchase.

When buying a car, applying a systematic decision-making process is a good approach to use to purchase a vehicle that meets personal needs and wants. Following this process can help analyze trade-offs and opportunity costs so that your purchasing decision stays within budget.

Knowing what you want and seeking out reliable consumer information can help you make the right spending choices. Using these strategies can make your car buying experiences rewarding rather than frustrating.

Focus on Finance

Automobile Recalls

There are times when automobile manufacturers issue recalls on certain vehicles. In recent years, defective automobile parts such as air bags and accelerator pedals have warranted recalls. If the vehicle is recalled, it can be brought to a dealer to repair or replace items that might pose a danger to the owner. There is no cost to the owner of the automobile when recall repairs are made by the dealer.

Information about recalls is available on the website of the National Highway Traffic Safety Administration (NHTSA). The NHTSA was established by the Highway Safety Act of 1970 and is dedicated to achieving the highest standards of excellence in motor vehicle and highway safety. It works daily to help prevent vehicle crashes and their attendant costs, both human and financial. By checking the NHTSA website on a regular basis, car owners can read the latest car recalls and keep their vehicle in safe condition at no cost to them.

College and Career Readiness

Reading Prep. Write all of the key terms for this chapter on a sheet of paper. Highlight the words that you do not know. Before you begin reading, look up the highlighted words in the glossary and write the definitions.

Sections

Rick Becker-Leckrone/Shutterstock.com

Section 13.1 Shopping for a Car

Essential Question

What decisions need to be made *before* buying a car?

Objectives

After studying this section, you will be able to:

- Describe the automobile marketplace.
- Identify sources of information that can be used when shopping for a pre-owned car.
- List major consumer protection laws for car buyers.

Terms

certified used car	vehicle identification number (VIN)	lemon law
depreciation		FTC Used-Car Rule

Automobile Marketplace

The automobile marketplace is competitive, offering many different ways for consumers to shop for a car. Traditional dealerships, auto superstores, and private sellers or auctions operate both in person as well as online. The benefits of purchasing and owning your own car include freedom of travel, lack of reliance on public transit, and establishing good credit. The disadvantages include cost of maintenance, insurance, gas, and loss of value due to depreciation.

Dealerships

welcomia/Shutterstock.com

A car dealership usually sells new cars produced by one or two manufacturers as well as used cars of various makes and models.

A car dealership usually sells new cars produced by one or two manufacturers as well as used cars of various makes and models. Traditional dealerships offer financing and take a used car as a trade-in. Dealers will usually offer trade-in customers one price that includes the new car with the trade-in value subtracted. However, consumers often get a better deal if the price of the trade-in and the price of the new car are negotiated separately.

Many dealerships also sell certified used cars with full warranties. A **certified used car** is a previously owned vehicle that has received a thorough mechanical and appearance inspection along with necessary repairs and replacements. Most certified vehicles meet age and mileage restrictions. They pass inspections that include checks for damage, top-off of fluids, and repair or replacement of damaged parts.

Employability Skills

Positive Attitude

Professionals exhibit a positive attitude in their job performance and workplace interactions. *Attitude* is how personal thoughts or feelings affect a person's outward behavior. It is a combination of how you feel, what you think, and what you do. Attitude is how an individual sees themsevles, as well as how they perceive others.

Once a vehicle passes this process, the dealer or manufacturer often extends the existing warranty or issues a new 12-month or 12,000-mile warranty.

Most manufacturers and many dealerships have online services. Also, a car-buying service such as Autobytel will find and price the car you want and put you in touch with a dealer near you.

Auto superstores are dealerships that sell both new and used vehicles that are inspected, serviced, and warranted. They typically carry huge used car inventories. However, prices are normally fixed and not negotiable.

Private Sellers or Auctions

Private sellers or auctions are other alternatives for buying a used car. Normally, there is no warranty coverage from private sellers or auctions unless the original warranty is still in effect. These cars are usually sold as-is, which offers no protection if problems arise with the vehicle. Before buying from private sellers or auctions, it is a good idea to have the vehicle checked by an independent, certified automotive technician.

Buying a previously used car from a private seller often costs less than buying from a dealer. Additionally, in many states retail sales tax is not paid when purchasing from private sellers.

Shopping for a Pre-Owned Car

For first-time buyers, the used car market can be the best place to satisfy both budget and transportation needs. Generally, it is a good idea to look for a two- to three-year-old car that has low mileage and is in good condition. It is a plus if the manufacturer's warranty is still in effect. Performance, safety, and service records for the make and model of a pre-owned car should be reviewed.

Used cars generally cost less to buy and to insure. They also depreciate more slowly, whereas a new car loses about 10 percent of its value through depreciation when it is driven off the lot. **Depreciation** is a decrease in the value of property as a result of use and age. It represents the difference between the amount paid for the car and the amount received when the car is sold or traded for another car.

hxdbzxy/Shutterstock.com

Buying a car at auction is an alternative to shopping at a dealership.

Although it is not an expense that is actually paid, depreciation can represent a sizable amount of money, particularly for new cars. For example, if you buy a new car this year and plan to sell or trade it in three years, its value is likely to drop by close to 50 percent. You lose less to depreciation if you buy a used car.

Buyers Guide Sticker

One source of information about a used car is the *Buyers Guide sticker.* The Federal Trade Commission's (FTC) *Used-Car Rule* requires a Buyers Guide sticker on the window of any used car sold by a dealer. This sticker describes warranty coverage or lack of it. It directs the buyer to ask that all promises from the dealer be in writing.

The sticker suggests the buyer ask to have the vehicle inspected by an independent automotive technician. It also lists some major defects that may occur in used cars.

VIN Check

The history of a used car can be checked online for a fee using its vehicle identification number (VIN). A **vehicle identification number (VIN)** is a unique number assigned by the automobile industry and used to identify an individual auto. This number is found in three places: on the dashboard, on a sticker on the driver's side doorjamb, and in the title documents of the car. The VIN history report will include information on accidents, flood damage, theft, recalls, liens on the vehicle, odometer records, and manufacturing details.

Fees for a VIN check range from about $15 to $30 for one report to $40 or more for several cars. Generally, this is a good investment if you are buying a used car.

Previous Owner

If you buy the car from the owner, ask questions. Normally, there is no warranty coverage, so it is important to learn all you can about the reliability of the car. Ask whether the seller is the original owner. Try to find out how the car was driven and maintained. Ask for service and other records on the car.

Consumer Protection for Car Buyers

Most states have consumer protection laws that prohibit car dealers from using deceptive and misleading practices to sell vehicles. A dealer must honestly answer all a consumer's questions. In addition, some states require that car dealers reveal any information they have concerning used vehicles, such as whether the vehicle was leased, a fleet vehicle, or a demonstrator. The dealer must reveal such information whether or not the buyer asks.

Truth in Lending Act

The *Truth in Lending Act* requires creditors to provide borrowers with a complete written account of credit terms and costs. According to this law, a loan contract must state this information:

- amount borrowed or financed
- total amount to be repaid

You Do the Math Units

When solving an equation, it is important to make sure the units match. For example, when calculating fuel economy in miles per gallon (MPG), the final unit must be miles over gallons. So, the equation must be the number of miles divided by the number of gallons. If the equation is incorrectly expressed as the number of miles *times* the number of gallons, the final unit would be mile-gallons, not miles/gallon.

Solve the following problems.

1. A business must calculate the number of sales dollars generated per sales representative ($/rep). Is this the correct equation for this calculation: dollars × reps? If this is not the correct equation, what is?
2. What is the final unit for this equation: 12.8 feet × 3.6 feet ÷ 7.6 seconds?
3. A shipping box is rated to hold 65 pounds. The company ships products that each weighs 1.3 pounds. It uses this formula to determine how many products can be placed in one box: pounds per product × pound per box. Is this the correct equation? If this is not the correct equation, what is?

- dollar cost of finance charges
- annual percentage rate or APR
- date charges begin to apply
- number, amount, and due dates of installment payments
- list and explanation of any penalties for late payment, default, or prepayment
- description of the security pledged, which is usually the car

A loan with a prepayment penalty does not allow the borrower to pay off the loan early and save on interest charges. These types of loans should be avoided. If the agreement is with the dealer, the contract must also state this information:

- full description of the car
- retail or cash price of the car
- deferred payment price which is the price with credit charges
- amount of the down payment

Before signing any loan agreement, as with other contracts, it is important to read it carefully and ask questions if any part of the contract is unclear. There should be no blank spaces or lines that could be filled in later. Pay special attention to the creditor's legal rights in case of late payment, default, or prepayment and be aware of any possible consequences. More information on buying a new or used car is available on the FTC website.

Lemon Laws

A *lemon* is a vehicle that has serious mechanical problems that the manufacturer has been unable to fix after a reasonable number of attempts. To protect consumers against such vehicles, federal and state lemon laws have been passed in recent years. A **lemon law** is a law that requires a seller or manufacturer of a defective vehicle either to replace or repair it or to refund the buyer's money. The defect must be extensive and must occur within a certain time or mileage period, usually 12 to 24 months or 12,000 miles. Lemon laws can be researched by searching for *lemon laws* and the name of your state.

Unfortunately, receiving help under a lemon law is not an automatic and straightforward process. The problem must be documented as well as the attempts to fix it. Your state may require arbitration, where a third party is involved in working out a solution. Some consumer experts recommend that the help of an attorney is sought at the start of the process. Figure 13-1 lists steps to take if you have purchased a car that is considered a lemon.

Magnuson-Moss Warranty Act

Lemon laws do not provide protection to buyers of used vehicles. However, there is a federal law that may. The *Magnuson-Moss Warranty Act* provides protection for purchasers of any product that costs over $25 and has a manufacturer's warranty. The act states that when a motor vehicle needs repairs three times or more for the same problem, the repairs provide proof of the ineffectiveness of the manufacturer's warranty. Under the act, buyers may have a right to receive damages for the reduced value of the vehicle. Unlike lemon laws, buyers may not only receive money but can also keep the vehicle. Additionally, if a buyer incurs legal expenses related to the problem, the manufacturer must pay the legal expenses.

FTC Used-Car Rule

Buyers of used vehicles are often concerned if the vehicle has hidden problems or defects that could result in costly repairs. The Federal Trade Commission's Used-Car Rule, commonly called the **FTC Used-Car Rule**, requires dealers to fully disclose to buyers what is and is not covered under a used vehicle's warranty. The rule covers cars, light trucks, vans, and certain

What to Do if You Buy a Lemon

1. Obtain copies of all repair orders.
2. Provide the dealer with a list of problems. Prepare a list identifying the problems, repairs performed, and dates that the car was in the dealer's repair shop.
3. Contact the manufacturer to report the problem. Some state laws require that the manufacturer be given an opportunity to fix the problem(s).
4. Contact your state or local consumer protection office for information on the laws in your state and the steps you must take to resolve your situation.
5. If the defect is serious and the car is a danger to drive, file for arbitration immediately.
6. If your car qualifies as a lemon, write a letter to the dealer and the manufacturer demanding that you receive a refund or replacement. Send a copy of the letter to your state or local consumer protection agency.
7. Contact an attorney if the dealer and manufacturer have not addressed your concerns to your satisfaction.

Goodheart-Willcox Publisher

Figure 13-1 If a recently purchased car turns out to be a lemon, follow these steps to resolve the situation.

Case Study: Choosing a Vehicle

David is a professional painter and has $3,000 to buy a car to carry equipment. The new vehicle needs to be used and in good condition, have room to carry equipment, be useful for personal driving, and be fuel-efficient. If the car is equipped with air conditioning and a radio, that would be great.

Two cars could meet the stated needs. One is a newer van in good condition that costs $6,000 and comes with a warranty. It would be perfect for carrying equipment, but awkward for personal use. It would also require financing if chosen.

The other is a station wagon priced at $2,500. A reliable dealer is selling the car with a used-car warranty. The car has the desired features and gets good mileage. The only drawback is its size. It is too small to meet the needs of the business. However, the car does have a luggage rack that could be used to carry equipment.

Case Review

1. How does the van meet the specified needs and wants?
2. How does the station wagon meet the specified needs and wants?
3. Based on the information provided, what are the potential advantages and disadvantages of purchasing each vehicle?
4. How would the systematic decision-making process help in making the decision?

demonstrators and program cars. Any dealer that sells five or more vehicles over a 12-month period is covered by the FTC Used-Car Rule.

The rule requires dealers to post a Buyers Guide sticker on all used vehicles before offering them for sale or permitting potential buyers to examine them. On a Buyers Guide, if the *AS IS–NO WARRANTY* box is checked, the buyer is responsible for all flaws and repairs after the sale. If the *WARRANTY* box is checked, the dealer pays for repairs as outlined in the warranty. The FTC Used-Car Rule does not apply to banks or financial institutions selling used vehicles, nor does it apply to private sellers.

Section 13.1 Review

Check Your Understanding

1. What is an auto superstore?
2. Approximately how much value does a new car lose when it is driven off the lot?
3. In what two ways are pre-owned cars less costly than a new car?
4. Where can a consumer locate a vehicle identification number (VIN)?
5. In terms of shopping for an automobile, what is a lemon?

Build Your Vocabulary

As you progress through this course, develop a personal glossary. This will help you build your vocabulary and prepare you for a career. Write a definition for each of the following terms and add it to your glossary.

certified used car
depreciation
vehicle identification number (VIN)
lemon law
FTC Used-Car Rule

Section 13.2 Car-Buying Decisions

Essential Question

Why should the decision-making process be applied when buying a car?

Objectives

After studying this section, you will be able to:

- Explain the decision-making process for buying a car.
- Identify the process for financing a car.

Terms

option
sticker price
manufacturer's suggested retail price (MSRP)

Decision-Making Process for Buying a Car

Buying a car typically is not a spontaneous purchase. Many people save money for months and even years before they accumulate enough to buy a car. When buying an auto, it helps to enter the marketplace knowing what you want and how much you can afford. It is necessary to determine your preferences and match your car choice to your transportation needs and budget. Using the systematic decision-making model in Figure 13-2 can help you through the car-buying process.

Step 1: Identify the Decision to Be Made

The decision-making process begins with identifying the decision that needs to be made. In this situation, it is a car. This will require analyzing your transportation needs and considering the features you want in a vehicle.

Needs

Think about why you *need* a car and how you will use it. Is a car primarily a necessity, convenience, or pleasure? Will you drive mostly on city streets, busy highways, or rugged country roads? Will you travel short or long distances? Will you drive frequently or only occasionally? Once you have identified your needs, then your wants can be established.

Wants

Before shopping begins, it is helpful to identify the features you *want* in a car. Then rank each in order of importance in meeting your needs. Some of the items to consider include:

- new or used
- domestic or imported

- hybrid or standard
- size
- appearance and styling
- performance and handling
- safety record and features
- model or body type
- features and options
- fuel efficiency
- warranty coverage

Step 2: Explore the Alternatives

After you have determined your needs and wants, it is time to explore the alternatives for the purchase and research choices. The first step is to evaluate what you can spend. Your income and overall budget will have a significant impact on the choices available to you. Next, setting priorities will help focus on what you can afford. Then, comparison shopping will help you evaluate the pros and cons as you make a decision.

Consider Cost

Your budget will have a significant impact on the car you choose. While exploring alternatives, review your overall financial situation and the value you place on responsible spending decisions. A cost-benefit analysis will weigh the costs of purchasing the car against the benefits of owning it.

Cost is a major component of the decision-making process. When buying a car, evaluate both the purchase price and the ongoing costs of car ownership. To determine how much you can afford to spend, start with the amount of cash you have on hand for a down payment and initial costs. If you own a car you can sell or trade, add its value to the amount you can spend. Calculate how large of a loan you will need and what the monthly payments will be. There are many loan calculators online that will help you estimate the monthly loan payment. Cash will also be needed for licensing, registration, taxes, and insurance.

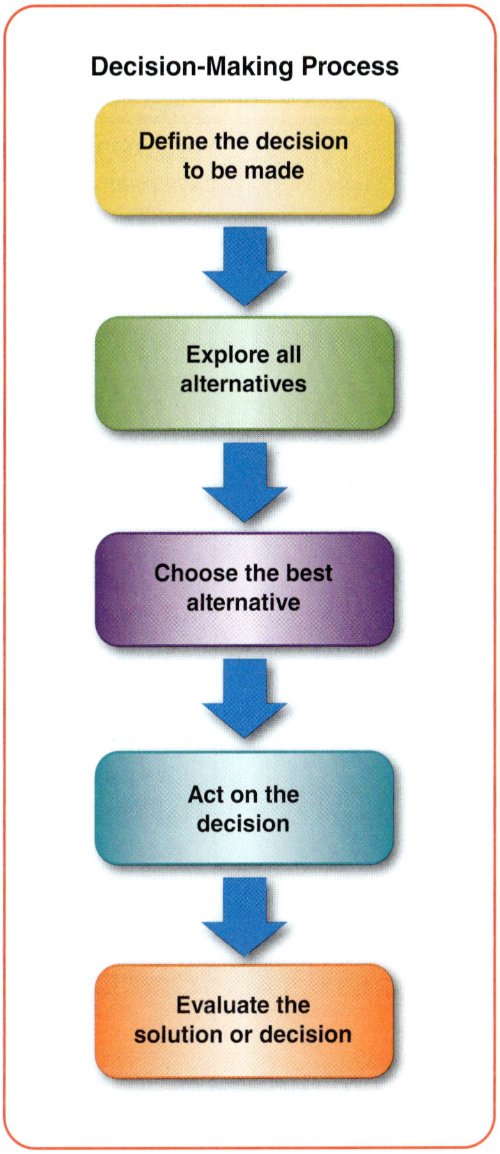

Goodheart-Willcox Publisher

Figure 13-2 Systematic decision-making can help a consumer through the car-buying process.

Next, determine how much you can spend each month to cover ongoing costs of car ownership. This amount should be factored into your monthly budget. Auto costs include many of these expenses:

- gasoline
- maintenance, including oil changes, batteries, tire rotations, and cleanings
- insurance premiums
- licensing and registration
- repair costs

- parking
- miscellaneous expenses

Some costs, like insurance premiums, will probably be fixed expense items in your monthly budget. Others, like gasoline and repair costs, will be variable expenses and should be budgeted for accordingly.

The worksheet in Figure 13-3 can help you calculate annual costs of owning and operating a car. Figure 13-4 illustrates how to calculate the cost of gas to arrive at an estimate for the worksheet.

Car Ownership Costs	
Ownership costs	**Amount**
Depreciation	$ ______
Insurance	$ ______
Sales tax	$ ______
License and registration	$ ______
Finance charges	$ ______
Total ownership costs	$ ______
Operating costs	**Amount**
Fuel and oil	$ ______
Maintenance and repairs	$ ______
Tires	$ ______
Parking	$ ______
City permits	$ ______
Total operating costs	$ ______
Total annual car costs Costs per mile (Divide total annual costs by number of miles driven.)	$ ______

Goodheart-Willcox Publisher

Figure 13-3 Use a worksheet similar to this one to help calculate the annual costs of car ownership.

Calculating Gas Costs		
Amount of Gas	**Cost**	**Mileage**
Full tank	—	Odometer 8,500
10 gallons	$35.00	Odometer 8,725
13 gallons	$46.15	Odometer 8,970
9 gallons	$31.32	Odometer 9,243
Total = 32 gallons	Total = $112.47	Total = 743 miles (9,243 – 8,500)
Miles per gallon: 743 miles ÷ 32 gallons = 23.22 **Cost of gas per mile:** total cost $112.47 ÷ 743 miles = $0.15		

Goodheart-Willcox Publisher

Figure 13-4 Starting with a full tank of fuel, record the mileage on the odometer. From that point on, record how many gallons of gasoline you buy, the price, and the odometer reading.

Ethics

Disclosing Information

To make a sale, some car sellers—both dealers and private sellers—fail to disclose to potential buyers all known defects in a vehicle. It is unethical for a seller to sell any vehicle without disclosing to the buyer all known defects. In most states, car sellers are legally liable to the buyer if it can be established that known defects were either covered up or undisclosed.

After you have determined the amount you think you need, you can compare it to Figure 13-5, which shows the average costs associated with owning a car. This will help you determine whether the amount you plan to spend is comparable with similar vehicles. The American Automobile Association (AAA) posts up-to-date figures on its website.

Set Priorities

Setting priorities will help you evaluate the pros and cons of each vehicle. For example, if you have a long commute to work, a priority might be finding a car with high fuel efficiency. If you need to transport cargo, the priority might be finding a pickup truck instead of a sedan. Prioritizing the car's style, options, and warranty coverage will help in the decision-making process.

Style. Cars come in a variety of standard sizes and styles. Compact, small, mid-size, and full-size cars are available in almost all styles and makes. Common body styles include two- and four-door sedans, station wagons, hatchbacks, convertibles, sport cars, pickups or light trucks, sport-utility vehicles (SUVs), minivans, and full-size vans. It will be necessary to decide how much space you will need for carrying passengers or cargo.

Options. An **option** is a feature available for a particular car. Some options contribute to safety, performance, and economy. Others are primarily for appearance and convenience. *Standard options* come at no additional cost. Different makes and models come with different sets of standard options or features. *Extra options* can add significantly to the price of a car. The chart in Figure 13-6 outlines common options and categorizes them according to purpose.

Average Driving Costs					
Cost	**Small Sedan**	**Large Sedan**	**Pickup Truck**	**Electric Vehicle**	**Minivan**
Cost per Mile	45.18 cents	65.36 cents	68.10 cents	55.89 cents	64.51 cents
Cost per Year	$6,777	$9,804	$10,215	$8,384	$9,677

Based on driving 15,000 miles annually

Goodheart-Willcox Publisher

Figure 13-5 The average costs of owning a car depend on the type of car.

Common Options			
Purpose	**Option**	**Purpose**	**Option**
Safety	• Air bags • Alarm system • Antilock brakes • Automatic restraint system • Child safety seats • Daytime running lights • Fog lights • Rear wiper and defrost • Rear-view camera	Security	• Antitheft alarm system • Bluetooth or Wi-Fi connectivity • Keyless entry • Single switch lock
Performance	• Automatic transmission • Cruise control • Front-wheel or four-wheel drive • Large engine • Power steering	Convenience and preference	• Adjustable steering column • Air conditioning • Electronic instrument panel • GPS (global positioning system) • Intermittent windshield wipers • Leather interior • Power mirrors • Power seats • Sound system • Sunroof • Trip computer

Goodheart-Willcox Publisher

Figure 13-6 These options are usually available at additional costs, although a few of these may be standard equipment for certain makes and models.

Every year, manufacturers add to the available options or features on new cars. Very often, option packages are offered at special prices. Try not to pay for any options you do not really want, and be sure you know the cost of each extra option.

Warranty. A *car warranty* is a written promise to the customer that should something break, malfunction, or otherwise go wrong with a vehicle within a stated period of time, the manufacturer will make necessary repairs at no cost. Normally, new cars carry full warranty protection on some parts and limited protection on others. Items such as the air conditioner, radio, and tires carry separate warranties.

Auto warranties usually run for three years or for the first 36,000 miles. Most warranties set forth specific maintenance requirements the owner must meet during the warranty period. If the car needs any repairs during that time, they must be made by a factory-authorized service department to keep the warranty valid. However, routine maintenance may be done by an independent service center as long as the work and the parts meet specifications in the owner's manual. Many manufacturers sell extended warranties.

Conduct Research

As in other decision-making situations, research is necessary before making a purchase. Shopping online and reading printed material can save time and help you become familiar with different car models, compare prices, and evaluate options.

The following resources are good references when shopping for a vehicle.

- *Kelley Blue Book* and *Edmunds* list the estimated resale value of new and used cars.

Exploring Careers

Loan Officer

Loan officers determine whether a person qualifies for a loan. They collect, verify, and evaluate data to assess an applicant's ability to pay back a loan. Loan officers can specialize in commercial, consumer, or mortgage loans. They can also work in collections or in underwriting, which is the process used in determining an applicant's ability to repay a loan. Loan officers typically:

- gather information from loan applicants
- explain different types of loans available to applicants
- obtain and verify credit scores, credit history, and income level
- analyze the applicant's finances
- approve or reject loan applications

Most loan officers work full time. They can work in a commercial bank, credit union, mortgage company, or other financial service company. Consumer loan officers typically have offices within the financial institution. Commercial and mortgage officers tend to work outside of the office to meet with clients. Loan officers must have a bachelor degree in a business or financial field. Mortgage officers must have a Mortgage Loan Originator license, which requires the completion of an examination. They must also have excellent decision-making, interpersonal, analytical, and mathematics skills.

- *Official Used Car Guide* from the National Automobile Dealers Association lists general information on cars by the make, model, and year.
- Auto Safety Hot Line, a toll-free number, gives safety data on various car models from the National Highway Traffic Safety Administration.
- Websites, such as Autobytel, Autotrader.com, Intellichoice, SmartMoney Auto Guide, and individual car manufacturers, provide new and used car information, such as pricing, safety, and more.
- Magazines, such as *Automobile Magazine*, *Car and Driver*, *Motor Trend*, and the auto issues of *Consumer Reports*, *Consumer Research*, and *Kiplinger's Personal Finance*, provide useful information on car buying and ownership.

Step 3: Make a Choice

Once the research is complete and you are ready to make a purchase, you can decide where to purchase the car. The next step will be to negotiate the price and determine the method of payment. Using credit will add to the overall cost of the purchase. Before making a commitment, figure out how much more money it will cost to buy using credit. You may decide to wait and save up until you can pay for the car with cash.

Negotiate Price

Wherever you shop, whether you buy or lease, you will have to negotiate the price. The **sticker price** is the price displayed on a vehicle as its selling price. For new cars, the sticker price is the **manufacturer's suggested retail price (MSRP)**, which is the price recommended by the manufacturer. On new cars, the advertised price is often lower than the MSRP to give the consumer the impression of a deal.

When you begin negotiating the price, start the process by offering less than the sticker price. Negotiate the cash price of the car first, and then negotiate the trade-in allowance, if any. Do not be afraid to walk away if you are not getting what you want. You can always come back.

If you are considering the purchase of a used vehicle, ask to see the service record. This will tell you how the vehicle has been maintained. Check out the VIN history as well. Be sure the title is in order and get all the figures and quotes in writing. Take a day or two to think over the deal you are offered before committing.

If you are financing the purchase, compare different loans and financial institutions. As explained in Chapter 8, the total amount paid for an auto loan is based primarily on three factors:

- interest rate charged
- amount of the loan
- length of the repayment period

Financing is covered in detail later in this section.

Conduct a Final Check

Check the car over carefully before completing the purchase. Sit in the driver's seat and see if you are within comfortable reach of the steering wheel, foot pedals, and controls. Adjust the seat, mirrors, and steering wheel position for comfort. Make sure you can see well out the front, side, and rear windows. Then start the engine. If you hear any strange noises, find out the cause. The car should idle smoothly and should not emit any burning odors.

History of Finance

Car Loans

In the early days of the automobile industry, dealers had to pay cash for all cars they purchased from manufacturers. This meant that most dealers could only buy a few cars at a time. However, with the development of the assembly line manufacturing process, manufacturers wanted dealers to buy vehicles in large quantities so they could keep the factories running regularly.

Automobile dealers today do not buy the cars they keep on their lots and in the showrooms. Instead, they acquire vehicles on a credit plan from the manufacturer, which is a process called *floor planning*. Dealers take possession of vehicles and pay the manufacturer interest until the inventory can be sold. This practice allows dealers to have a large inventory and, hopefully, generate more sales.

Since many people cannot afford to pay cash for cars, consumers can also buy cars using credit. The ability to finance cars brought the automobile into reach for many people who otherwise would have been shut out of the market. Founded in 1919, General Motors Acceptance Corporation (GMAC) was the first large nonbank financing source for automobile loans.

Test-drive the car to see how well it handles in traffic, on the open road, and when starting, stopping, turning, and parking. Is it comfortable and easy to drive? Also test all the equipment and controls, such as the emergency brake, turn signals, horn, radio, windshield wipers, and headlights. Also check the condition of the tires.

A careful check of the engine and working parts of a car is particularly important when buying a used car. Unless you know all about cars, ask an independent, certified automotive technician to take an overall look at the engine. Check the levels of all the fluids, including oil, brake fluid, and transmission fluid. If any fluid levels are low, it could be a sign of leakage or of poor maintenance.

Step 4: Implement the Decision

Once you become a car owner, you assume two major responsibilities. You are expected to carry adequate auto insurance and to operate and maintain your car properly and safely. Failing to carry out these responsibilities can endanger lives and financial resources of the car owner as well as passengers, other drivers, and pedestrians. Auto insurance is covered in Chapter 14.

Maintenance

You have much to gain by operating and maintaining your car properly. Rewards include better car performance, driving safety, and car reliability. You will have fewer breakdowns and repairs, better fuel economy, and greater trade-in value by keeping up with regular maintenance. Your car will also create less pollution.

Keeping your car in good driving condition is necessary for safety, economy, and performance. Study and follow the owner's manual for routine maintenance and service schedules. Manufacturer's instructions offer guidelines for lubrications, tune-ups, and other routine servicing. However, if you drive a car under severe conditions, your car may need more frequent attention than indicated in the owner's manual.

One key to long car life is anticipating and avoiding potential problems. Listen to your car and investigate strange noises and sluggish performance. Pay attention to warning lights, gauge readings, and any leaks, drips, or unusual odors. Check out irregularities promptly. If you ignore little sounds and changes in performance, a small problem may become major and costly.

For safer driving and better fuel economy, keep the tire pressure at the recommended level. Replace worn tires with the proper size as recommended in the owner's manual. Tires also need to be rotated periodically.

MBI/Shutterstock.com

The final check for buying a used car may include an inspection by a certified automotive technician.

Repairs

It is wise to investigate service centers before you need one. Look for a service shop or mechanic you can trust and go to the same place whenever your car needs service or repairs. Three choices of service centers are a dealer, a chain auto service center, or an independent, certified automotive technician. For warranty servicing, it may be necessary to go to the dealership. For routine repairs and maintenance, you may choose to shop around. Look for membership in such organizations such as the local Chamber of Commerce or Better Business Bureau.

Look for experienced, well-trained automotive technicians. Certification is one indication of competence. ASE-certified technicians have completed the training and passed the tests required by the *National Institute for Automotive Service Excellence.* Certified technicians receive credentials listing their areas of competence. They usually wear the blue and white ASE insignia. An ASE sign usually appears on the premises where these technicians are employed. An endorsement by the *American Automobile Association (AAA)* is another indicator of reliable servicing. Endorsed repair centers must meet the high standards of the association.

Time and gas can be saved by finding convenient locations when you need to leave your car for service. Business hours that suit your schedule may also be important when dropping off or picking up your car. Before taking your car in for service, call for an appointment and to ask how long you can expect the service to take.

Comparison shopping for fees and charges for routine maintenance jobs, such as a lubrication, a wheel alignment, and an oil change can save money in your budget. You can often make these comparisons on the telephone. It is likely that shops with reasonable charges for routine maintenance will be reasonable on bigger jobs as well.

Request written estimates, itemized bills, and written guarantees on the work performed. When you leave your car to be serviced, make it clear that the service center should contact you before any unexpected major repairs or services are performed. Keep your own file of auto records for purchases, maintenance, repairs, and insurance claims.

Step 5: Evaluate the Purchase

After you have used the goods or services for some time, evaluate the car and your decision-making process. Are you satisfied with your choice? What did you learn that will be helpful when you are ready to make another auto purchase? What would you do differently? Review the purchase to see if you met the goal that you intended and whether the car meets your expectations.

Financing a Car

Some purchases of new and used cars are made with cash, but most are financed. This means the buyer takes out a loan and pays for the car with monthly payments. Financing a car costs more than paying cash because interest is paid on the amount borrowed.

In general, the minimum age for obtaining a car loan is 18. When you apply for a car loan, the lender will want proof that you have a job and earn income. The lender will also look at your credit report or credit score to determine whether you are creditworthy.

The installment loan is the most common form of auto financing. The size of the monthly payments and the length of the repayment period for installment loans vary greatly. Loan periods are usually between three and seven years. This makes it relatively easy for car buyers to obtain loans they can afford to repay comfortably.

The following steps will help you prepare for the loan process.

1. *Obtain a copy of your credit report.* Your credit score plays a key role in determining the interest rate if you are approved for a loan. A high credit score can help you get a lower interest rate, which means lower monthly payments.
2. *Gather supporting documents.* In accordance with the USA PATRIOT Act, federal law requires all financial institutions to obtain, verify and record information that indentifies each individual when applying for a loan. Lenders require proof of employment, a checking account, and two forms of identification. You will also be asked for your social security number.
3. *Determine the amount you need to borrow.* A higher down payment means lower monthly payments and lower finance charges. Determine how much you can put down and how much you need to borrow.
4. *Decide the length of your loan.* The longer the loan, the lower the monthly payments. Financial experts recommend choosing the shortest loan payment schedule possible to save finance charges. The approximate monthly payment can be calculated using an online calculator.
5. *Shop around and get preapproved.* Check multiple banks, credit unions, and online lenders to find the best interest rate on the loan. Apply for the loan and get approved before you make an offer. Being preapproved makes you a cash buyer, which can get you a better price and simplifies the entire process.

NDAB Creativity/Shutterstock.com

When negotiating the price of a car, start the process by offering less than the sticker price.

Sources of Financing

Common sources of car loans include auto dealers, banks, credit unions, and finance companies. It is a good idea to shop around for loans before you go to the car dealer.

Dealer financing is a convenient, on-the-spot source of financing. Rates may also be attractive when dealers are overstocked and need to sell cars to reduce their inventories. When asking a dealer about auto financing, insist on separate quotes for the car and the financing. This is the only way you can accurately compare finance charges and terms with other loan sources. Be wary of a dealer who tries to package the car and the financing together. This can be a costly package.

After looking at the dealer's credit terms, check financing terms from other sources. Credit unions generally offer the lowest rates for auto loans. You can also investigate financing sources online and compare rates and terms.

To obtain an auto loan, the borrower pledges the car as security or collateral. This means the creditor will hold the title to the car until the loan is paid in full.

If the borrower fails to repay the loan, the lender may legally take back or *repossess* the car and sell it.

Interest	
Finance Charges	Loan Amount (Principal)
$ 99.28	$1,500
$132.37	$2,000
$198.56	$3,000

Goodheart-Willcox Publisher

Figure 13-7 This chart shows how much interest is paid on loans from $1,500 to $3,000. Each loan has an APR of 12 percent and is repaid in 12 monthly payments.

Cost of Financing

The overall cost of auto financing varies with the principal, which is the original amount borrowed, the annual percentage rate (APR), and the length of the repayment period. The more money you borrow, the more interest you pay, as illustrated in Figure 13-7. You want to make the biggest down payment you can and pay for taxes, title, and other fees up-front to lower the amount you need to borrow.

The higher the APR, the more money you will pay in interest. The longer the repayment period, the more interest is paid. A low monthly payment with a long repayment period is often no bargain.

You can use the principal, APR, and repayment period length to compare the cost of credit between different loans, as illustrated in Figure 13-8. Using the statistics in Figure 13-8 as a starting point, you can calculate the finance charges on different amounts of principal. For example, if you borrow $4,000, multiply the finance charge in the chart by four.

Leasing

Rather than buying, many consumers today prefer to lease. An auto lease is similar to an auto loan in that the lessee makes an initial payment and makes monthly payments for a set period of time. Generally, the lessee's initial costs and monthly payments are less than those of a buyer. However, the lessee does not own the car at the end of the lease term. Like buyers, lessees must also pay fees for registration, licensing, and other charges.

If you lease a car, the initial payment usually includes the first monthly payment, a security deposit, and a *capitalized cost reduction.* Familiarize yourself with the following terms before negotiating a car lease.

- *Capitalized cost* of a leased car is the price or value of the vehicle on which the lease is based. The lower the figure, the lower monthly payments will be.

Interest			
Repayment Period	6% APR	8% APR	10% APR
12 Months	$32	$43	$54
24 Months	$63	$85	$107
36 Months	$95	$128	$161

Goodheart-Willcox Publisher

Figure 13-8 This chart depicts the estimated finance charges for a $1,000 loan given different rates and repayment periods.

- *Capitalized cost reduction* may include a cash down payment, trade-in allowance, rebates, and other buying incentives. These factors reduce the capitalized cost which will lower the monthly payments.
- *Residual value* is the worth of a car at the end of the lease. The higher the residual value, the lower monthly payments will be. The residual value is based on depreciation estimates. Consult the *Automotive Lease Guide* at your local library or bookstore for a list of the residual values of leased cars.
- *Lease term* is the length of the lease, which is usually 24, 36, or 48 months. The lease term should be limited to the length of the car warranty.
- *Mileage limitations* are stated in the lease and is usually limited to 12,000 or 15,000 miles annually. There will be extra charges for excess mileage and wear and tear.
- *Money factor* is the interest that is paid, usually stated as a decimal such as .00265. To convert this to an annual interest rate, multiply by 24 (for example, $.00265 \times 24 = 6$ percent). The money factor should be similar to or lower than new car loan rates.

All the terms of the lease, including the capitalized cost of the car, should be negotiated. Be prepared to negotiate the trade-in allowance or capitalized cost reduction if you are trading a car or making a down payment. It also is important to be aware of the penalties if you terminate the lease early. It can be very costly to do this.

Check the lease for turn-back condition requirements and car care packages you may be required to purchase. Review the warranty and be sure it is good for the entire term of the lease. Consider buying *gap insurance*, which covers you if the car should be stolen or totaled in an accident. It pays the difference between what you owe on the lease and what the car is worth. Finally, look for a fixed residual price option to buy at the end of the lease if you think you may want to own the vehicle rather than lease a new car.

Get answers to any questions you have and be sure you understand all the terms of the agreement before you sign a lease contract. Review all the charges you must pay up front and at the termination of the lease. Get all the figures and promises in writing.

Section 13.2 Review

Check Your Understanding

1. Outside of the purchase price, what are three expenses related to owning an automobile?
2. Name two sources where you can find the estimated resale value of cars.
3. What are the rewards of properly maintaining a car?
4. List four common sources of car loans.
5. What does gap insurance cover?

Build Your Vocabulary

As you progress through this course, develop a personal glossary. This will help you build your vocabulary and prepare you for a career. Write a definition for each of the following terms and add it to your glossary.

option

sticker price

manufacturer's suggested retail price (MSRP)

Review and Assessment

Chapter Summary

Section 13.1 Shopping for a Car

- There are multiple ways to shop for a vehicle in the automobile marketplace. Traditional dealerships, auto superstores, and private sellers or auctions operate both in person as well as online.
- The used-car market can be the best place to satisfy both budget and transportation needs. Used cars cost less to buy and to insure and depreciate more slowly than new cars. The history of a used car can be checked online using its vehicle identification number (VIN). If buying the car from a private owner, ask to see the service and other records for the car.
- Most states have consumer protection laws that prohibit car dealers from using deceptive and misleading practices to sell vehicles. It is important to understand your consumer rights before making a purchase.

Section 13.2 Car-Buying Decisions

- Using the systematic decision-making model is a good practice when making a purchase, especially a major purchase such as an automobile. The five steps of this process are: identify the decision to be made; explore the alternatives; make a choice; evaluate the purchase; and implement the decision.
- Some purchases of new and used cars are for cash, but most are financed. Financing a car requires that the borrower apply for a loan and go through the steps of the loan process. Common sources of car loans include auto dealers, banks, credit unions, and finance companies. Rather than buying, many consumers today prefer to lease. An auto lease is similar to an auto loan in that the lessee makes an initial payment and makes monthly payments for a set period of time.

Review Your Knowledge

1. Describe the automobile marketplace.
2. What restrictions must be met for a car to be considered a certified used car?
3. Identify sources of information that can be used when shopping for a pre-owned car.
4. What is included in a VIN history report?
5. List and describe major consumer protection laws for car buyers.
6. Explain the decision-making process for buying a car.
7. When establishing priorities while car shopping, what factors should be considered?
8. Identify the process for financing a car.
9. What is the difference between buying and leasing a vehicle?
10. What does the first payment of a leased car include?

Apply Your Knowledge

1. Buying a used car requires research and comparison shopping. How would you prepare to purchase a used car and ensure you are getting the right car for you? Describe the resources you might use and the actions you might take when searching for the right used car to fit your needs and wants.
2. *Caveat emptor* is a Latin phrase that means "let the buyer beware." How can a consumer who is shopping for a pre-owned car act with caution in the automobile marketplace?

3. Multiple laws have been enacted to protect consumers who have purchased cars. Which of the consumer protection laws described in this chapter do you think is the most important for a teen or young adult making his or her first car purchase?
4. The systematic decision-making process can guide you through the process of buying a car. The first step in the process is to identify the decision to be made. Choose the car of your dreams that you would purchase if you were financially able. List the make, model, and year. Now, you must determine your needs and wants. First, create a list of the *needs* that must be met by this car purchase. Then, create a list of the features you *want* in a car.
5. Setting priorities will help you evaluate the pros and cons of each vehicle you consider when buying a car. Using the lists of needs and wants you created in the last activity, rank your needs and wants in order from most to least important. The most important items will be your priorities.
6. Most people obtain a loan when purchasing a car. Using cash might be an option if you have it available. Analyze whether you think getting a loan for the purchase of a car is a financially sound idea.
7. There are many factors to consider when financing a personal asset such as a car. Make a list of the information you would need to provide to the lender if you applied for a loan. Analyze each of those items. Do you currently have the documentation necessary to get a car loan?
8. Owning a car is costly and impacts the budget of an individual or family. Make a list of the costs that are associated with owning a car. Include items such as oil changes, tire rotations, repairs and any other expenses you think you would incur. Create a checklist of these items and insert an amount of money that you think each would cost on a monthly or yearly basis.
9. Categorize each expense you listed in the last activity as either fixed or variable. Analyze each line item. What do you think your monthly expenses would be for owning a car?
10. Some people prefer to lease a car rather than buy one. Make a list of the pros and cons of leasing a car. Would you prefer to buy or lease?

Apply Your Math Skills

1. Louisa wants to purchase a used SUV that costs $12,750 from an automobile superstore. After a $4,000 down payment, the rest must be financed. A credit union has approved the car loan application for 36 months at 2.9%. The superstore will offer financing for 48 months at 1.9%. Calculate the monthly payment for each loan.
2. Michael is leasing a new car for two years. The lease requires a down payment of $1,999 plus a security deposit of $1,000. The monthly payment is $500 a month for two years. What is the total cost for Michael to lease the car for two years?

Communication Skills

College and Career Readiness

Writing. Rhetoric is the study of writing or speaking as a way of communicating information or persuading someone. Identify rhetoric that could be used to persuade a loan officer to give you a loan. Write a script in a step-by-step format for presenting the item to an officer at a financial institution.

Listening. Listening requires discipline. When listening to your instructor, you must show you are listening by making eye contact, taking notes, or asking questions. As you listen to your teacher present this chapter, use a listening technique to make sure you understand what is being said.

Reading. *Scanning* is done when you know the information you need is in a document, you just have to find it. Scan this chapter for AAA and read the information around it. Did scanning work for you? How long did it take you to find AAA?

Teamwork

Arrange to visit an auto service center or repair facility on your own. Take note of the experience and qualifications of the technicians; equipment and facilities; guarantees on parts and servicing; charges for routine jobs such as an oil change; and the attitude of the employees toward answering questions and complaints of customers. After your visit, discuss with your team how everyone's individual experiences compare. Did one service facility seem preferable to the others? If so, why?

Internet Research

Automobile Loan Application. Visit the website of a financial institution in your area, such as a bank or credit union. Find out what information you would need to provide when applying for an automobile loan at this financial institution. Make a list of the documentation required. Print and complete the loan application. Organize the completed application and the supporting documentation as you would if you were to actually apply for a loan. Submit your loan application to your instructor.

Automobile Loan Calculator. The purchase of a car usually requires that an individual obtain a loan. Conduct an Internet search for an automobile loan calculator. Assume you are buying a car for $19,999 with a 10 percent down payment and a loan term of 4 years. Use a current interest rate. What is the monthly payment amount? Create a car loan payment schedule for the life of the loan.

Portfolio Development

College and Career Readiness

Social Responsibility. *Social responsibility* is a trait that many businesses support and encourage from their employees. Workplace studies show that socially responsible employees are, by nature, productive, generally ethical, and loyal.

Social responsibility is demonstrated in many ways, and you can start with activities at your current job or school. For example, you may have organized a green team at your school to initiate a recycling program.

Or, you may have participated in a campaign to "turn off the lights" and conserve energy at home or school. Documentation of these activities reflects social responsibility.

Participating in community service is an example of social responsibility. This can sometimes be criteria used by employers or universities when vetting potential candidates. Serving the community shows a candidate is well-rounded, socially aware, and capable of teamwork. For some individuals, volunteer work could substitute for actual paid employment. In some situations, showing that you spent regular hours supporting a social cause is as valuable as paid work experience. By including evidence of these kinds of activities, a candidate can attract the attention of a person reviewing job applicants and climb the list of interviewees.

For a digital portfolio, consider creating a video that informs viewers about it. Suppose you volunteer with a group that helps repair homes for elderly homeowners. The video could show scenes from the worksites and comments from the residents. Be sure you have permission to include other people in your video before doing so.

1. Using word-processing software, create a document that lists socially responsible projects in which you have taken part at school, work, or in your community. Use the heading "Service Projects," or something similar, along with your name. List the name of the programs, date(s) of service, and activities that you performed. If you received an award related to this service, mention it here.
2. Update your master portfolio spreadsheet to include your service projects. Back up your files on your flash drive.

CTSOs

Event Prep

Business Law. Business law is a competitive event you might enter with your CTSO. Business law is an individual event in which participants take an objective test that covers multiple legal topics. Participants are usually allowed one hour to complete the event. One of the topics that may be included on the test is *insurance as a means of risk management*. To prepare for a business law event, complete the following activities.

1. Visit the organization's website well in advance of the date of the event.
2. Download any posted practice tests.
3. Conduct research on the Internet regarding the legal topics that will be covered on the test. Print out the information you find to use as study material.
4. Visit the organization's website often to make sure information regarding the event has not changed.

CHAPTER

14 Risk Management and Insurance for Homes and Autos

Risk management is used to minimize or eliminate personal financial loss. Four risk management strategies can be applied: avoidance, reduction, transference, and assumption.

Insurance is an example of a risk management strategy that is used to help protect a person's financial well being. It is a way of transferring part of the risk to another entity such as an insurance company. By purchasing insurance, the insurance company helps offset some of the loss that an individual may encounter.

Home and auto insurance are two important types of insurance that the average consumer needs. Any losses to either of these assets could cause major financial and personal losses. Purchasing home and auto insurance can help eliminate the worry of loss that an individual might experience.

Focus on Finance

Renters Insurance

Many renters do not worry about property insurance because it is widely assumed that the owner of the rental property carries insurance. However, the property owner's policy does not cover the personal possessions of a tenant or damage that tenants may cause to the property.

Financially competent individuals consider purchasing renters insurance when living in a rented space. Renters insurance typically provides coverage for:

- damage to personal property from fire or wind;
- theft of property;
- personal liability in the event the insured is sued over accidental injury to others who are in the rented apartment;
- accidental damage to the property of others in the rented apartment; and
- living expenses if the renter must live elsewhere due to damage to the rented property.

College and Career Readiness

Reading Prep. Before reading this chapter, read the opening pages and section titles for this chapter. These can help prepare you for the topics that will be presented. What does this tell you about what you will be learning?

Sections

Monkey Business Images/Shutterstock.com

Section 14.1 Risk Management

Essential Question

Why does an individual or family need to purchase insurance?

Objectives

After studying this section, you will be able to:

- Define risk.
- Explain risk management.
- Discuss insurance protection.

Terms

risk	insurance	deductible
pure risk	insurance policy	policy limit
speculative risk	premium	
risk management	claim	

Risk

Life involves risk. **Risk** is the possibility of loss, damage, or injury. Some risks are predictable: you will sometimes get sick, and you will grow old. Other risks are unpredictable. These include serious illnesses or injuries, car accidents, house fires, and theft. Some events can limit your ability to earn a living or wipe out your assets. When you earn income, own property, and accumulate savings, these things are too important to lose.

You will likely face various types of risk in your lifetime. Some risks have little consequences, such as planning a trip to the beach on a day when there is only a 10 percent chance of rain. Other risks can have much more serious consequences, such as driving a car without insurance. Risks can be classified as pure risks and speculative risks.

photofriday/Shutterstock.com

Buying and trading stock is a speculative risk because the outcome is unpredictable.

Pure Risk

A **pure risk** is a risk with a possibility of loss but no possibility of gain. In such situations, insurance protection is clearly needed. Pure risk can be categorized as personal risk, property risk, and liability risk.

Ethics

Truthful Insurance Claims

Filing false insurance claims is unethical and illegal. It is important to report the most truthful and accurate information to an insurance company. Purposely using ıalse information to make an insurance claim could be considered fraud. Only file a claim for insurance assistance when it can be proven. Supplying false or misleading information can result in insurance coverage being canceled.

- *Personal risks.* Personal risks are those that affect you directly, such as illness or disability or the illness or disability of an immediate family member.
- *Property risks.* Property risks are those that affect your personal or real property. A car theft and a house fire are examples of property risk. A lightning strike that burns out your electronic equipment is another example of property risk.
- *Liability risks.* Liability risks, also called *legal risks,* result from the possibility of losing money or other property as a result of legal proceedings. For example, suppose Kyle King frequently texts while driving. This practice increases Kyle's liability risk because legal responisbility for damages belongs to a person who hits another person's car. Likewise, if you invited friends over for a party and the weight of everyone on your deck caused it to collapse, you would be legally liable for any injuries sustained by your friends.

Speculative Risk

Speculative risk differs from pure risk. A **speculative risk** is a risk that may result in either financial gain or financial loss. For example, if you buy gold, silver, land, or the stocks of companies, you could either make or lose money when the property is sold. When the stock of Google was first offered for sale to the public on August 19, 2004, the issue price was $85 per share. The stock soared in value, reaching $714.87 a share on December 3, 2007. Those who bought it when it was first offered speculated that it would go higher and they would make a profit when they sold their shares. Those who bought the stock at higher levels speculated that it would go even higher. However, in late 2008, the world economy fell into a recession, and the market value of Google shares dropped to under $300 a share.

As the economy slowly improved, the value of Google shares again soared, reaching $1,100 a share in the spring of 2014. By late summer 2015, the stock, before adjustment for a stock split, had climbed to over $1,300 a share. Some investors who speculated made money on their Google stock. Other investors who speculated lost money on their Google stock. This is the nature of speculative risk; you may make money, or you could lose money.

Speculative risks generally result in a higher frequency of loss than pure risks. However, most speculative risks are not insurable because they are taken willingly in hopes of making a gain.

Risk Management

Financial security depends in part on risk management. **Risk management** is the process of measuring risk and finding ways to minimize or manage loss. There are various ways to manage personal risk. Four common methods of risk management include avoidance, reduction, transference, and assumption, as shown in Figure 14-1.

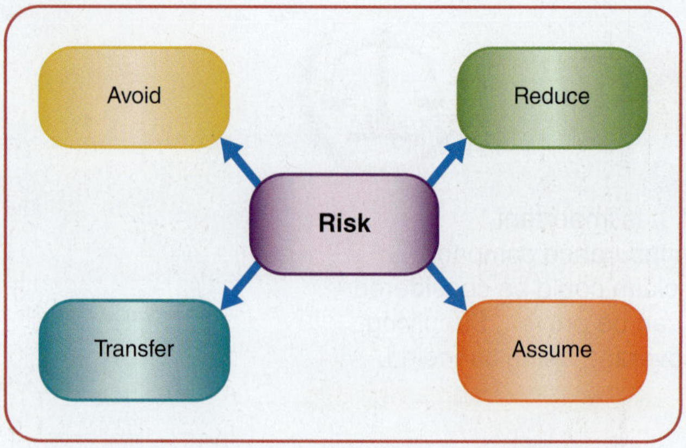

dizain/Shutterstock.com

Figure 14-1 Consumers can take any of these actions to manage identified risks.

- *Avoid* risk by taking steps to eliminate the risk. For example, suppose a trail marker warns "Do not go beyond this point!" Hikers may avoid injury by obeying the warning.
- *Reduce* risk by developing a strategy of minimizing risks that cannot always be avoided. For example, wearing a seat belt while driving reduces the chance of injury or death in the event of an accident.
- *Transfer* risk by shifting the risk to someone else. The most common way to do this is to buy insurance. By purchasing insurance, the insured becomes a member of a large pool of people and risk is transferred to the insurance company. Insurance is a common method of risk management.
- *Assume* risk by assessing the risk and making financial preparations for possible future loss. It is also called *self-insuring* or *retaining risk*. For example, a person may set aside money in a savings account to use in case of unemployment. By setting aside extra money before a loss occurs, that money will be available when needed.

The systematic decision-making process is one risk-management tool that can be used to assess risk. This process is illustrated in Figure 14-2 and involves the following steps.

Step 1. Identify risks. To begin the decision-making process, identify the possible or probable risks that in some way can affect you or your family. For example, if you live close to a moving stream of water, the risk is the potential flooding of your home. If you leave your locker unlocked, the risk is that your personal property may be stolen.

Step 2. Assess risks. Assess the seriousness of the risks and the likelihood of loss. Focus your attention and resources on the risks that can have serious consequences. If the risk is the flooding of your home, the loss could be financially devastating. If the risk is a stolen textbook from your locker, the loss may be costly but not devastating.

cbpix/Shutterstock.com

One way risk can be managed is by avoiding it, such as by obeying a warning sign.

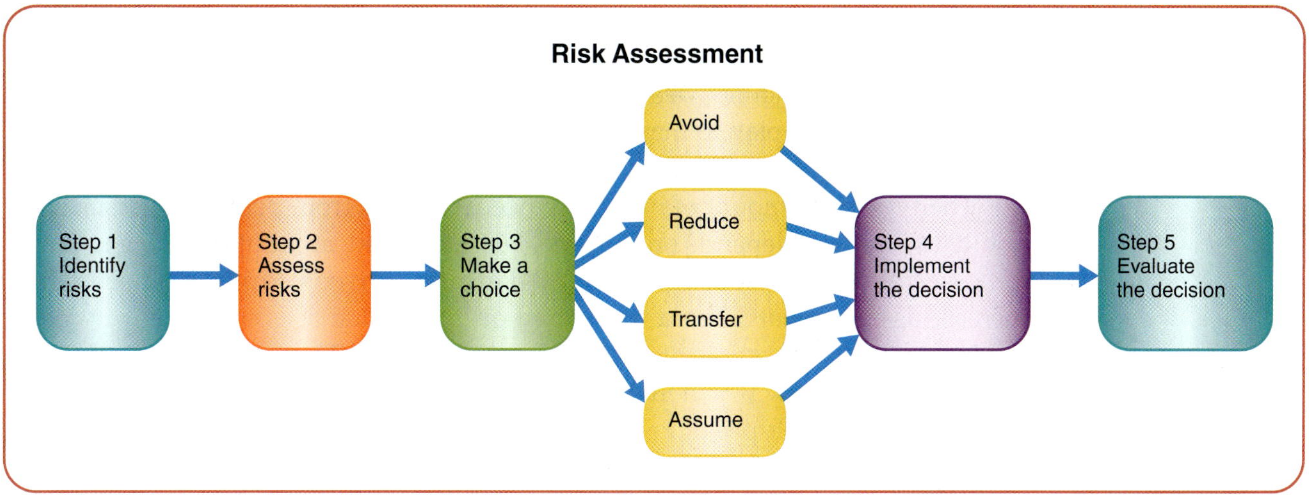

Goodheart-Willcox Publisher

Figure 14-2 Systematic decision-making can help consumers assess risks and determine their insurance needs.

Step 3. Make a choice. The ways of handling risk are avoidance, reduction, transference, and assumption. Serious risk, such as the flooding of your home, can be transferred by purchasing insurance. Less serious risks, such as leaving your textbooks in an unlocked locker, can be avoided by locking your locker.

Step 4. Implement the decision. After completing a thorough risk assessment, you can decide the best ways to protect yourself and your property. Consider the losses that could damage or destroy your financial security. If insurance is the solution, take steps to protect yourself with appropriate insurance.

Step 5. Evaluate the decision. After a decision has been implemented, it is important to evaluate the decision to determine whether it led to the desired outcome. This involves comparing the results of a decision with the problem, and deciding if the results are acceptable.

Insurance Protection

Insurance is a financial service used to protect against loss. The insurance company, the *insurer*, protects the *insured*, the policyholder. For a fee, the insurer provides the insured with protection against economic loss. An **insurance policy** is a contract that defines the type of losses that are covered, amount of coverage in dollars, and other conditions to which the two parties agree.

By purchasing insurance, a policyholder becomes a member of a large pool of customers. Each customer's risk is transferred to the insurance company. The insurance company charges its customers premiums to assume their risk. The **premium** is the amount the insured pays for insurance coverage. The money collected from premiums is invested by the insurance company, and the earnings are used to pay claims of insured persons.

When the insured suffers a loss, a claim is made. A **claim** is the process of documenting a loss against an insurance policy. Most policies have a deductible when a claim is made. The **deductible** is the amount the insured is responsible for paying when a claim is made. In general, the higher the amount of the deductible, the lower the premium.

The main purpose of insurance is to provide protection against specific types of financial losses. Events that could put an individual's finances at risk include illness or injury, accidents, death, and property losses. Taking a careful look at risks and making a plan to manage them with insurance and other resources are basic steps in any financial plan.

The type and amount of insurance needed varies from person to person and family to family. It depends on the risks being covered, amount available to pay for losses, and financial obligations of the insured persons. Protection needs also increase as additional assets are acquired or if the value of assets already owned has increased. For example, if a couple bought a house 20 years ago for $125,000 and the house is now worth $190,000, insurance is needed to cover the current value of the house. Types of insurance that protect against financial risks include health, disability, life, home, and automobile insurance.

Selecting a Company

Many different types of insurance programs are available through a multitude of insurance companies. Before purchasing insurance, it is wise to comparison shop. Requesting quotes from multiple companies will enable you to compare prices and how much coverage you can get for your money. The premium must fit in your budget.

However, the price of a policy is only one factor to consider when selecting an insurance company. Customer service is a key factor. Assistance and information from the company should be readily available to customers. Selecting a company that has a reputation for honoring claims and processing them promptly should be a part of the decision-making process. An efficient

Dragon Images/Shutterstock.com

Quotes from multiple insurance companies enable consumers to compare prices and evaluate coverage amounts.

process for filing claims is important. If a loss occurs, customers should be able to easily navigate the claims process to make use of their policy coverage.

It is worth taking the time to find a company that is respected within the insurance industry, by its policyholders, and by people in the financial field. Friends and relatives may be able to recommend a company. Insurance companies can be compared by reviewing *Best's Insurance Reports*. You can also research an insurance company through the Department of Insurance for your state.

Selecting an Agent

When purchasing insurance, select an agent that is respected within the insurance industry. A reputable agent can clearly explain the different types of coverage and benefits available. A good agent advises clients honestly about the type of coverage they need. Responsible agents handle policy changes, questions, and claims promptly.

Selecting a Policy

An informed, reputable insurance agent can advise the type and amount of coverage you need today and as your needs change. The insurance materials provided by the agent will describe the benefits and options that are being offered. It is wise to comparison shop and evaluate premiums and amounts of coverage with other insurance companies.

When selecting a policy, the policy limits should be considered. The **policy limit** is the highest amount an insurance company will pay for a claim. Any cost above the limit is the responsibility of the insured.

Exploring Careers

Insurance Broker

An insurance broker is a client's first contact person when buying insurance. They sell one or more types of insurance for the insurance company and act as a contact person between the company and the client. They may sell insurance to consumers or to businesses. They also explain the differences between various policies and offer advice for their clients. Insurance brokers typically:

- help determine customer needs, types of insurance, and levels of insurance that fit the customer's requirements
- facilitate the application process and submit the information to an underwriter
- prepare reports and maintain records
- find potential customers

Insurance brokers spend most of their time working with clients. The insurance environment is professional, and agents will generally dress in business attire. Clients may come to the insurance business office, or agents may travel to meet the client. Hours may be flexible and include evenings and weekends. A bachelor degree is preferred, and a professional license is required. Insurance brokers must have excellent communication, computer, and customer-service skills. They should also have above-average financial knowledge and the ability to work without direct supervision.

Once a policy is purchased, it should be reviewed and read carefully. It is important to confirm that the policy you are given is the one you chose. If the policy does not meet your expectations, most companies will allow you to return it within ten days without obligation. As you review the policy, check to see that it states the following information.

- name of the company
- name of the insured and the beneficiaries
- type of coverage
- amount of coverage and benefits
- amount and due dates of premiums
- benefits and options of the policy

Once you are insured, inform your family and beneficiaries of the coverage and the location of the policy. As a good recordkeeping practice, the policy and records of premium payments and claims should be kept together in one place.

Section 14.1 Review

Check Your Understanding

1. Name the two types of risks.
2. What are three categories of pure risk?
3. List common methods of risk management and provide an example for each.
4. What is the main purpose of insurance?
5. What information is typically stated on an insurance policy?

Build Your Vocabulary

As you progress through this course, develop a personal glossary. This will help you build your vocabulary and prepare you for a career. Write a definition for each of the following terms and add it to your glossary.

risk
pure risk
speculative risk
risk management
insurance
insurance policy
premium
claim
deductible
policy limit

Section 14.2 Home and Auto Insurance

Objectives

After studying this section, you will be able to:

- Outline the key factors to consider when buying home insurance.
- Outline the key factors to consider when buying auto insurance.

Essential Question

Why is it important to buy home insurance as well as auto insurance?

Terms

homeowners insurance
property insurance
homeowners liability insurance
umbrella policy
depreciation
endorsement
insurance settlement
automobile insurance
bodily injury liability insurance
property damage liability insurance
no-fault auto insurance

Home Insurance

Once you invest in a home of your own, you will want to protect it with insurance. If you have a mortgage on your home, you will be required by the lender to have insurance. **Homeowners insurance** is insurance that provides coverage for liability and damage to property under certain conditions. Homeowners insurance provides two basic types of coverage: property protection and liability protection.

Property insurance is insurance that insures the policyholder against financial loss due to damage to or loss of a dwelling and personal property and possessions, such as clothes and furnishings. It may also pay for additional living expenses if you should need to move out of your home because of damage to the property. The specific losses covered depend on the type of policy you buy. The cost of property insurance is determined primarily by the location of the property and the cost to rebuild or replace it.

If you live in an area that may be susceptible to floods or earthquakes, supplementary insurance should be considered. Floods and earthquakes are not covered by property insurance and must be purchased separately. Many homeowners make the mistake of thinking that their homeowners insurance covers these situations. It is important to evaluate the specific needs for the area of the country in which you live before an incident occurs. You may find it necessary to purchase flood insurance or earthquake insurance where you live.

Homeowners liability insurance, sometimes referred to as *personal liability insurance*, is insurance that protects a homeowner if others are injured on the policyholder's property. For example, if someone falls and is hurt in your home,

Jaroslav Moravcik/Shutterstock.com

Flood insurance is supplementary insurance that must be purchased separately from a homeowners policy.

liability coverage pays for any loss incurred. This coverage also protects you if you, your family, your pets, or your property accidentally damages the property of others. It pays for the legal costs of defending yourself if you are sued because of injuries or damages.

Additional coverage can be purchased through an umbrella policy or extended liability policy. An **umbrella policy** is an insurance policy that covers loss amounts that are higher than those covered by primary policies.

Amount of Coverage

The first step in buying the right homeowners coverage is to find out how much it would cost to rebuild your home. This may be more or less than the price you paid for the home or the amount it would bring if you sold it today. The cost of rebuilding your home depends on local building costs and the type of home you own. Today, most insurance companies recommend enough insurance coverage to rebuild your home if it should be completely destroyed.

To keep insurance coverage up to date, inform your insurance agent of any major home improvements you make. You may also want to add an inflation-guard clause to your policy. This automatically adjusts policy renewal coverage to reflect current rebuilding costs.

Read the policy to learn about the coverage provided for personal possessions. Compare the contents limit with the total value of your possessions. If coverage is not adequate, you should talk to your insurance agent about increasing protection.

Knowing whether your personal property is insured for replacement cost or actual cash value is also important.

- *Actual cash value* is the replacement cost minus depreciation. **Depreciation** is a decrease in the value of property as a result of age or wear and tear.
- *Replacement value* covers the cost of replacing what you lose without deducting depreciation.

For example, a five-year-old TV, even in good condition, is no longer worth what you paid for it or what a new similar set would cost. If the set were stolen, actual cash value recovery would not pay for a new one of comparable quality. If it were insured for replacement value, you could recover the full cost of a new TV set of comparable quality. Obviously, it pays to insure possessions for replacement rather than actual cash value.

Smart homeowners make a complete inventory of personal property. The inventory should include the purchase date and price for costly items. It is a good idea to take photos or videos of each room that will help identify the contents and establish a claim in case of major losses.

wavebreakmedia/Shutterstock.com

Insurance with a replacement value clause covers the cost to replace an item.

Cost of Home Insurance

The cost of protecting a home and personal possessions depends primarily on the following factors.

- *Type and amount of coverage.* The higher the amount of protection purchased and the more perils covered, the higher the premium will be. A policy with replacement value coverage is more expensive than one with cash or market value protection.
- *Size of the deductible.* The higher the deductible is, the lower the insurance premium will be.
- *Risk factors where you live.* The type of home you own and its location influence premium rates. For example, fire protection on a frame house is higher than on a brick house. Protection against theft and vandalism in high-crime areas is more costly than in low-crime areas.
- *The insurance company.* The cost of insurance premiums varies from company to company.
- *Opportunity for discounts.* Some policy holders qualify for premium reductions for having more than one policy with the company, such as home and auto coverage. Discounts may also be available for devices such as a smoke detector or burglar alarm, for nonsmoker policyholders, or for long-term policyholders.

Renters Insurance

Many renters mistakenly believe they do not need insurance because their property owner's policy will cover any loss they may suffer. However, the property owner's policy does not cover the personal items of a renter. As a result, it is a good idea for renters to purchase a renters insurance policy. Renters insurance covers losses due to damage or loss of personal property and possessions. These include electronics, furniture, bedding, and so forth. The property owner carries coverage on the dwelling itself.

You Do the Math

Problem-Solving and Reasoning

Insurance is a financial service used to protect against loss. The insurance company charges its customers to assume their risk. The charge is called a premium. When a claim is made, the policyholder is responsible to pay a certain amount toward the loss before the insurance company begins to pay. This amount is called a deductible. Once the deductible is met, the insurance company begins to pay for covered losses above the deductible amount.

Solve the following problems.

1. Scott has auto insurance with a deductible of $500. Scott is in an accident that affects only the car, but requires $3,000 worth of repairs. How much will both Scott and the insurance company pay toward the repairs?
2. Angela pays an auto insurance premium of $1,500 annually and wants to increase the property damage coverage limit from $100,000 to $150,000. The insurance agent says this will raise the premium by 6 percent. How much more will Angela pay each month with the new premium?
3. Ahmed's car insurance premium is $1,889.50. The company is offering a 15% discount. After the discount is applied, how much will Ahmed's premium be?

gpointstudio/Shutterstock.com

Renters insurance should be purchased when living in a dorm or apartment to cover the potential loss of personal belongings.

Renters should look for a policy with liability insurance. If guests were harmed in a rented home or apartment, liability insurance would cover any expenses incurred by the resident.

College students living in a dorm or renting an apartment may need renters insurance to protect their possessions. However, an endorsement to their parents' homeowners insurance may be necessary to cover a child's personal possessions while living in a dorm. An **endorsement** is an attachment to existing insurance coverage, such as a family policy, to protect a computer, a television, and other expensive items taken to college.

The cost of renters insurance is determined mainly by the amount of coverage, the location of the rented property, and the amount of the deductible. Riders also increase the cost of renters insurance. A *rider* is extra coverage added to a policy. Examples are coverage for identity theft and extra coverage for valuable items such as jewelry.

Filing an Insurance Claim

When a loss occurs, it will be necessary to file an insurance claim in order to receive a settlement. An **insurance settlement** is the amount of money or other services to which you are entitled under the terms of your insurance policy. The insurance claim settlement process is shown in Figure 14-3. Individual insurance companies have their own specific steps for reporting a loss, so it will be necessary to understand their processes before an incident occurs.

Insurance Claim Settlement Process	
Damage	**Theft**
If your home is damaged by a natural disaster or other accident, follow these steps. 1. If there is a fire, accident, or natural disaster, make sure everyone is safe. 2. Call your insurance agent or the company's 800 number. Report the claim and confirm the claim-filing process. If temporary repairs are needed to keep further damage from happening, such as rain, ask how you should proceed. 3. Take pictures of the damage. Then prevent further damage from weather or other hazards by covering affected areas of the house. Don't repair anything until the insurance company has been contacted. 4. Make a list of the damaged property items. Gather receipts and documentation for items that were damaged. This will be a part of the claim paperwork. 5. When the adjuster arrives, make sure that all damages are evaluated. Ask for a copy of the adjuster report and instructions on how and when repairs can begin. Once you have approval, you can secure estimates for the repairs. These will be sent to the insurance company for their approval. 6. If it is necessary to live in another location until damages are repaired, confirm what is covered by your policy. Keep all receipts for filing with your insurance company. 7. Work with your agent to file the claim.	If a personal item that you insure is stolen, follow these steps. 1. File a police report as soon as you learn of the theft. A police report will be requested by your insurance company. 2. Call your insurance agent or the company's 800 number. Report the claim and confirm the claim-filing process. 3. Create a detailed description of the stolen item. Gather receipts and documentation for the item that was stolen. This will be a part of the claim paperwork. 4. Work with your agent to file the claim.

Goodheart-Willcox Publisher

Figure 14-3 These guidelines can be helpful when filing a homeowners insurance claim.

Before filing a claim, it is important to know if you have insurance for replacement cost or actual cash value. There may be other limitations on your policy, so be prepared before you need the insurance assistance. As part of the settlement process, an insurance adjuster or other insurance official will evaluate damages. The time period for settling a claim depends on the seriousness of the incident such as damage to the structure as well as personal belongings.

To find out the status of your claim, follow up with the insurance company a few weeks after it has been filed. As a general rule, it will take several exchanges between you and the insurance company in order to receive payment.

If you are dissatisfied or have questions concerning the final settlement, discuss matters with your agent or the claims adjuster. If you find a settlement unsatisfactory or are not satisfied with your insurance company's handling of your complaint, you can contact the department of insurance for your state or call the National Insurance Consumer Helpline for assistance.

Employability Skills

Self-Esteem

Self-esteem is how individuals feel about their value as people. It is a sense of self-worth and what a person sees when looking in the mirror. The more comfortable people are with themselves as people, the more self-confidence will be exhibited.

Auto Insurance

Automobile insurance is insurance that covers passenger vehicles and protects the beneficiary against the financial aspects of a traffic accident. It is often referred to as *auto insurance* or *car insurance*. It gives policyholders coverage for liability and property damage under specified conditions. Drivers must carry proof of insurance coverage in their vehicles in most states.

Auto accidents are an unfortunate reality of life. According to the National Highway Traffic Administration, an auto accident happens every 60 seconds, resulting in upwards of 40,000 highway deaths annually in the United States. In addition, car accidents are a leading cause of permanent disability in the United States and the world, and the number one cause of teen deaths in the US.

When you own or lease a car, you take certain personal and financial risks. If you are involved in a car accident, you may be required to pay thousands of dollars for injuries and property damage. If you are in an accident where you are at fault or claims are filed against you, it can cost thousands of dollars in legal fees as well as damages. Practically no one can afford the financial risks of extensive property damage, serious injury, or death without insurance coverage.

All 50 states have *financial responsibility laws* that require drivers to show proof of their ability to pay stated minimum amounts in damages after an accident. Most states also have compulsory auto insurance laws that require car owners to buy a minimum amount of bodily injury and property damage liability insurance in order to legally drive their cars.

Types of Auto Insurance

Auto insurance is typically classified as two broad categories, which are bodily injury liability and property damage liability. These types of insurance policies pay other parties for losses caused by the insured.

Bodily injury liability insurance is insurance coverage that protects the person who is responsible for an auto accident that results in the injury or death of others. Many states require $100,000 bodily injury coverage per person, up to $300,000 per accident. This is called 100/300 coverage.

Property damage liability insurance is insurance for the insured person's car. It can include collision coverage, comprehensive coverage, or both. *Collision insurance* pays you for damage to your car due to an auto accident or collision with another car or object. This coverage is usually required if you have a loan on your vehicle. *Comprehensive physical damage insurance* pays you for loss or damage to your car resulting from crashes, fire, theft, falling objects, explosions, earthquakes, floods, riots, civil commotions, and collisions with a bird or animal.

These policies cover the policyholder, family members, and any person driving the car with the owner's permission. They pay damages to the other parties involved in an accident you cause. Both types of liability coverage pay the legal fees for settling claims. They also pay for damages assessed against you, up to limits stated in the policy. These damages include injuries to other parties or damage to the property of others.

Some states require that insurance companies offer *uninsured motorist liability insurance* and *underinsured motorist liability insurance.* This insurance pays you for injuries caused to you by an uninsured or underinsured driver or a hit-and-run driver. It covers insured persons driving, riding, or walking. It also covers passengers in the insured person's car.

Medical payment or *personal injury protection (PIP)* pays for medical expenses resulting from an accident in your car, regardless of who is at fault. It covers you and any person injured in or by your car. It is sometimes called *no-fault* coverage because claims are paid regardless of who is at fault. It is mandatory in some states.

There are additional types of insurance that a driver may purchase. These include roadside assistance and rental reimbursement insurance.

Cost of Auto Insurance

Auto insurance is a costly service. Coverage for young drivers is particularly high because they have more accidents. Premium rates and service for the same coverage may vary greatly from company to company.

The guidelines in Figure 14-4 can help you select the automobile insurance you need. The cost of auto insurance depends on the following factors.

Driver Classification

Driver classification is determined by the age, sex, and marital status of the driver. Driving record and habits are also considered. A poor driving record tends to increase premiums as does a record of previous claims and costly settlements.

Suggestions for Buying Automobile Insurance

- Decide the types and amounts of coverage you need. If you now have a policy, review your coverage and its cost before renewal time.
- Check with several reputable insurers. Keep in mind that the least expensive coverage is not necessarily the best for you. Consider such things as the company's reliability and its reputation for service, including claims handling. If you are in doubt about a company, check with the department of insurance for your state.
- Consider the amount you would save by paying a higher deductible. You may find it pays in the end to take care of small losses yourself.
- Check with your agent regarding your eligibility for premium discounts.
- Consider special coverages or higher policy limits if you frequently drive other commuters to work or groups of children to school or other events.
- Consider reducing or dropping collision coverage as cars get older.

Goodheart-Willcox Publisher

Figure 14-4 These guidelines can be helpful when making decisions about auto insurance.

It can be difficult for individuals with poor driving records to buy insurance. Insurers consider these drivers too great a risk. In such cases, it may be possible to obtain coverage through an assigned risk plan. This is a state-supervised program in which high-risk drivers are assigned to insurance companies. The companies are required to provide coverage, but premiums are considerably higher than for drivers with better driving records.

Young, single males are involved in more serious accidents than other classes of drivers. Therefore, they tend to pay the highest insurance premiums. If a young man marries, insurance costs may decrease because married men usually have fewer serious accidents than single men. Rates for women, single and married, are lower than for males. When your driver classification changes, so might your insurance rates.

Rating Territory

The number and amount of claims an insurance company processes in your area determines rates for auto insurance. Premiums are higher in frequent claim areas, such as big cities and high traffic districts.

Premium Discount Eligibility

Some companies offer discounts to drivers for a variety of reasons. Examples of reasons you may be eligible for discounted car insurance include:

- safe driving record
- good grades (if still in school)
- antitheft devices installed in vehicle
- over a certain age
- two or more cars on a policy
- good credit score

Case Study *Auto Insurance*

Lucas' car is ten years old and is inexpensive to insure and maintain, but it will soon begin to need expensive repairs. Sheila has agreed to give up the family's older car at no cost if the insurance premiums continue to be paid. Because the car is a newer model, an insurance agent has recommended increasing the liability insurance currently carried and adding collision insurance to the policy.

Currently, the monthly cost for liability insurance on the car is $37. According to the family's insurance agent, liability and collision insurance on new car would bring the monthly premium to $92. Luckily, affording the higher premiums is not a problem.

Case Review

1. What would be the opportunity cost experienced to buy the new car?
2. Which specific questions should be asked of the insurance agent about discounts, such as a perfect driving record, that could make the premium less expensive?
3. What would be the trade-off to use the current car one more year, then accept the family's car?
4. What are the risks of buying the car now but not buying collision insurance?

Economics in Action

Liability Insurance

Liability insurance is a component of auto insurance policies and is required in most states. It is important to understand how the coverage is stated to ensure that you have the appropriate amount for your situation. When in doubt, purchase the minimum that is required by law and a higher amount than the value of the vehicle.

Liability coverage is stated as a series of numbers, such as 100/300/100. Each number is separated by a forward slash similar to how fractions are expressed. For example, the first number, 100, means $100,000. This is the maximum amount paid per person for injuries from one accident. The second number, 300, means $300,000. This is the maximum amount paid for the total cost of all injuries from one accident. The third number, 100, means $100,000. This is the maximum amount paid for the total property damage from one accident.

Paying for liability coverage can be expensive. However, paying for it now can help your finances in the future should you have an accident.

Insured Vehicle

Vehicles that are costly to repair or that are favorite targets of thieves cost more to insure. Premiums are higher for luxury, sports, and new models than for standard models and older vehicles. For older ones, collision insurance may not be cost-effective. Very popular models cost more to insure than more ordinary cars. Check the insurance costs for different models before buying a vehicle.

Coverage

The more protection that is purchased, the higher the premium will be. However, the cost per dollar of coverage is usually less for more coverage. For example, a $100,000 policy costs less per dollar of coverage than a $50,000 policy. It is important to buy the amount of coverage you need.

Deductible

The deductible is the amount that must be paid before the insurance company starts to pay. For example, if an insurance plan has an annual deductible of $1,000, the first $1,000 of repair expenses must be paid by the policyholder. Once the deductible is met, the insurance company begins to pay on qualified expenses above the deductible.

Increasing the deductible amount can reduce premiums for collision and comprehensive damage coverage. The higher the deductible is, the lower the premium will be.

No-Fault Auto Insurance

No-fault auto insurance is a type of insurance plan that eliminates the faultfinding process in settling claims. When an accident occurs, policyholders make claims to their own insurance companies. Each company pays its own policyholder regardless of who is at fault. No-fault insurance is designed to simplify and speed up payments to accident victims. It also acts to lower insurance rates by reducing costly court trials to determine fault.

State legislators decide whether their state adopts a no-fault insurance plan and what form it takes. Most states with a no-fault plan have a combination no-fault and liability insurance. The no-fault pays for claims up to a set amount, called a *threshold*. However, in most states individuals can sue for additional damages when an accident involves severe injuries, death, or major medical bills. Liability insurance pays for damages over and above the threshold amount.

Filing an Automobile Insurance Claim

If you are involved in an accident, there are certain procedures to follow at the scene of the accident and when filing an insurance claim. Those procedures are summarized in Figure 14-5.

<table>
<tr><th colspan="2">Auto Accidents and Insurance Claims</th></tr>
<tr><th>At the Scene of an Accident</th><th>Filing an Insurance Claim</th></tr>
<tr><td>If you are involved in an automobile accident, follow these steps at the scene.
• Stop your car safely and out of traffic. Turn on the vehicle's hazard lights.
• If anyone may be injured, call 911 immediately. Administer any first aid you are qualified and trained to provide. Do not move anyone unless absolutely necessary.
• Contact the police even if the accident is minor. Depending on the severity of the accident, an officer may or may not arrive. Provide police with information they request over the phone or in person. If the police do not come, an accident report can be filed through your state's Department of Motor Vehicles (DMV).
• Trade insurance and contact information with others involved in the accident, including other drivers and witnesses. Also collect the name and badge number of any police offers involved.
• Take photos of the accident scene and any damage, if possible.
• For a collision with an unattended or parked auto, try to find the owner. If unsuccessful, leave a note with your name, number, and address. Damages over a certain amount must be reported to the police in most states.</td><td>If your car is involved in an auto accident; damaged by fire, flood, or vandalism; or stolen, follow these steps in filing a claim for your losses.
• Call your insurance agent or the company's 800 number. Report the claim and confirm the claim-filing process.
• Ask the agent how to proceed and what forms or documents are needed to support your claim. Provide details of the incident. If another driver was involved, provide the personal and insurance information that you obtained at the scene of the accident. Submit any documentation you have, such as a police report or photos of the accident.
• An adjuster will evaluate the damage to the car. Ask for a copy of the adjuster's report and instructions on how and when repairs can begin. The insurance company may require you to use a specific auto company to make the repairs.
• Keep records of any expenses you incur as a result of an automobile accident. They may be reimbursed under the terms of your policy.</td></tr>
<tr><td colspan="2">Note: If involved in an accident, it is unlawful to leave the scene without proper notification of the authorities if there is injury, death, or property damage over a certain amount. Check the laws on reporting accidents in your state.</td></tr>
</table>

Goodheart-Willcox Publisher

Figure 14-5 These guidelines can be helpful when filing an automobile insurance claim.

You can reduce your chances of an auto accident by keeping your car in good running condition, driving within the speed limit, and minimizing distractions while driving, such as eating, drinking, texting, and talking on a cell phone.

The claim settlement process will involve an adjuster to evaluate the amount of damage that the vehicle has incurred. Photos will be taken for evidence.

If there are personal injuries, the insurance company will contact the individual's health care provider for the cost of the medical services before reimbursement is made.

Section 14.2 Review

Check Your Understanding

1. What two basic types of coverage does homeowners insurance provide?
2. What is the first step to consider when buying homeowners insurance?
3. Explain the costs of property insurance, including homeowners insurance and renters insurance.
4. What is auto liability coverage?
5. The cost of auto insurance depends on what factors?

Build Your Vocabulary

As you progress through this course, develop a personal glossary. This will help you build your vocabulary and prepare you for a career. Write a definition for each of the following terms and add it to your glossary.

homeowners insurance
property insurance
homeowners liability insurance
umbrella policy
depreciation
endorsement
insurance settlement
automobile insurance
bodily injury liability insurance
property damage liability insurance
no-fault auto insurance

Review and Assessment

Chapter Summary

Section 14.1 Risk Management

- Risk is a measure of the likelihood that something will be lost, and risks can be classified as pure risks and speculative risks.
- Financial security depends in part on risk management. Four strategies for dealing with risk are avoidance, reduction, transference, and assumption.
- Insurance is a form of risk management that pools the premiums of a large group of people to cover the expenses of the smaller number within the group who suffer losses.

Section 14.2 Home and Auto Insurance

- Once you own a home, you need insurance to protect it. When buying home insurance, factors to consider include the type and amount of coverage, deductible amounts, risk factors, premiums, and discounts.
- Carrying adequate auto insurance is a major responsibility for car owners. When buying auto insurance, factors to consider include the types and amounts of coverage, deductible amounts, policy limits, premiums, discounts, and the company's reputation for service.

Review Your Knowledge

1. What is risk?
2. Explain risk management.
3. Discuss insurance protection.
4. How is the amount of an insurance deductible related to the cost of the premium?
5. List and describe the steps in the decision-making process for purchasing insurance.
6. How should a consumer select an insurance company?
7. Outline the key factors to consider when buying home insurance.
8. Summarize the insurance claim settlement process.
9. Outline the key factors to consider when buying auto insurance.
10. How can the chances of an auto accident be reduced?

Apply Your Knowledge

1. Identify one or more speculative risks you would consider taking. Give reasons for your choices.
2. Four risk management strategies are illustrated in Figure 14-1. Identify how you utilize each of these risk management strategies in your daily life.
3. Create a two-column chart to examine various types of financial risk and risk management strategies. Label the first column *Financial Risks*. Label the second column *Risk Management Strategy*. In the first column, list financial risks that individuals or a family might encounter over the lifespan. In the second column, write the strategy that you would use to manage the risk: avoid, reduce, transfer, or assume.
4. As a high-school student preparing for a job or for college, you will need insurance coverage. List the types of insurance coverage you think you will need. Next to each type, explain why you feel the insurance is necessary based on the risks you might have to manage.
5. Insurance provides important financial protection for the assets of an individual or a family. List the types of insurance coverage you think a family would need.

Next to each type, explain why you think the insurance is necessary.

6. Renters often make the mistake of assuming they do not need to insure their personal possessions when living in a rental unit. However, the property owner's policy would not cover these items in the event of loss. Create an inventory of your important personal property and consider how much it might cost to replace each item. Then, total the values to determine how much your personal property is worth. Describe how an insurance policy to protect these items might be helpful in the event they are lost, stolen, or damaged.
7. Interview someone you know who owns a car about the automobile insurance coverage on the vehicle. What type of coverage does this person have? Does it meet or exceed legal requirements?
8. The claim settlement process is explained in Figure 14-3. Using that information, draw a flow chart. A flow chart depicts steps in a process using directional lines to show the order in which steps should be completed. Which illustration would help you better explain the claim settlement process to a friend, the figure in the chapter or your flowchart?
9. Your friend Joshua recently purchased a car using money from savings. A large portion of monthly income is spent on the car payments. Joshua does not think the costs of monthly insurance premiums are worth paying since a car crash is such a small possibility. Write a dialog between you and your friend in which you explain the reasons that automobile insurance is necessary. Also discuss the state requirement of buying bodily injury liability insurance.
10. Create a chart with three columns. Label the columns *Homeowners Insurance*, *Property Insurance*, and *Personal Liability Insurance*. In each column, list reasons a person should buy that type of insurance.

Apply Your Math Skills

1. Jeremiah signed a lease for an apartment and would like to obtain renters insurance. An insurance agent provided a quote for a monthly charge of $12.99 plus a $50 administrative fee. How much money will the insurance cost per year?
2. Eva's car insurance costs $580 if it is paid annually. If is is paid semiannually, it costs $300; quarterly, $175; monthly, $62.50. What is the annual cost for each option? How much more will it cost if Eva pays monthly rather than once per year?

Communication Skills

Writing. When making important financial decisions, it is important to learn how to communicate effectively using reason. Create an outline that includes information about risk management for a young adult. Consider your audience as you prepare the information. Once your outline is complete, share it with your class.

Speaking. What do you think of the old adage, "necessity is the mother of invention"? Find examples of how the need for various types of insurance has lead to the availability of different types of insurance today. Identify a need for a new type of insurance and present your idea to the class.

Listening. Ask a classmate to give you directions on how to drive to the nearest mall. Take notes as the directions are given.

Evaluate and summarize your notes. If necessary, ask the speaker to slow down or repeat a point. Use prior knowledge of the city to follow the directions that are given. How can careful listening help you avoid risks when driving?

Teamwork

In this chapter, you learned about how to assess risk. Working with a teammate, brainstorm all of the risks you encounter in your daily lives. For each risk you think of, determine the ways a person could manage that risk, such as by avoidance, reduction, transference, or assumption. Give examples of specific steps that would be taken to manage each risk.

Internet Research

Supplemental Insurance Coverage. People who live in different areas of the country are exposed to different types of risks. Use Internet resources to determine if your geographic area puts you at risk for earthquakes or floods. Then, visit the websites of several insurance companies to explore their flood and earthquake insurance policies.

Auto Insurance Requirements. Each state has different laws that require drivers to carry certain types and amounts of auto insurance. Using the Internet, research the legal requirements for automobile insurance in your state. Explain any changes you think would improve the insurance laws in your state.

Auto Insurance Costs. Select the make, model, and year of a car that you would like to own. Using the Internet, research how much it would cost to insure this type of car in your state. Make notes about the deductible, monthly premiums, and specific coverage options for each type of policy you research. Which policy would you choose if you owned the car?

Portfolio Development

College and Career Readiness

Skills and Talents. Candidates are evaluated based on their qualifications, including their skills and talents. Communication and interpersonal skills are often qualities that interviewers seek in applicants. These types of qualities are called *soft skills.* Soft skills, also called *employability skills* or *foundational skills*, are applicable skills used to help an individual find a job, perform in the workplace, and gain success in any job or career.

Acceptance committees also look for candidates who have the necessary skills to be successful in a position, such as the ability to use software programs or machinery. These abilities are called hard skills. *Hard skills,* or *job-specific skills*, are measurable, observable, and critical skills necessary to perform required, work-related tasks.

Additionally, you should showcase your *technical skills.* Examples of technical skills include working with computers and creating videos. Technical skills are very important for succeeding in school or at work.

Talents give insight into who an applicant is. In addition, some talents rely on different methods of processing information. For example, playing a musical instrument requires a different way of thinking than rebuilding an engine does. Depending on the purpose of the interview, your talents may be criteria used to evaluate your qualifications.

Include samples of your skills or talents in your portfolio. Talents may be challenging to prove. One way to document your talents is to create a video. For example, if you are a musician, create a video with segments from your performances. Obtain permission to include other people in your video before doing so.

1. Conduct research about soft skills and their value in helping people succeed.
2. Create a Microsoft Word document and list the soft skills you currently possess that are important for a job or career. Use the heading "Skills" and your name. For each skill, write a paragraph that describes your abilities. Include soft skills, hard skills, and technical skills. Give examples to illustrate your skills. Save the document.
3. Create a Microsoft Word document that lists your talents. Use the heading "Talents" along with your name. Next to each talent listed, write a description of an assignment and explain how your talent was involved in completing it.
4. Scan hard-copy documents related to your talents to serve as samples. Save the documents in an appropriate folder.
5. Place the hard copies in the container for future reference.
6. Update your master spreadsheet.

CTSOs

Event Prep

Community Service Project. Many competitive events for CTSOs include a community service project. This project is usually carried out by the entire CTSO chapter and will take several months to complete. This project will probably span the school year. There are two parts to this event, written and oral. The chapter will designate several members to represent the team at the competitive event.

To prepare for a community service project, complete the following activities.

1. Read the guidelines provided by your organization.
2. Contact the association immediately at the end of the state conference to prepare for next year's event.
3. As a team, select a theme for your chapter's community service project.
4. Decide which roles are needed for the team. There may be one person who is the captain, one person who is the secretary, and any other roles necessary to create the plan. Ask your instructor for guidance in assigning roles to team members.
5. Identify your target audience, which may include business, school, and community groups.
6. Brainstorm with members of your chapter. List the benefits and opportunities of supporting a community service project.

CHAPTER

15 Health, Disability, and Life Insurance

Purchasing insurance is one strategy that individuals use to manage personal risk in their everyday lives. Health insurance helps transfer the risk when a person suffers illness, injury, or an accident. Disability insurance helps supplement income when the insured becomes disabled and cannot work. Life insurance protects dependents from loss after the death of the insured person. Each type of coverage can help a person avoid financial disaster.

Many employers offer group insurance plans as a benefit. Typically, the employer and employee share the cost of the monthly premiums. For those who do not have access to a group insurance plan, the health insurance exchange can help with finding and selecting an affordable policy. In addition, there are multiple options for health care provided through the government for those who qualify.

Focus on Finance

Life Insurance Rates

Multiple factors impact the cost of life insurance premiums. The insurance company evaluates the risk a person poses and what the payout would be when the insurance claim is made. Based on this information, the price of the premium is determined.

One of the main factors is age. Younger individuals will pay lower premiums because young people will pay for life insurance over a long period of time. This enables the insurance company to collect a larger amount of money. Conversely, older individuals will pay over fewer years. For that reason, people who buy a new policy later in life might pay higher rates.

Gender is also a factor used to determine risk. Statistically, women tend to live longer than men. They will probably pay over a longer time period than males, so the cost of their premium might be less than that of a male.

Medical exams may be required when applying for life insurance. Family medical histories are evaluated to measure health risks. Unhealthy habits, such as smoking, may cause a person to pay more in premiums.

College and Career Readiness

Reading Prep. Arrange a study session to read the chapter aloud with a classmate. At the end of each section, discuss any words you do not know. Take notes of words you would like to discuss in class.

Sections

Goodluz/Shutterstock.com

Section 15.1 Health Insurance

Objectives

After studying this section, you will be able to:

- Explain the purpose of health insurance.
- Describe private health care plans.
- Identify governmental health care plans.
- Discuss how to take responsibility for your health care.

Essential Question

What risks are managed by health insurance?

Terms

health insurance	major medical insurance	indemnity plan
copayment	comprehensive medical insurance	health savings account (HSA)
coinsurance	dental insurance	managed care plan
exclusion	vision care insurance	supplemental insurance
preauthorization	health insurance exchange	cancer insurance
utilization review	shared responsibility payment	long-term care (LTC) insurance
regular medical insurance		

Health Insurance

Health insurance is insurance that provides protection against financial loss due to illness or injury. Purchasing health insurance is one way that individuals manage personal risk. Health insurance offers financial protection by covering specific medical expenses created by illness, injury, and disability of the insured person and dependents. A *dependent* is an individual who relies on someone else for financial support, such as a child, a spouse, or an elderly parent.

Health insurance is a necessity, but it should be remembered that health insurance does not cover all medical expenses. Depending on the plan, the insured, or policyholder, may be responsible for co-pays, deductibles, and coinsurance. A **copayment**, or *co-pay*, is a set fee paid each time you see a doctor or have a prescription filled. The amount of the co-pay is stated in the policy and printed on the health plan identification card.

A *deductible* is an annual amount that must be paid before the insurance starts to pay. For example, if a plan has an annual $500 deductible, the first $500 of medical expenses must be paid by the policyholder. Once the deductible is met, the insurance company begins to pay on qualified expenses above the deductible. In some plans, co-pays count toward meeting the annual deductible.

Coinsurance is a percentage of the service costs that patients pay after the annual deductible is met. For example, if a medical service costs $100 and the coinsurance is 20 percent, the patient's cost would be $20.

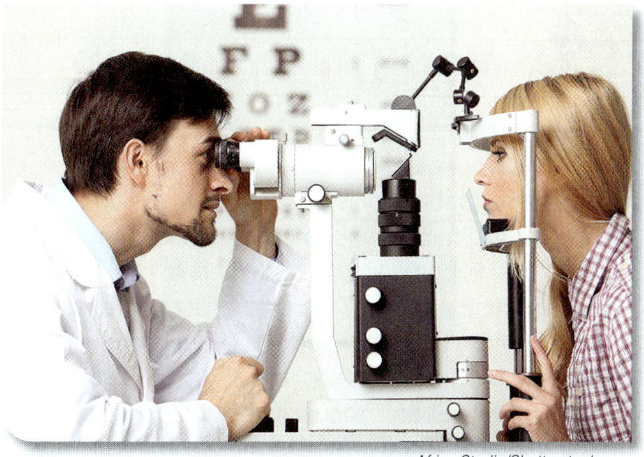

Africa Studio/Shutterstock.com

Health insurance offers financial protection by covering specific medical expenses, like an eye exam.

Some insurance plans may also contain exclusions. An **exclusion** is a medical service that is not covered in an insurance plan. Examples include elective cosmetic surgery or, in some cases, treatment of preexisting conditions. A *preexisting condition* is an illness or an injury a person has before signing up for health insurance.

Plans also may require preauthorization and utilization reviews for certain services. A **preauthorization** is an approval from the plan before receiving certain procedures and treatments. A **utilization review** is an insurance company's examination of requests for medical treatments and procedures to make sure they are covered and the patient truly needs them.

Health insurance plans include regular medical, major medical, comprehensive medical, dental, and vision care insurance.

- **Regular medical insurance** is insurance that covers prescriptions, hospital stays, and inpatient tests. An *inpatient* is a person whose care requires a stay in a hospital. It does not cover surgeries.
- **Major medical insurance** is insurance that typically covers the costs of serious illnesses and injuries as well as high-cost procedures.
- **Comprehensive medical insurance** is insurance that combines basic and major medical protection in one policy.
- **Dental insurance** is insurance that covers specified dental services, such as exams and teeth cleaning.
- **Vision care insurance** is insurance that covers specified eye care services, such as eye exams, glasses, and contact lenses.

No plan will pay for all your medical expenses or cover all the services you may need. *Maximum benefits* refer to the maximum paid for specific types of treatment or the maximum number of days care is covered. For example, payment for mental health care may be limited to $1,000 annually; the number of days in a hospital may be limited as well. Health insurance may be purchased as group health insurance or individual health insurance.

Group Health Insurance

Many health insurance plans are available through a group policy. *Group health insurance plans* are usually offered through an employer. However, group plans can also be offered through unions, trade associations, and other organizations.

You Do the Math Probabilistic Reasoning

Probability is the likelihood of an event occurring. In general, probability is stated as the number of ways an event can happen over the total number of outcomes. Flipping a coin, for example, can result in either heads or tails. The probability of the result being heads is one in two (1/2). There is only one side of the coin with heads, and there are two total possible outcomes. Probability can be expressed as a percentage. In the case of a flipped coin: 1/2 = .5 × 100 = 50% chance of being heads.

Solve the following problems.

1. A local office supply store offers a random discount to its regular customers. The discount may be 2 percent, 4 percent, 6 percent, or 25 percent. The discount is randomly selected by the cash register computer. What is the probability that a customer will receive the 25 percent discount?
2. Of 100 patients that a nurse treated in one week, 20 of them had the flu. What is the probability percentage that the next patient treated by the nurse will not have the flu?
3. At a combination supermarket and pharmacy, 47 customers purchased only groceries, 13 customers purchased groceries and items from the pharmacy area, and 62 customers purchased items only from the pharmacy area. What is the probability that a customer will purchase groceries?

Many organizations provide group coverage as an employee benefit, with the employer paying some or all the policy premiums. In most cases, the rates charged for group insurance plans are less than an individual policy for the same amount of coverage.

If you have access to a group plan through your employer or some other affiliation, you can usually sign up during an enrollment period. At this time, policyholders can also change plans or renew coverage. In evaluating health insurance plans, consider the services covered, the choice of health care providers, and the costs.

If you are covered by an employer-sponsored group plan and lose your job, you are likely to lose your health care coverage as well. In this case, you may be entitled to continue your health benefits under the *Consolidated Omnibus Budget Reconciliation Act (COBRA)*. This federal law enacted in 1986 gives covered workers the right to continue their group health care coverage for up to 18 months after job loss. In some cases, the coverage can be extended up to 36 months. However, the covered worker must pay the premiums for continuing coverage. A covered worker is anyone who is (or was) provided coverage under an employer's group plan.

COBRA generally applies to all group health plans maintained by private companies with at least 20 employees and by state and local governments. Employers may require individuals who elect continuation coverage to pay the full cost of the coverage plus a 2 percent administrative fee. The required payment for continuation coverage is usually more expensive than the amount that active employees pay for group health coverage. This is because the employer typically pays part of the cost of employees' coverage. However, the COBRA payment is usually less expensive than individual health coverage.

Individual Health Insurance

People who are not eligible for group insurance may purchase health insurance on their own for themselves and their families. Many health insurance companies sell individual plans. However, individual policies are more expensive and may offer fewer benefits than group plans. Premiums for an individual can be as much as $800 a month or more. Families often pay more than $1,000 a month.

Some plans allow the insured to choose doctors regardless of where they practice or their hospital affiliation. Other plans limit choices to participating health care providers. When selecting an individual plan, calculate the total cost of the premiums you would pay together with the deductible. Certain plans have lower premiums but higher copayments or deductibles. Other plans may have the reverse. Very often, monthly premiums can be reduced by choosing a plan with a higher deductible. This can save you money if you typically require only routine health care services. Figure 15-1 lists questions to ask when selecting an individual health insurance plan.

An application process for individual health insurance includes completing a medical history questionnaire and sometimes submitting to medical tests or a complete physical exam. Healthy, young applicants can usually qualify for reasonable premiums. However, people suffering from serious injuries, illnesses, or chronic physical or mental health problems may pay high premiums.

Health Insurance Exchange

People who purchase an individual health insurance plan might choose to do so through the federal health insurance exchange. The **health insurance exchange**, also called the *Health Insurance Marketplace*, is a government-sponsored price-comparison website where consumers can shop for, and purchase, government-regulated and standardized health care plans eligible for federal subsidies. For individuals who do not have health insurance through a job, Medicare, Medicaid, the Children's Health Insurance Program (CHIP), or another source that provides qualifying coverage, the Marketplace can help them find coverage. HealthCare.gov is the source for complete information.

Questions to Ask When Selecting an Individual Health Insurance Plan
• Do you want to choose your own doctor and hospital or continue with the providers you already use? • What health care providers, including doctors, hospitals, and labs, participate in the plan? Where are they located? • What are the provisions for seeing a specialist? • Can you change doctors without prior approval? • What premiums must you pay? • Is there a deductible? If so, how much is it? Which services are subject to the deductible? • What are the costs of using nonparticipating providers and facilities? • What health costs should you be prepared to pay? Check any exclusions, service limitations, or restrictions that may apply. • Do copayments apply to every medical service or only to specific ones, such as office visits and prescriptions? • In a managed care program, find out whether copayments are higher if you go outside your health care plan for treatment.

Goodheart-Willcox Publisher

Figure 15-1 Ask these questions when selecting an individual health insurance plan.

The Affordable Care Act's Ten Essential Health Benefits

- Ambulatory patient services
- Emergency services
- Hospitalization
- Maternity and newborn care
- Mental health and substance use disorder services, including behavioral health treatment
- Prescription drugs
- Rehabilitative and habilitative services and devices
- Laboratory services
- Preventative and wellness services and chronic disease management
- Pediatric services, including oral and vision care

Note: some plans may have limitations on certain benefits.

Goodheart-Willcox Publisher

Figure 15-2 All major medical plans sold through the Health Insurance Marketplace offer services from ten categories of essential benefits.

In some states, the Marketplace is run by the state. In others, it is run by the federal government. All major medical plans sold after 2014 offer services from ten categories of essential benefits. However, the scope and quantity of services offered under each category can vary. The ten essential health benefits are shown in Figure 15-2.

The health insurance exchange was created as a provision of the *Patient Protection and Affordable Care Act (PPACA)*, which was signed into law by President Obama in 2010. The Patient Protection and Affordable Care Act was created to ensure that all Americans have access to quality, affordable health care and create the transformation within the health care system necessary to contain costs.

The law was enacted in two parts: The Patient Protection and Affordable Care Act was signed into law on March 23, 2010 and was amended by the Health Care and Education Reconciliation Act on March 30, 2010. The *Affordable Care Act (ACA)* refers to the final amended version of the law.

Beginning in 2014, the ACA required every person in the US have health insurance. The idea was that if everyone buys health insurance, the overall cost of the insurance should decrease. By paying premiums, everyone would share the risk. A **shared responsibility payment** is a penalty imposed on those who did not purchase insurance. The penalty was due when the taxpayer filed a federal income tax return. However, the *Tax Cuts and Jobs Act (TCJA)* enacted in December 2017 reduced the shared responsibility payment to zero for tax year 2019 and beyond. Some states still impose a penalty for residents who do not purchase health insurance.

Private Health Care Plans

Private health care plans are offered by insurance companies. They include indemnity plans, managed care plans, and supplemental insurance.

Indemnity Plans

An **indemnity plan** is a health care plan that pays for covered medical services after treatment is provided, usually on a fee-for-service basis. It may also be referred to as a *fee-for-service plan*. An advantage of this type of plan is that the insured can usually go to a licensed health care provider or accredited hospital of choice. Any deductible or coinsurance payment is the responsibility of the insured. There are three common types of indemnity plans: preferred provider organization (PPO), point-of-service (POS) plan, and high-deductible health plan (HDHP).

Ethics

Accountability

It is ethical for both individuals and businesses to act with accountability. Accountability is the act of being responsible for activities and behavior. It is important to accept responsibility for mistakes, large and small. An innocent error is not considered unethical behavior; however, not taking responsibility for the error is unethical.

Preferred Provider Organization (PPO)

Preferred provider organizations (PPOs) are a common type of indemnity plan in which the insurance company contracts with specific doctors, hospitals, and other caregivers to provide services at reduced costs to plan members. The insured may choose providers outside the plan for an extra out-of-pocket cost.

Point-of-Service (POS) Plan

Point-of-service (POS) plans allow the insured to choose the doctor, hospital, or clinic, and the insurance pays part or all the costs according to a schedule laid out in the policy. POS plans are normally more expensive than other plans.

High-Deductible Health Plan (HDHP)

High-deductible health plans (HDHPs) are a type of health care plan in which the insured must pay a high deductible before the insurance begins to pay. However, the monthly premiums are usually lower than for other types of plans. A **health savings account (HSA)** is a tax-advantaged savings account available to people enrolled in qualified HDHP to help defray the costs. People who have a HSA may contribute pre-tax dollars into the account to pay for health care costs. Unused funds in the account may accumulate tax-free. However, if the funds are used for purposes other than health care costs, there are tax penalties. An HSA can save you money three ways.

- Having a high deductible makes monthly premiums less expensive.
- Contributions are tax-deductible, which reduces the amount paid in taxes overall.
- Unspent savings in the account are allowed to accumulate tax-free until they are needed to pay health care expenses.

You may be able to set up an HSA through your employer. Employer-sponsored plans result in pre-tax deductions. This means that your employer deducts your plan contributions from your pay before taxes are determined, reducing the amount of your income subject to taxes. If your employer does not offer an HSA account, you may be able to establish one on your own.

Managed Care Plans

A **managed care plan** is a type of health care plan in which the insurance company contracts with specific doctors, hospitals, and other health care providers to deliver medical services and preventive care to members at reduced cost.

Burlingham/Shutterstock.com

A doctor's appointment or prescription may require a copayment at the time of service.

The choice of service providers is limited to those who participate in the plan, except for referrals to necessary specialists outside the plan.

The insured and/or the employer pay a set amount in monthly premiums. The insured also pays any required deductibles, coinsurance payments, or copayments. Copayments are due at the time of service. For example, a doctor's appointment or a prescription may require copayment at the time of service.

A common form of managed care is *health maintenance organizations (HMOs).* These plans provide a list of participating physicians from which the insured selects a primary care doctor. This doctor coordinates the patient's health care and carries out routine exams and treatments. The primary care doctor makes referrals to a specialist for specialized treatments, consultations, or procedures. The plan normally covers only the treatments provided by doctors who participate in the plan.

Supplemental Insurance

Supplemental insurance is additional insurance that can be purchased to pay for medical expenses that standard health insurance does not cover or does not fully cover. Some individuals choose to buy supplement insurance to cover the treatment costs of a specific illness. Cancer insurance and long-term care insurance are examples of supplemental insurance.

Cancer insurance is insurance that helps manage the risks that occur when an insured has cancer. It is not intended to replace a standard health insurance policy, but to complement it by covering expenses not covered by the standard policy. For example, cancer insurance may pay for experimental treatments, transportation costs to and from medical facilities, and the insured's monthly home mortgage payment if unable to work during treatment. Cancer insurance may also cover expenses if the insured seeks treatment outside the health plan network.

Another common supplemental policy is long-term care insurance. **Long-term care (LTC) insurance** provides coverage for personal and custodial care during periods when an individual is unable to perform essential daily living activities. Essential daily living activities include feeding, dressing, bathing, and walking. Care can be provided in a variety of settings, such as in the insured's home, a nursing home, a skilled nursing facility, an assisted living facility, or a mental hospital. LTC insurance is usually purchased to care for elderly, chronically ill, disabled, or seriously injured individuals. It can also cover disabilities caused by mental disease.

The cost of long-term care insurance is determined primarily by the insured's age at the date coverage starts, health, gender, and amount of benefits. Women usually pay more than men because women have a longer life expectancy.

Employability Skills

Resilience

Resilience is a person's ability to cope with and recover from change or adversity. Resilient people are able to handle challenges in one aspect of their lives while not letting it affect other aspects. They can bounce back even when they feel as if they have been knocked down. People who have positive attitudes are generally more resilient than those who are not positive. You can learn to be resilient by looking at the good things rather than dwelling on the bad.

Governmental Health Care Plans

The government offers health insurance to certain eligible people, including older adults, people with disabilities, low-income families, and children. What each person pays, if anything, depends on various factors.

Medicare

Medicare covers specific health care expenses for eligible citizens age 65 and older. It also covers those under age 65 with certain diseases or disabilities. The governmental funding for Medicare comes from payroll taxes. Four different parts of Medicare provide coverage for specific services: Part A (hospital insurance), Part B (medical insurance), Part C (Medicare Advantage health plans), and Part D (prescription drug costs).

Part A helps pay for inpatient care in hospitals and skilled nursing facilities up to a specified number of days. It does not cover long-term care, but it covers some home health care and hospice care. *Hospice care* is for people with a terminal illness. A deductible must be met before Medicare will pay for hospital stays. If a patient needs care beyond the specified number of days allowed for home health, hospice, and skilled nursing care, the patient is responsible for paying certain costs.

Part B is a voluntary program that helps pay for a variety of health care costs. These include doctors' fees, outpatient hospital services, home health services, certain tests, and other health care costs. To obtain Part B coverage, enrollees must pay a monthly premium.

Part C, Medicare Advantage Plans, combines Parts A and Part B benefits under one plan. Some people prefer this type of plan because it simplifies enrollment and payment procedures. In most cases, prescription drug coverage is also included.

Part D helps to lower prescription drug prices and protect against higher future drug prices. Those who enroll in this program pay a monthly premium. Private insurance companies provide the coverage. There are a variety of plans offered, and subscribers choose the one that best suits their medical needs.

Medigap insurance helps pay for health care costs not covered by Medicare, such as copayments and deductibles. Private insurance companies sell this type of protection, not the government. Usually, this insurance is only available for patients who have both Medicare Parts A and B.

Medicaid

Medicaid is a health insurance program for eligible low-income persons and those with certain disabilities. It is a state-administered program financed by federal and state tax revenues.

Patients apply for Medicaid at public aid offices within their state. The services provided vary from state to state. Most Medicaid programs pay for inpatient and outpatient hospital services, clinic care, X-rays, and laboratory services. Some states also pay for family planning, home health care services, dental care, eye care, and other medical needs.

Pressmaster/Shutterstock.com

The government offers health insurance to certain eligible people, such as children ages 18 and younger.

Children's Health Insurance Program (CHIP)

Many American families earn too much to qualify for Medicaid but not enough to afford private health insurance premiums. The Children's Health Insurance Program (CHIP) gives federal funds to states to provide health insurance coverage for children ages 18 and younger. The program rules vary slightly among states. Taxes on the sales of cigarettes and other tobacco products are used to fund the program.

Taking Responsibility for Your Health Care

Individuals should be responsible for their health care. Purchasing insurance is a first step. Healthy, young people may not want to pay for health insurance, but serious illness or injury is always a possibility. In addition, accidents are a leading cause of injury and death among young adults and insurance is needed to cover these costs.

Being responsible involves carrying proof of insurance with you at all times in the event that medical care is needed. It also requires keeping receipts for paid medical bills and the purchase of medications for filing insurance claims and tax returns.

Up-to-date health and medical records should be kept in your personal recordkeeping system. If you switch doctors or health care plans or are hospitalized, the new care providers will request a thorough history of your medical background. Health and medical records can help doctors with the diagnosis and treatment of illnesses as well as with the prevention of certain diseases. Having health facts readily available is very important for anyone with health conditions that would require special treatment in an emergency.

Regular physical and dental checkups may help you avoid serious illnesses or at least identify them in their early stages. Knowing how to evaluate health care professionals and medical facilities can help you get adequate health care when you need it. The best time to choose a health care provider is when you are healthy. Look for providers who are graduates of approved medical or dental schools and who are licensed and board certified. Licensing requirements vary from state to state. Many medical professionals are members in one or more professional societies and associations. Choose providers who are well established in their practice with a good reputation among both patients and fellow professionals. Friends, relatives, employers, and coworkers can offer recommendations for qualified health care providers. If you move to a new area, your former doctor may be able to refer you to a new physician. Medical or dental schools often provide a list of faculty doctors and graduates who practice in the area. National and state medical associations operate referral services. Local hospitals often can recommend qualified licensed providers. The information in Figure 15-3 can help you understand important terms you will need to know when seeking medical care.

Being responsible for your health also includes controlling your health care costs by developing healthy habits. Quality self-care involves eating healthy and avoiding illegal drugs, tobacco products, and alcohol consumption. Getting adequate rest and physical activity and finding ways to deal with life's stressful situations are critical.

To encourage healthy living, fewer illnesses, and fewer claims, many insurance companies are developing incentives for their policyholders to stay healthy. By participating in documented physical fitness programs, health assessments, and other healthy-living activities, the insured can earn points and rewards. These points can be used for merchandise, travel, or even reduced insurance premiums. For example, some health insurance companies will lower

Medical Terms	
Term	**Description**
primary care physician	Physician trained to diagnose and treat a variety of illnesses in all phases of medicine; oversees general treatment for most patients
specialist	Physician who has additional education and training in a specific branch of medicine, qualified and licensed to practice general medicine or dentistry, but focuses on specialties
walk-in clinic	Health care facility that provides routine medical attention; offers quick, economical service with short waiting times
hospital emergency room or urgent care center	Health care facility that provides emergency care for injuries or sudden illnesses that require immediate attention
alternative medicine	Health care practices and products that are not presently a part of conventional medicine; includes behavioral counseling, hypnosis, homeopathic therapies, manipulation by chiropractors, and acupuncture
prescription drug	Medication obtained with a physician's orders
over-the-counter drug	Nonprescription medication available on store shelves
generic drug	Drug that is sold by its common name, chemical composition, or class and usually costs considerably less than a similar brand-name drug
dietary supplement	Product that is intended to enhance a person's diet such as vitamins, minerals, herbs, or amino acids

Goodheart-Willcox Publisher

Figure 15-3 It is important to know the meaning of these terms when making health care decisions.

your monthly premiums if you attend regular wellness visits, track exercise with an activity tracking device, and log healthy eating with a smartphone app. Insurance companies hope that preventive activities will reduce the number of claims made by the insured. Insured individuals should take advantage of the "get healthy" plans offered their insurance company. See Figure 15-4 for ways to lower health care costs.

Ways to Lower Health Care Costs
• Make good health a priority. Follow a balanced approach to diet, exercise, sleep, stress control, and accident prevention. • Find out what free or low-cost health services and programs are available through your school, employer, community, and government. • Know exactly what expenses your health insurance covers, keep accurate records, and file claims promptly for covered expenses. • Discuss fees and prices with health care providers. Cost-conscious patients can often avoid unnecessary expenses. • Lower hospital costs by asking for outpatient care, if possible, and minimum hospital stays. • Get a second opinion before agreeing to nonemergency surgery or costly procedures. • Obtain necessary authorizations before receiving treatments to be sure they are covered by your insurance. • Keep track of out-of-pocket spending on health care expenses. If these are more than a certain percentage of your income, they may be tax deductible.

Goodheart-Willcox Publisher

Figure 15-4 Individuals can lower the cost of health care by following these recommendations.

Section 15.1 Review

Check Your Understanding

1. In health insurance plans, what is the difference between copayments, deductibles, and coinsurance?
2. List examples of coverage that is often included in health insurance plans.
3. Name three types of indemnity plans.
4. Who is eligible for Medicaid?
5. How can you control your health care costs?

Build Your Vocabulary

As you progress through this course, develop a personal glossary. This will help you build your vocabulary and prepare you for a career. Write a definition for each of the following terms and add it to your glossary.

health insurance
copayment
coinsurance
exclusion
preauthorization
utilization review
regular medical insurance
major medical insurance
comprehensive medical insurance
dental insurance
vision care insurance
health insurance exchange
shared responsibility payment
indemnity plan
health savings account (HSA)
managed care plan
supplemental insurance
cancer insurance
long-term care (LTC) insurance

Section 15.2 Disability and Life Insurance

Objectives

After studying this section, you will be able to:

- Explain the purpose of disability insurance.
- Describe types of life insurance.
- Explain how to select appropriate life insurance coverage.

Essential Question

Why do individuals buy life insurance?

Terms

disability insurance
workers' compensation insurance
life insurance
beneficiary
term life insurance
whole life insurance
endowment insurance

Disability Insurance

Disability insurance is an insurance plan that pays a portion of income lost to a worker who is unable to work for a prolonged period because of illness or injury. Many people do not think they need disability insurance. However, the loss of income because of an inability to work can be financially devastating.

Disability insurance may replace as much as 60 to 70 percent of the income normally earned. The two types of disability insurance are short-term plans and long-term plans. Short-term coverage normally requires a waiting period of up to 14 days and provides coverage for up to two years. Long-term coverage may have a waiting period of several weeks or months, and it pays for a number of years or for life.

Many employers provide limited disability insurance to their workers as a benefit. The employer pays the premium for these group plans. If a higher level of insurance is desired through the group plan, an employee may be able to pay for it. The cost of disability insurance is determined primarily by your age, overall health, and type of occupation as well as the benefit period, waiting period, and amount of benefit.

Consumers may buy disability coverage independently if they are not part of employer health care plans or other insurance programs.

SpeedKingz/Shutterstock.com

When workers are permanently disabled, they may receive benefits for life.

Case Study Disability Insurance

Aaron is a single, healthy, 30-year old landscaper who owns a business with annual net income of $54,000 after expenses. Recently, purchasing health insurance through the federal health exchange seemed like a good idea.

The selected health insurance policy is inexpensive and provides minimal health coverage. The company's financial advisor warned that suffering an illness or injury that prevented work would negatively affect the business and Aaron's personal income. For that reason, the advisor suggested purchasing disability insurance as a precaution.

Case Review

1. What advantages does disability insurance provide?
2. What types of questions should the insurance agent be asked about disability insurance?
3. Are there any ways that the cost of the premium could be controlled?
4. What risk will be faced if no disability insurance is purchased?

Important questions to ask when buying disability insurance include the following.

- What benefits are promised? How much money will you receive?
- What is the waiting period if benefits do not start immediately? Is there is a waiting period of weeks or months? If you opt for a longer waiting period, your insurance premium will often be lower.
- How long are benefits available? The length of time a person can receive benefits varies. This can be a few years, until retirement, or for a lifetime.
- Can the policy be canceled by the insurer? A noncancelable clause means that the insurance company cannot cancel your coverage so long as you pay the premiums. A guaranteed renewable clause means that you can renew the coverage with the same benefits but usually at a higher cost.

You may have to give up some of the features you want to get an affordable premium. For example, lowering the amount of the benefit or lengthening the waiting period will reduce the premium you must pay.

Workers' compensation insurance is another type of disability insurance that helps pay for medical care, rehabilitation, and lost wages for an employee who suffers an injury or illness as a direct result of performing a job. It provides a safety net for workers with work-related illnesses or injuries. The entire cost of workers' compensation insurance is usually paid by the employer. The cost depends on several factors, including the number of employees, risk factors associated with the job, and the company's past history of accidents.

When workers are permanently disabled, they may receive benefits for life. If injuries and illnesses are fatal, workers' compensation provides death benefits to survivors.

Employers in every state are required to provide some form of workers' compensation insurance. Employees must file claims through their employers to apply for workers' compensation. Each state has its own laws and time limits for filing claims. Applicants must prove they are disabled and usually must submit to examinations by insurance company doctors. To find out more about your state's workers' compensation laws, check with the state Workers' Compensation Board.

Life Insurance

Denis Tabler/Shutterstock.com

A beneficiary is a person or organization named by a policyholder to receive the death benefit of an insurance policy after the policyholder's death.

The right life insurance choices can help provide financial security for you and your family. **Life insurance** is insurance that protects dependents from loss of income and helps pay expenses after the death of the insured person. The larger your financial responsibilities, the more important it is to have adequate coverage. Life insurance is especially important if you have a spouse, children, or elderly parents who depend on your income.

When an insured person dies, the face value of the policy is paid to the beneficiary. The face value is the amount for which the policy is written. A **beneficiary** is a person or group who receives a deceased person's assets. The beneficiary of a life insurance policy is a person or organization named by a policyholder to receive the death benefit of an insurance policy after the policyholder's death.

The three traditional types of life insurance are term life, whole life, and endowment. Each type is available in slightly different forms and with different features.

Term Life

Term life insurance is a type of insurance that provides protection only for a specific period of time. This time period may be 1, 5, 10, or 20 years or until a specified age. When the term ends, so does the protection. Term policies often include a renewable option that allows you to renew the coverage at the end of the term, usually at higher rates. The cost of term life insurance is based mainly on the amount of coverage, age of the insured, and gender.

The advantage of term insurance is that it offers the most protection for an individual's insurance dollars. Policies offering only protection cost less than policies with savings features. For those people who really need insurance and cannot afford high premiums, term coverage may be the best choice.

Whole Life

Whole life insurance is a type of insurance that provides basic lifetime protection so long as premiums are paid. Whole life insurance is also called *straight life insurance*. The face amount is paid to the beneficiaries upon death of the insured. The coverage builds cash value over the years. *Cash value* is the amount of money a policyholder would receive if the policy were surrendered before death or maturity.

You may be able to borrow against the cash value of whole life insurance at a relatively low interest rate. However, until repaid, benefits are reduced by the amount of the loan. You can also surrender the policy for its cash value if you want to change or eliminate coverage. New types of whole life insurance were developed in recent years to meet today's needs and demands. The new types include limited payment policies, variable life, adjustable life, and universal life.

The cost of whole life insurance is determined by the amount of coverage, age, gender, medical history, and nicotine use. A person's driving record can also affect the cost of whole life insurance.

Limited-Payment Life

Limited-payment life insurance offers lifetime protection. These plans require premium payments over a stated period of time, such as 20 years, or until you reach a certain age. During the payment period, premiums are higher and cash value builds faster than for standard whole life coverage.

Variable Life

Variable life insurance provides insurance protection that is combined with an investment feature. The premiums are fixed and the face value varies with the performance of the fund in which the premiums are invested. However, the face amount cannot fall below the original amount of the insurance. These policies guarantee a minimum death benefit. The benefit may be higher than the guarantee, depending on the earnings of the premium dollars invested. The advantage of this type of life insurance is the potential of earnings when the value of the fund rises. The main disadvantage is it may not offer the best of either insurance or investment opportunities.

Adjustable Life

Adjustable life insurance is an insurance policy that can be revised by the insured as individual needs change. Coverage may start with term insurance for a given amount, premium, and term. Within limits, the premium's face value and premium payment period may be raised or lowered. Flexibility is the key advantage of adjustable life coverage. However, the need to constantly monitor coverage may be a disadvantage.

Universal Life

Universal life insurance permits the adjustment of premiums, face value, and level of protection. In addition, it offers an investment feature. The cash value is invested to earn interest at current market rates. An annual statement shows the current level of protection, cash value, and interest earned. The statement also includes a breakdown of how premiums are allocated to protection, investment, and expenses.

An advantage of universal life is flexibility, both in the amount of the premiums and in the level of protection. Earnings also keep pace with current market rates. If interest rates go down, however, your earnings decrease. Taxes are not paid on the accumulated interest until the policy is cashed. This can be an advantage for persons in high income tax brackets.

hvostik/Shutterstock.com

All states require a special license to sell life insurance.

Endowment Insurance

Endowment insurance is insurance that pays the face value of the policy to beneficiaries if the insured dies before the endowment period ends. However, it pays the face amount to the insured if the endowment period ends and the insured is still living. The advantage of endowment insurance is the combination of protection and savings. The disadvantage is high premiums.

Exploring Careers

Patient Account Representative

Patient Account Representatives work in hospitals, doctors' offices, or other medical facilities. They help patients understand their medical expenses. They also aid patients in finding ways to pay for their charges. They process bills, collect payments, and contact collection agencies to assist with collecting past-due bills. Patient Account Representatives typically:

- keep and update financial records
- calculate charges and issue bills
- provide customer assistance
- perform financial transactions

Patient Account Representatives can work either part- or full-time depending on where the office is located and how many patients use that office. They work in an office and spend a great deal of time on the phone and computer. Patient Account Representatives require a high school diploma or equivalent. Most employers would prefer the representative have a certification or 2- or 4-year degree, but it is not always required. Patient Account Representatives must have the ability to work independently and possess excellent communication, customer-service, organizational, and mathematic or financial skills.

Choosing a Life Insurance Plan

Each person's needs are unique. The life insurance coverage that is right for one person or family may be wrong for another. Finding the right life insurance protection that works best for you requires careful planning.

Compare the premiums charged by different companies for the same types and amounts of coverage. If you are considering whole life insurance, compare the cash value accumulation rates. Additional information on buying life insurance is available from a number of financial publications and online.

Very often, the agent is the key to the quality of service you receive. All states require a special license to sell life insurance. Initials following an agent's name indicate completion of specific studies in the insurance field. *CLU* indicates a Chartered Life Underwriter. *ChFC* indicates a Chartered Financial Consultant. *LUTCF* indicates a Life Underwriters' Training Council Fellow. Members of the National Association of Life Underwriters subscribe to the ethical standards of that group. The amount and type of life insurance protection you need depends on two key factors: your present and future earning power and your financial responsibilities and obligations.

Amount of Protection

Protection is often based on the amount of earnings that would be lost if the insured died prematurely. It is also matched to the needs of survivors for whom the insured is financially responsible. These needs depend on an individual's number of survivors, marital status, earning power, and lifestyles.

History of Finance

Life Insurance

Ancient Rome is credited with being the birthplace of life insurance. The first policies were granted by burial clubs. These clubs, called *Fratres*, covered the cost of funeral expenses for members and provided financial assistance to surviving family members. Money left over after the cost of the funeral was typically given to the surviving family members to help them with financial problems that often accompanied the loss of a family member. Members who were behind with their club dues did not qualify for help with the funeral costs.

Life insurance was available for purchase in England in the early 18th century. The Amicable Society for a Perpetual Assurance Office, founded in 1706, offered the policies. With these plans, each member paid the same amount every year depending on the person's age. At the end of the year, if any members had died, a portion of the payments was divided among their families.

The first insurance company in the United States was formed in Charleston, South Carolina, in 1732. However, life insurance was not added to its product line until the late 1760s. In the beginning, many opposed the concept of life insurance because it was viewed as benefiting from death.

Other factors to consider include the share of family income provided by the insured and income available from other sources. Careful analysis is needed to determine the amount of protection to buy. Consider the following questions to decide how much coverage you need.

- What are the ages and financial needs of those depending on your income? Dependents may include aging parents or relatives as well as a spouse and young children.
- What amount of money would your dependents need to maintain their standard of living without your income? Ideally, money would be left to cover a home mortgage and everyday living expenses. It might also cover major future expenses, such as college educations for children.
- What other sources of income would be available for dependents? Would dependents be able to draw on Social Security benefits, savings, employee benefits, or their own earnings? You want enough coverage to fill the gap between what is available from other sources and what your dependents would need.
- What amount of cash would be needed to pay burial costs and unpaid debts? Even if you are single with no dependents, you need enough life insurance to take care of these costs. Then your financial obligations will not burden your parents or other relatives.

Types of Protection

Life insurance can be purchased in a variety of forms and with many special benefits. The decision depends on how much coverage is needed, what the individual can afford to spend, and the special features desired.

Group life insurance is a form of term insurance that covers a large number of people under a single policy. Group insurance may be available through your employer, union, or another group to which you belong. As a rule, group coverage costs less than an individual policy for the same amount of coverage. Very often, group coverage is provided as a benefits package through an employer. The employer may pay all or part of the premium. If you rely on group protection, look for a conversion clause. This permits you to convert to an individual policy without proof of insurability if you should leave the group.

Individual life insurance, though more expensive, generally can be tailored to the policyholder's needs. Features to consider when choosing life insurance protection include the following.

- *Guaranteed renewability* allows the insured to keep coverage in force at the end of a term without new evidence of insurability. Premium rates increase with each new term.
- *Double indemnity* provides for double benefits if death is the result of an accident. This may also be called an *accidental-death benefit*.
- A *disability benefit* provides for a waiver of premiums if the insured becomes permanently and totally disabled. While this is often available as a provision on a life insurance policy, separate disability coverage is usually more desirable.
- A *convertible provision* permits the insured to convert or exchange a term policy for another form of protection without new evidence of insurability.

Finally, consider how life insurance fits into your overall plan for future security and eventual retirement. Future financial security depends on the right mix of savings, insurance, and investments. Some people plan to use insurance as a form of savings. In this case, the earnings on your insurance should match or exceed those on other forms of savings and investments.

Section 15.2 Review

Check Your Understanding

1. List some of the important questions to ask when buying disability insurance.
2. What are the primary factors that determine the cost of (a) term life insurance and (b) whole life insurance?
3. Name four types of whole life insurance policies.
4. The amount and type of life insurance protection you need depends on what two key factors?
5. What is group life insurance?

Build Your Vocabulary

As you progress through this course, develop a personal glossary. This will help you build your vocabulary and prepare you for a career. Write a definition for each of the following terms and add it to your glossary.

disability insurance
workers' compensation insurance
life insurance
beneficiary
term life insurance
whole life insurance
endowment insurance

Review and Assessment

Chapter Summary

Section 15.1 Health Insurance

- Health insurance pays for medical expenses of an insured person and dependents. It does not cover all medical expenses, however, and the insured may need to pay a deductible and coinsurance. Health insurance is often provided by an employer as group health insurance or purchased as individual health insurance. Individual health insurance can also be purchased through the Health Insurance Marketplace.
- Private health care plans offered by insurance companies include indemnity plans, managed-care plans, and supplemental insurance. An indemnity plan is a health care plan that pays for covered medical services after treatment is provided, usually on a fee-for-service basis. A managed care plan is a type of health care plan in which the insurance company contracts with specific doctors, hospitals, and other health care providers to deliver medical services and preventive care to members at reduced cost. Supplemental insurance plans provide coverage that is usually not available with other health insurance plans.
- Governmental health insurance plans include Medicare, Medicaid, and the Children's Health Insurance Program (CHIP). Medicare covers health care expenses for eligible citizens age 65 and older. It also covers those under age 65 with certain diseases or disabilities. Medicaid is for eligible low-income persons and those with certain disabilities. CHIP gives federal funds to states to provide health insurance coverage for children ages 18 and younger.
- Individuals should be responsible for their health care. Purchasing insurance is a first step. Being responsible includes carrying proof of insurance, keeping medical records, and keeping medical receipts for insurance claims and taxes. It also includes finding a doctor before one is needed, maintaining up to date health records, and having regular checkups.

Section 15.2 Disability and Life Insurance

- Disability insurance pays a portion of income lost to a worker who is unable to work for a prolonged period because of illness or injury. Short-term coverage may pay a portion of a person's income for up to two years. Long-term coverage pays for a number of years or for life. Workers' compensation insurance is another type of disability insurance.
- Life insurance protects dependents from loss of income and helps pay expenses after the death of the insured person. The three traditional types of life insurance are term life, whole life, and endowment.
- Each person's life insurance needs are unique. Finding the right life insurance protection requires careful planning. The amount and type of life insurance protection needed depends on two key factors: the person's present and future earning power and the person's financial responsibilities and obligations.

Review Your Knowledge

1. Explain the purpose of health insurance.
2. What is the purpose of COBRA?
3. Describe private health care plans.
4. Identify government-sponsored health care plans.
5. Discuss how to take responsibility for your health care.
6. Explain the purpose of disability insurance.

7. Why is workers' compensation insurance considered a type of disability insurance?
8. What is the primary purpose of life insurance?
9. Describe types of life insurance.
10. Explain how to select appropriate life insurance coverage.

Apply Your Knowledge

1. The law requires that individuals purchase health insurance or pay a penalty. However, responsible individuals purchase health insurance for other reasons. Make a list of the personal reasons why you would purchase health insurance.
2. Some people decide to purchase various types of supplemental insurance in addition to regular health insurance. Cancer insurance is a type of supplemental insurance. For what reasons would a healthy individual purchase cancer insurance?
3. Long-term care (LTC) insurance is a supplemental insurance that individuals purchase to manage risk. Discuss reasons why long-term insurance would be a part of a financial plan for a person's future.
4. One type of disability insurance is short-term disability insurance. Discuss reasons why employers might provide short-term disability insurance for their employees.
5. Individuals who receive short-term disability insurance as a benefit from an employer can usually purchase additional long-term disability insurance themselves. Discuss reasons why employees would buy additional liability long-term disability insurance if their employers already provide short-term.
6. Life insurance protects dependents from loss of income and helps pay expenses after the death of the insured person. There are different types of life insurance that are available to purchase. Compare and contrast the different types of life insurance that are discussed in this chapter. For each type, state the reasons that an individual might choose a particular policy.
7. Whole life insurance is a long-term commitment for providing life insurance coverage. As a teen, discuss the reasons why you would consider buying whole life insurance rather than term insurance.
8. Purchasing insurance is a method of risk management that can pay big dividends. However, insurance is expensive and should be budgeted for in your monthly budget and financial plan. Create a checklist that you might use for choosing a life insurance plan when you become independent and make your own financial decisions about insurance. List your criteria in its order of importance to you.
9. The Patient Protection and Affordable Care Act (PPACA) had an impact on the way people look at health insurance and its importance. How has this new law affected citizens in your state?
10. When you begin working a full time job, your employer will probably provide options for you to purchase health insurance as an employee benefit. Some employers offer managed care programs. Three forms of managed care are health maintenance organizations (HMOs), preferred provider organizations (PPOs), and point-of-service (POS) plans. Compare and contrast each of these forms of managed care. If given a choice of these forms of managed care, which would you choose?

Apply Your Math Skills

1. Chauntal pays $115 per month for health insurance premiums for a family of three. The plan also requires a $30 copayment for each doctor visit and a $4 copayment for prescription medicines. If each person in the family visits the doctor twice this year and they require a total of 4 prescriptions, what is their total medical expense for the year?
2. Kristoff is injured in an accident at work and is unable to work for 15 months. The workers' compensation insurance carried by Kristoff's employer provides 100% salary reimbursement for the first year and 60% salary reimbursement after that. Assuming an annual salary of $55,000, what is the total amount of money that will be received through workers' compensation benefits?

Communication Skills

College and Career Readiness

Writing. Generate ideas that relate to the importance of accurate information. Make a list of reasons you would provide to a coworker while explaining why health insurance is necessary for every individual.

Reading. Now that you have completed reading multiple chapters in this text about financial literacy, analyze the themes and structures that the authors used. Create a concept map that illustrates how the themes of this text are related.

Speaking. Financial literacy requires that individuals be able to participate and contribute to one-on-one discussions that exhibit financial competency. Developing interpersonal communication skills is one way to achieve this goal. As your instructor lectures on this chapter, contribute thoughtful comments when participation is invited.

Teamwork

Together with your team, create a digital media presentation about a current event or recent trend in the insurance industry. Include information that describes the trend or event as well as how it may affect insurance in the future. Use examples that will enhance understanding and add interest to your presentation. Present your findings to the class.

Internet Research

Patient Protection and Affordable Care Act. Conduct an Internet search for *Patient Protection and Affordable Care Act*. After you have read information on the website, describe what you learned about young people age 26 and their options for health care coverage.

Governmental Health Care Eligibility. The US government subsidizes health care for eligible citizens with the Medicare, Medicaid, and CHIP programs. Use the Internet to research the eligibility requirements for one of these programs. Eligibility requirements may vary by state. Write a paragraph to summarize the requirements for the program you chose to research.

Portfolio Development

College and Career Readiness

Diversity Skills. As part of an interview with a school or business, you may be asked about your travels or experiences with people from other cultures. Many different organizations serve people from a variety of geographic locations and cultures. Some have offices or facilities in more than one region or country. Representatives of these organizations may travel to facilities in different countries. You may need to interact with people from diverse cultures.

When applying for both work and school, the interviewer will want to know that you have the ability to work or get along with any person you may encounter. Therefore, having traveled, studied, or worked in other countries can be valuable assets. It is in the school's or company's best interest to have culturally competent representatives. In an academic setting, you could work as an English as a second language (ESL) instructor. In a professional setting, you may be able to understand the needs and wants of diverse people. You may also be better able to communicate and get along with others.

1. Identify travel or other educational experiences that helped you learn about another culture, such as foreign languages studied or trips taken
2. Create a Microsoft Word document that describes the experience. Use the heading "Diversity Experience" and your name. Explain how the information you learned might help you better understand classmates, customers, or coworkers from this culture. Save the document in an appropriate folder.
3. Place a printed copy in the container for future reference.
4. Update your checklist to reflect the file format and location of the document.

CTSOs

Event Prep

Event Preparation. No matter which CTSO competitive events you participate in, you have to be well organized and prepared. Of course, you will have studied the content exhaustively before the event. You must also make sure all the tools you need for the event have been secured and travel arrangements to the event have been made. Confirming details well in advance of an event decreases stress and leaves you free to concentrate on the event itself.

To prepare for a competition, complete the following activities.

1. Pack appropriate clothing, including comfortable shoes and professional attire.
2. Prepare all technological resources, including anything that you might need to prepare or complete. Double check to make sure that any electronic presentation material is saved in a format that is compatible with the machines that will be available to you at the event.
3. If the event calls for visuals, make sure you have them prepared in advance and that they are packed and ready to take with you.
4. Bring registration materials, including a valid form of identification.
5. Bring study materials, including flash cards and other materials you have used to study for the event. If note cards are acceptable when making a presentation, make sure your notes are complete and easy to read. Have a back-up set in case of an emergency.
6. At least two weeks before you go to the competition, create a checklist of what you need for the event. Include every detail down to a pencil or pen. Use this checklist before you go into the presentation so that you do not forget anything.

UNIT

5 Exploring Economics

Chapters

Financial Literacy

Why It Matters

It is important to understand the basics of economics and its impact on your personal finances. Economic systems are based on choices—choices of what to produce, how to produce it, and how to distribute what is produced. These choices are necessary because wants and needs are unlimited while the resources to meet them are limited. Choices create scarcity and require decisions about which needs or wants to satisfy.

In a market economy, buyers and sellers (consumers and producers) make free economic choices. These choices determine what will be produced, how productively resources will be used, and who will receive the benefits of this productivity. The economic choices you make connect you to millions of other consumers in the United States and around the world.

2121fisher/Shutterstock.com

Big Idea

The economic decisions of consumers impact the overall economy. Smart consumers avoid the pitfalls that a market economy can create.

CHAPTER

16 Economic Principles

The world is based on economics. Money is involved every time you buy a snack, ride a bus, or see a doctor. Economic wheels turn to keep schools open, maintain streets and parks, and provide police and fire protection. Your home receives electricity, your television receives broadcasts, your computer or mobile device has Internet access, and your favorite stores are stocked with items to buy. Without realizing it, you use and depend on items every day that are generated by the US economy.

The United States is a free enterprise system in which individuals can make their own economic decisions. Market forces of competition, profit motive, and supply and demand create a vast marketplace for sellers and buyers.

Focus on Finance

Why Study Economics?

As the saying goes, knowledge is power. Studying economics will help you have a better understanding about the nation's economy. It will help you become an informed citizen and make better choices.

Economics is a science that examines how goods and services are produced, sold, and used. *Economic literacy* gives you power to make decisions about how world events influence you. It helps you decide as a consumer if you should buy a house, invest in stocks, or save money. It influences the career you choose, your role as a worker, and the part you play as a contributing citizen. When you understand the importance of economics in your day-to-day life, you can make wiser personal choices for you and your family.

College and Career Readiness

Reading Prep. Before reading this chapter, review the table of contents for this text. Create a graphic organizer that traces the content from simple to complex ideas.

Sections

leedsn/Shutterstock.com

Section 16.1 What Is Economics?

Essential Question

What role does economics play in our society?

Objectives

After studying this section, you will be able to:

- Compare the four basic types of economic systems.
- Explain the problem of scarcity that nations face.
- Describe the factors of production.

Terms

economics	command economy	labor
economic system	mixed economy	human resource
traditional economy	scarcity	productivity
market economy	factors of production	capital
marketplace	land	entrepreneurship
producer	natural resource	

Economic Systems

Throughout much of history, families were relatively self-sufficient. The family was the basic economic unit. It provided its members with food, shelter, protection, clothing, and other needs. *Needs* are items a person must have to survive. Food is a need. Needs differ from *wants,* which are items a person would like to have but that are not essential to life. A cell phone is a want.

goodluz/Shutterstock.com

Economics examines how goods and services are produced, sold, and used.

As families formed communities and moved away from an agricultural base, life became more complex. Families were no longer self-sufficient. They became consumers who looked beyond the family to meet many of their needs. They began to trade with one another. Artisans and tradesmen became experts in a particular type of work.

As individuals and communities provided specialized labor, a wider variety of goods and services became available. *Goods* are physical items, such as food and clothing. *Services* are activities that another person usually performs for a fee, such as preparing tax returns.

Economics is a science that examines how goods and services are produced, sold, and used. The interdependence of providers and users of goods and services marks the beginning of an economic system.

An **economic system** is the structure in which limited resources are turned into goods and services to address unlimited needs and wants. Every nation has an economic system. Economists have defined four basic types of economic systems: traditional, market, command, and mixed economies.

A circular flow of goods, services, and money takes place within the economy, as shown in the circular flow model in Figure 16-1. The outer circle shows the flow of consumer goods and services from producers and sellers to consumers and workers. It also shows the flow of the economic resources from consumers and workers to producers and sellers. The inner circle shows the flow of payments for goods and services from consumers to producers. It also shows the flow of payments for resources from producers to workers and suppliers. This model is a snapshot of how consumers and producers interact in the economy. However, it does not show the whole picture. For example, producers and sellers also are consumers. Businesses buy the goods and services that other businesses produce.

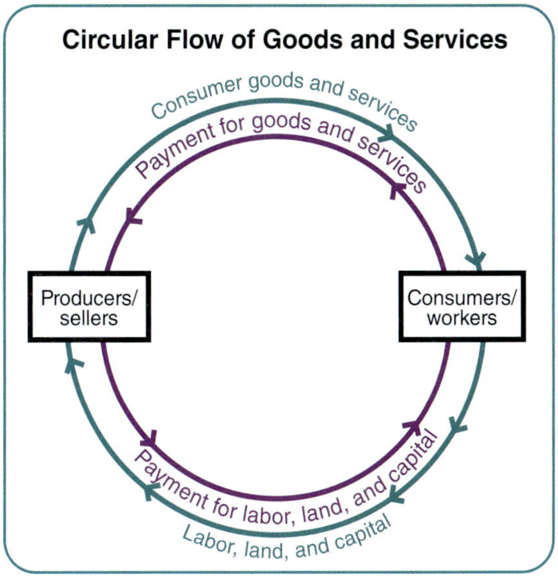

Figure 16-1 The circular flow model shows the circular flow of goods, services, and money between producers/sellers and consumers/workers.

Traditional Economy

A **traditional economy** is a system in which economic decisions are based on a society's values, culture, and customs. This type of economy mostly exists in developing countries or nations governed by strong cultural, religious, or tribal leadership.

In these areas, change comes slowly. People tend to stick with what they know and do as they have always done. For example, if you lived in a traditional economy and your parents raised sheep, chances are that you would, too. You would likely grow your own food and make your own clothing. You might barter or exchange goods and services rather than using money as a means of exchange.

In recent years, some traditional economies have begun to develop a new approach to economics. The advantages of technology and other advances of the modern world have been recognized. In these situations, there is a desire both to keep the old and to accept some of what is new.

Market Economy

A **market economy** is a system in which privately owned businesses operate and compete for profits with limited governmental regulation or interference. It is also called a *free-enterprise system* or *capitalism*.

In economic terms, the marketplace, or *market*, is not just a physical place, such as a mall or a grocery store. The **marketplace** is anywhere buyers and sellers meet to exchange goods, services, and money. It is an arena in which consumers and producers meet to exchange goods, services, and money. A *consumer* is a buyer and user of goods and services. A **producer** is an individual or business that provides the supply of goods and services to meet consumer demands.

Case Study Living in a Market Economy

Anita and Juan are in their twenties and plan to marry in six months. They have decided to buy their first home in the city and move to the suburbs once they have school-age children. They tour several small apartments in their price range, but their favorite is a higher-priced loft apartment they found online.

The cost of the loft is a small percentage over their spending budget, but its high ceilings, hardwood floors, and brand-new appliances tempt them. Their real estate agent says the loft should have an excellent resale value when they decide to sell and move in a few years, as long as the demand for housing in the city stays high.

Case Review

1. Describe the potential benefits of Anita and Juan staying in their price range.
2. What are Anita and Juan risking by buying out of their price range?
3. What would the trade-off be if Anita and Juan chose to buy a smaller apartment and stay in budget? What would the trade-off be if they chose to buy the more expensive loft?
4. How could Anita and Juan's investment in the loft be affected by changes in the economy?

The term "market" may refer to all goods and services in an economy or to a limited number of goods in a selected segment. For example, there are markets for children's clothes, luxury cars, and electronics. There also is a global market that encompasses trade among all nations of the world.

In a market economy, consumers are important, and businesses react to their demands. The United States is often considered to have a market economy. A market economy, with its freedom of choice, offers many advantages. However, living in a market economy also can present problems and challenges. Making wise choices and carefully managing money are important skills for consumers in the marketplace.

The economic activities of all consumers play a vital role in a market economy. Consumers earn, spend, borrow, and save. They invest their money. They share financial risks through insurance. They pay taxes and vote for the candidates who support policies and programs that will affect the economy. The way consumers perform these activities determines how well they live and how well the economic system works.

Consumer choices create market demand, which largely determines which goods and services businesses will produce and sell. The characteristics of a market economy are shown in Figure 16-2 and include the following.

- *Private property.* Individuals have the right to own property.
- *Profit.* Individuals and businesses have the right to make a profit.
- *Economic freedom.* Individuals are free to make their own economic decisions and can decide what to buy, when to buy, and how to use what they bought.
- *Voluntary exchange.* Individuals have the right to buy and sell in a marketplace where prices are freely set by the forces of supply and demand.
- *Competition.* Businesses can compete to sell goods and services and decide what to produce, how to produce, and for whom to produce.
- *Economic incentives.* Financial rewards may be offered to influence consumer behavior. An example is federal income tax credit for buying electric vehicles.

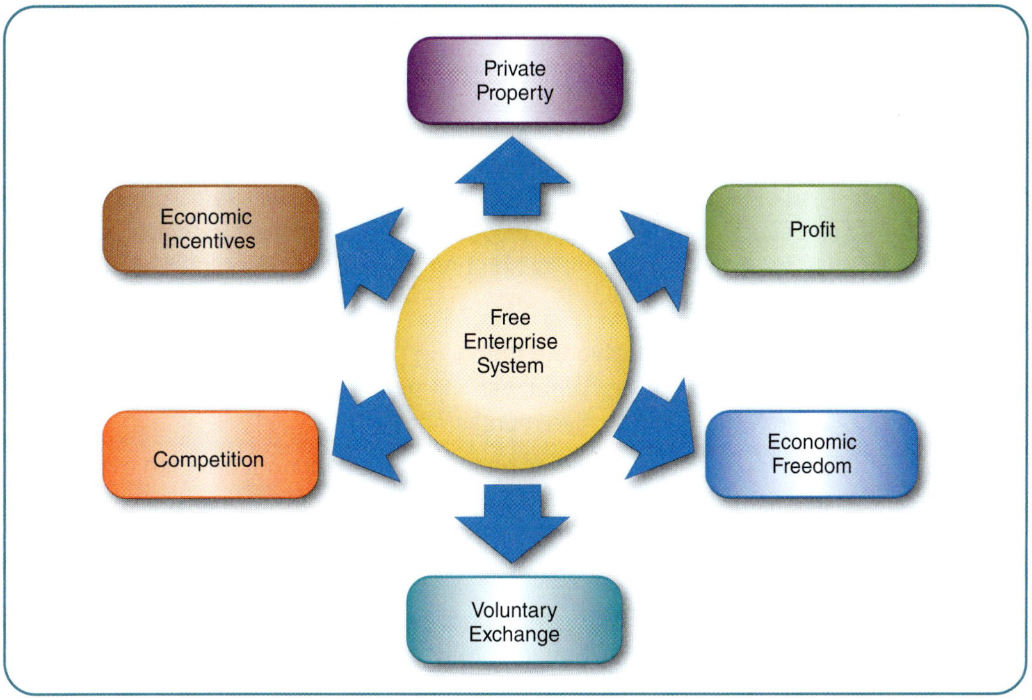

Goodheart-Willcox Publisher

Figure 16-2 The characteristics of a free-enterprise system enable consumers in the marketplace to make decisions.

A market economy offers many opportunities for businesses to grow and profit by meeting consumer demands. It also offers education and training opportunities to hardworking individuals to develop their talents and succeed in fields of their choice.

Command Economy

A **command economy** is a system in which a central authority, usually the government, controls economic activities. A central authority decides how to allocate resources. It determines what and how much to produce and sets the prices of goods and services. It also decides who will produce what.

In this type of system, the needs and wants of consumers are not generally a driving force in the decision-making process. Consumers do not have a broad freedom of choice. They often cannot decide for themselves how to earn and spend income. A command economy frequently exists in countries with socialist or communist governments.

Mixed Economy

Most economies are mixed. A **mixed economy** is a combination of the market and command systems. For example, a mixed economy may function through a marketplace, although the government or central authority regulates the prices and supply of goods and services. The government may regulate certain industries, such as utilities and airlines, in an otherwise market system.

The US economy is technically a mixed economy; however, it is usually called a market or free-enterprise economy. The government's limited role in the US economy is varied and important. Compared with other mixed economies, the economy of the United States has minimal governmental involvement.

You Do the Math Interpreting Line Graphs

Graphs are used to illustrate data in a picture-like format. Many times, it is easier to understand the data if they are shown in a graphical form instead of a numerical form in a table. For example, a line graph can be used to show the trend of financial markets over time. A line graph also organizes information on vertical and horizontal axes; however, data are graphed as a continuous line rather than a set of bars. Line graphs are often used to show trends over a period of time.

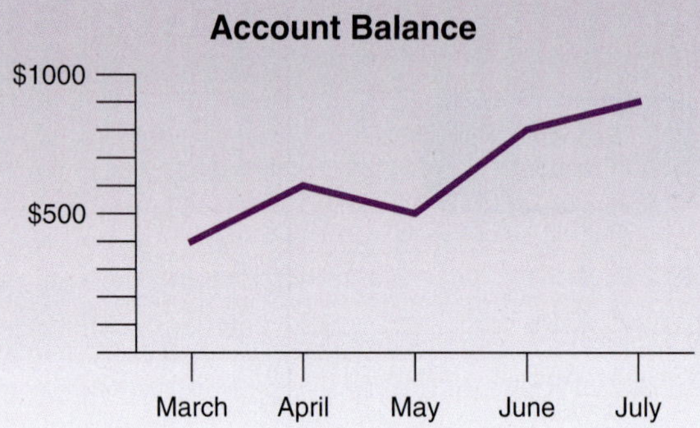

Solve the following problems using the line graph.

1. What was the highest account balance over the five months shown?
2. What was the lowest account balance over the five months shown?
3. In which month did the lowest account balance occur?
4. How much did the account balance increase between May and June?

Scarcity

All economic systems attempt to resolve the basic economic problem of unlimited needs and wants and limited resources. *Resources* are any input used to generate other goods or services. The challenge of stretching resources to cover needs and wants is called scarcity. **Scarcity** is the basic economic problem that arises because there are unlimited human wants and needs but limited resources.

Deciding how to deal with scarcity is the basis for the study of economics and an element of a market economy. Individuals, families, companies, and nations are all limited in the resources available to meet needs and wants. The *problem of scarcity* leads to three economic questions every nation must answer:

- What to produce and how much?
- How to allocate resources in producing goods and services?
- For whom are the goods and services produced?

Governments make economic choices that affect everyone. Major political and economic decisions center on how governments will divide limited resources among unlimited needs. These needs may include crime control, health care, environmental protection, education, national defense, and aid to the poor and homeless. At the local level, governments make many choices in allocating limited resources. For example, a local government may need to choose between using funds to build a public swimming pool or to repave the streets.

Scarcity forces people, businesses, and governments to make choices in the use of resources and the needs to be met, as shown in Figure 16-3. Society must make tradeoffs while considering opportunity costs. A *trade-off* is the choice given up when one choice is made over another. Making a choice results in a trade-off, and a trade-off results in an opportunity cost. As a result of the free-enterprise market in the United States, consumers have many choices and,

Goodheart-Willcox Publisher

Figure 16-3 Scarcity is the result of an imbalance of limited resources and unlimited wants.

by extension, trade-offs. In this sense, scarcity, choice, and trade-offs are all aspects of decision making.

Similar to trade-offs, opportunity cost is also an aspect of making sound financial decisions. *Opportunity cost* is the value of the option that was given up. If you turn down an after-school job because you have to be at soccer practice, there is an opportunity cost. The opportunity cost of playing soccer is the after-school job and the money you could have earned. The opportunity cost of working instead of playing soccer would be the pleasure and advantages you get from playing a team sport you love.

Opportunity cost can be measured in terms of dollars, time, enjoyment, or something else of value. These costs apply to economic choices of families, businesses, and governments as well as individuals. Weighing opportunity costs is a valuable decision-making tool.

Factors of Production

Factors of production are the economic resources a nation uses to make goods and supply services for its population. The factors of production are land, labor, capital, and entrepreneurship, as shown in Figure 16-4.

Land is all of the natural resources of a nation. A **natural resource** is a raw material, such as soil, water, minerals, plants, animals, and climate. All goods are made from natural resources. All services use natural resources in some form. Most natural resources are limited.

Factors of Production			
Land	**Labor**	**Capital**	**Entrepreneurship**
• Soil • Water • Minerals • Plants • Animals • Climate	• Agricultural workers • Construction workers • Factory workers • Miners • Professionals • Service workers	• Tools • Equipment • Machinery • Buildings • Vehicles • Transportation systems • Utilities	• Business owners

Goodheart-Willcox Publisher

Figure 16-4 The factors of production include the economic resources of land, labor, capital, and entrepreneurship.

Labor is the work performed by people who turn resources into products. Products can be goods or services. **Human resources** are qualities or characteristics that a person has. **Productivity** is a measure of the amount of work a person can do in a specific amount of time. A nation can make up for a lack of natural resources if its people are very productive.

Capital is all the tools, equipment, and machinery that are used to make final products. Capital is used by labor to transform land into goods and services.

Entrepreneurship is the willingness and ability to start a new business. Inventors, innovators, and entrepreneurs have always played an important role in the US economy. They are the engines that drive progress and prosperity. Together, inventions, innovations, and entrepreneurship lead to new or improved goods and services, higher productivity, more jobs, and higher wages overall. These are the keys to job creation, growth, and ongoing prosperity. The entrepreneur creates a way to produce and market a product or process, puts the necessary time and effort into its development, and accepts the financial and other risks involved in selling the idea. This hard work requires an ongoing commitment. The rewards include personal satisfaction, independence, and profits.

Taina Sohlman/Shutterstock.com

Kwangmoozaa/Shutterstock.com

rodho/Shutterstock.com

Monkey Business Images/Shutterstock.com

Nations must choose how to use their scarce resources of land, labor, capital, and entrepreneurship to create goods and services.

Exploring Careers

Economist

Economic activity is essential for businesses to succeed, but it can be difficult to predict. Economists study, analyze, and interpret economic issues. They observe financial markets, employment rates, and government economic policies. Economists typically work with statistics, charts, and surveys to organize economic data. Based on their studies, they make recommendations to a business or government. Examples of tasks that economists perform include:

- predict market trends by using sampling to collect data
- compare current and historic economic conditions
- advise businesses on economic trends and problems

Economists are required to have a bachelor degree. Coursework in economics, calculus, and statistics is required for entry-level jobs. A master degree or doctorate degree in economics is needed for higher-level positions. Economists should have advanced computer and math skills.

Section 16.1 Review

Check Your Understanding

1. What are the four basic economic systems?
2. Name the characteristics of a market economy.
3. List the three economic questions that must be answered as a result of scarcity.
4. Describe opportunity cost.
5. What are the four factors of production?

Build Your Vocabulary

As you progress through this course, develop a personal glossary. This will help you build your vocabulary and prepare you for a career. Write a definition for each of the following terms and add it to your glossary.

economics
economic system
traditional economy
market economy
marketplace
producer
command economy
mixed economy
scarcity
factors of production
land
natural resource
labor
human resource
productivity
capital
entrepreneurship

Section 16.2 How the US Economy Works

Essential Question

How does supply and demand influence our economy?

Objectives

After studying this section, you will be able to:

- Describe economic competition.
- Explain the profit motive.
- Discuss how supply and demand affect prices.

Terms

market forces	profit	law of supply and demand
economic competition	supply	equilibrium
innovation	demand	
profit motive		

Competition

A market economy is controlled by market forces. **Market forces** are economic factors that affect the price, demand, and availability of a good or service. Individuals are free to make economic decisions, but the market forces influence those decisions. A free-enterprise economy, such as the one in the United States, is characterized by three market forces:

- competition;
- profit motive; and
- supply and demand.

Within the framework of these three characteristics, the forces of supply and demand create a vast arena of sellers and buyers.

Economic competition occurs when two or more sellers offer similar goods and services for sale in the marketplace. Each seller tries to do a better job than the other in order to attract more customers, make more sales, and earn more profits. Businesses compete with each other in many ways. They compete in the areas of price, quality, features, service, and new products.

The companies providing the best goods and services at the lowest prices generally achieve the highest sales and profits. Ideally, this results in higher quality at lower prices for consumers. Competition encourages competence and efficiency in the production and sale of goods and services.

In a market economy, innovation is the engine that sparks growth and prosperity. **Innovation** is the process of creating something, such as new or

Economics in Action

Marginalism

Marginalism is the added value versus the additional cost of one more unit or item. For example, suppose you buy two pairs of jeans at $65 and consider buying a third pair. Will the added pair bring you as much satisfaction as the first two? As you buy more jeans, the price per unit stays the same, but the "marginal," or extra, value of one more pair decreases.

You can also approach economic choices through a cost-benefit analysis, which is similar to marginalism. The cost-benefit principle states that you should take an action or make a purchase only if the benefit is at least as great as the cost. Using the jeans example, suppose you see a casual jacket that complements the first two pairs of jeans. With the jacket and those jeans, you could coordinate several outfits. A third pair of jeans, on the other hand, would not benefit your wardrobe to the same degree as the jacket. These principles apply to economic decisions of individual consumers, businesses, and governments.

improved products and new ways to do things and solve problems. Research and development (R&D) is the key to realizing the potential of innovation. It is an investment in the future. In simple terms, the innovator comes up with a new idea, explores its practicality, and turns it into a new good or service. Businesses, universities, and governmental agencies all participate in research and development, both independently and in cooperation with each other.

Historically, the United States has invested more money in research and development than any other country. This is one reason America is among the most prosperous nations. The same is true of businesses. Those that invest the most in research and development tend to be the most competitive and successful.

There is also competition in the job market. The highest incomes go to the most educated, trained, and skilled workers who produce the goods and services in greatest demand. This demand increases the competition among workers. Workers try to update their skills and education in order to qualify for better jobs and be able to earn higher incomes and better benefits. This situation, in turn, improves a company's ability to compete.

Kobby Dagan/Shutterstock.com

Innovation sparks growth and prosperity in a market economy.

Profit Motive

The **profit motive** is the desire to make and maximize a profit. It drives both individuals and businesses to produce goods and services to meet consumer demand. For businesses and investors, **profit** is the difference between the income earned and expenses incurred by a business during a specific period of time.

Employability Skills

Team Player

To be a *team player* means to work cooperatively with others to achieve one goal. The ability to work productively with others is an important skill that employers desire for their employees. In many work situations, employees are assigned to work as teams. Recognizing that a group's goals outweigh those of the individual team players, establishing good working relationships with coworkers, and performing individual roles with efficiency are necessary skills for being a team player.

Income is the amount of money generated from sales. Expenses are costs involved in operating a business. Expenses include items such as rent, employee wages, and utilities.

For individuals, profit comes in the form of income. Individuals sell their productive resources, such as labor, ideas, land, and capital. In return, they receive income or a return on their investments. This is what brings people into the workforce and motivates investors to put their money to work. The promise of earning money inspires the worker, shop owner, manufacturer, and investor to engage in economic activity.

All businesses depend on profits, from a corner grocery store to a worldwide corporation. If there were no opportunities to earn profits, the US economy would falter. Individuals would be less motivated to work. Investors would not invest in businesses and provide the money needed to turn resources into goods and services. Businesses would not grow or try to increase sales.

Supply and Demand

Remember the economic problem common to all societies? In short, the challenges are: what and how much to produce, how, and for whom. The US economic system addresses these questions largely by letting the forces of supply and demand operate in competitive markets. **Supply** is the amount of a good or service producers are willing to provide. **Demand** is the amount of a good or service consumers are willing to buy. The **law of supply and demand** says that the price of a product is determined by the relationship of the supply of a product and the demand for the product.

Supply and demand are closely connected to price. For example, suppose you own a company that sells tennis shoes. When you price shoes at $80 a pair, you sell 1,000 pairs. At $40 each, you sell 3,000 pairs.

When the prices and quantities demanded are plotted on a graph and connected, they form a line called the *demand curve*. Price and demand move in opposite directions, so the curve has a negative slope, as shown in Figure 16-5. This illustrates the law of demand: the higher the price of a good or service, the lower the level of consumer demand. The demand curve shows how much people will buy at different prices.

As a producer, you want to sell your goods for the highest possible price. If you think you can get $80 for each pair of sneakers, you would want to produce more. If you think you can only get $20 a pair, you would decide to produce less.

When the prices and quantities supplied are plotted on a graph and connected, they form a line called the *supply curve.* Price and supply tend to move in the same direction, so the curve has a positive slope. This illustrates the law of supply: the higher the price of a good or service, the higher the supply from producers. The supply curve shows how much product will be produced at different prices.

Supply and demand work together. When supply and demand are relatively balanced, the market is said to be in equilibrium. **Equilibrium** is the point at which the demand and supply curves intersect, as shown in Figure 16-5. The intersection is the price at which the quantity supplied equals the quantity demanded. At this point, the market is operating at maximum efficiency. Equilibrium is more of an idea than a reality. Markets are usually not in equilibrium. Changes in supply or demand trigger price adjustments. When a price for a product is set too high, products stack up on store shelves. When a price is set too low, there are shortages.

What conditions might cause prices to increase? Prices rise when the demand for an item is greater than the supply or when demand rises and supply remains

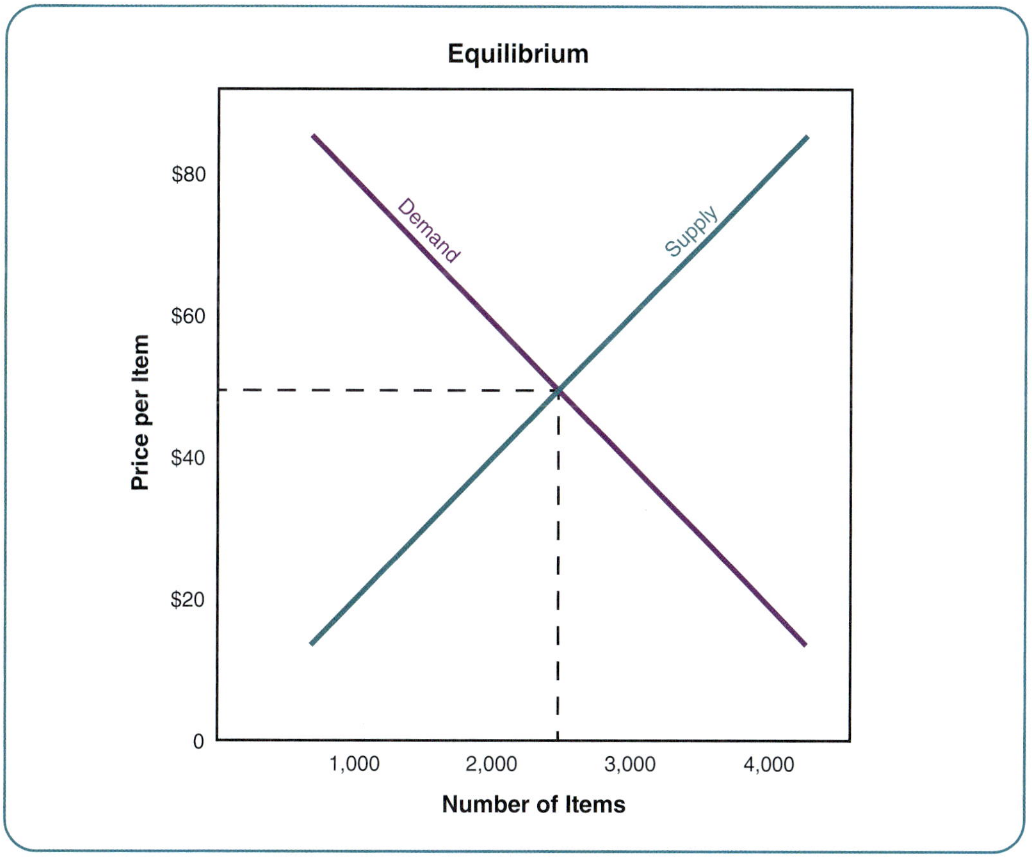

Goodheart-Willcox Publisher

Figure 16-5 The demand curve shows how many items people will buy (X axis) at different prices (Y axis). The supply curve shows how many products will be produced (X axis) at different prices (Y axis). Equilibrium is the point at which the demand and supply curves intersect, which is $50 in this case.

Ethics

Sourcing

Ethical businesses purchase raw materials or goods from reputable suppliers where products are created in safe conditions. Factories in which products are created should be clean and safe for workers. Manufacturers in other countries may have different work safety standards than the United States. Purchasing products at the expense of others to save money is unethical.

the same. For instance, airline ticket prices are highest during peak travel times. Seasonal foods become more expensive when the season ends because they become less plentiful. Food prices also rise when crops are lost to severe weather.

What conditions might cause prices to decrease? Prices fall when the supply for an item is greater than the demand or when supply rises and demand remains the same. For instance, at the end of winter, the demand for coats and gloves drops. Stores drop prices and hold end-of-season clearance sales.

MBI/Shutterstock.com

In the United States, marketplace demand determines what and how much is produced.

To a large extent, demand in the marketplace determines *what* and *how much* is produced. Demand is expressed by the spending choices of consumers, businesses, and governments. These choices determine what and how much producers will bring to the marketplace. In many cases, consumer demand leads to new and improved products.

Businesses generally own and control productive resources. They determine the right mix of productive resources and their use when they make goods and deliver services to meet consumer demands. They decide how to produce goods and services.

The forces of supply and demand in the job market largely determine how to divide the goods and services produced. Those who can offer the skills, knowledge, materials, or capital needed for production receive income or profits. In job markets, those who have the qualifications to perform the work that is in demand generally earn higher incomes and can buy more of the goods and services they need. This helps determine how production is divided.

Section 16.2 Review

Check Your Understanding

1. List the three market forces in a free-enterprise economy.
2. What are the five areas in which businesses compete with each other?
3. In the job market, which workers receive the highest incomes?
4. What is the demand curve?
5. What is the supply curve?

Build Your Vocabulary

As you progress through this course, develop a personal glossary. This will help you build your vocabulary and prepare you for a career. Write a definition for each of the following terms and add it to your glossary.

market forces
economic competition
innovation
profit motive
profit
supply
demand
law of supply and demand
equilibrium

Review and Assessment

Chapter Summary

Section 16.1 What Is Economics?

- Every nation has an economic system. Economists have defined four basic types: traditional, market, command, and mixed economies. A market economy is also called a free-enterprise system or capitalism.
- All economic systems attempt to resolve the problem of unlimited needs and wants and limited resources. This is called the basic economic problem. The challenge of stretching resources to cover needs and wants is called scarcity. Scarcity forces people, businesses, and governments to make choices in the use of resources and the needs to be met.
- Factors of production are the economic resources a nation uses to makes goods and to supply services for its population. These factors include land, labor, capital, and entrepreneurship. When used effectively, the factors of production can lead to new or improved goods and services, higher productivity, more jobs, and higher wages. This in turn leads to job creation, growth, and prosperity.

Section 16.2 How the US Economy Works

- Market forces are economic factors that affect the price, demand, and availability of a good or service. A market economy is controlled by three market forces: competition, profit motive, and supply and demand.
- Individuals and businesses are driven by the profit motive. The profit motive is the desire to make a profit and maximize it. Profit is the total amount of money earned after expenses are subtracted from income.
- The law of supply and demand states that the price of a product is determined by the relationship of the supply of a product and the demand for the product. Supply is the amount of a good or service producers are willing to provide. Demand is the amount of a product or service consumers are willing to buy.

Review Your Knowledge

1. Compare the four basic types of economic systems.
2. Explain the economic problem that nations face.
3. Describe the concept of scarcity and how it applies to individuals, families, and the government.
4. Explain the concept of trade-off.
5. Describe each of the four factors of production.
6. Use the circular flow model to identify how households, firms, and governments interact in both resource markets and product markets.
7. Describe economic competition.
8. Why is the profit motive important to the economy?
9. Explain the concept of equilibrium.
10. How do the laws of supply and demand relate to the prices of goods and services in the marketplace?

Apply Your Knowledge

1. Make a list of 25 goods and services. Identify whether each is a want or a need in your life. For each, write one or two sentences to explain why you consider it a need or a want.

2. Compare and contrast the four basic types of economic systems. Create a Venn diagram or other graphic organizer to visually display how these systems are the same and how they are different. Summarize your findings in two or three paragraphs.
3. In a traditional economy, people might barter or exchange goods and services rather than using money as a means of exchange. Write a dialogue between two friends who are bartering for goods and services rather than using money. For example, you might offer to wash your sister's car in exchange for letting you borrow a designer jacket for the evening.
4. In your opinion, what are the benefits of the US free-enterprise system?
5. Scarcity requires that choices be made. Name one item that has been scarce in your lifetime, like gasoline or water. Describe the decisions you or your family had to make because this resource was scarce.
6. Demonstrate the concept of scarcity as it influences your own life. Make a list of 10 items you want and need over the next year of your life. Include both short-term and long-term needs and wants, such as a movie ticket (short-term) or funding a college education (long-term). Identify the resources you will use to get these items. Will you be able to satisfy all of your wants?
7. How do you and your family decide which needs and wants to satisfy? Make a list of trade-offs that have been made to meet needs and wants. For each trade-off, write one or two sentences to explain the opportunity costs of the trade-off.
8. The four factors of production are land, labor, capital, and entrepreneurship. Identify examples of each factor of production being used in your community.
9. Identify a product innovation that has occurred during your lifetime. Describe how this innovation has sparked economic growth and prosperity in your community.
10. Explain the law of supply and demand. What effect do you think this law has on human behavior? Provide an example in which the supply and demand result in positive behavior. Then, provide an example in which behavior becomes negative.

Apply Your Math Skills

1. The Fortunate Sneaker and Shoe Company had total sales of $25,853 in this quarter. During the quarter, it spent $9,489 on creating products, $1,438 on marketing, $5,675 on rent, and $2,820 on wages. What was its profit or loss for the quarter?
2. Bella has two part-time job offers for the summer. The lifeguard job pays $9.75 per hour and will require 17 hours of work per week. The second job as a movie critic for the local newspaper pays $45 per article and will require reviewing 10 movies each month. Both jobs will last for three months (12 weeks). Bella loves movies and wants to accept the job as a movie critic. What is the opportunity cost of this decision?

Communication Skills

Writing. Generate ideas for writing a paper that describes the concept of economic freedom as you interpret it. Gather information to support your thoughts and ideas. Keep careful and accurate records of any sources that you use as references. Create the notes that you could use to write a paper to distribute for discussion with your classmates.

Speaking. Rhetoric is the study of writing or speaking as a way of communicating information or persuading someone. It is important to be prepared when you are speaking to an individual or to an audience. Style and content influence how the listener understands your message. Make an informal presentation to your class about an economic principle, such as the law of supply and demand or opportunity costs. Adjust your presentation length to fit the attention of the audience.

Listening. When taking notes in class, discretion must be used to decide which keywords and main ideas are important so they can be recorded. It is not necessary to write down every word you hear. A first rule of note taking is to practice active listing. You must not only hear what is said, but comprehend the information. One way to determine importance is to listen to repetition by the instructor. If information is repeated, it must be important. Listen closely to the lectures by your instructor. What have you noticed that they consistently repeat?

Teamwork

Working as a team, interpret the following quote: "One person's wage increase is another person's price increase." What was the consensus from the group as to the meaning of this quote?

Internet Research

Economic Systems. Select a country that you would be interested in learning more about. Research the economic system of that country. Using the Internet, visit the website of the Central Intelligence Agency (CIA) of the US government and select the library tab. The World Factbook on the page provides information on countries of the world. Summarize the information that you find about the country you select. How does the country you selected compare with the United States?

Factors of Production. The natural resources available for the production of goods and services vary from place to place. Conduct an Internet search for *natural resources available in [your state]*. What is the most abundant natural resource where you live? Describe how it is used as a factor of production and what goods and services are produced as a result.

Portfolio Development

Foreign-Language Skills. In some situations, individuals who are fluent in a foreign language may have an advantage over other candidates in an application process or other competitive situations. As part of an interview with an organization, you may be asked about your ability to speak multiple languages or experience with people who speak a language other than your own. Many organizations are interested in this information for good reasons. They often serve people from a variety of geographic locations, cultures, and languages.

People who speak more than one language or have traveled, studied, or worked in other countries can be valuable assets to an organization.

For example, an employer may have offices or factories in more than one region or country. A candidate who notes multilingual skills may be considered to have a competitive edge over other candidates with similar experience.

It is important to be specific and accurate when you list the language skills you possess. By being proactive and noting any experiences you have in working with people in other cultures, you may catch the eye of the interviewer even before the interviewing process begins.

1. If you are fluent in another language, create a document that describes the language in which you are proficient, where you received your training, and your level of fluency. Use the heading "Languages Spoken" and your name.
2. If you have limited language proficiency, create a document that says "Limited Language Proficiency" and list each language and your ability to communicate using it. For example, you may have only a limited proficiency in German that could be helpful in a business situation.
3. Update your master portfolio spreadsheet to include your foreign-language skills documentation.

CTSOs

Event Prep

Business Calculations. The business calculations event is an objective test that covers multiple problems related to various business applications. Participants are usually allowed one hour to complete the event.

To prepare for a business calculations test, complete the following activities.

1. Well in advance of the date of the event, visit the organization's website.
2. Download any posted practice tests.
3. Time yourself taking the tests with the aid of a non-graphing calculator. Check the answers and correct any mistakes you may have made.
4. Review the Math Skills Handbook in this text.
5. Visit the organization's website often to make sure information regarding the event has not changed.

CHAPTER

17 Functioning of the Economy

The economy keeps the country and the world functioning. In our economic system, the most fundamental role of government is to provide the legal and institutional environment and the economic policies that permit and encourage productive economic activity. The system is based on the rule of law and leads to political and economic stability. This is what gives businesses and individual citizens the confidence to enter the marketplace as producers, workers, and consumers.

The government controls the money supply and levies taxes to pay for governmental operations and public services. These monetary and fiscal policies work to keep our economy stable and prosperous. The government also enacts legislation to promote open and fair competition and to protect consumer interests. Laws and regulations cover everything from the purity of your food and water to the air you breathe and the money you borrow.

Focus on Finance

National Debt

In 2020, the national debt reached $26.9 trillion. The national debt is the total amount the government owes. In recent years, governmental spending exceeded its revenues each year by over $1 trillion. This deficit is added to the national debt, which means that the debt is growing by over a trillion dollars annually.

The annual interest on all this debt comes to approximately $376 billion, which is about the same as spending for education, the environment, and international affairs combined. Interest on the debt is expected to grow faster than any other item in the federal budget in coming years. This is money we cannot spend on other needs.

The Bureau of the Fiscal Service is responsible for accounting for and reporting the national debt in accordance with statutory direction. However, the Bureau does not have any public policy decision-making authority.

College and Career Readiness

Reading Prep. Arrange a study session to read the chapter with a classmate. After you read each section independently, stop and tell each other what you think the main points are in the section. Continue with each section until you finish the chapter.

Sections

Syda Productions/Shutterstock.com

Section 17.1 Basics of the Economy

Essential Question

How do business cycles affect your day-to-day life?

Objectives

After studying this section, you will be able to:

- Identify the five characteristics of money.
- List the four phases of the business cycle.
- Describe five common economic indicators.

Terms

money
medium of exchange
unit of value
store of value
prosperity
depression
economic indicator
gross domestic product (GDP)
consumer spending
GDP per capita
consumer price index (CPI)
stagflation
deflation
labor force
unemployment rate
underemployment
labor productivity

Role of Money in the Economy

Money is anything of value that is accepted in return for goods or services. Money is also known as *currency*. Currency can be in the form of paper bills or coins. In the United States, the dollar is the official currency used for financial exchange. It is *legal tender* that must be accepted "for all debts, public and private." Paper money is produced by the US Treasury, and coins are produced by the US Mint. Paper money is also referred to as *banknotes*.

As you learned in Chapter 6, government bonds, treasury notes, and treasury bills are also types of currency issued by the US government. They represent money the government has borrowed from investors, including individuals, businesses, and other governments.

isak55/Shutterstock.com

In the US economy, money serves as a medium of exchange, unit of value, and store of value.

Functions of Money

Money allows business transactions to take place and goods and services to be exchanged.

Case Study Supply and Demand

Jake owns a successful bakery that produces high-quality breads and rolls. Demand for baked goods has soared in the last year, and the current supply from the bakery is no longer adequate. It seems necessary to enlarge the bakery, buy new equipment, and hire more employees to increase production. However, the expansion will make the bakery subject to more governmental regulations about safety, materials, employee benefits, nutritional labeling, packaging specifications, and health department inspections.

To cover the cost of implementing these regulations, prices will have to be increased immediately. If the demand for the products falls due to the higher prices, customers may be lost. On the other hand, if supply is not increased, customers may still be lost.

Case Review

1. How is the business affected by the laws of supply and demand?
2. The plan was to increase prices immediately, which may drive customers away. How would you suggest approaching price increases?
3. Explain how Jake's business influences the consumer price index (CPI).
4. What is the opportunity cost of not expanding the bakery?

In this way, money has a *function*, or serves a purpose. As shown in Figure 17-1, money serves three functions in the economy:

- As a **medium of exchange**, money is used in exchange for goods and services needed by individuals, businesses, and governments.
- As a **unit of value**, money is a common measure of the worth or price of a good or service.
- As a **store of value**, money can be saved and used for purchases at a later date.

An item that holds its value over a period of time is said to have a good store of value. The value of currency is generally stable. However, money received today is worth more than the same amount received in the future. This is because money received today can be invested or deposited in the bank to earn interest. This concept is called the *time value of money*.

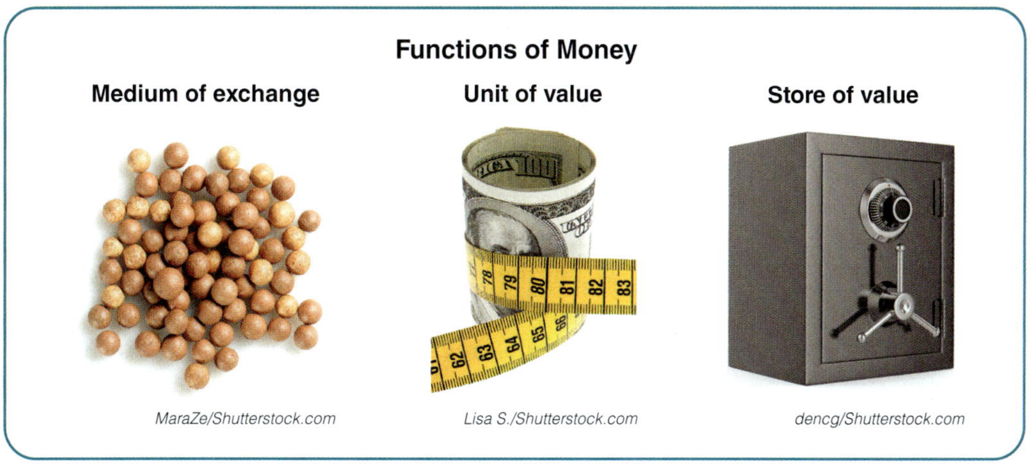

Goodheart-Willcox Publisher

Figure 17-1 Money serves three functions in the economy.

Properties of Money

To be useful and meaningful in an economy, money must have the following properties.

- *Stability.* The value of money must be stable over time in order for it to be widely accepted. People in an economy are confident to use and accept money that has a consistent value.
- *Recognizability.* To be accepted, money must be immediately recognizable. The US dollar is the most widely recognized currency around the world.
- *Divisibility.* There must be a way to divide money into smaller units. In US currency, paper and coin money allow dollars to be divided into smaller units of currency.
- *Portability.* To make purchases, people must be able to carry money with them. Therefore, money must be portable.
- *Durability.* Physical money is handled many times by many people and machines. It needs to be strong and last a long time. US paper bills are made out of a special blend of cotton and linen rather than paper. US coins are made with a blend of metals.

Business Cycle

The US economy fluctuates between periods of economic growth and slowdown. This is true of economies in other industrialized nations as well. The *business cycle* is fluctuations between periods of economic growth and slowdown, as shown in Figure 17-2. Some economists prefer the term *business fluctuations* because there are not predictable patterns to the ups and downs. There are four stages in the business cycle: expansion, peak, contraction, and trough. Each part of the business cycle can last months or even years.

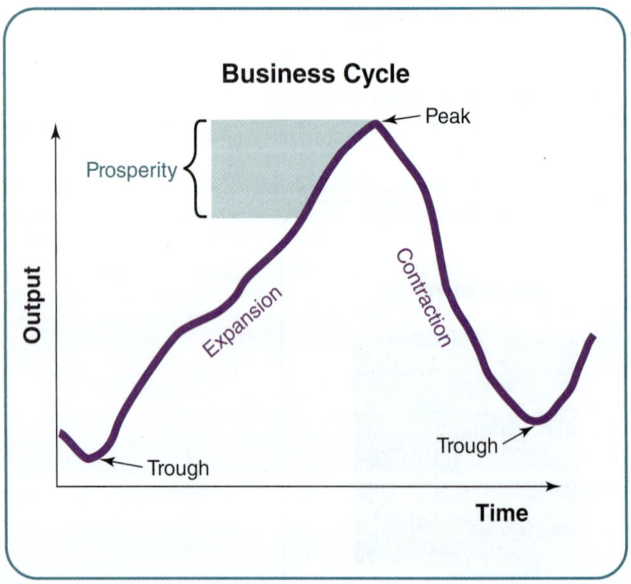

Goodheart-Willcox Publisher

Figure 17-2 One business cycle consists of the time from one trough to the next.

Expansion

Expansion is a period when business activity is growing. The longest economic expansion in modern US history occurred during the 1990s and lasted ten years. However, the average length of an expansion is about three years. Expansion and economic growth help achieve the greater goals of the United States by expanding the size of the economy, strengthening fiscal conditions, and reducing unemployment.

Consumer confidence is a key factor in determining the state of the economy. *Consumer confidence* is an assessment of the optimism or pessimism of consumers regarding current economic conditions. When consumers believe the economy is strong or improving, they tend to be optimistic and spend more. This creates a sense of prosperity. **Prosperity** is a time period of growth and financial well-being. These periods of prosperity are marked by high employment, job security, and overall stability.

Peak

The peak phase is the height of expansion. Economic activity reaches the highest level of growth. When the economy is at its peak, growth has slowed, but prices may continue to increase. Businesses may see lower sales or fewer opportunities to expand. Spending also slows. Consumers may put off large purchases. The peak generally is identified following one month of slowing growth. The peak lasts until the economy starts a downward trend.

Contraction

When the economy starts a downward trend, it enters the contraction phase of the business cycle. When consumers are doubtful about the economic future, they spend and borrow less. This lowers the demand for goods and services. Business slows down because sales decline. Jobs are harder to find. Workers are laid off.

These conditions can lead to a recession, which is a period of contraction of at least six months. A *recession* is a period of slow or no economic growth. A recession is marked by:

- high unemployment;
- declining retail sales;
- lowered average personal incomes;
- decreases in consumer spending; and
- reduced spending by businesses on equipment and expansion.

Overall economic activity declines to a greater degree in a recession than in normal contraction. Many workers lose their jobs and businesses fail. It may also be difficult to obtain a mortgage for a home or to start a new business. When a recession goes on for several years, which is rare, the economy is said to be in a depression. A **depression** is a period of economic contraction that is severe and lasts a long time.

During the Great Depression in the 1930s, one out of four workers was unemployed. Pay cuts were common among those who had jobs. People lost their savings and investments. Hunger and homelessness were common. Families migrated across the country looking for work. The depression lasted for about ten years.

More recently, between 2007 and 2009, the economy went into the Great Recession. Again, many people lost their jobs and homes, businesses failed, and the value of savings and investments fell dramatically. Unemployment exceeded 10 percent among unskilled and uneducated workers. In 2009, the economy again entered the expansion phase of the business cycle.

Trough

The trough phase is the low point of contraction. Economic activity reaches its lowest level. When the economy is in a trough, contraction has slowed. However, it is when the most business closures occur in the cycle. Unemployment is also at its highest level for this cycle. Consumers are reluctant to spend, businesses are reluctant to hire or to invest, and overall confidence in the economy hits bottom.

The trough lasts until the economy starts an upward trend. Recovery usually begins slowly. As the trough ends, businesses may start seeing higher sales or opportunities to expand. Spending starts to increase. Consumers once again begin to consider purchasing cars, houses, and other high-dollar items. The trough is identified after the fact as the economy begins to improve.

Economic Indicators

The economy is incredibly complex and difficult to understand and predict. Governmental policies attempt to provide stability in prices, economic growth, full employment, and ongoing prosperity. Existing economic conditions dictate the policies the government follows. The tools the government uses to influence the economy include monetary and fiscal policies, which are discussed later in this chapter.

In making policy decisions, the government looks to economic indicators. An **economic indicator** is a piece of significant economic data that economists use to evaluate the overall health of the economy. Economists use specific indicators to measure economic conditions and predict highs and lows. The common examples of these indicators include the gross domestic product, consumer price index, rate of inflation, interest rates, and labor figures.

Gross Domestic Product

The best indicator of economic growth is the gross domestic product. The **gross domestic product (GDP)** is a measure of the value of all goods and services produced by a nation during a specified period of time, usually one year. GDP is usually adjusted for inflation and stated in dollars. The GDP includes:

- personal consumption expenditures;
- gross private domestic investment;
- net exports of goods and services; and
- governmental spending.

Personal consumption expenditures is a measure of consumer spending. **Consumer spending** is the purchasing of goods and services by consumers. Gross private domestic investment is a measure of the money businesses invest in buildings, equipment, technology, innovation, and

tcly/Shutterstock.com

A country's net exports of goods and services is included in its GDP.

inventory. Net exports of goods and services is the value of the goods and services exported minus the value of goods and services imported from other countries. Governmental spending is a measure of governmental consumption expenditures and gross investment.

A rising GDP indicates economic growth or the beginning of a recovery from contraction. An unexpected increase in GDP may indicate that the economy is overheating and inflation could result. *Overheating* occurs when demand exceeds the capacity of the economy. A falling GDP indicates a weakening economy.

The US GDP dropped by 0.3 percent in 2008 and by 3.5 percent in 2009, as shown in Figure 17-3. These were the first declines in 16 years. They were evidence of the severe economic problems the United States faced during the Great Recession.

The US Department of Commerce's Bureau of Economic Analysis (BEA) calculates the GDP for the United States each quarter. The growth or decline in production is measured by the change in the GDP from one quarter to the next. Although the GDP is calculated quarterly, it is expressed as an annual rate.

GDP per capita is the market value of final goods and services produced per person. *Per capita* simply means "per person." GDP per capita is found by dividing the national GDP by the number of people in the country. When GDP per capita is high or rising, incomes are rising and more goods and services are available to each citizen. People are consuming more, and their standards of living are rising. On the other hand, when GDP per capita is falling, it indicates falling incomes. Fewer goods and services are being produced. A lower GDP per capita signals a lower standard of living. *Standard of living* is the degree to which one can obtain goods and services desired.

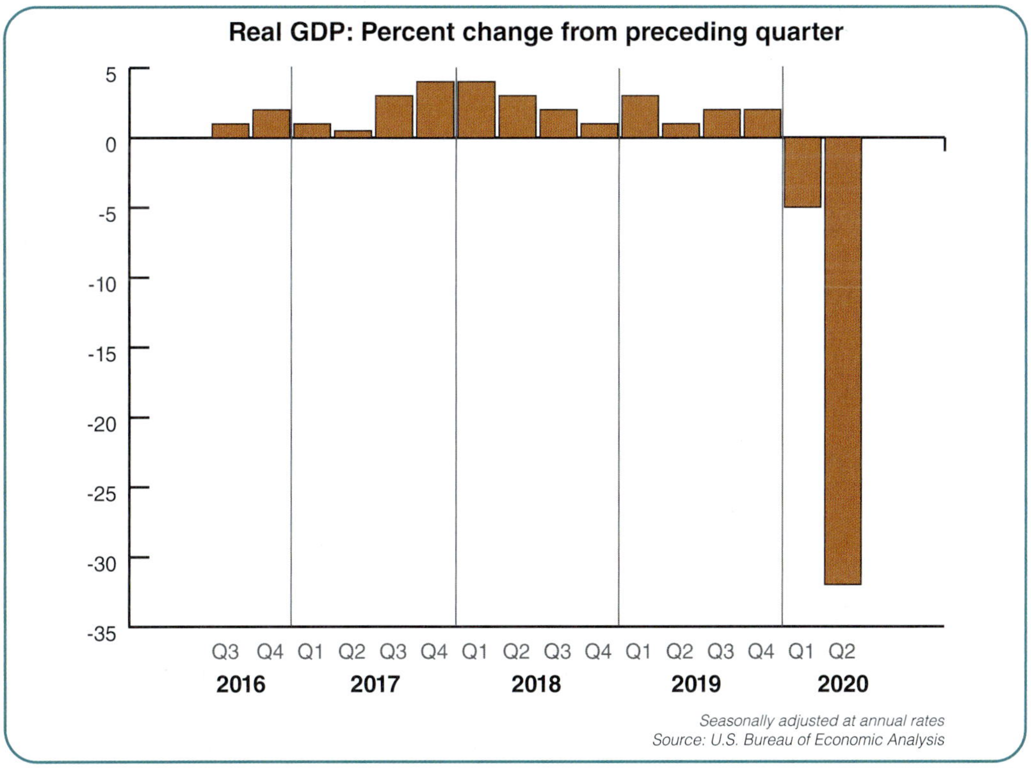

Goodheart-Willcox Publisher

Figure 17-3 The coronavirus pandemic (COVID-19) that started in early 2020 caused a 32.9 percent drop in the US GDP during the second quarter, the sharpest economic contraction in modern American history.

History of Finance

Adam Smith and John Maynard Keynes

Two economists instrumental in shaping modern economics were Adam Smith (1723–1790) and John Maynard Keynes (1883–1946). The ideas of Smith and Keynes continue to foster debate about the role of government in the economy today.

Adam Smith lived at the dawn of the industrial revolution. Previously, most people lived in rural areas and produced most of what they needed themselves. The industrial revolution brought people to cities to work in factories. Factory workers became part of an assembly line, each specializing in a small task that contributed to a finished product.

In the book, *The Wealth of Nations*, Smith hails specialization, or division of labor, that created greater economic efficiency, mass production, and markets for goods. Smith argued that a free market economic system was superior to other systems because it harnessed a powerful force that motivated people: self-interest. In a free market economy, people have the freedom to do what is best for themselves and wind up doing what is best for the economy.

For example, in order to maximize profits, producers avoid wasting resources. To increase earnings, workers learn new skills. This give and take between people acting on their own self-interest is the "invisible hand" that runs the economy. Smith opposed government interference in the economy.

John Maynard Keynes witnessed World War I and the Great Depression. Many people saw the Great Depression as a failure of Smith's "invisible hand" theory. The economy was damaged and only governmental intervention saved it. New governmental programs created jobs and stimulated the economy. Spending on World War II created new demand that finally lifted the United States out of the depression.

In the book, *The General Theory of Employment, Interest, and Money*, Keynes argued that economic stability and prosperity depends on government playing a role in the economy.

There are some problems with using GDP to measure standard of living. GDP per capita assumes that everyone gets an equal share, although that is not the case in reality. Also, GDP as a measure of output does not account for unpaid work, such as housework, childcare, and volunteer work. However, despite these omissions, GDP per capita is the most common way to measure standard of living.

Consumer Price Index

The **consumer price index (CPI)**, sometimes called the *cost of living index*, is a measure of the average change in prices over time for selected goods and services. It charts the ups and downs in the prices of consumer goods and services. The CPI measures annual price changes for a bundle of goods and services that average consumers purchase. It does not include changes in real estate prices, income tax and other taxes, or Social Security taxes paid by individuals and businesses. The CPI charts price changes by collecting data from over 50,000 households and 23,000 establishments in 87 areas across the country.

One use of the CPI is to measure cost of living changes and to adjust wages for workers who are covered by collective-bargaining agreements. The CPI is also used to determine the cost of living increases applied to Social Security and pension benefits.

Inflation

Inflation is an overall increase in the price of goods and services. It threatens the nation's prosperity because it decreases the value of a dollar. Due to inflation, today's dollar buys less than dollars from past years. For example, you would need $15.64 in 2015 to buy what would have cost $10 in 1995. Inflation is especially difficult for individuals and families who live on fixed incomes. With a fixed income, the amount of money received stays the same over the years, while costs climb. This results in the necessity to make trade-offs when making purchases of goods and services. When dollars are limited, choices have to be made based on what is actually needed rather than what is wanted.

The CPI Inflation Calculator on the Bureau of Labor Statistics' website can be used to calculate the cost of inflation in the United States. The US inflation rate is fairly low, especially when compared with the rates of many other countries. For example, in 2015, the estimated rate of inflation in the United States was about 0.2 percent. In India, it was about 4.5 percent. In Russia, it was about 15.7 percent. In China, it was about 1.6 percent.

Demand-Pull Inflation

Demand-pull inflation occurs during expansion and peak periods of the business cycle. When the economy is growing, consumers are more likely to be employed and spending money. Spending increases at a faster rate than supply. Put another way, there are too many dollars chasing too few goods. According to the laws of supply and demand, as demand goes up, so do prices.

Cost-Push Inflation

Cost-push inflation is triggered by an increase in the price of a widely used product. For example, when the price of oil rises, consumers pay more for fuel to power their cars and heat their homes. Many other goods and services increase in price as well, from food and flowers to building materials and airfares. This increase happens because many businesses require fuel to operate and bring goods to market. Petroleum (oil) is also a necessary ingredient in other products, such as plastics.

Stagflation

Stagflation is a period of slow growth (economic stagnation) and high inflation. The best-known episode of stagflation took place during the 1970s. Oil producers raised oil prices, which triggered inflation because the costs of many goods and services rose. This occurred at a time of slow growth and high unemployment.

Deflation

Deflation is an overall decrease in the price of goods and services. When prices continue to fall, consumers and businesses tend to defer spending while they wait for still lower prices. Eventually demand falls off, causing business failures, unemployment, and lower incomes. Extended deflationary periods can lead to an economic recession or depression.

Interest Rates

Consumer borrowing has two important effects on the economy. It increases the amount of money in circulation, and it increases the current demand for consumer goods and services. For example, when you borrow, you have more money to spend. As you and other consumers use borrowed money, consumer demand is increased in the marketplace. This is why the Federal Reserve Board may lower interest rates to encourage the use of credit (borrowed money) during a recession. Lower interest rates help stimulate growth.

However, consumer borrowing can have a negative impact on the economy during periods of inflation because it increases the supply of money. When the supply of money grows faster than the supply of goods and services, demand increases. This causes prices to rise, and inflation is the result. The Federal Reserve Board may raise interest rates to discourage borrowing, which reduces the money supply and controls price increases. The money supply is discussed later in this chapter.

Labor

All of the people in a nation who are capable of working and want to work are called the **labor force**. A nation's prosperity and stability depend on full use of its productive resources, including the labor force. This is one of the goals the government seeks to achieve through its economic policies.

The earning activities of individuals, plus those of all others in the job market, make a huge impact on the economy. At the same time, the state of the economy affects your earning potential. Economic conditions influence the number of jobs that are available, the type of work in demand, and salary levels. Demand in job markets is ever-changing.

kurhan/Shutterstock.com

The labor force includes all civilian workers in an economy.

Unemployment

The **unemployment rate** is the percentage of the labor force that is out of work and seeking employment. The unemployment rate in the United States is reported by the Bureau of Labor Statistics. This figure is closely tied to business fluctuations. The highest unemployment rates occur during periods of contraction.

Unemployment hurts workers and their families. When family breadwinners are unemployed, the entire family suffers. Some families must move because they lose their homes or cannot afford to make rent or mortgage payments. Some people go into debt or lose health benefits that are usually provided through an employer. Unemployment is also associated with health problems, such as stress-related illnesses, depression, and substance abuse.

Historically, from 1950 through 2019, the unemployment rate in the United States averaged 5.8 percent. The unemployment rate was trending downward, averaging 4.24 percent from 2015 to 2019. However, the shutdown of businesses caused by COVID-19 in the spring of 2020 caused a spike in the rate. In January of 2020, it was 3.6 percent. In April of 2020, it peaked at 14.7 percent. Figure 17-4 shows the unemployment rate between July of 2010 and July of 2020.

Some workers will be temporarily unemployed even in a strong and growing economy. *Frictional unemployment* is short-term unemployment that affects people who are between jobs. These are people who have moved or changed jobs or careers. Frictional unemployment is, in large part, why the unemployment rate will never be zero.

Structural unemployment refers to unemployment among workers who drop out of the labor force or do not enter it. There may be a mismatch between their skills and available jobs. Structural unemployment tends to be long-term, difficult to correct, and the most damaging to both workers and the economy. Examples of structural unemployment include jobs lost because of technological advances, failure of a major employer in an area, and outsourcing of jobs to cheaper labor markets.

Cyclical unemployment occurs when the economy slows or is in a recession. It is normally tied to the business cycle. Demand falls and workers are laid off. There are more job seekers than available jobs. When the economy moves into the growth phase, workers are rehired.

Seasonal unemployment is related to jobs that depend on seasonal activities. These jobs include those for the extra workers hired for the holidays, vacation seasons, and crop harvesting. Seasonal jobs end when the short-term demand for workers ceases.

In addition to the unemployed, a percentage of the labor force will be underemployed. **Underemployment** is a condition in which workers are employed only part-time or are overqualified for their jobs. An overqualified

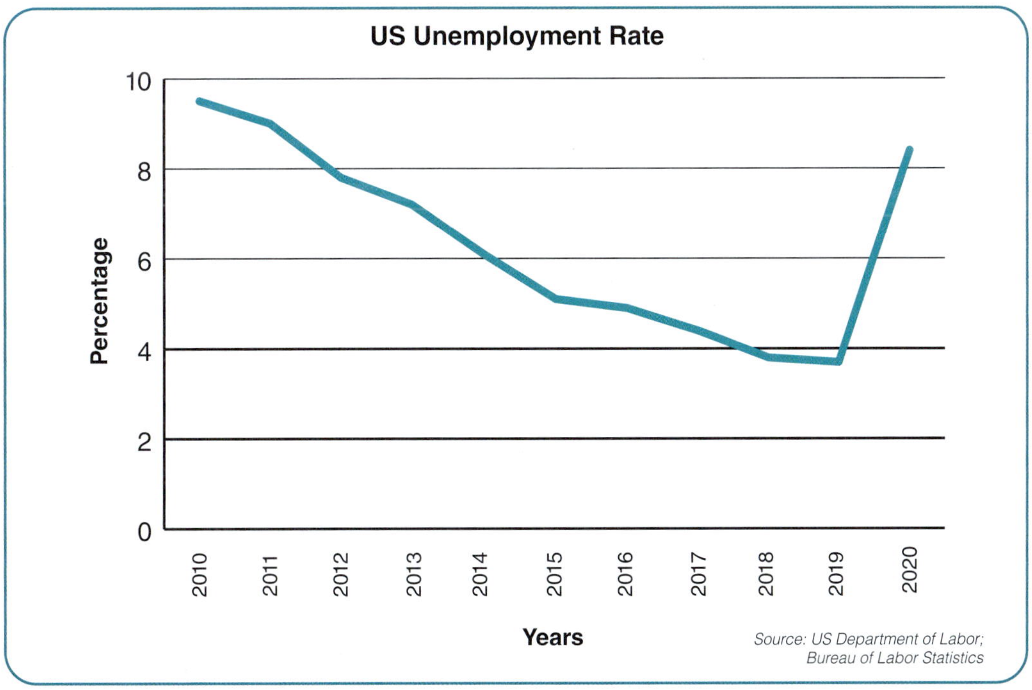

Goodheart-Willcox Publisher

Figure 17-4 The unemployment rate fell steadily from 2010 to 2019, then took a dramatic jump in 2020 due to the shutdown of businesses caused by the COVID-19 pandemic.

worker has far greater education or skills than is required of a job. Some underemployed workers are so by choice, but most are workers who cannot find work at their skill or educational levels.

Labor Productivity

Economists also use labor productivity as an indicator of a nation's economic health or prosperity. **Labor productivity** is the value of the goods and services a worker creates in a given time. High labor productivity indicates a healthy economy. To raise labor productivity, businesses and governments need to invest in productive resources, such as technology, infrastructure, factories, and the education and training of workers. Top-performing workers use efficient tools and technology to increase their own earnings. In turn, their high productivity also boosts the nation's wealth.

Section 17.1 Review

Check Your Understanding

1. What are the three functions of money?
2. List the four phases of the business cycle.
3. What does the gross domestic product measure?
4. Why does the dollar today purchase less than it did ten years ago?
5. How does underemployment differ from unemployment?

Build Your Vocabulary

As you progress through this course, develop a personal glossary. This will help you build your vocabulary and prepare you for a career. Write a definition for each of the following terms and add it to your glossary.

money
medium of exchange
unit of value
store of value
prosperity
depression
economic indicator
gross domestic product (GDP)
consumer spending
GDP per capita
consumer price index (CPI)
stagflation
deflation
labor force
unemployment rate
underemployment
labor productivity

Section 17.2 Government and the Economy

Objectives

After studying this section, you will be able to:

- Identify the function of the Federal Reserve System.
- Explain the meaning of fiscal policy.
- Describe the government's role in the economy.

Essential Question

How large of a role should the federal government play in the regulation of the economy?

Terms

Federal Reserve System	subsidy	market structure
monetary policy	deficit spending	perfect competition
monetary system	surplus	monopoly
money supply	national debt	monopolistic competition
discount rate	price competition	oligopoly
fiscal policy	nonprice competition	collusion

Function of the Federal Reserve

The **Federal Reserve System,** also called the *Fed*, regulates the nation's money supply and the banking system. Created by Congress in 1913 as our nation's central bank, its role is to regulate banks in the country. The system is composed of the Board of Governors, 12 Federal Reserve Banks, and the Federal Open Market Committee. The Federal Reserve System is divided in twelve districts as shown in Figure 17-5. Each of these districts has a Federal Reserve bank.

The Fed is responsible for the monetary system for the country. One of its core functions is to establish monetary policy. **Monetary policy** is the actions the Fed takes to manage the supply of money and credit in the economy. The Fed uses monetary policy to avoid sudden and severe ups and downs in the price levels of goods and services.

Managing the Monetary System

A **monetary system** is the mechanism a nation uses to provide and manage money for itself. The Fed looks at economic indicators and an analysis of economic conditions to determine what actions to take. The **money supply** is the total amount of money available at a given time in an economy.

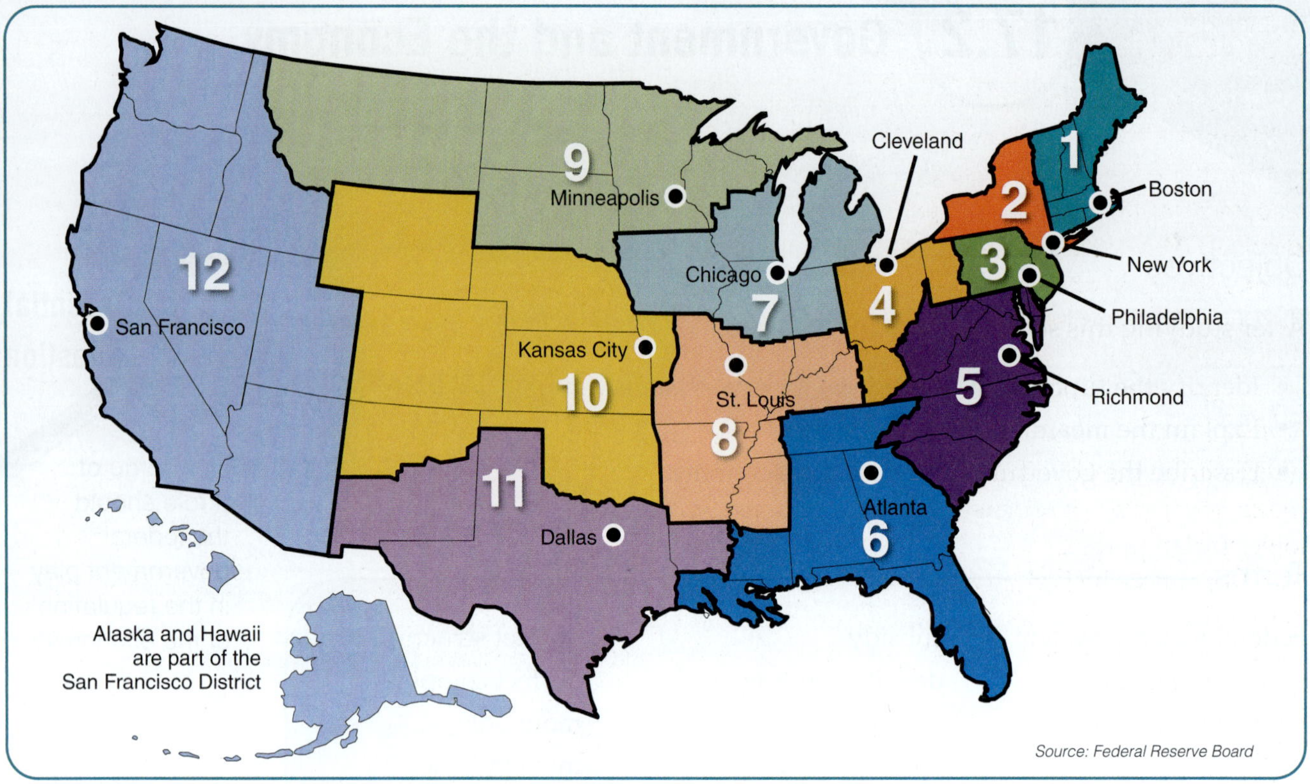

Goodheart-Willcox Publisher

Figure 17-5 The twelve Federal Reserve System districts cover the entire country.

Measures of the Money Supply	
Measure	**Description**
Monetary Base	Sum of currency in circulation and reserve balances.
M1	Sum of currency held by the public and deposits at depository institutions, such as funds deposited in checking accounts.
M2	M1 plus savings deposits; small-denomination certificates of deposit less than $100,000; and retail money market mutual fund shares less than $100,000.

Source: Board of Governors of the Federal Reserve System; Goodheart-Willcox Publisher

Figure 17-6 There are several standard measures of the money supply, including the monetary base, M1, and M2.

There are several standard measures of the money supply, including the monetary base, M1, and M2, as shown in Figure 17-6. M1 is the most liquid and what is used for everyday transactions. The Fed uses three tools to manage the supply of money and credit: reserve requirements, the discount rate, and open-market operations.

Reserve Requirements

The level of bank reserves mandated by the Fed is the cash reserves that banks and other financial institutions must set aside rather than lend to customers. It is expressed as a percent of their deposits. For example, suppose the reserve requirement is 10 percent. A bank that has $10 million in deposits from its customers can only lend $9 million. The other $1 million must stay on deposit. High reserve requirements reduce the amount of money available for lending. As a result, the supply of money and credit falls. Low reserve requirements have the opposite result.

Discount Rate

The **discount rate** is the interest rate the Federal Reserve charges commercial banks for loans. The discount rate affects the rates that banks and other lending institutions charge consumers and businesses. The higher the discount rate, the higher the rate consumers and businesses pay. The lower the discount rate, the lower the rate consumers and businesses pay.

The Fed uses the discount rate to help stabilize the economy. One of the first steps taken to address an economic slowdown is to lower the discount rate. Lower interest rates increase the money supply and stimulate the economy. They also encourage businesses to expand and consumers to buy more goods and services. Increased production and consumer demand lowers unemployment. During the Great Recession, the Fed lowered the discount rate to 0.25 percent. At the beginning of the COVID-19 pandemic, the discount rate was again lowered to 0.25 percent.

The Fed does the opposite during periods of high inflation. The interest rate is raised in an attempt to slow down the economy and reduce inflation. Higher interest rates result in less expansion by businesses. Consumers borrow less and make fewer credit purchases. The result is downward pressure on prices and a lower inflation rate.

Normally, the Fed increases the rate in stages. If rates rise too quickly, demand may decline to the point where businesses reduce output and cut jobs. To combat double-digit inflation in the early 1980s, the discount rate was raised to over 15 percent.

Open-Market Operations

Open-market operations refer to the Fed's buying or selling of treasury securities in the marketplace. Treasury securities are debt obligations of the US Department of the Treasury. They include treasury bonds, notes, and bills. When the Fed buys these securities, it increases the money supply and available credit. When the Fed sells government securities, the money supply shrinks because the dollars paid for these securities are no longer in circulation.

Easy Versus Tight Money

When the Fed follows an *easy monetary policy,* money and credit are readily available. Interest rates are relatively low. Under these conditions, consumers and businesses tend to spend. They buy or build more homes because interest rates for home mortgages are lower. Companies borrow more money for expanding their businesses. Entrepreneurs borrow money to start new businesses. Farmers borrow to buy machinery and land to produce more crops. All of these activities stimulate the economy and create jobs. However, if too much money is pumped into the economy through the Fed's policies, inflation may result.

In times of inflation, the Fed turns to a *tight monetary policy.* It increases reserve requirements, raises the discount rate, and sells government securities. These actions reduce the money supply and discourage the use of credit. As economic activity slows, price increases tend to level off or prices fall.

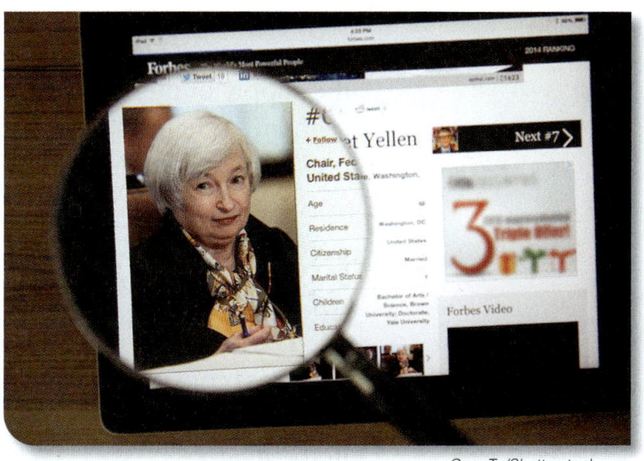

GongTo/Shutterstock.com

In 2014, Janet Louise Yellen became the first woman to hold the office of Chair of the Board of Governors of the Federal Reserve.

You Do the Math — Order of Operations

The *order of operations* is a set of rules stating which operations in an equation are performed first. The order of operations is often stated using the acronym *PEMDAS*. PEMDAS stands for parentheses, exponents, multiplication and division, and addition and subtraction. Anything inside parentheses is computed first. Exponents are computed next. Then, any multiplication and division operations are computed. Finally, any addition and subtraction operations are computed to find the answer to the problem. Equations are solved from left to right when applying PEMDAS.

Solve the following problems.

1. $8 - (4 \times 3) + 23 \div 2 =$
2. $3 + 4.5 - 27 \div 9 =$
3. $11^2 + (45 \times 2) =$

It may sound simple for the Fed to speed up or slow down the economy, but maintaining a balance between supply and demand is not an easy task. All parts in the puzzle are constantly changing. When facing stagflation, the Fed's job becomes even more challenging. If it tightens the money supply, which is the sure cure for inflation, it risks further slowing the already contracting economy. In addition, it can take months for monetary policies to bring about the desired changes. Finding the right balance and the right timing is critical and complicated. Governmental policymakers must be extremely careful in wielding their power.

Sometimes the government enacts policies that make a bad situation worse. For example, during part of the 1930s, the government followed a tight monetary policy. Some economists say this may have led to a deepening of the economic troubles that became the Great Depression. This depression did not end until the government pumped millions of dollars into the economy through a vast jobs program. The entry of the United States into World War II boosted demand for military weapons, uniforms, machinery, and many other goods and services that created jobs and economic growth.

During the Great Recession, the Fed followed an easy money policy to stimulate the economy by increasing the money supply. It lowered interest rates and reserve requirements imposed on banks. In addition, the Fed bought financial assets from banks and other institutions. These purchases increased the supply of money available for lending, spending, and investment. Many economists believe that the prompt action by the Fed early in the recession prevented a complete economic collapse and the start of a depression.

Fiscal Policy

Fiscal policy is the federal government's taxing and spending decisions. Congress controls taxing and spending decisions. Overall, the government's fiscal and monetary policies are intended to moderate the ups and downs in the business cycle. The government's goal is to create longer periods of prosperity and full employment with fewer severe downturns and upswings in the economy. The government's attempts to control recession and inflation are outlined in Figure 17-7.

Fiscal and Monetary Policies			
Economic Conditions	**Likely Fiscal Policy**	**Likely Monetary Policy**	**Expected Results**
Inflation A period of rising prices	• Increase tax rates, leaving consumers and business less money to spend • Reduce government spending to cut the amount of cash flowing into the system	• Raise reserve requirements so less money and less credit are available • Increase the discount rate, making credit more expensive • Sell government securities, drawing money out of circulation	• Decreased credit availability • Less money in circulation • Decreased spending • Decreased demand • Decreased production • Slowing economy
Recession A period of economic slowdown and unemployment	• Lower taxes, giving consumers and businesses more money to spend • Increase government spending to pump more money into the economy	• Lower reserve requirements, permitting banks to lend more money • Lower the discount rate, making credit more affordable • Buy government securities, pumping money into the economy	• Increased availability of money and credit • Increased spending • Increased demand • Increased production • Business expansion and job creation

Source: US Bureau of Economic Analysis; Goodheart-Willcox Publisher

Figure 17-7 The government uses fiscal and monetary policies to alter economic conditions.

The government often uses fiscal policy to stimulate the economy in periods of recession and high unemployment. When the government increases spending, it puts more money in circulation and stimulates greater economic activity, which creates more jobs.

Fiscal policy can also slow economic activity in periods of inflation or rising prices. Tax increases take money out of the economy and tend to dampen an overheated economy.

Taxing and Spending

The circular-flow diagram shown in Figure 17-8 illustrates the government's role in the economy. The inner circles show how the government participates in the flow of goods, services, and money. Producers and sellers provide goods and services to the government and receive payment in return. Consumers and workers provide labor and capital for the government and receive payment in return.

Governmental taxing and spending decisions make a significant impact on the overall economy. These decisions determine the amount of taxes individuals and businesses will pay. The decisions also determine the services that the government will provide in return.

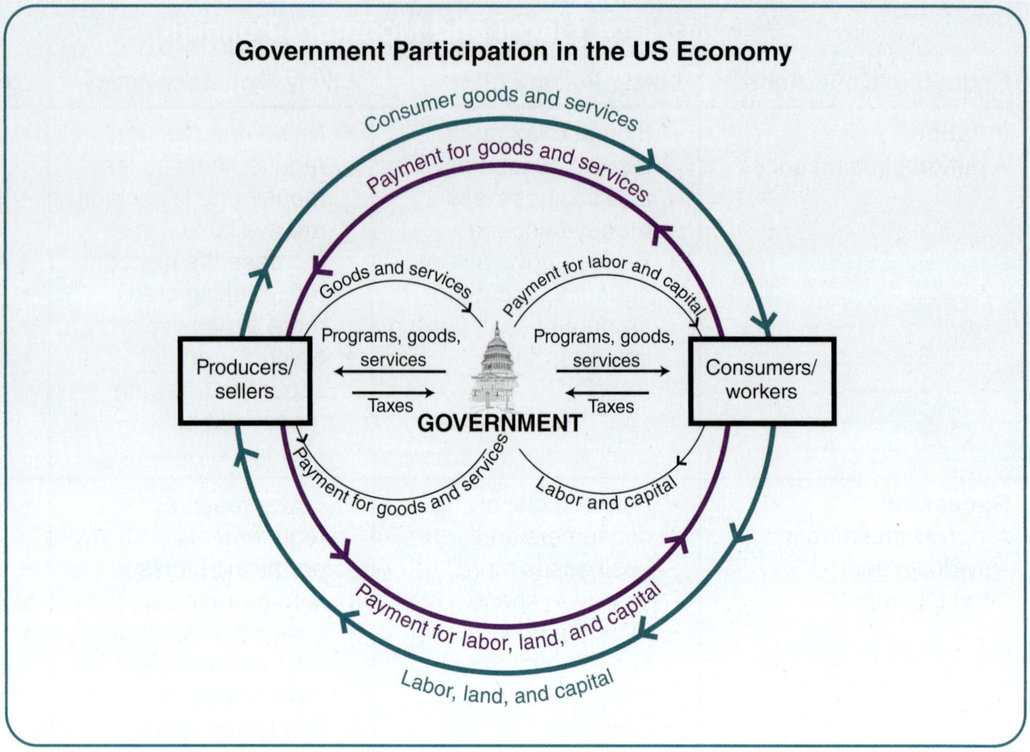

Figure 17-8 A circular flow of goods, services, and money takes place within the economy. Notice how the government participates.

Taxes

Local, state, and federal governments provide a wide variety of services for citizens. Citizens and businesses pay taxes to support these services. A *tax* is a fee imposed by a government on income, products, or activities and paid by citizens and businesses. The types of taxes governments levy to pay for their services and programs include:

- income tax;
- sales tax;
- property tax;
- excise tax; and
- estate tax.

Income tax is a tax individuals and corporations must pay on their earnings. The federal government, most states, and some city governments levy income tax. Consumers pay sales tax on the price of goods and services they buy. Owners must pay property tax on the assessed value of their property. Excise tax is levied by federal and state governments on the sale and transfer of certain items, such as air travel, telephone services, gasoline, and certain luxury items. Estate tax is a tax heirs must pay on the value of an estate that is greater than the exemption the law allows.

A tax may be direct or indirect. A *direct tax* is paid directly to the government by the taxpayer. Personal income tax is a direct tax. An *indirect tax* is levied on

Employability Skills

Self-Confidence

Self-confidence is being certain and secure about one's own abilities and judgment. Self-confident people believe in their abilities to perform in a given situation. They know what they are good at, and they trust their instincts. Self-confidence is affected by *self-talk*, which is the practice of talking to one's self. Positive self-talk includes reinforcement of one's appearance to abilities and boosts a person's self-confidence. Negative self-talk disparages a person and reduces self-confidence.

one person or entity, but shifted to or paid by another. Sales tax is one example. It is imposed on the seller of goods and services, but paid by the consumer.

Tax revenues pay for governmental operations. These operations include expenses connected with Congress, the court system, presidential offices, law enforcement, and a host of federal agencies and commissions. Taxes also pay for public goods and services that private citizens and businesses cannot or do not produce.

At the federal level, these goods and services include national defense, social-welfare programs, highways, transit systems, environmental protection, and certain areas of research and development. At the local and state levels, tax revenues pay for governmental operations and for public goods and services closer to home. These goods and services include schools, libraries, hospitals, roads, airports, parks, and fire and police protection. Citizens and businesses "buy" these goods and services from the government with tax dollars.

In the United States, voters indirectly decide what they want to "buy" from the government. They decide the level of taxes they will pay for their purchases through elections. They vote for higher taxes every time they vote for a candidate who advocates new governmental programs without reductions in governmental spending.

Spending

Governmental spending of tax revenues creates demand for goods and services. For example, the government pays for public schools with tax dollars. Private contractors build the schools with materials produced by private industries. This spending feeds money into the economy, sparks business activity, creates jobs, and in general creates demand for goods and services.

The government has the power to increase taxes in order to pay for its spending. This tends to depress the economy because it reduces the amount of money available for business activity. During a recession, the government may cut taxes to help stimulate the economy.

Excessive governmental spending can harm the economy. It can drive up prices and cause inflation. It also can contribute to the national debt. During periods of inflation, governmental spending has a negative impact on the economy. It increases demand in the marketplace. When the combined demands of the government and consumers are greater than the economy's capacity to produce, prices go up. This is why reductions in governmental spending help fight inflation, by reducing demand.

Redistribution of Income

When the government chooses to tax those who have more money in order to provide for those who have less, it redistributes income. Figure 17-9 illustrates the effect of three different taxation strategies on the redistribution of income. These three taxation strategies are progressive taxation, regressive taxation, and proportional taxation.

With a *progressive tax,* the higher the value of something, the higher the tax rate is on it. The income tax systems at the federal and state levels are examples of progressive taxes. Those with lower incomes pay a lower tax rate than those with higher incomes. The rate progressively rises as income rises. An estate tax is also progressive. The larger the value of an estate, the higher the estate tax. Progressive taxes are important to the economy because they generate more revenue, reduce economic volatility, and result in a more equitable distribution of income.

On the other hand, with a *regressive tax,* everyone pays the same tax rate regardless of income level. A sales tax is an example of a regressive tax. An individual with a lower income pays the same amount of sales taxes on a purchase as an individual with a higher income. This imposes a greater tax burden on lower-income individuals. The Social Security tax is a regressive tax because all taxpayers pay the same rate. The tax also stops after income reaches a higher level. Regressive taxes are important to the economy because they generate revenue and simplify the tax collection system. However, they are often considered an unfair tax.

A *proportional tax* imposes the same tax on all individuals or entities regardless of differences in income or ability to pay. This is sometimes called a *flat tax.* A vehicle sticker can be considered a proportional tax because the fee is the same dollar amount for everybody. Regressive and proportional taxes have the opposite effect on redistribution of income as a progressive tax because they impact lower incomes to a greater degree than higher incomes.

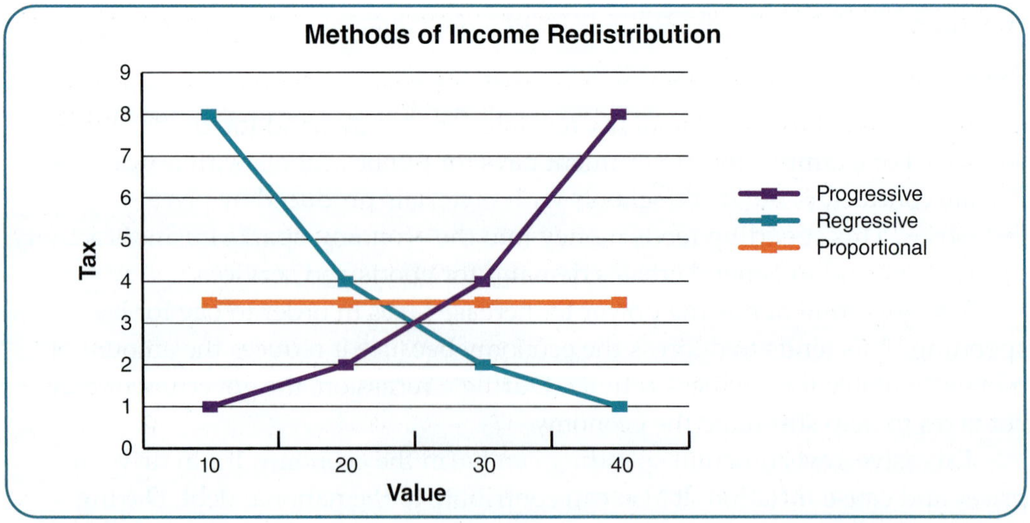

Goodheart-Willcox Publisher

Figure 17-9 A progressive tax increases as the value of the taxed item increases. A regressive tax decreases as the value increases. A proportional tax is the same regardless of value.

The government also redistributes income through transfer payments. Transfer payments include income and benefits that the government provides for individuals and households in the form of social programs. Three of the most familiar social programs are Social Security, unemployment compensation, and Temporary Assistance to Needy Families (TANF). These program benefits are paid largely by taxing those who do not receive them, thus redistributing income.

The government pays billions of dollars in subsidies each year. A **subsidy** is a form of transfer payment that gives financial assistance to a business or entity, such as those in education, agriculture, the arts, or health care. It may come in the form of a direct payment, tax benefit, or some other advantage. The principal goal of subsidies is to benefit the public in some way. For example, government may subsidize small farmers so they can compete with corporate farms. A subsidy paid to milk producers guarantees them a reasonable profit and ensures a supply of affordable milk for consumers. Many farmers who grow subsidized crops, including corn, wheat, cotton, soybeans, and rice, also get money from the government. The flow of money in these cases is from taxpayers, through the government, to those receiving the payments or benefits. To date, the federal government supports over 2,000 programs involving some form of subsidy. Critics of subsidies claim this gives the businesses receiving the incentives an unfair competitive advantage.

ndoeljindoel/Shutterstock.com

Farmers who grow subsidized crops, such as soybeans, receive money from the government.

Deficit Spending and the National Debt

Often, the cost of governmental programs and services is greater than the tax revenues the government collects. Just as consumers borrow or use credit to pay their bills, the government borrows money to cover its expenses. The money is raised by the sale of treasury and savings bonds to individuals, companies, and other countries.

When the government borrows excessively, there is less credit available for business expansion, home mortgages, and other business and consumer needs. Dollars spent by the government are dollars that are not available to the private sector where growth generally is created.

Deficit spending occurs when the government spends more than the amount it receives in revenues. When the government receives more than it spends, it is called a **surplus.**

Over the years, deficit spending and governmental borrowing have created a huge national debt. The **national debt** is the total amount of money the government owes at a given time. Each year's deficit increases this debt.

Like consumers, the government must pay interest to borrow money. The money paid in interest on the national debt leaves less to spend for health care, education, environmental protection, defense, and other needs.

You and other taxpayers must pay for the national debt. As governmental spending and debt increase, revenues and taxes must also increase. High levels of governmental spending and national debt threaten future economic growth and represent a huge burden on future generations.

Government's Role in the Economy

The US economic system is a *market* or a *free-enterprise system.* Compared with many other nations, the US government plays a small role in the economy. However, the economy could not function without certain types of governmental participation.

For example, the government provides the legal and institutional environments that permit and encourage economic activity. It does this by protecting individual liberties and private-property rights and enforces contractual agreements. It also provides the political stability and the rule of law that are necessary for economic interaction. These two elements are what enable individuals and businesses to carry out productive economic activities.

Governmental participation is necessary to maintain fair competition in the marketplace. In addition, governmental regulations provide a legal framework to also keep the marketplace fair and safe for all.

Fair Competition

Fair competition is one of the hallmarks of a market economy. It works best when there are many sellers offering similar products. Competition between producers results in more innovation, better products and services, and lower prices for consumers.

Businesses compete for customers using price or nonprice competition. **Price competition** is competing for business based on the prices of goods and services. Although lowering prices may attract more customers, it may have a negative effect on overall business profits. **Nonprice competition** is a competitive advantage based on factors other than price. Better service or more convenient store hours are ways businesses engage in nonprice competition and potentially increase sales.

Market structure is how a market is organized based on the number of businesses competing for sales in an industry. In a free-enterprise system, competition is the backbone of the economy. As shown in Figure 17-10, there are four basic market structures that represent varying degrees of competition:

- perfect competition
- monopoly
- monopolistic competition
- oligopoly

Perfect competition is a condition in which no single seller can significantly influence the market price of a good or service. It exists as a goal, but is never fully achieved. Perfect competition is also called *pure competition.*

Monopoly is a situation in which there is a single seller or producer of a given product or service. Since it has no competition, a monopolistic business can charge high prices, and it has little incentive to improve productivity or products and services. A monopoly is the opposite of perfect competition.

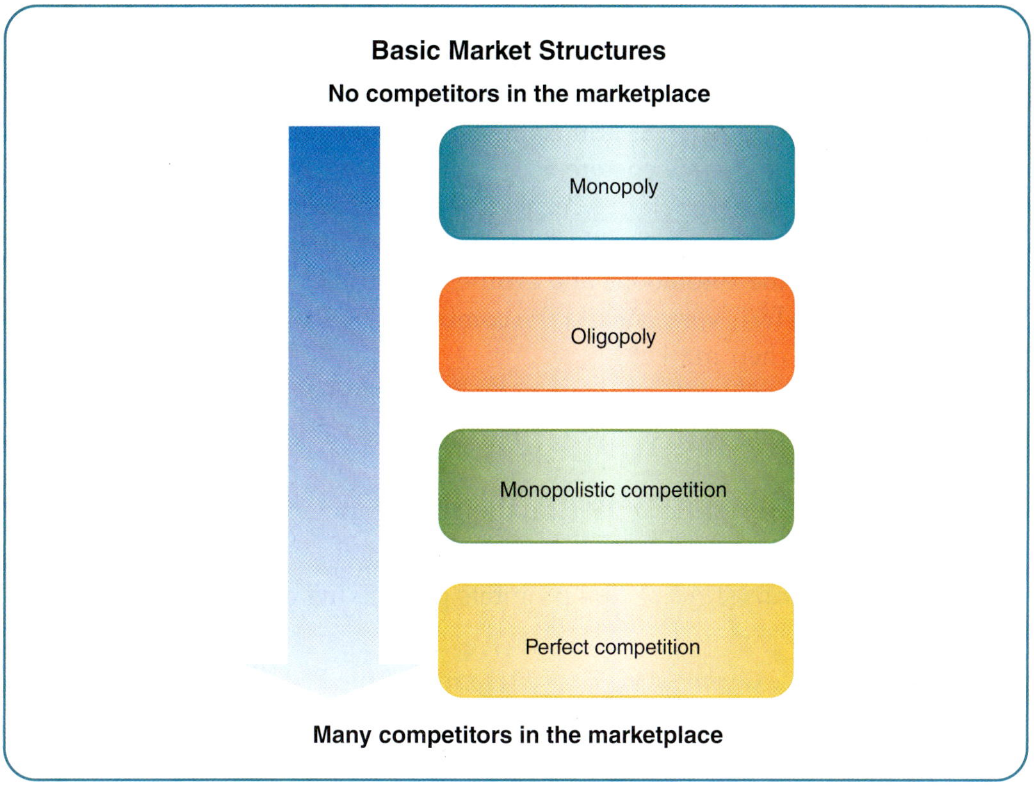

Goodheart-Willcox Publisher

Figure 17-10 The four basic market structures represent various levels of competition in an economy.

Exploring Careers

President of the United States

The President of the United States is the highest position in the US government. The position is given to the winner of a national presidential election, held every four years. The president is the head of state, the head of the government, and the commander-in-chief to the US armed forces. The US president typically:

- leads the executive branch of the US government;
- influences Congress when laws are being made; and
- inspires Americans as a role model and leader.

The US president often works in an office environment, but travels around the globe to meet with other world leaders. The job of US president comes with much responsibility and many challenges. US presidents also have a high level of notoriety and respect. US presidents have extremely long workdays in a very stressful work environment. To be President of the United States, you should have a strong background in politics or law, but a degree is not required. Experience working in government at the local, state, and national levels is preferred. By law, you have to be a natural-born citizen of the United States, be a permanent resident of the United States for 14 years, and be at least 35 years old. Public speaking, managerial, and organizational skills are essential.

Monopolistic competition is a situation in which a large number of businesses sell similar, but not the same, products and at different prices. Restaurants are examples of monopolistic competition. They offer different menus and other things, such as atmosphere, that make each unique. However, they all compete for the same customers.

An **oligopoly** is a situation in which a few large companies dominate an industry. The oligopoly is another threat to perfect competition. Examples of oligopolies include the automobile and airline industries. Wireless providers are another example. AT&T, Verizon, and the combined T-Mobile and Sprint control about 90 percent of their market.

Laws known as *antitrust laws* were passed to promote competition and fair trade and to prevent trade restraints in the marketplace. The best-known antitrust laws are as follows.

- The *Sherman Antitrust Act of 1890* prohibits anticompetitive activities, such as monopolies.
- The *Clayton Antitrust Act of 1914* prohibits price fixing and other unfair trade practices.
- The *Federal Trade Commission Act of 1914* created the Federal Trade Commission, which was given the power to investigate unfair or deceptive trade practices and to enforce compliance with lawful practices.

Although monopolies are illegal, exceptions have been made for some industries. For example, cable television companies were allowed to monopolize cable service in particular areas. It was impractical to have two or more companies rigging wires and cables throughout a community. In addition, this practice encouraged companies to make the large investment to bring cable service to a community, assured there would be no competitors.

Jonathan Weiss/Shutterstock.com

AT&T, Verizon, and the combined T-Mobile and Sprint control about 90 percent of the cell-phone provider market, forming an oligopoly.

Ethics

Collusion

It is unethical and illegal for a business to participate in acts of collusion. Collusion occurs when competing businesses work together to eliminate competition by misleading customers, setting prices, or other fraudulent activities. Unethical businesses sometimes collude with other businesses so that they can dominate the marketplace. Collusion is unethical, and it is also illegal.

Oligopoly is legal, but the companies in an oligopoly are not allowed to collude. **Collusion** is making a secret agreement to engage in illegal or dishonest activities, in this case to shut out smaller competitors and to engage in price fixing. *Price fixing* occurs when two or more businesses in an industry agree to sell at a set price and eliminate price competition.

Governmental Regulations

The US government did not always play a role in the regulation of business and industries. Some of the first major governmental regulation laws were passed in 1906. In that year, Congress passed laws regulating the labeling of food and drugs. It also passed laws to ensure that meat was inspected before it could be sold. Soon after, in 1913, the Federal Reserve System was established to oversee banking activities.

The need for governmental regulation increased in the 1930s. The Great Depression brought widespread unemployment and business failures. In response, Congress passed new laws that increased the government's power to intervene in the economy. New legislation provided for unemployment benefits, retirement income, and insurance of bank deposits. Congress also regulated the sale of securities and gave workers the right to form unions.

Today, there are more than 100 federal regulatory departments. Each department includes many regulatory agencies within it. The same types of regulation exist in every state, county, and municipality. Almost every aspect of public life falls under some form of governmental regulation. Laws that ensure public well-being and safety cover a number of key areas, including:

- equal opportunity;
- fair labor practices;
- workplace safety;
- environmental protection;
- pure foods, drugs, and cosmetics;
- product safety;
- truth in advertising and labeling;
- truth in lending and saving; and
- homeland security.

Governmental regulations have a major impact on the economy. For example, they cover every phase of the auto industry, from the manufacturer to your local service garage. The government provides a legal framework that allows regulation of working conditions, employee benefits, car warranties, auto financing, servicing, registration and licensing, insurance, and advertising, among other things.

Historically, governmental regulations were directed at a specific product or industry. Today, laws, such as the *Occupational Safety and Health Act (OSHA),* the *Consumer Product Safety Act (CPSA),* and the *National Environmental Policy Act (NEPA),* apply to almost every existing business and product.

Some regulations may be necessary to protect consumers and to ensure fair business practices. However, as the number of regulations and regulatory agencies increases, so do the costs to the government, businesses, and consumers. The scope of regulations and the paperwork they require increases the cost of complying with the laws enacted. In addition, regulations require far more recordkeeping and paperwork than in the past. It is costly for businesses to comply with governmental regulations. These costs make it difficult for businesses to compete in world markets and increase the prices they must charge for their goods and services.

Governmental agencies assist consumers by establishing and enforcing laws and regulations at the local, state, and federal levels. They protect consumers from unsafe products and unethical business practices. These agencies represent consumer interests in many areas. They regulate food standards and sanitation practices, credit and insurance transactions, and business and trade practices. They also govern the licensing and certification of groups, such as medical professionals, hospitals, nursing homes, funeral homes, lawyers, and others who serve the public.

The *Department of Agriculture (USDA)* provides various programs and services related to the food supply, natural resources, economics, and international trade. In the interests of consumers, the USDA researches the nutrient content of food and ways to improve the quality and safety of food, crops, and livestock. It also provides food assistance to needy consumers and nutrition education to the public.

The *Department of Energy (DOE)* works toward a reliable, affordable, and clean energy supply for the nation. To achieve that goal, current programs focus on energy, environmental, and nuclear challenges. DOE priorities include the development of alternative fuel sources and better fuel economy.

The *Department of Labor (DOL)* promotes the welfare of wage earners and retirees, improved working conditions, and better job opportunities. This department enforces labor laws that include minimum wage, child labor, antidiscrimination, maximum working hours, and safety and health regulations. It also administers the Bureau of Labor Statistics and the Occupational Safety and Health Administration.

The *Food and Drug Administration (FDA)* protects the public against impure and unsafe foods, drugs, cosmetics, and other hazards. It operates national centers for drug evaluation and research, food safety and applied nutrition, and veterinary medicine. The FDA aims to promote public health and food and drug safety.

The *Social Security Administration (SSA)* promotes economic security by managing the federal government's retirement, survivors, and disability insurance. It also manages the supplemental security income programs.

The *Department of Housing and Urban Development (HUD)* supervises programs related to housing needs, fair housing opportunities, and community development. It administers mortgage insurance to promote home ownership, rental assistance for low- and moderate-income families, housing safety standards, urban-renewal programs, and federal real estate laws.

Section 17.2 Review

Check Your Understanding

1. Identify the three components of the Federal Reserve System.
2. Explain the impact the Federal Reserve System's policies have on interest rates, inflation, and unemployment.
3. How are the services provided by local, state, and federal governments funded?
4. List the four basic market structures.
5. Describe price fixing.

Build Your Vocabulary

As you progress through this course, develop a personal glossary. This will help you build your vocabulary and prepare you for a career. Write a definition for each of the following terms and add it to your glossary.

Federal Reserve System
monetary policy
monetary system
money supply
discount rate
fiscal policy
subsidy
deficit spending
surplus
national debt
price competition
nonprice competition
market structure
perfect competition
monopoly
monopolistic competition
oligopoly
collusion

Review and Assessment

Chapter Summary

Section 17.1 Basics of the Economy

- Money is anything of value that is accepted in return for goods or services. Money allows business transactions to take place and goods and services to be exchanged. It serves as a medium of exchange, unit of value, and store of value.
- The business cycle is fluctuations between periods of economic growth and slowdown. There are four stages: expansion, peak, contraction, and trough.
- An economic indicator is a piece of significant economic data that economists use to evaluate the overall health of the economy. Common examples of these indicators include the gross domestic product, consumer price index, rate of inflation, interest rates, and labor figures.

Section 17.2 Government and the Economy

- The Federal Reserve System regulates the nation's money supply and the banking system. It is composed of the Board of Governors, 12 Federal Reserve Banks, and the Federal Open Market Committee. The Fed looks at economic indicators and an analysis of economic conditions to determine what actions to take.
- The government's fiscal and monetary policies are intended to moderate the ups and downs in the business cycle. The government uses fiscal policy to stimulate the economy in periods of recession and high unemployment or to slow economic activity in periods of inflation or rising prices.
- The economy could not function without certain types of governmental participation. It is necessary to maintain fair competition in the marketplace. In addition, governmental regulations provide a legal framework to also keep the marketplace fair and safe for all.

Review Your Knowledge

1. Identify the five characteristics of money.
2. List the four phases of the business cycle.
3. How is a depression different from a recession?
4. Describe five common economic indicators.
5. How does demand-pull inflation result in higher prices?
6. Which type of unemployment describes those who are between jobs?
7. Explain the importance of monetary policy in the economy.
8. Compare and contrast the easy and tight monetary policies, including interest rate fluctuations.
9. List and describe three types of taxes used to redistribute income.
10. Describe the government's role in the economy.

Apply Your Knowledge

1. Compare and contrast the following types of currency: paper money, coins, banknotes, government bonds, and treasury notes. What are the differentiating characteristics of each?
2. The properties of money state that money should be stable, easily recognized, divisible, portable, and durable. Noticeably absent from this list is *available*. How important is it to regulate how much money is printed and available for consumer use?

3. There are four stages in the business cycle: expansion, peak, contraction, and trough. Analyze the current economy in the United States. Which cycle is our economy in at present? On what did you base your opinion? Explain how this current cycle influences personal spending decisions you make.
4. The gross domestic product (GDP) is an economic indicator that measures the value of all goods and services produced by a nation during a specified period of time. GDP includes consumer spending. Analyze the measure of consumer spending as a part of the GDP. Explain why, when consumers spend money, the health of the economy is impacted.
5. The inflation rate has a direct impact on decisions that individuals make. Assume the inflation rate for the country is 3 percent. Analyze how inflation would affect these activities in your personal life: amount of your paycheck; gas prices for your auto; cost of college; and spending money.
6. Unemployment affects workers, their families, and the economy. Using the information in this chapter, make a list of the various ways the unemployment rate impacts a nation's economy. Next, add your opinion as to how unemployment affects the economy.
7. Create a list of the various responsibilities of the Federal Reserve. Rank your list in the order of importance according to your opinion. Next to each responsibility, analyze why it plays an important role in the economy.
8. There are many types of taxes at the local, state, and federal levels. Create a chart with three columns. In the first column, write *local taxes*. In the second column, write *state taxes*, and in the last write *national taxes*. In each column, identify specific taxes and their purpose. Why do we need these taxes? Explain the economic importance each tax has to the public.
9. Monetary policy requires a balance between pumping enough money into the economy and slowing down the amount of spending. Money supply is measured by monetary base, M1, and M2. Of these three, which is the most accurate measure of a nation's money supply? Explain your reasoning.
10. Governments use fiscal policy to combat inflation and recession in the economy. Analyze the relationship between inflation and recession and explain how a change in fiscal policy affects a nation's economy.

Apply Your Math Skills

1. Tanita purchased a new three-ring notebook last year for $3.29. This year, the same notebook is priced at $3.48. What is the rate of inflation for this product?
2. Jacque owns a home assessed by the county to be valued at $158,032. The property tax rate for the current year is 2.7%, and the tax is paid in equal semiannual installments. How much is one payment for Jacque's property tax?

Communication Skills

College and Career Readiness

Reading. After you have read this chapter, determine the central ideas and review the conclusions made by the author. Take notes to identify the chapter's purpose and intended audience. Demonstrate your understanding of the information by retelling or summarizing what you read.

Speaking. Informal speaking takes place in a casual environment and generally without a prepared dialogue. Participate in an informal conversation with a classmate about the benefits of a free-market economy. Keep in mind that your style of presentation can influence the opinion of the listener.

Writing. Writing style is the way in which a writer uses language to convey an idea. Select a page or pages of notes you have taken during a class. Evaluate your writing style and the relevance, quality, and depth of the information. Once you have done so, write a one page paper that synthesizes your notes into complete sentences and thoughts. Organize your material so that it is logical to the reader.

Teamwork

Work with a classmate and discuss why you think state, local, and federal taxes are important. What purpose do taxes serve in the economy? Could our economy exist without them? Summarize your conclusions and present them to the class.

Internet Research

Gross Domestic Product (GDP). Select a 10-year period at any point in history, such as 1987 to 1997. Use the Internet to locate the gross domestic value figures for those years. Plot this information on a graph showing the GDP over time. Try to determine what lead to any periods of expansion or contraction and any peaks and troughs.

Inflation Rate. Use the Internet to research the inflation rate over the last ten years. Make a list of years that had the greatest inflation rates. Next, make a similar list of the years that had the highest unemployment rates. Compare the two lists. Did you notice any trends? Using your lists, analyze the relationship between inflation and unemployment.

Unemployment Rate. Determine how the unemployment rate is calculated. Do you believe this calculation accurately reflects how many people are unemployed? Prepare a slide show to illustrate your findings and defend your position.

Monetary Policy. Monetary policy requires a balance between pumping enough money into the economy and slowing down the amount of spending. Conduct Internet research on monetary policy. Analyze how the Fed has used monetary policy in the current economy.

Portfolio Development

College and Career Readiness

Certificates. A *certificate* is a document that serves as evidence of completion of an activity, training, or other accomplishment. For example, a certificate might show that you passed an examination testing your knowledge of cybersecurity. Another one might show that you can key data at a certain speed.

Certificates are sometimes awarded to an individual as proof of receipt of scholarships, grants, or other recognition. For example, those who participated in competitive events for a Career and Technical Student Organization (CTSO) will probably have certificates that reflect leadership positions, awards, or other honors that were earned.

Some certificates provide evidence of specialized training without a degree being granted. These programs are designed for individuals who are not seeking a degree, but are looking to update their current skills or taking courses specifically for employment.

Certification is a professional status earned by an individual after passing an exam focused on a specific body of knowledge. Some jobs *require* certification. For example, a position as an information technology specialist may require industry specific hardware or software certifications. Already having and displaying a certification makes it more likely you will be seriously considered for the position.

1. Collect certificates of accomplishment that you have earned that are not associated with a degree or certification. You can arrange them in order of importance or dates earned.
2. Collect diplomas, proof of certification, and other examples that relate to educational accomplishments. This could mean making photocopies or digital scans of the original documents. If scanning, be sure to follow the naming conventions you established for your digital portfolio. These documents should be arranged in a logical order.
3. Update your master portfolio spreadsheet.

CTSOs

Event Prep

Promoting the Benefits of Entrepreneurship. Some Career and Technical Student Organizations (CTSOs) have competitive events where the chapter spends the school year developing and carrying out a marketing campaign that promotes entrepreneurship. This event provides chapters with the opportunity to demonstrate knowledge of entrepreneurial concepts while making presentations to audiences in their community. For the competition, the chapter is required to prepare a report detailing a marketing campaign and present the report to a panel of judges.

To prepare for an entrepreneurship marketing campaign chapter project, complete the following activities.

1. Read the guidelines provided by your organization. Make certain that you ask any questions about points you do not understand. It is important to follow each specific item that is outlined in the competition rules.
2. Contact the association immediately at the end of the state conference to prepare for next year's event.
3. As a team, select a theme for the marketing campaign to promote entrepreneurship.
4. Decide which roles are needed for the team. There may be one person who is the captain, one person who is the secretary, and any other roles that will be necessary to create the plan. Ask your instructor for guidance in assigning roles to team members.
5. Identify your target audience, which may include business, school, and community groups.
6. Brainstorm with members of your chapter. Make a list of the benefits and opportunities available through entrepreneurship that can be communicated beyond your chapter membership.
7. This project will probably span the school year. During regular chapter meetings, create a draft of the report based on direction from the CTSO. Write and refine drafts until the final report is finished.

CHAPTER

18 Business in the Free Enterprise

In a free enterprise system, privately owned businesses are in competition with one another to meet consumer demands and generate profit. Businesses can take on multiple forms in order to meet these goals. A business might be profit or not-for-profit. It can act as a producer, intermediary, or service business. Its ownership might be that of a sole proprietorship, partnership, or corporation. The decisions about how a business will function are often made by those who establish the business. These people are entrepreneurs who start a business to become self-employed and work for themselves.

Being self-employed offers many advantages, but it comes with much responsibility, and some drawbacks. As with all else in the work world, becoming self-employed should be a decision that has been well-researched and thought about carefully.

Focus on Finance

Consumer Emotions and the Economy

Since it is often described with data and charts, the economic system appears to function according to logic, science, and cold, hard facts. However, human emotions play a huge role in the economy. The best example of this is the ups and downs of the stock market. It can be highly volatile, fluctuating with consumer confidence and anxiety. The feelings and behaviors of consumers can cause economic upturns and downturns. When consumers are optimistic about the economy, they spend more money, which boosts the economy. When they are feeling anxious or pessimistic, they curtail their spending, which depresses the economy.

The US economic system is built on faith and trust. For example, millions of people put their money into banks because they trust that it will be safe there. The banks make money by taking in deposits and lending to businesses and other consumers. If anything should happen to frighten large numbers of depositors, they can demand their money and a bank failure can result.

College and Career Readiness

Reading Prep. The summary at the end of the chapter highlights the most important concepts. Read the chapter and write a summary of it in your own words. Then, compare your summary to the summary in the text.

Sections

Asier Romero/Shutterstock.com

Section 18.1 Business in the Private Sector

Essential Question

Why is it important that citizens understand the basics of business in the free enterprise?

Objectives

After completing this section, you will be able to:

- Identify business basics.
- Describe the three basic forms of business ownership.
- Explain alternative ways a business can be organized.

Terms

business
revenue
expenses
profit
for-profit business
not-for-profit organization
North American Industry Classification System (NAICS)
extractor
manufacturer
intermediary
wholesaler
retailer
service business
consumer market
business-to-consumer (B2C)
business market
business-to-business (B2B)
government market
institution
proprietorship
liability
partnership
partnership agreement
corporation
limited liability company (LLC)

Business Basics

Business is the term for all the activities involved in developing and exchanging products.

The primary goal of business is to generate revenue. **Revenue** is the earnings that a business receives for the goods and services it sells. Revenue is also called *income*. **Expenses** are the costs involved in operating a business. Examples include rent expenses and salaries expenses. **Profit** is the difference between the income earned during a specific period of time and the expenses incurred during the same period. Profit is also called *net income*. In a free enterprise system, business can operate and compete for profits with limited government regulation or interference.

There are three core goals of successful businesses. Each of these goals relates to generating adequate revenue. The three goals are as follows.

- *Pay debts.* Banks and other entities that have extended loans to the business must be repaid on time.

- *Provide return for investors.* Those who have a stake in a business expect to get returns on their investments.
- *Finance future growth.* For a business to continue operating, money must be available to finance future growth.

To generate revenue, businesses produce goods and services to sell to customers. Economic decisions must be made to maximize profit. Three *economic questions* must be answered about producing and distributing products:

- What should we produce?
- How should we produce it and with what resources?
- For whom should we produce it?

Businesses that meet the needs of the customer generally are successful and meet their core goals. However, the economy can have a direct impact on revenue and expenses as well as profit. As you recall from Chapter 17, the US economy fluctuates between periods of economic growth and slowdown. The *business cycle* also follows fluctuations between periods of economic growth and slowdown. When consumers believe the economy is strong or improving, they tend to be optimistic and spend more. Revenue and profits have the potential to increase. When the economy is at its peak, growth has slowed, but prices may continue to increase. The opportunity to increase prices may increase profits. Or, it may discourage consumers from purchasing, which decreases profits. At this time, a business must decide how to control expenses and maximize revenue.

In general, when consumers are doubtful about the economic future, they spend and borrow less. Interest rates, unemployment, and other factors must be considered. In order for a business to meet its goals, it must learn how to manage economic factors that influence its success.

Types of Business

In the United States, there are many different types of businesses that provide goods and services to customers. A **for-profit business** is an organization that generates revenue. One of its sole purposes is to be productive and generate money for its owners. A **not-for-profit organization** is an organization that exists to serve some public purpose. The money it raises is used to support a cause rather than make money for its owners.

Businesses are classified by industry. An *industry* is a group of businesses that produce the same type of goods or services. One way to distinguish businesses is to use NAICS codes. The **North American Industry Classification System (NAICS)** (pronounced nākes) is a numeric system used to classify businesses and collect economic statistics. This system was developed by the United States, Canadian, and Mexican governments for trade purposes. Figure 18-1 lists the major industrial categories of NAICS. More information on NAICS is available through the US Census Bureau.

Organizations are either part of the public sector or private sector. Governmental organizations are part of the *public sector.* Schools, the military, and the Internal Revenue Service are part of the public sector. Their purpose is to serve the public.

NAICS Business Classifications	
Code	**Industry Title**
11	Agriculture, Forestry, Fishing and Hunting
21	Mining, Quarrying, and Oil and Gas Extraction
22	Utilities
23	Construction
31–33	Manufacturing
42	Wholesale Trade
44–45	Retail Trade
48–49	Transportation and Warehousing
51	Information
52	Finance and Insurance
53	Real Estate Rental and Leasing
54	Professional, Scientific, and Technical Services
55	Management of Companies and Enterprises
56	Administrative and Support and Waste Management and Remediation Services
61	Educational Services
62	Health Care and Social Assistance
71	Arts, Entertainment, and Recreation
72	Accommodation and Food Services
81	Other Services (except Public Administration)
92	Public Administration

Source: US Census Bureau

Goodheart-Willcox Publisher

Figure 18-1 The North American Industry Classification System (NAICS) is a numeric system used to classify businesses and collect economic statistics.

The *private sector* consists of all other organizations that provide goods and services. In general, businesses in the private sector can be divided into three categories, as shown in Figure 18-2.

- producers
- intermediaries
- service businesses

Producers

Producers are businesses that create goods and services. Producers are important in the economy because they create products that can be used by individuals, businesses, and government.

Businesses in the Private Sector		
Producers	**Intermediaries**	**Service Businesses**
• Organic farmer • Logging contractor • Automobile manufacturer	• New car dealership • Floral supply wholesaler • Grocery store	• Tax accounting firm • Beauty salon • Currency exchange

Goodheart-Willcox Publisher

Figure 18-2 Businesses in the private sector can be divided into three categories.

Extractors are an example of producers. **Extractors** are businesses or people that remove natural resources from the land. Natural resources are also called *raw materials*. Extractors sell natural resources to manufacturers.

Manufacturers are businesses that use materials from other producers to make products. Some manufacturers use raw materials purchased from extractors. These businesses are called *raw-materials manufacturers*. They are also known as raw-materials producers. Manufacturers generally use assembly lines to mass-produce identical products. They create an end product that is sold for use by individuals, businesses, or governmental agencies.

Ekaterina Pokrovsky/Shutterstock.com

Farmers are producers who raise crops and livestock that are sold to either end users or other producers.

Farmers are another type of producer. They raise crops and livestock that are sold to either end users or other producers.

Intermediaries

People and businesses that sell the goods and services from producers to customers are called **intermediaries**. Intermediaries make sure goods and services are in the right place at the right time to meet consumer needs and wants. Wholesalers and retailers are the most common intermediary businesses.

A **wholesaler** is a business that purchases large quantities of products directly from producers and sells the products in smaller quantities to retailers. An example of a wholesaler is a business that purchases truckloads of lumber from a producer. The wholesaler divides the lumber into smaller quantities. These smaller quantities are sold to retailers like Lowe's or Home Depot.

Wholesalers are often called *distributors*. In addition to providing retailers with the products to sell to customers, wholesalers may offer product storage and transportation services. These services may be used by both producers and retailers.

Retailers are businesses that earn income by buying products from wholesalers or directly from producers and selling them to consumers. Consumers are also called *end users*. In the private enterprise system, retailers directly provide consumers with the products that meet their needs and wants. Food, clothing, and electronics are some of the products provided by retailers.

F8 Studio/Shutterstock.com

A service business earns income by providing consumers with services that meet their needs and wants.

Service Businesses

A **service business** is a business that sells services to consumers or other businesses. These businesses earn income primarily by selling services that meet the needs and wants of consumers. These businesses perform activities and provide expertise for their customers. Examples of service businesses include moving companies, law firms, and interior design firms.

Types of Customers

Each type of business works to meet the needs of its customers. A customer is an individual or group who buys products. The customer of a service business is often called a *client*. The types of customers served by businesses can be separated into three categories, as shown in Figure 18-3.

- Consumer market
- Business market
- Government and institutions

The **consumer market** consists of customers who buy products for their own use. Consumers are actually the end-users of the products. Businesses that sell primarily to individual consumers are in the **business-to-consumer (B2C)** market. Businesses in the consumer market are some of the most familiar

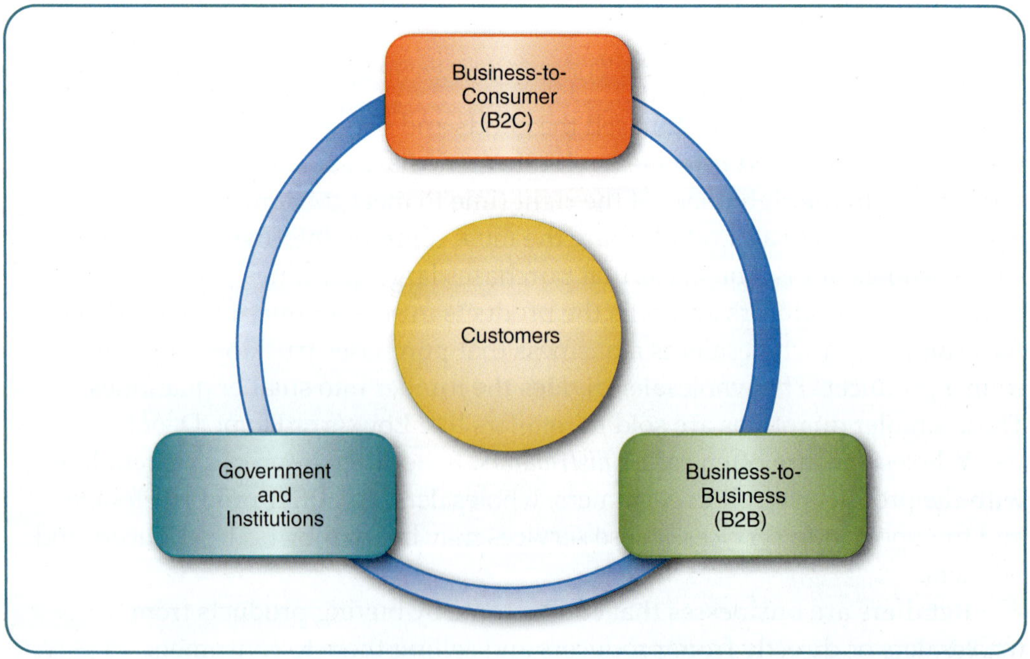

Goodheart-Willcox Publisher

Figure 18-3 Businesses can serve any of the three types of customers or multiple types of customers.

You Do the Math

Measurement Reasoning

Different systems of measurement are used throughout the world. The United States uses a system called the US Customary System that consists of feet, pounds, and degrees Fahrenheit. However, most of the world uses a variation of the metric system called the *Système International d'Unités* (SI), or International System of Units. The SI system consists of meters, grams, and degrees Celsius. The following are some common conversions:

- To convert degrees Fahrenheit to degrees Celsius, subtract 32, multiply by 5, and divide by 9.
- One inch is equal to 25.4 millimeters.
- One pound is equal to 0.45 kilogram.

Solve the following problems.

1. If a carton ready for shipping weighs 18.7 kilograms, how many pounds does it weigh?
2. Marion must ship a temperature-sensitive good to a country that uses the metric system. The product cannot be exposed to temperatures below 0 degrees Fahrenheit. A label must be placed on the package indicating this temperature in Celsius. What temperature must be written on the label?
3. Luis must order a length of specialized steel rod from a company in Germany. The rod must be 0.3 feet long. However, the rod must be ordered in increments of 10 millimeters. What length of rod must be ordered?

and well-known businesses. Customers in the consumer market buy clothes, cars, gifts, and many other products and services. Most of the commercials on television are aimed at the consumer market.

Syda Productions/Shutterstock.com

The consumer market consists of customers who buy products for their own use.

The **business market** consists of customers who buy products for use in a business. A customer in the business market is a *business* that buys products from another *business*. Businesses that sell primarily to other businesses are in the **business-to-business (B2B)** market. For example, a computer-sales business sells computer systems to a law firm. The employees of the law firm will use the computers for various business activities. This is a B2B sale.

The **government market** includes national, state, and local governmental offices and agencies. Government customers buy a wide variety of products. These products range from airplanes and ground vehicles to office supplies and electronics. Governments also buy services, such as food preparation, education, security, and medical care.

Institutions are nonprofit organizations that may be either public or private. A nonprofit organization is an entity that exists to serve a public purpose. These include schools, hospitals, museums, and organizations such as United Way and the American Cancer Society. Like government customers, institutions also buy a wide variety of products and services to support their activities.

Forms of Business Ownership

Private businesses can be structured, or owned, in different ways. The number of owners and size of the business are important factors when choosing the best form of ownership. There are three basic forms of business ownership:

- proprietorship
- partnership
- corporation

Each type of business ownership has unique characteristics, as shown in Figure 18-4.

Proprietorships

A **proprietorship** is a business that is owned and often operated by a single individual. This individual is called the *sole proprietor.* A proprietorship is the simplest and most common form of business ownership. It is also the easiest to establish because no formal action is necessary. In most cases, the owner simply decides to start a business. As long as there is only one owner, the status of "proprietorship" automatically comes from business activities.

A proprietorship can operate under the name of its owner or under a business name. However, a proprietorship cannot be named in a way that implies more than one owner or another ownership structure. For example, names such as Gordy and Associates or Gordy Corp. cannot be used. Also, a sole proprietor cannot choose a business name that is already in use.

Licenses or permits may be required in the locality where the business operates. A *doing business as (DBA)* license may be required if using a business name other than the owner's name. The DBA license, also known as *fictitious name registration*, allows the owner to officially register the business. Some types of business activities may require certain licenses or permits from the local or

Common Forms of Business Ownership

Characteristic	Proprietorship	Partnership	Corporation
Limited liability	No	No	Yes
Number of owners restricted	Yes	No	No
Limited life	Yes	Yes	No
Easy to transfer ownership	No	No	Yes
Double taxation	No	No	Yes
Formation costs	None	Low	High

Goodheart-Willcox Publisher

Figure 18-4 When choosing a form of ownership, the number of owners and size of the business should be considered.

Ethics

Integrity

Integrity is defined as the honesty of a person's actions. Integrity and ethics go hand-in-hand in both personal and professional lives. Employees and employers help establish the reputation of a business in the community. Company employees who display integrity helps create a positive culture for the business, customers, and the community.

state government. For example, hair stylists are typically required to have a state-issued cosmetology license to provide their services to customers.

Advantages of Proprietorships

There are several advantages of the proprietorship form of business ownership:

- *Easy to start.* Once the owner opens the business, a proprietorship is formed.
- *Easy to close.* The business can be closed simply by making the decision to do so. There is no formal or legal process to close operations.
- *Retain all profits.* Since a proprietorship has only one owner, all the profits from the business belong to the owner. Profits do not have to be shared with anyone else.
- *Complete control of operations.* The owner has complete control over all business decisions. A sole proprietor is not required to consult with anyone else when making decisions about the business.
- *Simple tax structure.* A proprietorship is not taxed separately from the business owner. The profit of the business is added to the personal tax return of the business owner. This makes tax preparation simple.

Disadvantages of Proprietorships

Many of the advantages of a proprietorship involve the fact that there is only one owner. However, being the sole owner of a business also has disadvantages:

- *Unlimited liability.* **Liability** means legal responsibility. *Unlimited liability* means the business owner is held personally responsible for all debts and losses of the business. If a business fails, a sole proprietor could lose personal property, savings, investments, and other personal items of value.
- *Limited expertise.* A sole proprietor is in charge of every aspect of operating a business. While the sole proprietor may be extremely good at a trade, the person may not have enough business skills and experience to run a successful business alone.
- *Limited life of business.* A *limited life* means a proprietorship business exists only as long as the owner wants or is able to run the business. A change in ownership automatically dissolves a proprietorship. For the business to continue, the new owner must form a new proprietorship.

Employability Skills

Writing Etiquette

Writing etiquette is the art of using good manners when communicating in written form. It involves careful selection of language and tone. Your professional image is at stake each time you write a letter, send an e-mail, or post a comment or video on a social media site. Writing etiquette involves deciding when it is appropriate to send a letter or e-mail. It also includes writing thank-you notes and responding to RSVPs.

Partnerships

A **partnership** is an association of two or more persons who co-own a business with the objective of earning a profit. There must be at least two parties involved to form a partnership. However, there is no limit to the maximum number of partners involved in a business. Partnerships are businesses created for the purpose of earning a profit. If the objective of an organization is something other than profit, such as a charity or a religious activity, the partnership form of business ownership cannot be used.

There are two common types of partnerships: general partnerships and limited partnerships. A *general partnership* is a business that is co-owned by two or more general partners who are responsible for business operations and obligations. The general partners and the partnership are considered to be one and the same. Typical responsibilities of a *general partner,* or *managing partner,* include:

- authority to make decisions
- active in the day-to-day business operations
- unlimited liability for all partnership debts

A *limited partnership* is a business co-owned by at least one general partner and one or more limited partners. A *limited partner* is a business partner who does not participate in managing the business. The liability of general partners is limited to the amount of investment they have made in the business. Limited partners invest money in the business, but have no authority to make decisions.

Partnership Agreement

A partnership is formed when two or more persons voluntarily enter into an agreement or a legally-binding contract. The **partnership agreement**, also called the *articles of partnership*, is a written contract that establishes a partnership. Partnership agreements can be prepared by the business partners or by an attorney. Most experts recommend the services of an attorney.

There is not a standard format for the articles of partnership, but it should contain the following common details:

- date of the agreement
- names of the partners
- name and location of the business

- nature of the business activity
- duties of each partner
- investment of each partner
- division of profit and losses
- plan for dissolving the partnership
- signatures of the partners

Rido/Shutterstock.com

There must be at least two parties involved to form a partnership, but there is no limit to the maximum number of partners involved in a business.

Advantages of Partnerships

Many of the advantages of a partnership are similar to those of a sole proprietorship:

- *Easy to start.* A partnership is easy to establish. The partnership agreement is created by the partners to define the important terms of the partnership.
- *Combined financial resources.* Several partners can usually contribute more money overall to a business than a single owner can alone.
- *Skills and resources.* Each partner brings skills and experience into the business. Business decisions are based on the combined knowledge, special skills, and experience of all the partners.
- *Simple tax structure.* A partnership is not taxed separately from the partners. Each partner pays income taxes based on that person's share of the business profit.

Disadvantages of Partnerships

The partnership business structure also has some disadvantages:

- *Unlimited liability.* General partners are personally liable for all debts of the partnership, including debts created by other partners.
- *Limited life.* A partnership is dissolved when a partner leaves the business, no matter the reason. A new partnership agreement is needed when a new partner enters the business.
- *Potential disagreements.* All of the partners will not always agree when making important business decisions. This can lead to disagreements, which could weaken the partnership.

Corporations

A **corporation** is defined by the US Supreme Court as "an artificial being, invisible, intangible, and existing only in contemplation of the law." It is a business that is legally separate from its owners. A corporation has been described an "artificial person" because it has most of the legal rights of an actual person. A corporation can:

- buy and sell property;
- hire and fire employees;
- borrow money;

- enter into binding contracts;
- sue or be sued; and
- make gifts to charitable causes.

A corporation exists only on paper. However, the law recognizes a corporation as a separate legal entity that can act on its own behalf.

Establishing a Corporation

Forming a corporation is more complex than starting a proprietorship or partnership. To form a corporation, articles of incorporation must be filed with the Secretary of State's office in the state of operation. The *articles of incorporation* are a document that includes the names of the corporation's founders, name of the corporation, and type of business that will be conducted.

In the United States, a business does not have to incorporate in the same state where the company headquarters are located. The choice is usually based on two factors:

- the cost of incorporating in a particular state compared to other states
- how favorable a state's incorporation laws and taxes are compared to other states

The corporation's founders create *corporate bylaws* that explain the practices and procedures to be followed in conducting business. The bylaws typically include the name and address of the business, the type of stock that will be issued, the number of shares of stock that will be issued, and procedures for stockholder meetings. *Stock* is a share of ownership in a corporation. Those who own stock are stockholders, or shareholders, of the corporation. Some corporations pay dividends. A *dividend* is a portion of the corporation's earnings distributed to stockholders.

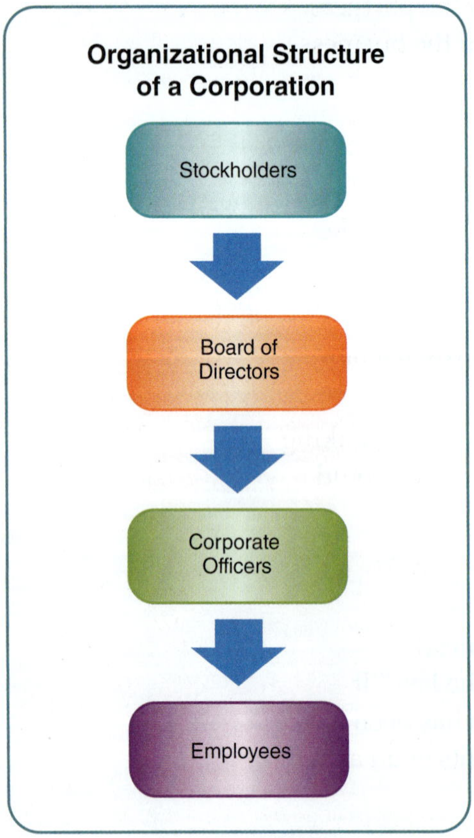

Goodheart-Willcox Publisher

Figure 18-5 The organizational structure of a corporation is more complex than most other business types.

The stock of public corporations is listed on an organized stock exchange. A *stock exchange* is where securities are bought and sold through stockbrokers. The New York Stock Exchange (NYSE) is a well known example. Anyone who wishes can buy stock of a public corporation. All financial information of public corporations must be made public. Private corporations do not sell company stock on stock exchanges. All the stock is privately owned and sales or profit information does not have to be released to the public.

Stockholders are the owners of the corporation. They participate in managing the business by electing a board of directors. The *board of directors* is a group of individuals who make high-level management decisions for the business and establish company policies. The board also selects a chief executive officer (CEO) and other corporate officers to run the day-to-day operations of the company. Figure 18-5 shows the typical organizational structure of a corporation.

Exploring Careers

Chief Executive

Businesses are run by people in a variety of management levels. In many businesses, the chief executive is the person in charge. Chief executives are responsible for creating policies for a business. They hold the highest position within the company and often have the most authority. Their responsibilities include overseeing the overall direction of their company established by a company's board of directors.

Typical job titles for this position also include *chief executive officer (CEO)*, *chief financial officer (CFO)*, and *president*. Examples of tasks that chief executives perform include:

- direct financial activities
- appoint department heads and managers
- analyze operations
- determine areas of cost reduction, program improvement, and policy change

Chief executive positions require a bachelor degree, but a postgraduate degree may be preferred. Chief executives must also have effective leadership and communication skills, as well as strong analytical and problem-solving abilities.

Advantages of Corporations

The corporation form of businesses offers a number of advantages that are not available to proprietorships or partnerships. Many businesses choose to incorporate once the business is large enough to justify the costs of forming a corporation. The advantages of forming a corporation include:

- *Limited liability.* Limited liability means stockholders are not personally responsible for the debts and obligations of the business. The corporation is responsible for business debts and obligations.
- *Ability to raise capital.* A corporation can raise large sums of capital by selling stock. The ability to raise money helps corporations grow and become more profitable.
- *Continued life.* Corporations continue to operate as long as the business is profitable and the majority of the stockholders want the corporation to continue.
- *Transferring ownership.* The stock of a corporation can be transferred to another investor without affecting the operations of the business.
- *Professional management.* Stockholders elect a board of directors to govern the corporation. The board appoints knowledgeable corporate officers to run the daily business activities.

Disadvantages of Corporations

With all its advantages, the corporation form of business ownership also has a number of disadvantages:

- *Expensive to form.* Forming a corporation requires a great deal of paperwork. In addition to attorney fees, there are application fees, registration fees to sell stock, publication fees, and many others. The fees involved usually total several thousands of dollars.

- *Many governmental regulations.* There are many standards and regulations a corporation must follow to sell stock, which require annual financial reports to be filed with the federal and state governments.
- *Double taxation.* Since a corporation is a separate legal entity, it must pay state and federal income taxes on its profit. Stockholders must add stock dividends to their personal income tax returns. Because of this, the profit of a corporation is taxed twice.

Alternative Forms of Ownership

There are certain business ownership structures that combine elements of proprietorships, partnerships, and corporations. Depending on the goals of the business and the individuals involved, an alternative ownership structure may be beneficial. As with other forms of ownership, tax and legal requirements must be evaluated when considering an alternative business ownership structure.

Three examples of alternative business ownership structures are S corporations, limited liability companies, and cooperatives. The characteristics of these alternative forms of ownership are compared in Figure 18-6.

An *S corporation* is a form of business ownership that provides limited liability to its owners, but is taxed as a partnership. S corporations are restricted to no more than 100 shareholders. All shareholders must be US citizens or residents.

A **limited liability company (LLC)** is a form of business ownership that combines the benefits of a corporation with those of proprietorships and partnerships. Like stockholders of a corporation, owners of an LLC have limited liability. Also, there is no limit to the number of business owners.

Alternative Business Ownership Structures			
Characteristic	**S Corporation**	**Limited Liability Company**	**Cooperative**
Limited liability	Yes	Yes	Yes
Double taxation	No	No	No
Board of directors	Yes	No	Yes
Number of owners restricted	Yes	No	No
Limited life	No	Yes	No
Formation cost	High	Low	Low

Goodheart-Willcox Publisher

Figure 18-6 Limited liability companies and cooperatives combine many of the characteristics of proprietorships, partnerships, and corporations.

Other features of an LLC are more like those of a partnership or a proprietorship. These advantages make the LLC form of business ownership popular with owners of new businesses.

A *cooperative*, or *co-op*, is a nonretail association owned and operated by a group of members for their own benefit rather than for profit. These types of businesses are owned and operated by those using its services. The members of a co-op pool their resources and work together to produce quality goods and services. For example, several supermarkets may join together to pool their resources and operate as a wholesaler. When purchasing in larger quantities, they may be able to get better prices on the goods their businesses need to operate.

Co-ops are run democratically and usually have an elected board of directors. All members of a co-op have voting rights when deciding the actions of the organization. This democratic form of operation ensures that the needs of all members are met.

Section 18.1 Review

Check Your Understanding

1. Describe the primary goal of business.
2. What are the three categories into which customers can be separated?
3. List five details commonly found on a partnership agreement.
4. What are some disadvantages of the corporation form of business ownership?
5. List three alternative forms of business ownership.

Build Your Vocabulary

As you progress through this course, develop a personal glossary. This will help you build your vocabulary and prepare you for a career. Write a definition for each of the following terms and add it to your glossary.

business
revenue
expense
profit
for-profit business
not-for-profit organization
North American Industry Classification System (NAICS)
extractor
manufacturer
intermediary
wholesaler
retailer
service business
consumer market
business-to-consumer (B2C)
business market
business-to-business (B2B)
government market
institution
proprietorship
liability
partnership
partnership agreement
corporation
limited liability company (LLC)

Section 18.2 Entrepreneurship

Essential Question

Why would a person aspire to become an entrepreneur?

Objectives

After studying this section, you will be able to:

- Describe advantages and disadvantages of becoming an entrepreneur.
- Identify major parts of a business plan.

Terms

entrepreneur	franchisor	business plan
franchise	franchisee	

Becoming an Entrepreneur

An **entrepreneur** is a person who owns and operates a business. Entrepreneurs have always played a key role in the growth and success of the American economy. A few of the most successful entrepreneurs have names you will probably recognize. Bill Gates, Walt Disney, and Mark Zuckerberg are all well-known entrepreneurs. Most major corporations were started by one or two people who had an idea and a plan. These individuals started with a dream and a willingness to work hard and take risks.

You may think big businesses dominate the marketplace, but small businesses are the backbone of the US economy. Since the mid-1970s, more than two-thirds of the new jobs in the nation have been created by small businesses. Small firms employ approximately 60 percent of the nongovernmental workforce. Approximately 30.7 million small businesses exist in America today. Most of these employ fewer than 20 workers. The definition of a small business varies by industry, but is based on either the number of employees or the annual revenue.

The rewards of starting and owning a business can be huge. Large and successful corporations that started out as small businesses include Apple, Facebook, Google, YouTube, Amazon, and the Walt Disney Company. However, starting and owning a business can be risky. Thousands of small businesses fail each year. To succeed in a business of your own, it is a good idea to have previous work experience with the product you plan to sell or produce. Entrepreneurs need to know how to manage a business, make sales, and deal with customers and suppliers. They must be able to keep accurate financial records and know the legalities involved in running a business. You will require enough money to get started and operate until the business begins to pay for itself.

Establishing a business requires long hours and hard work. Unfortunately, there is no sure income and no guarantee of success. There is very little financial security at the beginning. However, for those who do succeed, the advantages and rewards can be great. They include not only income and profits, but also independence and personal satisfaction.

Case Study Entrepreneurship

Emelie is the primary owner of a business, and Griffin is a limited partner. Currently, their business is on the verge of bankruptcy. They owe approximately $400,000 on their business loan. Emelie owns 75 percent of the business, while Griffin owns 25 percent. Griffin thinks that they should close the business and liquidate assets to pay off the loan.

A former colleague of Emelie's has shown interest in coming on as a silent partner. This person has business experience and resources to help save the company. The silent partner wants a 40 percent stake, which would require the current partners to both take a cut on their ownership.

Case Review

1. How much money would Emelie owe the bank should they decide to close the business and pay off the loan?
2. How much money would Griffin owe the bank if they close the business and pay off the loan?
3. If they decide to keep the business open and take on a silent partner, what percentage would each now have?
4. What are the pros and cons of taking on a third business partner?

As a business owner, your business can take on four basic forms. You can organize the business as a:

- sole proprietorship;
- partnership;
- limited liability company (LLC); or
- corporation.

Once the form of ownership has been established, the next step is to consider *start-up strategies.* Will the business be a service business, producer, manufacturing business, or retail business? The next strategy is to decide to start a new business, purchase an existing business, or buy a franchise.

To start a business from scratch, entrepreneurs need a new product, service, or operating strategy that sets the business apart from the competition. To buy an established business removes some of the risks typically involved in opening a new business. An existing business has an established location and customer base, as well as relationships with suppliers.

Many new businesses start out as franchised operations. A **franchise** is the right to sell a company's goods or services in a specific area. The **franchisor** is the parent company that sells the rights for another business to operate using its brand. The **franchisee** is the person or company that buys a franchise.

Buying a franchise can be less risky than starting a business from scratch. Franchising enables a business owner to enter a market where a product or service is already known and has an established customer base. However, buying a franchise can be expensive. Additionally, policies and procedures established by the franchisor must be followed by the franchisee. Examples of popular franchise businesses include Subway restaurants, Anytime Fitness, The UPS Store, H&R Block, Ace Hardware, and 7-Eleven stores.

Business Plan

A **business plan** is a formal document that states the goals of a business and includes a detailed strategy of how to achieve the goals and grow the business.

History of Finance

Levi Strauss

In the United States, cotton denim jeans were first made by entrepreneurs Levi Strauss and Jacob Davis. They received a patent for their pants in 1873. The first jeans were created for miners working in California's gold rush. The popularity of denim jeans spread to others who sought durable and comfortable work pants.

Perhaps more than any other garment, jeans are associated with an attitude and a lifestyle. In the 1940s, they became synonymous with freedom and the Wild West because of their popularity among cowboys. During the 1950s, some parents and educators prohibited teenagers from wearing jeans because of their association with rebellion and delinquency.

During the 1970s, jeans became canvases of the wearer. Young people painted, embroidered, and beaded their jeans. Cutoff jeans were also popular. During the 1980s, designer jeans and stonewashed denim were popular. Jean styles became baggy and were worn below the hip. Ribbed, faded, decorated, and designer labeled, denim jeans have been a favorite wardrobe item for generations of Americans.

A business plan will be necessary if you need to obtain a loan or other funding to start the business.

The *US Small Business Administration (SBA)* provides a wealth of information and resources for businesspeople and entrepreneurs. These resources include an online training course in business planning and business plan samples. These samples can be very helpful when writing a business plan.

A business plan serves several purposes. It helps an entrepreneur think through ideas and set goals and objectives. An effectively written business plan can help convince investors and bank loan officers to put money into a new or already existing company.

Writing a business plan should be the first step in creating a business. According to the SBA, a business plan consists of multiple sections.

1. *Executive Summary.* The executive summary is a succinct one- to two-page description of the business. It should grab the reader's attention and make the reader want to learn more. Although it comes first in the plan, it is written last.
2. *Company Description.* The company description gives details about the business and who will run it. It should include mission and vision statements, which are brief descriptions of the business's purpose and its plan for future growth. It should also include company goals and objectives, a company history, and a list of company principals, or key employees.
3. *Market Definition.* The market definition section provides an overview of the industry and market. This includes the current and projected size of the entire market and who the competitors are and how much of the market the business hopes to capture. Characteristics of target customers are given, as well as the customer needs the business will satisfy.
4. *Products.* The products section describes the goods or services the business offers as well as prices charged. The business plan must address the issue of competitiveness by explaining why the goods and services offered will be successful despite competition from other companies.

5. *Organization and Management.* The organization and management section details how the company is organized, including its legal structure (proprietorship, partnership, or corporation). It may include an organizational chart that shows the relationships among various departments and employees. Biographies of company leaders and any special licenses and permits held by the business are given.

takasu/Shutterstock.com

A business plan is necessary to obtain a loan or other funding to start the business.

6. *Marketing and Sales Strategy.* The target market was defined in the market definition section. How the business will reach this market is outlined in the marketing and sales strategy section. It includes information on the four Ps of marketing: positioning, pricing, promotion, and place. The positioning information describes the niche the goods or services will fill relative to goods and services already available. The pricing information describes what competitors charge and what customers are willing to pay. It gives a rationale for pricing. The promotion information outlines advertising, sales events, and other strategies to get product information to consumers. The place information discusses how the products will be distributed or put into the hands of consumers.
7. *Financials.* The financials section gives a balance sheet, income statement, and cash-flow statement for the business. A balance sheet measures the net worth or value of a business at a particular time. An income statement reports the revenue and expenses of a business and shows a net income or net loss. A cash flow statement reports how cash moves in and out of a business. Financial statements for a proposed business should contain estimates of these costs over one year as well as a summary of start-up costs and budgets.
8. *Appendices.* Appendices may be included in the business plan. Some items that may be in the appendices include company brochures, résumés of those in leadership roles, copies of published articles about the business, photographs of products, and contracts. Include any important information that does not fit in the other sections of the business plan.

A business plan should be updated as a business grows. Goals and objectives, as well as strategies to achieve them, may change over time.

Section 18.2 Review

Check Your Understanding

1. What is an entrepreneur?
2. The definition of a small business is based on what information?
3. What is the purpose of a business plan?
4. List the sections of a business plan.
5. What financial statements should be included in a business plan?

Build Your Vocabulary

As you progress through this course, develop a personal glossary. This will help you build your vocabulary and prepare you for a career. Write a definition for each of the following terms and add it to your glossary.

- entrepreneur
- franchise
- franchisor
- franchisee
- business plan

Review and Assessment

Chapter Summary

Section 18.1 Business in the Private Sector

- Business is all the activities involved in developing and exchanging products. Their customers are the consumer market, business market, and government and institutions. Successful businesses have three core goals: pay debts, provide return for investors, and finance future growth. Three general types of businesses in the private sector are producers, intermediaries, and service businesses. Producers are businesses that create goods and services.
- Businesses can be structured in different ways. The number of owners and size of the business are important factors in determining the best form of ownership. Three basic forms of business ownership are proprietorship, partnership, and corporation. Each form has unique advantages and disadvantages.
- Alternative forms of business ownership combine elements of proprietorships, partnerships, and corporations. These alternative forms include S corporations, limited liability companies, and cooperatives. Like other forms of ownership, each of these has advantages and disadvantages.

Section 18.2 Entrepreneurship

- An entrepreneur is a person who owns and operates a business. The business can take one of four basic forms: sole proprietorship, a partnership, a limited liability company, or a corporation. For entrepreneurs who succeed, the advantages and rewards can be great. They include not only income and profits, but also independence and personal satisfaction.
- A business plan helps an entrepreneur think through his or her ideas and set goals and objectives. These parts are typically included in a business plan: executive summary, company description, market definition, products and services, organization.

Review Your Knowledge

1. What are the three economic questions that are answered by businesses?
2. Describe three core goals of successful businesses.
3. What is the purpose of the North American Industry Classification System?
4. Explain the three basic forms of business ownership.
5. Name three alternative ways a business can be organized.
6. Describe advantages and disadvantages of becoming an entrepreneur.
7. Explain the three start-up strategies an entrepreneur could choose.
8. Why is a business plan needed when starting a business?
9. What is one resource for entrepreneurs looking for help with business plan writing?
10. Identify the major parts of a business plan.

Apply Your Knowledge

1. Make a list of four natural resources. Give examples of products that are created from each resource. What role do producers, intermediaries, and service businesses play in creating the products you listed?

2. Create a chart listing ten businesses in your community. Identify which businesses are for-profit and which are not-for-profit. For each business, indicate if it is part of the public sector or the private sector.
3. Identify an example of a not-for-profit organization with which you are familiar. What services does this organization provide? How does this organization raise funds?
4. Compare the forms of business ownership discussed in this chapter. What characteristics do they have in common? How are the ownership structures different? Create a chart that compares the features of the forms of business ownership.
5. A group of students plans to start a delivery service. Which business ownership structure should they choose? Consider the size of the business, the type of business activities performed, and the number of owners. Write a paper explaining your answer.
6. In this chapter, the names Bill Gates, Walt Disney, and Mark Zuckerberg are mentioned as well-known entrepreneurs. Compare other well-known entrepreneurs and the businesses they started. Then create a list of characteristics that are common to all of the entrepreneurs on your list.
7. Create a list of 10 small businesses in your city and surrounding area. Describe the types of products they sell and their operating hours. Note any similarities and differences.
8. Create a chart listing the pros and cons of three different start-up strategies. Which strategy involves the most amount of risk? Which involves the least amount of risk? Make a decision as to which strategy you would feel most comfortable with if you were to start a business.
9. In this chapter, you learned that an effectively written business plan can help convince investors and bank loan officers to put money into a new or already existing company. Why do you think a well-written business plan can help sway a loan officer? Should it be required for an entrepreneur to provide a business plan when applying for a loan? Why or why not?
10. A business plan is a formal document that states the goals of a business and includes a detailed strategy of how to achieve the goals and grow the business. What are the consequences of putting misleading or fictitious information in one's business plan?

Apply Your Math Skills

1. Kevin and Ethan are looking to buy a franchised restaurant. The franchise requires an initial investment of $750,000. Between them, they have $230,000 in savings and another $100,000 in assets. They have been approved for a business loan of $275,000. Will they have enough money to apply for a franchise? If not, how much more money will they need to raise?
2. Maeghan, Mary, and John are siblings who have decided to open a business as a three-person partnership. Their ownership percentages are based on their individual investment to the company. Mary invested the most, providing $62,000. Maeghan invested $23,750, and John invested $6,500. Based on their investments, what are their ownership percentages?

Communication Skills

College and Career Readiness

Speaking. A presentation is usually a speech given to a group of people. This chapter discussed different ways to start a business. Plan and deliver a speech to a group of business people about an idea you have to start a business. Be clear in your perspective for the idea and demonstrate solid reasoning.

Listening. *Informative listening* is the process of listening to gain specific information or instructions from the speaker. Ask a classmate to give you directions to the school cafeteria. Take notes as the directions are given. If necessary, ask the speaker to slow down or repeat a point. Summarize your notes and retell the directions to your classmate to confirm your understanding of them. Follow the directions as they were given. Did you arrive at the cafeteria?

Writing. Becoming a business owner in your community would require that you model integrity, ethical leadership, and effective management. Make a list of actions that you could take to meet these requirements.

Teamwork

Working with your team, discuss the three major types of business in the private sector. Which type of business does your team think is most important to the economy? Make a list of reasons why the team thinks their choice is most important to the economy. Did everyone agree?

Internet Research

Business Ownership. Primary research is conducted by the writer in preparation for writing a report. The most common types of primary research are interviews, surveys, and experiments. Before research begins, questions should be formulated. Using the Internet as a resource, formulate research questions that should be answered when investigating types of business ownership. Next, decide how you would approach getting answers to these questions. Would it be interviews, surveys, or experiments? Explain your reasoning.

Economic Questions. Conduct Internet research on the basic economic questions. Summarize how these questions relate to economic systems, including the traditional, command, market, and mixed economic systems.

Businesses in the US Economy. The state of the economy can have a direct impact on the profit, revenue, and expenses of business. Use the Internet to conduct research on the state of the US economy today. Identify factors that affect the profit, revenue, and expenses of businesses operating in the United States.

Portfolio Development

College and Career Readiness

Clubs and Organizations. Participation in an organization, academic club, or sport demonstrates that you have the skill set to work with others and be a team player. Many soft skills, such as appreciation for diversity, leadership, and social responsibility, are learned from participating in a club or group. Documenting that you have been a member of an organization shows an employer that you are responsible, a hard worker, and a team player.

Showing evidence that you have participated in competitive events, such as those organized by CTSOs, is a valuable addition to a portfolio. These competitions support lifelong learning and the application of the skills learned in real-world situations. Participation in competitive events encourages leadership, teamwork, and career development. If you have participated in an event for a club or sports team, write a summary of your role and what you learned from the experience.

1. Identify organizations, academic clubs, or sports teams to which you belong. Create a document that lists each membership using word-processing software. Include the name of each organization, its contact information, and the dates that you were active. Use the heading "Clubs and Organizations," or another appropriate title, and your name. Save the document, and update your master portfolio spreadsheet. Remember to back up each document on your flash drive.

CTSOs

Business Financial Plan. Creating a business financial plan is a competitive entrepreneurship event that may be offered by your CTSO. This may be an individual or team event. There may be two parts to this event: the written plan and the oral presentation of the plan. The event calls for the development of a written business plan that will likely be judged prior to the competition. Written events can be lengthy and take a lot of time to prepare. Therefore, it is important to start early. The rules for this event are similar to other business plan presentations. However, writing this plan requires research on the means of financing a business and the institutions and individuals that provide such financing.

To prepare for writing a financial plan, complete the following activities.

1. Read the guidelines provided by your organization. There will be specific directions given as to the parts of the business plan and how each should be presented. All final format guidelines will also be given, including how to organize and submit the business plan. Be sure to ask any questions about points that you do not understand.
2. Read the research topic assigned by your CTSO. Do your research early. Research may take days or weeks, and you do not want to rush the process.
3. Study this chapter to learn about financial plans.
4. Visit the website of your CTSO and create a checklist of the guidelines you must follow. Ask yourself: Does this event still interest me? Can I do what is necessary to be successful at the event? If you answered "yes," move forward with the writing process.
5. Set a deadline for yourself so that you write at a comfortable pace.
6. After you write your first draft, ask a teacher to review it and give you feedback.
7. Once you have the final version of your finance plan, review the checklist you prepared. Make sure you have addressed all the requirements. Your score will be penalized if a direction is not followed exactly.
8. Practice presenting the presentation.

CHAPTER

19 Global Trade and the Economy

Economic globalization is the economic connections among governments, businesses, and citizens of the world. It is the flow of goods, services, money, labor, technology, and ideas across national borders.

As a major force behind globalization, international trade plays an essential role in every nation's economic system. It influences supply, demand, prices, competition, consumer choice, and governmental policies. It affects job opportunities and living standards around the world.

Globalization has its benefits, such as providing a large selection of product at low prices. However, it does come at the cost of some Americans losing employment. Understanding the global economy can help you find your place in the job market. It can also help you learn to manage your personal finances in a competitive marketplace.

Focus on Finance

Antiglobalization Movement

The term *antiglobalization* describes individuals and groups who oppose globalization. The basic goal of the antiglobalization movement is to promote social justice and human rights. Antiglobalization groups also work for the elimination of inequities between the poor and the rich around the world.

Many in this movement are not against globalization in general. Rather, they object to a type of globalization driven by the needs of wealthy countries and multinational corporations. They believe that international trade agreements and global economic institutions put corporate profits above the well-being and livelihood of people. For example, opponents of organizations such as the World Trade Organization and the World Bank contend they enable large global economic institutions to support their own corporate and financial interests. These organizations put in place policies and practices that are not available to small businesses and individuals.

College and Career Readiness

Reading Prep. Scan this chapter and look for information presented as fact. As you read this chapter, try to determine which topics are fact and which are the author's opinion. After reading the chapter, research the topics and verify which are facts and which are opinions.

Sections

racorn/Shutterstock.com

Section 19.1 Economic Globalization

Essential Question

How does globalization impact your personal finances?

Objectives

After studying this chapter, you will be able to:

- Describe the flow of goods and services in the global economic system.
- Explain the flow of labor among countries.
- Analyze the effect of multinational corporations on the global economy.

Terms

economic globalization	trade deficit	multinational corporation
international trade	specialization	subsidiary
culture	absolute advantage	outsourcing
import	comparative advantage	offshore outsourcing
export	economy of scale	onshoring
trade surplus	migrant	cartel

Flow of Goods and Services

Consider this scene. After silencing an alarm clock manufactured in China, a consumer in the United States gets dressed in jeans produced in Thailand and a T-shirt made in Israel. Breakfast is cereal sprinkled with California raisins made from grapes picked by migrant farmworkers. Before leaving, the consumer uses toothpaste made in a Nigerian factory by employees of an American corporation. Once outside, the drive to work at a multinational corporation with offices in 30 countries begins in a vehicle made in the United States by a Japanese automaker. Like this fictitious consumer, you live in a world that is globalized.

Globalization refers to the process of becoming worldwide in scope. **Economic globalization** is the flow of goods, services, labor, money, ideas, and technology across national borders. It is changing the way people communicate, shop, and conduct business, which impacts an individual's personal finances.

International trade is one of the major forces behind globalization. **International trade** is the buying and selling of goods and services across national borders and among the people of different nations. It has been going on for thousands of years. Many of the earliest travelers were traders looking for natural resources, new products, and new markets for their goods. They created trade routes that crisscrossed continents and oceans. Most trade today occurs between individuals and businesses in different nations. The government in each nation regulates and sets the parameters for international trade.

Culture is an important consideration for international trade. **Culture** is the shared beliefs, customs, practices, and social behavior of a particular group or nation. Culture influences how people respond to the communication and behavior of individuals and organizations. It affects how people think, work, and interact with others. For example, in the United States a topic is "tabled" if it is put off for another time. In contrast, the same phrase in Great Britain means to "bring it to the table" for discussion. Additionally, the concept of time may be interpreted differently in some cultures. The workday may not be the eight-hour workday common in the United States. In the United States, many companies work Monday through Friday and are closed on Saturday and Sunday. This may not be the case in other countries.

Imports and Exports

International trade is discussed in terms of imports and exports. **Imports** are the goods and services that come into a given country from other countries. The *importer* is the business or consumer who buys these goods and services. **Exports** are the goods and services grown or made in a given country and then sold in world markets. The *exporter* is the party who sells goods or services in foreign countries. Much of what is consumed in the United States is produced in the United States. However, products and services that cannot be provided in sufficient quantity or quality at the desired price are imported.

chungking/Shutterstock.com

Goods are sent all around the world to fuel the global market.

Imports represent money flowing out of the country, while exports represent money flowing into the country. *International capital flows* refer to the purchase or sale of financial or real assets across national borders. Money flows into a country when foreigners invest in that country's assets. Money flows out of a country when its citizens, businesses, or governments invest in assets in other countries.

The United States is a dominant power in global economic markets. It is the world's largest importer and a major market for more than 60 countries. Millions of people across the globe depend on the United States for their livelihoods. When the US economy falters and consumers decrease spending, workers at home and around the world lose their jobs.

The United States is the world's third largest exporter of manufactured goods followed closely by Germany. China is the world's largest exporter and one of the major global trading partners of the United States. According to the US Census Bureau, the United States imported about $435 billion worth of goods from China in 2020 while exporting about $124 billion in goods to China. This is a $311 billion trade imbalance with China.

What Is Traded

For many people, the subject of international trade conjures images of giant containers being loaded onto and unloaded from ships at US ports. These containers hold trade goods, which are physical items such as food, furniture, toys, computers, and car parts. World imports and exports also include intermediate goods, such as lumber and oil, that are used to produce other goods. Figure 19-1 lists some of the goods imported into and exported from the United States. The United States imports more products than it exports.

Trade in services accounts for a sizeable piece of imports and exports. These services are provided by businesses, including banking, transportation, insurance, law, telecommunication, and entertainment companies. This sector is rapidly increasing as the world seeks more professional services in research, consulting, and information processing. The United States exports more services than it imports. Figure 19-2 lists some of the services exported from the United States.

The United States has a trade surplus in services. A **trade surplus** is a favorable balance of trade. Overall, the United States has a trade deficit. A **trade deficit** is an unfavorable balance of trade. Top import and export trading partners for the United States are listed in Figure 19-3.

Imports and Exports of the United States

Category	Imports	Exports
Industrial supplies	Oil	—
Consumer goods	Automobiles	Vehicles
Capital goods	Electronic equipment	Machines, engines, electrical equipment
Agriculture	Fruit, coffee products, sugar-related products	Soybeans and poultry meat

Goodheart-Willcox Publisher

Figure 19-1 The United States has a trade deficit for goods, meaning it imports more than it exports.

US Service Exports

Financial services—investing services, insurance services
Information services—computer consulting, data processing
Other services—architectural design, construction, engineering, legal services, advertising, marketing, accounting, management, technical training, travel, tourism, entertainment, transportation services

Goodheart-Willcox Publisher

Figure 19-2 The United States exports more services than it imports.

Why Trades Occur

Two parties trade with each other because each expects to benefit from the transaction. One party receives a product or service and the other receives a payment. You probably make dozens of trades every day. For example, you might go to a restaurant, give the clerk some money, and receive lunch in return. In this case, you have traded money for a good, and the restaurant has traded a good for money.

Buying what you need can be easier and more efficient than trying to make all of the items yourself. The same is true for countries. No country can produce all of the goods and services that its people and businesses need and want. However, it can provide a range of products and services. Then it can trade these for whatever it cannot produce. This is called specialization. **Specialization** is a method of production in which a particular range of products and services is produced. The types of goods and services that countries specialize in depend on factors such as climate, geography, and natural resources; human resources; and consumer preferences.

Top Import and Export Trading Partners for the United States

Exports	Imports
Canada	China
Mexico	Mexico
China	Canada
Japan	Japan
South Korea	Germany
Germany	Vietnam
United Kingdom	South Korea
Netherlands	Ireland
Brazil	Taiwan
India	India
Taiwan	Switzerland
Singapore	Italy
Belgium	Malaysia
Hong Kong	United Kingdom
France	France

https://www.census.gov/foreign-trade/statistics/highlights/toppartners.html

Goodheart-Willcox Publisher

Figure 19-3 This table lists the current top nations with which the United States trades in the world market.

Climate, Geography, and Natural Resources

Climate, geography, and access to natural resources vary from one country to another. In part, these factors determine what a particular country can and cannot produce. Even the United States, a country with varied climate and geography, cannot produce enough of certain items, such as coffee and cocoa, to meet consumer demand.

For example, the tropical climate of Costa Rica makes it an ideal place to grow bananas, but in the United States there is a limited area in which bananas will grow. Thailand, China, and Indonesia produce most of the world's rubber. Bolivia has the largest stores of lithium in the world, which is used in batteries. The vast natural gas fields of Russia supply that country with more natural gas than it needs. Likewise, Saudi Arabia and other countries have vast reserves that can produce an excess of oil. The climate and geography in parts of the United States make it well suited to grow much of the world's corn, wheat, and soybeans. Each country exports what it produces in excess of its needs.

Human Resources

The quality of the labor force in a particular country determines what it can and cannot produce. What is the literacy rate? Does a large share of the population have computer skills? How many colleges, universities, and specialized training programs are available?

Case Study *Global Economy*

Timothy is a freshman in college. The ability to speak Spanish would be an advantage in any future career. According to the career counselor, the best way to become fluent in the language is to complete a study-abroad program in Spain for a semester.

Unfortunately, the value of the US dollar has weakened and living expenses are no longer affordable. The airfare to Spain has also increased more than 20 percent because fuel prices have risen. It looks like a semester in Spain is no longer an option.

Though disappointed, Timothy is still determined to study abroad and is considering a summer study-abroad program in a South American country where the US dollar is stronger and would buy more. The airfare would also be lower.

Case Review

1. Why would a weak US dollar be a disadvantage while studying abroad?
2. Why would a strong US dollar be a disadvantage while studying abroad?
3. How do global issues beyond a person's control have a personal affect?
4. How would travel plans be impacted by the value of the US dollar increasing rather than decreasing?

Industries that require a highly skilled workforce would not take root in a country where most workers are uneducated and unskilled. In these countries, most jobs would be low paying, such as those in the garment-making industry and in factories that do not require highly skilled workers.

Other labor-force factors include pay scale and cost of living. Shoes and clothing are examples of labor-intensive products that often are made in countries where labor is plentiful and pay is relatively low. The workers generally earn less than workers in the United States who do the same jobs. For example, a factory worker in a developing country may make only $5 for a 14-hour workday.

Some companies move their manufacturing operations overseas to take advantage of lower labor costs along with more favorable tax laws and regulations. Their products are then shipped to the United States and sold here.

Consumer Preferences

Some products are imported because they are specialties of particular countries or regions. These products can be made just as efficiently in the importing country. However, the foreign-made products offer style and performance qualities that consumers prefer. This has been the case in high-fashion clothing from European designers; high-performance automobiles from Japan and Germany; and a variety of electronic products, primarily from Asia.

Absolute and Comparative Advantage

The climate, geography, natural resources, and human resources in a country can give it an advantage over other countries. An **absolute advantage** exists when a country can produce goods more efficiently and at a lower cost than another country. The United States has an absolute advantage over Costa Rica in the production of wheat. On the other hand, Costa Rica has an absolute advantage over the United States in producing bananas. Both countries can benefit from trading wheat for bananas.

Even if a nation could produce all of the goods and services its citizens and businesses need and want, there are still advantages to trading with other nations to due comparative advantages. A **comparative advantage** exists when a country specializes in producing a product more efficiently than another country. The country with the comparative advantage will have a lower opportunity cost in producing the product.

When individuals, businesses, or nations specialize in the activities for which their opportunity costs are lowest, everyone benefits. Countries tend to export what they produce most efficiently. They import the goods and services produced more efficiently in other countries. When nations trade with each other, consumers gain more choices and lower prices.

One of the reasons for comparative advantage is a concept called the economy of scale. **Economy of scale** means the cost of producing one unit of something decreases as the total number of units produced increases. This is because the costs of production are spread over more units. If a business can sell more of a product by expanding into overseas markets, it can take advantage of the economy of scale.

Flow of Labor

In addition to increasing the movement of goods and services between countries, globalization increases the flow of labor. Suppose an American business opens an office in another country. If American workers staff this new office, that is American labor flowing to another country. On the other hand, many workers come to the United States seeking jobs. In these cases, labor is flowing into the United States. The gap between wealth and poverty in countries

Aleksandar Dickov/Shutterstock.com

The United States has an absolute advantage over many countries in the production of wheat.

is a major cause of migration and immigration. Developed countries such as the United States draw people seeking economic opportunities.

Migrants

A person who temporarily moves from one place to another is a **migrant**. Migrants may move within a country or between countries. For example, there are many migrant farmworkers who move from place to place as crops grow and require labor. Today, approximately three in every 100 people in the world are migrants.

When workers migrate, labor flows from one place to another. In many cases, migrant workers send money back to their families. This represents money flowing out of the location to another location, such as from one country to another.

Many migrants are people seeking better opportunities to work and earn a living wage. For example, a person can earn on average about five times more working in the United States than working in Mexico.

Immigrants

People who permanently move from one country to another are *immigrants.* They are called *emigrants* when they leave one country and *immigrants* when they enter another country. There are many reasons people immigrate, including political and economic reasons or due to natural disasters. When people immigrate for economic reasons, they move to countries that offer better opportunities for work and higher wages. These are the same reasons that people migrate.

When people immigrate, labor flows from one country to another. In some cases, immigrants will send money back to their families in the home countries. However, since immigrants are permanently relocating, often the money they earn stays with the immigrants and there is no flow of money out of the country.

More than 44 million people, or 14.7 percent of the US population, are immigrants. When the US-born children of the immigrants are included, that population is 80 million or about one-quarter of the total population of the United States.

Impact of Multinational Corporations

Much of globalization is driven by the growth of multinational corporations. A **multinational corporation** is a business that has facilities or other assets in more than one country. Multinational corporations often are created when several companies in different countries are combined. Some multinational corporations are so large that their assets are greater than the GDPs of some countries. These large companies have greatly increased the amount of global trade.

An example of a multinational corporation is Johnson & Johnson, which was founded in 1886. With corporate headquarters in New Jersey, it is comprised of more than 265 subsidiary companies in more than 60 countries. A **subsidiary** is a business that is controlled by another business. Johnson & Johnson employs more than 125,000 people worldwide.

Multinational corporations with headquarters in the United States employ millions of people around the world. Also, millions of Americans work for US-based subsidiaries of multinational corporations headquartered elsewhere. For example, the Japanese automaker Toyota employs thousands of workers in the United States. Foreign multinational corporations can be found in all 50 states. Approximately three to four percent of all workers in the United States are employed by foreign multinational corporations. Many companies and brand names that are thought to be American are actually subsidiaries of foreign multinational corporations, as shown in Figure 19-4.

American Subsidiaries of Foreign Multinational Corporations	
Company or Brand	**Owner**
7-Eleven	Seven and I Holdings (Japanese)
Adidas	Adidas AG (German)
Alka-Seltzer	Bayer Schering Pharma AG (German)
AMC Theaters	Dalian Wanda Group (Chinese)
Anheuser-Busch	AB InBev (Belgian)
Ben & Jerry's	Unilever (British-Dutch)
Breyers	Unilever (British-Dutch)
Caribou Coffee	JAB Holding Company (German)
Dial Corporation	Henkel KGaA (German)
Firestone Tire & Rubber	Bridgestone (Japanese)
Frigidaire	AB Electrolux (Swedish)
Gerber	Nestlé (Swiss)
Holiday Inn	InterContinental Hotels Group (British)
Puma	Groupe Artémis S.A. (France)
Purina	Nestlé (Swiss)
Reebok	Adidas (German)
Shell	Royal Dutch Shell (Dutch)
Sunglass Hut	Luxottica Group (Italian)
T-Mobile	Deutsche Telekom (German)
Trader Joe's	Aldi Nord (German)

Goodheart-Willcox Publisher

Figure 19-4 A vast majority of the companies whose products you use every day are actually multinational corporations.

History of Finance

Silk Road

One of the most famous trade routes was called the Silk Road, created around 100 BC. Named for the lucrative silk industry in China, the Silk Road was a network of roads that connected Europe, North Africa, and Asia. The Silk Road extended 10,000 km (6,400 miles), and there were several routes that those looking to trade could take. The main traders were of Chinese, Persian, Somali, Greek, Syrian, Roman, Armenian, Indian, and Bactrian decent. Caravans of traders exchanged gold, glass, perfumes, and other Western goods for the East's silk, ceramics, spices, and iron. People, plants, animals, ideas, knowledge, and culture also flowed back and forth. The spread of Christianity and Buddhism in Asia are both attributed to the Silk Road, as is the influence of Hellenistic, Iranian, Indian, and Chinese cultures on the visual arts. In 2014, the United Nations Educational, Scientific, and Cultural Organization (UNESCO) named a 5,000 km portion of the Silk Road called the Chang'an-Tianshan Corridor a World Heritage Site, which designated it as physically and culturally significant.

One Product, Many Origins

A product label that reads "Made in the USA" or "Made in China" only tells part of the story. Many of the world's largest companies operate in several countries. Today, the parts and labor that go into the production of almost any product come from many different countries. The idea of "country of origin" for manufactured goods has lost its meaning in a globalized world.

Electronic products, for example, require components from suppliers all over the world. American companies buy these components chiefly from India, Philippines, Russia, China, Canada, Taiwan, and Ireland. An estimated 90 percent of iPhone parts are made in other countries. The phones are assembled largely in China. Even so, Apple is credited with creating well over 300,000 jobs in the United States while outsourcing thousands of jobs to other countries as well.

Outsourcing is moving sections of a business to other companies or to subsidiaries in other locations. **Offshore outsourcing**, or *offshoring*, is moving sections of a business to another country. Labor is cheaper in many other nations than in the United States. In addition, foreign manufacturers often offer the flexibility and skills companies seek. Workers in other countries may have longer workdays and workweeks than in the United States. This can help companies meet production deadlines.

While outsourcing may offer a company cost savings and greater productivity, it also results in job losses for workers at home. This job loss may be in the form of jobs not added or, in some cases, existing jobs may be eliminated. If existing jobs are cut, the displaced workers must find new jobs. For some workers, they may need to upgrade their skills and seek retraining to find new jobs.

US-based subsidiaries of foreign companies account for over five million jobs in America. These companies are engaged in offshore outsourcing because the jobs are in America, not in the company's home country. For example, Volvo and BMW are foreign car manufacturers with factories located in South Carolina. Toyota, Nestlé, T-Mobile, and Sony Corporation are just a few of the other foreign companies that outsource jobs to the United States. These companies provide jobs to American workers in the United States.

Onshoring is outsourcing within the country where the company is located. For example, a New York City–based magazine publisher may choose to use a printer located in the United States rather than one located in China. In doing so, the publisher has outsourced the printing, but has engaged in onshoring because the printer is located in the United States. In another example, when an American company returns operations from another country to the United States, it has changed from offshoring to onshoring.

Flow of Capital Investment

The growth in the number of multinational corporations has increased the flow of capital investments around the world. *Capital investments* are money used to generate income or to invest in a business or asset. Many economists believe that the flow of capital investments, rather than the flow of goods and services, is the most powerful force driving globalization today.

Money flows from one country to another when a parent company builds a factory overseas or lends money to a foreign subsidiary for expansion. A large share of global trade today is the movement of raw materials, goods, services, and product parts from one subsidiary of a multinational corporation to another.

Another type of international investment occurs when investors buy or sell the stocks and bonds of foreign companies. Investors include individuals, businesses, and groups of people who pool their money in pension and mutual funds. These funds are then used for international investments.

Cartels

A **cartel** is a group of countries or firms that controls the production and pricing of a product or service. It has the same economic effect as a monopoly. An example of a cartel is the Organization of Petroleum Exporting Countries (OPEC). OPEC nations work to set prices for oil by controlling the supply. Their decisions largely determine market prices for crude oil and, ultimately, the amount you pay for fuel to run your car and heat your home.

PhotoStock10/Shutterstock.com

The Organization of Petroleum Exporting Countries (OPEC) acts as a cartel by setting prices for oil and controlling the supply.

Many multinational corporations have achieved worldwide dominance in their industries. For example, some large agribusiness companies control the world market for seeds and other agricultural products. While these may not be outright cartels, their enormous wealth and power can give them significant influence over governments and global trade policies.

You Do the Math — Currency Conversion

It may be necessary to convert currency when doing business with another country. To determine the exchange, you can use one of the many currency converters found on the Internet.

Solve the following problems.

1. You want to buy two books published only in the UK. The prices of the books are listed in British pounds (GBP or £). The cost of the books is £17.98. The current exchange rate is $1.00 = £0.60797.
   A. What is the cost of the books in US dollars? (Round up to the nearest cent.)
   B. Shipping from the UK is £9.97. What is the total cost of your purchase including shipping in US dollars?
2. An Indian student attending school in the United States is going to make a $3,500 tuition payment to the school. The money that was saved up for school is in Indian rupees (INR or ₹). The current exchange rate is $1.00 = ₹66.00. What is the cost of the tuition payment in rupees?

Section 19.1 Review

Check Your Understanding

1. What is the difference between economic globalization and international trade?
2. What role does culture play in international trade?
3. Why do people trade?
4. Explain the influence of capital in globalization.
5. What is the difference between offshoring and onshoring?

Build Your Vocabulary

As you progress through this course, develop a personal glossary. This will help you build your vocabulary and prepare you for a career. Write a definition for each of the following terms and add it to your glossary.

economic globalization
international trade
culture
import
export
trade surplus
trade deficit
specialization
absolute advantage
comparative advantage
economy of scale
migrant
multinational corporation
subsidiary
outsourcing
offshore outsourcing
onshoring
cartel

Section 19.2 International Monetary System

Objectives

After studying this chapter, you will be able to:

- Describe the relationship between currency strength and the balance of trade.
- Explain the government's role in global trade.
- List examples of trade organizations and the purposes of each.
- Describe what you can do to develop the skills needed to succeed in a global economy.

Essential Question

How does the exchange value of money influence global trade?

Terms

foreign exchange market (FOREX)	trade barrier	World Trade Organization (WTO)
exchange rate	currency manipulation	General Agreement on Tariffs and Trade (GATT)
balance of trade	free trade agreement (FTA)	International Monetary Fund (IMF)
balance of payments	European Union (EU)	
free trade		

Foreign Exchange Market

When people buy and sell goods to one another in the same country, they use the same currency. In the United States, that currency is the dollar. However, when buyers and sellers are in countries that use different currencies, they must first determine the value of one currency in relation to the other. This involves the foreign exchange market, or *foreign currency market.* The **foreign exchange market (FOREX)** is a financial marketplace for buying and selling the currencies of different countries. It works like a stock market for foreign currencies. Figure 19-5 shows examples of international currencies.

The foreign exchange market affects your life every day. It determines how much you pay for the goods and services you rely on. However, most people only learn of the foreign exchange market when they travel to another country. A currency, like a product, has a price. The **exchange rate** is how much one currency buys in another currency. It can be thought of as the price of the second currency stated in the first currency.

International Currencies		
Country	**Currency**	**Abbreviation**
United States	dollar	USD
European Union	euro	EUR
United Kingdom	pound	GBP
Australia	Australian dollar	AUD
Canada	Canadian dollar	CAD
Mexico	peso	MXN
Japan	yen	JPY
South Korea	won	KRW
China	renminbi	CNY
Brazil	real	BRL
Saudi Arabia	Saudi riyal	SAR
Venezuela	bolivar fuerte	VEF
India	rupee	INR
South Africa	rand	ZAR

Goodheart-Willcox Publisher

Figure 19-5 There are multiple currencies used in the world as reflected in this table.

For example, if you go to Canada, you may need to exchange US dollars (USD) for Canadian dollars (CAD). If the exchange rate is CAD 1.10 for USD 1.00, a traveler should get CAD 110 for each USD 100. The bank or currency exchange may charge a fee for converting currency. Figure 19-6 shows a sample of five currency exchange rates. You can exchange money at banks, airports, and currency exchanges. Airports usually charge the highest fees. A number of online currency conversion calculators is available.

Exchange rates are constantly changing. Supply and demand drive the exchange rates. The more desirable a currency, the greater the demand for it.

Currency Exchange Rates (value per USD)			
Currency	**2018**	**2019**	**2020**
British Pound	£0.750148 GBP	£0.783652 GBP	£0.779494 GBP
Canadian Dollar	$1.296654 CAD	$1.327074 CAD	$1.340771 CAD
European Union Euro	€0.847541 EUR	€0.892882 EUR	€0.876819 EUR
Japanese Yen	¥110.430067 JPY	¥109.007953 JPY	¥106.72534 JPY
Mexican Peso	$19.227887 MXN	$19.246267 MXN	$21.46617 MXN

https://www.ofx.com/en-us/forex-news/historical-exchange-rates/

Goodheart-Willcox Publisher

Figure 19-6 The exchange rate determines how much one US dollar will buy of another currency.

There are several factors that determine the desirability of a currency. The currencies of countries that are politically and economically stable are more desirable to investors. The value of a nation's currency also can be affected by changes in its interest rates. The higher an interest rate, the greater the return on an investment. Higher interest rates draw foreign investors, and this increases the demand for the domestic currency. A country's rate of inflation, debt, and import-export balance can also affect its currency's desirability.

Businesses must also use the foreign exchange market when conducting business in other countries. For example, suppose a business located in China wants to buy road-building equipment from an American company in Peoria, Illinois. The equipment costs USD 500,000. To make the purchase, the Chinese firm needs to convert its currency, the yuan renminbi (CNY), into USD. How much will this purchase cost in Chinese currency? Suppose the foreign exchange rate on the day of purchase is:

USD 1.00 = CNY 6.21
then the cost is calculated as:
USD 500,000 × 6.21 = CNY 3,105,000

When American businesses buy Chinese products, they may be able to trade in dollars rather than converting to the yuan renminbi. This is because many countries, including China, accept the USD due to its stability relative to other currencies. The USD is the strongest *international reserve currency,* which means it is considered a safe and stable currency. However, converting to domestic currency may be less costly than conducting business in USD as the companies accepting USD may not use the current exchange rate on the foreign exchange market.

spectrumblue/Shutterstock.com

When the dollar is strong, goods and services imported into the United States cost less. When the dollar is weak, goods and services imported into the United States cost more.

Exchange Rates and Trade

When the dollar is strong, or its value is high, goods and services imported into the United States cost less. This raises demand for imports. On the other hand, buyers in other countries must pay more for exports from the United States. This lowers the demand for US exports. When the dollar is strong, foreign investors must pay more for US companies, real estate, and stock, so they tend to invest less.

When the dollar is weak, or its value is low, goods and services imported into the United States cost more. This lowers demand for imports. On the other hand, buyers in other countries pay less for exports from the United States. This raises demands for US exports. Foreign investors pay less for US companies, real estate, and stock, so they tend to invest more. A weak dollar also attracts more tourists to the United States because they will get more for their money.

Balance of Trade

To understand international trade, you need to know the meaning of balance of trade. **Balance of trade** is the difference between total imports and total exports of goods and services. These numbers are recorded in the balance of payments. The **balance of payments** is an account of the total flow of goods, services, and money coming into and going out of the country. When a country buys, or imports, more products than it sells, a *trade deficit* develops. If it sells, or exports, more than it buys, the country has a *trade surplus*.

The United States has had a trade deficit every year since 1976. Figure 19-7 shows the deficit between 2000 and 2020. Currently, the United States runs the largest trade deficit among worldwide trading nations, and China runs the largest surplus. This balance of trade makes it possible for China and other nations to accumulate US dollars. With accumulated dollars, these nations can buy more US goods, services, and assets such as real estate, securities, and businesses.

The United States needs more foreign investors to buy treasury bills, corporate securities, and real estate to help pay off the growing national debt. Most economists think that, in the long run, this situation is not healthy for the economy. They think that a trade deficit coupled with the growing national debt weakens the US economy and its leadership position in the world.

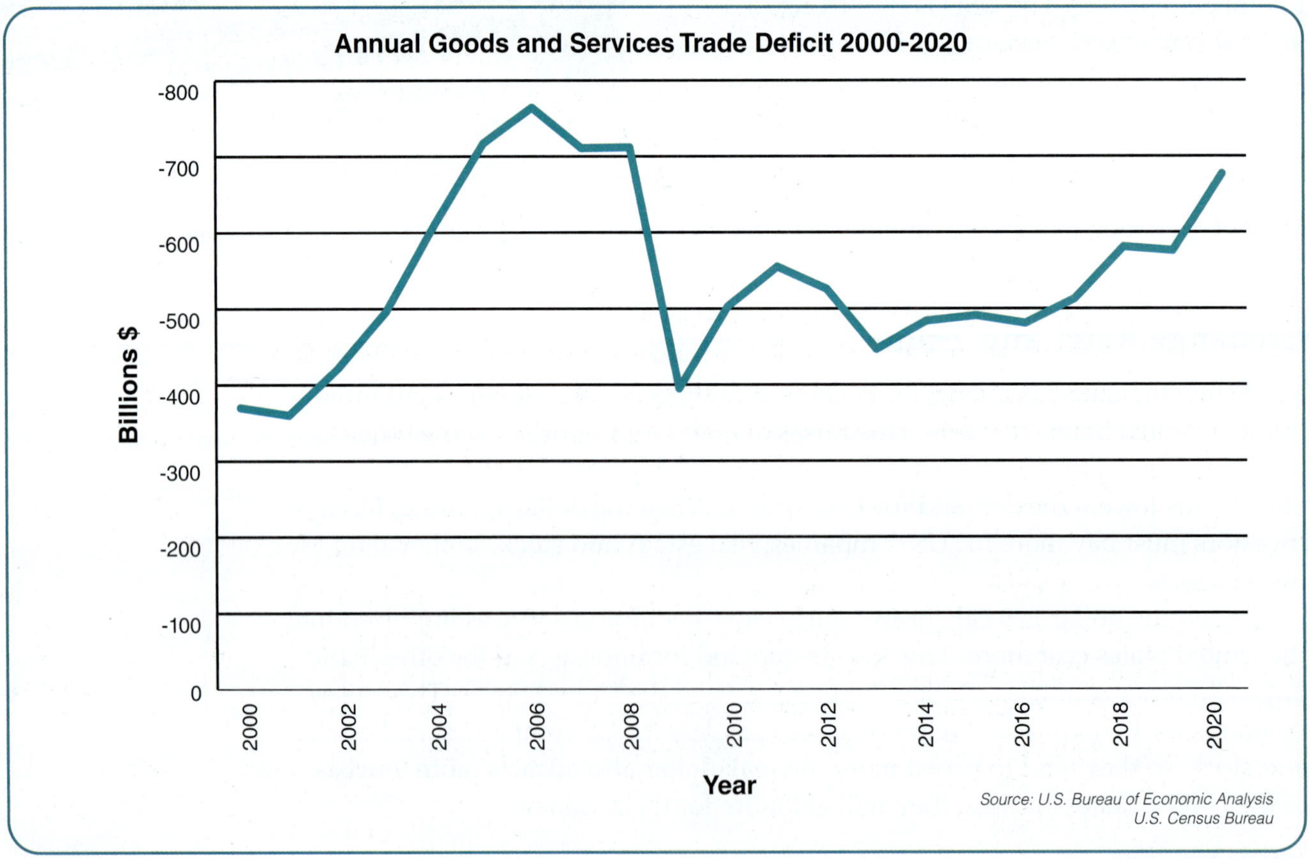

Goodheart-Willcox Publisher

Figure 19-7 Every year since 1976, the United States has had a trade deficit, meaning its imports were greater than its exports.

Employability Skills

Appropriate Dress

The workplace requires appropriate dress. Most businesses have a dress code that employees are required to follow. Some jobs require uniforms or protective clothing. If your company requires business attire, clarify with your manager what is expected. Remember that *business casual* does not mean jeans or shorts. Always dress appropriately and do not push the limits on the appearance that is expected from you.

Government's Role in Global Trade

Governments regulate trade. Governmental trade policies are often described as either free trade or protectionism. **Free trade** is a policy of limited governmental restrictions on trade. Individuals and businesses are relatively free to buy and sell goods and services from people and businesses in other countries. Governments generally favor free trade that opens markets for the goods and services they export.

However, there are critics of free trade. In the United States, critics claim that free trade increases the US trade deficit in world markets as the United States continues to import more than it exports. Others say free trade benefits larger companies and developed nations at the expense of smaller businesses and emerging nations. Many people think that free trade threatens cultural identity and individuality as large multinational corporations replace small local businesses. These critics feel multinational corporations create a "worldwide sameness" as they become a dominant presence around the globe. In many countries, there is a fear that imports bring foreign values and cultural identities with them at the expense of local traditions, values, and culture.

A policy of setting trade restrictions is often called *protectionism*. These trade restrictions are designed to protect businesses at home from foreign competition. Imports are restricted to make domestic products more attractive to consumers. However, protectionist policies can backfire as other countries retaliate by imposing their own trade restrictions.

Why Nations Favor Free Trade

Theoretically, trade among nations benefits all of the trading nations. Therefore, everyone benefits when tariffs and other barriers to trade are kept to a minimum. Free trade stimulates growth and raises productivity and living standards in the countries that open their economies to world markets.

Free trade also allows countries to specialize in those goods and services they produce more efficiently and trade for those that they produce less efficiently. This is the comparative advantage.

Free trade generates more innovation and product improvements as a result of competition and the international exchange of ideas and technologies. The

Ethics

Online Sellers

Unethical individuals might set up a website, accept electronic payments, and then disappear without shipping products to the buyer. Before purchasing anything online, consumers should verify the seller. The Better Business Bureau evaluates sellers and informs consumers about sellers' trustworthiness.

worldwide competition and innovation free trade promotes result in a greater variety of goods and services at lower prices.

Free trade creates new investment opportunities stemming from capital flows across international borders. It also promotes cooperation and peaceful relations among nations who become trading partners. When a country needs and wants goods and services produced in other nations, there is a strong incentive to maintain working relationships between those nations.

Why Nations Favor Restricted Trade

Nations, including the United States, restrict trade for various reasons. Some of these reasons include to:

- protect domestic industries;
- protect the jobs of workers;
- reduce dependence on foreign sources;
- control distribution; and
- address unfair trade practices.

Governments often seek to protect domestic industries from foreign competition. Foreign competitors may be able to produce products for much less than can domestic companies. To protect domestic companies, governments may restrict imports or impose tariffs to make the price of imported products closer to similar domestic products.

Protecting domestic industries from foreign competition also protects domestic jobs. If less-expensive imports are allowed into the US marketplace, domestic companies making similar goods may not be able to compete. This could drive them out of business and lead to job losses.

Countries may want to avoid dependence on single sources of necessary items. For example, about one-third of the oil imported into the United States comes from OPEC nations. If OPEC cuts the production of oil, the price of oil will rise, causing serious economic problems in the United States. If restrictions were placed on oil imported from OPEC nations, the United States would have to look for other sources of oil to compensate. These other sources may be domestic or foreign.

Countries may want to control the distribution of products or technologies that threaten national security or provide a competitive advantage. For example, the United States restricts the export of technological know-how and materials that could be used to build weapons. Encryption technology is also restricted, and a license must be granted to export it.

Trade restrictions are often put in place to prevent unfair trade practices by foreign companies. An example of an unfair trade practice is importers engaging in "dumping." This refers to the sale of imported products at artificially lower prices than those charged in the domestic market for similar products. Once the imported products dominate the market and drive the domestic producers out of business, the importer raises the price. To combat dumping, governments may tax these imports to raise their prices so domestic companies can compete.

How Governments Restrict Trade

There are many reasons governments may restrict trade, and there are many ways to do so. Some common methods of restricting trade include several types of trade barriers, subsidies, and currency manipulation. However, these are not the only ways to limit trade.

Adisa/Shutterstock.com

Fruits and vegetables are not permitted to be brought into some countries due to potential diseases they may carry.

Trade Barriers

Governmental policies can discourage imports through trade barriers. A **trade barrier** is any action taken to control or limit imports. There are several types of trade barriers.

- A *tariff* is a tax on imports, which can make the price of domestic products more competitive with imports.
- An *import quota* is a limitation on the number or quantity of imports allowed into the country.
- A *nontariff barrier* is a type of regulation, such as environmental-quality standards or safety requirements, that prevents certain imports.
- An *embargo* is a legal action prohibiting trade with a particular country, usually for political reasons.

Subsidies

A *subsidy* is money paid by an organization, usually the government, to a business or industry to help it remain in operation. Subsidies allow businesses to offer their goods for sale at lower prices. This can restrict trade by making domestic products less expensive than similar foreign products.

For example, suppose an electronics company in another country can produce products at a lower price than American companies making similar products. To restrict the imports, the US government gives the American manufacturers a subsidy that makes the domestic products less expensive than the imported products. The demand for the domestic products goes up, while the demand for the imported products goes down. In effect, the subsidy has restricted the importing of the foreign products.

Currency Manipulation

Currency manipulation refers to action taken, usually by a government or central bank, to increase or decrease the value of the nation's currency. The forces of supply and demand in the currency exchange markets usually determine the value of currency. However, a nation can set the value of its currency without regard for the market. This is currency manipulation.

For example, in late 2015, China devalued its currency by about 2 percent. This was the largest drop in value in nearly 20 years. It was followed by additional drops of 1.6 percent and 1.1 percent on the two subsequent days. One of the reasons for the devaluation was to make China's exports more attractive by effectively decreasing their prices. Another reason was increasing pressure from the global community to allow the currency's value to be determined by the foreign exchange market. The first devaluation was the result of currency manipulation by the Chinese government, but the devaluations on the two following days were controlled by market forces in the foreign exchange market.

When a nation's currency is weak, its exports become less expensive in world markets. What it imports, however, becomes more expensive. As a result, the country tends to increase its exports and decrease its imports. This creates a trade surplus. A weak currency also invites more foreign investment into the country. This often translates into new factories, new jobs, and more products for export. For trading partners, the consequences include trade deficits and increased price competition in domestic markets.

If a nation artificially lowers the value of its currency, it can gain competitive trade advantages. The International Monetary Fund (IMF) prohibits currency manipulation for the purpose of gaining unfair trade advantages.

International Trade Organizations and Agreements

The United States has trade agreements and partnerships with a number of nations and regions of the world. An *international trade organization* deals with the rules and regulations related to trade between member nations. A **free trade agreement (FTA)** is a partnership between two or more countries in which certain requirements related to specific trade goods are outlined. These agreements are also called *international trade agreements*. The goal of free trade agreements is to create economic benefits and opportunities for all participating nations as a result of free trade and investment across their borders. Figure 19-8 lists some of the many international trade organizations and agreements in the world today.

European Union (EU)

The **European Union (EU)** is an economic and political organization consisting of 27 nations, most of which are in Europe. It has the largest economy in the world, surpassing any individual country, although some sources report it as second to the United States or China. Most of the EU member nations share a

International Trade Organizations and Agreements		
Abbreviation	**Organization**	**Country Members**
ASEAN	Association of South East Asian Nations	Brunei Darussalam, Cambodia, Indonesia, Laos, Malaysia, Myanmar, Philippines, Singapore, Thailand, and Vietnam
CAFTA-DR	Central America-Dominican Republic	Costa Rica, Dominican Republic, El Salvador, Guatemala, Honduras, and Nicaragua
EU-27	European Union-27	Austria, Belgium, Bulgaria, Croatia, Cyprus, Czech Republic, Denmark, Estonia, Finland, France, Germany, Greece, Hungary, Ireland, Italy, Latvia, Lithuania, Luxembourg, Malta, Netherlands, Poland, Portugal, Romania, Slovakia, Slovenia, Spain, and Sweden
USMCA	United States-Mexico-Canada Agreement	United States, Canada, and Mexico
OPEC	Organization of the Petroleum Exporting Countries	Algeria, Angola, Congo, Equatorial Guinea, Gabon, Iran, Iraq, Kuwait, Libya, Nigeria, Saudi Arabia, United Arab Emirates, and Venezuela
SADC	South African Development Community	Angola, Botswana, Comoros, Democratic Republic of Congo, Eswatini, Lesotho, Madagascar, Malawi, Mauritius, Mozambique, Namibia, Seychelles, South Africa, Tanzania, Zambia, and Zimbabwe

Goodheart-Willcox Publisher

Figure 19-8 This table lists some of the many trade organizations around the world.

common currency called the euro. The main trading partners of the EU include the United States, China, Russia, and Switzerland.

United States-Mexico-Canada Agreement (USMCA)

In 2018, President Donald Trump signed the *United States-Mexico-Canada Agreement (USMCA)*, which supports mutually beneficial trade leading to freer markets, fairer trade, and robust economic growth. The USMCA replaced the *North American Free Trade Agreement (NAFTA)* after the president deemed NAFTA unfair to the US and pushed for a repeal.

NAFTA was a treaty implemented in 1994 to lower trade barriers and increase trade between the United States, Canada, and Mexico. NAFTA significantly increased trade between the countries, but also resulted in manufacturing jobs being moved from the US to Mexico.

World Trade Organization (WTO)

The **World Trade Organization (WTO)** is a 164-member international organization that establishes trade practices between its member nations for trade that is as free and smooth as possible. It works to ensure agreements are acceptable and fair to all and mediates trade disputes. Practically every trading nation in the world is a member of the WTO. Besides trade in goods, the WTO is also involved in the regulation of trade in services, inventions, and intellectual property. The WTO was created in 1995 to expand the work of the GATT.

The **General Agreement on Tariffs and Trade (GATT)** is a set of international agreements that promotes free and fair trade among nations. This agreement was created after World War II by the Allied nations to aid post-war recovery. GATT agreements attempted to reduce the use of tariffs, quotas, and other trade restrictions.

Other Important Global Organizations

Many of the world's nations have come together in various organizations and forums to achieve mutual goals. These goals often include the establishment of world peace; elimination of hunger, poverty, and disease; and sustainable growth and development. Many of the groups, which often work together, directly or indirectly influence trade and global economics. Some of these organizations include the World Bank, International Monetary Fund, Group of Twenty (G20), United Nations, and Organisation for Economic Co-operation and Development. Many of these groups have similar or overlapping goals.

World Bank

The *World Bank* has as its primary mission to fund specific projects that promote economic development, reduce poverty, and raise living standards. To this end, it provides financial and technical assistance to developing countries. Financial assistance consists of grants and low- or no-interest loans. The World Bank was founded in 1944 and has a membership of 189 countries, which are called shareholders.

International Monetary Fund

Created in 1945, the **International Monetary Fund (IMF)** is an organization that works to stabilize exchange rates and eliminate trade barriers. The mission of the IMF is to oversee the international monetary system. Its 189 member countries are advised on how to better manage their economies. The IMF also helps member nations head off and resolve economic crises.

Like the World Bank, the IMF provides loans and technical assistance to countries. However, unlike the World Bank, the loaned money is not intended to fund specific projects. Rather, the money is meant to help stabilize the overall economy of the country and promote growth.

Group of Twenty

The *Group of Twenty (G20)* is a forum for 19 countries plus the European Union for promoting economic cooperation and decision-making between the member nations. The heads of state of G20 countries meet annually to discuss issues ranging from health to the environment, trade, and terrorism. Throughout the year, the finance ministers and central bank governors of the member nations meet to discuss economic regulations and reforms needed in each member country. Besides the United States, the G20 members are: Argentina, Australia, Brazil, Canada, China, European Union, France, Germany, India, Indonesia, Italy, Japan, Mexico, Russia, Saudi Arabia, South Africa, South Korea, Turkey, and United Kingdom. The leadership role rotates among the member countries.

Stuart Monk/Shutterstock.com

The United Nations is headquartered in New York City, New York, on international territory.

United Nations

The *United Nations (UN)* is an international organization of 193 member countries that addresses worldwide issues such as security, climate change, sustainable development, human rights, disarmament, terrorism, humanitarian and health emergencies, gender equality, and food production. The UN provides a forum where member countries can condemn political aggression and human rights violations. Its programs promote better living standards for people around the world.

When it was created after World War II, the primary purpose of the UN was to maintain peace and security in the world. Today, its most visible activities are providing humanitarian assistance in areas ravaged by war and natural disasters and peacekeeping in areas of conflict.

Organisation for Economic Co-operation and Development

The *Organisation for Economic Co-operation and Development (OECD)* was established in 1961 to promote policies that improve the economic and social well-being of people around the world. It addresses critical global issues and helps governments deal with the economic, social, and governance concerns of globalized economies. It has 37 member nations from around the world. In addition, there are countries in the process of becoming a member and other countries that are key partners. The OECD also has cooperative relationships with several nonmember countries.

Globalization and You

In the future, the citizens of every nation will become, in a sense, citizens of the world. Common interests will include policies governing the use and sharing of resources, environmental concerns, and controlling terrorism. Other issues include broad access to necessary health care, alleviating poverty, and educating citizens for life in a global society.

As the perception of the world gets smaller, the United States will have to decide whether it will become more involved with other nations in a variety of areas. Nations will need to cooperate with one another in addressing issues such as the environment, poverty, terrorism, disease, and disaster recovery. Peacekeeping in areas of conflict will continue to call for international cooperation.

The future is likely to hold both more cooperation and more competition in global markets. There will need to be international agreements on the use of world resources. You will also likely see a continued increase in the exchange of ideas and developments in the fields of science and technology.

Globalization presents advantages and disadvantages, hopes and fears, and pros and cons. It dramatically affects economic conditions and trade in every nation. Both consumers and producers operate in world markets. You are already buying goods and services from other countries.

As a worker, the goods or service your company produces may be sold in other countries or the resources it uses may come from other countries. You may work for a multinational corporation at some point in your life. Your managers and coworkers may be born in other countries. You will be competing for jobs with workers around the world. For all of these reasons, it is important to understand the role of globalization in your life. There are many actions you can take now as a student to better prepare yourself for working in the global community.

As a consumer, international activities will impact your personal financial decision-making. The activities of workers around the world affect the prices of products where you live. In addition, events that take place around the globe have an impact on the economy at home. It is important to consider international and domestic current events and their impact on your personal decisions regarding money.

As a Worker

Globalization influences the demand for both goods and services. This, in turn, influences job creation and opportunities. Increased exports mean growth, and growth means jobs. However, globalization also affects the flow of labor, which may mean jobs are lost.

You may be favorably affected by globalization by an increase in available jobs. When an American company gains access to foreign markets and competes successfully in the sale of its products and services, the company will grow and expand. It will need more workers. There will be more jobs. This also is true when foreign companies open plants or offices in the United States. New jobs are created in the United States.

Africa Studio/Shutterstock.com

Studying math and science is one step a person can take to prepare to be successful in the global market.

You may be unfavorably affected by globalization if you work in an area that is subject to foreign competition. When American companies must compete with popular imports, American workers may lose their jobs as demand for the American products decreases.

In some industries, there may also be layoffs and shifts in employment as a result of offshore outsourcing. Jobs commonly outsourced offshore are those in the manufacturing industries. However, service and professional jobs, especially those in information technology, are also being outsourced offshore.

Exploring Careers

Freight Forwarder

Producers of goods ship their products to businesses who, in turn, sell those products to end users. On each end of these transactions is a freight forwarder. Freight forwarders advise clients on transportation and payment methods for shipping merchandise, both domestically and internationally. They research and estimate shipping rates, arrange delivery of shipments, and track shipments. In addition, they prepare bills, invoices, and other shipping documents.

Typical job titles for this position also include *export agent*, *export coordinator*, and *route specialist*. The following are examples of tasks that freight forwarders perform:

- record shipment costs and weights
- keep records of all goods shipped, received, and stored
- check import or export documentation
- estimate shipping costs
- arrange transport of goods with shipping companies

Freight forwarders are required to have a high school diploma, though a college degree is preferred. Excellent organization skills, attention to detail, and the ability to work cooperatively with diverse groups are necessary. Good technology and math skills are also required.

For example, when you call a computer company's service department, the person who answers is often half a world away. Accountants living in another country may prepare your tax returns. X-rays and other test results can be read and interpreted by medical professionals in distant locations. These all represent jobs that could be in the United States, but are not.

To be successful, prepare for employment in a global market and for the changing cultural and political landscape that lies ahead. Some suggestions are as follows.

- Continue your education.
- Increase your science- and math-related knowledge.
- Improve your skills and knowledge.
- Learn a foreign language.
- Learn about world affairs.
- Travel or live abroad.

Completing high school and getting postsecondary education and training are more important than ever. With offshore outsourcing and the Internet, competition for jobs is global. Jobs that do not require a high level of education or skill are moving to places where workers are paid a small percentage of an American worker's salary. The more education and professional and technical skills you have, the more opportunities and job security you will gain.

The United States currently imports workers to fill many jobs that require science and math backgrounds. There is a great need for workers who have solid foundations in these subject areas. Considering careers in these areas can help you prepare for working in a global environment.

After you enter the work world, keep the door open to education. Stay informed about trends in your field. Take advantage of retraining and educational opportunities on and off the job. Go back to school to learn new skills.

Fluency in almost any foreign language can be a key asset in the work world. Becoming proficient in Mandarin, Russian, Hindi, or Arabic may open doors to job opportunities around the world.

Regularly read newspapers, magazines, and websites that report on international affairs and foreign-policy issues. Seek out books about areas of the world that interest you. Tune in to radio and television programs broadcast from other countries. Find out about international organizations and their function in the world economy.

Enroll in a student-exchange program. Spend a summer working, studying, or doing volunteer work abroad. Visit relatives and friends who live in other countries. Learn about other cultures while having the adventure of your life. As the world grows more interconnected, global issues will become more important to everyone.

As a Consumer

In the global economy, events in other countries can have a serious effect on social and economic conditions where you live. They influence the prices and availability of consumer goods and services, the types and availability of career opportunities, and saving and investment opportunities.

Labor issues have a great impact on the supply of products. If there is a shortage of labor, certain products may not be made in a high enough quantity to meet demand. This drives the prices of those products higher. In this case, it may be a better financial decision to wait to buy the product. Once there is enough labor to make the product in sufficient quantity, the price of the product usually will come down. It may be a better financial decision to wait until this happens to purchase the product.

On the other hand, if there is a surplus of labor, the price of the product is often lower than if there is a labor shortage. This is because the cost of labor often decreases when there is a surplus. By examining the labor situation, you can see that the price of the product is at a low point, so making a purchase may be a wise decision.

Labor is only one factor that can affect the price of products you wish to purchase. International current events related to environmental conditions, political situations, and overall supply and demand all can impact price. For example, the Paris Climate Conference in 2015 was an international event that gradually affects the way you live and spend money. Over 12 days of negotiating between the 195 participating countries, the conference produced an international agreement with pledges from all participants to cut carbon emissions and to take other measures to slow global warming and climate change. The costs of addressing these issues will reach trillions of dollars.

The cost of transitioning to renewable energy sources will impact agriculture and food production, processing, and delivery. This will mean higher prices at the grocery store and in restaurants. Costs will rise for transportation, utilities, travel, energy-efficient products, and production methods. All of these increasing costs affect you as a consumer.

As an individual, you must evaluate what impact international events have on prices now and in the future. For example, as a result of the Paris Climate Conference, the price of cars may increase as more pollution-control measures are added to vehicles. On the other hand, an energy-efficient product may be expensive now because few units are manufactured. However, as the measures dictated by the Paris Climate Conference go into effect, more units of this product may be made, thus decreasing the price of the product even as demand increases.

Evaluate all of the factors affecting price, both here in the United States and globally, before making purchases. Additionally, international and domestic issues can affect the stock market, interest rates for savings accounts and loans, and other economic areas. Wise financial decisions are made when all of the facts are evaluated.

Section 19.2 Review

Check Your Understanding

1. How does a strong US dollar affect US exports?
2. What are some reasons nations restrict trade?
3. Explain the purpose of a tariff.
4. What is currency manipulation?
5. What is the World Bank's mission, and how is it achieved?

Build Your Vocabulary

As you progress through this course, develop a personal glossary. This will help you build your vocabulary and prepare you for a career. Write a definition for each of the following terms and add it to your glossary.

- foreign exchange market (FOREX)
- exchange rate
- balance of trade
- balance of payments
- free trade
- trade barrier
- currency manipulation
- free trade agreement (FTA)
- European Union (EU)
- United States-Mexico-Canada Agreement (USMCA)
- World Trade Organization (WTO)
- General Agreement on Tariffs and Trade (GATT)
- International Monetary Fund (IMF)

Review and Assessment

Chapter Summary

Section 19.1 Economic Globalization

- Economic globalization is the flow of goods, services, labor, money, innovative ideas, and technology across borders. International trade is one of the major forces behind globalization. World imports and exports include both goods and services.
- Globalization increases the flow of labor among countries. Many people are economic migrants seeking better opportunities to work and earn a living. The developed countries, such as the United States, are beacons for people seeking economic opportunities.
- Multinational corporations have greatly increased the amount of global trade. Multinationals employ millions of people. They greatly affect the origins of parts and labor for products, the flow of capital around the world, and the pricing and availability of products.

Section 19.2 International Monetary System

- A nation's currency strength can affect its balance of trade. Foreign buyers must pay more for exports from a country when its currency is strong, so they buy less. Foreign buyers pay less for exports when the currency is weak, so they buy more exports.
- Governments regulate trade. Government trade policies are often described as free trade or protectionism. Theoretically, trade among nations benefits all the trading nations. However, some nations restrict trade for various reasons.
- The United States has existing trade agreements and partnerships with a number of individual nations and regions of the world. The goal of these agreements is to create economic benefits and opportunities for all participating nations as a result of free trade and investment across their borders.
- It is important to prepare for employment in a global market and for changes in the cultural and political landscape. Continuing your education, learning a foreign language, learning about world affairs, and traveling abroad are examples of things you can do to develop the skills needed to succeed in a global economy.

Review Your Knowledge

1. Describe the flow of goods and services in the global economic system.
2. How does comparative advantage affect trade with other nations?
3. Explain the flow of labor among countries.
4. What are migrants and what role do they play in globalization?
5. What is the role of multinational corporations in globalization?
6. Explain the relationship between currency strength and the balance of trade.
7. Explain the difference between a trade deficit and a trade surplus.
8. Explain the government's role in global trade.
9. List examples of trade organizations and their purposes.
10. Describe what you can do to develop the skills needed to succeed in a global economy.

Apply Your Knowledge

1. List three ways international trade affects you.
2. Describe how you think the world would be different with minimal or no globalization.
3. Describe the climate, geography, and natural resources of your state. What is your state known for producing? How do these three factors make your state ideal for production of these goods or services?
4. Conduct an interview with someone who moved to the United States from another country. Be sure to ask why the person decided to move and what the similarities and differences are between the United States and the country of origin. Record your answers and share the interview with the class.
5. Offshore outsourcing is moving business to another country. Assume a manufacturing company has decided to move its operations from the United States to China. What are some of the trade-offs and opportunity costs of this decision?
6. Refer to Figure 19-6, which lists the exchange rates of five foreign currencies compared to the US dollar. Using this table, examine how these exchange rates affect the trading relationship between the United States and the five nations listed in the figure.
7. Reflect on the value of the dollar in today's economy. Is the dollar weak or strong? What economic factors have led to its current value?
8. Explain the impact of imports and exports on the US economy. How does the population benefit? Are there negative aspects to participating in import and export activities? Write several paragraphs to support your opinion.
9. Describe the benefits and importance of globalization for workers, consumers, and citizens.
10. Communication includes verbal, nonverbal, and written forms of expression. Describe the communication barriers that you might encounter as a worker in the global marketplace. How can you prepare yourself for intercultural communication?

Apply Your Math Skills

1. Randy is staying in a hotel in Niagara Falls, Ontario for two nights. The hotel rate is 76.99 in Canadian dollars (CAD) per night. With the current exchange rate, 1 CAD is equal to 0.72 USD. How much will the hotel stay cost Randy in US dollars before tax?
2. Sophie runs an online business selling hand-knitted items. The prices are listed in US dollars. Sophie also charges a 7% tax on every purchase and $8 for shipping. A customer located in Europe wants to purchase a sweater that is priced at $119. The customer wants to know what the total cost of the sweater would be in euros before making the purchase. With the current exchange rate, 1 US dollar is equal to 0.91 euros. How much would the sweater cost in euros, including tax and shipping?

Communication Skills

College and Career Readiness

Reading. *Environmental print* refers to the words you come across in your daily life, such as signage, logos, and advertisements. Locate an example of environmental print in your classroom or school and read the words. What is the purpose or meaning of the environmental print?

Speaking. Participate in a collaborative classroom discussion about trade. Discuss why you think the United States has had a trade deficit since 1976 and imagine possible solutions to the trade deficit. Ask questions that connect your ideas to the relevant evidence that has been presented.

Writing. Choose one of the trade organizations mentioned in this chapter. Write a two- to three-page report that explores why the organization was formed, its history, and the trade-related issues that it handles. Keep careful and accurate records of any sources that you use as references. Be sure to support your thoughts and ideas with facts.

Teamwork

Working with a teammate, discuss international trade. One person should be for open markets and the other person against open markets. Create a chart with your opinions and discuss some of the problems and disputes that have arisen among nations over trade policies.

Internet Research

Global Current Events. Using the Internet, conduct research on global current events. How does globalization affect your personal finances? Explain the effect of globalization on your personal financial decision-making.

International Labor Issues. Labor conditions vary around the world. Conduct Internet research on domestic or international labor issues. Select an article or another resource that explores some of the current labor issues happening around the world. Examine how these issues might relate to the personal financial decision-making of someone living in the United States.

Portfolio Development

College and Career Readiness

Networking. Networking means talking with others and establishing relationships with people who can help you achieve career, educational, or personal goals. You have probably already begun to build one, even if you have not thought of it in these terms. People in your network include your instructors, employers, coworkers, or counselors who know about your skills and interests. Those who participate with you in volunteer efforts, clubs, or other organizations can also be part of your network. These people may help you learn about open positions and may be able to give you information that will help you get a position.

1. Identify people who are part of your network.
2. Create a spreadsheet that includes information about each person. Include each person's name, contact information, and relationship to you. For example, the person might be a coworker, employer, or fellow club member. Save the file. This will be used for your personal use and not included in your portfolio.

CTSOs

Personal Finance. Personal finance is a competitive event you might enter with your Career and Technical Student Organization (CTSO). The personal finance competitive event may include an objective test that includes banking topics. If you decide to participate in this event, you will need to review basic banking concepts to prepare for the test.

To prepare for a personal finance event, complete the following activities.

1. Read the guidelines provided by your organization. Make certain that you ask any questions about points you do not understand. It is important to follow each specific item that is outlined in the competition rules.
2. Review the vocabulary terms at the beginning of each chapter.
3. Review the Checkpoint questions at the end of each section of the text.
4. Review the end-of-chapter activities for additional practice.
5. Ask your instructor to give you practice tests for each chapter of this text. It is important that you are familiar with answering multiple choice and true/false questions. Have someone time you as you take a practice test.

CHAPTER

20

Environmental Responsibilities in an Economic System

Protecting the environment is a critical responsibility as a consumer, citizen, and taxpayer. Individuals, governments, and businesses share responsibility for preserving the environment and managing Earth's natural resources. Climate change, waste disposal, dwindling resources, and urban sprawl are some of the environmental challenges facing society today and in the future.

You can take an active role in protecting Earth. Stay informed about current environmental issues. Learn to conserve and reuse resources in your own life. Participate in community environmental-protection programs. Your tax dollars pay for research to find eco-friendly ways to meet basic human needs. Your votes for policymakers will decide how the country manages natural resources. Learning how your money is spent and what environmental choices you have is in your own best interest.

Focus on Finance

ENERGY STAR Program

The Environmental Protection Agency (EPA) ENERGY STAR program, which began in 1992, helps businesses and individuals save money and protect the environment through superior energy efficiency. The purpose of the program is to identify and promote energy-efficient products and buildings in order to reduce energy consumption and pollution. This is achieved through voluntary labeling of products and buildings that meet the highest governmental energy efficiency standards.

The ENERGY STAR program has increased the usage of energy-efficient goods and services. It has also increased the level of consumer education about environmental protection. American consumers, businesses, and organizations have invested in energy efficiency and are transforming the market for efficient products and practices. This is both creating jobs and stimulating the economy.

College and Career Readiness

Reading Prep. Before reading this chapter, write down everything you know about the topic. As you read, make a list of things you have learned that you did not know before. When you finish the chapter, compare the two lists and share with the class.

Sections

wavebreakmedia/Shutterstock.com

Section 20.1 Environment

Essential Question

Why is it important to preserve the environment?

Objectives

After studying this section, you will be able to:

- Discuss the importance of natural resources in modern society.
- Outline today's major environmental challenges.

Terms

ecology	nonrenewable energy	global warming
sustainable	food insecurity	climate change
conservation	environmental issue	landfill
renewable energy	environmental trend	hazardous waste

Natural Resources

The factors of production are land, labor, capital, and entrepreneurship. As discussed in Chapter 16, *land* is all of the natural resources of a nation. A *natural resource* is a raw material, such as soil, water, minerals, plants, animals, and climate. Natural resources must be balanced in order to preserve the environment. **Ecology** is the study of the relationship between living things and their environment. Scientists who study ecology have found that life on Earth exists in a delicate balance. When that balance is disrupted, the consequences can be serious, unpredictable, and irreversible.

Sustainable practices and conservation preserve natural resources. **Sustainable** means able to be kept in existence. As this term relates to the environment, it refers to using resources responsibly to prevent depletion or permanent damage. **Conservation** is the protection and management of the environment and natural resources to ensure they will exist in the future.

Most natural resources are limited. By 2030, the world's population is expected to increase by about one billion to reach 8.5 billion people. Scientists predict a future in which shortages of basic natural resources, such as energy, water, and food, will affect an increasing number of people.

Energy

Energy sources can be classified as renewable or nonrenewable. **Renewable energy** is a power source that is continually available or can be replenished. This includes solar (sunlight), wind, water, and biofuels, as shown in Figure 20-1. A *biofuel* is composed of or produced from a renewable biological raw material.

Renewable Energy Sources		
Renewable Energy Source	**Description**	**Disadvantages**
Solar	• Sun's radiation that reaches the earth • Can be converted to electricity and heat • Produces almost no undesirable side effects • Used most often and most effectively in warm climates • In cloudy areas, solar energy systems usually need to be used with other forms of power	• Cannot be concentrated into high-grade, usable fuel in large enough quantities • Limited use at night and on cloudy days unless new storage systems are installed to absorb, store, and release energy as needed
Wind	• Large windmill-like turbines turn wind energy into electricity • A wind farm is a business that generates power from multiple turbines at one location	• Many areas lack sufficient wind or space to set up wind turbines • Not a constant or dependable source of energy • Getting wind energy to places that need it requires creating a system of power lines across many miles • Equipment to harness wind energy requires an investment • People who live near wind farms complain about disturbances, such as light deflection off turbine blades
Hydro	• Captures the power of ocean waves or water flowing over a dam to create electricity	• Depends on the presence of enough water
Geothermal	• Uses hot water and steam produced deep inside the earth to create energy	• Sources of geothermal energy are very limited
Biofuels	• Made of biological matter from plants and animals that can be converted to energy • Ethanol is made from grains—corn, sorghum, wheat, sugar cane, etc. • Ethanol is usually mixed with gasoline • Biodiesel is made from plant and animal oils and fats	• Not yet possible to produce adequate quantities of usable energy from any of these sources • Depends on availability of farmland and forests • When land is used to grow sources of biofuels it cannot be used to grow food

Goodheart-Willcox Publisher

Figure 20-1 Renewable energy sources can be replenished.

Examples are ethanol made from corn or sugar beets and biodiesel made from used cooking oil or algae.

Nonrenewable energy is a power source that can be used up or cannot be used again. Nonrenewable energy sources are described in Figure 20-2. Once nonrenewable energy is gone, it cannot be replaced. Nuclear energy is a nonrenewable resource because it is created from uranium, a substance available in limited amounts. Fossil fuels are also nonrenewable energy sources. A *fossil fuel* is an organic substance, such as coal, petroleum, and natural gas, derived

Nonrenewable Energy Sources		
Nonrenewable Energy Source	**Description**	**Disadvantages**
Petroleum and natural gas	• Fossil fuels • Main forms of energy used in the United States today	• Use contributes to air pollution and climate change • Oil spills foul water and kill wildlife • United States is dependent on imports to meet demand • Supplies and prices are controlled by other governments, including those hostile to the United States
Coal	• Also a fossil fuel • Plentiful US source of energy and a major export • Likely to be a major source of energy well into the future	• Difficult to transport • Burning coal contributes to air pollution and climate change • Strip-mining causes long-lasting damage to the land • Converting coal to a gaseous or liquid form is a costly process
Nuclear	• Energy is produced from nuclear fission, (splitting apart) of uranium in nuclear power plants • Produces 20 percent of the electric power in the United States, which is 8 percent of the nation's total energy production • Releases few greenhouse gases • Used as the main source of energy in some countries, including France and Japan	• Questions persist about plant safety and safe waste disposal • Nonrenewable because uranium is scarce • Nuclear waste, improperly handled, could cause catastrophic environmental damage

Goodheart-Willcox Publisher

Figure 20-2 Dependence on nonrenewable energy sources will eventually use up remaining resources.

from the decomposed remains of animals and plants that lived in prehistoric times. Fossil fuels provide more than 80 percent of all energy consumed in the United States. This includes gasoline that powers cars, natural gas that heats homes, and coal that produces electricity.

In 2014, the United States depended on foreign sources for about 27 percent of its petroleum, which was the lowest level since 1985. Dependence on foreign sources of energy is a big concern. The more the United States has to import energy, the more other countries can influence the US economy. Achieving energy independence will require greater efficiency in the use of energy and conservation. It will also require development of new energy sources that are renewable, affordable, and environmentally safe.

Water

Most people in the United States take for granted that water is available, clean, and safe to drink. This natural resource, which is vital to all forms of life, is becoming more precious. In addition to drinking water, water is used in the production of many goods. It is part of the land factor of production.

Many of the common items you buy require a large amount of water to manufacture. For example, nearly two thousand gallons of water are used in the production of one pair of denim jeans, from growing the cotton to processing it into dyed fabric.

Both the availability and quality of water are important environmental issues. Water scarcity creates severe problems. Demands for fresh water increase dramatically with population growth. Conserving water and keeping the water supply clean is vitally important to maintaining a healthy society and economy.

Food

Labor is the work performed by people who turn resources into products. Enough food must be available to support the labor force. The United States is very wealthy and has an abundance of food. In fact, food is one of the major exports of the United States. However, this does not mean that everyone in the United States is well-fed. Roughly 1 in 6 Americans faces food insecurity. **Food insecurity** is the lack of enough food at least part of the time to support an active and healthy life.

Exploring Careers

Environmental Scientist

Environmental scientists work to protect the environment by identifying problems and finding solutions that minimize hazards to the health of the environment and the population. They determine what is in the air, water, and soil to make sure that the environment is safe. These professionals also give advice on how to clean the environment. Environmental scientists typically:

- determine data collection methods for research projects
- collect environmental data for scientific analysis
- analyze samples, surveys, and other information to identify and assess threats to the environment
- develop plans to prevent, control, or fix environmental problems
- develop plans to restore polluted or contaminated land or water
- provide information and guidance to government officials, businesses, and the general public on environmental hazards and health risks
- prepare technical reports and presentations that explain their research and findings

Most environmental scientists work 40 hours per week. The work environment is typically an office or laboratory. They may also spend time in the field gathering data and monitoring environmental conditions. Environmental scientists also travel to meet with clients.

A bachelor degree in environmental science or another natural science, such as biology, chemistry, earth science, or physics, is usually required, and a master degree may increase chances for advancement. Environmental scientists must have excellent analytical, interpersonal, problem-solving, and communication skills. Math and computer skills, as well as attention to detail, are also important characteristics.

Employability Skills

Prompt Response

Business requires prompt responses to customers or coworkers. When people try to reach you via phone or e-mail, respond as soon as possible. If you are not able to do what the person is asking you right away, acknowledge that you have received the call and will follow up at a later time. It is important that the sender knows that the message was received and not lost in transmission.

In many urban areas, there are so-called *food deserts*. These are areas without grocery stores or other sources of affordable, nutritious food. In some cases, the only food available in these areas is from fast-food restaurants or convenient stores that generally do not offer healthy and nutritious options. Some rural areas may also be considered food deserts. Food deserts can lead to undernourishment for those who live in those areas. More information on food deserts can be found on the US Department of Agriculture's website.

In many other countries, food insecurity affects a larger percentage of the population than in the United States. In developed regions, around 5 percent of the population or less faces food insecurity. However, in developing regions, about 15 percent of the population may face food insecurity.

Having a well-fed labor force is essential to maintaining a healthy economy. As the population of the world grows, keeping it fed becomes a greater challenge. Better distribution of food, more efficient methods of growing, and reducing food waste are all ways in which this challenge can be addressed.

Environmental Issues and Trends

An **environmental issue** is a harmful problem that arises as a result of human activities in the environment. Environmental issues are problems that affect the planet's air, water, and soil. Oil spills and air pollution are examples of such problems that affect individuals and families today, as well as future generations of people. The Environmental Protection Agency (EPA) helps consumers and business learn how to protect our planet against these issues.

An **environmental trend** is the progression of human actions toward being more eco-friendly. Consumers and businesses have become more involved in respecting the environment through positive actions and conserving limited natural resources. Reducing a carbon footprint or choosing a renewable resource are examples of how to be responsible for the environment. Governmental programs, such as ENERGY STAR, help businesses and individuals save money and protect the planet through energy efficiency.

The choices you make about the environment involve trade-offs and opportunity costs. Reviewing the examples of environmental issues and trends in Figure 20-3 can help you evaluate how to be socially responsible. Climate change, water and air pollution, and the depletion of natural resources are some of the topics that are important in today's news.

Environmental Issues and Trends	
Issues	**Trends**
Climate change	Alternative energy sources (solar, wind)
Deforestation	Biodegradable products and packaging
Pollution	Efficient energy use
Hazardous waste removal	Energy-saving appliances
Depletion of natural resources	Fuel-efficient vehicles
Urban sprawl	Recycling
Food contamination	Reduction of greenhouse gases
Waste disposal	Local shopping
Water shortages	Water conservation

Goodheart-Willcox Publisher

Figure 20-3 These environmental issues and trends affect individuals and families today, as well as future generations.

Climate Change

Global warming is the steady rise in average temperatures near Earth's surface. Warming temperatures are causing climate change throughout the world. **Climate change** is the shifts in measurements of climate, such as temperature, precipitation, or wind, that last decades or longer.

Both natural processes and human activity contribute to climate change. Activities such as driving cars and generating electricity by burning coal release carbon dioxide. Carbon dioxide (CO_2) is a *greenhouse gas (GHG)*. Like the roof on a greenhouse, greenhouse gases form a layer in the atmosphere that prevents heat from escaping. The burning of fossil fuels is the major source of greenhouse gases in the United States, according to the EPA.

Adding to climate change is *deforestation*, which is the clearing of forests. Trees and other plants filter carbon dioxide from the air, using it and sunlight to grow. When large tracts of trees are cut down by loggers and removed by farmers, fewer plants exist to absorb carbon dioxide. The CO_2 remains in the atmosphere. If carbon dioxide and other greenhouse gases continue to collect in the atmosphere, experts predict serious consequences, as shown in Figure 20-4. Climate change can have a negative impact on the world's economy.

Water and Air Pollution

In 1960, the average American generated about 2.5 pounds of garbage, or waste, each day. Today, the average American generates about 4.5 pounds of garbage each day. Some of this waste is disposed through burning, but most household waste is buried in a landfill. A **landfill** is a permanent waste-disposal site for most solid, nonhazardous waste.

Special sites are devoted to the disposal of hazardous waste. **Hazardous waste** is a substance that is dangerous or potentially harmful to human health or the environment. It can be liquid, solid, or gas. Hazardous wastes are discarded by-products of agricultural, manufacturing, medical, electricity generation, and other sources. Households discard hazardous waste, too. Some examples are paint, cleaners, automotive products, pesticides, and flame-retardants.

Possible Implications of Climate Change		
Possible Climate Change	**Environmental Implications**	**Economic Implications**
Rising sea levels	Ice in arctic region and high altitudes would melt faster if temperatures rise. This would release large volumes of water, possibly flooding many coastal areas.	The rise in sea level could cause damage to many shipping docks, slowing the process of trading internationally. Levees may also have to be constructed to reduce the regular occurrence of flooding.
Weather pattern changes	Some regions would suffer water shortages and drought. Warmer oceans would trigger more hurricanes, which could cause flooding.	A shortage of water could cause crops to die, leading to a decline in food production.
Famine	Extreme weather changes would threaten crop production in many regions, causing food shortages.	A decline in the production of food could cause the prices of these items to go up, making it harder on the consumer to purchase them.
Animal and plant extinction	Weather would probably change faster than many plants and animals could adjust. In the short term, animals would probably try to migrate to more comfortable climates that supported familiar food supplies. Plants, however, would likely die off.	Animal extinction could cause a change in the food chain that could cause people to lose their jobs, such as fishermen not being able to catch the fish they intend to sell. The extinction of bees could also cause problems with medicine and agriculture due to the loss of pollinators.
Human migration	Flooded coastal areas plus shortages of food and safe water could force millions of people from their homes. This might lead to regional conflict.	Regional conflict might lead to war, which could have a significant effect on the economy.

Goodheart-Willcox Publisher

Figure 20-4 Climate change has both environmental and economic implications worldwide.

Also hazardous are fluorescent lamps, batteries, consumer electronics, and anything containing mercury, such as fever thermometers.

Existing landfills are filling up, and building new landfills is costly. Few communities are willing to permit landfills in their area, so new sites are located further from the areas they serve. This requires transporting waste for long distances at considerable cost. The disposal fees are passed along to consumers in the form of higher prices for products and services.

Improper disposal of waste poses serious threats to human health and the environment. If hazardous waste is placed in regular landfills, it can pollute groundwater and cropland. Without proper controls, burning waste can release greenhouse gases that pollute the air and contribute to climate change.

The economic impact of pollution can be great. The cost of cleanup is paid by taxpayers and industry. Additionally, governmental regulations may be placed on businesses and industries that can increase the cost of doing business. This cost is passed on to consumers in the form of higher prices. In some cases, pollution can

kosmos111/Shutterstock.com

The job of an environmentalist involves working to improve environmental issues such as water and air pollution, natural resources, climate change, and land use.

lead to serious health problems for the population. This can place an economic burden on the individuals and the community.

Depletion of Natural Resources

Many of Earth's natural resources are being depleted. For example, crude oil is needed to produce gasoline, which the world needs for commerce and transportation. It is also needed to create plastic products. However, there is a limited amount of oil that can be extracted from the earth.

There are many other natural resources that society relies on to produce goods and services. Iron is needed in the production of many products, including automobiles, household appliances, buildings, surgical instruments, and industrial equipment. Coal is needed to generate electricity and other fuels.

As essential as they are, most natural resources are of limited supply. For some, the existing reserve is down to a few years. For example, the reserves of antimony, an element used in the production of batteries, credit cards, and car parts, are projected to last only five to ten years. The reserves of silver, most of which is used in industry, are limited to 10 to 15 years.

The economic impact of depleting natural resources can be high. As a resource becomes more scarce, its cost increases. In turn, the goods created with that resource cost more. In many cases, the best and least expensive resource is being used to create goods. Alternative resources may exist, but might be inferior in quality or performance or may be more expensive. However, as the current resource becomes economically unfeasible, the alternative may need to be used even if the quality is lower or the cost higher than what is used today.

Land Use

Before the invention of cars, most people worked and went to school within walking distance of their homes. Everything a person needed was concentrated in a compact town center. If public transportation was available, most people used it.

Cars gave people more mobility, and by the mid-20th century, America became a commuter nation. Homes and businesses were built along highways that led to and from city centers. Open land was converted into housing developments, roads, malls, and business parks. This spread-out development, which continues to this day, is described as *urban sprawl*. Many environmental groups oppose urban sprawl, especially when it replaces forests or farmland. They argue that sprawl requires more roads, more driving, and more services than well-planned, concentrated business and residential developments.

As urban areas increase in size, land becomes more valuable as residential or business developments than as a natural resource. Farmland that becomes a residential subdivision or shopping center no longer can produce food or commodities such as cotton. Houses and businesses may be built on land that could hold minerals or other resources, which then are not accessible. All of these factors have an impact on the economy, from reduced natural resources to increased distances goods have to travel to consumers.

Section 20.1 Review

Check Your Understanding

1. List two examples of natural resources.
2. What is a *food desert*?
3. How does deforestation add to climate change?
4. What is the economic impact of depleting a natural resource?
5. Why do some environmental groups oppose urban sprawl?

Build Your Vocabulary

As you progress through this course, develop a personal glossary. This will help you build your vocabulary and prepare you for a career. Write a definition for each of the following terms and add it to your glossary.

ecology
sustainable
conservation
renewable energy
nonrenewable energy
food insecurity
environmental issue
environmental trend
global warming
climate change
landfill
hazardous waste

Section 20.2 Addressing Environmental Challenges

Objectives

After studying this section, you will be able to:

- Explain steps individuals can take to conserve natural resources and protect the environment.
- Identify the role of government in protecting the environment.
- Explain steps businesses can take to reduce their impact on the environment.

Essential Question

How can one individual address environmental challenges?

Terms

environmentalist	home energy audit	composting
biodegradable	recycle	

What You Can Do

An **environmentalist** is a person who is concerned with the quality of the environment and how to maintain it. "Think globally, act locally" is a saying often used to address environmental challenges. There are many steps you and your family can take in your home and community to improve and protect the world environment. Reduce, reuse, and recycle are commonly called the "three Rs of environmentalism." Making a few small changes in your shopping habits, reducing your water and energy use at home, reducing and reusing waste, and conserving fuel all make a positive impact on sustaining the environment. Your actions can be as an individual, a family, or part of a citizen group. These efforts also have an economic impact. You save money, create a demand for environmentally friendly products, and help ensure natural resources will be around for future generations.

SpeedKingz/Shutterstock.com

Reduce, reuse, and recycle are commonly called the "three Rs of environmentalism."

Shop Wisely

Green has become the symbolic color of Earth-friendly products, policies, and lifestyles. Many products now carry "green" labels identifying them as Earth friendly, eco-friendly, or environmentally friendly. However, these terms have no official definition. A careful examination of the manufacturer's goals and accomplishments can help you judge if the company's practices actually benefit the environment.

When buying products such as appliances, furnaces, air conditioners, and electronic equipment, look for energy-saving features. The ENERGY STAR label on a product means it has been independently certified to save energy. When buying dishwashers, clothes washers, toilets, faucets, and showerheads, look for water-saving features. Install low-flow water fixtures. Purchase vehicles that are fuel efficient. Also look for automakers that use environmentally friendly manufacturing processes.

Buy pre-owned consumer goods when they address your needs. You can buy pre-owned items at resale shops, garage sales, and online auction and sales sites. By purchasing pre-owned items, not only are these items kept out of landfills, but the number of new items that must be manufactured is reduced.

Look for products with packaging that is biodegradable. **Biodegradable** means able to be broken down naturally by microorganisms into harmless elements. Cardboard is an example of a biodegradable material.

Support businesses and manufacturers that operate recycling and take-back programs. Many businesses that sell electronics accept old devices, sometimes for a credit, when consumers purchase a new model. Ink and toner printer cartridges often come with a prepaid shipping label to send the cartridge being replaced to a recycling center.

Economics in Action

Pollution Credits

The US government uses market incentives to tackle environmental problems. New programs create markets where "pollution credits" are bought and sold like stocks and bonds. The laws of supply and demand set credit prices.

For example, conservation banking programs reward landowners and local governments for preserving open space, endangered species, and habitats. They earn credits that can be sold. Other people or businesses must buy credits to offset environmental damage they cause. Having to buy credits is costly and discourages practices that are harmful to the environment.

Another example is a cap-and-trade program for greenhouse gas (GHG) emissions. The government sets a cap, or maximum allowable amount, for GHG emissions. Businesses get an initial allowance of credits from the government. They are awarded additional credits for good environmental stewardship, such as planting trees.

If a business exceeds the emission cap, it must pay the government with credits. If a business doesn't have enough credits, it can buy them from lower-polluting businesses. Having to purchase credits is like paying a fine.

These programs, especially the cap-and-trade program, are controversial. Program promoters say they minimize the cost of governmental regulation. Business owners, not governmental regulators, decide how to keep their emissions under the cap. However, some environmentalists say the programs do not do enough to curtail fossil fuel burning and other environmental damage. Other critics say they create undue hardship for businesses and will boost energy prices for consumers.

Ethics

Gossip

As an employee, you may hear confidential information about employees or the company business. It is unethical to share any confidential information you learn, and doing so may cost you your job. Repeating information is sometimes known as gossiping. Television shows present taking part in "water cooler" talk and listening to the "grapevine" as fun office activities. However, sharing information may be considered slander. Always protect any confidential information you learn and respect the situation in which you learned it.

When possible, shop locally. Not only does this support your local economy, it can have a great impact on the environment. Transporting food and other products uses fuel. Locally grown food or locally made products are not transported as far, so less fuel is used to bring these items to the consumer. Locally grown food can be found at farmer's markets and grocery stores. Also, bring your own reusable bags when you shop. This cuts down on the need for plastic bags. Plastic bags are not biodegradable and, if not disposed of properly, can harm the environment.

Some major energy suppliers offer green energy sources as an alternative or as a supplement to conventional energy. *Green power* is electricity generated by renewable energy, such as wind and solar. If available, purchase green power instead of electricity generated by a conventional energy source, such as coal, natural gas, oil, or nuclear power.

Conserve Energy

Most people can conserve a considerable amount of energy without major inconvenience. Often, it simply involves a new mindset to get into the habit of using less, economizing, and saving. Some ways to reduce personal and family energy use include conducting a home energy audit, monitoring heating and cooling, insulating your home, conserving hot water, and wisely using appliances and electrical devices.

Conduct a Home Energy Audit

A **home energy audit** is an assessment of how much energy your home uses. It also identifies ways to reduce consumption. However, you must follow through and take the steps recommended by the audit in order to save energy. The audit merely tells you what you can do to save energy.

Your house, condo, or apartment has meters that measure the amounts of electricity and gas you use each month. These meters are used by the utility companies to determine how much you used and what to charge in your bill. Look at your bills or visit utility company websites to learn how to read your electric and gas meters. Compare your usage from year to year to see how well your energy-saving efforts are working.

A utility company may provide free or low-cost energy auditing services. You can also hire a company that provides this service.

Monitor Heating and Cooling

On average in the United States, space heating consumes the greatest share of energy in the home at about 42 percent. You can use the thermostat in your home to conserve energy. Consider saving energy by setting the thermostat no higher than 68°F in winter and no lower than 78°F in summer. Programmable or smart thermostats can be installed. These devices help save energy by reducing heating or cooling while nobody is home.

When heating or cooling equipment is in use, close the vents in unused rooms. Keep all outside doors and windows tightly closed. Also, keep heating and cooling vents clear of furniture, rugs, and other obstacles.

You can conserve energy by keeping heating and cooling equipment clean and in good working order. Be sure to regularly change or clean filters. Clean the coils on the exterior part of the air conditioning system to remove leaves or other debris.

Christina Richards/Shutterstock.com

Home insulation is necessary to slow the movement of hot or cool air.

Insulate Your Home

Well-fitted storm doors and windows help reduce heat loss in the winter and the escape of cool air in the summer. Inexpensive weather-stripping kits and materials can be used to stop drafts through loose-fitting windows and doors.

Insulation is necessary in all homes, especially older homes. Insulation is a material used to slow the movement of hot or cool air. It is installed in ceilings, walls, and floors to help maintain the desired indoor air temperature. Although insulating a home can be costly, it more than pays for itself in lower fuel costs over time.

Insulation has an R value, or resistivity rating. The higher the R value of insulation, the more it resists the movement of heat or cold. The recommend amount of insulation varies by region and by where the insulation will be placed. For example, in the South, the recommended R value for attic insulation may be as low as R30. However, in the North, the recommendation for attic insulation may be as high as R60.

Conserve Hot Water

The water heater is a major energy user in the home, in most homes second only to space heating. Insulating a tank-type unit cuts energy use. Less energy will be needed to keep the water hot. If you buy a new water heater, look for one with a high energy-efficiency rating.

Installing a tankless water heater can result in a large energy savings. This is especially true for a small family. A tankless water heater only uses energy to heat water as hot water is needed. There is no tank full of water that must be constantly kept hot.

Water heaters have an adjustable thermostat. Most tank-type water heaters are set at the factory to 140°F. However, the Department of Energy recommends consumers turn the water heater thermostat down to 120°F to save energy. This temperature is high enough for washing hands and comfortable bathing. Tankless water heaters also have an adjustable temperature setting.

When washing clothes, use the cold-water setting. Purchase a laundry detergent designed for cold-water washing. Using this detergent and the cold-water setting allows your clothes to be cleaned without using any hot water.

Wisely Use Appliances and Electrical Devices

Electrical appliances and equipment account for about 23 percent of energy used in the home. Some strategies for reducing the energy use of these items are as follows.

- Replace incandescent bulbs with compact fluorescent lightbulbs (CFLs) or LED lightbulbs.
- Turn off the television, computer, lights, and other electrical equipment when not in use.
- Unplug electronic devices when not in use, including the television, DVR, and cable or satellite box, as many of these units consume electricity even when "off."
- Keep appliances and equipment in good working condition.
- Open refrigerator and freezer doors for only as long as necessary; periodically check and clean door seals to make sure they fit tightly.
- Use dishwashers only for full loads, and select the shortest cycle able to do the job well.

Conserve Water

There are many ways you can cut down on water usage. This will help you save on your water bill as well as conserve a valuable resource. The four primary areas in which water is used in the home are the bathroom, kitchen, laundry, and outdoors.

Take shorter showers and install a low-flow showerhead. Take a bath instead of a shower as a bath uses less water. Turn off the water while brushing your teeth or shaving instead of letting it run.

While washing or rinsing dishes or cleaning vegetables and fruits, do not let the water run. Turn on the water only as needed. Repair leaky faucets promptly. When using the dishwasher, wash only full loads to reduce the number of times you have to run the dishwasher.

High-efficiency (HE) clothes washers are available that use much less water than traditional washers. Be sure to purchase laundry detergent designed for HE washers. Since they use less water, traditional laundry detergent will not work as well as it should. HE washers also use less electricity to operate.

Water the garden and lawn in the early evening or after dark. This prevents evaporation due to sunlight and the heating of the day. Use a soaker hose, which waters more efficiently than sprinklers. Or, do not water the lawn and garden at all.

Multiart/Shutterstock.com

Composting is a natural process that transforms organic materials into a nutrient-rich material that can be added to soil to improve it.

Reduce and Reuse Waste

Reducing trash involves an overall sense of economizing: buying less, using less, reusing, and recycling. To **recycle** means to reprocess resources so they can be used again. For example, paper products can be washed to remove ink, mixed with water to create a *slurry*, and the slurry pressed between rollers to form "new" paper. Recycling reduces waste in landfills, conserves resources, and saves energy. Almost every community provides some type of recycling programs.

To *reuse* means to use an item again for the same or different purpose as it was designed. Many families pass clothes down as they are outgrown. This is a form of reuse. Another form of reuse is to use empty paint cans or other containers as flowerpots.

Some communities encourage composting as a way to recycle yard waste and other organic waste. **Composting** is a natural process that transforms organic materials, such as food waste, leaves, and grass clippings, into a nutrient-rich material that can be added to soil to improve it. Find out whether your local government sponsors a composting project or offers information on home-composting measures.

Conserve Fuel

Transportation accounts for almost 70 percent of the petroleum used in the United States. There are many opportunities for energy conservation in this area. Make each mile count. The greatest difference you can make is switching from driving to biking, walking, or taking public transportation. Limiting airplane travel can also help reduce petroleum use. Drivers can conserve fuel and cut down costs by following these tips:

- Consider buying a small car to reduce fuel needs.
- Carefully plan trips, combining errands when possible.
- Carpool when possible.
- Decrease the speed at which you drive.
- Maintain your car for optimal performance.
- Ensure your tires are inflated to the proper pressure.

Citizen Groups

Citizen groups are nongovernmental organizations that pursue action that is in the best interest of a certain sector. Some of these groups promote actions for a healthy environment. At the local level, citizen action is often the driving force that protects a community's environment. The efforts of citizens working together have led to investigations of polluting industries and the establishment of local air- and water-quality standards. Citizen groups also help launch recycling and composting centers. In some communities, they promote programs for recycling electronic products and the safe disposal of hazardous waste.

You Do the Math — Word Problems

Word problems are exercises in which the problem is set up in text rather than presented in mathematical notation. Many word problems tell a story. You must identify the elements of the math problem and solve it.

Solve the following problems.

1. Assume a car gets 20 miles per gallon (mpg) going 70 miles per hour (mph). If the car gets 20 percent better fuel economy going 55 mph, how much farther does it travel per gallon of fuel at the lower speed?
2. How many total miles per gallon does the previously mentioned car travel at 55 mph?
3. Assume the previously mentioned car's miles per gallon drops by 15 percent at 80 miles per hour. How many total miles per gallon does the car travel at 80 miles per hour?

Some communities have managed to turn solid waste into an asset by producing energy from the gas that builds up in landfills. Other landfills, once full, are turned into golf courses and recreational areas. Many times, these projects are the result of the efforts of a citizen group.

Many citizen groups sponsor a variety of programs to protect and enhance the environment. These include restrictions on land use, emissions controls, and environmental education and awareness programs. To reduce air pollution from cars, some citizen groups lobby for restrictions on downtown parking, banning vehicle traffic in certain parts of the city, and improvements in public transportation. Other citizen groups encourage carpooling by lobbying the municipal government to establish express lanes for cars with two or more passengers.

Local action is the speediest, most direct way to deal with problems in and near your community. The organizations listed in Figure 20-5 are good sources for information on environmental issues.

What Governments Can Do

An important function of government is to ensure a safe and healthy environment for citizens. Both the environment and the economy are critical issues. Many environmental problems, such as climate change, deforestation, and water pollution, are global. The federal government frequently pursues environmental interests at the international level. The methods used to protect and conserve the environment and its resources need to be cost effective at the local, federal, and international levels.

Regulation and Legislation

In 1970, the federal government passed legislation creating the Environmental Protection Agency (EPA). The agency serves as the national watchdog and coordinating bureau for matters affecting the environment. The EPA focuses on air and water quality, noise, solid waste, hazardous waste, toxic substances, and other ecological issues.

Sources of Environmental Protection Information
Government
• National Aeronautics and Space Administration (NASA) on Global Climate Change • US Department of Energy and US Environmental Protection Agency ENERGY STAR Program • US Department of Energy Office of Energy Efficiency and Renewable Energy • US Environmental Protection Agency • US Fish & Wildlife Service Endangered Species Program • United Nations Environment Programme
Consumer Groups and Nonprofits
• Basel Action Network • Center for Resource Solutions • Consumers Union • Natural Resources Defense Council • The Nature Conservancy • Ocean Conservancy • World Wildlife Federation
Business/Industry Groups
• American Council for an Energy-Efficient Economy • Association of Home Appliance Manufacturers • Consumer Electronics Association • E-Cycling Central, Telecommunications Industry Association • US Chamber of Commerce Institute for 21st Century Energy

Goodheart-Willcox Publisher

Figure 20-5 Information about the environment can be found on the websites of these organizations.

Under a 1975 law, the Department of Energy (DOE) was required to set efficiency standards for major home appliances and several other commercial products. The goal of the standards was to reduce the nation's energy use. Since then, the list of products under the DOE's review has grown. Besides setting minimum efficiency standards, it also sets maximum water-use standards for certain products. The DOE is charged with periodically reviewing opportunities for more energy and water savings from the items under its authority. These reviews involve input from manufacturers and consumers.

In addition to federal regulations, many state and local regulations govern environmental activities. To find out how your state is involved, go to your state website and look for the department or agency that deals with environmental issues.

Taxation

Taxes can be a tool in fighting pollution. *Green taxes*, also known as environmental or pollution taxes, offer a way to charge the cost of pollution to the polluter, whether a producer or consumer. Examples of possible items subject to a green tax include excess household waste and vehicle emissions. The *Gas Guzzler Tax* is another example of a green tax. It applies to vehicles that do not meet the requirements for fuel economy. People who buy these vehicles pay the Gas Guzzler Tax.

Case Study Recycling

Maxine is president of the city council. A major problem the community needs to address is that the landfill is almost full. A sanitation report calls for it to be closed in three years. To extend the landfill's use, Maxine and the other council members proposed the following ideas.

- Promote voluntary recycling programs with curbside collection.
- Establish mandatory recycling with curbside pickup, and charge a fee-per-pound of solid waste over a specified minimum to encourage recycling and composting.
- Assist households with composting of yard and food waste.
- Designate convenient recycling drop-off containers around the city.
- Levy a specific tax per household to pay for solid waste disposal.
- Organize an awareness campaign to encourage residents to recycle more.

Case Review

1. Which ideas would you recommend that Maxine encourage the council to employ?
2. Which of these suggestions would be the most convenient for the residents of Maxine's city?
3. Which of these suggestions would be the least convenient for the residents of Maxine's city?
4. What other suggestions could Maxine propose to the city council to solve this problem?

Green taxes could take the form of direct tax, fines, or user fees. They provide greater incentive and pressure to find cost-effective ways of reducing and controlling pollution. Green taxes also produce revenues that can be used to help clean up waste and pay for governmental pollution-control services.

In some cases, a government can use tax incentives to reward and encourage good environmental stewardship by consumers and business. Examples include tax benefits for insulating homes, using solar energy, or purchasing fuel-efficient cars and energy-efficient appliances.

Clean-Energy Development

Energy policies and choices affect jobs, prices, industries, the environment, and lifestyles here and around the world. There is increasing interest in reducing dependence on nonrenewable and polluting sources of energy. Harnessing the energy of the sun, wind, and water may provide a large share of the energy used in the future. Scientists and entrepreneurs are also developing other sources of energy. The government is heavily involved in these efforts both through its own laboratories and through funding of private research. Other actions the government can take on energy issues include the following.

- Tax fossil fuels to encourage greater efficiency and discourage excessive energy consumption.
- Provide incentives for industries to conduct comprehensive clean-energy research.
- Create cooperative policies with other nations for the development, allocation, and efficient and safe use of world energy resources.

Water Conservation

Governments can enact bans, restrictions, and rationing for different types of water usage. These normally are temporary measures taken during periods of severe shortages, but can be long term. More permanent conservation measures governments can take include:

- passing local building codes that require water-efficient faucets, toilets, showerheads, and appliances in new construction;
- instituting billing that imposes higher rates for excess water usage;
- requiring recycling of industrial water;
- conducting educational programs to encourage voluntary reductions in water usage; and
- requiring testing of water meters for accuracy and leaks.

What Businesses Can Do

Manufacturers and retailers share responsibility for the environmental impact of the production, use, and disposal of their products. "Product stewardship" is a concept that calls on businesses to take a leadership role in reducing the health and environmental impacts of consumer products. For example, producers should try to:

- design products to be upgraded instead of discarded;
- incorporate energy-saving features in products;

Levent Konuk/Shutterstock.com

Many businesses manufacture products using recycled materials and energy-efficient machinery.

- use recycled materials in the product or its packaging;
- avoid excess packaging;
- use renewable energy and recycled water in the manufacturing process;
- upgrade machinery and vehicles to energy-saving models; and
- minimize the discharge of pollutants into the environment.

Manufacturers and retailers can encourage recycling by providing free pickup of used goods, such as old appliances. They can sponsor educational programs to identify the efforts being made to preserve natural resources.

Some businesses take back products that are no longer usable and offer free recycling to customers. Others refurbish used products for resale or donation. By planning for disposal during product design, producers can also minimize disposal problems.

Section 20.2 Review

Check Your Understanding

1. What are some steps you can take in your home and community to improve and protect the world?
2. Describe green power.
3. What is a home energy audit?
4. What are two ways you can reduce paper trash?
5. What are the issues on which the Environmental Protection Agency (EPA) focuses?

Build Your Vocabulary

As you progress through this course, develop a personal glossary. This will help you build your vocabulary and prepare you for a career. Write a definition for each of the following terms and add it to your glossary.

environmentalist
biodegradable
home energy audit
recycle
composting

Review and Assessment

Chapter Summary

Section 20.1 Environment

- Modern society relies on natural resources to produce the products and services needed to maintain good health and a high standard of living. Most natural resources are of limited supply. Scientists predict a future in which shortages of basic natural resources, such as water, food, and fuel, will affect a growing number of people.
- Environmental issues and trends affect individuals and families today, as well as future generations of people. Climate change, water and air pollution, depletion of natural resources, and land use are some of the environmental challenges faced today.

Section 20.2 Addressing Environmental Challenges

- There are many steps you can take in your home and community to improve and protect your world. Making small changes in your shopping habits, reducing your water and energy use at home, reducing waste, and conserving fuel all make an impact on sustaining the environment. Participation in citizen groups can also help protect a community's environment.
- An important function of government is to ensure a safe and healthy environment for its citizens. Governments can use regulation, legislation, taxation, energy development programs, and water conservation programs to help achieve this goal.
- Businesses share responsibility for the environmental impact of the production, use, and disposal of their products. Companies can take a leadership role in reducing the health and environmental impacts of consumer products. They can also encourage recycling of used goods and proper disposal of hazardous products.

Review Your Knowledge

1. Describe the importance of natural resources in modern society.
2. What are three examples of renewable energy sources?
3. What are some factors that contribute to climate change?
4. List some of today's major environmental challenges.
5. What are some examples of household hazardous wastes?
6. Explain steps individuals can take to conserve natural resources and protect the environment.
7. What are three ways that you can conserve water in the kitchen?
8. Identify the role of government in protecting the environment.
9. Under a 1975 law, the Department of Energy (DOE) was required to set efficiency standards for major home appliances and several commercial products. What was the goal of these standards?
10. Explain steps businesses can take to reduce their impact on the environment.

Apply Your Knowledge

1. Environmental issues like pollution, depletion of natural resources, and land use affect families today as well as future generations. Summarize your opinion of current environmental issues that affect you today. Then list environmental issues that will affect future generations.
2. Create a list of five environmental trends that you have observed in your community. Summarize each and explain how you think they affect you today and future generations.

3. As consumers, you and your family are responsible for the ways in which your actions impact the environment. Analyze the daily activities of yourself and those in your household. Are there any activities that are negative and contribute to environmental issues? If so, what can be done to change these actions? What activities does your family do that have a positive impact on the environment?
4. Individuals and families can demonstrate behaviors to protect the environment by creating a family "green policy." Make a list of habits that you and your family can practice at home to conserve, reuse, and recycle resources. Create your own "green policy" and post it in a place that reminds each of you of behaviors that should happen every day.
5. Limiting the amount of fresh water used during daily routines is an easy way to begin to help the environment. Monitor how much water you and your family members use throughout one day. Analyze and keep track of how long the water is running for each activity. Estimate how much water was actually used versus how much was wasted. As a family, discuss what can be done to lower the amount used.
6. Limiting the amount of electricity used during daily routines is another easy way to begin to help the environment. Monitor how much electricity you and your family members use throughout one day. Analyze and keep track of how long lights, electronics, and appliances are on for each activity. Estimate how much electricity was actually used versus how much was wasted. As a family, discuss what can be done to lower the amount used.
7. The federal government frequently pursues environmental interests at the national and international levels. Since 1970, the US government has established multiple laws and regulations to help preserve the environment. Create a time line that explains each regulation in chronological order.
8. What are some environmental problems that exist in your community? How might they be solved?
9. In your opinion, what are the most important factors that contribute to pollution in your state?
10. By the year 2040, the world population is expected to exceed 9 billion people. Do you think the resources of the world can adequately sustain a population that large?

Apply Your Math Skills

1. The O'Conner family decided to purchase a solar panel to put on their rooftop to provide the house with some electricity. The solar panel costs $1,000, but has a rent-to-own option. They will rent the solar panel for $42 each month for 2 years. At the end of the 2 years, they have the option of buying the panel for half of its original price. How much money will they end up spending on the panel if they elect to buy the panel at the end of the 2-year contract?
2. Adir's electricity provider currently uses a nuclear power supply to generate electricity. This supply costs $.07 per kilowatt hour, and Adir uses, on average, 900 kilowatt hours each month. After doing some research, Adir finds that a local wind-powered electricity supplier costs $.01 per kilowatt hour. How much would be saved annually if Adir switched to the wind-powered supplier?

Communication Skills

College and Career Readiness

Reading. Active reading is processing the words, phrases, and sentences you read. To actively read, you must consider the writer's purpose for writing, consider your purpose for reading, relate what you read to your prior knowledge, and evaluate information as your read to ensure understanding and form judgments. Using this technique, read an article about recent environmental research and write a one-page summary that describes the research and offers an opinion. Be prepared to present your findings to the class.

Speaking. There will be many instances when you will be required to persuade the listener. When you persuade, you convince a person to take a proposed course of action. Prepare for a conversation with a person in the community about who should be responsible for paying for a clean environment. Ask for assistance to help you plan a focused presentation that argues your case and shows solid reasoning that will influence the listener's understanding of the topic.

Listening. Informative listening is the process of listening to gain specific information from the speaker. Interview a person who is responsible for the recycling program in a household, business, or other organization. Ask that person to explain recycling policies followed by the people in the household, business, or organization. Make notes as the policies are described. Evaluate the speaker's point of view and reasoning. Did you listen closely enough to write accurate facts?

Teamwork

Work with other students in research teams to investigate one of the following sources or types of energy: nuclear, natural gas, coal, solar, geothermal, petroleum, wind, water, or underwater technology. Prepare a report on its use, cost, safety, effectiveness, availability, and impact on the environment.

Internet Research

Urban Sprawl. Visit the website of the Environmental Protection Agency, the Department of Energy, or another governmental agency. Conduct a search for articles about urban sprawl versus smart growth. Summarize your findings. Make an effort to present a balanced view covering both sides of the issue. Cite authorities, events, dates, figures, pros, and cons.

Energy Audit. The government's Home Energy Saver calculator is an easy way to get a quick assessment of the energy used at a residential address. The calculator also computes greenhouse gas emissions. You can visit the government's ENERGY STAR website. The Home Energy Yardstick can help you see how your home's energy use compares with similar homes across the country.

Local Landfills. Use the Internet to research the number of active landfills that operate in your area. What is the time estimated for each to reach full capacity? Does your community have a plan to extend the life of the landfill?

Portfolio Development

College and Career Readiness

Portfolio Introduction. After you have collected materials for your portfolio, you are ready to start organizing the content inside the portfolio. The first document in your portfolio should be an *introduction* that gives an overall snapshot of who you are. This will set the tone for your presentation, so you want to make a good impression. Tell the reader who you are, your goals, and any relevant biographical information, such as schools attended, titles or certifications earned, or degrees completed. You may want to highlight information by referencing specific sections or page numbers of items in the portfolio.

This document should also include links regarding your online presence. If you are creating an electronic portfolio, create a home page to house the introduction. This should be the first page a visitor to your portfolio site will encounter. In addition to the introduction, provide live links to your pages. You should also link to any pages containing documents of importance.

1. Create a thorough, comprehensive document that introduces yourself, outlines your goals and qualifications, and entices the employer to continue reading your portfolio. Include the heading "Introduction" and your name.
2. Update your master portfolio spreadsheet.

CTSOs

Event Prep

Proper Attire. Some Career and Technical Student Organization (CTSOs) require appropriate business attire from all entrants and those attending the competition. This requirement is in keeping with the mission of CTSOs: to prepare students for professional careers in business.

To be sure that the attire you have chosen to wear at the competition is in accordance with event requirements complete the following activities.

1. Visit the organization's website and look for the most current dress code.
2. The dress code requirements are very detailed and gender specific. Some CTSOs may require a chapter blazer to be worn during the competition.
3. Do a dress rehearsal when practicing for your event. Are you comfortable in the clothes you have chosen? Do you present a professional appearance?
4. In addition to the kinds of clothes you can wear, be sure the clothes are clean and pressed. You do not want to undermine your appearance or event performance with wrinkled clothes that may distract judges.
5. Make sure your hair is neat and worn in a conservative style. If you are a male, you should be clean-shaven. Again, you do not want anything about your appearance detracting from your performance.
6. As far in advance of the event as is possible, share your clothing choice with your organization's advisor to make sure you are dressed appropriately.

UNIT

6 Preparing for Your Career

Chapters

Personal Finance

Why It Matters

As a young adult, one of the keys to personal financial success will be your ability to transition from school to career. Now is the time to begin creating a financial plan to fund the training and education that you will need to open doors to future opportunities. Adequate planning for funding will affect the quality of your choices of careers.

The career you choose will determine the people you meet, the places you travel, and the amount of money that you make. It is one of the most important decisions you will make in your lifetime. Waiting until you graduate from high school to create a plan to pay for tuition might be too late to enable you to make the choices that you prefer. By investigating funding options, scholarships, and other resources now, you can help ensure that the future choices you make are the ones that will make you happy. Life is not all about making money. However, selecting the career that is a good fit for you will lead to personal and financial success.

Evgeny Karandaev/Shutterstock.com

Big Idea

The way in which you use your limited resources to achieve your goals will require good decision-making skills.

CHAPTER

21 Planning for Your Career

People work primarily to earn money for life's necessities and a few extra wants. Most people begin working during their teens or early 20s and continue until retirement age. Because you will likely be working for many years, it pays to get the training and education that will lead to good jobs and good pay.

If you are like most young people, entering the workforce will be a major step. It calls for thoughtful choices. You will spend about one-third of your waking hours at the occupation you choose. Therefore, you should find work you can do well and enjoy.

Some people seem to know from an early age what they want to do with their lives. Most people have to search for jobs that bring adequate income and job satisfaction. For high school students who plan to go on to college or enter a training program after graduation, the world of work may seem far away. However, it is not too early to begin thinking about your future and the career choices that will bring you satisfaction.

Focus on Finance

529 College Savings Plan

A 529 College Savings Plan is a state-sponsored, tax-advantaged investment vehicle that allows parents, grandparents, other relatives, and even friends to plan and invest for a child's college education. The plans are usually sponsored by a state. However, participation in a 529 plan is not restricted to residents of that state. For example, if a 529 investor does not like the plan of the state in which he or she lives, a plan of another state can be chosen.

All money invested under the plan grows tax-free. Your investment can grow at a faster pace than it would in a taxable account. Withdrawals from the plan are also tax-free, as long as the funds are used to pay for qualified higher-education expenses of the specified beneficiary. Qualified expenses include tuition, fees, supplies, tutoring, rooming, and transportation.

Most states allow contributions up to $380,000 to be made to a 529 College Savings Plan. Unused funds of a beneficiary can be transferred to a sibling.

College and Career Readiness

Reading Prep. The summary at the end of the chapter highlights the most important concepts. Read the chapter and write a summary in your own words. Then, compare your summary to the summary provided in the text.

Sections

Paul Matthew Photography/Shutterstock.com

Section 21.1 Choosing a Career

Essential Question

How do a person's skills contribute to career success?

Objectives

After studying this section, you will be able to:

- Determine the skills needed for the workplace.
- Explain how to create a career plan.
- Identify sources of career information.
- Summarize how CTSOs can prepare a student for a career.
- Explain the importance of staying current on industry trends.

Terms

job	career ladder	networking
career	career plan	informational interviewing
skill	aptitude	career and technical student organization (CTSO)
job-specific skills	ability	
employability skills	values	
career cluster	interest	
career pathway		

Skills for the Workplace

A **job** is the work a person does regularly in order to earn money. A **career** is a series of related jobs in the same profession. A job may be a part-time position you work after school. A career is a position for which you prepare by attending school or completing specialized training. Over time, a job can turn into a career.

All employment opportunities require skills. A **skill** is something an individual does well. Skills are the foundational elements of all career fields. **Job-specific skills** are critical skills necessary to perform the required work-related tasks of a position. Job-specific skills are acquired through work experience and education or training. Without them, an individual will be unlikely to perform the job successfully.

Employability skills are applicable skills used to help an individual find a job, perform in the workplace, and gain success in a job or career. Employability skills are known as *foundation, transferrable* or *soft skills*. You have already acquired many of these skills. However, some of them are gained through life experience. Others may be gained from working at a job. Some of these may be gained in social situations. These skills are not specific to one career but are transferrable to

Case Study *Career Preparation*

Marco always wanted to be a professional counselor, which is a career in the Family & Community pathway of the Human Services career cluster. During sophomore year, the guidance counselor recommended setting SMART goals and writing a career plan. The guidance counselor also recommended attending a professional conference and networking with professionals. People at the conference suggested getting a part-time job to gain experience and confirm if this is a future career worth pursuing. Marco applied for a job as an assistant in a counselor's office and as a customer service representative in a retail setting. After interviewing and being offered both jobs, there was still uncertainty about which to choose. The customer service job was interesting, but the assistant job would better fit the career plan previously created.

Case Review

1. What are some advantages of taking a job as an assistant in a counselor's office?
2. What are some advantages of taking the customer service representative job?
3. What will be gained by taking a job that is not in the career plan?
4. How can working as an assistant in a counselor's office improve Marco's résumé?

many different jobs and professional positions. Examples of employability skills are shown in Figure 21-1.

Career Clusters

Studying career clusters is a good way to begin analyzing the principles of career fields. **Career clusters**, shown in Figure 21-2, are groups of occupational and career specialties. Career clusters are centered on related career fields.

Within each of the career clusters are multiple career pathways. **Career pathways** are subgroups within the career clusters that reflect occupations requiring similar knowledge and skills. These pathways include careers that range from entry-level to those that require advanced college degrees and many years of experience. All the careers within the pathways share a foundation of common knowledge and skills.

Employability Skills			
Basic skills	Reading Writing	Speaking Listening	Technology Mathematics
Thinking skills	Decision-making Creative thinking	Problem solving Visualization	Reasoning
People skills	Social perceptiveness Leadership	Teamwork Cultural competence	
Personal qualities	Self-management Integrity	Honesty Social responsibility	

Goodheart-Willcox Publisher

Figure 21-1 Employability skills can help lead to success in the workplace.

Career Clusters			
Career Cluster	**Description**	**Career Cluster**	**Description**
Agriculture, Food & Natural Resources	Careers involving the production, processing, marketing, distribution, financing, and development of agricultural commodities and resources.	Hospitality & Tourism	Careers involving management, marketing, and operations of foodservice, lodging, and recreational businesses.
Architecture & Construction	Careers involving the design, planning, managing, building, and maintaining of buildings and structures.	Human Services	Careers involving family and human needs.
Arts, A/V Technology & Communications	Careers involving the design, production, exhibition, performance, writing, and publishing of visual and performing arts.	Information Technology	Careers involving the design, development, support, and management of software, hardware, and other technology-related materials.
Business Management & Administration	Careers involving the planning, organizing, directing, and evaluation of functions essential to business operations.	Law, Public Safety, Corrections & Security	Careers involving the planning, management, and providing of legal services, public safety, protective services, and homeland security.
Education & Training	Careers involving the planning, management, and providing of training services.	Manufacturing	Careers involving the planning, management, and processing of materials to create completed products.
Finance	Careers involving the planning and providing of banking, insurance, and other financial-business services.	Marketing	Careers involving the planning, management, and performance of marketing and sales activities.
Government & Public Administration	Careers involving governance, national security, foreign service, revenue and taxation, regulation, and management and administration.	Science, Technology, Engineering & Mathematics	Careers involving the planning, management, and providing of scientific research and technical services.
Health Science	Careers involving planning, managing, and providing health services, health information, and research and development.	Transportation, Distribution & Logistics	Careers involving the planning, management, and movement of people, materials, and goods.

Source: States' Career Clusters Initiative 2008

Figure 21-2 Each of the career clusters contains multiple career pathways.

Levels of Careers

In each career area, positions are generally grouped by skill level or education. A **career ladder** is an outline of progressively higher positions achieved through education and experience that lead to greater responsibility and career success. Often each job in an individual's career ladder requires more education and experience than the previous one. There are five levels of careers that make up a career ladder, as illustrated in Figure 21-3.

- An *entry-level* position is usually a person's first or beginning job. It requires very little previous training.
- A *career-level* position requires an employee to have the skills and knowledge for continued employment and advancement in the field.
- A *specialist-level* position requires specialized knowledge and skills in a specific field of study. However, someone in this position does not supervise other employees.
- A *supervisory-level* position requires specialized knowledge and skills. It also includes management responsibility over other employees.
- An *executive-level* position is the highest level. This position is responsible for the planning, organization, and management of a company.

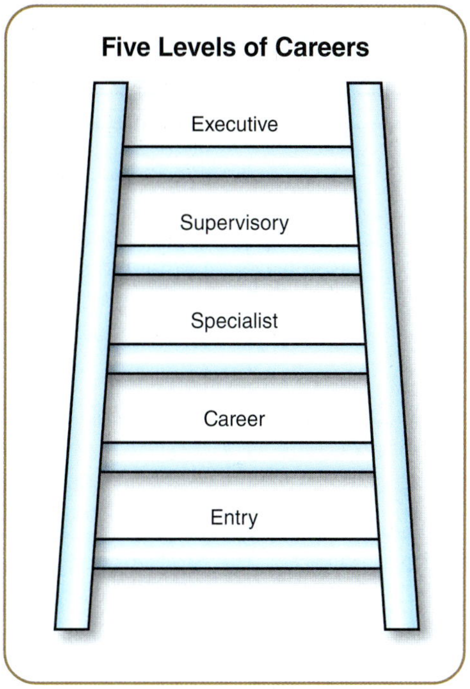

Goodheart-Willcox Publisher

Figure 21-3 Most careers have different levels of positions based on years of experience, education, and technical skills.

Career Plan

A **career plan** is a list of steps on a timeline an individual can follow to reach personal career goals. It is also known as a *postsecondary plan.* A career plan should include education options. Education options include four-year colleges, two-year colleges, or technical schools. It should also address current job opportunities in your career of interest.

There is no set format for writing a career plan. Many free career plan templates can be found on the Internet. To create a plan, you should first conduct a self-assessment and then set SMART goals. You will continue revising the career plan as you achieve your goals and set new ones.

Figure 21-4 illustrates some of the action items needed for a career plan. This action plan provides an overview for a financial advisor, which is a position in the Consumer Services pathway of the Human Services career cluster. This illustration is based on the education and training requirements for the career. The role of a Consumer Services position is to assist individuals with decisions and problems relating to finance, real estate, insurance, and consumer goods. Examples of positions in the Consumer Services pathway include banker, real estate service representative, insurance representative, and event specialist. Positions in the Human Services career cluster share many job titles with the Finance career cluster. These careers fulfill similar functions of assisting individuals with personal finance issues.

Action Items for a Career Plan: Financial Advisor Human Services Cluster, Consumer Services Pathway			
Life Stage	**Extracurricular and Volunteer Activities**	**Work Experience**	**Education and Training**
During High School	• Network with business professionals to learn about the financial advisor position • Participate in a CTSO	• Work as an intern in an investments office	• Enroll in Human Services course and Accounting course • For optional or extra credit work, select topics and projects related to consumer services
During College	• Help student, nonprofit, or local groups evaluate their financial needs	• Work as a part-time clerk in an accounting firm or bank	• Follow the bachelor degree path for a degree in Finance, Economics, or Business
After College	• Become a member of a professional organization for students • Attend local business professionals and chamber of commerce events	• Work as an entry-level financial advisor	• Research certification opportunities, such as Certified Financial Planner (CFP) • Consider obtaining a master degree in Finance or Business Administration

Goodheart-Willcox Publisher

Figure 21-4 This table illustrates action items to use for a potential career plan in the Human Services career cluster.

Conducting a Self-Assessment

A *self-assessment* is the first step in evaluating your aptitudes, abilities, values, and interests. By conducting a self-assessment, you can focus your energy on what is necessary for you to become successful in a career. Some self-assessment techniques are thinking or writing exercises. Others are in the form of tests, such as a personality test. Your career counselor can help you conduct a self-assessment.

Consider what you like to do and what you do well. This can give you clues to aid your self-assessment. If you always do well in math class, you may find success in a career that requires working with numbers. On the other hand, if you do not do well in English class, a career that requires writing may not be your best match. Identifying a career that you will enjoy and excel in begins with finding out what you like to do.

What is your *work style*? Some individuals prefer to work independently. Others need constant direction to accomplish a task. Mornings are more productive for some workers, while others perform better in the afternoons. Casual dress influences some people to perform well. Business dress makes others more effective on the job.

When taking a self-assessment, strive to identify your aptitudes, abilities, values, and interests. Learning this information can reveal careers for which you are well suited.

Aptitudes

An **aptitude** is a characteristic that an individual has developed naturally. Aptitudes are also called *talents*. When an individual naturally excels at a task without practicing or studying, that person has an aptitude for it. For example, a person with an aptitude for music may be very good at accurately humming a tune or keeping a beat, even never having studied music. Some examples of aptitudes include:

- mathematics
- drawing
- writing
- sports

Goodluz/Shutterstock.com

By conducting a self-assessment, an individual can focus on what is necessary to become successful in a desired career.

Abilities

An **ability** is the mastery of a skill or the capacity to do something. Having aptitudes and skills are supported or limited by a person's abilities. For instance, a student who has musical aptitude and skill might not have the ability to perform under pressure in musical concerts. Examples of abilities are:

- teaching others
- multitasking
- thinking logically
- speaking multiple languages

While an aptitude is something a person is born with, an ability can be acquired. Often, it is easier to develop abilities that match your natural aptitudes. For example, someone with an aptitude for acquiring languages may have the ability to speak French. A person without an aptitude for acquiring language can also learn to speak French, but it may be more difficult. Aptitudes and abilities do not always match. Someone with an aptitude for repairing machines may not enjoy doing this type of work and never develop the ability.

Values

The principles and beliefs that an individual considers important are values. **Values** are beliefs about the things that matter most to an individual. They are developed as people mature and learn. Your values will affect your life in many ways. They influence how you relate to other people and make decisions about your education and career.

Your work values can provide great insight into what kind of career will appeal to you. For some individuals, work values include job security. For others, the number of vacation days is important. Everyone has a set of work values that are taken into consideration when choosing a career path. Examples of values include:

- perfection
- equality

- harmony
- status

Closely related to values are family responsibilities and personal priorities. These can have a direct impact on career choice. For example, if you expect to have a large family, you may decide that time is a family responsibility. You may want to spend as much time as possible with your children as they grow. This may mean choosing a career that does not typically require travel or working long hours. On the other hand, it may be important to you to live in an expensive house and drive an expensive car. This personal priority will require a career with an income level that supports these choices.

Interests

An **interest** is a feeling of wanting to learn more about a topic or to be involved in an activity. Your interests might include a subject, such as history. Your interests can also include hobbies, such as biking or cooking. There is a good chance there is a career that would allow you to do what you enjoy as a profession.

Your interests may change over time. Try to determine if there is a uniting theme to your interests. When considering your interests, look at the "big picture." For example, you may enjoy being on the cross-country team right now. In a few years, a career as an arborist might suit you because you enjoy physical activity and being outdoors. Examples of interests include:

- art and creativity
- technology
- sports and adventure
- collecting

Setting SMART Goals

Another step in the career-planning process is to set goals. A *goal* is something a person wants to achieve in a specified time period. There are two types of goals: short term and long term. A *short-term goal* is one that can be achieved in less than one year. An example of a short-term goal may be getting

Ethics

Applications and Résumés

When applying for a job, to a college, or for a volunteer position, it is important to be truthful in your application and résumé. Fabricating experience or education is unethical and could cost you the opportunity to be a part of that organization. This means always telling the truth about your skills, experience, and education. Do not embellish. Play up your strengths without creating the illusion of being someone you are not. Present your information in a positive light, but be honest.

an after-school job for the fall semester. A *long-term goal* is one that will take a longer period of time to achieve, usually more than one year. An example of a long-term goal is to attend college to earn a four-year degree.

Goal setting is the process of deciding what a person wants to achieve. Your goals must be based on what you want for your life. Well-defined career goals follow the SMART goal model. Recall that *SMART goals* are specific, measurable, attainable, realistic, and timely, as illustrated in Figure 21-5.

Specific

A career goal should be specific and straightforward. For example, "I want to have a career" is not a specific goal. Instead, you might say, "I want to have a career in consumer services." When the goal is specific, it is easier to track progress.

Measurable

It is important to be able to measure progress so you know when you have reached your goal. For example, "I want to earn a bachelor degree in finance." This goal can be measured. When you earn the degree, you will know the goal has been reached.

Attainable

Goals need to be attainable. For example, "I want to be a consumer service director when I graduate from college." This is not reasonable for that point in a person's career. Gaining work experience is necessary before obtaining an executive position. This goal becomes more attainable when coupled with a plan to gain the necessary aptitudes, skills, and experience.

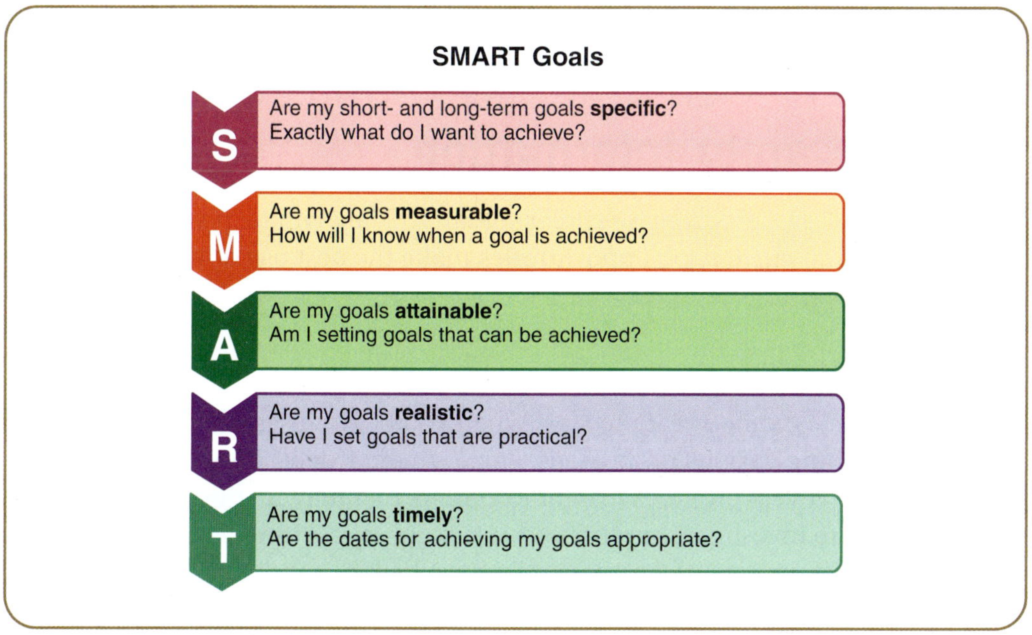

Goodheart-Willcox Publisher

Figure 21-5 Well-defined career goals follow the SMART goal model.

You Do the Math — Geometric Reasoning

Slope is the angle of a line measured in relation to a horizontal axis. It is the ratio of rise over run (rise/run). The *rise* is the distance of a line above or below the horizontal axis. The *run* is the length of a line measured along the horizontal axis. The greater the slope, the steeper the line. Two lines are parallel if their slopes are identical. If the slopes are not identical, the lines will intersect.

Solve the following problems.

1. Line A has a run of 2 inches and a rise of 1 inch. Line B has a run of 12 inches and a rise of 6 inches. Are these parallel or intersecting lines?
2. The roof on house A has a slope of 4/12. What is the rise of this roof? What is the run?
3. Hill A has a slope of 8/4. Hill B has a slope of 8/6. Which hill is steeper?

Realistic

Goals must be realistic. Obtaining a position as a Certified Financial Planner (CFP) at an investment firm may be practical with proper planning. It is not realistic for a new college graduate. Finding an entry-level position as a personal banker and working your way up to CFP over a period of years makes this a realistic goal.

Timely

A goal should have a starting point and an ending point. Setting a time frame to achieve a goal is the step most often overlooked. An end date can help you stay on track. For example, you may want to be a consumer services director by the time you are 35 years old. Aiming to get the experience and education necessary to achieve this position by a specific age will help you remain motivated to reach the goal on time.

Finding Career Information

There are many resources for career research. They will help you evaluate which careers and current job opportunities make the best use of your talents, skills, and interests.

Internet Research

The Internet is a good place to start when you begin researching your future career. Researching various professions, employment trends, industries, and prospective employers provides insight to careers that may interest you. It is also important to investigate current and future job opportunities for various occupations. Certain potential careers may have low demand now, but may be increasing in the future. And the opposite may be true: there are jobs that are plentiful now but will be phased out in the future.

The Occupational Information Network (O*NET) is a valuable resource for career information. The most comprehensive database of occupational information, O*NET Online, was created by the US Department of Labor and is updated regularly. This website contains data on salary, growth, openings, education requirements, skills and abilities, work tasks, and related occupations for more than 1,000 careers. The database can be searched by career cluster.

The Internet is also a great tool to use when you begin applying for jobs. You can search for available jobs in almost any career field. When you find a job that interests you, you can submit a résumé, job application, and cover letter via the Internet.

Career Handbooks

The US Bureau of Labor Statistics publishes the *Occupational Outlook Handbook* and the *Career Guide to Industries*. An *industry* is a group of businesses that produce the same type of goods or services. These handbooks describe the training and education needed for various jobs. They provide up-to-date information about careers, industries, employment trends, and even salary outlooks. The average person spends 30 percent of his or her time working every day. Understanding the industry of a chosen career is an important step to take. Career handbooks offer a great place to begin researching specific careers, their industries, and the areas of the country or world in which these industries thrive.

wavebreakmedia/Shutterstock.com

There are many resources for information on careers.

Networking

Networking means talking with people you know and making new contacts. Networking with family and friends can lead to job opportunities. The more contacts you make, the greater your opportunities for finding career ideas. Talking with people you know can help you evaluate career opportunities. It also may lead to potential jobs.

There are many professional organizations that encourage students and professionals to join and interact with other professionals. Professional organizations typically provide networking events, job opening notification, and continuing education opportunities for members. Examples of professional organizations for Consumer Services careers include:

- Event Service Professionals Association
- National Association of Insurance and Financial Advisors
- National Association of Realtors
- National Customer Service Association

Informational Interviews

Informational interviews can give you unique insight into a career. **Informational interviewing** is a strategy used to interview a professional to ask for advice and direction, rather than for a job opportunity. This type of interview will help you get a sense of what it is like to work in that profession.

It can also be a valuable networking opportunity. By talking with someone in the field, you can learn more about what is expected. You can also learn what types of jobs are available and other information about an industry.

At informational interviews, be as professional and polite as you would in any other interview situation. Follow up with your contact after an interview. Send a thank-you message to show appreciation for the person taking time to meet with you.

Career and Technical Student Organizations

Career and technical student organizations (CTSOs) are national student organizations with local school chapters that are related to career and technical education (CTE) courses. CTSO programs are tied to various course areas. Internships and other cooperative work experiences may be a part of the CTSO experience. CTSOs can help prepare high school graduates for their next step, whether it is college or a job.

CTSO Goals

The goal of CTSOs is to help students acquire knowledge and skills in different career and technical areas. They also help students develop leadership skills and gain work experience important for professional development. These organizations guide student members to become competent, successful members of the workforce.

Support for local CTSO chapters is often coordinated through each state's education department. Local chapters elect officers and establish a program of work. The CTSO advisors help students run the organization and identify the best programs that meet the goals of the educational area.

Dragon Images/Shutterstock.com

Participating in CTSO program activities can promote a lifelong interest in community service.

CTSO Opportunities

Competitive events are a main feature of most CTSOs. Competing in various events enables students to show mastery of specific content. These events also measure the use of decision-making, problem-solving, and leadership skills. Students may receive recognition awards for participating in events. In some cases, scholarships may be awarded if students win at state- and national-level competitions.

Participating in a CTSO program and its activities can promote a lifelong interest in community service and professional development. Student achievement in specific areas, such as leadership or patriotism, is recognized with certificates or award ceremonies. Other professional development opportunities may include:

- completing a school or community project related to the field of study

Exploring Careers

Financial Analyst

Financial analysts study the economy and the financial information of a business in order to advise its leaders. They analyze the financial affairs of a business and develop a plan to meet its financial goals for the future. Financial analysts advise businesses on investments, insurance, and taxes. They may be a member of a private practice or provide services through an investment firm, bank, or financial service firm.

Other typical job titles for a financial planner are *investment planner* and *financial consultant*. Some examples of tasks that financial analysts perform include:

- analyze financial statements
- advise businesses on ways to achieve their financial goals
- provide investment and tax advice
- monitor investments, tax strategies, and risk management for the business

Financial analyst jobs often require a bachelor degree in finance, economics, or business or law school. They must also pass the General Securities Representative Qualification Examination Series 7 and any additional exams required by individual states. Two or more years of work experience in financial services or a related field are needed.

- training in the field
- supporting a local or national philanthropic organization
- attending CTSO state meetings
- participating in leadership conferences

Your participation in a CTSO can help you learn more about a profession. These organizations give students firsthand experience with the demands of a career.

Employment Trends

In the workplace, it is very possible that today's opportunity will become tomorrow's dead end. It is important to stay abreast of new technology and to follow industry trends. Consider where the best jobs are likely to surface given current trends and developments.

New technology requires highly trained and skilled workers in a variety of fields. Untrained workers will either be unemployed or remain at bottom-level, low-paying jobs. Not only is initial training important, the willingness to continue training over the years is equally important. Technology makes dramatic and sometimes sudden changes. These changes often lead to a demand for workers with different types of skills and training. It also leads to the elimination of jobs. For example, fewer cashiers are needed in grocery stores because self-check registers enable customers to check out without assistance.

Economic and political factors, both at home and around the world, can seriously affect employment in different fields. Recession, inflation, tax policies, and international trade all have an impact on what and how many jobs are available.

Downsizing is the elimination of jobs generally because the economy is suffering. Downsizing means there are fewer jobs and competition increases for the jobs that are available. When unemployment is high and jobs are hard to find, training, education, and competence become even more important in finding and keeping a job. When taxes and interest rates are high, there may be fewer jobs because businesses are less likely to expand and are more likely to cut back on hiring. However, when the economy is stable or growing, more jobs may be available.

Social conditions, such as crime levels in a community, can impact the type of available jobs for workers. If the working environment is not safe, workers may look for jobs outside their neighborhood. Cultural conditions, such as the ability to speak specific languages, directly impact the ability to become employed. The income earning potential decreases when jobs are not available within a community.

Economic, social, cultural, and political conditions can vary around the world and from one part of the country to another. Supply and demand in the job market varies greatly from one field of employment to another and from one area to another.

Section 21.1 Review

Check Your Understanding

1. Explain the difference between a job and a career.
2. Describe the relationship between career clusters and career pathways.
3. Explain the importance of setting SMART goals.
4. What is the goal of CTSOs?
5. What is the effect of dramatic changes in technology?

Build Your Vocabulary

As you progress through this course, develop a personal glossary. This will help you build your vocabulary and prepare you for a career. Write a definition for each of the following terms and add it to your glossary.

- job
- career
- skill
- job-specific skills
- employability skills
- career cluster
- career pathway
- career ladder
- career plan
- aptitude
- ability
- values
- interest
- networking
- informational interviewing
- career and technical student organization (CTSO)

Section 21.2 Preparing for Your Education

Objectives

After completing this section, you will be able to:

- Discuss the role of education, training, and certification on career choices.
- Explain the term *college access*.
- Identify sources of funding for pursuing an education.

Why is planning for education, training, or certification worthwhile?

Terms

formal education	occupational training	529 plan
postsecondary education	internship	grant
not-for-profit school	apprenticeship	scholarship
for-profit school	certification	work-study program
	college access	need-based award

Education, Training, and Certification

There are many steps you will take as you plan your career. Your educational needs will depend on your career interests and goals. Some careers require a high school diploma followed by technical training or a bachelor degree. Others require a master degree or doctorate, as well. Still others require professional certification. Early career planning can help you make decisions about your education. Investigating the opportunities and costs of future education, training, and certification is an investment in your future.

Education, training, and certification have a direct effect on income and career potential. Some employers pay increased salaries for those individuals who continue training in their positions and become more skilled in their areas. Certain positions may require additional training in order to advance career potential.

Blend Images/Shutterstock.com

A person's education, training, and certification needs depend on personal career goals.

Education

Formal education is the education received in a school, college, or university. Most careers require a college degree.

Employability Skills

Workspace Etiquette

Whether you are in an office, a cubicle, or an open room, chances are you will have to share your workspace with others. Always allow your neighbors their privacy. Knock before entering a room or speaking to someone. Walk around walls or partitions to communicate; do not shout over or around them. Wait to be invited into a conversation rather than jumping in just because it is within earshot. Be respectful of social distancing when at work and leave adequate space between you and your coworkers.

However, for an entry-level position, a high school diploma may get you in the door. Jobs higher on the career ladder often require additional formal education.

High School

During high school, a variety of subjects are covered. This gives students a well-rounded education to serve as a foundation for lifelong learning. English, history, and science are some of the subjects all students study in high school. At the end of four years, students graduate and receive a *high school diploma*.

Postsecondary Education

Postsecondary education is any education achieved after high school. This includes all two- and four-year colleges and universities. Common postsecondary degrees are an associate degree and a bachelor degree. An associate degree is a two-year degree. A bachelor degree is a four-year degree.

Area of Study. Students in postsecondary schools choose an area of study that suits an interest or meets a career goal. This is referred to as a *major.* For example, a student who wants to become an elementary school teacher may major in education.

When considering a major, research the income potential of the related careers. Some careers start at a low salary and steadily increase over the course of the career. Other careers may start high and continue to increase. In addition to income potential, look into the number of jobs that are available in the area of study, both for new graduates and for those with experience.

In addition to major areas of study, postsecondary students are typically required to take a wide variety of classes in other subjects. These courses are referred to as *general education courses.* They cover many of the same subject areas as high school courses. The courses also cover subjects not often offered at the high-school level, such as political science and psychology.

Not-for-Profit and For-Profit Schools. A postsecondary school may be either a not-for-profit school or a for-profit school. A **not-for-profit school** is one that returns the money it earns back into the school. These schools receive funding from student tuition and fees, donations, and governmental programs. A not-for-profit school is what most people think of in terms of "college." It may be public, such as a state university. Others may be private, such as a private college or university.

Not-for-profit schools tend to encourage academic exploration and personal growth beyond the specific requirements of a student's major.

A **for-profit school** is one that is set up to earn money for investors. It provides a product, which is education. In return for providing education, for-profit schools receive money from their customers, who are students. For-profit schools are also known as *proprietary schools.* They tend to focus on specific skills and do not require general education courses. A trade school is an example of a for-profit school. They typically offer a two-year degree specialized in a field of trade, such as automotive repair or cosmetology. Some for-profit schools offer bachelor degree programs.

Requirements and Costs. When considering a college or university, be aware of what is needed to apply. Requirements may include official transcripts, college exam test scores, essays, and interviews. For all requirements, be sure to know the deadlines for completing and submitting the information. Missing a deadline can mean not being accepted to the school.

The costs of a postsecondary education must be considered. In addition to tuition, there are fees for many classes. Some majors include many laboratory classes. These classes can have more fees than other courses. Living expenses must also be considered as part of the cost of a postsecondary education.

Graduate and Postgraduate Education

Education received after an individual has earned a bachelor degree is *graduate education*. Master degrees are graduate degrees. Education beyond a master degree is called *postgraduate education*. Doctorate degrees are postgraduate degrees.

Graduate study often builds on the same subject area, or a closely related subject, in which the bachelor degree was earned. For example, a student who earned a Bachelor of Science in accounting may pursue a Master of Business Administration (MBA) degree.

Continuing Education

Some careers that have professional licenses require *continuing education* classes. These classes are completed to maintain the license. Completing these classes earns the student *continuing education units (CEUs).* If you are a teacher, for example, your school system may require that you earn a specified number of CEUs every year.

Another form of continuing education is more commonly called *adult education* or *adult ed*. These classes are for people age 18 or older and traditionally focus on basic skills. Classes are offered in a wide variety of topics ranging from learning computer skills to the English language.

Quality of Education

Colleges, universities, and training programs can vary significantly in the quality and type of education offered. There are many resources that rank schools and provide tools to help you evaluate an institution. As you begin to make decisions about your education after high school, analyze the quality of the education that institutions offer. This can ensure that the education you receive will be well worth the investments of both time and money. Some of the criteria include academic reputation, credentials of the faculty, graduation statistics, potential earning power of graduates, and student activities and opportunities on and around the campus.

Training

A college degree is not necessary for all career paths. Before taking on the expense of college classes, decide if college is right for you and your goals. There are many options for career training, including occupational training, internships, apprenticeships, and military service.

Occupational Training

Training for a specific career can be an option for many technical, trade, and technology fields. **Occupational training** is education that prepares you for a specific type of work. This type of training typically costs less than a traditional college education. It can also be completed in less time.

Internships

An **internship** is a short-term position with a sponsoring organization that gives the intern an opportunity to gain on-the-job experience in a certain field of study or occupation. Internships can be paid or unpaid. Often, high schools, colleges, and universities offer school credit for completing internships. Internships are an opportunity to gain work experience while working on an education.

Apprenticeships

An **apprenticeship** is a combination of on-the-job training, work experience, and classroom instruction. Apprenticeships are typically available to those who want to learn a trade or a technical skill. The apprentice works on mastering the skills required to work in the trade or field under the supervision of a skilled tradesperson.

Military Service

Service in the military can provide opportunities to receive skilled training, often in highly specialized technical areas. In addition to receiving this training, often it can be translated into college credit or professional credentials. After completing military service, there are many benefits available to veterans. For example, the *GI Bill* is a law that provides financial assistance for veterans pursuing education or training. Other forms of tuition assistance are also available.

Some people choose to enter the armed forces through the *Reserve Officers Training Corps (ROTC)*. Each branch of the military has an ROTC program at selected colleges and universities. Some high schools have Junior ROTC programs. The purpose of the ROTC program is to train commissioned officers for the armed forces. It can provide tuition assistance in exchange for a commitment to military service. Students enrolled in this program take classes just like other college students. The program is considered an elective. However, students also receive basic military and officer training. Information is available on the Today's Military website sponsored by the US Department of Defense. Opportunities available in the armed forces are also outlined in the *Occupational Outlook Handbook*.

Professional Certification

Some professional organizations offer certifications. **Certification** is a professional status earned by an individual after passing an exam focused on a specific body of knowledge. The individual usually prepares for the exam by taking classes and studying content that will be tested.

Some jobs require a professional certification. There are many types of certifications in most industries and trades, as shown in Figure 21-6. For example, a financial planning agency might require a financial planner to be certified as a qualification for the job. Other employers may prefer, but not require, certification. Certification requirements should be considered when creating a career plan.

There are certifications that must be renewed on a regular basis. For example, many certifications sponsored by Microsoft are only valid for the specific version of software. When the next version is released, another exam must be taken to be certified for the update. Other certifications require regular continuing education classes to ensure individuals are current with up-to-date information in the profession.

Some certifications are not subject-specific. Instead, they verify that an individual has employability skills. These certifications confirm that the person possesses the skills to be a contributing employee. The focus of these certifications is on workplace skills. Individuals who earn this type of certification have demonstrated they possess the qualities necessary to become effective employees.

Certifications by Industry

Industry	Certification(s)	Industry	Certification(s)
Auditing	Certified Internal Auditor (CIA) Certified Government Auditing Professional (CGAP) Certified Financial Services Auditor (CFSA)	Information Technology	Cisco Certified Network Professional (CCNP) Microsoft Certified Systems Engineer (MCSE) CompTIA A+ Certification Certified Information Systems Auditor (CISA)
Financial Planning	Certified Financial Planner (CFP)	Project Management	Certified Associate in Project Management (CAPM) Project Management Professional (PMP)
Health Support	Certified EKG/ECG Technician (CET) Certified Pharmacy Technician (CPhT)	Real Estate	Seller Representative Specialist (SRS) Accredited Buyer's Representative (ABR) Certified Residential Specialist (CRS)
Hospitality	Certified Hospitality Accountant Executive (CHAE) Certified Hospitality Supervisor (CHS) Certified Hotel Administrator (CHA)	Workplace Safety	Occupational Health and Safety Technologist (OHST) Certified Safety Professional (CSP) Safety Trained Supervisor (STS)
Human Resources	Professional in Human Resources (PHR) Senior Professional in Human Resources (SPHR)	Workplace Skills	ACT National Career Readiness Certificate (NCRC™)

Goodheart-Willcox Publisher

Figure 21-6 Certifications are available in many different industries.

College Access

College access refers to building awareness about college opportunities, providing guidance regarding college admissions, and identifying ways to pay for college. College access includes access to many types of postsecondary institutions. This includes colleges, universities, and trade schools. Attending a postsecondary school to further your education can be a critical step in your career plan. However, preparing to go to college can present challenges to students and families, both academically and financially. The sooner you begin planning, the better. It is never too early.

Academic preparation includes taking the right classes and doing your best. If you have always been a good student, keep up the good work. If you have not been performing to your potential, demonstrate your abilities and commitment by showing improvement. Along with strong academics, involvement in organizations at your high school or in your community will also provide greater access to college. Most schools are looking for well-rounded individuals. As you plan for your education, learn as much as possible about what it takes to be admitted to the college of your choice.

Many websites provide information to help you gain access to college. You can begin by searching the Internet for resources offered in your state. Search using the term *college access* plus the name of your state. If you have already been thinking about a specific school, visit its official website to learn about admission requirements and to find out what financial help might be available to you. The US Department of Education, the College Board, and the National College Access Network have websites that include a wealth of information about college access. Topics include applying to college and paying for college. If you have not already done so, talk to your family, friends, and guidance counselor today for information to begin planning for college.

Funding Your Education

As you make decisions about your education, you will need to create a financial plan for paying for your education. Whether you attend a trade school, community college, or university, someone has to pay the cost of the education. Funds to pay for education can come from a variety of sources. Each student's financial situation is different. Many online college-cost calculators can help you estimate how much money you will need to fund your education. Once you have an idea of how much it will cost to go to college, you need to figure out how you will pay for it.

Some families can afford to pay for college with current income, savings, or investments. If your parents or other family members are able and willing to pay for a college education for you, take advantage of their generosity. Thank them by studying hard and earning your degree.

Saving money for a college education is an investment strategy for the future. Someone in your family may have established a 529 plan to fund your college education. A **529 plan** is a savings plan for education operated by a state or educational institution. These plans are tax-advantaged savings plans and

History of Finance

Practical Education

The original purpose of college was not practical education designed to prepare students for a career. Originally, college was for the enlightenment of the mind. Students went to college to study the arts, literature, philosophy, history, and law. The growth and expansion of the nation following the Civil War led to the need for practical education. The apprentice system was no longer able to provide as many skilled workers as the nation needed. As a result, private business colleges were founded to fill the void. One of the original such schools was Folsom's Mercantile College, which opened in 1848 in Cleveland, Ohio. Among the courses offered by the school were penmanship, bookkeeping, and drawing. Schooling lasted only two to three months, and night classes were offered for those who worked during the day.

Folsom became the model for the national chain of Bryant & Stratton Business Schools. Many other proprietary business schools sprang up, and the for-profit education industry played a significant role in preparing Americans for the workforce well into the twentieth century.

By the mid-twentieth century, most colleges offered degrees in business and other practical fields. Most high schools were also offering practical education. Around 1960, public vocational/trade schools were starting to open in many states. These schools offered courses of study ranging from accounting to welding, and they were designed to put students in the workforce within a year.

By 1975, community colleges offered practical as well as academic courses of study. Four-year and two-year schools continue to expand offerings in practical education. With the advent of online education, the trend is likely to continue.

encourage families to set aside college funds for their children. These funds may be used for qualified colleges across the nation. Each state now has at least one 529 plan available. Plans vary from state to state because every state sets up its own plan. There are restrictions on how this money can be used, so make sure you understand how the plan works. There are penalties if money invested in a 529 plan is used for anything other than college expenses.

Even if your family has a 529 plan, the amount saved might not be enough to pay for all your college expenses. Many families pay for college using savings, current income, and loans. Parents, other family members, and students often work together to cover the cost of college. You might contribute money you have saved, money you earn if you work while attending school, and money for loans you will have to repay. More than half of students attending college get some form of financial aid. Figure 21-7 shows potential sources of funding for your education.

Financial aid is available from the federal government, as well as from nonfederal agencies. There is more than $100 billion in grants, scholarships, work-study, need-based awards, and loans available each year. Some states also offer college money to attend a state school, if you have good grades in high school.

A **grant** is a financial award that does not have to be repaid and is typically provided by a nonprofit organization. Grants are generally need-based and usually tax exempt. A Federal Pell Grant is an example of a government grant.

Potential Sources of Funding a College Education		
Source	**Brief Description**	**Repayment**
529 plan	Tax-advantage savings plan designed to encourage saving for future college costs. Plans are sponsored by states, state agencies, and educational institutions.	No repayment.
Grants	Money to pay for college provided by government agencies, corporations, states, and other organizations. Most grants are based on need and some have other requirements.	No repayment.
Scholarships	Money to pay for college based on specific qualifications including academics, sports, music, leadership, and service. Criteria for scholarships vary widely.	No repayment.
Work-study	Paid part-time jobs for students with financial need. Work-study programs are typically backed by government agencies.	No repayment.
Need-based awards	Aid for students who demonstrate financial need.	No repayment.
Government education loans	Loans made to students to help pay for college. Interest rates are lower than bank loans.	Repayment is required. Repayment may be postponed until you begin your career.
Private education loans	Loans made to students to help pay for college. Interest rates are higher than government education loans.	Repayment is required.
Internships	Career-based work experience. Some internships are paid and some are not. In addition to experience, you will likely earn college credit.	No repayment.
Military benefits	The US Military offers several ways to help pay for education. It provides education and training opportunities while serving and also provides access to funding for veterans. The US Reserve Officers' Training Corps (ROTC) programs and the military service academies are other options to consider.	No repayment, however a service commitment is required.

Goodheart-Willcox Publisher

Figure 21-7 There are multiple alternatives for funding a college education.

A **scholarship** is financial aid that may be based on financial need or some type of merit or accomplishment. There are scholarships based on standardized test scores, grades, extracurricular activities, athletics, and music. There are also scholarships available for leadership, service, and other interests, abilities, and talents.

It is surprising how many scholarships and grants go unused because no one has applied for them. Do not fail to apply for help just because you do not want to write the essay or fill out the application. Talk to your school counselor. Be persistent if you think you might qualify for a scholarship.

Work-study programs are part-time jobs on a college campus. They are subsidized by the government. Wages earned at a work-study job go toward paying for tuition and other college expenses such as rent or dormitory expenses.

Need-based awards are financial-aid awards available for students and families who meet certain economic requirements. Income and other demographics are used to determine if a student qualifies for this assistance.

The *Free Application for Federal Student Aid (FAFSA)* is the application form used to determine your eligibility for federal financial aid. Many institutions require the FAFSA form if you are applying for any type of financial aid. You can file your application online at the Federal Student Aid website, which is an office of the US Department of Education. In addition to the financial aid application, the FAFSA website has resources to help you plan for college. The website suggests these steps to complete the FAFSA.

1. Create a Federal Student Aid ID. By creating a FAS ID, you can sign the FAFSA electronically and access other important information online.
2. Gather necessary financial documents, such as your social security number, federal income tax returns, W-2s, and any other records of money you have earned.
3. Start the FAFSA for the desired year. You will need to complete a FAFSA for each year you attend school.
4. Follow the instructions carefully and make sure all information you provide is accurate. There are seven sections to be completed: student demographics, name and location of high school and colleges interested in attending, dependency status, demographics of your parents, financial information, signature, and confirmation.
5. Sign and submit your FAFSA. Once the application is processed, you will receive a copy of your Student Aid Report that will list your Expected Family Contribution.

Financial resources are a major consideration when selecting postsecondary education or training. However, it is also important to analyze the quality of education the institution can offer you. Research the school's academic reputation, quality of courses offered in your chosen area of study, and types of degrees offered. Does the school offer the rigor you need to meet the qualifications for your chosen career? Also consider the likelihood of employment after graduation from that institution, as well as potential starting salaries if employment is found.

Section 21.2 Review

Check Your Understanding

1. What are three ways to fulfill personal education needs for a career?
2. Describe the role formal education can play in career preparation.
3. Discuss the importance of continuing education.
4. Describe how military service provides career training.
5. Give examples of financial aid that might be available for high school students.

Build Your Vocabulary

As you progress through this course, develop a personal glossary. This will help you build your vocabulary and prepare you for a career. Write a definition for each of the following terms and add it to your glossary.

formal education
postsecondary education
not-for-profit school
for-profit school
occupational training
internship
apprenticeship
certification
college access
529 plan
grant
scholarship
work-study program
need-based award

Review and Assessment

Chapter Summary

Section 21.1 Choosing a Career

- Employers require both job-specific skills and employability skills. Job-specific skills are those that are specific to the tasks related to a position. Employability skills are not specific to one career, but rather transferrable to any career. Studying career clusters is a good way to learn about the different types and levels of careers.
- Creating a career plan will help you reach your goals. Conducting a self-assessment is the first step to discover who you are and what your interests are. Next, setting SMART goals will help you as you write your career plan.
- There are many resources for career research to help evaluate which careers would make the most of your talents, skills, and interests. The Internet is a good place to start. Career handbooks and informational interviews are also ways to gain insight into a career.
- Career and technical student organizations (CTSOs) are national student organizations that are related to career and technical education (CTE) courses. The goal of CTSOs is to help students acquire knowledge and skills in different career and technical areas, as well as related leadership skills and work experience.
- When evaluating career opportunities, it is important to stay current with industry trends and developments. Changes in technology, as well as economic, social, cultural, education, and political conditions can affect income and career potential.

Section 21.2 Preparing for Your Education

- Your educational needs will depend on your career interests and goals. Most careers require a college education. However, there are many options for career training, including occupational training, internships, and apprenticeships. The military is also a career option.
- College access refers to building awareness about college opportunities, providing guidance regarding college admissions, and identifying ways to pay for college. It includes access to many types of postsecondary institutions, including colleges, universities, and trade schools.
- As you are making decisions on your education, it is important to create a financial plan for paying for your education. A 529 plan is a savings plan and is one way to pay for an education. There are also grants, scholarships, work-study, need-based awards, and loans available to help students and their families.

Review Your Knowledge

1. Describe types of skills needed for the workplace.
2. What information should be included when creating a career plan?
3. Explain the relationship between aptitudes and abilities.
4. Name some sources of career information.
5. Summarize how CTSOs can prepare you for a career.
6. What is the goal of informational interviewing?
7. Describe the impacts of education, training, and certification on career choices.
8. Explain the importance of college access.
9. College access is important to any student considering educational opportunities. What are some sources of information for building college awareness?

10. Identify sources of funding for pursuing an education.

Apply Your Knowledge

1. Two important types of skills that are foundational to your career are job specific skills and employability skills. Create a chart with two columns. In column one, list the job-specific skills you currently possess. In column two, list the employability skills that you possess. Use this chart as a source of information when you create a career plan.
2. What types of experiences in high school do you think would be helpful in getting full-time employment? Explain.
3. Conduct an informal self-assessment by defining your work style, aptitudes, values, and interests. Next, evaluate your individual talents, abilities, and skills. This will help prepare you to write a career plan.
4. Your interests and abilities can be a first step in determining career opportunities that would be a good fit for you. Take time to analyze your interests and abilities and how you can turn these into SMART career goals. Write three of your career goals as SMART goals. Specify how each of these goals is specific, measurable, attainable, realistic, and timely.
5. Analyzing various clusters will help you select a career in which you are interested. Refer to the career clusters in Figure 21-2. Review the Human Services career cluster, Business Management career cluster, and Finance career cluster. Select a career cluster to analyze. How are the different careers within the cluster related to one another?
6. A career plan is a list of steps to reach a career goal. Write a list of action items for a career plan for the next five years that you might consider following. Use Figure 21-4 as an example. Include your career objectives and the strategies you will use to accomplish your goals.
7. Discuss the key advantages and disadvantages of going from high school to each of the following: college, occupational training, an internship, an apprenticeship, the military.
8. There are many careers that require or suggest that individuals obtain certification for their chosen field. For the career you have chosen to investigate, are there any certification requirements that will be necessary to stay in the chosen field? If yes, describe what is needed. If no, explain why you think it is not necessary to have certification in that career.
9. Think about your future career plans. They may involve a career in finance, human services, or another career cluster. Consider how your personal priorities and family responsibilities would influence the type of career you would pursue. Make a list of the priorities and responsibilities that would have the most influence on a future career.
10. Economic, social, cultural, and political conditions impact an individual's career potential. Create a chart with four columns. Label the columns *Economic Influences*, *Social Influences*, *Cultural Influences*, and *Political Influences*. In each column, list ways your future career and income potential might be impacted. When you are finished, analyze your findings. How do you think these factors could affect your income and career potential?

Apply Your Math Skills

1. Gerald was accepted to two different universities. One is a state university, and the other is a private, liberal arts college. The state university costs $16,572 per year, and the private college costs $35,200 per year. The estimate for the cost of books is around $1,200 each year. How much would tuition and books cost over four years at each school?
2. Susanne's parents have set aside $10,000 for college expenses with eligibility for another $10,000 in scholarships and grants for the academic year. If tuition is $1,450 per credit hour and a full-time student enrolls in 12 credits, how much more money will be needed for a year of tuition?

Communication Skills

College and Career Readiness

Speaking. The way you communicate with others will have a lot to do with the success of the relationships you build. Create a speech that will introduce you to a counselor at a local college. The counselor should be a person you have never met. Deliver the speech to your class. How did the style, words, phrases, and tone you used influence the way the audience responded to the speech?

Writing. Postsecondary applications, such as applications to colleges, often require an essay as part of the application process. Write a 500-word essay that describes the role and function of an individual who is in a Consumer Services or a Finance career. Identify the audience and determine an effective approach and technique that will clearly state your purpose. Edit your writing for proper voice, tense, and syntax, assuring that it conforms to Standard English, when appropriate.

Reading. Service in the military can provide opportunities to receive skilled training that often can be translated into college credit or professional credentials. Ask your guidance counselor for pamphlets or other materials about military service opportunities. Read the information. What did you learn?

Teamwork

By joining a CTSO, you can participate in student leadership and learn how to prepare for school and career opportunities. Working with your team, make a list of the CTSOs that are available at your school. What leadership activities are provided for students in each organization? What professional development activities are available? How can your school CTSOs help you prepare for life after graduation? Share your findings with the class.

Internet Research

Employment Opportunities. Conduct Internet research about a career of interest to you in a career cluster such as human services or finance. Summarize the education, training, and certification requirements of the career. Explain the role that a person in this position would provide. Next, compare this career with a second career in the same career cluster. What opportunities are currently available for each career? Evaluate salaries, career paths, and demand for the careers. Does the future look promising for either pathway?

Career Plan. It is important that you take ownership of a career plan that matches your interests and skills. Using the Internet, research how to create a career plan. Select a template that meets your needs. Create a career plan that aligns a career pathway to your educational goals. List any application, testing, or certification requirements and note any associated deadlines. State the potential beginning earnings and expected future earnings, and any other information that will help you create a viable post secondary plan. Using your list of SMART goals, create a career plan for the next five years.

Costs of College. Use the Internet to research the costs in tuition and fees of a college, university, or training program you would like to attend. Include living expenses in your projected amounts. Next, research scholarships and grants for which you may be eligible. Finally, locate a copy of the Free Application for Federal Student Aid (FAFSA) form. Print the form and practice filling it out (use 123-45-6789 as your Social Security number). Build a plan to fund your first year of attendance and present your plan to the class.

Quality of Education Investment. Research information about a college or university that interests you. Analyze the quality of the education it offers by reading about its academic reputation, selectivity and rigor, average starting salary of students graduating in chosen field, and likelihood of student graduation. What did you learn?

Professional Organizations. Investigate professional organizations for a Consumer Services, Finance, or other career of your choice. Select an organization that interests you. Write several paragraphs that describe the organization and how it serves its members.

Completing the FAFSA. It is important that every student understand how, why, and when to complete grant and scholarship applications and the Free Application for Federal Student Aid (FAFSA) provided by the U.S. Department of Education. Perform an Internet search for the FAFSA form. Your state may have also have a specific site to use for guidance to complete this application, so consider performing the search with your state in front of the search phrase. Read the directions and practice completing the form. Make notes of information that you need when completing the official form for submission. What did you learn from this practice exercise?

Portfolio Development

College and Career Readiness

Presenting the Print Portfolio. Once you have collected items for your portfolio, it is time to organize the contents. Select and print the documents to include in your final portfolio. Opt for quality over quantity, and remove working documents such as your checklist. Next, create divider pages for each section. For example, a page that says *Work Samples* helps organize the material. Prepare a title page, which should consist of the word *Portfolio* followed by the phrase *Prepared by* and your full name. Next, create a table of contents.

Conclude your portfolio with a résumé and generic cover letter followed by references and letters of recommendation. Consider adding a photo to help the interviewer connect a name and a face during the evaluation process.

Decide what you want to use to house your portfolio. Remember, a portfolio is a living document and updated regularly. If you create too many initial versions, you may find yourself discarding them.

1. Review the documents and select the items you want to include. Make copies of certificates and other important documents. Keep the originals in a safe place.
2. Organize the documents.
3. Place the items in a folder, binder, or other container.
4. Submit the portfolio to an instructor or other person who can give constructive feedback.

CTSOs

Event Prep

Careers. Many competitive events for CTSOs competitions offer events that include various careers. This competitive event may include an objective test that covers multiple topics. Participants are usually allowed one hour to complete the event.

To prepare for the careers component of an event, complete the following activities.

1. Read the careers features in each chapter of the text. As you read about each career, note an important fact or two that you would like to remember.
2. Conduct an Internet search for *careers*. Review careers that may be a choice for the event. Make notes on important facts about each.

CHAPTER

22 Applying for and Accepting Employment

Finding a job is often a lengthy process. A job-seeker can enhance the chances of success by becoming aware of standard employment practices, such as the proper way to apply for a job and good interviewing skills.

Once you earn your first job, it is important to be prepared for the career that lies ahead. Entering the workplace is a major step for most people. Being employed not only provides a person with the means to obtain what is needed and wanted in life, it also gives an individual a sense of identity and security. For many people, a career defines who they are.

Well-developed employability skills are important for individual success in the workplace. Knowing how to act professionally and be a contributing team member are necessary employability skills in the business world.

Focus on Finance

Citizenship

Being a good citizen is important to your personal and financial success. Personal ethics and social responsibility are keys to a well-lived life.

Good citizens are ethical. Personal ethics serve as a moral compass that helps an individual decide what is right and wrong. Ethical behavior centers on honesty, fairness, integrity, and well-defined values. Ethical behavior is expected when representing yourself and the business for which you work. Avoid the temptation to "twist the truth." Always keep your communication honest.

Good citizens are socially responsible. *Social responsibility* involves concern for the welfare of others in the community and around the world. You show your concern for others through participation in community life, shared problem solving, and good citizenship. Examples include staying up-to-date on local issues, voting in elections, and volunteering.

College and Career Readiness

Reading Prep. Before reading the chapter, skim the photos and their captions. As you read, determine how these concepts contribute to the ideas presented in the text.

Sections

Mix and Match Studio/Shutterstock.com

Section 22.1 Résumés, Cover Messages, and Employment Applications

Essential Question

What can a person's résumé reveal about potential career success?

Objectives

After completing this section, you will be able to:

- Summarize how to write a résumé.
- Write a persuasive cover message to accompany a résumé.
- Explain how to apply for a job in person and online.

Terms

résumé
career objective
chronological résumé
reference
portfolio
cover message
job application

Writing a Résumé

When looking for employment, you must sell your talents and skills to a potential employer. A job applicant must persuade the hiring manager that the person's personal skills and experience match the qualifications of the job being sought. A **résumé** is a document that profiles a person's career goals, education, and work history. Think of a résumé as a snapshot that shows who you are and why you would be an asset as an employee.

A résumé is the first impression that potential employers will have of you. It must be well-written and free of errors. A résumé that contains typographical errors or poor language usage reflects negatively on the applicant. The *four Cs of communication* are clarity, conciseness, courtesy, and correctness. These should be applied when writing for employment. When finished, each line should be proofread and checked for correct grammar, vocabulary, and punctuation.

A general rule of thumb is that a résumé should be one page. Résumés have standard parts that employers expect to see. A typical résumé is shown in Figure 22-1. This student is applying for a job as an accountant's assistant, which is a consumer services position in the human services career cluster. Positions in the human services career cluster share many job titles with the finance cluster, including accountant positions.

Name and Personal Information

The top of the résumé should present your name, address, telephone number, and e-mail address. Use an e-mail address that is your real name, or at least a portion of it. E-mails with nicknames or screen names do not make a professional impression.

Jake Barton
123 Eastwood Terrace
Saratoga Springs, NY 60123
518-555-9715
jbarton@e-mail.edu

CAREER OBJECTIVE
A mature and responsible individual seeks an entry-level job as an accountant's assistant.

WORK EXPERIENCE
Saratoga Springs City Online Newspaper, Saratoga Springs, NY
September 20-- to present
Accounting Clerk

- Track subscriptions revenue for newspaper.
- Assist with the setup of billing processes.
- File invoices as needed.
- Prepare accounts receivable and payable schedules.

Hunter High School, Saratoga Springs, NY
September 20-- to September 20--
Student Office Volunteer

- Answered telephone calls.
- Sorted and filed vendor invoices as they were received.
- Updated spreadsheets to track student fees.
- Recorded fees for parking permits.

EDUCATION
Hunter High School, Saratoga Springs, NY
Graduation date: May 20--
Relevant coursework: Accounting I and II, Financial Math

HONORS

- Hunter High School Honor Roll, 8 quarters
- FBLA Most Valuable Student of the Year, 20--

ACTIVITIES

- Saratoga High School FBLA, two years

Goodheart-Willcox Publisher

Figure 22-1 A chronological résumé has standard sections that employers expect to see.

Case Study *Writing a Résumé*

Lucy graduates from college this semester and needs to write a résumé. It is well known that fellow classmates have impressive résumés, and it is important to be just as impressive.

Without a lot of work experience, Lucy compensates by listing job duties in great detail, embellishing responsibilities and suggesting that previous positions were more important than they were. As for references, listing friends prevents previous supervisors from contradicting claims in the résumé. After all, what is the harm in slight exaggeration?

Case Review

1. Is it ethical to list job duties in great detail?
2. Is it ethical to embellish job responsibilities on a résumé?
3. What problems may Lucy face if hired based on an inaccurate resume?
4. What information should be included on a résumé when experience is limited?

Before you begin applying for jobs via e-mail, set up an e-mail address that you will use only for professional communication.

Career Objective

A **career objective** is a summary of the type of job for which the applicant is looking. An example of an objective is, "To gain industry experience as a sales associate while earning my business degree." The career objective should match or be related to the position for which you are applying.

Work Experience

The work experience section of a résumé includes details about the jobs you have held in the past as well as your current job. The information in this section is typically the main focus of the employer's attention.

As you begin composing this section, list your current or most recent employer first. This format is known as a chronological résumé. A **chronological résumé** lists information in reverse chronological order, with the most recent employer listed first.

For each work experience entry, include the company name, your job title, and the duration of time you worked there. List the responsibilities and details about the position you held. Do not list the addresses or telephone numbers of previous employers. This information will be provided on a job application.

Volunteer work may also be listed as work experience. Employers are especially interested in community-oriented applicants who do volunteer work. Be certain to list any volunteer activities and the length of time you have participated in the activities.

Education

The education section should list the name of your high school and where it is located. Indicate the year in which you will graduate. Briefly describe any courses you have taken that are relevant to the job for which you are applying. List any certifications you have earned, special courses or training programs completed, and any other educational achievements related to the job you are seeking.

Honors, Activities, and Publications

Employers look for well-rounded individuals. Include information on your résumé that shows your involvement in activities outside of work or school. These can be separate sections, or they can be combined into one section. List applicable honors, activities, or publications with the corresponding year in which each occurred. If you have been a leader in an organization, note that experience. If you are a member of career and technical student organization (CTSO), include the name of the organization and number of years you have been a member.

References

It is customary for references to be provided only when requested by the employer. For that reason, references should not be included on your résumé. Instead, create a separate list of references.

A **reference** is a person who can comment on the qualifications, work ethic, personal qualities, and work-related aspects of another person's character. Your list of references should include three or four people for whom you have worked and one person who knows you socially. Do not include relatives. Ask permission from the people you intend to use as references. Include each person's name, title, and contact information.

To be prepared, bring copies of your list of references to the job interview. Employers who require references in advance usually indicate this in the job advertisement. Otherwise, you will be told during the interview process when references are needed.

MBI/Shutterstock.com

A teacher or mentor is a good choice to ask to be a reference when applying for a position.

Portfolio

In some cases, candidates may be asked to submit a portfolio as part of the application process. A **portfolio** is a selection of related materials that an individual has created to show qualifications, skills, and talents to support a career or personal goal. For example, a technical writer may have a portfolio of published articles or other written pieces. A fashion designer may have a portfolio with drawings or photographs of designs.

You have been creating a portfolio throughout this course. Each chapter in this text has a Portfolio Development activity as part of the end-of-chapter exercises. Your finished portfolio may be part of the materials you need to apply for a job.

Writing a Cover Message

A **cover message**, or *cover letter,* is a letter or e-mail sent with a résumé to introduce the applicant and summarize reasons for applying for a job. It is a sales message written to persuade the reader to grant an interview. A cover message provides an opportunity to focus a potential employer's attention on your background, skills, and work experience that match the job you are seeking. Writing a cover message is an important part of applying for a job. It sets the tone for the résumé that follows. Figure 22-2 shows an example of a cover letter that is sent by e-mail.

Introduction

The cover message should begin with an introduction. The introduction should tell the employer who you are and why you are applying. If applying for a specific position, state the title of the position.

If responding to an advertisement, mention where you found the ad. For example, you might be responding to a posting on the company's website. Mention this in the introduction.

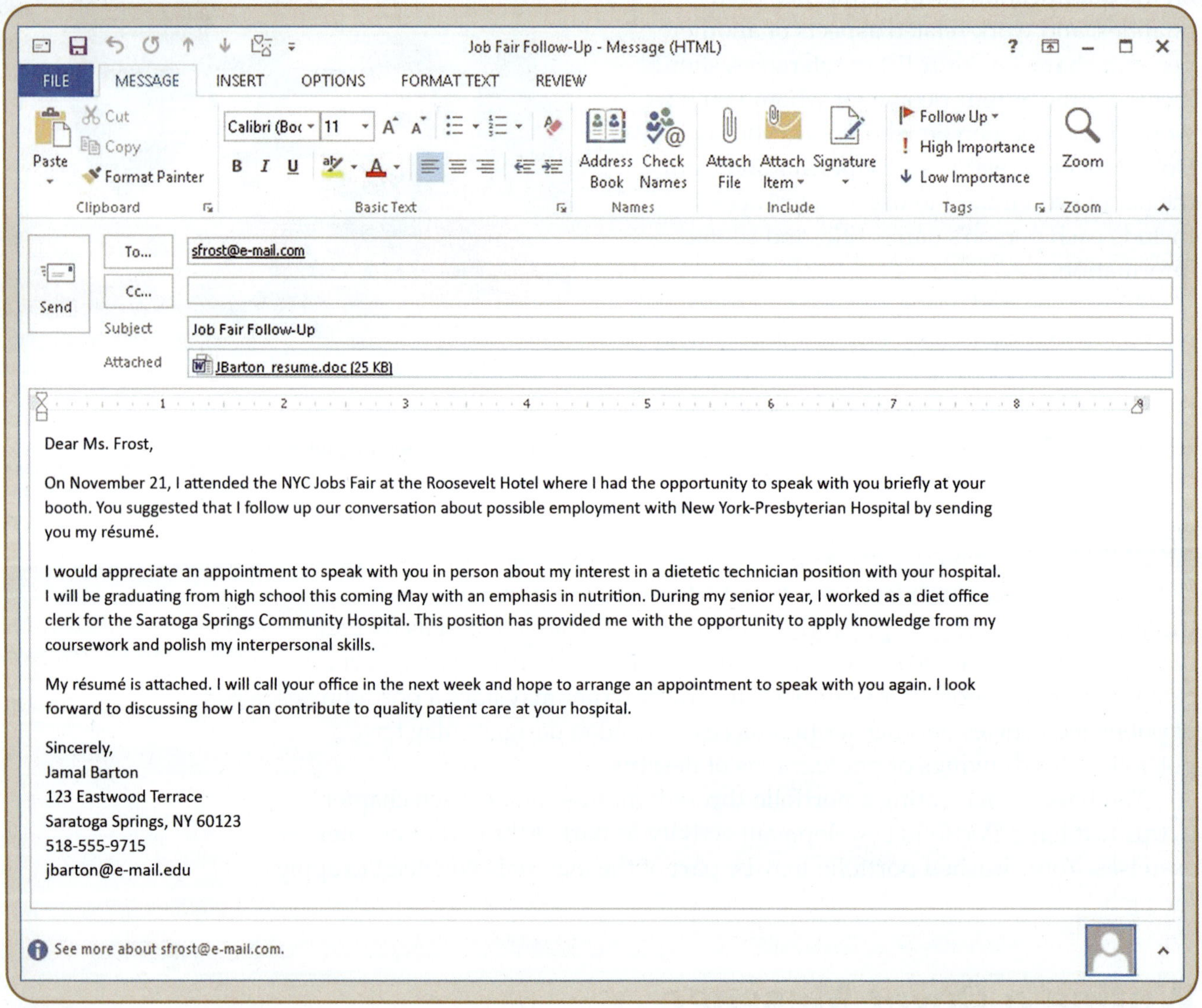
Job Fair Follow-Up - Message (HTML)

To... sfrost@e-mail.com

Cc...

Subject: Job Fair Follow-Up

Attached: JBarton resume.doc (25 KB)

Dear Ms. Frost,

On November 21, I attended the NYC Jobs Fair at the Roosevelt Hotel where I had the opportunity to speak with you briefly at your booth. You suggested that I follow up our conversation about possible employment with New York-Presbyterian Hospital by sending you my résumé.

I would appreciate an appointment to speak with you in person about my interest in a dietetic technician position with your hospital. I will be graduating from high school this coming May with an emphasis in nutrition. During my senior year, I worked as a diet office clerk for the Saratoga Springs Community Hospital. This position has provided me with the opportunity to apply knowledge from my coursework and polish my interpersonal skills.

My résumé is attached. I will call your office in the next week and hope to arrange an appointment to speak with you again. I look forward to discussing how I can contribute to quality patient care at your hospital.

Sincerely,
Jamal Barton
123 Eastwood Terrace
Saratoga Springs, NY 60123
518-555-9715
jbarton@e-mail.edu

See more about sfrost@e-mail.com.

Goodheart-Willcox Publisher

Figure 22-2 A cover message sent in an e-mail should also have the résumé included as an attachment.

If sending a general letter of application, explain in specific terms how you identified the company and why you are interested in working there. If someone gave you the name of the employer to contact, mention the person and the connection that person has to the company.

Body

The body of the cover message is where to demonstrate your positive work behaviors and qualities that make you employable. This may include illustrating your ambition, determination, and skills. Examine the job description for the position and identify the positive traits and skills the employer seeks. Then, focus on these traits and skills. Explain why you are qualified and how your skills and experience make you the best candidate for the job.

Conclusion

The cover message should end with a conclusion. The conclusion has two purposes:

- request an interview
- make it easy for the reader to grant an interview

Leave no doubt in the reader's mind about your desire to be contacted for an interview. Specifically request an interview. State how and when you can be reached to schedule an interview. Provide the information necessary to arrange an interview. You may also state how and when you will follow up to schedule an interview.

Applying for Employment

Applying for employment may involve completing a form, submitting a résumé, or both. This may be done in person, by mail, or online. However, before applying, it is important to do one final review of your résumé and cover message. Make sure both are accurate and free from errors. If you are submitting an application by mail, follow the rules for formatting a letter.

Applying in Person

The traditional way to apply for employment is to print your résumé, cover message, and portfolio and hand deliver them to a potential employer. All documents should be on the same high-quality white or off-white paper and printed using a laser printer. Do not fold or staple the documents. Instead, use a large envelope or paperclip the pages together. If using an envelope, print your name on the outside and list the components included.

eurobanks/Shutterstock.com

Blue or black ink should be used when completing a job application by hand.

Be prepared to complete a job application. A **job application** is a form with spaces for contact information, education, and work experience. Even though much of this information may be repeated on your résumé, many companies require a job application to be completed. Use blue or black ink and your best penmanship. Like a résumé or cover message, an employment application needs to be free of spelling, grammar, and usage errors. Carefully review the form before submitting it.

Applying Online

Today, most people submit résumés online. The first step in submitting may be to complete an online application. Next, you may be required to upload a résumé, copy and paste information into a form on the site, or send it as an e-mail attachment. Do not forego a cover message just because you are submitting online.

Singkham/Shutterstock.com

A job application can be filled out and submitted online.

Be aware that copying and pasting into a form usually strips out formatting, such as tabs, indentations, and bold type. Avoid pasting text that is formatted in any way. Even if the formatting holds, it can make the information difficult to read when the employer accesses the application. You may need to adjust the layout of your résumé after uploading it or pasting it into an online application form.

Carefully review everything before clicking the submit button. Just because you are applying online does not mean you can ignore proper spelling, grammar, and usage. What you submit will be the employer's first impression of you. Submitting an application with misspellings or other errors may encourage an employer not to consider you as a serious candidate.

Section 22.1 Review

Check Your Understanding

1. What is the purpose of a résumé?
2. What should be included in the name and personal information section of a résumé?
3. Explain the purpose of a cover message.
4. Name two ways to apply for a job.
5. What information is normally asked for on a job application?

Build Your Vocabulary

As you progress through this course, develop a personal glossary. This will help you build your vocabulary and prepare you for a career. Write a definition for each of the following terms and add it to your glossary.

- résumé
- career objective
- chronological résumé
- reference
- portfolio
- cover message
- job application

Section 22.2 Job Interviews and the Employment Process

Objectives

After completing this section, you will be able to:

- Discuss how to prepare for a job interview.
- Explain the employment process.

Essential Question

Which job interview questions are the most important to be prepared to answer?

Terms

job interview
etiquette
telephone etiquette
verbal communication
mock interview
hypothetical question
behavioral question
employment verification
background check

Job Interview

A **job interview** is a meeting in which an applicant and the employer discuss the job and the candidate's skills. It is the employer's opportunity to review you résumé with you and ask questions to see if you are qualified for the position. This is your opportunity to sell yourself in person and to demonstrate professionalism. Your answers to interview questions are important in the employer's decision-making process. Most job interviews are conducted face to face, but it is common to have a preliminary phone interview before the in-person meeting.

mentatdgt/Shutterstock.com

The job interview is an opportunity to convince the employer that you are a match for the position.

Preparing for the Interview

The first step in preparing for a job interview is to learn as much as you can about not only the position, but the company as well. There are several ways to do this. If the company has a website, thoroughly study the site. Pay special attention to the About Us section for an overview of the company. Look for press releases, annual reports, and information on its products or services.

While a company website can be a valuable source of information, do not limit your research to just the company site. Use your network of friends and relatives to find people who are familiar with the employer. Get as much information as you can from them.

Call the company's human resources department. The human resources department often has materials specifically for potential employees. Use your best telephone etiquette while speaking with the person who answers the phone. **Etiquette** is the art of using good manners in any situation. **Telephone etiquette** is using good manners while speaking on the telephone. Introduce yourself, state your purpose for calling, and be prepared with a list of questions to ask. Be polite and say "please" and "thank you" when speaking with each person so that you project a positive impression.

Depending on the position, there may be a performance test as part of the interview. For example, a graphic artist may be asked to create a simple design using the software the company utilizes. This will test not only the person's design abilities, but also the person's ability to use the software. Be prepared to take a performance test if needed.

Dressing for the Interview

Phase4Studios/Shutterstock.com

Professional dress is a must for a job interview.

A face-to-face interview is typically the first time you are seen by a company representative. First impressions are important, so dress appropriately. You should be well-groomed and professionally dressed. Your appearance communicates certain qualities about you to the interviewer. When dressing for an interview, consider what you wish to communicate about yourself.

The easiest rule to follow is to dress in a way that shows you understand the work environment and know the appropriate attire. It is better to dress more conservatively than to dress in trendy clothing. Employers understand that interviewees want to put their best foot forward. Dressing more conservatively than needed is not likely to be viewed as a disadvantage. However, dressing too casually, too trendy, or wearing inappropriate clothing is likely to cost you the job. Additionally, personal expressions such as visible tattoos or piercings may be seen as inappropriate for the workplace by the employer.

Preparing for Interview Questions

Interview questions are intended to assess your skills and abilities and to explore your personality. Your answers to these questions will help determine whether you will fit in with the company team and the manager's leadership style. Interviewers also want to assess your critical-thinking skills. They may ask you to cite specific examples of projects you have completed or problems you have solved.

Communicating effectively in an interview requires specific skills to be mastered. **Verbal communication** is speaking words to communicate. It is also known as *oral communication*. In the course of a workday, most people spend at least some portion of time talking with coworkers, supervisors, managers, or customers. This communication involves a variety of situations, such as conversations about work tasks, asking and answering questions, making requests, giving information, and participating in meetings.

Employability Skills

Leadership

You do not have to be in a leadership position to exhibit leadership skills. Leadership is the ability to influence others to reach a goal. Common leadership characteristics include honesty, competence, self-confidence, communication skills, problem-solving skills, and dependability. Leaders have the ability to set goals, follow through on tasks, and be forward-thinking. Individuals who possess leadership skills are people who influence others, have ideas and solutions for challenges, and set examples for behavior.

During the interview, your communication skills will be observed. Communicate as clearly and effectively as you can.

Common Questions

Before the interview, try to anticipate questions the interviewer is likely to ask you. The following are some common interview questions.

- What are your strengths?
- What are your weaknesses?
- What about this position interests you?
- What do you plan to be doing five years from now?
- Why do you want to work for this organization?

Write down your answers to these questions. Practice answering the questions while in front of a mirror. An important part of the communication process is nonverbal communication. Practicing in front of a mirror will allow you to see your nonverbal communication.

Another way to prepare for an interview is to conduct a mock interview with a friend or instructor. A **mock interview** is a practice interview conducted with another person. Practice until you can give your planned responses naturally and without reading them. The more prepared you are, the more relaxed, organized, competent, and professional you will appear to the interviewer.

Hypothetical Questions

Interviewers may also ask hypothetical questions. **Hypothetical questions** require candidates to imagine a situation and describe how they would act. Frequent topics of hypothetical questions relate to working with and getting along with coworkers. For example, "How would you handle a disagreement with a coworker?" You cannot prepare specific answers to these questions, so you need to rely on your ability to think on your feet.

For these types of questions, the interviewer is aware that you are being put on the spot. In addition to what you say, other aspects of your answer are considered as well. Body language is first and foremost. Avoid fidgeting and looking at the ceiling while thinking of your answer. Instead, look at the interviewer and calmly take a moment to compose your thoughts. Keep your answer brief. If your answer runs on too long, you risk losing your train of thought. Try to relate the question to something that is familiar to you and answer honestly.

Do not try to figure out what the interviewer wants you to say. Showing that you can remain poised and project confidence carries a lot of weight, even if your answer is not ideal. In many cases, the interviewer is not as interested in *what* your response is as much as *how* you responded. Was your response quick and thoughtful? Did you ramble? Did you stare blankly at the reviewer before responding?

Bronwyn Photo/Shutterstock.com

Prepare for the questions asked in an interview by rehearsing your answers. The more prepared you are, the more relaxed and professional you will appear to be.

Behavioral Questions

Interviewers may ask behavioral questions. **Behavioral questions** are questions that draw on an individual's previous experiences and decisions. Your answers to these types of questions indicate past behavior, which may be used to predict future behavior and success in a position. The following are some examples of behavioral questions.

- Tell me about a time when you needed to assume a leadership position in a group. What were the challenges, and how did you help the group meet its goals?
- Describe a situation where you needed to be creative in order to help a client with a problem.
- Describe a situation when you made a mistake. How did you correct the mistake and what measures did you put in place to ensure it did not happen a second time?

Again, you cannot prepare specific answers to these questions. Remain poised, answer honestly, and keep your answers focused on the question. Making direct eye contact with the interviewer can project a positive impression.

Questions an Employer Should Not Ask

State and federal laws prohibit employers from asking questions on certain topics. It is important to know these topics so you can be prepared if such a question comes up during an interview. It is illegal for employers to ask questions about a job candidate's religion, national origin, gender, or disability. Questions about age can only be asked if a minimum age is required by law for a job. The following are some examples of questions an employer is not permitted to ask a candidate.

- What is your religion?
- Are you married?
- What is your nationality?
- Are you disabled?
- Do you have children?
- How much do you weigh?

If you are presented with similar questions during the interview, remain professional. You are not obligated to provide an answer. You could respond,

Exploring Careers

Credit Counselor

Credit counselors advise individuals on how to manage their debt. They determine the best types of loans and explain requirements and restrictions. They analyze their clients' credit and debt situations, create a plan that best suits the clients' needs, and implement and manage the plan. The goal of a credit counselor is to avoid advising bankruptcy. Some of the tasks credit counselors typically perform include:

- develop debt management plans
- provide advice regarding credit problems
- prioritize client debt repayment
- provide budget counseling
- provide mortgage and bankruptcy advice

Credit counselors often work in an office at a financial institution. They typically work full time. They spend a good amount of time on the phone or in face-to-face meetings with clients, so the ability to work with the general public is a necessity. A bachelor degree is often required for these positions. Credit counselors must have excellent listening, communication, and analytical skills.

"Please explain how that relates to the job." Or you could completely avoid the question by saying, "I would rather not answer personal questions."

Questions to Ask the Employer

Keep in mind that the questions you ask reveal details about your personality. Asking questions can make a good impression. Questions show that you are interested and aware. Good questions cover the duties and responsibilities of the position. Be aware of how you word questions.

Some questions are not appropriate until after you have been offered the job. In the early stages of the interview process, your questions should demonstrate that you would be a valuable employee and are interested in learning about the company. The following are some questions you may want to ask.

- What are the specific duties of this position?
- What is company policy or criteria for employee promotions?
- Do you have a policy for providing on-the-job training?
- When do you expect to make your hiring decision?
- What is the anticipated start date?

Usually, questions related to pay and benefits, such as vacation time, should not be asked in the interview unless the employer brings them up. These can be asked after an offer of employment is made to you. Sometimes, however, an interviewer asks what salary you want or expect. It is also common for salary requirements to be requested in the job posting, in which case you would need to address that in your cover message. Prepare for questions about salary by researching the industry. If you are unsure, you can simply tell the interviewer that the salary is negotiable.

Evaluating the Interview

Evaluate your performance as soon as you can after the interview. Asking yourself the following questions can help in evaluating your performance.

- Was I adequately prepared with knowledge about the company and the position?
- Did I remember to bring copies of my résumé, list of references, portfolio, and any other requested documents to the interview?
- Was I on time for the interview?
- Did I talk too much or too little?
- Did I honestly and completely answer the interviewer's questions?
- Did I dress appropriately?
- Did I display nervous behavior, such as fidgeting, or forget things I wanted to say?
- Did I come across as composed and confident?
- Which questions could I have handled better?

Every job interview is an opportunity to practice. If you discover that you are not interested in the job, do not feel as though your time was wasted. Make a list of the things you feel you did right and things you would do differently next time.

Writing Follow-Up Messages

Immediately after the interview, write a *thank-you message* to each person who interviewed you. Thank the interviewer for taking the time to talk with you about the job and your career interests. A thank-you may be in the form of a printed letter sent through the mail or an e-mail. Keep the letter brief and to the point. Remind the interviewer of your name and reiterate your enthusiasm, but do not be pushy. An example of a thank-you message is shown in Figure 22-3.

Employment decisions can take a long time. Some companies notify all applicants when a decision has been made, but some do not. If you have not heard anything after a week or two, it is appropriate to send a brief follow-up

Dear Ms. Frost:

Thank you for the opportunity to discuss the position of accountant assistant.

I am very excited about the possibility of working for Frost and Roberts CPA firm. The job is exactly the sort of challenging opportunity I had hoped to find. I believe my educational background and internship experience will enable me to make a contribution, while also learning and growing on the job.

Please contact me if you need any additional information. I look forward to hearing from you.

Sincerely,

Goodheart-Willcox Publisher

Figure 22-3 A thank-you message is an appropriate way to follow up the interview.

message. Simply restate your interest in the job and politely inquire whether a decision has been made.

Employment Process

The employment process can take a substantial amount of time. There are tasks that the employer completes to make sure a candidate is a fit for the position. In addition, there are forms that the employee must complete before starting a position. Reference checks are also made at this time.

Employment Verification

The employer will complete an employment verification using the information on your application or résumé. **Employment verification** is a process through which the information provided on an applicant's résumé is checked to verify that it is correct. A person's past employers typically verify only the dates of employment, position title, and other objective data. Most companies will not provide opinions about employees, such as whether or not the employee was considered a good worker.

Another important part of the employment process is a background check. A **background check** is an investigation into personal data about a job applicant. This information is available from governmental records and other sources, including public information on the Internet. The employer must inform you that a background check will be conducted, and you must grant permission before the employer can do so. Sometimes employers also run a check of your credit. Employers must have your permission to conduct this check as well.

wavebreakmedia/Shutterstock.com

Employment verification can include a background check, credit check, and completing a variety of forms.

Many employers use Internet search engines, such as Google, to search for your name. Employers may also check social networking websites, such as Facebook and Twitter. Be aware of this before posting any personal information or photos. These checks might work to your advantage or against you, depending on what the employer finds. It is up to you to ensure that the image you project on social networking sites, which is your *digital footprint*, is not embarrassing or, more importantly, does not prevent you from reaching your career goals.

Accepting an Offer

If an employer decides to offer you a position after the interview process and employment verification, someone will contact you with an official offer of employment. Sometimes this offer is extended via mail, e-mail, or telephone. Be sure to evaluate the offer before making a decision. If you have any questions regarding salary or benefits, this is the time to ask them. Take the time to apply critical thinking skills to evaluate opportunities before you accept the offer.

Consider the position and whether it is right for you. Are you looking for a short-term position or one that is long term? Is the job a correct fit for you in terms of hours, location, and responsibilities? If you have taken a self-assessment, you have already identified your aptitudes, abilities, values, and interests. Does the position match these?

Compare salary and benefits before accepting the offer of employment. Evaluate what the starting salary is and what future pay increases may be expected. Ask about career rewards, such as job promotions or pay bonuses for outstanding performance. Verify whether the position is salaried or hourly. Be sure to understand what demands will be placed on you. Will you be expected to work outside of the scheduled hours? How does the employer allow employees to maintain a good work-life balance? Compare the demands with the rewards, and decide if the position is right for you. The employer should also outline the responsibilities and demands of the job. Some positions require supervising other employees. Many salaried positions require work weeks that go beyond the typical 40-hour week.

Many companies offer benefits. Health insurance is offered by most companies, but some also offer dental and vision care insurance. Other benefits that may be offered include paid time off (vacation and sick time), short-term disability insurance, tuition assistance, and flexible work hours. Opportunities for continuing education can be a big benefit, allowing you to improve your lifelong learning while enhancing chances for advancement in your career. Depending on the type of position, a company car or expense account may be offered. Evaluate the benefits offered as compared to what is standard for the type of position.

Employment Forms

The first day on the job, you will spend a considerable amount of time in the human resources department completing necessary forms for your employment. Come prepared with the personal information required for the many forms you will need to complete. You will need your social security number, contact information for emergencies, and other personal information.

Form I-9

A *Form I-9 Employment Eligibility Verification* is used to verify an employee's identity and authorization to work in the United States. This form is from the US Citizen and Immigration Services, a governmental agency within the US Department of Homeland Security. Both citizens and noncitizens are required to complete this form. An example of a Form I-9 is shown in Figure 22-4.

The Form I-9 must be signed in the presence of an authorized representative of the human resources department. Documentation of identity must be presented at the time the form is signed. Acceptable documentation commonly used includes a valid driver's license, a state-issued photo ID, or a passport.

Form W-4

A *Form W-4 Employee's Withholding Allowance Certificate* is used by the employer for the information needed to withhold the appropriate amount of taxes from an employee's paycheck. Withholdings are based on marital status and the number of dependents claimed, including the employee. The amounts withheld are forwarded to the appropriate governmental agency.

Employment Eligibility Verification
Department of Homeland Security
U.S. Citizenship and Immigration Services

USCIS
Form I-9
OMB No. 1615-0047
Expires 10/31/20--

►START HERE: Read instructions carefully before completing this form. The instructions must be available, either in paper or electronically, during completion of this form. Employers are liable for errors in the completion of this form.

ANTI-DISCRIMINATION NOTICE: It is illegal to discriminate against work-authorized individuals. Employers **CANNOT** specify which document(s) an employee may present to establish employment authorization and identity. The refusal to hire or continue to employ an individual because the documentation presented has a future expiration date may also constitute illegal discrimination.

Section 1. Employee Information and Attestation *(Employees must complete and sign Section 1 of Form I-9 no later than the **first day of employment**, but not before accepting a job offer.)*

Last Name *(Family Name)*	First Name *(Given Name)*	Middle Initial	Other Last Names Used *(if any)*

Address *(Street Number and Name)*	Apt. Number	City or Town	State	ZIP Code

Date of Birth *(mm/dd/yyyy)*	U.S. Social Security Number	Employee's E-mail Address	Employee's Telephone Number
	☐☐☐ - ☐☐ - ☐☐☐☐		

I am aware that federal law provides for imprisonment and/or fines for false statements or use of false documents in connection with the completion of this form.

I attest, under penalty of perjury, that I am (check one of the following boxes):

☐ 1. A citizen of the United States

☐ 2. A noncitizen national of the United States *(See instructions)*

☐ 3. A lawful permanent resident (Alien Registration Number/USCIS Number): ____________

☐ 4. An alien authorized to work until (expiration date, if applicable, mm/dd/yyyy): ________
Some aliens may write "N/A" in the expiration date field. *(See instructions)*

Aliens authorized to work must provide only one of the following document numbers to complete Form I-9: An Alien Registration Number/USCIS Number OR Form I-94 Admission Number OR Foreign Passport Number.

1. Alien Registration Number/USCIS Number: ____________

OR

2. Form I-94 Admission Number: ____________

QR Code - Section 1
Do Not Write In This Space

Source: US Department of Homeland Security

Goodheart-Willcox Publisher

Figure 22-4 The Employment Eligibility Verification Form I-9 confirms an employee's identity.

At the end of the year, the employer sends the employee a *Form W-2 Wage and Tax Statement* to use when filing income tax returns. This form summarizes all wages and deductions for the year for an individual employee.

Benefits Forms

The human resources department will provide a variety of forms that are specific to the compensation package offered by the employer. Health insurance forms will need to be completed. If the position involves driving, you may need to fill out additional forms related to your driving record. Other benefits offered by the employer may also have forms that need to be completed.

Section 22.2 Review

Check Your Understanding

1. Explain the purpose of a job interview for both the employer and the applicant.
2. How can a job seeker prepare for questions that an interviewer might ask?
3. What is the easiest rule to follow when dressing for an interview? Explain.
4. What should be included in a follow-up message after an interview?
5. List the forms that must be completed by a newly hired employee.

Build Your Vocabulary

As you progress through this course, develop a personal glossary. This will help you build your vocabulary and prepare you for a career. Write a definition for each of the following terms and add it to your glossary.

job interview
etiquette
telephone etiquette
verbal communication
mock interview
hypothetical question
behavioral question
employment verification
background check

Section 22.3 Success in the Workplace

Objectives

After studying this section, you will be able to:

- Identify examples of skills that exhibit professional behavior.
- Define workplace ethics.
- Discuss safety practices in the workplace.

Essential Question

How can you prepare for success at a new job?

Terms

team
diversity
stereotype
communication skills
problem-solving skills
critical-thinking skills
verbal skills
nonverbal skills
listening skills
collaboration skills
time management
customer service
Occupational Safety & Health Administration (OSHA)

On the Job

Landing the job you want is just a beginning. You should do all you can to succeed and advance in your chosen field. Exhibiting *professional behavior* means taking responsibility for your behavior and your work. Certain work habits and traits demonstrate professionalism in almost any job in business and industry, from stock clerk to top executive. These habits and traits include promptness, reliable attendance, dependability, a positive attitude, and eagerness to do the work as best you can. Meeting the dress standards of your work environment will help you fit in and move ahead. If there is no dress code to guide you, take your cue from reliable coworkers or ask superiors what is appropriate. This applies to "casual Fridays," too.

fizkes/Shutterstock.com

Business etiquette applies to interaction with customers as well as other employees.

Etiquette is the art of using good manners in any situation. *Business etiquette* is required in the workforce. You will need to master basic communication skills, such as meeting and greeting clients and customers, interacting with other employees and superiors, and handling

You Do the Math Interpreting Circle Graphs

Graphs are used to illustrate data in a picture-like format. Many times, it is easier to understand the data if they are shown in a graphical form instead of a numerical form in a table.

A circle graph looks like a divided circle and shows how a whole object is cut up into parts. Circle graphs are also called *pie charts* and are often used to illustrate percentages.

Monthly Expenses

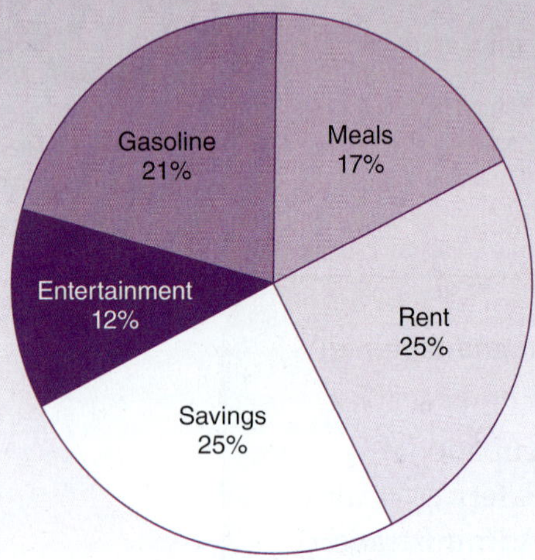

Solve the following problems.

1. Using the circle graph, determine how much of the monthly expenses is for meals.
2. Using the circle graph, determine how much of the monthly expenses is spent on entertainment.
3. Using the circle graph, what accounts for the highest monthly expense?
4. Using the circle graph, determine the difference between the percentage of money spent on gasoline and the percentage spent on meals.

business telephone calls and e-mails. Face-to-face communication requires eye contact and an easy conversational manner. Listening to what other people say is important as well. Concentrate on important names, dates, information, and instructions.

A businesslike approach to the job will take you a long way. This means taking job responsibilities seriously. Stick to the work you have to do, and try not to be idle during working hours. If you find yourself with time on your hands, ask for more work to do. If you end up with more work than you can complete, discuss the situation with your superior before falling hopelessly behind.

There are some behaviors you should avoid on the job. Do not send and receive personal e-mail and phone calls on company time. Do not let friends drop by to see you at your workplace. Keep breaks and lunches to the amount of time allowed.

Team Member Skills

A **team** is a group of two or more people who work together to achieve a common goal. In business, the terms *team* and *group* are used interchangeably. Teams may be located under one roof, or they may have members located around the world.

Effective teams are those that accomplish the defined goals. This can happen only when the members are cooperative and focused on the assigned tasks. Effective team members are individuals who collaborate and contribute both ideas and personal effort. They are cooperative and work well with others on their team and outside of the team. Successful team members are productive and work to see the team achieve its goals.

A diverse workplace is valued in society. **Diversity** is having people from different backgrounds, cultures, or demographics come together in a group. Elements of diversity include age, race, nationality, gender, mental ability, physical ability, and other qualities that describe an individual. Diversity should never create situations of stereotyping. A **stereotype** is a belief or generalization about a group of people with a given set of characteristics. Stereotyping is not acceptable in any situation.

Communication Skills

Members must interact with each other in a positive manner for the team to be successful. Acquiring positive communication skills helps an employee be effective within the team and with customers of the business. A skill is something a person does well. **Communication skills** are skills that help people communicate and work well with each other. These skills are important when working with team members, an employer, or customers. Some examples of important communication skills necessary to be an effective employee are:

- problem-solving skills
- critical-thinking skills
- verbal skills
- nonverbal skills
- listening skills
- collaboration skills

Problem-solving skills are the ability to use the mind to solve a problem by working through specific steps. The systematic decision-making model in Figure 22-5 is a guideline that can be used when a problem needs to be solved.

Critical-thinking skills are the ability to interpret and make reasonable judgments and decisions by analyzing a situation. Then, a solution or process can be applied so that a productive action can be taken. Applying critical-thinking skills can help you problem-solve in a more efficient manner.

Verbal skills are the ability to communicate effectively using spoken or written words. Possessing good verbal skills helps to make communication with other team members and customers successful.

Nonverbal skills are the ability to communicate effectively using body language, eye contact, touch, personal space, behavior, and attitude. Nonverbal skills can be used to send messages.

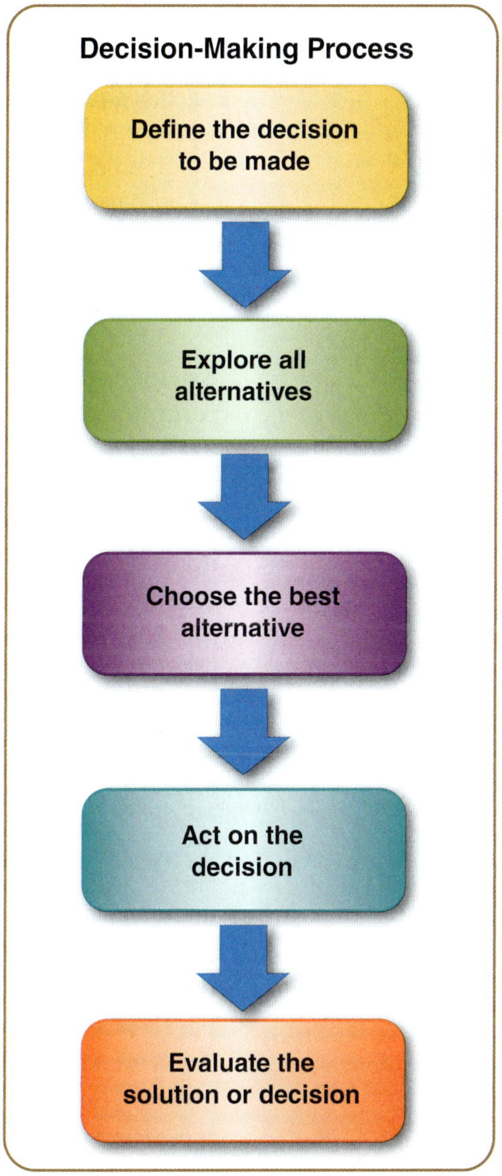

Goodheart-Willcox Publisher

Figure 22-5 The systematic decision-making model can help when choosing a course of action, whether working alone or as part of a team.

Economics in Action

Financing Education

In an extended economic downturn, many families find it difficult to save money for college or job training. Normal sources of cash for college become scarce. Grants and loans become harder to get. Investments in savings programs lose value. State governments are often forced to cut funding for state schools, which means increases in tuitions and fees.

Demand for financial aid becomes stronger, which makes it difficult to qualify for available assistance. While financial aid becomes more limited, college costs rise. At the same time, education has never been more important for individual students and for the country.

In order to finance an education, families need to start planning and saving as early as possible. As a student, you should work toward a high school record of achievement that will appeal to college admissions boards. Explore every possible source of money for college—scholarships, grants, loans, savings, work/study programs, and part-time work. Also remember to complete and submit a Free Application for Federal Student Aid.

Listening skills are the ability of an individual to not only hear what a person says, but also understand it. Listening is required for all positive communication.

Communication skills—verbal, nonverbal, and listening—may be applied in person or through digital means. Communicating digitally may take the form of e-mail, video conferencing, message boards, or forums. In many cases, nonverbal communication is difficult when communicating digitally, so the other communication skills become more important.

Collaboration skills are being able to work with others to achieve a common goal. This includes sharing ideas and compromising when the greater good of the team is at stake. To *compromise* is to give up an individual idea so that the group can come to a solution. Collaboration and compromise are two important skills to learn in the workplace.

Time-Management Skills

Effective teams achieve great accomplishments. In order to be productive and accomplish the goals that are set, time-management skills are needed. **Time management** is the practice of organizing time and work assignments to increase personal efficiency. Team members often work on several tasks at the same time. Tasks must be prioritized by determining which ones should be completed before others. The difference between average and excellent workers is often not how hard they work, but how well they prioritize assignments.

A *personal information management (PIM)* system is technology that individuals use to acquire, organize, maintain, retrieve, and use information. An example of a PIM system is Microsoft Outlook. This software can be used to keep a schedule, record contact information, and complete other activities that help organize personal information. Productivity tools are important in one's personal and professional life. A PIM system can help you have the right information at the right time.

Customer Service Skills

All businesses require good customer service skills from their employees. **Customer service** is the ability to provide a product or service in a way it has been promised to a customer. *External customers* are the people and businesses who purchase product from an organization. *Internal customers* are the coworkers within the business with whom each employee works and collaborates. As an employee, it is necessary to apply relationship building with both types of customers.

Listening to customers, hearing their concerns, and meeting their needs are necessary for a company to exist and be profitable. Learning how to resolve complaints from outside customers can help ensure that product is sold and customers return for future transactions. Understanding and collaborating with internal customers helps a business create product that meets customer needs and generates profits. Both types of customers are necessary for a successful business.

Workplace Ethics

Ethics are a set of moral values that guide a person's behavior. They help a person determine what is right and wrong in given situations. Ethics are based on traits such as trustworthiness, honesty, loyalty, respect, responsibility, and fairness. Ethics in the workplace is a significant issue in the business world.

michaeljung/Shutterstock.com

Listening is an important part of providing customer service.

Ethics

Confidential Information

It is unethical for an employer to share personal information about a job applicant. Information that appears on a résumé or discussed during an interview is confidential. It is unethical to share confidential information about employees and doing so may end in a lawsuit. Depending on the confidentiality of the topic, sharing the information may be considered slanderous.

Over 90 percent of business schools now require ethics courses as part of their curriculum.

An employee with strong ethics will always try to do the right thing. Employees demonstrate their ethics through honesty, integrity, and loyalty. *Honesty* is the quality of being truthful and sincere. *Integrity* is strong moral character. Employees with integrity will consistently refuse to compromise their ethical principles, regardless of any outside influence, punishment, or reward. *Loyalty* is faithfulness to a commitment. In the business world, loyalty is faithfulness to an employer or a supplier.

Companies differ in their approach to workplace behavior. Some companies simply assume that employees bring their own standards to the job, and management offers very little guidance. Some companies rely on an informal corporate culture that guides job-related decisions and actions. Other businesses follow a carefully developed program. This program may include a statement of corporate values and a code of ethics to guide employees.

A company may convey its expectations for ethics on the job in different ways. These may include employee handbooks, training sessions or seminars, or printed formal statements of company values and ethics. A stated *code of ethics* generally addresses relationships of the business with employees, customers, suppliers, investors, creditors, competitors, and communities. A business code of ethics frequently relates to issues such as fair treatment of employees, teamwork, competition, and conflicts of interest. Other issues include use of business resources and assets, confidentiality, and environmental concerns.

Workplace Safety

Individuals should be aware of workplace safety for themselves as well as for those with whom they work. Employers, schools, and other organizations and facilities are responsible for providing an environment that is safe for everyone on the premises.

Maintaining a safe workplace is the joint responsibility of the employer and employee. The employer makes sure the facility and working conditions are such that accidents are unlikely to occur. The employee uses common sense and care while at the office. Always read and understand equipment safety manuals, follow safety instructions, and abide by safety requirements.

The US Department of Labor enforces laws that protect workers. There are over 180 federal laws that apply to the workplace. Figure 22-6 shows a brief summary of laws that protect the rights of workers.

In 1970, the *Occupational Safety and Health Act* was passed. The Occupational Safety and Health Administration was established a year later. The **Occupational Safety & Health Administration (OSHA)** is a federal agency that sets and enforces safety and health regulations in the workplace. OSHA's efforts have led to a significant decline in workplace injuries and deaths since the 1970s.

Accidents

Workplace safety guidelines are of no use if they are not properly communicated. Workplace safety signs warn employees and visitors of dangerous situations. OSHA suggests guidelines for creating signs to help decrease workplace accidents. Falling hazards, lifting hazards, and material-storage hazards account for most of the workplace accidents that occur in offices.

Worker Protection Laws

Law	Year	Description
Fair Labor Standards Act	1938	Supports workers rights by establishing the federal minimum wage, 40-hour workweek, requirements for overtime pay, and restrictions on child labor
Equal Pay Act	1963	Requires that women and men receive equal pay for equal work
Civil Rights Act	1964	Outlaws discrimination and segregation based on race, color, religion, sex, or national origin
Age Discrimination in Employment Act	1967	Protects employees age 40 and older from discrimination on the basis of age in hiring, promotion, discharge, and compensation
Occupational Safety and Health Act	1970	Requires employers to provide a workplace free of hazards that could affect the health and safety of workers
Americans with Disabilities Act	1990	Prohibits discrimination against people with disabilities in employment, transportation, public accommodation, communications, and governmental activities
Family and Medical Leave Act	1993	Requires certain employees be granted temporary, job-protected leave based on qualifying events

Goodheart-Willcox Publisher

Figure 22-6 It is essential that employers follow current laws and regulations that protect workers.

Falling Hazards

Falls are the most common workplace accident in an office setting. Preventing workplace falls is relatively simple. Some guidelines for helping to prevent falls include:

- close drawers completely
- do not stand on a chair or box to reach
- secure cords, rugs, and mats
- obey safety signs

Lifting Hazards

Lifting hazards are sources of potential injury from improperly picking up or carrying items. Most back injuries are caused by improper lifting. To avoid injuries from lifting:

- make several small trips with items rather than one trip with an overly heavy load
- use dollies or handcarts whenever possible
- lift with the legs, not with the back
- never carry an item that blocks vision
- obey safety signs

©iStock.com/martin meehan

It is important to know workplace safety protocol and emergency procedures.

Material-Storage Hazards

Material-storage hazards are sources of potential injury from the improper storage of office equipment or other items. A cluttered workplace is an unsafe workplace. Material stacked too high can fall on employees. Paper and files that are stored on the floor or in a hall are a fire risk. To prevent material-storage injuries:

- do not stack boxes or papers on top of tall cabinets
- store heavier objects on lower shelves
- keep aisles and hallways clear
- obey safety signs

Emergencies

There are many types of emergencies that can happen at school, at work, or in a social environment. Individuals are responsible for understanding how to react in an emergency at work, school, or another facility. Some emergency situations for which you should be prepared are:

- fire
- natural disasters such as a tornado, earthquake, or hurricane

- medical emergencies such as heart attack, stroke, fainting, burns, or cuts
- bomb threats and other threats of violence

If emergency procedures or guidelines have not been given to you at school or work, request that they be reviewed.

Emergency procedures are a series of actions taken to minimize risks in the event of an emergency. The first line of defense in all emergencies is to stay calm. This makes it easier to follow the emergency procedures established by the organization. The seriousness of the emergency should be evaluated in order to determine what type of help is required. Be aware of exits and how to evacuate the premises if necessary. If there is a medical emergency, follow established procedures to give appropriate assistance, and call for help if needed.

Section 22.3 Review

Check Your Understanding

1. Name examples of communication skills.
2. How can etiquette be used in the workplace?
3. What are ethics?
4. What federal agency promotes and enforces safety and health standards in the workplace?
5. What is the first line of defense in all emergencies?

Build Your Vocabulary

As you progress through this course, develop a personal glossary. This will help you build your vocabulary and prepare you for a career. Write a definition for each of the following terms and add it to your glossary.

team
diversity
stereotype
communication skills
problem-solving skills
critical-thinking skills
verbal skills
nonverbal skills
listening skills
collaboration skills
time management
customer service
Occupational Safety & Health Administration (OSHA)

Review and Assessment

Chapter Summary

Section 22.1 Résumés, Cover Messages, and Employment Applications

- A résumé is a document that provides potential employers with a profile of a person's career goals, work history, and job qualifications. The most important part of a résumé is the listing of work experience and achievements. Other parts of the résumé, however, are essential to presenting a complete profile for the employer.
- A cover message is a selling or persuasive message. A cover message provides an introduction to who you are and why you are the right person for the position you are seeking. Writing a cover message provides an opportunity to focus a potential employer's attention on the fact that you are the best candidate for the job.
- Most job applicants apply for a job either in person or online. The traditional way to apply for employment is in person by hand delivering a printed version of a résumé, cover message, and portfolio. Applying online can vary by employer, but it typically includes uploading documents and completing forms on a company website.

Section 22.2 Job Interviews and the Employment Process

- The job interview is your opportunity to sell yourself. To prepare for the interview, rehearse answers to questions likely to be asked during the interview. At the interview, it is important to dress appropriately and professionally. Immediately after your interview, follow up with a thank-you letter or e-mail to the person who interviewed you.
- The employment process can take a substantial amount of time. Employers must conduct employment verification and a background check to make sure the candidate is qualified for the position. In addition, employment forms must be completed by an employee when beginning a new job.

Section 22.3 Success in the Workplace

- Some work habits and traits will be important for success in almost any job. These habits and traits include promptness, reliable attendance, dependability, and a positive attitude. You will need to master basic communication skills, take job responsibilities seriously, and be able to work as a team member.
- Ethics in the workplace is a significant issue in the business world. Some companies rely on an informal corporate culture to guide job-related decisions and actions. Other businesses follow a carefully developed ethics program.
- The US Department of Labor enforces laws that protect workers. These laws are set in place and enforced to help ensure safety and health in the workplace. Accidents involving falling hazards, lifting hazards, and material-storage hazards pose common safety concerns in the office.

Review Your Knowledge

1. List the standard sections of a résumé.
2. How can a cover letter act as a persuasive message?
3. Why is the cover message important?
4. How can a person apply for employment online?
5. Describe steps that should be taken to prepare for a job interview.
6. What steps should be taken by an applicant after a job interview?
7. Describe the employment process.
8. List and describe examples of interpersonal skills.

9. Explain how mastering the following skills can lead to success in the workplace: team member, time management, and customer service skills.
10. Summarize safety practices necessary in the workplace.

Apply Your Knowledge

1. Prepare to write a personal résumé for a Human Services or Finance position of your choice. Make a list of all your past work experiences. Write a brief description of your job responsibilities to demonstrate positive work behaviors and qualities that make you employable. If you have any special licenses or certifications, note them. Next, list your educational background and any other information you think should be included on your résumé. Then, create a draft of your résumé. After your draft is complete, format the document. Using Figure 22-1 as an example, create your final résumé. Demonstrate use of appropriate content, concepts, and vocabulary. Check the final document for grammar.
2. Write a cover message that you would attach with your résumé if applying for a Human Services or Finance position. Use Figure 22-2 as an example. Explain how your positive work behaviors and other qualities make you employable. Mention any special licenses or certifications you have earned. Note that your professional portfolio will contain samples of your work. Demonstrate use of appropriate content, concepts, and vocabulary. Check the final document for grammar and formatting.
3. Write an answer for each of the following potential interview questions.
    - What makes you a good employee?
    - What are your strengths?
    - What are your weaknesses?
4. Assume you have recently been interviewed for the position of customer service representative. Write a thank-you message to the interviewer.
5. Customer-service skills are a professional behavior necessary for the workplace. Make a list of five activities that an employee can perform to build customer relationships. Next, make a list of five activities that an employee can perform to resolve customer complaints. How do the two lists compare?
6. Acquiring interpersonal skills will help you be a successful team member and productive employee. This chapter introduced problem solving, critical-thinking, listening, and collaboration as interpersonal skills. For each skill, evaluate your own interpersonal skills. How could you apply these skills to solve problems in a job situation?
7. When communicating with coworkers, employers, and customers, common courtesies must be applied. Create an outline for communication with others in the workplace. Your outline should include these methods of communication: verbal skills, nonverbal skills, and digital means. Under each category, identify communication situations and which method of communication is appropriate.
8. Applying time-management skills as an employee is important in order to accomplish daily tasks. If an employee fails to meet daily goals, there can be a ripple effect to others on the team. Make a list of outcomes that may occur if an individual does not practice time management on the job. What impact does this have on the profitability of a business?
9. There are times when situations in the workplace border the edge of being unethical or illegal. Next to each of the situations that follow, indicate if you think the behavior in the workplace is ethical or unethical and legal or illegal.

- Using a company telephone to make a personal phone call.
- Stopping work tasks to take a planned lunch break.
- Downloading pirated music onto a company computer.
- Revealing private information about a friend that you were only able to learn through your work tasks.
- Working fifteen minutes late because you arrived fifteen minutes late that morning.

10. Put yourself in the role of a supervisor in a business situation. Identify examples of ethical and professional behavior that you would expect from employees. Write a script that you would use to explain your expectations to an employee.

Apply Your Math Skills

1. Rosalyn was offered two different jobs. The first job is located about 17 miles from home, but would only require travel 2 days each week. The other three days would be worked from home. The second job is located approximately 7 miles from home, but would require traveling to the office every day. If Rosalyn wanted to base the decision solely off of mileage driven per week, which job should be chosen?
2. Johnny is concerned about spending too much in gas traveling to work. The car gets 30 miles per gallon, but the commute is 75 miles round trip each day. Taking the train is an option, but it would cost $55 each month, and the commute would take an additional 35 minutes. Assuming gas is steady at $2.09 per gallon, which method of transit would be most cost effective for Johnny?

Communication Skills

College and Career Readiness

Reading. Read a magazine, newspaper, or online article about the importance of professional communication. Take notes to identify the purpose of the article and the intended audience. Determine the central ideas of the article and review the conclusions made by the author. Demonstrate your understanding of the information by summarizing what you read, making sure to analyze the audience, purpose, and message of the article.

Speaking. Business careers require that individuals be able to participate and contribute to one-on-one discussions. Developing interpersonal communication skills is one way to achieve career opportunities. As your instructor lectures on this chapter, contribute thoughtful comments when participation is invited.

Writing. As a student, you will be planning for your future career. It is important that you take ownership of a career plan that matches your interests and skills. Review and update your plan to align your personal educational goals to a career path. Consult with counselors or other professionals who can help guide you in the process.

Teamwork

Work in pairs or teams as assigned by your teacher to conduct mock interviews. Dress as you would for an actual job interview. Take turns acting as the interviewer and the interviewee. Refer to the typical interview questions given in this chapter, but come up with your own questions as well. As you answer questions, demonstrate your professionalism by applying appropriate oral skills and conducting yourself in a manner that is acceptable in the workplace. Apply your presentation skills as you communicate what you know about the job for which you are interviewing. After you finish, write a thank-you message to the interviewer. When all interviews are completed, write a brief summary evaluating how you performed in the interview. Describe what you could do better in the future.

Internet Research

Evaluate and Compare Employment Options. Using the Internet, locate job advertisements for positions that interest you. Select two or more that would fit your criteria if you were to apply for them. Summarize the demands of each job. How do the demands compare with the rewards, including salary (or other wages) and benefits? Determine which of the positions you selected would be your preferred job.

Lawful Interview Questions. Use the Internet to research the term *lawful interview questions*. Give examples of federal laws regarding employment interviews. Write several paragraphs explaining how you would use problem-solving and critical-thinking skills if you were asked an unlawful question during a job interview.

Portfolio Development

College and Career Readiness

Presenting the Electronic Portfolio. After your print portfolio is assembled, decide how to present your electronic portfolio. Review the files you have collected and select the ones you want to include. Next, decide how you want to present the materials. You could create a slideshow and store it on a flash drive or create a portfolio website. The method in which you choose to present your electronic portfolio may dictate the file types you use.

Your electronic portfolio will contain documents you created digitally as well as scanned, hard-copy documents. Before you begin, consider the technology that you might use for creating and scanning documents. This may require access to desktop-publishing software, scanners, cameras, or other digital equipment or software.

For hard-copy files you are scanning, consider saving them in PDF format. For documents you create, consider using the default format to save the files. For example, you could save letters and essays created in Microsoft Word in the default DOCX format. If your presentation includes graphics or video, verify the native file formats for each item.

Keep in mind that the person reviewing your electronic portfolio will need programs that open these formats to view your files. One option is to save *all* files as PDF files. Having all of the files in the same format can make viewing them easier for those who need to review your portfolio.

1. Create the slide presentation, website, or other vehicle for presenting your electronic portfolio.
2. View the completed electronic portfolio to check the appearance and functionality.
3. Write a short summary about the format of your electronic portfolio. Include brief instructions on how to navigate or view the portfolio.
4. Give the portfolio to an instructor, counselor, or other person who can give constructive feedback. Make necessary adjustments and revisions.

CTSOs

Event Prep

Job Interview. Job interviewing is an event you might enter with your CTSO. By participating in the job interview, you will be able to showcase your presentation skills, communication talents, and ability to actively listen to the questions asked by the interviewers. For this event, you will be expected to write a letter of application, create a résumé, and complete a job application. You will also be interviewed by an individual or panel.

To prepare for a job interview event, complete the following activities.

1. Use the Internet or textbooks to research the job application process and interviewing techniques.
2. Write your letter of application and résumé, and complete the application form (if provided for this event). You may be required to submit this before the event or present the information at the event.
3. Make certain that each piece of communication is complete and free of errors.
4. Solicit feedback from your peers, instructor, and parents.

CHAPTER

23 Digital Citizenship

Our daily lives revolve around using technology in many shapes and forms. However, using technology comes with rights as well as responsibilities. It is necessary to learn to communicate ethically and appropriately in the digital world. Becoming a good digital citizen can help you be successful in your personal life as well as your career.

It is important to take your digital responsibilities seriously. Cyberbullying, abuse of intellectual property, and violating digital security are unacceptable behaviors. These are unethical, potentially illegal, and should be avoided. Anything posted on the Internet creates a digital footprint. Your online communications will never really go away. They can follow you when you are applying for college entrance or looking for employment.

Focus on Finance

Intellectual Property

Laws exist to protect the owners of intellectual property, such as written works, music, art, and other original material. The author of an original work is given certain rights when a copyright or patent is registered for the work. Protecting intellectual property can be worth the money and time involved.

A copyright protects the owner of an original work for a term consisting of the life of the author and 70 years after the author's death. A copyright can be applied for by completing an application provided by the United States Copyright Office and paying a fee. The online registration fee in 2021 for a single author of a work was $45. The fee for a paper registration was $125.

A patent protects the creator of an invention. A patent is applied for through the United States Patent and Trademark Office. Applying for a patent is a more complicated process than filing for a copyright. In addition to filing fees, there are patent search and examination fees.

College and Career Readiness

Reading Prep. Arrange a study session to read the chapter aloud with a classmate. Take turns reading each section. Stop at the end of each section to discuss what you think its main points are. Take notes of your study session to share with the class.

Sections

Section 23.1 Communicating in a Digital Society

Section 23.2 Internet Use in the Workplace

Mirexon/Shutterstock.com

Section 23.1 Communicating in a Digital Society

Essential Question

What implications does digital citizenship have for society as a whole?

Objectives

After completing this section, you will be able to:

- Describe the elements of digital communication.
- Explain intellectual property and what it includes.
- Discuss the importance of the Electronic User's Bill of Rights.

Terms

digital communication	netiquette	plagiarism
digital citizen	slander	piracy
digital literacy	libel	infringement
digital citizenship	digital footprint	public domain
cyberbullying	intellectual property	open source

Digital Communication

Digital communication is the exchange of information through electronic means. Using technology to communicate in the workplace, as well as in one's personal life, requires users to be responsible. A **digital citizen** is someone who regularly and skillfully engages in the use of technology, such as the Internet, computers, and other digital devices. This requires the knowledge and skills to successfully navigate the Internet to interact with individuals and organizations. Digital communication is composed of digital literacy and digital citizenship.

Digital Literacy

Digital communication requires digital literacy skills. **Digital literacy** is the ability to use technology to locate, evaluate, communicate, and create information. According to the US federal government, digital literacy skills include the following:

- using a computer or mobile device, including the mouse, keyboard, icons, and folders
- using software and applications to complete tasks, such as word processing and creating spreadsheets, tables, and databases
- using the Internet to conduct searches, access e-mail, and register on a website

- communicating online, including sharing photos and videos, using social media networks, and learning to be an informed digital citizen
- helping children learn to be responsible and make informed decisions online

To learn more about digital literacy skills, visit the Digital Literacy website for information, resources, and tools. This website is supported by various departments of the US government.

StockLite/Shutterstock.com

Digital literacy skills are necessary when working in a business environment.

Digital Citizenship

Digital citizenship is the standard of appropriate behavior when using technology to communicate. Good digital citizenship focuses on using technology in a positive manner rather than using it for negative or illegal purposes. People who participate in the digital society have a legal responsibility for their online actions, whether those actions are ethical or unethical. *Ethics* are the principles of what is right and wrong that help people make decisions. Ethical actions are those that apply ethics and moral behavior. Unethical actions are those that involve immoral behavior, crime, or theft while online. These actions can be punishable by law.

It is important to understand the difference between ethical and unethical electronic activities. For example, it is sometimes difficult for a reader to know where joking stops and bullying starts. **Cyberbullying** is using the Internet to harass or threaten an individual. It includes using social media, text messages, or e-mails to harass or scare a person with hurtful words or pictures. A target of cyberbullying cannot be physically seen or touched by the bully. However, this does not mean the person cannot be harmed a bully's actions. Cyberbullying is unethical and can be prosecuted.

Case Study *Cyberbullying*

Keith is the author of a popular comic strip that was published regularly in the high school newspaper. After graduation, the comic strip continues online in the form of a web comic. The web comic becomes even more popular and gains a considerable following.

Jeremy also had a comic strip published in the same newspaper. However, the comic is not continued after graduation. Jeremy grows jealous of Keith's success, and begins positing mean and hurtful comments on the comic's website using a screen name. The comments suggest that Keith's art is unoriginal and plagiarized from the work of others. Keith is shocked and humiliated at these false statements.

Case Review

1. Explain why Keith may be a victim of cyberbullying.
2. Explain whether Jeremy's behavior is ethical or unethical.
3. What actions can be taken to stop these false statements from being made?
4. How can Keith handle this cyberbullying situation while maintaining good digital citizenship?

wavebreakmedia/Shutterstock.com

Digital citizens respect their employer and only use office equipment for business purposes.

Another unacceptable behavior is flaming. *Flaming* is purposefully insulting someone and inciting an argument on social media. Spamming is equally unethical. *Spamming* is sending unwanted mass e-mails or intentionally flooding an individual's social media site or e-mail inbox with unwanted messages.

Etiquette is the art of using good manners in any situation. **Netiquette** is etiquette used when communicating electronically. It is also known as *digital etiquette*. Netiquette includes accepted social and professional guidelines for Internet communication. These guidelines apply to e-mails, social networking, and other contact with customers and peers via the Internet during work hours. For example, using all capital letters in a message, which has the effect of yelling, is not acceptable. Always use correct capitalization, spelling, and grammar.

Having poor netiquette can also have legal ramifications. **Slander** is speaking a false statement about someone that causes others to have a negative opinion of that person. **Libel** is publishing a false statement about someone that causes others to have a negative or untrue opinion of that person. Slander and libel can be considered crimes of defamation. It is important to choose words carefully when making comments about others, whether online or in person.

What you post on the Internet never really goes away. A **digital footprint** is a data record of all an individual's online activities. Even if you delete something you have posted on the Internet, it is still stored in your digital footprint. Always think before posting to social media sites or sending an e-mail. What you post online today could risk your future college and job opportunities.

Intellectual Property

The Internet provides countless sources for obtaining text, images, video, audio, and software. Even though this material is easily obtainable, this does not mean it is available for you to use any way you choose. Laws exist to govern the use of media and creative works. The creators or owners of this material have certain legal rights. **Intellectual property** is something that comes from a person's mind, such as an idea, invention, or process. Intellectual property laws protect a person's or a company's inventions, artistic works, and other intellectual property.

Plagiarism is claiming another person's material as one's own, which is both unethical and illegal. If you must refer to someone else's work, follow intellectual property laws to ethically acquire the information. Use standard methods of citing sources. Citation guidelines in *The Chicago Manual of Style* and the Modern Language Association's *MLA Handbook* can be helpful.

Ethics

Intellectual Property

Any information you use that was written by someone else must be cited. Intellectual property is anything that belongs to someone else, such as copyrighted material, trademarks, and music. If you quote material for a blog, website, or even a presentation, you must give the owner credit for that material. It is unethical to present information as your own when it is not and can be illegal. It is also unethical to misrepresent data. Search the Internet for the proper use of intellectual material.

Piracy is the unethical and illegal copying or downloading of software, files, and other protected material. Examples of protected material include images, movies, and music. Piracy carries a heavy penalty, including fines and incarceration.

Copyright

A *copyright* acknowledges ownership of a work and specifies that only the owner has the right to sell the work, use it, or give permission for someone else to sell or use it. Any use of copyrighted material without permission is called **infringement**. The laws cover all original work, whether it is in print, on the Internet, or in any other form of media. Scanning a document does not make the content yours.

Copyrighted material is indicated by the © symbol or the statement "copyright by." Lack of the symbol or statement does not mean the material is not copyrighted. All original material is automatically copyrighted as soon as it is in a tangible form. An idea cannot be copyrighted. A copyright can be registered with the US Copyright Office, which is part of the Library of Congress. However, original material is still legally protected whether or not the copyright is registered.

Most information on the Internet is copyrighted, whether it is text, graphics, illustrations, or digital media. This means it cannot be reused without obtaining permission from the owner. Sometimes, the owner of the material places the material on the Internet for others to reuse. However, if this is not explicitly stated, assume the material is copyrighted and cannot be freely used.

lightpoet/Shutterstock.com

Reusing material without permission, such as photocopying pages out of a textbook, is unethical.

Many websites list rules, called the *terms of use*, which must be followed for downloaded files. The agreement may come up automatically, for example, if you are downloading a file or software application. If, however, you are copying an image or a portion of text from a website, you will need to look for the terms of use information. Unless the terms of use specifically state that you are free to copy and use the material provided on a website, assume the material is copyrighted. You cannot reuse the material without permission.

Fair use doctrine allows individuals to use copyrighted works without permission in limited situations under very strict guidelines. Fair use doctrine allows copyrighted material to be used for the purpose of describing or reviewing the work. For example, a student writing about the material in an original report is an example of fair use. Another example is a product-review website providing editorial comment. Fair use doctrine does not change the copyright or ownership of the material used under the doctrine.

In some cases, individuals or organizations may wish to allow others to use their intellectual property without needing permission. This type of use assignment may be called *copyleft*, which is a play on the word *copyright*. One popular method of allowing use of intellectual property is a Creative Commons license.

A *Creative Commons (CC) license* is a specialized copyright license that allows free distribution of copyrighted work. If the creator of the work wants to give the public the ability to use, share, or advance original work, a Creative Commons license provides that flexibility. The creator maintains the copyright and can specify how the copyrighted work can be used. For example, one type of Creative Commons license prohibits commercial use.

Public domain refers to material that is not owned by anybody and can be used without permission. Material can enter the public domain when a copyright expires and is not renewed. Much of the material created by federal, state, or local governments is often in the public domain. This is because taxpayer money was used to create it. Additionally, the owner of the material may choose to give up ownership and place the material in the public domain.

Patent

A *patent* gives a person or company the right to be the sole producer of a product for a defined period of time. Patents protect an invention that is functional or mechanical. The invention must be considered useful and inoffensive, and it must be operational. This means that an idea may not be patented. A process can be patented under certain conditions. The process must be related to a particular machine or transform a substance or item into a different state or thing.

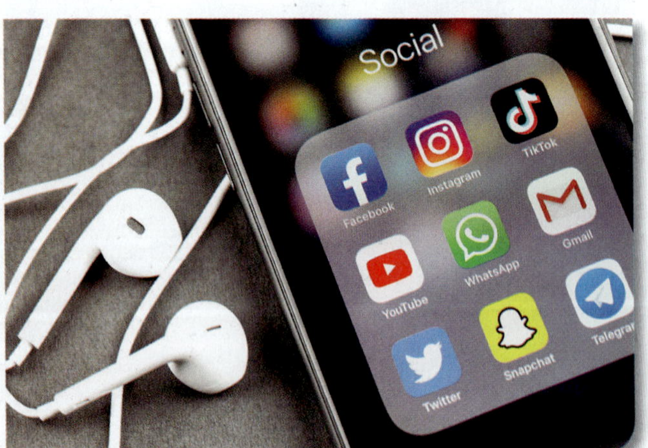

Primakov/Shutterstock.com

Most brand logos, such as those seen on social media websites, are trademarks.

Trademark

A *trademark* protects taglines, slogans, names, symbols, and any unique method to identify a product or company. A *service mark* is similar to a trademark, but it identifies a service rather than a product. Trademarks and service marks do not protect a work or product. They only protect the way in which the product is described.

You Do the Math — Margin of Error

The margin of error is an allowance permitted to account for changes in circumstances or miscalculations. Margin of error is commonly seen in surveys, but may also be applied to calculations to allow for rounding errors. For example, a political survey may compare the percentage of voters favoring one candidate over another. These surveys, called polls, almost always state a margin of error, such as ±3 percent. In this case, the stated percentages may be 3 percent too high or too low.

Solve the following problems.

1. A business calculates its weekly expenses as $12,054 with a margin of error of ±2.5 percent. What is the maximum the weekly expenses should be?
2. A survey states that 45.6 percent of American households will purchase a new smartphone in the next year. The survey has a margin of error of ±8 percent. When estimating how many smartphones will be sold, what is the lowest percentage of households that can be assumed to make this purchase within the next year?
3. A survey of families planning to take a vacation over the upcoming holiday weekend states that 73.6 percent will drive at least 500 miles. The margin of error is ±4.6 percent. Allowing for the margin of error, what is the range of percentages of families that will drive at least 500 miles?

The term "trademark" is often used to refer to both trademarks and service marks. Trademarks never expire.

The symbols used to indicate a trademark or service mark are called *graphic marks*. Some graphic marks can be used without being formally registered, as shown in Figure 23-1.

Correct Usage of Graphic Marks

Graphic Mark	Meaning
™	Trademark, not registered
SM	Service mark, not registered
®	Registered trademark

Goodheart-Willcox Publisher

Figure 23-1 Graphic marks are symbols that indicate legal protection of intellectual property.

License Agreement

A *licensing agreement* is a contract that gives one party permission to market, produce, or use the good or service owned by another party. The agreement grants a license in return for a fee or royalty payment. When buying software, the purchaser agrees to follow the terms of a license. A *license* is the legal permission to use a software program. All software has terms of use that explain how and when the software may be used. Figure 23-2 explains the characteristics of different software licensing.

Alternative usage rights for software programs are typically covered by the *GNU General Public License (GNU GPL).* The GNU GPL guarantees all users the freedom to use, study, share, and modify the software. The term **open source** applies to software that has had its source code made available to the public at no charge. Open-source software can be downloaded and used for free and can be modified and distributed by anyone. However, part or all of the code of open-source software may be owned by an individual or organization.

Software Licensing Permissions			
Characteristics	**For-Purchase**	**Freeware**	**Shareware**
Cost	• Must be purchased to use • Demo may be available	• Never have to pay for it	• Free to try • Pay to upgrade to full functionality
Features	• Full functionality	• Full functionality	• Limited functionality without upgrade

Goodheart-Willcox Publisher

Figure 23-2 Each type of software has specific licensing permissions.

Electronic User's Bill of Rights

The *Electronic User's Bill of Rights* details the rights and responsibilities of both individuals and institutions regarding the treatment of digital information. It was originally proposed in 1993 by Frank W. Connolly of American University. It is modeled after the original United States Bill of Rights, although it contains only four articles. The articles are not legally binding, but contain guidelines for the appropriate use of digital information. The articles in the Electronic User's Bill of Rights include the following.

- *Article I: Individual Rights* focuses on the rights and freedoms of the users of computers and the Internet. It states "citizens of the electronic community of learners" have the right to access computers and informational resources. They should be informed when their personal information is being collected. They have the right to review and correct the information that has been collected. Users should have freedom of speech and rights of ownership for their intellectual property.
- *Article II: Individual Responsibilities* focuses on the responsibilities that come with those rights outlined in Article I. A citizen of the electronic community is responsible for seeking information and using it effectively. It is also the individual's responsibility to honor the intellectual property of others. This includes verifying the accuracy of information obtained electronically. A citizen of the digital community is expected to respect the privacy of others and use electronic resources wisely.
- *Article III: Rights of Educational Institutions* states the right of educational institutions to access computers and informational resources. Like individuals, an educational institution retains ownership of its intellectual property. Each institution has the right to use its resources as it sees fit.
- *Article IV: Institutional Responsibilities* focuses on the responsibilities that come with the rights granted in Article III. Educational institutions are held accountable for the information they use and provide. Institutions are responsible for creating and maintaining "an environment wherein trust and intellectual freedom are the foundation for individual and institutional growth and success."

Exploring Careers

Fundraising Manager

Fundraising managers direct campaigns that aim to bring money into an organization. This money is donated to the organization, not generated through profits. They manage the entire fundraising process to achieve the organization's goals. Fundraising managers typically:

- create and perform fundraising strategies
- identify and contact potential donors
- plan fundraising events that can generate donations
- meet important donors
- apply for grants
- manage the activities of the staff

Fundraising managers often work with public relations managers. They usually work in an office environment, but many travel to deliver speeches and attend community activities. They often work full time, and they regularly work more than 40 hours per week. Their work environment can be highly stressful. A bachelor degree in public relations, communications, English, or a similar field is often required for these positions. Obtaining a certification through CFRE International is not mandatory, but is often preferred. Fundraising managers must have excellent communication, leadership, organizational, public-speaking, problem-solving, and finance skills.

Section 23.1 Review

Check Your Understanding

1. List the components of digital communication.
2. What actions are considered cyberbullying?
3. Name two unethical uses of another person's intellectual property.
4. What does a licensing agreement allow?
5. What does the Electronic User's Bill of Rights provide?

Build Your Vocabulary

As you progress through this course, develop a personal glossary. This will help you build your vocabulary and prepare you for a career. Write a definition for each of the following terms and add it to your glossary.

digital communication
digital citizen
digital literacy
digital citizenship
cyberbullying
netiquette
slander
libel
digital footprint
intellectual property
plagiarism
piracy
infringement
public domain
open source

Section 23.2 Internet Use in the Workplace

Essential Question

How can unacceptable Internet use by an employee affect a company as a whole?

Objectives

After completing this section, you will be able to:

- Explain how employers ensure appropriate Internet use in a professional setting.
- Describe the importance of digital security.

Terms

acceptable use policy	cookies	firewall
cloud computing	phishing	identity theft
Internet Protocol address	malware	authentication
hacking	spyware	
	software virus	

Using the Internet

An important aspect of digital citizenship is respecting your employer's property and time. Internet access provided by the company should be used only for business purposes. For example, checking personal e-mail or playing a game online is not acceptable. Most companies have an established acceptable use policy. An **acceptable use policy** is a set of rules that explains what is and is not acceptable use of company-owned and company-operated equipment and networks. Employees are typically made aware of acceptable use policies during training, before they are allowed access to the company's computers and network.

Many organizations allow cloud computing to support collaboration and working remotely. **Cloud computing** is using remote servers to store and access data over the Internet rather than on a personal computer or local server. This allows users to access personal content, such as saved files, from anywhere with a Wi-Fi connection. Cloud computing makes private digital information accessible from any device. However, before using Internet access for cloud computing at work, make certain that your employer has given you permission to do so. Some companies and schools use *filters* that prevent unauthorized Internet surfing or visiting selected websites during working hours. If you have not been given explicit permission before accessing the cloud at work, it may be considered unauthorized use in the workplace.

Censorship is the practice of examining material, such as online content, and blocking or deleting anything considered inappropriate. Employers are legally allowed to censor information that employees read on the Internet during work hours.

Whether at work or home, each time you access a search engine or visit a web page, the computer's identity is revealed. The **Internet Protocol address**, known as an *IP address*, is a number used to identify an electronic device connected to the Internet. While your personal information cannot be easily discovered, an IP address can reveal your approximate geographic location. Any e-mails you send from your computer or mobile devices have an IP address attached to them. Use caution when doing so.

One way to protect yourself online is to ensure that you are transmitting data over secure web pages. When transmitting private information to a website, check that the site is secure. A secure URL begins with https. The s stands for secure. This is not 100 percent foolproof, but generally is a sign of protection. Secure websites may also display an icon somewhere in the browser to indicate that the communication is secure. Be wary of uploading personal information to sites that do not display the protection icon.

Public Wi-Fi hotspots should be avoided. While convenient, these networks are generally not secure and put your devices at risk of inadvertently exposing data. One definition of **hacking** is illegally accessing or altering digital devices, software, or networks.

Hackers can also create illicit hotspots in locations where free or paid public Wi-Fi exists. Users unknowingly connect to the incorrect network, which allows the hacker access to any data being transmitted over that connection. The signal with the best strength may not always be the legitimate hotspot. An easy way to avoid illicit hotspots is to check with an employee of the business providing

History of Finance

Automated Teller Machines

An *automated teller machine (ATM)* is an electronic banking machine that allows a person to perform basic banking activities around the clock from locations outside the bank. The first ATM in the United States was invented by Donald Wetzel, an engineer. Customers used his machine by inserting plastic cards with magnetic strips, just as customers do today. Wetzel's invention was installed at a Chemical Bank branch in Rockville Centre, New York, in 1969.

By 1970, scores of other banks were installing ATMs. However, during the early 1970s, people were wary of the new technology. Customers felt that using a machine was cold and impersonal. Banks tried to get customers interested with heavy advertising, including television commercials.

Surprisingly, ATMs finally gained a foothold with American consumers as a result of a blizzard. In 1977, Citibank spent more than $100 million (almost $400 million today) to install ATMs around New York City. Then, in February 1978, a major blizzard covered the city in 17 inches of snow in 24 hours. Banks were closed for days, while ATM use soared. Shortly after, Citibank launched a famous ad campaign featuring the slogan "The Citi Never Sleeps" alongside photos of customers using Citibank ATMs during the blizzard. ATMs had finally earned the trust of the American consumer.

it. Ask the employee for the name of the network and the access key. If a Wi-Fi authentication screen asks for credit card information, confirm that the Wi-Fi connection is legitimate.

Cookies

Cookies are bits of data stored on your computer that record information about the websites you have visited. Cookies may also contain the personal information you enter on a website. Most cookies are from legitimate websites and will not harm your computer. Some advertisers place them onto your computer without your knowledge or consent. Marketers use the information for research and selling purposes. If a hacker gains access to your cookies, you are at risk. The cookies can be used to steal personal information you have entered on a website. Cookies also can be used to target you for a scam based on your Internet history.

As a precaution, there are ways to protect your computer from cookies. One way is to prevent them from being accepted by the browser. Most Internet browsers allow you to set a preference to never accept cookies. Check your browser for specific instructions. Another way to protect your computer is to delete cookies on a regular basis. Cookies can also be removed by running a disk cleanup utility.

Misha Beliy/Shutterstock.com

Use caution and protect your privacy when using technology to communicate.

Phishing

Phishing is the use of fraudulent e-mails and copies of valid websites to trick people into providing private and confidential data. A common form of phishing is sending a fraudulent e-mail that appears to be from a legitimate source, such as a bank. The e-mail asks for certain information, such as a Social Security number or bank account number. Sometimes it provides a link to a web page. The linked web page looks real, but its sole purpose is to collect private information that will be used to commit fraud.

Most legitimate organizations do not use e-mail to request this type of information. Never provide confidential information in response to an unsolicited e-mail. Avoid clicking a link to a website in an e-mail. It is better to manually enter the website URL into a web browser. Never open an e-mail attachment that you are not expecting.

Malware

Malware, short for *malicious software*, is a term given to software programs that are intended to damage, destroy, or steal data. Beware of an invitation to click on a website link for more information about an advertisement, as the link may trigger malware. One click can activate a code, and your computer could be hacked or infected. Malware comes in many forms including spyware, Trojan horses, worms, and viruses.

Employability Skills

Etiquette

Etiquette is the art of using good manners in any situation. Professional etiquette is applying the rules of good manners in the workplace and in other work-related situations. This includes putting away your personal digital device when in the workplace. *Netiquette* is etiquette used when communicating electronically. It is also known as *digital etiquette*. Netiquette includes accepted social and professional guidelines for Internet-based communication. These guidelines apply to e-mails, social networking, and other contact with customers and peers via the Internet.

- *Spyware*. **Spyware** is software that spies on a computer. Spyware can capture private information, such as e-mail messages, usernames, passwords, bank account information, and credit card information. Often, affected users are not aware that spyware is on their computer.
- *Trojan horses* are malware usually disguised to appear as a useful or common application in order to convince people to download and use the program. However, the Trojan horse performs malicious actions on the user's computer, such as destroying data or stealing information. Trojan horses do not self-replicate, nor do they infect other files.
- *Worms* are similar to Trojan horses, except they do self-replicate. Worms self-replicate so they can infect other computers and devices. Like Trojan horses, worms do not infect other files.
- *Software virus*. A **software virus** is a computer program designed to negatively impact a computer system by infecting other files. A virus may destroy data on the computer, cause programs to malfunction, bring harm to a network, or steal information. Viruses can be introduced to a computer in many ways, such as by downloading infected files from an e-mail or website.

Virus-protection software helps safeguard a computer and should be used on any computer or electronic device that is connected to the Internet or any type of network. Virus-protection software is also referred to as *antivirus* or *antimalware* software.

Virus-protection software should also have a firewall. A **firewall** is a program that monitors information coming into a computer. It helps ensure that only safe information gets through.

Digital Security

Do not be lulled into a false sense of security when communicating with others online. Be especially careful with those whom you do not know personally. Avoid opening e-mails that look suspicious. Use common sense when deciding what personal details you share, especially your address and Social Security number. Resist the urge to share too much information that could be stolen.

Avoid Identity Theft

Identity theft is an illegal act that involves stealing someone's personal information and using that information to commit theft or fraud. There are many ways that your personal information can be stolen without your knowing. A lost credit card or driver's license can provide thieves with the information they need to steal a person's identity. Criminals also steal physical mail to commit identity theft. This method is often called *dumpster diving*. However, computer technology has made identity theft through digital means the most prevalent.

Be wary of how much information you share on social networking websites. If you suspect your identity has been stolen, visit the Identity Theft website provided by the Federal Trade Commission for resources and guidance. Time is of the essence, so if this unfortunate situation happens to you, act immediately.

Create a Security Plan

A security plan should be in place for your computer in general, any databases you maintain, and any mobile devices you have. Your employer will assist in creating a plan for your workplace equipment. If you have any suspicions about communicating with someone or giving your information via a website, do not proceed. Investigate the person or the company with whom you are dealing. You may be able to avoid a scam before it is too late.

Consider downloading and running antivirus software for your mobile device. Many people rely on mobile devices. It is important to guard them against viruses that would disrupt a primary means of communication and expose personal data.

You must also plan to protect your mobile devices from theft. If you become careless and leave your smartphone or other device in an unexpected location, your identity can be stolen. You may also be stuck with a large telephone bill. If it is an employer-issued device, you may be responsible for replacing it using your personal funds. To protect your mobile device from use by a thief, create a password to lock it. Have the number of your mobile device in a safe place so that if the unexpected happens, you can contact your service provider.

Kues/Shutterstock.com

A security plan includes storing backup of important digital files in a fireproof container.

Security Settings

Become familiar with the security settings and features of your browser when accessing the Internet from your computer. Change your settings to protect your computer and your information. Enabling a *pop-up blocker* prevents your browser from allowing you to see pop-up ads, which can contain malware.

Back Up Your Computer

An important part of a security plan is backing up the data on your computer. If a virus invades your computer or the hard disk crashes, it may be too late to retrieve your files and computer programs.

Your employer will request regular backups of files on your work computer. For your personal computer, put a plan in place to perform regular backups. Decide on a storage device and method for backing up your files. Place the backup in a fireproof container and store it at a location other than your home.

Authentication

Authentication is the process of verifying a user's identity. Authenticating a user profile is the first line of defense in online protection.

Multifactor authentication is the use of multiple authentication techniques to verify a person's identity. There are three categories of authentication:

- *Something you know*
- *Something you have*
- *Something you are*

Something You Know

A *password* is a secret word or phrase consisting of alphanumeric characters that provides a user access to a computer, network, or profile. A password is considered as *something you know.* A PIN (personal identification number) is similar to a password.

Unfortunately, many people have weak passwords for even their most important accounts, such as banking or credit card accounts. Your employer will have guidelines for creating passwords for work accounts.

Something You Have

Something you have is an item that contains security information. For example, a smart card is considered as *something you have.* A smart card, such as a credit card, typically has a chip that holds personal information.

Something You Are

Biometrics are physical characteristics that a person possesses that are used to identify a person digitally. Using a person's fingerprints for digital entry to a building is an example of *something you are.*

Section 23.2 Review

Check Your Understanding

1. Explain why following an acceptable use policy is an example of ethical behavior.
2. Why should a digital citizen be aware of a personal computer's IP address?
3. Discuss the importance of digital security.
4. Explain how to protect a mobile device from theft.
5. Why should a computer be backed up on a regular basis?

Build Your Vocabulary

As you progress through this course, develop a personal glossary. This will help you build your vocabulary and prepare you for a career. Write a definition for each of the following terms and add it to your glossary.

acceptable use policy
cloud computing
Internet Protocol address
hacking
cookies
phishing
malware
spyware
software virus
firewall
identity theft
authentication

Review and Assessment

Chapter Summary

Section 23.1 Communicating in a Digital Society

- Digital communication is the exchange of information through electronic means. It requires digital literacy skills and appropriate digital citizenship behavior.
- Intellectual property is something that comes from a person's mind, such as an idea, invention, or process. Copyrights, patents, and trademarks can protect intellectual property rights. Material that is in the public domain refers to material that is not owned by anyone and can be used without permission. Goods or services can be protected by issuing a licensing agreement which is a contract that gives one party permission to use a good or service owned by someone else.
- The Electronic User's Bill of Rights details the rights and responsibilities of both individuals and institutions regarding the treatment of digital information.

Section 23.2 Internet Use in the Workplace

- Internet access provided by a company should be used only for business purposes. Most companies have an acceptable use policy that explains what is and is not acceptable use of company-owned and company-operated equipment.
- Digital security is important because it guards against identity theft. Identity theft is an illegal act that involves stealing someone's personal information and using that information to commit theft or fraud. It is important to protect equipment, data, and your digital footprint against theft by putting a security plan in place.

Review Your Knowledge

1. Give examples of the elements of digital communication.
2. Explain the importance of digital citizenship.
3. Explain what intellectual property is and what it includes.
4. What is the importance of the Electronic User's Bill of Rights?
5. How does open-source software differ from other forms of software?
6. Describe measures companies put in place to ensure their employees use the Internet appropriately while at work.
7. Why should a digital citizen protect personal computers and other devices?
8. Describe the most common form of phishing.
9. How does virus protection software help safeguard a computer?
10. Why is it important to back up a computer?

Apply Your Knowledge

1. Create a list of acceptable behaviors that are considered to be good examples of netiquette. Next to each, explain why these behaviors are necessary in a digital society.
2. Prepare a presentation to illustrate your understanding of digital citizenship and its implications for individuals, society, and business. Explain to your audience how digital citizenship can be exhibited by an individual in any personal or professional situation.

3. Analyze the legal and ethical responsibilities for digital citizenship that you have as a student.
4. Your digital footprint is important to your personal life as well as your future professional career. List examples of activities that may have a negative impact on your life if you posted about them on a social media website. After putting these actions in writing, will you think more seriously about what you post? Explain your answer.
5. Photocopying copyrighted material is illegal and unethical. What is your opinion of a friend photocopying a textbook chapter instead of buying the textbook? Demonstrate your understanding of ethical and legal issues by writing a letter to your friend about whether the fair use doctrine would apply in this situation.
6. Review the citation guidelines in a style guide such as *The Chicago Manual of Style* or the *MLA Handbook*. Use these guidelines to cite a book, newspaper article, or copy on a website. How is the citation unique for each type of source?
7. Locate your school or district's policy on acceptable Internet use. This is often located in the student handbook. What policies does your school have in place regarding appropriate Internet use? How are these policies enforced?
8. When shopping online, you may notice that with each new site you browse, you see advertisements for previous sites and products that you have searched. This is due to the presence of cookies on your computer. Marketers use this information for selling purposes. That is why you are likely to see those products appear repeatedly when shopping online. Is this an ethical practice? Why or why not?
9. Secure passwords are crucial to digital security. Describe your experiences creating passwords for various online accounts or electronic devices, such as an e-mail account, social media website, or cell phone. What were the requirements for these passwords? How do you keep track of them?
10. Create your own digital security plan. Make a list of the actions you will take to protect your online identity as well as your private information.

Apply Your Math Skills

1. Spencer is purchasing antivirus software for a laptop computer. Antivirus A costs $7.49 per month for the duration of a two-year contract. Antivirus B costs $79.99 for a one-year subscription. Which antivirus software is less expensive to purchase for two years of virus protection?
2. Alexandria has been the victim of identity theft. The following charges were found on a monthly credit card statement: $48.75 for utilities; $74.80 for groceries; $376.30 at a department store; and $94.55 at an online retailer. Alexandria never shopped at the department store or the online retailer. What percentage of the total credit card bill is for charges someone else made? Round your answer to the nearest percentage.

Communication Skills

College and Career Readiness

Reading. Imagery is descriptive language that indicates how something looks, feels, smells, sounds, or tastes. After you have read this chapter, find an example of how the author used imagery to appeal to the five senses. Analyze the presentation of the material. Why did you think this appealed to the senses? How did this explanation create imagery? Did it influence the reader's mood?

Writing. Generate your own ideas relevant to using digital technology in the appropriate manner. Use multiple authoritative print and digital sources and document each. Write several paragraphs about your findings to demonstrate your understanding of digital citizenship.

Speaking. Most people in the United States act as responsible and contributing citizens. How can a person demonstrate social and ethical responsibility in a digital society? Can you think of ways that are not discussed in this chapter? Share your opinions with the class.

Teamwork

Working with your team, identify and analyze examples of ethical responsibilities that a working professional has to society. Make a list of applicable rules your team thinks is appropriate for professional conduct. How can a professional exhibit ethical conduct?

Internet Research

Copyright. Copyright laws protect intellectual property. Conduct an Internet search for *copyright law violation example.* Select an example and discuss the law and how it was violated. What copyright issues were at stake? Write your findings and cite your sources using *The Chicago Manual of Style* or your choice of reference guide.

Multifactor authentication. Multifactor authentication is the first line of defense to secure personal data. Using the Internet, conduct a search on *multifactor authentication.* What did you learn about the importance of this security technique for protecting your personal data?

Portfolio Development

College and Career Readiness

Reflection. When your portfolio is complete, take time to reflect on your accomplishment. To reflect is to review your work and take an objective view of your actions. You spent a lot of time working on this personal project and after a few weeks or months pass, you can review your work with new objectivity.

1. If you received feedback from an instructor, employer, or friend, now is the time to analyze their comments and decide if you should make adjustments in your documents.

2. Take a fresh look at your work. Was it your best writing? How was your grammar and sentence structure?
3. Were you honest in each word that you wrote? You want to be proud but not boastful. Above all, never embellish what you are capable of doing.

CTSOs

Event Prep

Day of the Event. You have practiced all year for this CTSO competition, and now you are ready. Whether it is for an objective test, written test, report, or presentation, you have done your homework and are ready to shine.

To prepare for the day of the event, complete the following activities.

1. Get plenty of sleep the night before the event so that you are rested and ready to go.
2. Use your event checklist before you go into the presentation so that you do not forget any of your materials that are needed for the event.
3. Find the room where the competition will take place and arrive early. If you are late and the door is closed, you will be disqualified.
4. If you are making a presentation before a panel of judges, practice what you are going to say when you are called on. State your name, your school, and any other information that will be requested. Be confident, smile, and make eye contact with the judges.
5. When the event is finished, thank the judges for their time.

Contents

Getting Started

Math skills are needed in everyday life. You will need to be able to estimate your purchases at a grocery store, calculate sales tax, or divide a recipe in half. This section is designed to help develop your math proficiency for better understanding of the concepts presented in the textbook. Using the information presented in the Math Skills Handbook will help you understand basic math concepts and their application to the real world.

Using a Calculator

There are many different types of calculators. Some are simple and only perform basic math operations. Become familiar with the keys and operating instructions of your calculator so calculations can be made quickly and correctly.

Shown below is a scientific calculator that comes standard with the Windows 10 operating system. To display this version, select the **Settings** pull-down menu and click **Scientific** in the menu.

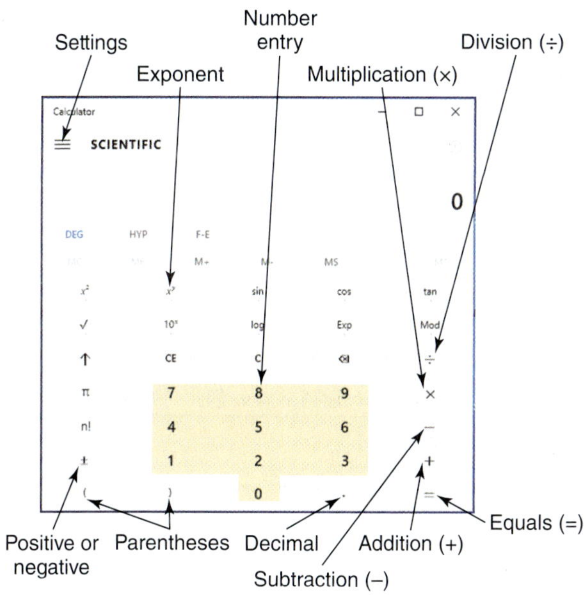

Solving Word Problems

Word problems are exercises in which the problem is set up in text, rather than presented in mathematical notation. Many word problems tell a story. You must identify the elements of the math problem and solve it.

Strategies for Solving Word Problems	
Strategy	**How to Apply**
List or table	Identify information in the problem and organize it into a table to identify patterns.
Work backward	When an end result is provided, work backward from that to find the requested information.
Guess, check, revise	Start with a reasonable guess at the answer, check to see if it is correct, and revise the guess as needed until the solution is found.
Substitute simpler information	Use different numbers to simplify the problem and solve it, then solve the problem using the provided numbers.

There are many strategies for solving word problems. Some common strategies include making a list or table; working backward; guessing, checking, and revising; and substituting simpler numbers to solve the problem.

Number Sense

Number sense is an ability to use and understand numbers to make judgments and solve problems. Someone with good number sense also understands when a computations is reasonable in the context of a problem.

Example

Suppose you want to add three basketball scores: 35, 21, and 18.

- First, add 30 + 20 + 10 = 60.
- Then, add 5 + 1 + 8 = 14.
- Finally, combine these two sums to find the answer: 60 + 14 = 74.

Example

Suppose your sibling is 72 inches tall and you want to convert this measurement from inches to feet. Suppose you use a calculator to divide 72 by 12 (number of inches in a foot) and the answer is displayed as 864. You recognize immediately that your sibling cannot be 864 feet tall and realize you must have miscalculated. In this case, you incorrectly entered a multiplication operation instead of a division operation. The correct answer is 6.

Numbers and Quantity

Numbers are more than just items in a series. Each number has a distinct value relative to all other numbers. They are used to perform mathematical operations from the simplest addition to finding square roots. There are whole numbers, fractions, decimals, exponents, and square roots.

Whole Numbers

A whole number, or integer, is any positive number or zero that has no fractional part. It can be a single digit from 0 to 9, or may contain multiple digits, such as 38.

Place Value

A digit's position in a number determines its *place value.* The digit, or numeral, in the place farthest to the right before the decimal point is in the *ones position.* The next digit to the left is in the *tens position,* followed by the next digit in the *hundreds position.* As you continue to move left, the place values increase to thousands, ten thousands, and so forth.

Example

Suppose you win the lottery and receive a check for $23,152,679. Your total prize would be *twenty-three million, one hundred fifty-two thousand, six hundred seventy-nine dollars.*

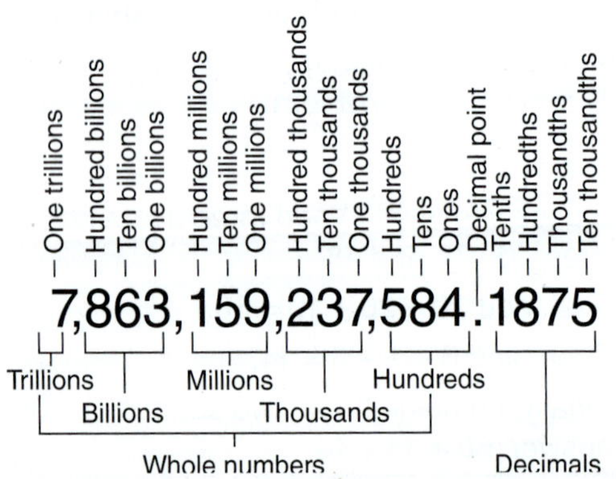

Addition

Addition is the process of combining two or more numbers. The result is called the *sum.*

Example

A plumber installs six faucets on the first job and three faucets on the second job. How many faucets were installed in total?

$$6 + 3 = 9$$

Subtraction

Subtraction is the process of finding the *difference* between two numbers.

Example

A plumber installs six faucets on the first job and three faucets on the second job. How many more faucets were installed on the first job than the second? Subtract 3 from 6 to find the answer.

$$6 - 3 = 3$$

Multiplication

Multiplication is a method of adding a number to itself a given number of times. The multiplied numbers are called *factors,* and the result is called the *product.*

Example

Suppose you are installing computers and need to purchase four adaptors. If the adaptors are $6 each, what is the total cost of the adaptors? The answer can be found by adding $6 four times:

$$\$6 + \$6 + \$6 + \$6 = \$24$$

However, the same answer is found more quickly by multiplying $6 times 4.

$$\$6 \times 4 = \$24$$

Division

Division is the process of determining how many times one number, called the *divisor,* goes into another number, called the *dividend.* The result is called the *quotient.*

Example

Suppose you are installing computers and buy a box of adaptors for $24. There are four adaptors in the box. What is the cost of each adaptor? The answer is found by dividing $24 by 4:

$$\$24 \div 4 = \$6$$

Decimals

A decimal is a kind of fraction with a denominator that is either ten, one hundred, one thousand, or some power of ten. Every decimal has three parts: a whole number (sometimes zero), followed by a decimal point, and one or more whole numbers.

Place Value

The numbers to the right of the decimal point indicate the amount of the fraction. The first place to the right of a decimal point is the tenths place.

The second place to the right of the decimal point is the hundredths place. As you continue to the right, the place values move to the thousandths place, the ten thousandths place, and so on.

Example

A machinist is required to produce an airplane part to a very precise measurement of 36.876 inches. This measurement is *thirty-six and eight hundred seventy-six thousandths* inches.

36.876

Addition

To add decimals, place each number in a vertical list and align the decimal points. Then add the numbers in each column starting with the column on the right and working to the left. The decimal point in the answer drops down into the same location.

Example

A landscaper spreads 4.3 pounds of fertilizer in the front yard of a house and 1.2 pounds in the backyard. How many pounds of fertilizer did the landscaper spread in total?

```
  4.3
+ 1.2
-----
  5.5
```

Subtraction

To subtract decimals, place each number in a vertical list and align the decimal points. Then subtract the numbers in each column, starting with the column on the right and working to the left. The decimal point in the answer drops down into the same location.

Example

A landscaper spreads 4.3 pounds of fertilizer in the front yard of a house and 1.2 pounds in the backyard. How many more pounds were spread in the front yard than in the backyard?

```
  4.3
- 1.2
-----
  3.1
```

Multiplication

To multiply decimals, place the numbers in a vertical list. Then multiply each digit of the top number by the right-hand bottom number. Multiply each digit of the top number by the bottom number in the tens position. Place the result on a second line and add a zero to the end of the number. Add the total number of decimal places in both numbers you are multiplying. This will be the number of decimal places in your answer.

Example

An artist orders 13 brushes priced at $3.20 each. What is the total cost of the order? The answer can be found by multiplying $3.20 by 13.

```
   $3.20
×     13
--------
     960
+   3200
--------
  $41.60
```

Division

To divide decimals, the dividend is placed under the division symbol, the divisor is placed to the left of the division symbol, and the quotient is placed above the division symbol. Start from the *left* of the dividend and determine how many times the divisor goes into the first number. Continue this until the quotient is found. Add the dollar sign to the final answer.

```
   3.20
3 ) 9.60
   -9       Product of 3 × 3
    0 6     Bring down the 6
      6     Product of 2 × 3
      0     No remainder
```

Example

An artist buys a package of three brushes for $9.60. What is the cost of each brush? The quotient is found by dividing $9.60 by 3.

```
   3.20
3 ) 9.60
   -9
    0 6
     00
```

Rounding

When a number is rounded, some of the digits are changed, removed, or changed to zero so the number is easier to work with. Rounding is often used when precise calculations or measurements are not needed. For example, if you are calculating millions of dollars, it might not be important to know the amount down to the dollar or cent. Instead, you might *round* the amount to the nearest ten thousand or even hundred thousand dollars. Also, when working with decimals, the final answer might have several more decimal places than needed.

To round a number, follow these steps. First, underline the digit in the place to which you are rounding. Second, if the digit to the *right* of this place is 5 or greater, add 1 to the underlined digit. If the digit to the right is less than 5, do not change the underlined digit. Third, change all the digits to right of the underlined digit to zero. In the case of decimals, the digits to the right of the underlined digit are removed.

Example

A company's utility expense last year was $32,678.53. The owner of the company is preparing a budget for next year and wants to round this amount to the nearest 1,000.

Step 1: Underline the digit in the 1,000 place.

$3<u>2</u>,678

Step 2: The digit to the right of 2 is greater than 5, so add 1.

2 + 1 = 3

Step 3: Change the digits to the right of the underlined digit to zero.

$33,000

Fractions

A fraction is a part of a whole. It is made up by a numerator that is divided by a denominator.

$$\frac{\text{numerator}}{\text{denominator}}$$

The *numerator* specifies the number of these equal parts that are in the fraction. The *denominator* shows how many equal parts make up the whole.

Proper

In a *proper fraction,* the numerator is less than the denominator.

Example

A lumber yard worker cuts a sheet of plywood into four equal pieces and sells three of them to a carpenter. The carpenter now has 3/4 of the original sheet. The lumber yard has 1/4 of the sheet remaining.

Improper

An *improper fraction* is a fraction where the numerator is equal to or greater than the denominator.

Example

A chef uses a chili recipe which calls for 1/2 cup of chili sauce. However, the chef makes an extra-large batch that will serve three times as many people and uses three of the 1/2 cup measures. The improper fraction in this example is 3/2 cups of chili sauce.

Mixed

A mixed number contains a whole number and a fraction. It is another way of writing an improper fraction.

Example

A chef uses a chili recipe that calls for 1/2 cup of chili sauce. However, the chef makes an extra-large batch that will serve three times as many people and uses three of the 1/2 cup measures. The improper fraction in this example is 3/2 cups of chili sauce. This can be converted to a mixed number by dividing the numerator by the denominator:

The remainder is 1, which is 1 over 2. So, the mixed number is 1 1/2 cups.

$$\begin{array}{r} 1 \\ 2\overline{)3} \\ -2 \\ \hline 1 \end{array}$$

Reducing

Fractions are reduced to make them easier to work with. Reducing a fraction means writing it with smaller numbers, in *lowest terms.* Reducing a fraction does not change its value.

To find the lowest terms, determine the largest number that *evenly* divides both the numerator and denominator so there is no remainder. Then use this number to divide both the numerator and denominator.

Example

The owner of a hair salon asks ten customers if they were satisfied with the service they recently received. Eight customers said they were satisfied, so the fraction of satisfied customers is 8/10. The largest number that evenly divides both the numerator and denominator is 2. The fraction is reduced to its lowest terms as follows.

$$\frac{8}{10} = \frac{8 \div 2}{10 \div 2} = \frac{4}{5}$$

Addition

To add fractions, the numerators are combined and the denominator stays the same.

However, fractions can only be added when they have a *common denominator.* The *least common denominator* is the smallest number to which each denominator can be converted.

Example

A snack food company makes a bag of trail mix by combining 3/8 pound of nuts with 1/8 pound of dried fruit. What is the total weight of each bag? The fractions have common denominators, so the total weight is determined by adding the fractions.

$$\frac{3}{8}+\frac{1}{8}=\frac{4}{8}$$

This answer can be reduced from 4/8 to 1/2.

Example

Suppose the company combines 1/4 pound of nuts with 1/8 cup of dried fruit. To add these fractions, the denominators must be made equal. In this case, the least common denominator is 8 because $4 \times 2 = 8$. Convert 1/4 to its equivalent of 2/8 by multiplying both numerator and denominator by 2. Then the fractions can be added as follows.

$$\frac{2}{8}+\frac{1}{8}=\frac{3}{8}$$

This answer cannot be reduced because 3 and 8 have no common factors.

Subtraction

To subtract fractions, the second numerator is subtracted from the first numerator. The denominators stay the same. However, fractions can only be subtracted when they have a *common denominator.*

Example

A snack food company makes a bag of trail mix by combining 3/8 pound of nuts with 1/8 pound of dried fruit. How much more do the nuts weigh than the dried fruit? The fractions have common denominators, so the difference can be determined by subtracting the fractions.

$$\frac{3}{8}-\frac{1}{8}=\frac{2}{8}$$

This answer can be reduced from 2/8 to 1/4.

Example

Suppose the company combines 1/4 pound of nuts with 1/8 cup of dried fruit. How much more do the nuts weigh than the dried fruit? To subtract these fractions, the denominators must be made equal. The least common denominator is 8, so convert 1/4 to its equivalent of 2/8. Then the fractions can be subtracted as follows.

$$\frac{2}{8}-\frac{1}{8}=\frac{1}{8}$$

This answer cannot be reduced.

Multiplication

Common denominators are not necessary to multiply fractions. Multiply all of the numerators and multiply all of the denominators. Reduce the resulting fraction as needed.

Example

A lab technician makes a saline solution by mixing 3/4 cup of salt with one gallon of water. How much salt should the technician mix if only 1/2 gallon of water is used? Multiply 3/4 by 1/2:

$$\frac{3}{4}\times\frac{1}{2}=\frac{3}{8}$$

Division

To divide one fraction by a second fraction, multiply the first fraction by the reciprocal of the second fraction. The *reciprocal* of a fraction is created by switching the numerator and denominator.

Example

A cabinet maker has 3/4 gallon of wood stain. Each cabinet requires 1/8 gallon of stain to finish. How many cabinets can be finished? To find the answer, divide 3/4 by 1/8, which means multiplying 3/4 by the reciprocal of 1/8.

$$\frac{3}{4}\div\frac{1}{8}=\frac{3}{4}\times\frac{8}{1}=\frac{24}{4}=6$$

Negative Numbers

Negative numbers are those less than zero. They are written with a minus sign in front of the number.

Example

The number –34,687,295 is read as *negative thirty-four million, six hundred eighty-seven thousand, two hundred ninety-five.*

Addition

Adding a negative number is the same as subtracting a positive number.

Example

A football player gains nine yards on the first running play (+9) and loses four yards (–4) on the second play. The two plays combined result in a five yard gain.

$$9 + (-4) = 9 - 4 = 5$$

Suppose this player loses five yards on the first running play (–5) and loses four yards (–4) on the second play. The two plays combined result in a nine yard loss.

$$-5 + (-4) = -5 - 4 = -9$$

Subtraction

Subtracting a negative number is the same as adding a positive number.

Example

Suppose you receive a $100 traffic ticket. This will result in a –$100 change to your cash balance. However, you explain the circumstance to a traffic court judge, and the fine is reduced by $60. The effect is to subtract –$60 from –$100 change to your cash balance. The final result is a –$40 change.

$$-\$100 - (-\$60) = -\$100 + \$60 = -\$40$$

Multiplication

Multiplication of an odd number of negative numbers results in a *negative* product. Multiplication of an even number of negative numbers results in a *positive* product.

Example

If you lose two pounds per week, this will result in a –2 pound weekly change in your weight. After five weeks, there will be a –10 pound change to your weight.

$$5 \times (-2) = -10$$

Suppose you have been losing two pounds per week. Five weeks ago (–5) your weight was 10 pounds higher.

$$(-5) \times (-2) = 10$$

Division

Division of an odd number of negative numbers results in a *negative* quotient. Division of an even number of negative numbers results in a *positive* quotient.

Example

Suppose you lost 10 pounds, which is a –10 pound change in your weight. How many pounds on average did you lose each week if it took five weeks to lose the weight? Divide –10 by 5 to find the answer.

$$-10 \div 5 = -2$$

Suppose you lost 10 pounds. How many weeks did this take if you lost two pounds each week? Divide –10 by –2 to find the answer.

$$-10 \div -2 = 5$$

Percentages

A percentage (%) means a part of 100. It is the same as a fraction or decimal.

Representing Percentages as Decimals

To change a percentage to a decimal, move the decimal point two places to the left. For example, 1% is the same as 1/100 or 0.01; 10% is the same as 10/100 or 0.10; and 100% is the same as 100/100 or 1.0.

Example

A high school cafeteria estimates that 30% of the students prefer sesame seeds on hamburger buns. To convert this percentage to a decimal, move the decimal point two places to the left.

$$30\% = 0.30$$

Representing Fractions as Percentages

To change a fraction to a percentage, first convert the fraction to a decimal by dividing the numerator by the denominator. Then convert the decimal to a percentage by moving the decimal point two places to the right.

Example

A high school cafeteria conducts a survey and finds that three of every ten students prefer sesame seeds on hamburger buns. To change this fraction to a percentage, divide 3 by 10, and move the decimal two places to the right.

$$3 \div 10 = 0.30 = 30\%$$

Calculating a Percentage

To calculate the percentage of a number, change the percentage to a decimal and multiply by the number.

Example

A car dealer sold ten cars last week, of which 70% were SUVs. How many SUVs were purchased? Change 70% to a decimal by dividing 70 by 100, which equals 0.70. Then multiply by the total number (10).

$$0.70 \times 10 = 7$$

To determine what percentage one number is of another, divide the first number by the second. Then convert the quotient into a percentage by moving the decimal point two places to the right.

Example

A car dealer sold 10 cars last week, of which seven were SUVs. What percentage of the cars purchased were SUVs? Divide 7 by 10 and then convert to a percentage.

$$7 \div 10 = 0.70$$

$$0.70 = 70\%$$

Ratio

A ratio compares two numbers through division. Ratios are often expressed as a fraction, but can also be written with a colon (:) or the word *to.*

Example

A drugstore's cost for a bottle of vitamins is $2.00, which it sells for $3.00. The ratio of the selling price to the cost can be expressed as follows.

$$\frac{\$3.00}{\$2.00} = \frac{3}{2}$$

$$\$3.00{:}\$2.00 = 3{:}2$$

$$\$3.00 \text{ to } \$2.00 = 3 \text{ to } 2$$

Measurement

The official system of measurement in the United States for length, volume, and weight is the US Customary system of measurement. The metric system of measurement is used by most other countries.

US Customary Measurement

The following are the most commonly used units of length in the US Customary system of measurement.

- 1 inch
- 1 foot = 12 inches
- 1 yard = 3 feet
- 1 mile = 5,280 feet

Example

An interior designer measurers the length and width of a room when ordering new floor tiles. The length is measured at 12 feet 4 inches (12′ 4″). The width is measured at 8 feet 7 inches (8′ 7″).

Example

Taxi cab fares are usually determined by measuring distance in miles. A recent cab rate in Chicago was $3.25 for the first 1/9 mile or less, and $0.20 for each additional 1/9 mile.

Metric Conversion

The metric system of measurement is convenient to use because units can be converted by multiplying or dividing by multiples of 10. The following are the commonly used units of length in the metric system of measurement.

- 1 millimeter
- 1 centimeter = 10 millimeters
- 1 meter = 100 centimeters
- 1 kilometer = 1,000 meters

The following are conversions from the US Customary system to the metric system.

- 1 inch = 25.4 millimeters = 2.54 centimeters
- 1 foot = 30.48 centimeters = 0.3048 meters
- 1 yard = 0.9144 meters
- 1 mile = 1.6093 kilometers

Example

A salesperson from the United States is traveling abroad and needs to drive 100 kilometers to meet a customer. How many miles is this trip? Divide 100 kilometers by 1.6093 and round to the thousandth place.

```
              62.138
1.6093.)100.0000.000
       − 96 558
          3 4420
        − 3 2186
            2234 0
          − 1609 3
             624 70
           − 482 79
             141 910
           − 128 744
              13 169
```

Estimating

Estimating is finding an *approximate* answer and often involves using rounded numbers. It is often quicker to add rounded numbers, for example, than it is to add the precise numbers.

Example

Estimate the total miles a delivery truck will travel along the following three segments of a route.

- Detroit to Chicago: 278 miles
- Chicago to St. Louis: 297 miles
- St. Louis to Wichita: 436 miles

The mileage can be estimated by rounding each segment to the nearest 100 miles.

- Detroit to Chicago: 300 miles
- Chicago to St. Louis: 300 miles
- St. Louis to Wichita: 400 miles

Add the rounded segments to estimate the total miles.

300 + 300 + 400 = 1,000 miles

Accuracy and Precision

Accuracy and precision mean slightly different things. *Accuracy* is the closeness of a measured value to its actual or true value. *Precision* is how close measured values are to each other.

Example

A machine is designed to fill jars with 16 ounces of peanut butter. The machine is considered accurate if the actual amount of peanut butter in a jar is within 0.05 ounces of the target, which is a range of 15.95 to 16.05 ounces. A machine operator tests a jar and measures the weight to be 16.01 ounces. The machine is accurate.

Suppose a machine operator tests 10 jars of peanut butter and finds the weight of each jar to be 15.4 ounces. The machine is considered precise because it fills every jar with exactly the same amount. However, it is not accurate because the amount differs too much from the target.

Algebra

An *equation* is a mathematical statement that has an equal sign (=). An *algebraic* equation is an equation that includes at least one variable. A *variable* is an unknown quantity.

Solving Equations with Variables

Solving an algebraic equation means finding the value of the variable that will make the equation a true statement. To solve a simple equation, perform inverse operations on both sides and isolate the variable.

Example

A computer consultant has sales of $1,000. After deducting $600 in expenses, the total profit equals $400. This is expressed with the following equation.

sales – expenses = profit

$1,000 – $600 = $400

Example

A computer consultant has expenses of $600 and $400 in profit. What are the total sales? An equation can be written in which sales are the unknown quantity, or variable.

sales – expenses = profit

sales – $600 = $400

Example

To find the value for sales, perform inverse operations on both sides and isolate the variable.

sales	–	$600	=	$400
	+	$600	+	$600
sales			=	$1,000

Order of Operations

The order of operations is a set of rules stating which operations in an equation are performed first. The order of operations is often stated using the acronym *PEMDAS*. PEMDAS stands for parentheses, exponents, multiplication and division, and addition and subtraction. This means anything inside parentheses is computed first. Exponents are computed next. Then, any multiplication and division operations are computed. Finally, any addition and subtraction operations are computed to find the final answer to the problem. The equation is solved from left to right by applying PEMDAS.

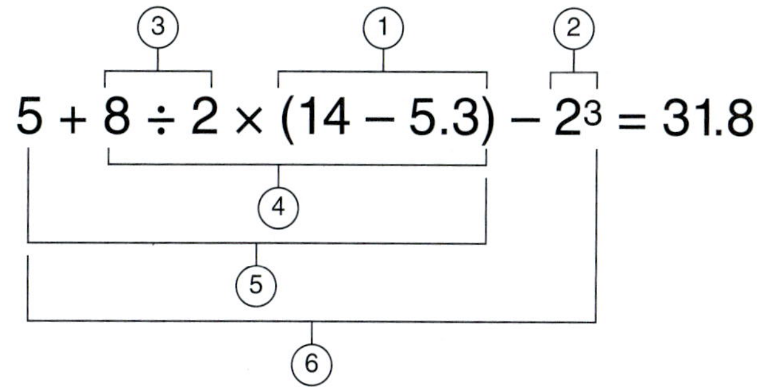

Recursive Formulas

A *recursive formula* is used to determine the next term of a sequence, using one or more of the preceding terms. The terms of a sequence are often expressed with a variable and subscript. For example, a sequence might be written as a_1, a_2, a_3, a_4, a_5, and so on. The subscript is essentially the place in line for each term. A recursive formula has two parts. The first is a starting point or seed value (a_1). The second is an equation for another number in the sequence (a_n). The second part of the formula is a function of the prior term (a_{n-1}).

Example

Suppose you buy a car for $10,000. Assume the car declines in value 10% each year. In the second year, the car will be worth 90% of $10,000, which is $9,000. The following year it will be worth 90% of $9,000, which is $8,100. What will the car be worth in the fifth year? Use the following recursive equation to find the answer.

$$a_n = a_{n-1} \times 0.90$$

where $a_1 = \$10,000$

a_n = value of car in the nth year

Sample Recursive Formula

Year	Value of Car
n = 1	$a_1 = \$10,000$
n = 2	$a_2 = a_{2-1} \times 0.90 = a_1 \times 0.90 = \$10,000 \times 0.90 = \$9,000$
n = 3	$a_3 = a_{3-1} \times 0.90 = a_2 \times 0.90 = \$9,000 \times 0.90 = \$8,100$
n = 4	$a_4 = a_{4-1} \times 0.90 = a_3 \times 0.90 = \$8,100 \times 0.90 = \$7,290$
n = 5	$a_5 = a_{5-1} \times 0.90 = a_4 \times 0.90 = \$7,290 \times 0.90 = \$6,561$

Geometry

Geometry is a field of mathematics that deals with shapes, such as circles and polygons. A *polygon* is any shape whose sides are straight. Every polygon has three or more sides.

Parallelograms

A *parallelogram* is a four-sided figure with two pairs of parallel sides. A *rectangle* is a type of parallelogram with four right angles. A *square* is a special type of parallelogram with four right angles (90 degrees) and four equal sides.

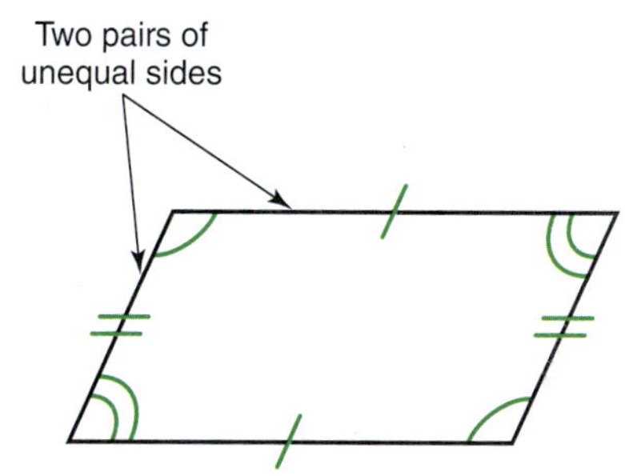

Parallelogram

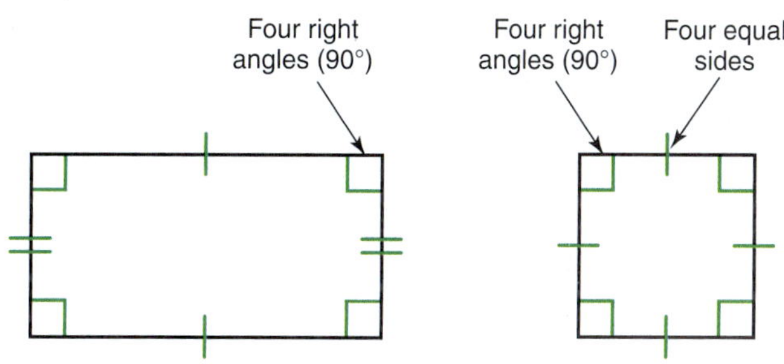

Rectangle **Square**

Example

Real-life examples of squares include ceramic floor and wall tiles, and each side of a die. Real-life examples of a rectangle include a football field, pool table, and most doors.

Triangles

A three-sided polygon is called a *triangle*. The following are four types of triangles, which are classified according to their sides and angles.

- *Equilateral:* Three equal sides and three equal angles.
- *Isosceles:* Two equal sides and two equal angles.
- *Scalene:* Three unequal sides and three unequal angles.

- *Right:* One right angle; may be isosceles or scalene.

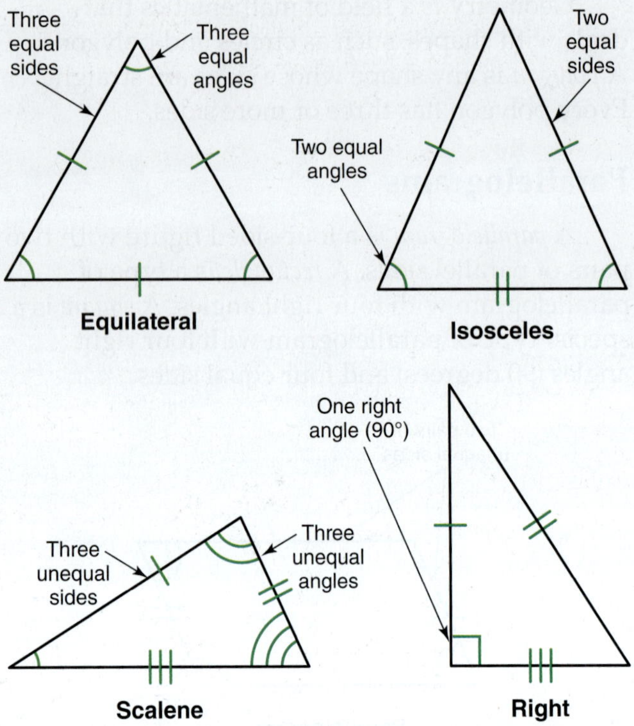

Example
Real-life examples of equilateral triangles are the sides of a classical Egyptian pyramid.

Circles and Half Circles

A *circle* is a figure in which every point is the same distance from the center. The distance from the center to a point on the circle is called the *radius.* The distance across the circle through the center is the *diameter.* A half circle is formed by dividing a whole circle along the diameter.

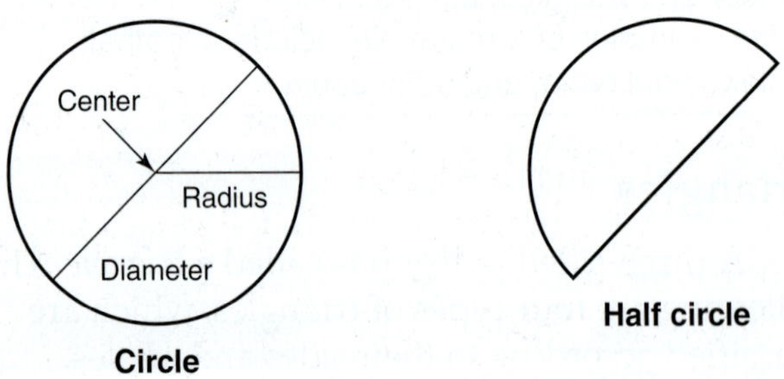

Example
Real-life examples of circles include wheels of all sizes.

Perimeter

A *perimeter* is a measure of length around a figure. Add the length of each side to measure the perimeter of any figure whose sides are all line segments, such as a parallelogram or triangle. The perimeter of a circle is called the *circumference.* To measure the perimeter, multiply the diameter by pi (π). Pi is approximately equal to 3.14. The following formulas can be used to calculate the perimeters of various figures.

Perimeter Equations

Figure	Perimeter
parallelogram	2 × width + 2 × length
square	4 × side
rectangle	2 × width + 2 × length
triangle	side + side + side
circle	π × diameter

Example
A professional basketball court is a rectangle 94 feet long and 50 feet wide. The perimeter of the court is calculated as follows.

$$2 \times 94 \text{ feet} + 2 \times 50 \text{ feet} = 288 \text{ feet}$$

Example
A tractor tire has a 43 inch diameter. The circumference of the tire is calculated as follows.

$$43 \text{ inches} \times 3.14 = 135 \text{ inches}$$

Area

Area is a measure of the amount of surface within the perimeter of a flat figure. Area is measured in square units, such as square inches, square feet, or square miles. The areas of the following figures are calculated using the corresponding formulas.

Area Equations

Figure	Area
parallelogram	base × height
square	side × side
rectangle	length × width
triangle	1/2 × base × height
circle	π × radius^2 = π × radius × radius

Example

An interior designer needs to order decorative tiles to fill the following spaces. Measure the area of each space in square feet.

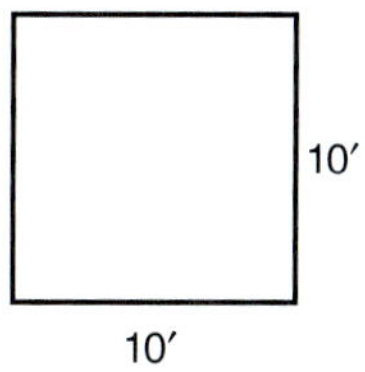

10 × 10 = 100

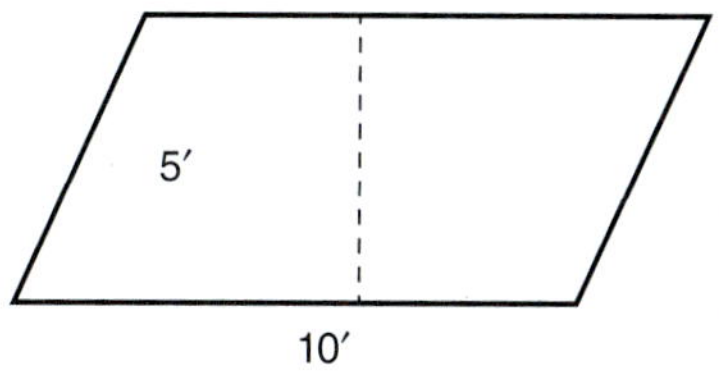

10 × 5 = 50

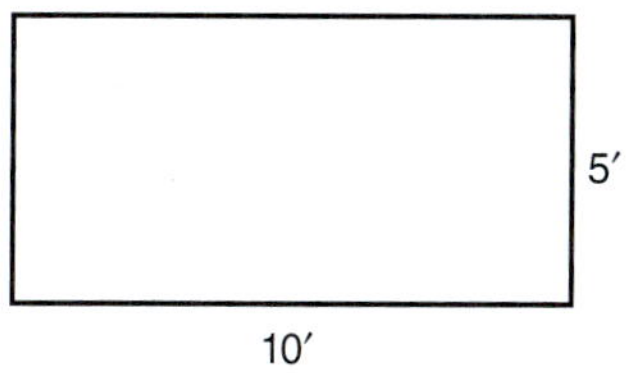

10 × 5 = 50

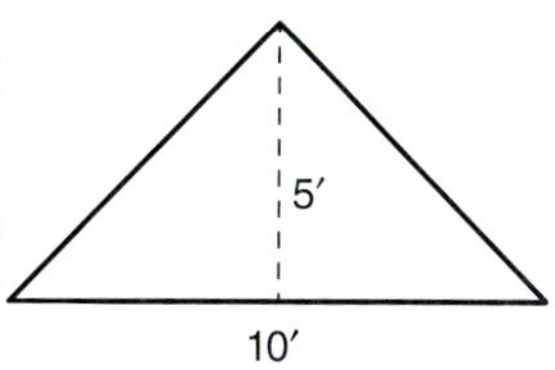

½ × 10 × 5 = 25

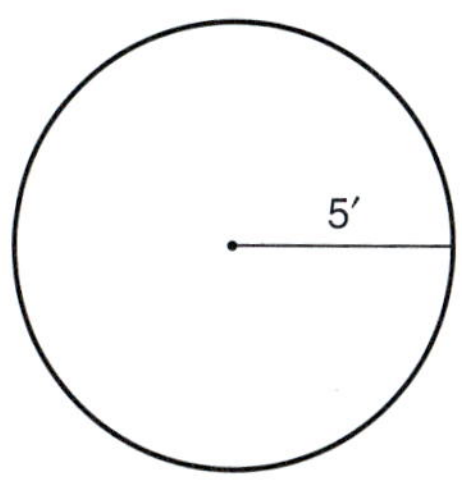

$3.14 \times 5^2 =$

3.14 × 5 × 5 = 78.5

Surface Area

Surface area is the total area of the surface of a figure occupying three-dimensional space, such as a cube or prism. A *cube* is a solid figure that has six identical square faces. A *prism* has bases or ends which have the same size and shape and are parallel to each other, and each of whose sides is a parallelogram. The following are the formulas to find the surface area of a cube and a prism.

Surface Area Equations	
Object	**Surface Area**
cube	6 × side × side
prism	2 × [(length × width) + (width × height) + (length × height)]

Example

A manufacturer of cardboard boxes wants to determine how much cardboard is needed to make the following size boxes. Calculate the surface area of each in square inches.

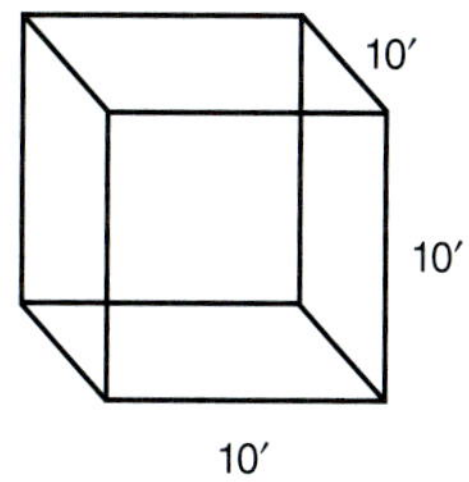

6 × 10 × 10 = 600

Cube

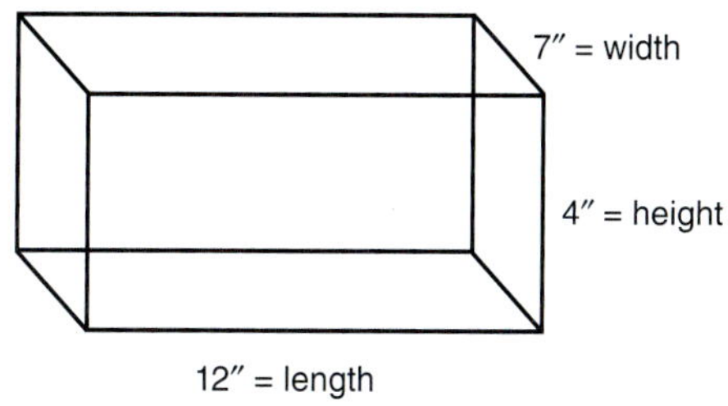

2 [(12 × 7) + (7 × 4) + (12 × 4)] =

2 [84 + 28 + 48] = 320

Prism

Volume

Volume is the three-dimensional space occupied by a figure and is measured in cubic units, such as cubic inches or cubic feet. The volumes of the following figures are calculated using the corresponding formulas.

Volume Equations	
Solid Figure	**Volume**
cube	$side^3$ = side × side × side
prism	length × width × height
cylinder	$\pi \times radius^2 \times height = \pi \times radius \times radius \times height$
sphere	$4/3 \times \pi \times radius^3 = 4/3 \times \pi \times radius \times radius \times radius$

Example
Find the volume of packing material needed to fill the following boxes. Measure the volume of each in cubic inches.

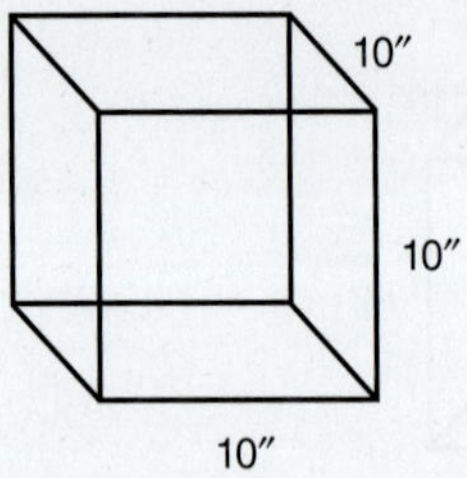

$10 \times 10 \times 10 = 1{,}000$

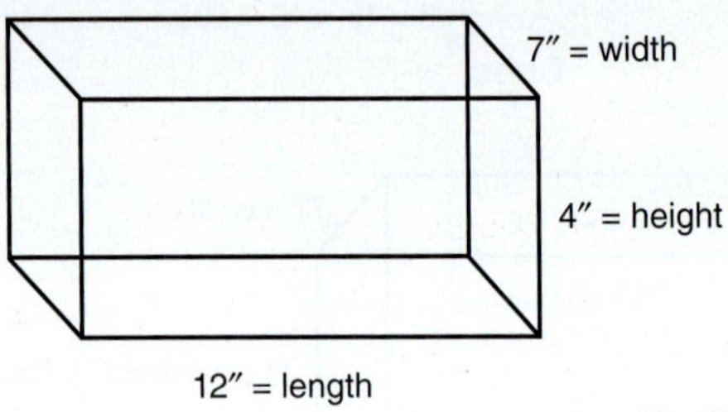

$12 \times 7 \times 4 = 336$

Example
Find the volume of grain that will fill the following cylindrical silo. Measure the volume in cubic feet.

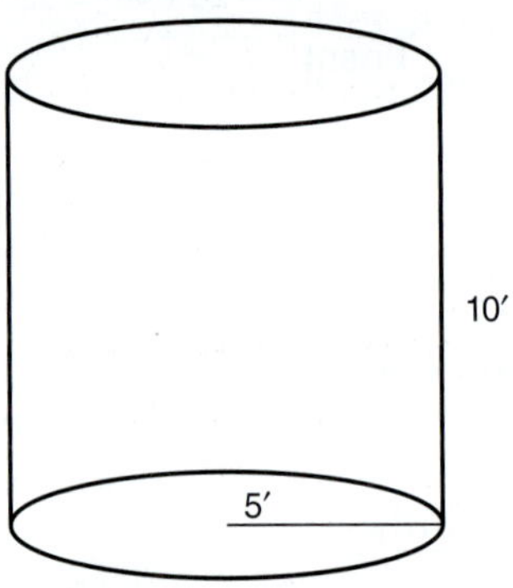

$3.14 \times 5 \times 5 \times 10 = 785$

Example
A manufacturer of pool toys wants to stuff soft material into a ball with a 3 inch radius. Find the cubic inches of material that will fit into the ball.

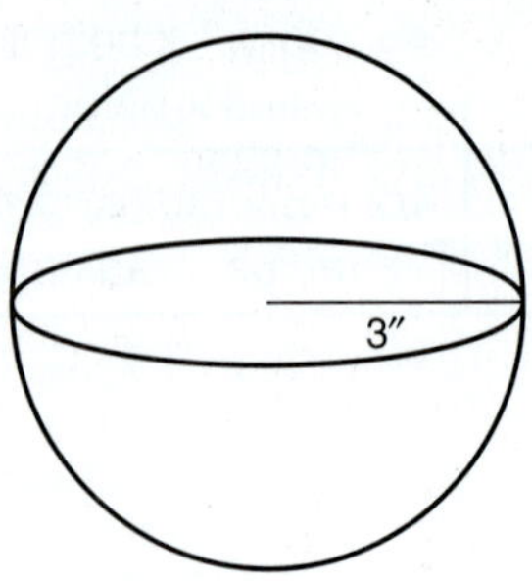

$\frac{4}{3} \times 3.14 \times 3 \times 3 \times 3 = 113$

Data Analysis and Statistics

Graphs are used to illustrate data in a picture-like format. It is often easier to understand data when they are shown in a graphical form instead of a numerical form in a table. Common types of graphs are bar graphs, line graphs, and circle graphs.

A *bar graph* organizes information along a vertical axis and horizontal axis. The vertical axis runs up and down one side; the horizontal axis runs along the bottom.

A *line graph* also organizes information on vertical and horizontal axes; however, data are graphed as a continuous line rather than a set of bars. Line graphs are often used to show trends over a period of time.

A *circle graph* looks like a divided circle and shows how a whole object is cut up into parts. Circle graphs are also called *pie charts* and are often used to illustrate percentages.

Example
A business shows the following balances in its cash account for the months of March through July. These data are illustrated in the following line graph.

Sample Business Cash Account Balances

Month	Account Balance	Month	Account Balance
March	$400	June	$800
April	$600	July	$900
May	$500	—	—

Account balance

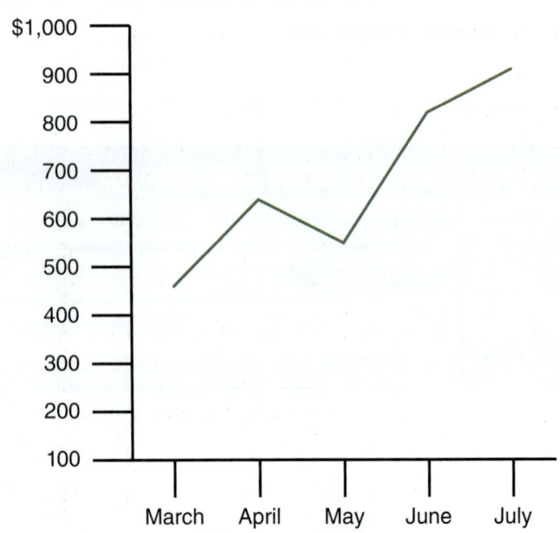

Line Graph

Example

A business lists the percentage of its expenses in the following categories. These data are displayed in the following circle graph.

Sample Business Expenses	
Expenses	**Percentage**
Cost of goods	25
Salaries	25
Rent	21
Utilities	17
Advertising	12

Circle Graph

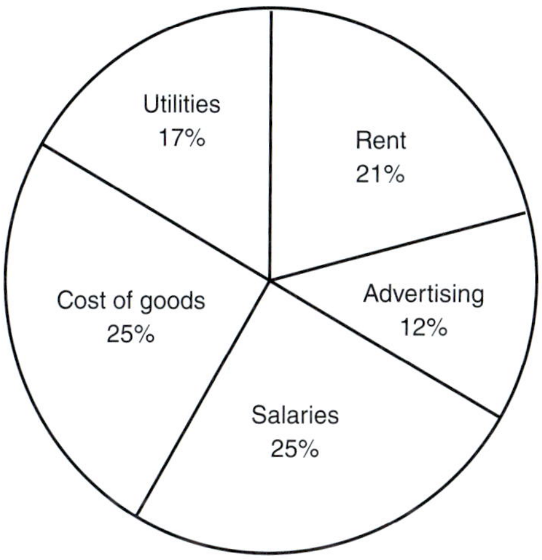

Monthly expenses

Math Models for Business and Retail

Math skills used in business and retail are the same math skills required in everyday life. The ability to add, subtract, multiply, and divide different types of numbers is very important. However, this type of math is often focused on prices, taxes, profits, and losses.

Markup

Markup is a retailing term for the amount by which price exceeds the cost. One way to express markup is in dollars. Another way to express markup is percentage. The *markup percentage* is the amount of the markup as a percentage of the cost.

Example

A retailer pays $4 for a pair of athletic socks and prices them for sale at $7. The dollar markup is $3.

selling price – cost = dollar markup

$7 – $4 = $3

Example

A pair of athletic socks, which cost $4, is priced at $7. The dollar markup is $3. To find the markup percentage, divide $3 by $4. The markup percentage is 75%.

markup dollars ÷ cost = markup percentage

$3 ÷ $4 = 0.75 = 75%

Percentage Markup to Determine Selling Price

The selling price of an item can be determined if you know the markup percentage and the cost. First, convert the markup percentage to a decimal. Next multiply the cost by the decimal. Then, add the markup dollars to the cost to determine the selling price. Another way to find the selling price is to convert the markup percentage to a decimal and add 1.0. Then multiply this amount by the cost.

Example

A pair of athletic socks costs $4, which the retailer marks up by 75%. Find the selling price.

1. Convert the markup percentage to a decimal.

   75% = 0.75

2. Multiply the cost by the markup.

   cost × markup = dollar markup

   $4 × 0.75 = $3

3. Add the $3 markup to the $4 cost to find the selling price. The selling price is $7.

   $4 + $3 = $7

Example

A pair of athletic socks costs $4, which the retailer marks up by 75%. Find the selling price.

1. Convert the 75% markup percentage to 0.75 and add 1.0.

   0.75 + 1.0 = 1.75

2. Multiply 1.75 by the $4 cost to find the selling price.

   $4 × 1.75 = $7

Markdown

A *markdown* is the amount by which the selling price of an item is reduced. Sometimes a markdown is also called a *discount.* To find the amount of a markdown, subtract the new or discounted price from the original price. A markdown can also be expressed as a percentage of the original price. Sometimes this is called a *percentage discount.*

Example

A package of meat at a supermarket is originally priced at $10. However, the meat has not sold and is nearing its expiration date. The supermarket wants to sell it quickly, so it reduces the price to $6. This is a markdown of $4.

selling price – discounted price = dollar markdown

$10 – $6 = $4

Example

A package of meat at a supermarket is originally priced at $10. However, the meat has not sold and is nearing its expiration date. The supermarket wants to sell it quickly, so it marks down the price by $4. The markdown percentage is determined by dividing the $4 markdown by the original $10 price.

markdown ÷ selling price = markdown percentage

$4 ÷ $10 = 40%

Gross Profit

Gross profit is a company's net sales minus the cost of goods sold. *Gross margin* is often expressed as a percentage of revenue.

Example

A wristband manufacturer generated net sales of $100,000 last year. The cost of goods sold for the wristbands was $30,000. The net sales of $100,000 minus the $30,000 cost of goods sold leaves a gross profit of $70,000.

net sales – cost of goods sold = gross profit

$100,000 – $30,000 = $70,000

Example

The gross profit of $70,000 divided by the net sales of $100,000 is 0.70, or 70%.

gross profit ÷ net sales = gross margin percentage

$70,000 ÷ $100,000 = 0.70 = 70%

Net Income or Loss

Net income or loss is a company's revenue after total expenses are deducted from gross profit. Total expenses include marketing, administration, interest, and taxes. A company earns a *net income* when gross profit exceeds expenses. A *net loss* is incurred when expenses exceed gross profit.

Example

A wristband manufacturer had a gross profit of $70,000. In addition, expenses for marketing, administration, interest, and taxes were $50,000. Net profit is calculated by subtracting the total expenses of $50,000 from the gross profit of $70,000. The net profit was $20,000.

gross profit on sales – total expenses = net income or loss

$70,000 – $50,000 = $20,000

Break-Even Point

A *break-even point* is the number of units a company must sell to cover its costs and expenses and earn a zero profit. Use the following formula to find a company's break-even point.

total costs ÷ selling price = break-even point

Sales Tax

Sales tax is a tax collected on the selling price of a good or service. The sales tax rate is usually expressed as a percentage of the selling price. Sales tax is calculated by multiplying the sale price by the tax rate.

Example

Suppose you buy a T-shirt for $10.00. How much is the sales tax if the tax rate is 5%? Convert 5% to a decimal (.05) and multiply it by the sale price.

sale price × sales tax rate percentage = sales tax

$10 × 0.05 = $0.50

Return on Investment

Return on investment (ROI) is a calculation of a company's net profit as a percentage of the owner's investment. One way to determine ROI is to divide net profit by the owner's investment.

Example

Suppose you start a dry-cleaning business with a $100,000 investment, and you earn a $20,000 net profit during the first year. Divide $20,000 by $100,000, which equals a 20% return on your investment.

net income ÷ owner's investment = return on investment (ROI)

$20,000 ÷ $100,000 = 0.20 = 20%

Glossary

20/10 rule. States that an individual's maximum debt load should never be more than 20 percent of the annual take-home pay and monthly payments should be less than 10 percent of the monthly take-home pay. (9)

401(k) plan. Employer-sponsored retirement plan that allows an individual to deposit earnings into a tax-deferred investment. (7)

403(b) plan. Retirement plan available to employees of nonprofit organizations. (7)

457 plan. Type of defined-contribution retirement plan that does not have required minimum distribution rules and is available primarily to governmental employees. (7)

529 plan. Savings plan for education operated by a state or educational institution. (21)

A

ability. Mastery of a skill or the capacity to do something. (21)

absolute advantage. Exists when a country can produce goods more efficiently and at a lower cost than another country. (19)

acceleration clause. Statement in a contract that allows the creditor to require full and immediate payment of the entire balance if a payment is missed or the individual fails to abide by the terms of the contract. (8)

acceptable use policy. Set of rules that explains what is and is not acceptable use of company-owned and company-operated equipment and networks. (23)

adjustable-rate mortgage (ARM). Mortgage with an interest rate that can be adjusted up or down periodically. (12)

adjusted gross income. Calculated by subtracting adjustments from total income. (3)

advertising. Any paid public announcement promoting the sale of a good or service. (10)

amortization. Process of paying back a loan in equal monthly installments. (12)

annual percentage rate (APR). Annual cost of credit a lender charges for an installment loan. (8)

annual percentage yield (APY). Rate of yearly earnings from an account, including compound interest. (5)

annuity. Contract with an insurance company that provides regular income for a set period of time. (7)

apartment. Group of rooms designed for use as a private living space. (12)

appraisal. Written estimate of the value of real estate. (12)

appreciation. Increase in the value of an investment. (6)

apprenticeship. Combination of on-the-job training, work experience, and classroom instruction. (21)

aptitude. Characteristic that an individual has developed naturally; also called *talent*. (21)

asking price. Price the seller wishes to receive from the sale of the property. (12)

assessed value. Dollar amount assigned to a residence for tax purposes. (12)

asset. Item of value that is owned. (2)

audit. Review of financial records and statements to make sure the information is accurate as reported. (3)

authentication. Process of verifying a user's identity. (23)

automobile insurance. Covers passenger vehicles and protects the beneficiary against the financial aspects of a traffic accident. (14)

B

background check. Investigation into personal data about a job applicant. (22)

bait and switch. Illegal strategy that involves advertising one item and then substituting another item. (11)

balance of payments. Account of the total flow of goods, services, and money coming into and going out of the country. (19)

balance of trade. Difference between total imports and total exports of goods and services. (19)

bank. Financial institution that receives, lends, exchanges, and safeguards money. (4)

bank reconciliation. Process of comparing a check register with a bank statement. (4)

bank statement. Record of checks, ATM transactions, deposits, and charges on an account. (4)

bankruptcy. Legal state in which the courts excuse a debtor from repaying some or all debt; in return, the debtor must give up certain assets and possessions. (9)

bear market. Extended period of falling stock prices, which comes with uncertainty and pessimism. (6)

behavioral question. Interview question that draws on a person's previous experiences and decisions. (22)

beneficiary. Person or group who receives a deceased person's assets. (7) Also, person or organization named by a policyholder to receive the death benefit of an insurance policy after the policyholder's death. (15)

binding arbitration. Method of settling disagreements through an objective third party. (11)

biodegradable. Able to be broken down naturally by microorganisms into harmless elements. (20)

bodily injury liability insurance. Protects the person who is responsible for an auto accident that results in the injury or death of others. (14)

bond. Certificate of debt issued by a corporation or government. (6)

bonus. Money added to an employee's base pay. (3)

brick-and-mortar store. Retail store that sells directly from a physical location. (10)

brokerage firm. Financial institution that facilitates the purchase and sale of financial securities by buyers and sellers and savings accounts can be opened. (5, 6)

budget. Plan for the use of money over time based on goals, expenses, and expected income. (2)

bull market. Extended period of rising stock prices, which comes with high consumer confidence and optimism. (6)

business. All the activities involved in developing and exchanging products. (18)

business cycle. Fluctuations between periods of economic growth and slowdown. (6)

Note: The number in parentheses following each definition indicates the chapter in which the term can be found.

business market. Consists of customers who buy products for use in a business. (18)

business plan. Formal document that states the goals of a business and includes a detailed strategy of how to achieve the goals and grow the business. (18)

business-to-business (B2B). Business that sells primarily to other businesses. (18)

business-to-consumer (B2C). Business that sells primarily to individual consumers. (18)

buying incentive. Special offer by sellers designed to help sell goods and services. (10)

C

cancer insurance. Insurance that helps manage the risks that occur when an insured has cancer. (15)

capital. All the tools, equipment, and machinery that are used to make final products. (16)

capital gain. Income that results from selling an asset for more than the purchase price. (3, 6)

capital loss. Loss of money that occurs when the selling price of an investment is less than the purchase price. (6)

capitalism. See *market economy*.

career. Series of related jobs in the same profession. (21)

career and technical student organization (CTSO). National student organizations with local school chapters that are related to career and technical education (CTE) courses. (21)

career cluster. Group of occupational and career specialties. (21)

career ladder. Outline of progressively higher positions achieved through education and experience that lead to greater responsibility and career success. (21)

career objective. Summary of the type of job for which a person is looking. (22)

career pathway. Subgroup of a career cluster that reflects occupations requiring similar knowledge and skills. (21)

career plan. List of steps to reach a career goal; also called postsecondary plan. (21)

cartel. Group of countries or firms that controls the production and pricing of a product or service. (19)

cash advance. Loan against the available credit on an individual's account. (8)

cash flow statement. Summary of the amount of money received and the amount paid for goods and services during a specific period. (2)

caveat emptor. Latin phrase that means *let the buyer beware*. (11)

certificate of deposit (CD). Savings account that requires a deposit of a fixed amount of money for a fixed period of time. (5)

certification. Professional status earned by an individual after passing an exam focused on a specific body of knowledge. (21)

certified used car. Previously owned vehicle that has received a thorough mechanical and appearance inspection along with necessary repairs and replacements. (13)

chain letter. Letters, e-mails, or social media posts that solicit money or gifts from others on an ever-growing list in the hopes that the sender will receive more gifts or money in return. (11)

Chapter 13 bankruptcy. Permits debtors with regular incomes to pay all or a portion of their debts under the protection and supervision of the court; also called *Wage Earner's Bankruptcy*. (9)

Chapter 7 bankruptcy. Eliminates most types of debt and stays on a credit report for ten years; also known as *straight bankruptcy* or *liquidation bankruptcy*. (9)

charitable contribution. Donation of money, gifts, or personal time. (2)

charity. Organization that aids those in need. (2)

charter. License authorizing a bank to operate. (4)

check. Written order for the bank to pay a specific amount to the person to whom the check is written. (4)

check register. Record of account deposits, withdrawals, checks, fees, and interest.

checking account. Bank account that allows the owner to make deposits, write checks, and withdraw money. (4)

chronological résumé. Résumé that lists information in reverse chronological order, with the most recent employer listed first. (22)

claim. Process of documenting a loss against an insurance policy. (14)

class-action lawsuit. Legal court action brought by a group of individuals who have been similarly wronged. (11)

climate change. Shifts in measurements of climate that last decades or longer. (20)

closed-end credit. Loan for a specific amount that must be repaid with interest by a specified date or according to a specified schedule. (8)

closing costs. Fee or settlement charge that must be paid before the sale of a home is final. (12)

cloud computing. Using remote servers to store and access data over the Internet rather than on a personal computer or local server. (23)

codicil. Document that explains, changes, or deletes provisions in a will. (7)

coinsurance. Percentage of the service costs that patients pay after the annual deductible is met. (15)

collateral. Property that a borrower promises to give up in case of default. (8)

collection agency. Business that specializes in debt collection. (9)

college access. Building awareness about college opportunities, providing guidance regarding college admissions, and identifying ways to pay for college. (21)

collusion. Making a secret agreement to engage in illegal or dishonest activities. (17)

command economy. System in which a central authority controls economic activities. (16)

commercial bank. Business in which the primary function is to receive, transfer, and lend money to individuals, businesses, and governments. (4)

commission. Income paid as a percentage of sales made by a salesperson. (3)

common stock. Stock that has voting rights and receives dividends when declared by a company. (6)

communication skills. Skills that help people communicate and work well with each other. (23)

community bank. Type of commercial bank that is locally owned and operated. (4)

comparative advantage. Exists when a country specializes in producing a product more efficiently than another country. (19)

comparison shopping. Process of gathering information about products to find the best option among similar products. (10)

compensation. Wages or salaries and benefits paid to employees. (3)

composting. Natural process that transforms organic materials into a nutrient-rich material that can be added to soil to improve it. (20)

compound interest. Amount calculated using the principal plus the interest it earns. (5)

comprehensive medical insurance. Insurance that combines basic and major medical protections in one policy. (15)

conflict of interest. Situation in which a buyer and a seller have competing goals. (10)

conservation. Protection and management of the environment and natural resources to ensure they will exist in the future. (20)

consumer advocate. Group or individual who promotes consumer rights. (11)

consumer cooperative. Nonretail association owned and operated by a group of members for their own benefit rather than for profit. (10)

consumer credit. Credit granted to individual consumers by a retail business. (8)

consumer fraud. Deceptive business practice that causes consumers to lose money or other property. (11)

consumer market. Consists of customers who buy products for their own use. (18)

consumer price index (CPI). A measure of the average change in prices over time for selected goods and services; sometimes called the cost of living index. (17)

consumer protection laws. Laws that govern sales and credit practices involving consumer goods and services. (11)

consumer spending. The purchasing of goods and services by consumers. (17)

consumer. Individual who purchases goods and services for personal use. (1)

contingency clause. Part of a contract that calls for certain requirements to be met before the contract is binding. (12)

contract. Legally binding agreement between a borrower and a creditor. (8)

cookies. Bits of data stored on a computer that record information about the websites visited. (23)

copayment. Flat fee the patient must pay for medical services. (15)

corporation. Business that is legally separate from its owners; defined by the US Supreme Court as "an artificial being, invisible, intangible, and existing only in contemplation of the law." (18)

cosigner. Responsible person who signs the loan with the person to whom the loan is granted. (8)

cost-benefit analysis. Method of weighing the costs against the benefits of an action, a purchase, or a financial decision. (1)

coupon. Printed or electronic offer giving a discount for goods or services bought before a certain date. (10)

cover message. Letter or e-mail sent with a résumé to introduce an applicant and summarize his or her reasons for applying for a job. (22)

credit. Agreement between two parties in which one party lends money or provides goods or services to another party with the understanding that payment will be made at a later date. (8)

credit bureau. Organization that collects information about the financial and credit transactions of consumers. (8)

credit card. Card that allows the holder to make credit purchases up to an authorized amount. (4)

credit counseling service. Organization that provides debt and financial management advice and services to people with debt problems at little or no cost. (9)

credit fraud. Fraudulent use of someone else's credit information. (9)

credit history. Individual's credit and financial behavior over a period of years. (8)

credit rating. Creditor's evaluation of an applicant's willingness and ability to pay debts and is often expressed as a letter grade. (8)

credit report. Record of a person's credit history. (8)

credit score. Numerical measure of a loan applicant's creditworthiness at a particular point in time. (8)

credit union. Nonprofit financial cooperative owned by and operated for the benefit of its members. (4)

creditor. Party extending credit. (8)

creditworthy. Having the assets, income, and willingness to repay debt. (8)

culture. Beliefs, behaviors, and other characteristics common among members of a group or society. (1, 19)

currency manipulation. Refers to action taken, usually by a government or central bank, to increase or decrease the value of the nation's currency. (19)

cyberbullying. Using the Internet to harass or threaten an individual. (23)

D

data analysis. Process of studying data with the goal of discovering new information that can help with making decisions. (2)

data. Information. (2)

debit card. Card that allows the holder to electronically access funds in an account at an ATM or to pay for goods and services from a business. (4)

debt. Something that is owed that will decrease future earnings. (9)

debt load. Amount of debt a consumer has at a given point in time. (9)

debtor. Party receiving credit. (8)

deceptive advertising. Information that purposely misleads a consumer through dishonest claims. (10)

deductible. Amount the insured is responsible for paying when a claim is made. (14)

deficit spending. When the government spends more than the amount it receives in revenues. (17)

defined-benefit plan. Retirement plan that makes regular payments to a retiree until death; also known as a *pension plan*. (7)

defined-contribution plan. Retirement plan in which an employee and/or employer contributes to the employee's individual account under the defined plan. (7)

deflation. Overall decrease in the price of goods and services. (17)

demand. Quantity of a good or service consumers are willing to buy. (16)

demographics. Statistical characteristics of a population. (1)

dental insurance. Insurance that covers specified dental services. (15)

dependent. Individual who relies on someone else for financial support. (3)

depreciation. Decrease in the value of property as a result of use, age, or wear and tear. (13, 14)

depression. A recession that continues for several years. (17)

digital citizen. Someone who regularly and skillfully engages technology such as the Internet, computers, and other digital devices. (23)

digital citizenship. Standards of behavior when using technology to communicate. (23)

digital communication. Exchange of information through electronic means. (23)

digital etiquette. See *netiquette*.

digital footprint. Data record of all an individual's online activities. (23)

digital literacy. Ability to use technology to locate, evaluate, communicate, and create information. (23)

direct tax. Paid directly to the government by the taxpayer. (3)

disability insurance. Pays a portion of income lost to a worker who is unable to work for a prolonged period because of illness or injury. (15)

disability. Limitation that affects a person's ability to function in major life activities. (3)

discount rate. The interest rate Federal Reserve Banks charge commercial banks for credit when they borrow. (17)

discretionary expenditure. Expense item that can be adjusted according to needs and revenues. (3)

discretionary expense. Amount spent for an item that a person could do without. (2)

discretionary income. Money that remains after a person has paid all expenses. (2)

diversification. Spreading risk by putting money in different types of investments. (6)

dividend reinvestment plan (DRIP). Allows investors to reinvest cash dividends by purchasing additional shares of stock. (6)

dividend. Portion of a company's earnings that is paid to stockholders. (6)

dollar-cost averaging. Strategy of investing a fixed dollar amount at regular intervals without regard to the price of the investment at the time a person buys it. (6)

down payment. Portion of the purchase price paid up front. (8)

durable goods. Items that do not wear out quickly. (10)

E

earned income. Income received from employment, including self-employment. (3)

earnest money. Deposit made by a buyer when signing a purchase agreement to show that the offer is serious. (12)

easy-access credit. Short-term loan at a high interest rate that is granted regardless of the borrower's credit history. (8)

ecology. Study of the relationship between living things and their environment. (20)

e-commerce. Buying and selling goods and services over the Internet, as well as transferring money or data. (10)

economic competition. Occurs when two or more sellers offer similar goods and services for sale in the marketplace. (16)

economic conditions. State of the economy at a given time. (1)

economic globalization. Flow of goods, services, labor, money, ideas, and technology across national borders. (19)

economic indicator. A piece of significant economic data that economists use to evaluate the overall health of the economy. (17)

economic system. Structure in which limited resources are turned into goods and services to address unlimited needs and wants. (16)

economics. Science that examines how goods and services are produced, sold, and used. (16)

economy of scale. Cost of producing one unit of something decreases as the total number of units produced increases. (19)

electronic funds transfer (EFT). Movement of money over an online network from one financial institution to another. (4)

emergency fund. Amount of money that can easily be accessed in case of a job layoff, illness, or unexpected expense. (2, 5)

employability skills. Applicable skills used to help an individual find a job, perform in the workplace, and gain success in a job or career. (21)

employee benefit. Form of noncash compensation received in addition to a wage or salary; also known as *fringe benefit*. (3)

employment verification. Process through which the information provided on an applicant's résumé is checked to verify that it is correct. (22)

endorsement. Signature on the back of a check. (4) Also, attachment to existing insurance coverage. (14)

endowment insurance. Pays the face value of the policy to beneficiaries if the insured dies before the endowment period ends. (15)

entitlement. Government program that provides financial benefits to eligible citizens based on their legal rights. (1)

entrepreneur. Person who owns and operates a business. (18)

entrepreneurship. Willingness and ability to start a new business. (16)

environmentalist. Person who is concerned with the quality of the environment and how to maintain it. (20)

equilibrium. Point at which the demand and supply curves intersect. (16)

equity. Difference between the market value of the property and the amount owed on the property. (12)

escrow account. Account for holding money in trust for others. (12)

estate. Consists of the assets and liabilities a person leaves after death. (7)

ethics. Moral principles or beliefs that direct a person's behavior. (1)

etiquette. Art of using good manners in any situation. (22)

European Union (EU). Economic and political organization consisting of 28 nations, most of which are in Europe. (19)

eviction. Legal process of removing a tenant who is not paying rent from a rental property if the tenant does not leave voluntarily. (12)

exchange rate. How much one currency buys in another currency. (19)

exclusion. Medical service that is not covered in an insurance plan. (15)

expense. Cost of goods and services purchased. (2) Also, cost involved in operating a business. (18)

export. Goods and services grown or made in a given country and then sold in world markets. (19)

express warranty. Warranty that is clearly stated and can be written or verbal. (10)

extended warranty. Covers servicing and repairs that may be required after the initial warranty expires. (10)

extractor. Business or person that removes natural resources from the land. (18)

F

factors of production. Economic resources a nation uses to make goods and supply services for its population. (16)

family life cycle. Stages a family passes through over its lifetime. (2)

Federal Deposit Insurance Corporation (FDIC). Independent agency created by the federal government to protect bank customers by insuring their deposits. (4)

Federal Reserve System. Regulates the nation's money supply and the banking system; also called the Fed. (17)

fee-for-service plan. See *indemnity plan*.

FICA taxes. Taxes paid by the employee and employer that are used to finance the federal Social Security and Medicare programs; also known as Social Security and Medicare taxes. (3)

finance charge. Total amount paid by a borrower to a lender for the use of credit. (8)

financial competence. Ability to understand basic topics related to finance. (1)

financial exchange. Process of transferring money from one individual or organization to another. (4)

financial institution. Organization that provides services related to money. (4)

financial literacy. Possession of a body of financial knowledge, a set of basic skills, and the ability to apply knowledge and skills to making informed, responsible financial choices. (1)

financial personality. Combination of an individual's attitudes about money and spending patterns. (9)

financial plan. Overview of an individual's current financial position and strategies to meet future financial aspirations. (1)

firewall. Program that monitors information coming into a computer. (23)

fiscal policy. The federal government's taxing and spending decisions. (17)

fixed expense. Set amount that must be paid each budget period. (2)

fixed-rate mortgage. Mortgage with a guaranteed fixed or unchanging interest rate for the life of the loan. (12)

flat tax. See *proportional tax*.

food insecurity. Lack of enough food at least part of the time to support an active and healthy life. (20)

foreclosure. Forced sale of property because the debtor failed to make loan payments. (9)

foreign exchange market (FOREX). Financial marketplace for buying and selling the currencies of different countries. (19)

Form W-2. Wage and Tax Statement that shows earnings and the amounts of income, Social Security, and Medicare taxes withheld from earned income during the year. (3)

Form W-4. Employee's Withholding Allowance Certificate that helps an employer determine how much income tax to withhold from an employee's paychecks as payroll deductions. (3)

formal education. Education received in a school, college, or university. (21)

for-profit business. Organization that generates revenue. (18)

for-profit school. School that is set up to earn money for investors. (21)

franchise. The right to sell a company's goods or services in a specific area. (18)

franchisee. The person or company that buys a franchise. (18)

franchisor. The parent company that sells the rights for another business to operate using its brand. (18)

free trade agreement (FTA). Partnership between two or more countries in which certain requirements related to specific trade goods are outlined. (19)

free trade. Policy of limited governmental restrictions on trade. (19)

free-enterprise system. See *market economy*.

fringe benefit. See *employee benefit*.

FTC Used-Car Rule. Requires dealers to fully disclose to buyers what is and is not covered under a used vehicle's warranty. (13)

full warranty. Completely covers the repair or replacement of any defect in a product. (10)

future value. Value of an amount of money invested with compound interest at the end of a specified time period. (5)

G

game of chance. Participant must wager something to win. (10)

garnishment. Legal procedure requiring a portion of the debtor's pay to be set aside by the person's employer to pay creditors. (9)

GDP per capita. The market value of final goods and services produced per person. (17)

General Agreement on Tariffs and Trade (GATT). Set of international agreements that promotes free and fair trade among nations. (19)

global warming. Steady rise in average temperatures near Earth's surface. (20)

globalization. Worldwide spread and integration of production, markets, communications, and technology. (1)

goal. Objective to be attained in a specific amount of time. (1)

good. Tangible items that can be touched, used, and purchased, such as food or clothing. (1)

government market. Includes national, state, and local governmental offices and agencies. (18)

grace period. Time between the billing date and the start of interest charges. (8)

graduated payment mortgage. Mortgage that allows the buyer to pay low monthly payments at first and higher payments in the future. (12)

gratuity. See *tip*.

gross domestic product (GDP). A measure of the value of all goods and services produced by a nation during a specified period of time, usually one year. (17)

gross income. All the income an individual receives in a year including both earned and unearned income. (3)

gross pay. Total income before payroll deductions. (3)

H

hacking. Illegally accessing or altering digital devices, software, or networks. (23)

hazardous waste. Substance that is dangerous or potentially harmful to human health or the environment. (20)

health insurance exchange. Government-sponsored price-comparison website where consumers can shop for and purchase government-regulated and standardized health care plans eligible for federal subsidies; also called the *Health Insurance Marketplace.* (15)

Health Insurance Marketplace. See *health insurance exchange.*

health insurance. Provides protection against financial loss due to illness or injury. (15)

health savings account (HSA). Tax-advantaged savings account available to people enrolled in qualified high-deductible health plans (HDHPs). (15)

high-pressure selling. Attempting to convince a buyer to make a quick decision. (10)

high-yield savings account. Account that pays a higher interest rate than passbook and statement savings accounts. (5)

home energy audit. Assessment of how much energy a person uses in his or her home. (20)

home equity loan. Type of loan in which the borrower uses the equity in a home as collateral for the loan; also called a *second mortgage.* (12)

homeowners insurance. Provides coverage for liability and damage to property under certain conditions. (14)

homeowners liability insurance. Protects a homeowner if others are injured on the policyholder's property; sometimes referred to as *personal liability insurance.* (14)

human resource. Qualities or characteristics that a person has. (16)

hypothetical question. Question that requires a person to respond in a personal manner. (22)

I

identity theft. Illegal act that involves stealing someone's personal information and using that information to commit theft or fraud. (23)

implied fitness. Unwritten promise that a product must be fit for any performance or purpose promised by the seller. (10)

implied merchantability. Unwritten guarantee that a product is what it is called and does what its name implies. (10)

implied warranty. Unwritten promise about a product and its use. (10)

import. Goods and services that come into a given country from other countries. (19)

impulse buying. Making a purchase without first considering needs, goals, or the consequences of spending money. (10)

income. Any form of money received, such as an allowance, a paycheck, gifts, and gains from an investment. (2)

indemnity plan. Health care plan that pays for covered medical services after treatment is provided, usually on a fee-for-service basis; also referred to as a *fee-for-service plan.* (15)

indirect tax. Tax levied on one person or entity, but shifted to or paid by another. (3)

individual 401(k) plan. See *solo 401(k) plan.*

individual retirement account (IRA). Personal account for setting money aside for retirement. (7)

inflation. Overall rise in prices. (1, 6)

informational interviewing. Strategy used to interview a professional to ask for advice and direction, rather than asking for a job opportunity. (21)

infringement. Any use of copyrighted material without permission. (23)

initial public offering (IPO). Company's first sale of stock to the public. (6)

innovation. Process of creating something. (16)

installment loan. Loan for a specific amount of money that is repaid with interest in regular installments. (8)

institution. Nonprofit organization that may be either public or private. (18)

insurance policy. Contract that defines the type of losses that are covered, amount of coverage in dollars, and other conditions to which the two parties agree. (14)

insurance settlement. Amount of money or other services to which a person is entitled under the terms of his or her insurance policy. (14)

insurance. Financial service used to protect against loss. (14)

intellectual property. Something that comes from a person's mind. (23)

interest. Amount that is paid for using money. (1) Also, a feeling of wanting to learn more about a topic or to be involved in an activity. (21)

interest-bearing savings account. Type of demand deposit account that pays interest and allows for regular deposits and withdrawals. (5)

intermediary. Person or business that sells the goods and services from producers to customers. (18)

International Monetary Fund (IMF). Organization that works to stabilize exchange rates and eliminate trade barriers. (19)

international trade. Buying and selling of goods and services across national borders and among the people of different nations. (19)

Internet bank. Financial institution that provides banking services exclusively online; also known as *virtual bank.* (4)

Internet Protocol address. Number used to identify an electronic device connected to the Internet; also known as an *IP address.* (23)

internship. Short-term position with a sponsoring organization that gives the intern an opportunity to gain on-the-job experience in a certain field of study or occupation. (21)

investing. Purchasing a financial product or valuable item with the goal of increasing wealth over time in spite of possible loss. (6)

investment club. Group of people who work together to learn about securities and to invest their pooled funds. (6)

investment portfolio. Collection of the investments a person has made. (6)

IP address. See *Internet Protocol address.*

J

job. Work a person does regularly in order to earn money. (21)

job application. Form with spaces for contact information, education, and work experience. (22)

job interview. Meeting in which an applicant and an employer discuss the job and the applicant's skills. (22)

job-specific skills. Critical skills necessary to perform the required work-related tasks of a position. (21)

L

labeling law. Governmental regulation that requires certain information be placed on labels for certain products. (10)

labor. Work performed by people who turn resources into products. (16)

labor force. People age 16 and over who are employed or looking for and able to work. (17)

labor productivity. The value of the goods and services a worker creates in a given time. (17)

land. All of the natural resources of a nation. (16)

landfill. Permanent waste-disposal site for most solid, nonhazardous waste. (20)

last will and testament. See *will*.

law of diminishing marginal utility. States that the marginal benefit of using each additional unit of something tends to decrease as the quantity used increases. (1)

law of supply and demand. Says that the price of a product is determined by the relationship of the supply of a product and the demand for the product. (16)

lawsuit. Civil action brought by a person (plaintiff) against another party (defendant). (11)

lease. Contract that specifies the conditions, terms, and rent for the use of an asset. (12)

legal document. Paper that can be filed with a court officer or used to uphold an agreement in a court of law. (2)

lemon law. Requires a seller or manufacture of a defective vehicle to either replace or repair it or to refund the buyer's money. (13)

lessee. Person who rents the property. (12)

lessor. Person who owns and rents out the property. (12)

level of risk. Degree to which an investment may deviate from its rate of return. (6)

levy. To use legal authority to impose a payment. (3)

liability. Current or future financial obligation, such as unpaid bills, credit card charges, mortgages, personal loans, and taxes. (2) Also, legal responsibility. (18)

libel. Publishing a false statement about someone that causes others to have a negative opinion of that person. (23)

lien. Claim on a borrower's property by a creditor who is owed money. (9)

life insurance. Protects dependents from loss of income and helps pay expenses after the death of the insured person. (15)

life span. Time between birth and death. (2)

limited liability company (LLC). Form of business ownership that combines the benefits of a corporation with those of proprietorships and partnerships. (18)

limited warranty. Guarantee for service repairs, and replacements only under certain conditions. (10)

line of credit. Preapproved amount that an individual can borrow. (8)

liquidation bankruptcy. See *Chapter 7 bankruptcy*.

liquidity. Ease with which an asset can be converted into cash without losing value. (2)

living will. Statement of instructions for specific medical treatment if a person becomes unable to make medical decisions related to deathbed concerns. (7)

loan application package. Loan application and supporting documents for the loan. (12)

long-term care (LTC) insurance. Provides coverage for personal and custodial care during periods when an individual is unable to perform essential daily living activities. (15)

loss leader. Item priced at or below cost to attract buyers in the expectation that they will purchase other merchandise as well. (10)

lottery. Similar to sweepstakes except prizes are awarded to participants by chance in exchange for some form of payment. (11)

low-risk borrower. Borrower who is most likely to pay debts. (8)

M

major medical insurance. Insurance that covers the costs of serious illnesses and injuries as well as high-cost procedures. (15)

malicious software. See *malware*.

malware. Term given to software programs that are intended to damage, destroy, or steal data; short for *malicious software*. (23)

managed care plan. Type of health care plan in which the insurance company contracts with specific doctors, hospitals, and other health care providers to deliver medical services and preventive care to members at reduced cost. (15)

management. Process of organizing and using resources to achieve predetermined objectives. (1)

mandatory expenditure. Federal spending that Congress legislated into law. (3)

manufacturer. Business that uses materials from other producers to make products. (18)

manufacturer's suggested retail price (MSRP). Price recommended by the manufacturer. (13)

marginal benefit. Change in total benefit of using one additional unit. (1)

marginal cost. Change in total cost of using one additional unit. (1)

market economy. System in which privately owned businesses operate and compete for profits with limited governmental regulation or interference; also called a *free-enterprise system* or *capitalism*. (16)

market forces. Economic factors that affect the price, demand, and availability of a good or service. (16)

market structure. How a market is organized based on the number of businesses competing for sales in an industry. (17)

market value. Price at which something can be bought or sold at a given point in time. (6, 12)

marketplace. Arena in which consumers and producers meet to exchange goods, services, and money. (10, 16)

m-commerce. Any business activity that transpires using a mobile device. (10)

media. Forms of communication designed to reach a large number of people. (1)

Medicaid. Government program that pays certain health-care costs for eligible, low-income individuals and families. (3)

Medicare. Federal program that pays for certain health-care expenses for older citizens and others with disabilities. (3)

medium of exchange. Something used in exchange for goods and services needed by individuals, businesses, and governments. (17)

migrant. Person who temporarily moves from one place to another. (19)

minimum wage. Lowest hourly wage employers can pay most workers by law. (3)

mixed economy. Combination of the market and the command systems. (16)

mock interview. Practice interview conducted with another person. (22)

monetary policy. Actions taken by the Fed to manage the supply of money and credit in the economy. (17)

monetary system. The mechanism a nation uses to provide and manage money for itself. (17)

money. Anything of value that is accepted in return for goods or services. (4, 17)

money management software. Computer program used to organize daily finances and keep track of income, spending, saving, debts, investments, and other financial data. (2)

money market account. Type of savings account that typically pays a higher interest rate than regular savings accounts. (5)

money market mutual fund. Type of mutual fund that deals only in interest-paying, short-term investments. (6)

money supply. Total amount of money available at a given time in an economy. (17)

monopolistic competition. Situation in which a large number of businesses sells similar products at different prices. (17)

monopoly. Situation in which there is a single seller or producer of a given product or service. (17)

mortgage. Type of secured loan used for buying property. (12)

multinational corporation. Business that has facilities or other assets in more than one country. (19)

mutual fund. Investment created by pooling the money of many people and investing it in a collection of securities. (6)

mutual savings bank. Financial institution that is owned by its depositors. (4)

N

national debt. Total amount of money the government owes at a given time. (17)

natural resource. Raw material. (16)

nature of financial planning. Development of a strategy to meet a person's financial needs over the course of a lifetime. (2)

need. Necessities a person must have to survive. (1)

need-based award. Financial-aid awards available for students and families who meet certain economic requirements. (21)

negotiation. Discussion with the goal of reaching an agreement. (12)

net asset value (NAV). Total of the fund's assets minus its liabilities divided by the number of the shares the fund has outstanding. (6)

net income. Gross income minus the expenses of operating a business. (3)

net pay. Gross pay (plus bonuses) minus payroll deductions; also known as *take-home pay*. (3)

net worth statement. Written record of an individual's current financial situation. (2)

net worth. Difference between what is owned and what is owed. (2)

netiquette. Etiquette used when communicating electronically; also known as *digital etiquette*. (23)

networking. Talking with people a person knows and making new contacts. (21)

new-issues market. See *primary market*.

no-fault auto insurance. Eliminates the faultfinding process in settling claims. (14)

nondurable goods. Items that are used up immediately in one use or that will wear out in fewer than three years. (10)

nonprice competition. Competitive advantage based on factors other than price. (17)

nonrenewable energy. Power source that can be used up or cannot be used again. (20)

North American Industry Classification System (NAICS). Numeric system used to classify businesses and collect economic statistics. (18)

not-for-profit organization. Organization that exists to serve some public purpose. (18)

not-for-profit school. School that returns the money it earns back into the school. (21)

O

obsolete. Something that is no longer useful because a newer version exists. (10)

occupational training. Education that prepares a person for a specific type of work. (21)

offshore outsourcing. Moving sections of a business to another country; also called *offshoring*. (19)

offshoring. See *offshore outsourcing*.

oligopoly. Situation in which a few large companies dominate an industry. (17)

onshoring. Outsourcing within the country where the company is located. (19)

open source. Applies to software that has source code freely available to the public. (23)

open-end credit. Agreement that allows the borrower to use a specific amount of credit over a period of time. (8)

opportunity cost. Value of the option given up. (1)

option. Feature available for a particular car. (13)

oral communication. See *verbal communication*.

OTC market. Virtual markets where stockbrokers conduct business through an electronic network of computers and telephones. (6)

outsourcing. Moving sections of a business to other companies or to subsidiaries in other locations. (19)

overdraft. Check written for an amount greater than the balance of the account. (4)

overspending. Spending more money than a person can afford to spend. (10)

overtime wage. Amount paid for working time in a week that is beyond the standard 40-hour workweek. (3)

P

partnership agreement. Written contract that establishes a partnership; also called the *articles of partnership*. (18)

partnership. Association of two or more persons who co-own a business with the objective of earning a profit. (18)

pawnshop. Business that gives customers high-interest loans with personal property, such as jewelry, held as collateral. (8)

pay yourself first. Personal financial strategy that can help a person save money by paying oneself first and putting money aside for saving. (2)

payday loan. Short-term, high-interest loan that usually must be repaid on the borrower's next payday. (8)

payee. Person, business, or organization to whom the check is written. (4)

payroll deduction. Subtraction from gross pay. (3)

payroll savings plan (PSP). Program in which an employee authorizes the employer to make regular deductions from each paycheck to automatically deposit in a designated savings plan. (5)

pension plan. See *defined-benefit plan*.

perfect competition. Condition in which no single seller can significantly influence the market price of a good or service; also called pure competition. (17)

personal financial crisis. Major problem that changes a person or family's lifestyle and future. (2)

personal financial planning. Process of setting financial goals and developing plans to reach financial needs. (1)

personal information management (PIM). System that individuals use to acquire, organize, maintain, retrieve, and use information. (1)

personal investment plan. Outlines how to develop investment growth. (6)

personal liability insurance. See *homeowners liability insurance*.

philanthropy. Act of giving money, goods, or services to meet the needs of others and supporting organizations and causes that are important to an individual. (2)

phishing. Use of fraudulent e-mails and copies of valid websites to trick people in to providing private and confidential data. (23)

piecework. Wage based on a rate per unit of work completed. (3)

piracy. Illegal copying or downloading of software, files, or other protected material, including images, movies, and music. (23)

plagiarism. Unethical and illegal practice of claiming another person's material as one's own. (23)

point. Fee charges by lenders at closing and equals one percent of the mortgage. (12)

policy limit. The highest amount an insurance company will pay for a claim. (14)

Ponzi scheme. Investment operation in which money from new investors is used to pay earlier investors. (11)

portfolio. Selection of related materials that an individual collects and organizes to show qualifications, skills, and talents to support a career or personal goal. (22)

postsecondary education. Any education achieved after high school. (21)

power of attorney. Legal document that gives a person the power to act for another person regarding financial and legal matters. (7)

preauthorization. Approval from the plan before receiving certain procedures and treatments. (15)

preferred stock. Type of stock that pays a regular dividend at a fixed rate. (6)

premium. Amount the insured pays for insurance coverage. (14)

price. Amount of money requested in exchange for a product. (10)

price competition. Competing for business based on the prices of goods and services. (17)

primary market. Exists when a company first sells stock to the public, also called the *new-issues market*. (6)

principal. Amount of money originally borrowed or deposited. (5, 8)

priority. Value or goal that is given more importance than other values and goals. (1)

private mortgage insurance (PMI). Insurance policy that protects the lender from loss is the borrower defaults on the loan and the home goes into foreclosure. (12)

probate. Legal process of settling the affairs of an estate, paying final expenses, and distributing the balance of money and property to beneficiaries. (7)

producer. Individual or business that provides the supply of goods and services to meet consumer demands. (16)

productivity. Measure of the amount of work a person can do in a specific amount of time. (16)

profit motive. Desire for profit. (16)

profit. Difference between the income earned and expenses incurred by a business during a specific period of time. (16, 18)

progressive tax. Imposes a higher tax rate on those with higher incomes. (3)

promotion. Process of communicating with potential customers in an effort to influence their buying behavior. (10)

property damage liability insurance. Insurance for the insured person's car. (14)

property insurance. Insures the policyholder against financial loss due to damage to or loss of a dwelling and personal property and possessions. (14)

proportional tax. Imposes the same tax rate on all individuals or entities regardless of differences in income or ability to pay; also called *flat tax*. (3)

proprietorship. Business that is owned and often operated by a single individual. (18)

prospectus. Legal document that gives a detailed description of a security. (6)

prosperity. Time period of growth and financial well-being. (17)

proxy. Written authorization to have someone else cast a vote on the stockholder's behalf. (6)

public domain. Refers to material that is not owned by anybody and can be used without permission. (23)

purchase agreement. Contract between a homebuyer and a seller that includes a description of the real estate, its location, the purchase price, the possession date, and any other conditions and terms of the sale. (12)

pure risk. Risk with a possibility of loss but no possibility of gain. (14)

pyramid scheme. Fraudulent investment plan. (11)

R

rate of return. Amount earned on an investment for a given period of time. (6)

real estate investment trust (REIT). Company that owns income-earning real estate. (6)

rebate. Cash back offer. (10)

recession. Period of slow or no economic growth. (1)

reconcile. Comparing items to make sure they are in agreement with each other. (4)

recordkeeping. Process of setting up an organized system for important documents. (2)

recycle. Reprocess resources so they can be used again. (20)

redress. Set right or make up for a mistake. (11)

reference. Person who can comment on the qualifications, work ethic, personal qualities, and work-related aspects of another person's character. (22)

regressive tax. Imposing a higher tax rate on those with lower incomes. (3)

regular medical insurance. Insurance that covers prescriptions, hospital stays, and inpatient tests. (15)

renewable energy. Power source that is continually available or can be replenished. (20)

rental agreement. Written agreement that permits the tenant to move out at any time as long as the required notice is given. (12)

rental inventory checklist. Detailed list of property items and their condition. (12)

rent-to-own agreement. Arrangement in which a consumer pays rent for the use of a product and eventually owns it. (8)

repossession. Taking collateral when a borrower fails to repay a loan. (9)

required minimum distribution (RMD). Minimum amount that much be withdrawn from a retirement plan each year. (7)

research. Process of gathering information. (10)

resource. Supply of something that can be used when needed. (1)

résumé. Document that profiles a person's career goals, education, and work history. (22)

retailer. Business that buys products from wholesalers or directly from producers and sells them to consumers to make a profit. (18)

retirement. Period of life after ending a working or professional career; can also be used to refer to the money a person has saved to be used during this period of life. (7)

revenue. Earnings that a business received for the goods and services it sells. (18)

review. Critical report about an item. (10)

revolving credit account. Type of open-end credit agreement that offers a choice of paying in full each month or spreading payments over a period of time. (8)

risk. Measure of the likelihood that something will be lost. (6) In insurance, possibility of loss, damage, or injury. (14)

risk management. Process of measuring risk and finding ways to minimize or manage loss. (14)

risk tolerance. Amount of uncertainty a person is willing to handle. (6)

rollover. Process of moving retirement savings from one qualified account to another qualified account without incurring penalties and taxes. (7)

Roth 401(k). Employer-sponsored retirement plan in which contributions are made with after-tax earnings, but withdrawals are not taxed. (7)

Roth IRA. Individual retirement arrangement in which individuals contribute after-tax income, but qualified withdrawals are not taxed. (7)

Rule of 72. Equation that estimates how long it will take to double an investment with a fixed interest rate. (5)

S

salary. Fixed payment for work expressed as an annual figure. (3)

savings account. Bank account used by depositors to accumulate money for future use. (4, 5)

savings and loan association (S & L). Financial institution that offers most of the services commercial banks do. (4)

savings plan. Strategy for using money to reach important goals and to advance a person's financial security. (5)

scarcity. Basic economic problem that arises because there are unlimited human wants and needs but limited resources. (16)

scholarship. Financial aid that may be based on financial need or some type of merit or accomplishment. (21)

second mortgage. See *home equity loan.*

secondary market. Exists when investors purchase securities from other investors rather than from the issuing company. (6)

secured credit. Credit loans that require collateral. (8)

securities exchange. Secondary market where securities are bought and sold through stockbrokers. (6)

securities. Financial assets issued by corporations, governments, and other organizations. (6)

security deposit. Amount a renter pays to help protect the property owner against financial losses in case the renter damages the property or fails to pay rent. (12)

SEP IRA. Tax-deferred retirement plan that allows a business owner to open an IRA and make tax-deductible contributions; short for *Simplified Employer Pension Individual Retirement Account*. (7)

Series EE bond. Earns a fixed rate of interest for up to 30 years. (6)

Series I bond. Earns interest based on combining a fixed interest rate and the inflation rate. (6)

service. Intangible activities that another person usually performs for a fee, such as cleaning services or completing tax returns. (1)

service business. Earns income by providing consumers with services that meet their needs and wants. (18)

shared responsibility payment. Penalty paid by those who do not purchase health insurance. (15)

simple interest. Interest earned only on the principal. (5)

SIMPLE IRA. Tax-deferred retirement plan for businesses with 100 or fewer employees; short for *Savings Incentive Match Plan for Employees of Small Employers*. (7)

skepticism. Having a degree of doubt. (11)

skill. Something an individual does well. (21)

skill contest. Offers the opportunity to win prizes by skill, such as writing an essay or submitting a photo, rather than by chance. (11)

slander. Speaking a false statement about someone that causes others to have a negative opinion of that person. (23)

small claims court. Part of the court system that offers a simple, prompt, and inexpensive way to settle minor differences involving small amounts of money. (11)

SMART goal. Something a person wants to achieve stated in terms that are specific, measureable, achievable, realistic, and time related. (5)

social responsibility. Behaving with sensitivity to social, environmental, and economic issues. (2)

Social Security. Federal program that provides income when earnings are reduced or stopped because of retirement, serious illness or injury, or death. (3)

software virus. Computer program designed to negatively impact a computer system by infecting other files. (23)

Solo 401(k) plan. Self-employed retirement plan that allows tax-deductible contributions for employers and employees; also called an *individual 401(k) plan*. (7)

specialization. Method of production in which a particular range of products and services is produced. (19)

speculative risk. Risk that may result in either financial gain or financial loss. (14)

spending plan. Strategy to help an individual make smart choices and get the most of his or her money. (10)

spousal IRA. Type of individual retirement account that allows a working spouse to contribute to the retirement savings of a nonworking spouse. (7)

spreadsheet. Software program that formats data in columns and rows and can perform calculations. (2)

spyware. Software that spies on a computer. (23)

stagflation. Period of slow growth (economic stagnation) and high inflation. (17)

standard deduction. Dollar amount that non-itemizers may subtract from their income before income tax is applied. (3)

standard. Established measure of quality, value, or quantity. (1)

sticker price. Price displayed on a vehicle as its selling price. (13)

stock. Share in the ownership of a corporation. (6)

stock trade. Purchase or sale of shares of stock. (6)

stop-payment order. Request for a financial institution to refuse to honor a check written, if the check has not already cleared the account and been paid. (4)

store of value. Something that can be saved and used for purchases at a later date. (17)

straight bankruptcy. See *Chapter 7 bankruptcy*.

subprime credit card. Card offered to people who have a poor credit history. (8)

subprime mortgage. Mortgage made by lenders who charge higher-than-prime rates to borrowers who have poor or no credit ratings. (12)

subsidiary. Business that is controlled by another business. (19)

subsidy. Form of transfer payment that gives financial assistance to a business or entity. (17)

supplemental insurance. Additional insurance that can be purchased to pay for medical expenses that standard health insurance does not cover or does not fully cover. (15)

supply. Amount of a good or service producers are willing to provide. (16)

surplus. When the government receives more in revenues than the amount it spends. (17)

sustainable. Able to be kept in existence. (20)

sweepstakes. Promotional offer that gives participants the chance to win items of value or prizes. (11)

systematic decision-making. Process of choosing a course of action after evaluating available information and weighing the costs and benefits of alternative actions and their consequences. (1)

T

take-home pay. See *net pay*.

tax audit. Detailed examination of a tax return by the IRS. (3)

tax deferred. Taxes on the principal and/or earnings are delayed until the funds are withdrawn. (5)

tax exempt. Free of certain taxes. (5)

tax liability. Amount of total tax owed on income for the year. (3)

tax return. Report containing information used to calculate taxes owed by the taxpayer. (3)

tax table. Government issued tables that show a taxpayer's total tax obligation for a year based on the amount of total income. (3)

taxable income. Amount on which taxes are calculated. (3)

t-commerce. Buying and selling products and services using an interactive or smart television. (10)

technology. Application of science and research to human life and environments. (1)

telemarketing. Sale of merchandise by phone. (10)

telephone etiquette. Using good manners while speaking on the telephone. (22)

term life insurance. Provides protections only for a specific period of time. (15)

testing and rating service. Group or organization that tests products and rates them according to certain criteria. (10)

time value of money. Idea that money decreases in value over time. (5)

tip. Money paid for service beyond what is required; also known as *gratuity*. (3)

title. Legal document that proved ownership of property. (12)

title loan. Short-term loan made using a borrower's car as collateral. (8)

trade barrier. Any action taken to control or limit imports. (19)

trade deficit. When a country buys, or imports, more products than it sells. (19)

trade surplus. When a country sells, or exports, more than it buys. (19)

trade-off. Choice given up when making one choice over another. (1)

traditional economy. System in which economic decisions are based on a society's values, culture, and customs. (16)

traditional IRA. Individual retirement account in which contributions are tax-deductible, but withdrawals are taxed. (7)

transfer payment. Payment made to individuals from the federal government through various social benefit programs. (3)

Treasury bill. Short-term debts with maturities ranging from a few days to 52 weeks. (6)

Treasury bond. Long-term investments with maturities of 30 years. (6)

Treasury note. Short-term securities with maturities of two, three, five, seven, or ten years. (6)

trust. Arrangement through which a person transfers assets to a trustee, who then oversees and manages the assets on behalf of beneficiaries. (7)

trustee. Person or institution named to manage assets on behalf of the beneficiaries. (7)

U

umbrella policy. Covers loss amounts that are higher than those covered by primary policies. (14)

underemployment. A condition in which workers are employed only part time or are overqualified for their jobs. (17)

unearned income. Earnings from sources other than work. (3)

unemployment rate. The percentage of the labor force that is out of work and seeking employment. (17)

unit of value. Common measure of the worth or price of a good or service. (17)

unit price. Cost per unit, weight, or measure. (10)

unsecured loan. Credit granted based on a signed credit agreement. (8)

utilization review. Insurance company's examination of requests for medical treatments and procedures to make sure they are covered and the patient truly needs them. (15)

V

value system. Overall structure of values and goals that guides a person's behavior and provides a sense of direction in life. (1)

values. Principles and beliefs that a person considers important. (1, 21)

variable expense. Cost that changes both in the amount and time it must be paid. (2)

variance. In budgeting, the difference between the budgeted amount and the actual amount. (2)

vehicle identification number (VIN). Unique number assigned by the automobile industry and used to identify an individual auto. (13)

verbal communication. Speaking words to communicate; also known as *oral communication*. (22)

vesting. Process of determining when money that has been set aside in a retirement plan belongs to an employee. (7)

virtual bank. See *Internet bank.*

vision care insurance. Insurance that covers specified eye care services. (15)

volatility. Quick and unexpected changes in value or price. (6)

voluntary compliance. Government expects individuals and businesses to voluntarily report all income that is subject to the income tax. (3)

W

wage. Payment for work that is usually calculated on an hourly, daily, or piecework basis. (3)

want. Things that a person desires but can live without. (1)

warranty. Guarantee that a product will meet certain performance and quality standards. (10)

wealth. Abundance of money and other assets. (2)

whole life insurance. Provides basic lifetime protection so long as premiums are paid. (15)

wholesaler. Business that purchases large quantities of products directly from producers and sells the products in smaller quantities to retailers. (18)

will. Legal document that states a person's wishes for an estate after death; also called a *last will and testament*. (7)

workers' compensation insurance. Type of disability insurance that helps pay for medical care, rehabilitation, and lost wages for an employee who suffers an injury or illness as a direct result of performing a job. (15)

work-life balance. Amount of time an individual spends at work compared to the amount of time spent in a personal life. (3)

work-study program. Part-time job on a college campus that is subsidized by the government. (21)

World Trade Organization (WTO). 164-member international organization that establishes trade practices between its member nations for trade that is as free and smooth as possible. (19)

Y

yield. Amount of money earned on the investment, usually expressed as an annual percentage. (6)

Index

C

F

G

H

Q

R

V

W

Y